T0236507

# Lecture Notes
# in Business Information Processing

227

## Series Editors

Wil van der Aalst
*Eindhoven Technical University, Eindhoven, The Netherlands*
John Mylopoulos
*University of Trento, Povo, Italy*
Michael Rosemann
*Queensland University of Technology, Brisbane, QLD, Australia*
Michael J. Shaw
*University of Illinois, Urbana-Champaign, IL, USA*
Clemens Szyperski
*Microsoft Research, Redmond, WA, USA*

More information about this series at http://www.springer.com/series/7911

José Cordeiro · Slimane Hammoudi
Leszek Maciaszek · Olivier Camp
Joaquim Filipe (Eds.)

# Enterprise Information Systems

16th International Conference, ICEIS 2014
Lisbon, Portugal, April 27–30, 2014
Revised Selected Papers

 Springer

*Editors*

José Cordeiro
INSTICC
Polytechnic Institute of Setúbal
Setúbal
Portugal

Slimane Hammoudi
MODESTE/ESEO
Angers
France

Leszek Maciaszek
Wroclaw University of Economics
Wroclaw
Poland

Olivier Camp
MODESTE/ESEO
Angers
France

Joaquim Filipe
INSTICC
Polytechnic Institute of Setúbal
Setúbal
Portugal

ISSN 1865-1348          ISSN 1865-1356   (electronic)
Lecture Notes in Business Information Processing
ISBN 978-3-319-22347-6          ISBN 978-3-319-22348-3   (eBook)
DOI 10.1007/978-3-319-22348-3

Library of Congress Control Number: 2015944743

Springer Cham Heidelberg New York Dordrecht London

© Springer International Publishing Switzerland 2015
This work is subject to copyright. All rights are reserved by the Publisher, whether the whole or part of the material is concerned, specifically the rights of translation, reprinting, reuse of illustrations, recitation, broadcasting, reproduction on microfilms or in any other physical way, and transmission or information storage and retrieval, electronic adaptation, computer software, or by similar or dissimilar methodology now known or hereafter developed.
The use of general descriptive names, registered names, trademarks, service marks, etc. in this publication does not imply, even in the absence of a specific statement, that such names are exempt from the relevant protective laws and regulations and therefore free for general use.
The publisher, the authors and the editors are safe to assume that the advice and information in this book are believed to be true and accurate at the date of publication. Neither the publisher nor the authors or the editors give a warranty, express or implied, with respect to the material contained herein or for any errors or omissions that may have been made.

Printed on acid-free paper

Springer International Publishing AG Switzerland is part of Springer Science+Business Media
(www.springer.com)

# Preface

The present book includes extended and revised versions of a set of selected papers from the 16th International Conference on Enterprise Information Systems (ICEIS 2014), held in Lisbon, Portugal, during April 27–30, 2014. The conference was sponsored by the Institute for Systems and Technologies of Information, Control and Communication (INSTICC), held in cooperation with the Association for the Advancement of Artificial Intelligence (AAAI), IEICE Special Interest Group on Software Interprise Modelling (SWIM), ACM SIGART - ACM Special Interest Group on Artificial Intelligence, ACM SIGMIS - ACM Special Interest Group on Management Information Systems, ACM SIGCHI - ACM Special Interest Group on Computer–Human Interaction, and in collaboration with the Informatics Research Center (IRC).

The conference was organized in six simultaneous tracks: "Databases and Information Systems Integration, Artificial Intelligence and Decision Support Systems, Information Systems Analysis and Specification, Software Agents and Internet Computing, Human–Computer Interaction, and Enterprise Architecture". The book is based on the same structure.

ICEIS 2014 received 313 paper submissions from 50 countries in all continents. From these, after a blind review process, only 47 were accepted as full papers, of which 24 were selected for inclusion in this book, based on the classifications provided by the Program Committee. The selected papers reflect state-of-art research work that is often oriented toward real-world applications and highlight the benefits of information systems and technology for industry and services, thus forming a bridge between the worlds of academia and enterprise. These high-quality standards were maintained and reinforced at ICEIS 2015, which was held in Barcelona, Spain, and will continue to be reinforced in future editions of this conference.

Furthermore, ICEIS 2014 included five plenary keynote lectures given by Kecheng Liu (University of Reading, UK), Jan Dietz (Delft University of Technology, The Netherlands), Antoni Olivé (Universitat Politècnica de Catalunya, Spain), José Tribolet (INESC-ID/Instituto Superior Técnico, Portugal), and Hans-J. Lenz (Freie Universität Berlin, Germany). We would like to express our appreciation to all of them and in particular to those who took the time to contribute with a paper to this book.

On behalf of the conference Organizing Committee, we would like to thank all participants. First of all the authors, whose quality work is the essence of the conference, and the members of the Program Committee, who helped us with their expertise and diligence in reviewing the papers. As we all know, producing a conference requires

the effort of many individuals. We wish to thank also all the members of our Organizing Committee, whose work and commitment were invaluable.

February 2014

José Cordeiro
Slimane Hammoudi
Leszek Maciaszek
Olivier Camp
Joaquim Filipe

# Organization

## Conference Co-chairs

| | |
|---|---|
| Joaquim Filipe | Polytechnic Institute of Setúbal/INSTICC, Portugal |
| Olivier Camp | ESEO, MODESTE, France |

## Program Co-chairs

| | |
|---|---|
| Slimane Hammoudi | ESEO, MODESTE, France |
| Leszek Maciaszek | Wroclaw University of Economics, Poland and Macquarie University, Sydney, Australia |
| José Cordeiro | Polytechnic Institute of Setúbal/INSTICC, Portugal |

## Organizing Committee

| | |
|---|---|
| Marina Carvalho | INSTICC, Portugal |
| Helder Coelhas | INSTICC, Portugal |
| Bruno Encarnação | INSTICC, Portugal |
| Ana Guerreiro | INSTICC, Portugal |
| André Lista | INSTICC, Portugal |
| Filipe Mariano | INSTICC, Portugal |
| Andreia Moita | INSTICC, Portugal |
| Raquel Pedrosa | INSTICC, Portugal |
| Vitor Pedrosa | INSTICC, Portugal |
| Cláudia Pinto | INSTICC, Portugal |
| Cátia Pires | INSTICC, Portugal |
| Susana Ribeiro | INSTICC, Portugal |
| Rui Rodrigues | INSTICC, Portugal |
| Sara Santiago | INSTICC, Portugal |
| André Santos | INSTICC, Portugal |
| Fábio Santos | INSTICC, Portugal |
| Mara Silva | INSTICC, Portugal |
| José Varela | INSTICC, Portugal |
| Pedro Varela | INSTICC, Portugal |

## Senior Program Committee

| | |
|---|---|
| Balbir Barn | Middlesex University, UK |
| Senén Barro | University of Santiago de Compostela, Spain |
| Albert Cheng | University of Houston, USA |
| Jan Dietz | Delft University of Technology, The Netherlands |

| | |
|---|---|
| Schahram Dustdar | Vienna University of Technology, Austria |
| António Figueiredo | University of Coimbra, Portugal |
| Nuno Guimarães | Lasige/ISCTE-University Institute of Lisbon, Portugal |
| Jan Jürjens | TU Dortmund and Fraunhofer ISST, Germany |
| Kecheng Liu | University of Reading, UK |
| Pericles Loucopoulos | Harokopio University of Athens, Greece |
| Andrea de Lucia | Università degli Studi di Salerno, Italy |
| Yannis Manolopoulos | Aristotle University, Greece |
| José Legatheaux Martins | FCT/UNL, Portugal |
| Masao Johannes Matsumoto | Solution Research Lab, Japan |
| Alain Pirotte | Université catholique de Louvain, Belgium |
| Matthias Rauterberg | Eindhoven University of Technology, The Netherlands |
| Colette Rolland | Université Paris 1 Panthéon-Sorbonne, France |
| Narcyz Roztocki | State University of New York at New Paltz, USA |
| Abdel-Badeeh Mohamed Salem | Ain Shams University, Egypt |
| Bernadette Sharp | Staffordshire University, UK |
| Alexander Smirnov | SPIIRAS, Russian Academy of Sciences, Russian Federation |
| Ronald Stamper | Measur Ltd., UK |
| François Vernadat | European Court of Auditors, France |

## Program Committee

| | |
|---|---|
| Lena Aggestam | Region Västra Götaland, The Hospital in Alingsås, Sweden |
| Miguel Angel Martinez Aguilar | University of Murcia, Spain |
| Adeel Ahmad | Laboratoire d'Informatique Signal et Image de la Côte d'Opale, France |
| Antonia Albani | University of St. Gallen, Switzerland |
| Patrick Albers | ESEO - Ecole Superieure D'Electronique de L'Ouest, France |
| Abdullah Alnajim | Qassim University, Saudi Arabia |
| Mohammad Al-Shamri | Ibb University, Yemen |
| Rainer Alt | University of Leipzig, Germany |
| Andreas S. Andreou | Cyprus University of Technology, Cyprus |
| Wudhichai Assawinchaichote | King Mongkut's University of Technology Thonburi, Thailand |
| Tamara Babaian | Bentley University, USA |
| Cecilia Baranauskas | State University of Campinas - Unicamp, Brazil |
| Rémi Bastide | ISIS - CUFR Jean-François Champollion, France |
| Bernhard Bauer | University of Augsburg, Germany |
| Orlando Belo | University of Minho, Portugal |
| Jorge Bernardino | Polytechnic Institute of Coimbra - ISEC, Portugal |
| Frederique Biennier | INSA Lyon, France |

| | |
|---|---|
| Sandro Bimonte | Irstea, France |
| Jean-Louis Boulanger | CERTIFER, France |
| Coral Calero | University of Castilla – La Mancha, Spain |
| Daniel Antonio Callegari | PUC-RS Pontificia Universidade Catolica do Rio Grande do Sul, Brazil |
| Luis M. Camarinha-Matos | New University of Lisbon, Portugal |
| Manuel Isidoro Capel-Tuñón | University of Granada, Spain |
| Glauco Carneiro | Salvador University (UNIFACS), Brazil |
| Angélica Caro | University of Bio-Bio, Chile |
| Nunzio Casalino | Università degli Studi Guglielmo Marconi, Italy |
| Marco Antonio Casanova | PUC-Rio, Brazil |
| Luca Cernuzzi | Universidad Católica "Nuestra Señora de la Asunción", Paraguay |
| David Chen | Laboratory IMS, France |
| Ming-Puu Chen | National Taiwan Normal University, Taiwan |
| Shiping Chen | CSIRO ICT Centre Australia, Australia |
| Shu-Ching Chen | Florida International University, USA |
| Max Chevalier | Institut de Recherche en Informatique de Toulouse UMR 5505, France |
| Nan-Hsing Chiu | Chien Hsin University of Science and Technology, Taiwan |
| Witold Chmielarz | Warsaw University, Poland |
| William Cheng-Chung Chu | Tunghai University, Taiwan |
| Daniela Barreiro Claro | Universidade Federal da Bahia (UFBA), Brazil |
| Pedro Gouvêa Coelho | State University of Rio de Janeiro, Brazil |
| Francesco Colace | Università Degli Studi di Salerno, Italy |
| Cesar Collazos | Universidad del Cauca, Colombia |
| Antonio Corral | University of Almeria, Spain |
| Mariela Cortés | State University of Ceará, Brazil |
| Karl Cox | University of Brighton, UK |
| Sharon Cox | Birmingham City University, UK |
| Broderick Crawford | Pontificia Universidad Catolica de Valparaiso, Chile |
| Maria Damiani | University of Milan, Italy |
| Vincenzo Deufemia | Università di Salerno, Italy |
| Dulce Domingos | University of Lisbon, Portugal |
| César Domínguez | Universidad de La Rioja, Spain |
| António Dourado | University of Coimbra, Portugal |
| Juan C. Dueñas | Universidad Politécnica de Madrid, Spain |
| Alan Eardley | Staffordshire University, UK |
| Sophie Ebersold | Université Toulouse II-LeMirail, France |
| Hans-Dieter Ehrich | Technische Universität Braunschweig, Germany |
| Fabrício Enembreck | Pontifical Catholic University of Paraná, Brazil |
| Sean Eom | Southeast Missouri State University, USA |
| Hossam Faheem | Ain Shams University, Egypt |
| João Faria | FEUP, University of Porto, Portugal |

| Jamel Feki | University of Sfax, Tunisia |
| Edilson Ferneda | Catholic University of Brasília, Brazil |
| Maria João Silva Costa Ferreira | Universidade Portucalense, Portugal |
| Paulo Ferreira | INESC-ID/IST, Portugal |
| George Feuerlicht | University of Technology, Sydney (UTS), Australia |
| Barry Floyd | California Polytechnic State University, USA |
| Rita Francese | Università degli Studi di Salerno, Italy |
| Ariel Frank | Bar-Ilan University, Israel |
| Ana Fred | Instituto de Telecomunicações/IST, Portugal |
| Lixin Fu | University of North Carolina, Greensboro, USA |
| Mariagrazia Fugini | Politecnico di Milano, Italy |
| Maria Ganzha | SRI PAS and University of Gdansk, Poland |
| Mouzhi Ge | Technical University of Munich, Germany |
| Johannes Gettinger | University of Hohenheim, Germany |
| Daniela Giordano | University of Catania, Italy |
| Raúl Giráldez | Pablo de Olavide University of Seville, Spain |
| Pascual Gonzalez | Universidad de Castilla-La Mancha, Spain |
| Robert Goodwin | Flinders University of South Australia, Australia |
| Raj Gopalan | Curtin University, Australia |
| Feliz Gouveia | University Fernando Pessoa/Cerem, Portugal |
| Virginie Govaere | INRS, France |
| Janis Grabis | Riga Technical University, Latvia |
| Maria Carmen Penadés Gramaje | Universitat Politècnica de València, Spain |
| Gerd Groener | University of Koblenz-Landau, Germany |
| Sven Groppe | University of Lübeck, Germany |
| Tom Gross | Bauhaus University Weimar, Germany |
| Wieslawa Gryncewicz | Wroclaw University of Economics, Poland |
| Slimane Hammoudi | ESEO, MODESTE, France |
| Karin Harbusch | Universität Koblenz-Landau, Germany |
| Markus Helfert | Dublin City University, Ireland |
| Wladyslaw Homenda | Warsaw University of Technology, Poland |
| Wei-Chiang Hong | Oriental Institute of Technology, Taiwan |
| Miguel J. Hornos | University of Granada, Spain |
| Hesuan Hu | Nanyang Technological University, Singapore |
| Kai-I Huang | Tunghai University, Taiwan |
| Miroslav Hudec | University of Economics in Bratislava, Slovak Republic |
| Arturo Jaime | Universidad de La Rioja, Spain |
| Wassim Jaziri | College of Computer Science and Engineering, Saudi Arabia |
| Sabina Jeschke | RWTH Aachen University, Germany |
| Edson Oliveira Jr. | State University of Maringá, Brazil |
| Nikitas Karanikolas | Technological Educational Institute of Athens (TEI-A), Greece |

| Andrea Kienle | University of Applied Sciences, Dortmund, Germany |
| Marite Kirikova | Riga Technical University, Latvia |
| Alexander Knapp | Universität Augsburg, Germany |
| Natallia Kokash | Leiden University, The Netherlands |
| John Krogstie | NTNU, Norway |
| Rob Kusters | Eindhoven University of Technology and Open University of the Netherlands, The Netherlands |
| Wim Laurier | Université Saint-Louis, Belgium |
| Ramon Lawrence | University of British Columbia Okanagan, Canada |
| Jintae Lee | Leeds School of Business at University of Colorado, Boulder, USA |
| Alain Leger | France Telecom Orange Labs, France |
| Daniel Lemire | TELUQ, Canada |
| Joerg Leukel | University of Hohenheim, Germany |
| Lei Li | Hefei University of Technology, China |
| Da-Yin Liao | Applied Wireless Identifications, USA |
| Therese Libourel | University of Montpellier II (IRD,UR, UAG), France |
| Luis Jiménez Linares | University of de Castilla-La Mancha, Spain |
| Panos Linos | Butler University, USA |
| Stephane Loiseau | LERIA, University of Angers, France |
| João Correia Lopes | Universidade do Porto/INESC Porto, Portugal |
| Maria Filomena Cerqueira de Castro Lopes | Universidade Portucalense Infante D. Henrique, Portugal |
| Miguel R. Luaces | Universidade da Coruña, Spain |
| Wendy Lucas | Bentley University, USA |
| André Ludwig | University of Leipzig, Germany |
| Mark Lycett | Brunel University, UK |
| Jose Antonio Macedo | Federal University of Ceara, Brazil |
| Leszek Maciaszek | Wroclaw University of Economics, Poland and Macquarie University, Sydney, Australia |
| Cristiano Maciel | Universidade Federal de Mato Grosso, Brazil |
| Rita Suzana Pitangueira Maciel | Federal University of Bahia, Brazil |
| S. Kami Makki | Lamar University, USA |
| Pierre Maret | Université de Saint Etienne, France |
| Herve Martin | Grenoble University, France Katsuhisa Maruyama, Ritsumeikan University, Japan |
| Viviana Mascardi | University of Genoa, Italy |
| David Martins de Matos | L2F/INESC-ID Lisboa/Instituto Superior Técnico, Portugal |
| Wolfgang Mayer | University of South Australia, Australia |
| Zaamoune Mehdi | Irstea, France |
| Andreas Meier | University of Fribourg, Switzerland |
| Jerzy Michnik | University of Economics in Katowice, Poland |
| Marek Milosz | Lublin University of Technology, Poland |
| Michele Missikoff | IASI-CNR, Italy |

| | |
|---|---|
| Vladimír Modrák | Technical University of Košice, Slovak Republic |
| Ghodrat Moghadampour | Vaasa University of Applied Sciences, Finland |
| Pascal Molli | LINA, University of Nantes, France |
| Lars Mönch | Fern Universität in Hagen, Germany |
| Valérie Monfort | Université de Paris1 Panthéon Sorbonne, France |
| Francisco Montero | University of Castilla-la Mancha, Spain |
| Carlos León de Mora | University of Seville, Spain |
| João Luís Cardoso de Moraes | Federal University of São Carlos, Brazil |
| Fernando Moreira | Universidade Portucalense, Portugal |
| Nathalie Moreno | University of Malaga, Spain |
| Haralambos Mouratidis | University of East London, UK |
| Pietro Murano | University of Salford, UK |
| Tomoharu Nakashima | Osaka Prefecture University, Japan |
| Ovidiu Noran | Griffith University, Australia |
| Jose Angel Olivas | Universidad de Castilla-La Mancha, Spain |
| Andrés Muñoz Ortega | Catholic University of Murcia (UCAM), Spain |
| Samia Oussena | University of West London, UK |
| Sietse Overbeek | University of Duisburg-Essen, Germany |
| Mieczyslaw Owoc | Wroclaw University of Economics, Poland |
| Claus Pahl | Dublin City University, Ireland |
| Tadeusz Pankowski | Poznan University of Technology, Poland |
| Eric Pardede | La Trobe University, Australia |
| Rodrigo Paredes | Universidad de Talca, Chile |
| Massimiliano Di Penta | University of Sannio, Italy |
| Dana Petcu | West University of Timisoara, Romania |
| Yannis A. Phillis | Technical University of Crete, Greece |
| Josef Pieprzyk | Macquarie University, Australia |
| Luis Ferreira Pires | University of Twente, The Netherlands |
| Ángeles Saavedra Places | University of A Coruña, Spain |
| Malgorzata Plechawska-Wojcik | Lublin University of Technology, Poland |
| Geert Poels | Ghent University, Belgium |
| Michal Polasik | Nicolaus Copernicus University, Poland |
| Luigi Pontieri | National Research Council (CNR), Italy |
| Jolita Ralyte | University of Geneva, Switzerland |
| T. Ramayah | Universiti Sains Malaysia, Malaysia |
| Pedro Ramos | Instituto Superior das Ciências do Trabalho e da Empresa, Portugal |
| Francisco Regateiro | Instituto Superior Técnico, Portugal |
| Ulrich Reimer | University of Applied Sciences St. Gallen, Switzerland |
| Nuno de Magalhães Ribeiro | Universidade Fernando Pessoa, Portugal |
| Michele Risi | University of Salerno, Italy |
| Alfonso Rodriguez | University of Bio-Bio, Chile |
| Daniel Rodriguez | University of Alcalá, Spain |
| Oscar Mario Rodriguez-Elias | Institute of Technology of Hermosillo, Mexico |

| | |
|---|---|
| Erik Rolland | University of California at Merced, USA |
| Luciana Alvim Santos Romani | Embrapa Agriculture Informatics, Brazil |
| Jose Raul Romero | University of Cordoba, Spain |
| David G. Rosado | University of Castilla-la Mancha, Spain |
| Gustavo Rossi | Lifia, Argentina |
| Artur Rot | Wroclaw University of Economics, Poland |
| Francisco Ruiz | Universidad de Castilla-La Mancha, Spain |
| Belen Vela Sanchez | Rey Juan Carlos University, Spain |
| Luis Enrique Sánchez | Sicaman Nuevas Tecnologias S.L., Spain |
| Manuel Filipe Santos | University of Minho, Portugal |
| Jurek Sasiadek | Carleton University, Canada |
| Isabel Seruca | Universidade Portucalense, Portugal |
| Ahm Shamsuzzoha | University of Vaasa, Finland |
| Jianhua Shao | Cardiff University, UK |
| Mei-Ling Shyu | University of Miami, USA |
| Markus Siepermann | TU Dortmund, Germany |
| Alberto Rodrigues Silva | Instituto Superior Técnico, Portugal |
| Sean Siqueira | Federal University of the State of Rio de Janeiro, Brazil |
| Hala Skaf-molli | Nantes University, France |
| Michel Soares | Federal University of Sergipe, Brazil |
| Ricardo Soto | Pontificia Universidad Catolica de Valparaiso, Chile |
| Chantal Soule-Dupuy | University of Toulouse 1, France |
| Chris Stary | Johannes Kepler University of Linz, Austria |
| Stefan Strecker | University of Hagen, Germany |
| Vijayan Sugumaran | Oakland University, USA |
| Hiroki Suguri | Miyagi University, Japan |
| Lily Sun | University of Reading, UK |
| Jerzy Surma | Warsaw School of Economics, Poland |
| Miroslav Sveda | Brno University of Technology, Czech Republic |
| Ryszard Tadeusiewicz | AGH University of Science and Technology, Poland |
| Tania Tait | Maringá State University, Brazil |
| Mohan Tanniru | Oakland University, USA |
| Sotirios Terzis | University of Strathclyde, UK |
| Claudine Toffolon | Université du Maine, France |
| Ying-Mei Tu | Chung Hua University, Taiwan |
| Theodoros Tzouramanis | University of the Aegean, Greece |
| José Ângelo Braga de Vasconcelos | Universidade Atlântica, Portugal |
| Michael Vassilakopoulos | University of Thessaly, Greece |
| Christine Verdier | LIG - Joseph Fourier University of Grenoble, France |
| Bing Wang | University of Hull, UK |
| Dariusz Wawrzyniak | Wroclaw University of Economics, Poland |
| Hans Weghorn | BW Cooperative State University of Stuttgart, Germany |
| Hans Weigand | Tilburg University, The Netherlands |
| Viacheslav Wolfengagen | Institute JurInfoR, Russian Federation |

| | |
|---|---|
| Ouri Wolfson | University of Illinois at Chicago, USA |
| Stanislaw Wrycza | University of Gdansk, Poland |
| Ing-Long Wu | National Chung Cheng University, Taiwan |
| Mudasser Wyne | National University, USA |
| Hongji Yang | De Montfort University, UK |
| Eugenio Zimeo | University of Sannio, Italy |

## Additional Reviewers

| | |
|---|---|
| María Luisa Rodríguez Almendros | University of Granada, Spain |
| Almudena Sierra Alonso | Universidad Rey Juan Carlos, Spain |
| Pierluigi Assogna | Libera Università Internazionale Degli Studi Sociali (luiss), Italy |
| Alexander Bock | University of Duisburg-Essen, Germany |
| Emmanuel Desmontils | Faculté des Sciences et des Techniques, Université de Nantes, France |
| Adolfo Almeida Duran | Federal University of Bahia, Brazil |
| Fausto Fasano | University of Molise, Italy |
| Tiago Ferreto | PUCRS, Brazil |
| Francesco Folino | ICAR-CNR, Italy |
| Francisco Javier Gil-Cumbreras | Pablo de Olavide University, Spain |
| Massimo Guarascio | ICAR-CNR, Italy |
| Agnieszka Jastrzebska | Warsaw University of Technology, Poland |
| Paloma Cáceres García de Marina | Rey Juan Carlos University, Spain |
| Asmat Monaghan | Brunel University, UK |
| Luã Marcelo Muriana | UFF, Brazil |
| Aurora Ramirez | University of Córdoba, Spain |
| Monica Sebillo | Università degli Studi di Salerno, Italy |
| Panagiotis Symeonidis | Aristotle University of Thessaloniki, Greece |
| Pawel Szmeja | Polish Academy of Sciences, Poland |
| Francesco Taglino | CNR-IASI, Italy |
| Mahsa Teimourikia | Politecnico di Milano, Italy |

## Invited Speakers

| | |
|---|---|
| Kecheng Liu | University of Reading, UK |
| Jan Dietz | Delft University of Technology, The Netherlands |
| Antoni Olivé | Universitat Politècnica de Catalunya, Spain |
| José Tribolet | INESC-ID/Instituto Superior Técnico, Portugal |
| Hans-J. Lenz | Freie Universität Berlin, Germany |

# Contents

**Information Systems Analysis and Specification**

**Software Agents and Internet Computing**

## Human-Computer Interaction

## Enterprise Architecture

# Invited Papers

# Semiotics in Digital Visualisation

Kecheng Liu[✉] and Chekfoung Tan

Informatics Research Centre, University of Reading,
Whiteknights campus, Reading, RG6 6UD, UK
k.liu@henley.ac.uk, c.f.tan@pgr.reading.ac.uk

**Abstract.** Digital visualisation is a way of representing data and information with the aid of digital means, engages human interpretation on information in order to gain insights in a particular context. Digital visualisation is always purposeful that will illustrate relationships; discover patterns and interdependencies; or generate some hypothesis or theory. However, it is still bound to the semantic (interpretation of visual displays and the meaning in the context) and pragmatic (effect and intention to be achieved) issues. These two issues can be addressed by semiotics, a formal doctrine of signs introduced by Peirce back in the 1930s; where digital visualisation is seen as a process of abduction. Abduction is a key process of scientific inquiry, which involves norms. Norms are patterns, regulations, rules and laws which are the reflection of knowledge in a cultural group or an organisation; which has an effect on the human interpretation on information. This paper pioneers a new perspective of digital visualisation by positioning digital visualisation as a process of abduction and proposes the key principles in digital visualisation.

**Keywords:** Semiotics · Digital visualisation · Norms · Abduction process · Hypotheses formation

## 1 Introduction

Digital visualisation is a way of representing data and information with the aid of digital means. It ranges from a simple form such as a graph or chart to a complex form like animated visualisations that allows user to interact with the underlying data through direct manipulation [1]. The notion of digital visualisation engages human interpretation on information in order to gain insights in a particular context [2–4]. Hence, it is a complex process involving multiple disciplines, including the socio-technical element. The social element relates to human perception in interpreting information. The technical element on the other hand, refers to the technology used to enable visualisation, for example the SAS suite [5] that offers visual analytics to support interactive dashboard and reporting.

A typical process of digital visualisation starts from data collection, followed by data transformation and filtering, and finally the visual display [adapted from 4]. The primary goal of digital visualisation is enhance the efficiency of understanding of certain phenomenon through visualised data and information; but it also aims to address latent

© Springer International Publishing Switzerland 2015
J. Cordeiro et al. (Eds.): ICEIS 2014, LNBIP 227, pp. 3–13, 2015.
DOI: 10.1007/978-3-319-22348-3_1

aspects, such as semantic and pragmatic issues [6, 7]. The semantic issues are related to the interpretation of visual displays and the meaning in the context. The pragmatic issues are concerned with the effect and intention to be achieved on the users through digital visualisation.

Digital visualisation is always purposeful that will illustrate relationships; discover patterns and interdependencies; or generate some hypothesis or theory. The user's hypothesis would very much influence on what data would be interested in the analysis and be included in the visualisation. Therefore, there will be always a set of questions highly relevant in any visualisation, such as data availability, access, format (data itself and display format), meaning (i.e. interpretation), purpose of data presented, and effect of visualised data on the recipients. Such questions can be best answered by drawing input from semiotics.

This paper pioneers a new perspective on digital visualisation by positioning digital visualisation as a process of abduction. Section 2 illustrates the components, process and the challenges of digital visualisation. Section 3 describes the semiotics perspective to digital visualisation. Section 4 suggests a set of principles for digital visualisation aftermath of the notion of semiotics. This paper is concluded with the future research insights by intertwining the notion of semiotics, abduction process especially with digital visualisation.

## 2   Digital Visualisation

### 2.1   Components and Process

Digital visualisation deals with three components: data, information and knowledge [adapted from 8], in which can be explained by social and technical perspective (see Fig. 1). In the social facet, human users perceive data in the forms of e.g. figures, numbers and charts. Such a presentation of the data enables the human users to understand the data better and to obtain information efficiently through the processing of the data, which bring in the meaning and insight of the data to the user. In the technical facet, digital visualisation assists the users further to gain knowledge through interaction, interpretation and abstraction of data and information to produce generic types or patterns based on classifications of contexts and application domains. Table 1 summarises the description of the components of digital visualisation from the social and technical perspective.

The process of digital visualisation captures the intentions from users, exposes the effect of data and addresses the purposes of data analysis through graphical images. This is reflected in the four main stages in the process of digital visualisation [adapted from 4, 9] (see Fig. 2): (1) *data collection*, (2) *data transformation and filtering*, (3) *visual mapping* and, (4) *display and interaction*. In the *data collection* stage, data is gathered through various sources. The collected data can be structured or unstructured data. According to Baars and Kemper [10], the structured data is data that has predefined format and can be processed by computing equipment. Unstructured data is data that usually does not have a specific format such as social media data, images, and audio files [11]. The *data transformation and filtering* stage

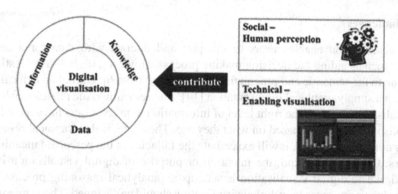

**Fig. 1.** Social and technical facet of digital visualization.

**Table 1.** Description of the digital visualisation components.

| Component | Social (Human Perception) | Technical (Enabling Visualisation) |
|---|---|---|
| Data | Figures, numbers, text | Representing abstracted data schematic form, including attributes or variables for the units of data (direct display, no deep processing) |
| Information | Processed data that answers *what*, *who*, *where*, *when*, *why* and *how* questions | Showing/emphasising on relationship between data items; with interpretation; show semantics |
| Knowledge | Application of data that explains the type or patterns of a situation or context | Representing the effect on organisation through visual analytics on social, on economy, e.g. drop on sales, decision-making by looking at alternatives |

explores the collected data through various techniques such as extract, transform and load (ETL) and data mining. Data are extracted from the source databases are transformed into a desired format for analysis purpose, and then loaded into the destination databases [12]. Some of the common data mining techniques in dealing with structured data are clustering and categorisation for visualisation purpose. The *visual mapping* stage contains a graphic engine that manipulate the process of transforming the focus data with their geometric primitives (e.g. points, lines) and attributes (e.g. colour, position, size) to image data. The *display and interaction* stage provides the user interface control that enables users to interact with data from multiple perspectives (e.g. drill down, expand), where visual analytics take place [13]. This is the stage where meaning is interpreted by uses when interacting with data.

## 2.2  Challenges

Digital visualisation enables users to interpret and interact with data for a certain purpose, such as aiding the decision making process. However, digital visualisation is still prone to the semantic and pragmatic issue [adapted from 6]. Digital visualisation is more than a simply graphical representation [14]. The semantic issue relates to whether the visualisation conveys the right level of information to users. Users have a tendency to establish a relationship based on what they see. Therefore, if the graphical representation is not pointedly used, it will exacerbate the fallacies of the perceived meaning by the users. On the other hand, the intention or purpose of digital visualisation is not reflected, where digital visualisation is seen as an analytical reasoning process [15]. There is always a purpose how digital visualisation should be designed. There are usually many data sources are required to achieve the purpose. Hence, this leads to challenges such as data reliability, selection of the right information and the selection of the right graphics to visualise information. Thus digital visualisation is only effective when there is a clear purpose (guided by the pragmatic instance) on how data should be visualised so it conveys a clear meaning to users (incorporated with the semantic aspect) [13].

## 3  Semiotics Perspective to Digital Visualisation

### 3.1  Signs and Norms

Semiotics, a formal doctrine of signs introduced by Peirce back in the 1930s [16], shows great relevance to digital visualisation. A special branch is organisational semiotics which has been developed by Stamper and his colleagues [17] to study the effective use of information in business context. Data, under the study through visualisation, are signs.

The human interpretation on information is closely related to the five types of norms (see Table 2 for the description of norms): perceptual, cognitive, evaluative, denotative and behavioural [18]. Norms as a generic term are patterns, regulations, rules and laws which are the reflection of knowledge in a cultural group or an organisation [19]. Norms and signs (data) are intertwined [20]. In this research context, norms are employed to interpret the signs; where a sign is a data object that conveys information and produces an effect towards users in directing or prescribing users' action, such as an action of making a decision.

### 3.2  Abduction in Piercean Logical System

Abduction is a reasoning approach introduced in Piercean logical system [16], together with induction and deduction. Abduction, according to Peirce [16], is a form of semiotics interpretation [21], that guides the process of forming a hypothesis, which leads to introducing new ideas. Deduction is the process of explaining the hypothesis; and induction, is the process of evaluating the hypothesis. Abduction aims to find the best explanation of the observed phenomenon [22]. In Piercean logical system, abduction contributes to the human understanding of a phenomenon, by making sense of the observed signs [adapted from 23].

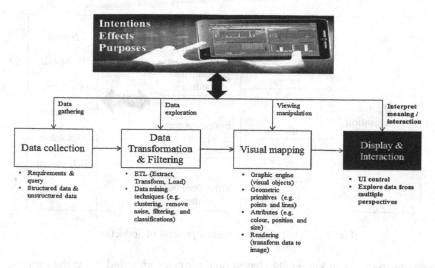

**Fig. 2.** The process of digital visualization.

Kovács and Spens's [24] and Thagard's [25] propose the abduction process based on Peirce's [16] definition on abduction. The abduction process starts by a puzzlement (an observed phenomenon) that leads to a search for explanation, followed by using prior knowledge to establish a hypothesis and validating the hypothesis by conducting more observations.

### 3.3  Digital Visualisation Is a Process of Abduction

From a semiotic perspective, digital visualisation is a process of abduction which is a key process of scientific inquiry, i.e. a process of generating new knowledge. Peirce's abduction is a reasoning approach to fashion a hypothesis of the observed phenomenon, hence the more clues that are collected, it is more likely the hypothesis leads to a truthful conclusion [21]. Digital visualisation is therefore seen as a process of abduction from a semiotics perspective; in which abduction is a key process of scientific inquiry for generating new knowledge. On the basis, the process of abduction involves the norms extensively. When encountering with a new phenomenon, prior knowledge will enable us to produce some initial, but often, plausible explanations. Abduction thus allows us to generate hypotheses (which should be plausible) and further to determine which hypothesis or proposition to be tested [23, 26]. This aligns with Peirce's definition on abduction as "the process of forming explanatory hypotheses", and the "only kind of argument which starts a new idea" (Peirce, 1935).

Figure 3 illustrates the four key stages in digital visualisation as a process of abduction: (1) *search for explanation,* (2) *generation of hypotheses,* (3) *evaluation and acceptance of hypotheses* and, (4) *effect from the hypotheses.* In the *search for explanation* stage, users establish an initial hypothesis based on what they see through digital visualisation (e.g. graphical display of abstract information). This stage commences the process of abduction. In the *generation of hypotheses* stage, users

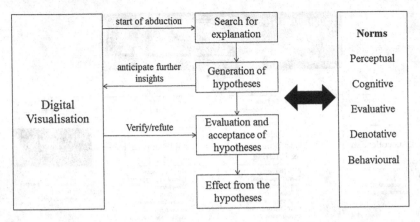

**Fig. 3.** Digital visualisation is a process of abduction.

derive some patterns of knowledge based on their prior knowledge. At the same time, users are anticipating for further insights grounded on what they see. Visual analytics take place here to enable users interact with data by providing navigations such as drill down for more information. In the *evaluation and acceptance of hypotheses* stage, users verify or refute the perceived visual objects based on their prior knowledge. This stage adopts Popper's [27] refutationism approach, where the formed hypothesis can be refuted by the observed facts. And lastly, in the stage of *effect from the hypotheses,* users reaffirm or refine the established hypothesis. The five types of norms (perceptual, cognitive, evaluative, denotative and behavioural) correspond with each stage in the process of abduction in digital visualisation, which will be illustrated in Sect. 4.2.

## 4    The Principles of Digital Visualisation

Research leads us to believe that the three principles are important in digital visualisation as illustrated in the following sub sections.

### 4.1    Digital Visualisation as Shared Semiosis

Digital visualisation is a sign-process that involves the production and consumption of signs. Any digital visualisation will begin with the awareness of context. The design of a digital visualisation is usually determined by certain purposes and effects that are intended to be achieved. On the production side of this process, the producer may wish to achieve a certain effect as he or she has certain intention and purposes through the visualisation. The producer of the visualisation may situate the visualisation in a context and relate it to some purposes. On the consumption side, a user, who could be any one who sees the visual display in a different context and for a different purpose, may be led to an effect that is same or totally different from what is intended by the producer. To ensure the success of the communication through the use of visual display, it is important

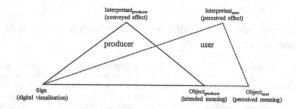

**Fig. 4.** Shared semiosis process engaging producer and user.

to understand the semiotics in the production and utilisation of visualisation. Figure 4 illustrates the shared semiotic processes (i.e. semiosis) engaging the producer and user. It is therefore vital to see digital visualisation as a shared semiosis; where there is an agreement made between the producer and user on how and what data should be visualised, and producer should understand what purpose (or context) user tries to achieve through digital visualisation.

### 4.2 Digital Visualisation as Norm-Centric Activities

Effective digital visualisation heavily relies on knowledge expressed as norms. Digital visualisation is seen as an interactive artefact, which is usually designed based on producer's reasoning [28]. As mentioned in Sect. 4.1, the design of digital visualisation should engage producer and user. Norms serve as the foundation and drive for the design of a digital visualisation for the producer. On the other hand, the user incorporates norms into the digital visualisation for discovering new knowledge. Both the producer and user will invoke their norms in production (design of the graphical display) and utilisation (use of the graphical display to gain new knowledge and perform certain actions). Table 2 illustrates the five types of norms and their effect on the producer (or the designer) and user by taking the digital visualisation design for the monthly sales report for a department store as an example. The graphical display should clearly indicate how the values relate to one another, represent the figure correctly and make it easy to navigate between figures. As digital visualisation is a process of abduction, the central role of the subject who is engaged in the process must be recognised. If the goal of the digital visualisation is to discover new knowledge, interactivity of digital visualisation to allow the user's manipulation of data in visualisation is essential.

### 4.3 Digital Visualisation as Artefacts as Well as Process

Digital visualisation is seen as an artefact, where it is a set of graphical displays (e.g. charts and graphs) that conveys information. The graphical displays produce effect towards designers (who determine the design of the graphical display) and users (who use the displayed data to perform certain actions). The graphical display should clearly translate the abstract information, that can be easily, efficiently, accurately and meaningfully perceived [29]. At the same time, there is an important feature (or it can be called affordance) of digital visualisation is that it is not just static display but allows (or affords) interactive inquiry. Digital visualisation hence is also seen as a process of

**Table 2.** Norms and their effect in Digital Visualisation (with an example of a monthly sales report for a department store).

| Types of norms | Descriptions | Effect on producer | Effect on user |
|---|---|---|---|
| Perceptual | Relate to how human perceive signs in an environment. For example, the distance between two bollards is wide enough to drive the car through | Relate to the perception on sales figures. For example, sales figures are described by month, categories of products and customer gender | Apply the prior knowledge to perceive the sales figures. For example, sales figures displayed on the chart are presented in month and categories |
| Cognitive | Relate to how human interpret the observed signs. For example, an illuminated red light above an orange and green means stop | Affiliate with the interpretation of the sales figures. For example, the low sales figure of product A means the product is not selling well in the particular month. This leads to a graphic representation to highlight the poor sales | Employ the prior knowledge to interpret the sales figures. For example, the lowest bar that represents product A in the bar chart means the poor sales of product A in the month |
| Evaluative | Explain why human have beliefs, values and objectives. For example, frankness in debating between employee and boss; openness in voicing personal views | Associate with the assessment of the sales figure. For example, lower sales figures should attract more attention in the display by certain distinctive shape or colour | Assess the performance. For example, the low sales figures identify poor performance through the aid of digital visualisation which otherwise may not be noticed |
| Denotative | Direct the choices of signs for signifying based on the cultural background. For example, stop signals are red and octagonal | Relate to the selection of the graphical display that best represents the sales figure. For example, red means under performance and green means acceptable performance that meets the expectation | Deploy the shared knowledge of shaping and colour coding between the producer and the user. For example, certain shape or colour represent certain meanings |
| Behavioural | Govern human behaviour within the regular patterns. For example, if a library book is overdue than the borrower must pay a fine | Relate graphic information with actions. For example, the poor performance will be linked with the production of some warning messages for attention | Adopt the business knowledge to perform actions. For example, poor sales lead to certain corrective actions such as strengthening marketing effort or reviewing the price |

abduction. Affordance, originated by Gibson [30], is extended to the study of the real world for understanding patterns of human behaviour. Digital visualisation can assist human to interact with data to enhance understanding of the meaning of data, e.g. to acquire more information. Furthermore, it will also enable one to discover pattern, regularities and norms from the visualised data, e.g. to obtain knowledge related to types of problems and situations. With such interactivity, a user is able to explore data visually to generate, refine and testify his or her hypothesis as an abductive reasoning process.

# 5   Conclusions and Future Research Insights

This paper initiates a new perspective on digital visualisation by positioning digital visualisation as a process of abduction; through the generation, verification, refutation and refinement of hypotheses. Some insights have been provided in the components and process of digital visualisation and the semantic and pragmatic challenges embedded within digital visualisation. Challenges in human perception and intention in digital visualisation have been addressed by incorporating norms into the semiotics of visualisation and visual analytics. This paper posits three key principles, i.e. digital visualisation is seen as: (1) a shared semiosis, (2) norm-centric activities and, (3) artefacts as well as process. These three key principles contribute to how digital visualisation should be designed (from the producer's perspective) and how digital visualisation helps in gaining new knowledge when new patterns and relationships are discovered (from the user's perspective).

This paper has established a vivid implication of semiotics to digital visualisation. There are three main future research insights proposed on this basis. First of all, researchers can adopt the three key principles suggested, especially the utilisation of norms to increase the interactivity of digital visualisation. The interactive feature should be able to draw and keep the attention of users, and enable users to drill down into data and customise reporting [6]. In addition, users should be able to interact with each other through information sharing.

The second potential area that researchers can look into is to understand the perspective anticipated by users in manipulating the data. In relation to the interactivity of digital visualisation, it is expected that the users will become more used to interpreting data and creating new knowledge. Researchers should look into the human factors, the norms in perceiving and reacting to visualisation result [14] (see Table 2).

The third area researchers can explore is the application of norms captured through the abduction process into the technical implementation. Apart from the technicality of the graphical display, researchers can focus on data collection, data processing and analysis, in conjunction with the trend of big data. Digital visualisation should enable users to do real time data analysis; and has the hold data in-memory in which it is accessible to multiple users.

**Acknowledgements.** We would like to thank Dr Huiying Gao, visiting scholar to the Informatics Research Centre of Henley Business School, University of Reading, from School of Management and Economics of Beijing Institute of Technology, for her valuable and insightful comments to this paper.

# References

1. Chen, C.-H., Hrdle, W., Unwin, A.: Handbook of data visualization. Springer-Verlag, Heidelberg (2008)
2. Czernicki, B.: Introduction to data visualizations. In: Czernicki, B. (ed.) Next-Generation Business Intelligence Software with Silverlight 3, pp. 127–164. A press, New York (2010)

3. Robert, S.: Information Visualization - Design for Interaction. Pearson Educated Limited, Essex (2007)
4. Ware, C.: Information visualization: perception for design. Elsevier, Somerville (2013)
5. SAS.: SAS Visual Analytics, 28 Feb 2014. http://www.sas.com/en_us/software/business-intelligence/visual-analytics.html
6. Azzam, T., et al.: Data Visualization and Evaluation. New Dir. Eval. **2013**(139), 7–32 (2013)
7. Tufte, E.R.: Beautiful evidence, vol. 1. Graphics Press, Cheshire (2006)
8. Chen, M., et al.: Data, information, and knowledge in visualization. IEEE Comput. Graph. Appl. **29**(1), 12–19 (2009)
9. Liu, S., Cui, W., Wu, Y., Liu, M.: A survey on information visualization: recent advances and challenges. Vis. Comput. 1–21 (2014)
10. Baars, H., Kemper, H.-G.: Management support with structured and unstructured data—an integrated business intelligence framework. Inf. Syst. Manage. **25**(2), 132–148 (2008)
11. Zikopoulos, P., et al.: Harness the Power of Big Data the IBM Big Data Platform. McGraw Hill Professional, New York (2012)
12. Singhal, A.: An Overview of Data Warehouse, OLAP and Data Mining Technology, In: Data Warehousing and Data Mining Techniques for Cyber Security, pp. 1–23. Springer, New york(2007)
13. Davenport, T., Merino, M.: State of the Art Practice with Visual Analytics. Harvard Business Review, New York (2013)
14. Alexandre, D.S., Tavares, J.M.R.: Introduction of human perception in visualization. Int. J. Imaging Robot. **4**(10), 45–69 (2010)
15. Thomas, J.J., Cook, K.A. (eds.): Illuminating the path: The research and development agenda for visual analytics. IEEE Computer Society Press, Los Alamitos (2005)
16. Peirce, C.S.: Collected Papers of Charles Sanders Peirce: Pragmaticisms and Pragnoaticism, Scientific Metaphysics, vol. 5-6. Belknap Press, Cambridge (1935)
17. Stamper, R.: Organisational semiotics: Informatics without the computer. In: Liu, K., et al. (eds.) Information, Organisation and Technology: Studies in Organisational Semiotics, pp. 115–171. Kluwer Academic Publishers, Boston (2001)
18. Stamper, R., et al.: Understanding the roles of signs and norms in organizations-a semiotic approach to information systems design. Behav. Inf. Technol. **19**(1), 15–27 (2000)
19. Liu, K.: Semiotics in information systems engineering. Cambridge University Press, Cambridge (2000)
20. Stamper, R.: Information systems as a social science. In: Bouissac, P. (ed.) Information System Concepts: An Integrated Discipline Emerging. IFIP — The International Federation for Information Processing, pp. 1–51. Springer, New York (2000)
21. Moriarty, S.E.: Abduction: a theory of visual interpretation. Commun. Theory **6**(2), 167–187 (1996)
22. Wirth, U.: What is abductive inference? In: Bouissac, P. (ed.) Encyclopedia of Semiotics, pp. 1–3. Oxford University Press: Oxford, New York (1998)
23. Yu, C.H.: Abduction? deduction? induction? is there a logic of exploratory data analysis?. In: Annual Meeting of the American Educational Research Association, ERIC Clearinghouse, New Orleans, LA (1994)
24. Kovács, G., Spens, K.M.: Abductive reasoning in logistics research. Int. J. Phys. Distrib. Logistics Manage. **35**(2), 132–144 (2005)
25. Thagard, P.: Abductive inference: from philosophical analysis to neural mechanisms. In: Feeney, A., Heit, E. (eds.) Inductive Reasoning: Experimental, developmental, and Computational Approaches, pp. 226–247. Cambridge University Press, Cambridge (2007)

26. Gregory, R. Muntermann, J.: Theorizing in design science research: inductive versus deductive approaches. In: Thirty Second International Conference on Information Systems (ICIS 2011), Shanghai (2011)
27. Popper, K.R.: Conjectures and Refutations, vol. 192. Routledge and Kegan Paul, London (1963)
28. de Souza, C.S.: Semiotic engineering: bringing designers and users together at interaction time. Interact. Comput. **17**(3), 317–341 (2005)
29. Few, S.: Data visualization for human perception. In: Soegaard, M., Dam, R.F. (eds.) The Encyclopedia of Human-Computer Interaction, 2nd edn, pp. 93–104. The Interaction Design Foundation, Aarhus (2013)
30. Gibson, J.J.: The Ecological Approach to Visual Perception. Lawrence Erlbaum Associates Inc, Hillsdale (1968)

# Data Fraud Detection: A First General Perspective

Hans-J. Lenz[✉]

Institute of Statistics and Econometrics, Freie Universität Berlin,
Boltzmannstr. 20 K30, 14195 Berlin, Germany
hans-j.lenz@fu-berlin.de

**Abstract.** We try to present a first broad overview on data fraud, and give hints to data fraud detection (DFD). Especially, we show examples of data fraud that happened at anytime of human mankind, all around the world, and affects all kind of human activities. For instance, betrayers are entities of the society, industry, banks, services, health-care, non-profit organizations, art, science, media or even a government or the Vatican. We consider four main areas of data fraud: spy out, plagiarism, manipulation and fabrication of data.

Of course, there is not only interest on data fraud itself but on its detection, too. Although improvements of data fraud detection is evident, it seems that the intellectual creativity and capacity of the betrayers is unlimited. Especially, the Internet with its various services and the mobile communication opened the Pandora box for criminal acts. Furthermore, one may state the hypothesis that while the ethics behavior of people decreases over time the data fraud rate is continuously increasing.

There does not exist an omnibus data fraud detector, and the author supposes there will be never one upcoming due to the heterogeneity of the domain. For instance, compare the domains "spy out" in industry and "data fabrication" of observational or experimental studies in science. It is a matter of fact that the interest and need of science, business and governmental authorities is increasing over time for improving tests of data fraud detection. This paper can be viewed as a modest attempt for stimulating research into this direction.

## 1  Introduction

One can best unfold the complexity of data fraud by classifying fraud into four classes. All of them are driven by three time-invariant features of the societies, business and human beings: Power, glory and money. As saying goes "Knowledge is Power" power is the driving force of **Spy out** in the military and secret service area, while knowledge and profit(money) are the main factors in business. The activities of the secret services of all countries like *Central Intelligence Service (CIA)* or *NSA* in USA, *Military Intelligence (MI6)* in UK, the *Russian secret service (CBP)* etc. go back far into history. No doubt, they have ever had influenced failure and success of military actions at any time. Less power and glory but more profit (money) has been the forcing power of industrial or business

© Springer International Publishing Switzerland 2015
J. Cordeiro et al. (Eds.): ICEIS 2014, LNBIP 227, pp. 14–35, 2015.
DOI: 10.1007/978-3-319-22348-3_2

spy out. There is no sharp boundary to the extensive "silent" storing and analytic analyses of customer's data, mostly without explicit permission. Consider only the massive accumulation of such data by *Amazon*, *Ebay* or *Google*. Together with nearly unlimited **memory** and **Big Data Analytics** it demonstrates the increasing risk of leaving *Recommendation Systems*, simple pull/push systems, and entering into a *Total Information World* with loss of any privacy of anybody, anywhere and anytime as an extension of *ubiquitous computing*.

The second domain of data fraud is related to **Plagiarism**. It concerns mainly the illegal usage of data of somebody else, sometimes existing as *self plagiarism*. Since the start of the digital era plagiarism M.Sc. or Ph.D. studies have gained more and more attention, although plagiarism is not limited to master or doctoral studies, cf. plagiarism happening in composing, drawing and painting. As we shall see later the main interest in *plag* detection in the domain *PhD dissertations* is caused by spectacular cases and the development of improved methods (citation based plag detection besides of substring matching), [4], and "swarm intelligence". The last approach makes use of the efficiency of many, more or less independently acting *plag hunters* pooling information about the same entity.

Our main interest, however, is devoted to **Data Manipulation**. Its main characteristic is given by the dishonest manipulation of existing own or foreign data. The objective is gaining prestige or making money. Evidently, data manipulation happened at any time, anywhere and every domain of life is influenced. For instance, the annual fraud rate of the new U.S. health care system is estimated to be about 10%, [29]. Consider the scandalous manipulation of clinical trails at the Medical University of Innsbruck (MUI), Austria, by Dr. H. Strasser, [19], or the Libor 3(5)-months interest rate manipulation jointly performed by a cartel of *Deutsche Bank, Royal Bank of Scotland (RBS), Union Bank of Switzerland (UBS)*, and *Barclays Bank*, UK, [20]. Greece fudged its annual depths-GDP rates in the years before the country applied for entering the Euro zone, [22]. In recent times the dishonest shuffling of ranks for TV shows by non-profit organizations like ADAC, [23], or ZDF, Germany, [24], or even black money transfers and money laundry by the Vatican, [25], caused much attention in the media.

A question of historical interest remains to be answered later: Who is known to be the first betrayer in science? It is a tragedy of science that that profession is more and more inclined to manipulate data gained from empirical (observational or experimental) studies. The causes are simple the pressure caused by the dominating principle "Perish or Publish", the increasing know-how needed for applying sophisticated methods of data science, and the need of fund raising for ongoing research. Yet, there exists a further variant of data fraud which is far beyond the "simple manipulation" we talked about.

**Data Fabrication.** seems to be the most awful or "mostly criminal" form of data fraud. Instead of manipulating data the betrayer selects an easier way of collecting data: He simply generates the artificial data he needs. Evidently, this safes cost and time, and, consequently, increases the chances of fund raising or early publication because application forms or research papers can be submitted with some time lead. Furthermore, the data will perfectly fit the betrayer's

# Ontology
## of Data Fraud

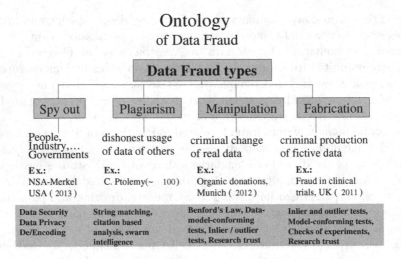

**Fig. 1.** Data fraud types, examples and detectors.

hypothesis or objective if 'professionally" created. A shocking case of such academic data fabrication is related to the Dutch psychologist D. Stapel, Univ. of Tilburg, [21] whose forgery finally was stopped in 2013.

In the following we shall give a short history of spectacular cases of data fraud. We pass by spying out, and turn to plagiarism with a special emphasis on doctoral dissertations.We deeply look at data manipulation, fabrication and the corresponding detection techniques. From the methodological point of view the domains *manipulation* and *fabrication* strongly overlap. Consequently, the same methods of detection can be used, i.e. **Statistics, Data Mining**, and **Machine Learning**. Today, that bundle is labeled **Data Analytics**.

An overview on the four types of data fraud is given in Fig. 1 where we limit ourselves to one example per each fraud type, and list some fraud detectors at the bottom line.

# 2  A Short History of Data Fraud

To best of the author's knowledge the first spectacular case of data fraud (data plagiarism) happened in ancient Egypt. **Claudius Ptolemy** ( 85 – 165 p. C.) was a leading astronomer and mathematician at Alexandria, the center of the antic world of science. He was the father of the Almagest, the famous Arabic star calendar. He used the astronomical data from **Hipparchos of Nicaea** ( 190 – 120 a. C.), but he did not refer to him, [6]. Historians may argue here that the current point of view of referencing might not be adequate for that science period. Today such kind of fraud is called **Data Plagiarism**. The lesson for detecting such a fraud is to carefully **Check the Provenance** of observational data referred to in a publication.

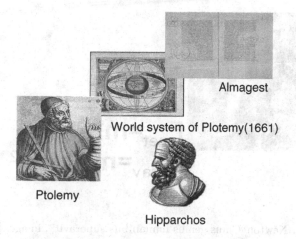

**Fig. 2.** Ptolemy, his centric world view, the Almagest, and Hipparchos, images: [10–13].

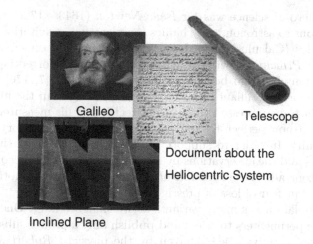

**Fig. 3.** Galileo, his heliocentric system, telescope and plane model, images: [14–17].

There is no doubt that *Galileo Galilei* (1564 – 1641) was one of the giants in science. For example, he made ingenious contributions to astronomy and physics. Especially, his astronomical research on the heliocentric system, and his experiments with bodies sliding down inclined planes are famous. At that time, the devices for measuring run time of moving objects produced "large" measurement errors. Galileo believed in the validness of his cinematic hypotheses, and for supporting them he decided to reduce the measurement errors. Today, there is no doubt that Galileo's experiments could not have been run in its way. As [7, 176] stated "The Genius was motivated by the objective of supporting the final break-through of his ideas." Refer to [8,27] for further details. Simply speaking, motivated by prestige Galileo used data manipulation thus violating the **Principle of Reproduceability** of well-performed experiments.

$$F_{net} = m*a$$
$$F_{grav} = m_1 * m_2 / d^2$$
...

**Fig. 4.** Newton "Cuius genius humanibus superavit", image: [18].

A further hero of science was *Sir Isaac Newton* (1643 - 1726) whose scientific contributions to astronomy, mechanics (acceleration, gravitation and forces) and mathematics (Calculus) opened a new era of physics, especially kinematics. In his book *Principia* Newton convinced due to the reported high precision of his observations far from being legitimate, [7,9]. Or as [7, 176] or [9, 1118] put it "Nobody was so brilliant and effective in cheating than the master mathematician." Newton suppressed the real imprecision of his measurements being anxious about a non perfect fit and casting doubts on his theory in the scientific community. In order to support his hypotheses he faked the output of his experiments and the observations by downsizing the errors. Accordingly, this manipulation contradicts the *Principle of Reproduceability*. His motive certainly was not profit, but fear of loss of prestige.

Data manipulation has many variants as we shall see later. One form is the trick used by experimenters to select and publish only a proper subset of results or runs. A "representative" case is given by the physicist *Robert Millikan*, US Nobel Price Winner, 1868 – 1953. The claim is his strikingly precise measurements of the charge of electrons in 1913 being quite better than those of his rival *Felix Ehrenfeld* who experienced large deviations, [7,8]. Milikan's lab protocols showed later that he published only the 'best 58 out of 140' experiments having smallest measurement variance, [8,34] and [7, 176–177]. Today such a misbehavior of running experiments is called **Experimental Selection Bias** and contradicts, of course, the *Principle of Reproduceability*. Here again *Prestige* combined with Nobel price winning expectations was presumable the driving force of data fraud.

We continue presenting historical cases of data fraud and turn to the *Deutsche Bank* as an example from the business sector. Alternatively, we could have selected from the U.S. economy the *Enron* case with falsification of balance sheets, [47]. *Josef Ackermann*, born 1948, was the chairman of the board of directors 2002–2012, and was responsible for all claims. Under his leadership the *Deutsche Bank* was involved in many scandals like manipulating the prices of

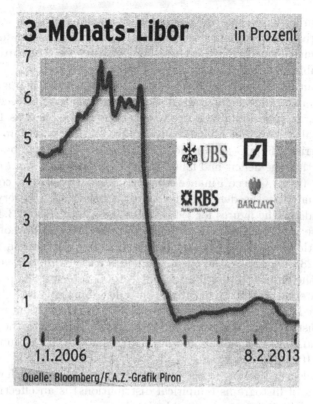

**Fig. 5.** Libor manipulation by the cartel, image: [20].

food products, unlawful $CO_2$-emission permits and financial derivatives trading, and, last but not least, manipulating the 3(6) months Libor interest rate within a bank cartel consisting of Barclays, Deutsche Bank, RBS and UBS, [20]. The legal task of the group was a"fair price fixing" of both interest rates, but the cartel used its economic power for down or upraising of the Libor for making moderate but continuous profits, cf. Fig. 5.

Another domain where forgery typically happens is health care, cf. [29] for fraud detection in the new U.S. medicare system. Especially medical universities are affected institutions because of the pressure to economically manage clinics, fund raising for research or corruption. The last motive was underlying extensive sport doping and manipulation of facts and figures at the Univ. of Freiburg, Germany, cf. [27]. Above we already mentioned the case of illegal experiments at the *Medical University of Innsbruck (MUI)*, Austria, as reported by *Nature*, [19]. In Germany tricksters manipulated the lists of organic transplantations at several of the 49 German transplantation centers like Göttingen, München, Münster, Regensburg etc. [26]. In order to detect fraud in such cases independent experts are employed who checked with diligence all mails, lab protocols, lists, reports, time-schedules and revenues and expenditures vouchers with respect to facts and prior knowledge in a qualitative and quantitative way. We call these (qualitative) manual activities assisted by analytical techniques **Manual Inquest of Data Fraud**. They are based on **Abductive Reasoning**, and are similar to trouble shooting from an investigation point view.

Next, we turn to economics. In this domain data fraud happens for gaining more economic influence or reward. As an example take Greece in the late nineties. The crucial period for Greece to enter the Euro zone was 1997 – 1999. Greece manipulated its official macro-economic statistics, and made the EC member countries, the EC authorities in Bruxelles and Luxembourg and the public believe that the deficit had fallen under the *Maastricht limit* of 3%. However, later the (new) Greece Finance Minister, Mr. *Aligoskoufis*, confessed: "It has been proven that the deficit had not fallen below 3% in every year since 1999." [22]. Indeed, the figures for 1997-1999 were 6.44, 4.13 and 3.38%.

Let us close with politics and consider governments who do not completely obey democratic rules. It is a matter of fact that the elections in Russia 2011 were fudged, [28]. Especially, the result of *Putin's* party *United Russia* is doubtful. Consider the empirical distribution of electoral votes on the percentages of votes in the interval [0, 100]. Typically, such a distribution is bell-shaped and is smoothly curved in the center and at both tails. Due to the evident manipulation of votes the distribution of *Putin's* party is heavily skewed to the right (large percentages), and shows small up-and-down spikes above 30% around the values 35, 40, 45, . . . , 100%, cf. Fig. 6.

The lesson learned from the last type of data manipulation that sometimes simply plotting of histograms (empirical distributions) is an effective "starter" for further investigations on suspectable data.

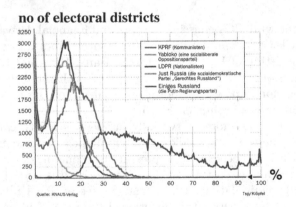

**Fig. 6.** Manipulation of Russian elections in 2011, image: [28] layout modified.

## 3   Spy Out

One can raise the question whether or not **Cheating** by copying text or formulas from neighbors during examinations at school is an entry into the world of spy out or plagiarism, and is abnormal or not. No doubt that kind of spying out is happening at a very low fraud level.

From a historical perspective massive **Spy out** is related to ancient and modern populations and their military actions against other countries. It may be considered as a prerequisite of any war and struggle, and aims for getting better information about the enemy for improving the success of their own attacks. Think only of the empires Greek and Persia, Egypt and Hittites, or Roman and Germanic. The secret services of all modern countries around the globe are expected to deliver information about the rest of the world. After 9/11 the National Security Agency (NSA), USA, has scaled-up its computing facilities for spying out everybody's data on an extreme large scale. The question arises whether "Big brother is watching you" is realized or not. Here any kind of world-wide communication by phone, email, Twitter or any other media is affected. Even encrypting is not at all safe and a guarantee for people's privacy. The fact that even the German chancellor's telephone is tapped by US authorities is a nasty perspective.

Let us leave this domain and turn to economics and business. Telephone fraud became roughly a problem at the end of the eighties. Legal telephone cards with or without a credit were stolen and manipulated by betrayers which made phone calls possible free of any charge. Corruption related to data fraud was recently reported by the German Press Agency and printed in *Der Tagesspiegel*, a leading newspaper in Berlin, Germany. Employees of the sanctuary health assurance company *Debeka* were accused of having tried to get data of state employees candidates from corruptive state employees targeting for new contracts, [5].

As buying and selling is an intrinsic part of daily life of consumers, tricksters and betrayers consider trade as their domain for data fraud. Each trade has a phase "selecting and putting an item into the shopper basket" and "paying". Paying is mostly done by cash, alternatively by EC or credit cards. Forget cyber money here due to its minimal market share. **Card Fraud** is concerned with card theft or the misuse of bank account and PIN data. Therefore, we have the following four classes of fraud, cf. [2]:

- Theft
- Duplicate Generation
- Skimming
- Pishing.

**Theft** is a real fraud if a credit card like VISA, AMERICAN EXPRESS or MASTER is stolen and used for money withdrawals. However, when a card theft is combined with **Card Cloning** (in the sense of duplicate production) things become more tricky and dangerous, and increase the card owner's risk of big monetary losses. The thief simply can withdraw money from various sites. **Skimming** starts at the other end of the buying chain just to say so. Before a consumer pays by cash he has to collect money, for instance, from a teller machine (ATM). Tricksters install a small web cam and a thin keyboard at the ATM's site for catching the bank account or credit card number together with

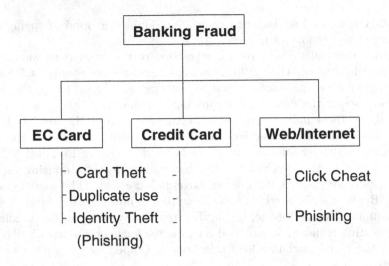

**Fig. 7.** Fraud of banking and internet banking.

the PIN from an innocent client. **Phishing** refers to sending faked emails to users with a subject like "Full mail box" or "Special offer", and asking them for delivering their account, password (PIN) and transaction number (TAN). In a similar way, novice surfers are redirected to false (criminal) links or attracted by special (low priced) offers for visiting specially prepared web pages. When such sites are entered the trickster fishes the bank account, PIN or name, credit card number and safety code for starting his own criminal transactions. Let us add **Advertising Click Fraud** where *Pay per click* systems are manipulated by artificially generating clicks by the betrayer for illegally making money at the expense of the advertising company, [2].

For an overview by a diagram of data fraud related to card usage or Internet banking have a look at Fig. 7. There exists a big bundle of **Multivariate Explorative Data Analysis Techniques** for detecting EC or credit card fraud, especially methods like *Generalized Linear Regression* and *Classification*.

## 4   Plagiarism

As noted above **Plagiarism** is considered to be the dishonest use of data of a second party. It has many facets and exists in many fields of human life like arts, business and science. The motives are either prestige or mostly profit. A short overview is given in the diagram in Fig. 8 below.

We present famous cases of plags: Pirating of documents ("Galileo Forgery") and doctoral dissertation plag of the former German minister of defense, *K.-T. von Guttenberg*. Both cases happened in Germany, and the forgery was proven in 2012 and 2011, respectively.

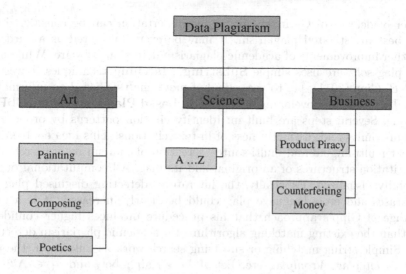

**Fig. 8.** Selected domains of plagiarism.

**Fig. 9.** Discrepancies between the original ("Sidereus Nuncius") and faked book, image: A Galileo Forgery.

Galileo's book "Sidereus Nuncius" was published in 1610, and it is a fact that 80 legal copies are known to exist worldwide. In 2005, surprisingly, a further (faked) copy including until then eighty unknown (faked) ink drawings was offered by art dealers on the international market. The German expert Horst Bredekamp, Humboldt Univ. Berlin, used the drawings from the faked copy in a book he published entitled "Galilei, der Künstler". Finally, in 2012 a British historian proved the forgery done by the Italian M.M. De Caro. His detection caused Bredekamp et al. to edit the book "A Galileo Forgery" where he compiles the events and explains what happened. It is interesting to note that besides of various material analytical techniques **Pattern Matching** of symbols (stars) and characters (L) helped discriminating between the original and faked document, cf. Fig. 9.

One of the most spectacular data plagiarism claims corresponding to doctoral dissertations was caused by the work of K.-T. von Guttenberg, the former minister of defense of Germany. Today his dissertation can be considered one of the best investigated plagiarism. It may be even considered as a yardstick for further improvements of academic plagiarism detection software. While most of the plag software uses simple **Substring Matching** techniques it was the idea of *B. Gipp* (2011), [4], to use a kind of *meta analysis* based on *information retrieval methods* for developing his **Citation based Plag Detection (CbPD)** technique. Several steps are built-in: Identify citation patterns by order, non-lexical proximity and distinctiveness of in-text citations. This idea enabled him to detect multi-lingual and multi-source detection plagiarism by cross-reference of the citation structures of an original and its plag. All computational output is carefully visualized. Especially, the hit rate of detecting disguised plag like paraphrases and cross-language plag could be clearly increased. It is a great advantage of Gipp's approach that his procedure produces higher confidence levels than the existing matching algorithms for academic plagiarism detection, [4, 30]. Simple string matching or substring search work as follows, cf. the plag platforms *citeplag*, *Vroniplag* etc. Let $A$ be an alphabet, and $s_1 \in A^m$ and $s_2 \in A^n$ literal text strings where $m \le n$. Prove $s_1 \subseteq s_2$ or $sim(s_1, s_2) > s_{low}$! We present a barcode representation of the thesis produced by manual inspection done by the members of the GuttenPlag Wiki project, see Fig. 10. The semantics of coloring is as follows:

- red bars: multiple sources plag pages
- black: single source plag pages
- white: no plag pages
- blue: content and bibliography pages.

It was found that 64 % of all lines of the text was plagiarized. More details of *v. Guttenberg's* plagiarism case can be unscrambled by using the plag location and visualization prototype *CitePlag* developed by Gipp(2013). The software offers five citation-based approaches using two documents as input - a plag candidate and the original - [30]. We present only one illustration here. In Fig. 11 the left image shows the dense citation patterns produced by the *Bibliographic Coupling* method in *v. Guttenberg's* thesis. The image to the right shows the concept of citation chunking. Numbers represent matching citations occurring in both documents, and the letter x indicates non-matches.

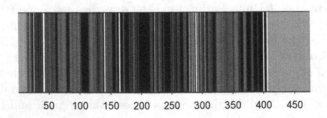

**Fig. 10.** Barcode of Guttenberg's thesis by plag type, image: [31].

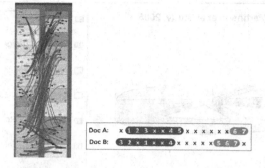

**Fig. 11.** Citation chunking of Guttenberg's thesis and its concept, images: [30].

- *Bibliographic Coupling* is a similarity measure between two reference lists
- *Citation Chunking* is a citation pattern matching irrespective of the order of matching citations
- *Greedy Citation Tiling* identifies longest citation patterns consisting entirely of matching citations in the exact same order
- *Longest Common Citation Sequence* searches for the longest string of citations matching in both documents in identical order
- *Longest Common Sequence of Distinct Citations* includes only the first occurrence of a matching citation. It ignores repeated citations of the same source regardless of occurring in the same order in both documents or not.

## 5    Data Manipulation and Fabrication

As mentioned above **Data Manipulation** and **Fabrication** overlap from a methodological point of view. Of course, the data generation process is quite different. Therefore it makes sense to present fraud detectors for both fraud kinds together.

Data manipulation is the dishonest change of the content of existing own or third party data, irrespectively, whether the content is encapsulated in text documents or not, i.e. tables, diagrams or photos. In most cases numbers are manipulated. Data fabrication is the criminal production of artificial figures driven by gaining power, prestige or profit ("Gier").

In the following we mainly focus on data fraud in science. There exists a lot of studies on the various types of fraud. A recent field study based on interviews and questionnaires was published in *Nature* in 2005, and was authored by *Martinson, Anderson* and *de Vries*, [32]. They addressed $N = 7760$ scientists who got a grant from the National Institutes of Health, USA. The final sample size was $n = 3247$, i.e. the response rate is only slightly less the 42%. The field study was designed as an anonymous self-report based on a standardized questionnaire with $(10+6)$ items of strong and medium fraud types. The study differed between early and mid-career researchers. Figure 12 summarizes the quite disappointing aggregated results.

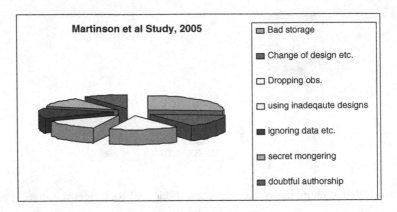

**Fig. 12.** Types of data manipulation, compiled in the Martinson et al. study, image: [32].

Empirical data is no longer accessible, designs are doubtful, and inappropriately application of statistical methods like sub-setting, sequential testing or manipulation of p-values. From the author's point of view the *Martinson* et al. report supports the conjecture of time-stability of such findings in psychology, social science and medicine. Further contributions supporting this hypothesis are due to J.P.A. Ioannidis and L. John, [33,34]. Again, remind yourself that data manipulation exists everywhere at any time in science. For instance, the Japanese stem-cell researcher H. Obokata, Kobe, was forced in 2014 to retract her co-authored papers in *Nature* because of four main allegations raised about her research, [35]:

- Irregularities of published images
- Identical text copied from another own paper without reference (self plag)
- Inconsistencies between published papers and later author's explanation
- Non Reproduceability of experimental results.

Next we present some few cases where statistical methods are not correctly used leading to surprising results. One has to confess that the borderline between non professional usage of statistics and data manipulation is fuzzy.

- Although the diastolic and systolic blood pressure are stochastical dependent, doctors use them independently of each other for their diagnoses worldwide.
- Nowadays, doctors generally consider the PSA value or the related 1 or 5% - confidence intervals as an important tumor marker of the prostate carcinoma. As the calcium, phosphate and PSA value are feedback controlled by the human body, it is doubtful to consider one-dimensional confidence intervals, thus ignoring correlation.
- Fixing a (nominal) probability of the error of first kind, $\alpha$ , and testing for various hypotheses based on the same data set increases strongly the effective underlying $\alpha$. For instance, checking 20 hypotheses and fixing $\alpha_{nom} = 5\%$ leads to $\alpha_{eff} \approx 64\%$. In the long run every hypothesis is "*accepted*". There exists a Bonferroni correction, but this must be handled with care, too.

## 5.1  Benford's Law

In the following we focus on numerical data fraud including manipulation and fabrication of figures. It should be stressed that we shall present only a real subset of statistical and related methods. Clustering, classification, Generalized Linear Models or even case-based reasoning truly belong to any anti-fraud tool box. For instance, the last methodology is treated in the context of fraud detection in [46].

Consider a "homogeneous" data set or corpus like revenue and expenditure transactions in business, assurance claims in health care, main economic indicators of an UNO membership country etc. It was *Newcomb* (1881) who first described the phenomena when detecting unexpectedly many usage spots at the digit 1 of some tables of logarithms at hand, [36]. *Benford* (1938) gave the first formal proof, [37], and later on, *Hill* (1995) added more technical details, [38]. Very interesting examples from a broad range of domains can be found in [39].

Simply speaking, the **Benford's Law** states that the distribution of the leading numeral $D_1$ with range $1, 2, \ldots, 9$ of figures from a well defined corpus **C** obeying the law is given by $P_C(D_1 = d)) = log(1 + 1/d)$. The formula can be generalized to the first k digits, i.e. $P_C(D_1 = d_1, D_2 = d_2, ..., D_k = d_k)) = log(1 + 1/(d_1d_2...d_k))$. Of course, not all data sets are distributed according to the Benford's Law. Sets of identifiers used in database systems or a taxonomy or house numbers are counter examples. Pinkham (1961) proved that for the distribution $f_X$ to be a *Benford* probability distribution it is equivalent to be scale and basis invariant [40]. Let us illustrate the law, and assume a betrayer manipulated a set of bookings by adding faked ones with amounts between Euro 6100 − 6900. A plot of the empirical and Benford's Law signals the forgery, see Fig. 13.

## 5.2  Data-Model Conforming Tests (DMCTs)

Functional relationships between main business indicators are mostly based on the four arithmetic operations. If we assume that the included variables are superimposed by observational or measurement errors they can be modeled as

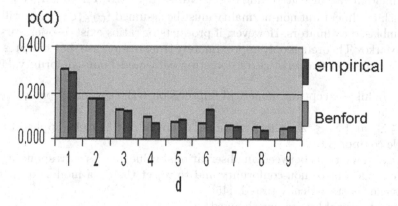

**Fig. 13.** Manipulated bookings with too many items between Euro 6100 − 6900.

random variables. Consequently, their functional dependency is captured by a (generalized) regression model with errors in the variables, [45]. In the linear case (addition and subtraction) the unobservable (true) values of the variables can be estimated exactly using the **Method of Generalized Least Squares (GLS)**. However, if the variables are linked by multiplication and division a *Taylor Approximation of first kind* developed around the mean vector becomes necessary.

Let $(x, z)_0 \in \mathbf{R}^{p,q}$ be noisy *observation vectors* of the state equation system $x = \xi + u$, and balance equation system $z = \zeta + v = H(\xi) + v$ where $H : \mathbf{R}^p \rightarrow \mathbf{R}^q$. Note, that we use small letters for random vectors. If the balance equations model linear relationships they reduce to the matrix equation $\zeta = H\xi$. For example, in the univariate case we have $Profit = Revenues - Expenditures = H\xi = (1, -1)\begin{pmatrix} Revenues \\ Expenditures \end{pmatrix}$ representing a linear equation. The fundamental economic relation $Turnover = Quantity \times Price = H(Quantity, Price)$ is of non-linear type.

As proven in [45], $(\xi, \zeta) \in \mathbf{R}^{p,q}$ can be estimated by GLS with maximum precision under the hypothesis of Gaussian noise, a linear system and uncorrelated noise, i.e. $(u, v) \sim N(0, \Sigma_{uv})$. From the computationally point of view the estimation problem reduces to minimizing a quadratic form:

$$\hat{\xi}_{GLS} = argmax\{(uv)^T \Sigma_{uv}^{-1} \begin{pmatrix} u \\ v \end{pmatrix}\} \tag{1}$$

and

$$\hat{\zeta}_{GLS} = H\hat{\xi}_{GLS}. \tag{2}$$

The variances on the diagonal of the covariance matrix $\Sigma_{uv}$ are assumed to be completely known due to prior information while the correlations are set to zero. This means that for each variable the observational or measurement error should be known. To some reasonable extent this can justified by the principle **Minimal Specifity** saying that the covariance matrix $\Sigma_{uv}$ has a block structure, and all correlations (off-diagonal-elements) vanish. The estimators above have minimal estimation variance according to the **Gauss-Markov Theorem**, [48]. If the relationship is linear but non-normality must be assumed $\hat{\xi}_{GLS}, \hat{\zeta}_{GLS}$ are still best linear unbiased estimators. However, if products or ratios exist as operators, the Gauss-Markov Theorem is only approximately true. In any case the estimates have some convenient characteristics for detecting data-model non-conformity, [45]:

1. $(\hat{\xi}, \hat{\zeta})$ fulfill – except for numerical imprecision – the system of balance equations and
2. $\hat{\Sigma}_{\hat{\xi}} \leq \Sigma_x$ and $\hat{\Sigma}_{\hat{\zeta}} \leq \Sigma_z$ where relational operator "$\leq$" is to be applied to each single component.
3. "Large" deviations between an observational value and its corresponding estimate are a hint to non-conformity and to reject the data-model consistency. This can be statistically tested, [45]
4. Error free variables are not changed.

| ▦ c:\qr\modelle\dupont.sht | | | |
|---|---|---|---|
| Umsatz<br>100 ± 5<br>? | | Kosten<br>80 ± 4<br>? | Kapital<br>80 ± 4<br>? |
| | Gewinn<br>30.0 ± 1.5<br>? | | Return on investment (%)<br>40.0 ± 2.0<br>? |
| Umsatzrendite (%)<br>20.0 ± 1.0<br>? | | | Kapitalumschlag (%)<br>?<br>? |
| | | | |

**Fig. 14.** Reduced DuPont-System as a spreadsheet.

Let us consider a simple illustrating example. We consider the famous **DuPont-Model** which is presented in Fig. 14. We focus on the (linear) balance equation $Sales = Cost + Profit$. Note that we used German labels for the variables of the model. More formally, $\zeta = \xi_1 + \xi_2$. Let the measurements be imprecise. The observations and the absolute errors of the three quantities are as follows: $Sales(z) = 100 \pm 5$, $Cost(x_1) = 80 \pm 4$ and $Profit(x_2) = 30 \pm 1.5$.

Evidently, the measurements $(x_1, x_2, z)$ do not satisfy the balance equation because $100 \neq 80+30$. GLS estimation using the software $Quantor$ ([49]), delivers the following consistent estimates and estimation errors: $\hat{\zeta} = 110 \pm 3$, $\hat{\xi}_1 = 85 \pm 3$ and $\hat{\xi}_2 = 25.6 \pm 0.9$. We confirm $110 \approx 85 + 25, 6$. As mentioned above data-model consistent estimates reduce the imprecision of a data set (or leave it unchanged) given levels of $90, 95, 99\%$-confidence. For instance, $\varepsilon_z = 5 > \hat{\varepsilon}_\zeta = 3$. Alternative approaches of $GLS$ are **Fuzzy Logic** or **MCMC Simulation**. Details can be found in [2].

## 5.3 Inlier Detection

The *Benford* Law makes clear that a trickster who tries to manipulate numerical data must be careful and skillful doing so because the law imposes logical restrictions on a "human number generator" as we have seen. Generally, further tests on data manipulation and fabrication exist implying more and more restrictions on fudged figures.

Some betrayers fearing to be detected because of generating too large numbers, prefer to do the opposite, i.e. produce "too many" numbers near the average. Such a value is called **Inlier** in Statistics. Roughly speaking, inliers represent a dense cluster of data items around the mean related to a different density.

A log-score approach of inlier detection under the quite strong assumption of independence among the random variables considered is due to *Weir* and *Murray* (2011) and leads to a "quick and dirty" treatment of the problem, [41]. The procedure is as follows.

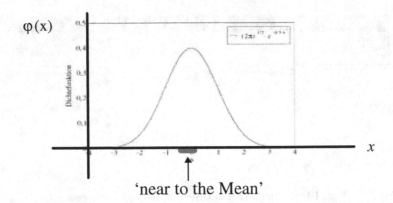

**'near to the Mean'**

**Fig. 15.** Potential inlier range under a Gaussian regime.

```
Procedure Inlier Test
  {Weir and Murray (2011)};
  Input: Problem size (n,p),
         confidence level (1-alpha),
         data matrix X_(nxp);
  Output: Scores szi^2, ln szi^2 for i=1,2,?,n
begin
      Standardize data by z=(x-my)/sigma
      for all p variables and n test objects;

      Compute squared score z_i^2 by summing z_ij
      over all p variables and n objects;

      Perform chi^2 test;
      Plot ln-scores ln z_i^2 against i=1,2,...,n
  end.
```

We illustrate the approach by a fictive case study: Consider the energy consumption (electric power and gas ) of Company X. Thus we have $p = 2$ variables of interest. The company runs five factories in each of five districts. Altogether, we have $n = 25$ objects of interest. As the management has suspicion whether or not the factories of a specific district falsify their figures the score test supports assessing the risk of data manipulation.

Figure 16 gives a hint that in district no 3 inliers are present, and that the reported data may be manipulated. While the overall mean of the five districts is $\overline{ln z^2} = +0,29$, we observe the mean of district no 3 to be exceptionally small, $\overline{ln z_3^2} = -1,53$. In such cases the management of company X should start trouble shooting for finding out the causality of what has happened.

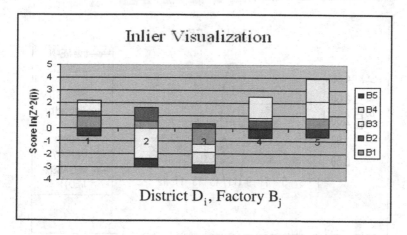

**Fig. 16.** Hint of inlier generation at all factories of district 3.

## 5.4   Outlier Tests

Now we turn to the problem of detecting outliers. The motive of tricksters producing outliers either by manipulation or fabrication of data is typical profit making when participating in investment banking, stock market selling or private borrowing.

A naive approach for detecting outliers is given by the "popular" **3-sigma Rule**. Let us assume that the amounts of transactions, say, have a normal distribution, i.e. $X \sim N(\mu, \sigma^2)$. Note, that generally the moments of the Gaussian distribution are unknown and must be estimated from the sample $x_1, x_2, \ldots, x_n$, mostly assuming *identically* and *independently distributed* (i.i.d) observations. The hypothesis of the test is $H_0 : x$ generated by $N(\mu, \sigma^2)$. The alternative hypothesis is $H_1 : x$ not generated by $N(\mu, \sigma^2)$. Under a Gaussian regime the confidence level is $(1 - \alpha) = 0,9973$ for a $3\sigma$-confidence interval. Consequently, the rejection area of the related outlier test given a suspectable observation $x \in \mathbf{R}$ is reject $H_0$ if

$$|x - \mu|/\sigma > 3. \tag{3}$$

As the unknown parameters must be estimated from the sample which possibly includes outliers the **Masking Effect** is caused, [42]. It leads to the masking of outliers by distorting the estimated mean and standard deviation. The masking effect can be quantified as follows. The $3\sigma$-rule is ineffective to locate outliers with the same sign at a rate $p_I = 1/(1 + \lambda^2)$, [42]. For example, let $\lambda = 3$. It follows $p_I = 10\%$. We visualize the masking effect in Fig. 17.

Evidently, the outlier $x_{11}$ can only be certainly located if the true value of $(\mu, \sigma)$ is known. Even using robust estimation by substituting the standard deviation $s$ by the median (MED) of the absolute deviations around the overall median $\tilde{x}$ as *Hampel* (1985) proposed, i.e. $MAD(x_\nu)_{\nu=1,2,\ldots,n} - \mathrm{MED}(|x_\nu - \tilde{x}|)_{\nu=1,2,\ldots,n}$, no convincing improvement of the outlier detection is recognizable.

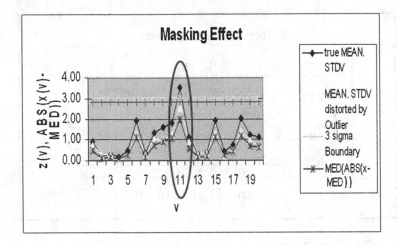

**Fig. 17.** Masking effect of outlier detection.

In our context, a more efficient outlier location rule is the *c-MAD Rule* proposed by [42]. The idea is to determine the proper $(1 - \alpha_n)$ percentile $c$ of the distribution of $MAD(x_\nu)_{\nu=1,2,...,n}$ by Monte-Carlo simulation. Reject $x \in \mathbf{R}$ if

$$|x - \tilde{x}| > c_{n,\alpha_n} MAD(x_\nu)_{\nu=1,2,...,n} \tag{4}$$

where $\alpha = \alpha_n = 1 - (1 - \tilde{\alpha})^{1/n}$ and $c_{n,\alpha_n}$ is simulated by solving the inequality

$$P_{n,\alpha_n}(X \notin \{x \in \mathbf{R} | |x - \tilde{x}| > c_{n,\alpha_n} MAD(x_\nu)_{\nu=1,2,...,n}\}) \geq 1 - \tilde{\alpha} \tag{5}$$

where $\tilde{\alpha} \in (0.5, 1)$ is given. Davies and Gather(1993) showed by example that for a nominal value of $\tilde{\alpha} = 5\%$ the critical values of $c_n$ should be set equal to $c_{20} = 3,02$, $c_{50} = 3,28$, and $c_{100} = 3,47$, [44]. This means that except for very small sample sizes the $3\sigma$-rule is misleading.

A straightforward generalization of outlier detection in multi dimensional data spaces is to use the Mahalanobis distance, cf. [45]. Assume $\mathbf{X} \sim N(\mu, \Sigma)$ with $\mu \in \mathbf{R}^p$ and $\Sigma \in \mathbf{R}^{p \times p}$ known. Then reject $x \in \mathbf{R}^p$ if

$$(x - \mu)^T \Sigma^{-1}(x - \mu) > \chi^2_{p,1-\alpha}. \tag{6}$$

Of course, the same problems as in the univariate case arise:

- unknown parameters $(\mu, \Sigma)$
- non normality (skewness, mixed distributions)
- outlier robustness.

Alternative approaches to be investigated are given by an *order statistics* or *convex hull confidence regions* approach. The bottleneck here will be the curse of high dimension.

# 6    Outlook and Perspectives

**Data Fraud Detection** is a hot topic not only since computers and the Internet dominate our daily life. We conjecture that the relation *fraud rate* $\propto$ $1/ethical$ *attitude* is true and there seems some evidence of continuously decreasing ethics in economics, business and society. All important domains like industry, science, public service, press, clinical and pharmaceutical research, health care, religious communities etc. are affected by data fraud. Therefore there exists a great need for improving methodologies and tools for data fraud detection. In science, one step into the right direction of increasing the transparency among the scientific community is by the notification of cross-referencing of ongoing related research. An example for such an authority is the start-up *ResearchGate* at Berlin, Germany.

Furthermore, independent, international scientific data centers are needed where published data must be deposited. The *Principles of Repeteability and Reproduceability* are to be obeyed in any case. *Observational and Experimental Selection Bias* should become a taboo. This implies checking the correctness and soundness of experimental designs, collecting data schemes, and applying sound statistical methods. However, such an inspection of data sets of a third party is not a very inspiring task for any researcher!

Finally, we have to admit that there exist vague boundaries between data fraud, fudge, falsification, appraisal, cheat, deception, and scouting. But this should not stop data fraud hunting at all. The scene reminds a bit of the relationship between betrayers and detectives. As the saying goes:"In the long run we get them all!" Or as Di Trocchio put it: "Fraud has been since ever an art. Recently it has become a science." [6].

# References

1. Akkaya, A.D., Tiku, M.L.: Robust estimation and hypothesis testing under short-tailedness and inliers. Test **14**(1), 129–150 (2005)
2. Müller, R.M., Lenz, H.-J.: Business Intelligence. Springer, Heidelberg (2013)
3. http://de.wissenschaftlichepraxis.wikia.com/wiki/Untersuchungen_zu_Datenfal schung_und_schlechter_Wissenschaft. Accessed: 19 June 2014
4. Gipp, B.: Citation-based Plagiarism Detection - Applying Citation Pattern Analysis to Identify Currently Non-Machine-Detectable Disguised Plagiarism in Scientific Publications. Doctoral Dissertation, Technical University Magdeburg (2013)
5. German Press Agency (dpa): DEBEKA Polizei im Haus. Der Tagesspiegel, Nr. 22106, July 17, (2014) 15
6. di Trocchio, F.: Der große Schwindel Betrug und Fälschung in der Wissenschaft. Campus-Verlag, New York (1994)
7. Sheldrake, R.: Sieben Experimente, die die Welt verändern. Scherz Verlag, Berlin (1996)
8. Broad, W.J., Wade, N.: Betrayers of the Truth. Oxford Paperback Reference, Oxford (1985)
9. Westfall, R.S.: Newton and the fudge factor. Sci. **179**(4079), 751–758 (1973)
10. World System. http://de.wikipedia.org/wiki/Almagest. Accessed 18 July (2014)

11. Plotemy. http://en.wikipedia.org. Accessed 18 July 2014
12. Almagest. http://ibiblio.org. Accessed 18 July 2014
13. Hipparchos. http://myastrologybook.com. Accessed 18 July (2014)
14. Galilei, G.: http://wundervollesrom.com. Accessed 18 July 2014
15. Galileo's document on heliocentric System. http://medienwerkstatt-online.de. Accessed 18 July 2014
16. Galileo's Telescope. http://www.museum.vic.gov.au/scidiscovery/images/mn0063 09w150.jpg. Accessed 18 July 2014
17. Galileo's inclined plane. http://sciencedemonstrations.fas.harvard.edu/icb/icb. do?keyword=k16940&pageid=icb.page80863&pageContentId=icb.pagecontent 341734&state=maximize&view=view.do&viewParam_name=indepth.html. Accessed 18 July 2014
18. Godfrey, K.: Newton Portrait. National Portrait Gallery, London (1702)
19. Nature: Austria's most serious report of scientific misconduct in recent memory must be handled properly. (The scandalous behavior of Dr. H. Strasser at MUI, Innsbruck, Austria) Nature 454, pp. 917–918, 21 August 2008
20. Ch. Siedenbiedel: Die Libor-Bande. Frankfurter Allgemeine Sonntagszeitung (FASZ), pp. 21–22, no 6, 10 February 2013
21. Tilburg Univ.: Prof. Diederik Stapel suspended. Press release Tilburg University, September 7, (2011). Accessed 17 September 2011
22. Howden, D.: St. Castle: Greece admits deficit figures were fudged to secure Euro entry. The Independent, 16 November 2004
23. Gennies, S.: ADAC gibt Manipulationen zu. Der Tagesspiegel, vol. 15, no. 21933, 20 January 2014
24. S. Alvarez, J. Huber: Mit dem Zweiten trickst man besser. Der Tagesspiegel, vol. 24, no. 22402, 13 July 2014
25. Sanderson, R.: The scandal at the Vatican bank. Financial Time magazine, 6 December 2013. http://www.ft.com/cms/s/2/3029390a-5c68-11e3-931e-00144feabdc0.html. Accessed 21 July 2014
26. Organ Transplantationen. Der Spiegel, pp. 42–44, no 3 (2013)
27. Hartmann, G.: Die Doping-Uni vertuscht ihre Doping-Vergangenheit. Zeit Online section Sport, 7 February 2013
28. Ziegler, G.M.: Keine Wahl. In: Der Tagesspiegel, Nr. 21816, vol. 31, 21 September 2013
29. Thornton, D., van Capelleveen, G., van Hillegersberg, J., Mueller, R.M.: Outlier-based health insurance fraud detection for u.s. medicaid data. In: Proceeding of CD on Special Session on Information Systems Security - ISS, ICEIS 2014, Lisboa (2014)
30. Gipp, B., Meuschke, N., Breitinger, C., Pitman, J., Nürnberger, A.: Web-based demonstration of semantic similarity detection using citation pattern visualization for a cross language plagiarism case. In: Proceeding of (CD) on Special Session on Information Systems Security - ISS, ICEIS 2014, Lisboa (2014)
31. GuttenPlag Wiki )2011). http://de.Guttenplag.wikia.com/wiki/GuttenPlag_Wiki. Accessed 22 July 2014
32. Martinson, B.C., Anderson, M.S., de Vries, R.: Scientists behaving badly. Nature 435, pp. 737–738, 9 June 2005. http://www.vub.ac.be/phd/doctoralschools/lsm/ docs/435737a.pdf. Accessed 20 February 2014
33. John. L.: Seven Shades of Grey. Psychological Science, April 2012
34. Ioannidis, J.P.A.: Why most published research findings are false. PLoS Med. **2**(8), 0696–0701 (2005)

35. Martin, A.: Five allegations against riken stem-cell researcher in Japan. Japan Realtime Technology, 12 March 2014
36. Newcomb, S.: Note on the frequency of use of the different digits in natural numbers. Am. J. Math. 4(1), 39–40 (1881)
37. Benford, F.: The law of anomalous numbers. Proc. Am. Phil. Soc. 78, 551–572 (1938)
38. Hill, T.P.: A statistical derivation of the significant-digit law. Stat. Sci. 10, 354–363 (1995)
39. Nigrini, M.J.: Benford's Law: Applications for Forensic Accounting, Auditing, and Fraud Detection. Wiley, New York (2012)
40. Pinkham, R.S.: On the distribution of first significant digits. Ann. Math.Stat. 32(4), 1223–1230 (1961)
41. Weir, C., Murray, G.: Fraud in clinical trials detecting it and preventing it. Signif. 8(4), 164–168 (2011)
42. Davies, L., Gather, U.: Robust statistics. In: Gentle, J., Härdle, W., Mori, Y. (eds.) Handbook of Computational Statistics Concepts and Methods, pp. 655–695. Springer, Heidelberg (2004)
43. Hampel, F.: The breakdown points of the mean combined with some rejection rules. Technometrics 27, 95–107 (1985)
44. Davies, L., Gather, U.: The identification of multiple outliers. J. Am. Stat. Assoc. 88, 782–801 (1993)
45. Lenz, H.-J., Röel, E.: Statistical quality control of data. In: Gritzmann, P., Hettich, R., Host, R., Sachs, E. (eds.) Operations Research 1991, pp. 341–346. Springer, Heidelberg (1991)
46. Wheeler, R., Aitken, S.: Multiple algorithms for fraud detection. Knowl. Based Syst. 13(2–3), 93–99 (2000)
47. Windolf, P.: Korruption, betrug und 'corporate governance' in den USA - anmerkungen zu enron. Leviathan 31(2), 185–218 (2003)
48. Anderson, T.W.: An Introduction to Multivariate Statistical Analysis. Wiley, New York (1958)
49. Schmid, B.: Bilanzmodelle. Simulationsverfahren zur Verarbeitung unscharfer Teilinformationen. ORL-Bericht No.40, ORL Institut, Universität Züich (1979)
50. Mosler, K., Lange, T., Bazovkin, P.: Computing zonoid trimmed regions in dimension d > 2. Comput. Stat. Data Anal. 53, pp. 2500–2510 (2009)

# Databases and Information Systems Integration

# ERP System Integration:
# An Inter-organizational Challenge
# in the Dynamic Business Environment

Tommi Kähkönen$^{(\boxtimes)}$, Andrey Maglyas, and Kari Smolander

Software Engineering and Information Management,
Lappeenranta University of Technology,
P.O. Box 20, 53851 Lappeenranta, Finland
{Tommi.Kahkonen,Andrey.Maglyas,Kari.Smolander}@lut.fi

**Abstract.** The number of ERP system integration challenges has recently increased as ERP systems need to be integrated not only with the other business information systems inside the organization but also with the systems of business partners. We examined the development and integration of a customized ERP system used by a global manufacturing enterprise by interviewing 21 industrial experts. By using Grounded Theory as the data analysis approach, four groups of factors influencing ERP system integration were revealed. Business environment sets the constraints for integration that is governed in a dynamic organizational landscape, hindered by political agendas. Besides the ERP system vendor, many other ERP development network partners contribute to ERP system integration. The complexity of system level can further distract the integration efforts. Our findings can help managers to guide their strategic decision making on integration issues.

**Keywords:** Information systems · Enterprise systems · Enterprise resource planning · ERP · Integration · ERP development network · Stakeholders · Affecting factors · Moderating factors · Grounded theory

## 1 Introduction

*"If you investigate IT and are searching for an easy integration between systems, there is no such thing. Or if there is, I'm very interested in hearing more about it."*

–Enterprise architect, adopting organization

This statement from one of our interviewees clearly describes the motivation of this study and highlights its relevance to practice. Indeed, integration remains a continuous challenge in organizations. Decades ago, as a partly solution to integration problems ERP systems were introduced to integrate the core business processes of an organization [1]. An ERP implementation is difficult because of variety of reasons. It is an expensive project and a socio-technical challenge that involves both social interactions between many stakeholders and technical aspects in development or customization of the ERP system [2]. After choosing the ERP system to be implemented, the project is constant

© Springer International Publishing Switzerland 2015
J. Cordeiro et al. (Eds.): ICEIS 2014, LNBIP 227, pp. 39–56, 2015.
DOI: 10.1007/978-3-319-22348-3_3

balancing between customization of the package and re-engineering of business processes to fit into the package [3]. ERP systems tend to change the organizational culture and way how people have been used to do their work [4]. ERP projects are prone to failures and some of them even led to total catastrophes [5].

As the field of ERP systems matured, it was soon realized that with an ERP system, a company could improve its operations and get rid of numerous legacy systems, but the need for other business information systems interacting with the ERP system did not vanish [6, 7]. Because of the collaborative nature of modern business, the boundaries between systems have become fuzzier as systems cross the organizational borders and integrate with business partners' systems [8]. Because of the extended role of the ERP system as the backbone enterprise business suite that connects with customers and business partners [9], integration becomes an important consideration during the ERP development.

However, it has been noted that ERP systems cannot be easily integrated with other systems [10, 11]. Moreover, it has been suggested that methods for enterprise systems integration have not been aligned with the advances on integration technologies [7]. Some studies state that integration is not well understood as a concept [12, 13]. A literature review on Information System (IS) integration research pointed out that we do not know much about moderating factors of IS integration [12]. In our previous study, we analyzed the existing literature on ERP system integration and concluded that integration has not been often studied by means of systematic research approaches [14].

We attempt to fill the gap and contribute to the knowledge on ERP system integration. In this paper, our interest is to study ERP system integration from the perspective of ERP Development network (EDN), by which we mean the involved organizations in the ERP system development. We used Grounded Theory [15] to observe and understand the practice of ERP system integration in a global manufacturing enterprise. The following research questions were set: (1) *what are the factors that have impact on ERP system integration?* And (2) *how can these factors be grouped?*

The next section introduces the key concepts used in this study: *ERP system integration* and *ERP development network*. Section 3 presents the research approach and Sect. 4 reports the findings by describing the four groups of factors influencing ERP system integration. The novelty of the findings is discussed in Sect. 5 before concluding the paper.

## 2 Background

### 2.1 ERP System Integration

*Integration* is a general term that has various dimensions and meanings in the domain of information systems. According to Linthicum [16], integration has technical, business process and strategic perspectives and it includes data exchange between systems, standardization of business processes and also cooperation and coordination between human actors. Integration can happen inside a single organization or it can cross organization boundaries, which can be considered external integration [17]. Gulledge [13] clarified the concept of integration related to enterprise systems by dividing integrationto "big I", in which business processes are integrated by a single software application such as ERP, and "little I", in which enterprise systems are linked together by different approaches, such as database-to-database and application server integration.

When examining integration from the perspective of an ERP system, it can be concluded that integration consists of various activities. Integration of business functions is the goal of an ERP implementation as the ERP system enables data flow between business processes [8]. However, numerous other information systems, such as Decision Support Systems (DSS) and Manufacturing Execution Systems (MES) are still needed, and application-level integration of ERP and these systems is often necessary [18], [19]. The functionality of an ERP is often enhanced by bolt-on applications, such as Customer Resource Management (CRM), and Warehouse Management System (WMS) [20]. Because the purpose of a contemporary ERP is to provide the backbone for business collaboration, external integration with business partners' systems is unavoidable [21]. Another form of ERP system integration is to provide interfaces for customers and clients to access the system through the Web or on mobile. This type of integration is called portal-oriented application integration where an interface is built to display the desired information needed by the intended user group [16]. In this paper we understand ERP system integration as *an activity that builds interfaces and manages interconnections between the ERP and other internal and external systems during the ERP system development as a collaborative effort by the ERP development network.*

## 2.2  ERP Development Network

Many groups of stakeholders are involved in ERP projects [22]. Besides the adopting organization, an ERP vendor can have the key role in the project by providing support and tools for development [23]. Consultants are often hired to ERP projects to solve problems that occur during the implementation [24]. The ERP community has been defined as a group consisting of an ERP vendor, consultant and implementing organization and it has been suggested that understanding the relationships and interactions within this group would be a key milestone in the ERP research [25]. Koch [26] uses the term "ERP network" in his work but mainly focuses on the complexity of organizational structures of ERP vendors.

However, it is often the case that this network of stakeholders involved in ERP development is even more complex if all the involved organizations are taken into account. The "flagship" organization, such as SAP or Microsoft can have a major role in the ERP development when a packaged ERP is adopted. The network also includes supply chain partners, suppliers of supporting software (databases, operating systems and tools), as well as vendors of the existing systems that are integrated with the ERP system. Multiple levels from the key organizations are involved, including the upper management, business process owners, mid-level managers, the IT-department, business representatives and end-users. Furthermore, the network is dynamic, which means that it constantly changes its shape during the ERP development. In this regard, we define the ERP Development Network (EDN) as *a dynamic group of stakeholders from different levels of all the involved organizations that are needed for ERP-related problem solving during the ERP system development.*

## 3 Research Approach

Qualitative research methods are essential for studies in information systems development (ISD) and software development, because of the central role of human behavior in them and due to the fact that they introduce, besides technological challenges, also numerous organizational and management issues [27]. Grounded Theory (GT), originally developed by Glaser and Strauss in 1967, was chosen as the research method for this study because ERP projects are complex and they include cooperation and collaboration of various stakeholders. As an inductive research method that is based on collecting research data primarily from interviews with practitioners, GT is suitable for approaching complex organizational phenomena [28]. ERP development is a sociotechnical endeavor making the role of network of stakeholders and human interactions evident [2]. Respectively, ERP system integration is not purely a technological challenge but includes also collaboration and knowledge sharing among various stakeholders [29].

Our specific focus on the integration challenges in ERP development networks required in-depth knowledge of different stakeholders involved in the ERP project. Therefore, we needed to approach the subject with an iterative inquiry into the EDN and with investigation of the challenges presented from different viewpoints. Without having a predefined theoretical model in mind, we investigated the EDN from the viewpoint of one stakeholder to another, iteratively collecting and analyzing the data, which GT supported well. This far GT has not been widely utilized to investigate the integration in ERP projects. However, we deemed it especially suitable when investigating broad phenomena, such as ERP system integration, in depth.

GT is a qualitative research method that allows to develop theory iteratively based on data that is systematically collected and analyzed [30]. Data is usually collected by interviewing or observing one or several cases, but other sources of evidence like written documentation or other archive material can be used as well [31]. GT is considered to be useful for creating context-based and process-oriented descriptions of organizational phenomena and it provides, in its Strauss and Corbin version, relatively clear guidelines for the data analysis [15]. The benefit of GT is that it allows a researcher to trace back to the original sources of data in order to observe how the theory has been developed and how different instances of data have emerged into concepts and relationships between them [30].

The data analysis in Strauss and Corbin's version of GT consists of three coding procedures: open, axial, and selective coding. In open coding, the transcribed data is first labelled with codes that capture the meaning of the current piece of data. The most important procedure in open coding is constant comparison between the pieces of data in order to find similarities and differences. In axial coding, the connections between categories are formed. Basically, this is the interpretation of codes, categories, and properties developed in open coding with the goal of refining the constructs and making them more abstract and theoretical [31]. In selective coding, the goal is to choose a core category and interpret its relationships to other categories and explain it as a theory.

As data is collected and analyzed iteratively, the main question is when to stop the process. As a theory emerges, more focus can be needed on some particular aspects of it. At the same time, categories, dimensions, and properties become more refined as more data collected. The situation when a researcher finds out that any new set of data will not bring significant new codes, categories and/or relationships is called theoretical saturation [30].

## 3.1 Context Description

The adopting organization (from now on referred as AO) is a large and global manufacturing enterprise with an annual turnover over 9 billion euros. AO decided to build a fully-customized ERP system for sales and logistics in order to replace several legacy systems and also to overcome the year 2000 problem without having to make the necessary updates to all the systems. The implementation started in the middle of 1990s and during that time, the existing ERP packages did not have the desired functionality to support business processes of the domain and control the complex supply chain in AO's specific business field. The ERP project went through major challenges, including redesigning the insufficient system architecture and a merger of companies. Eventually, the project greatly exceeded the intended budget. However, the system is currently in a global use and it was widely considered as successful in the interviews. The system is still under a constant development in 2014. The vendor of the system has remained the same from the beginning and has a long-term relationship with AO. Major parts of the development have been recently outsourced to Asia by the vendor to reduce development costs. Benchmarking against ERP products in the market is constantly being done, but for the time being, AO has decided to keep the system to handle its core business processes.

Integration of the ERP system has been a challenging endeavor during the early phases of the project, requiring a vast amount of resources, expertise and strict processes, and also being the major consideration of the current development. The system is integrated with a packaged ERP from SAP that is used for administrative processes such as financial controlling and human resources. According to AO's global ERP strategy the customized ERP system is taken into use in any new facility in order to achieve synergy benefits. This requires integrating the system with operative systems in facilities. In order to let customers and partners to access the relevant information, a web interface to the system has been built. Creating an infrastructure to support mobile use to access the system with mobile devices has also been under consideration. To ease the supply chain collaboration, e-business standardization with competitors and business partners within the same domain has been considered. Integration with customers' ERPs and supply chain partners' systems, including systems of warehouse and transportation operators as well as customs systems has also been made.

## 3.2    Data Collection and Analysis

The data collection included two interview rounds. In the first round we conducted 17 theme-based interviews between February and May 2013. Instead of determining a large number of fixed questions addressing specific areas of interest, the questions in the first round were open-ended, focusing on interviewees' experiences in the ERP project. The more detailed questions were asked based on responses of interviewees. For example, major challenges and successes experienced in the ERP development were asked. This way, we were able to get a rich set of data for further investigation.

The first round started with discussions with our key contact person from the upper management in AO. The goals of the research project were briefly presented to him in order to identify the right persons to interview. The snowballing technique [30] in which the next interviewee is a referral from the previous one was used for selecting the interviewees. Rather than interviewing random persons, we navigated through the ERP development network from one interviewee to another in order to get different viewpoints to the same issues. The interviewees had different positions, ranging from upper management to mid-level management and developers, and included people from the AO, an ERP vendor and a company providing the middleware to the system. Due to the long duration of the ERP system development, the roles and responsibilities of the interviewees have been constantly changing. Some of the interviewees have been intensively involved during the early implementation of the system whereas the others are currently working with the system. The duration of interviews ranged from 26 to 100 min, the average being 53 min.

The second data collection round was conducted between May and June 2014. This round focused more deeply on integration issues. In total, six experts from AO were chosen, based on the recommendations of the contact person. The question set included more detailed questions about integration issues, standards, technologies, organizations and stakeholders dealing with the issues. The list of interviewees' organizations and roles is presented in Table 1.

**Table 1.**  The roles and organizations of the interviwees and durations of the interviews.

| Representatives of adopting organization | | | | Representatives of vendor and middleware provider | | |
|---|---|---|---|---|---|---|
| ID | Role | R1 | R2 | ID | Role | R1 |
| AO1 | Business-IT negotiator | 62 | 100 | V1 | Software manager | 48 |
| AO2 | IT manager of business area | 49 | 65 | V2 | Service owner | 32 |
| AO3 | Programme manager | 32 | – | V3 | Continuous service manager | 56 |
| AO4 | Enterprise architect | 38 | – | V4 | Infrastructure manager | 56 |
| AO5 | Representative of sales | 58 | – | V5 | Project manager | 29 |
| AO6 | IT support manager | 32 | – | V6 | Lead Software Developer | 29 |
| AO7 | Representative of logistics | 31 | – | V7 | Service manager | 52 |
| AO8 | Project manager | 43 | – | MP1 | Middleware manager | 73 |
| AO9 | Manager of E-business and integration | – | 83 | MP2 | Technical consultant | 73 |
| AO10 | Head of E-business and integration | – | 60 | AO = Adopting organization | | |
| AO11 | Business support manager of a business area | – | 83 | V = Vendor<br>MP = Middleware provider | | |
| AO12 | Director of business process development | – | 34 | R1, R2 = duration of the first and the second round interviews in minutes | | |

**Open and Axial Coding.** After conducting the interviews, they were transcribed to text format and analyzed by using ATLAS.ti as the coding tool. The first step in GT is to open code the data by conceptually labelling the data based on its interpreted meaning. We grouped the open codes into categories. A category gives the context for the code and provides the data with more concrete meaning. For example, *structural change* is ambiguous if it appears without a category, but providing the code with the

**Table 2.** Caterogires and their relationships.

| Category | Description | Examples of codes | Relationships to other categories |
|---|---|---|---|
| ERP development network (EDN) | EDN consists of organizations involved in the ERP system development | -actor – database vendor<br>-AO–vendor relationship<br>-middleware provider–vendor relationship<br>-conflicting objective<br>-evolution<br>-global network | -carries out the ED |
| AO | The company that took the ERP system into use | -governance model<br>-organizational culture<br>-structural change<br>-enterprise architecture<br>-political agendas | -is a part of the EDN<br>-collaborates with other organizations in the EDN<br>-operates in the BE |
| Vendor | The company that implemented the ERP system | -involvement<br>-role in integration<br>-role in decision making | -is a part of the EDN |
| Middleware provider (MP) | The company involved to redesign the system architecture | -involvement<br>-expertise | -is a part of the EDN |
| Business partners (BP) | Customers and other value chain partners of AO | -different types<br>-setting integration requirements | -are a part of the EDN |
| Individuals | Besides the organizations, the EDN consisted of Individuals | -role in ERP development<br>-critical action<br>-viewpoint on system's success | -are a part of the EDN |
| ERP development (ED) | Included the development activities of the ERP system | -specifying the system<br>-testing<br>-deploying the system<br>-practices supporting integration | -partly targets integration |
| Integration | Consisted of different forms of integration | -target – internal systems<br>-target – external systems<br>-web interface<br>-standardization<br>-business processes | -is mainly determined by AO<br>-is done during the ED<br>-is affected by BP |
| ERP system (ES) | AO's customized ERP system for sales and logistics[a] | -scope<br>-architecture<br>-flexibility<br>-changed scope | -is the outcome of the ED<br>-is a part of the IA |
| IT-architecture (IA) | Other information systems and technologies of AO | -packaged ERP system<br>-facility systems<br>-middleware<br>-integration platform | -is determined by AO<br>-has connections to BP's systems |
| Business environment (BE) | The business environment and domain where AO operated | -business processes support of ERP products<br>-change<br>-cost cutting of AO | -determines BP<br>-can set constraints for ED |
| ERP strategy | AO had a certain strategy for its ERP systems | -road-mapping<br>-exception (local ERPs)<br>-synergy benefits | -is determined by AO<br>-targets the ERP system |

[a]From now on referred as *the system.*

category *Adopting organization* clarifies the meaning. The code *Adopting organiza-tion: structural change* makes it more meaningful.

In axial coding, the relationships between categories are identified and new categories may be formed based on them. Open and axial coding are not necessarily sequential steps in the analysis process, but are often done concurrently. In total, 12 categories were created during open and axial coding. Table 2 shows the categories created during open and axial coding, some of the codes and relationships between categories.

There were indications of theoretical saturation in the analysis of the last interviews. The data did not produce new codes and already observed phenomena and patterns repeated.

**Selective Coding.** In selective coding the core category is chosen and the relationships of other categories to this category are interpreted. The whole data can be revisited and looked from the perspective of the core category to support and explain the emerging theory. *Integration* was chosen as the core category, because integration issues emerged from the data as an important matter, and it appeared that integration was a

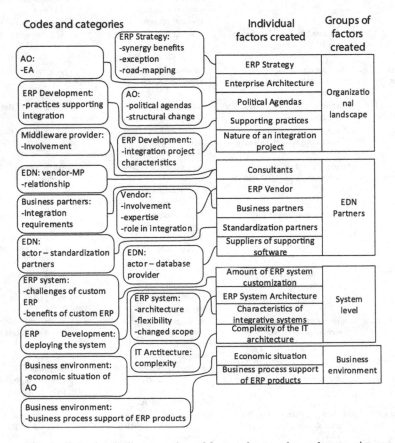

**Fig. 1.** Selective coding: creation of factors from codes and categories.

major challenge during the project phase of the ERP system development as well as being one of the current challenges.

By analyzing the relationships between other categories and integration, factors that have influence on integration were created. A factor can be based on a single code or it can be based on one or several codes in the same or different categories. For example, the factor "Consultants" is based on the codes in *EDN* and *Middleware provider*. When naming factors, general names were considered, for example "EDN: actor – database provider" was renamed to "Suppliers of supporting software". Finally, factors were divided into four groups. Figure 1 show factors emerged from codes and categories by displaying the most important codes that the factors are based on.

## 4   Factors Influencing ERP System Integration

This section describes how ERP system integration was affected by the identified factors, divided into four groups: *Organizational landscape, EDN partners, System level* and *Business environment*.

### 4.1   Organizational Landscape

Organizational landscape consists of the following factors that had impact on ERP system integration: ERP *strategy, enterprise architecture, political agendas, practices supporting integration* and *nature of an integration project*.

**ERP Strategy.** AO had an ERP strategy, which considered the two main ERP systems: the system handled the sales and logistics functionality and the packaged ERP that was utilized for administrative processes. This consequentially meant that an integration between these systems had to be made. New managers often questioned the strategy of having two main ERP systems. AO aimed to deploy these two ERP systems to any new facility worldwide in order to reach synergy benefits. However, sometimes the local ERP systems that were used in facilities were remained. This made the IT architecture more complex and led to further problems, such as difficult integration scenarios. AO had a 5-year roadmap for the system, but constant changes in the business and in the organization made it difficult to follow.

> *"You never reach the ideal world, you end up in having lots of [different systems] here and there, maybe all the possible ERP vendors in some way. Then you have this company-level roadmap and it constantly evolves." –AO1*

**Enterprise Architecture.** Because of the global organization and the challenging supply chain, the Enterprise Architecture (EA) of AO appeared to be very complex. When new features were introduced into the system, an internal architecture check was done first to see if there was a duplicate feature in the IT-architecture and if the new functionality could be achieved through integration. However, a single and integrated system used by different business units with different needs caused challenges when specifying new functionality for the system. Moreover, it was suggested that EA should have more central role in the early phases when making development decisions in order to reduce the complexity.

*"Whenever any kind of change to IT is planned, then the architecture is involved. It always looks to the future, so that it is ensured that the change is being done in as correctly as possible" –AO4*

**Political Agendas.** The organizational structure of the AO was constantly changing during the development of the system. For example, a big merger of two companies took place when the system was not yet taken into use. This changed the governance model and power structures inside AO: different functional areas became under a changed leadership. This led to decisions to take some of the functionality away from the ERP system, to be implemented in other systems, which required additional integrations with the ERP system. As a result, the original scope of the system changed. This was mentioned as one of the major challenges in the current state of the system because of the increased the costs. It was also pointed out that the increased complexity of systems introduced delays when querying order status information from the supply chain. Furthermore, the major structural change also prolonged the integration projects between AO and customers – it took years until these projects were carried out again under a new management that favored e-business.

*"[Logistics] started making separate islands, they wanted to "freeze" the system to a certain point and started to include all kinds of additional systems there. It has been ongoing for ten years now and we have ended up to serious problems and the costs have increased in that area. [Consultants] have evaluated the systems and made this great finding that it's a spaghetti and a new transportation management system needs to be built there." –AO1*

**Practices Supporting Integration.** The system replaced several legacy systems. The parallel run with the legacy systems could take from several months to one year of time. Appropriate practices to manage the master data while running the system in parallel with the legacy systems needed to be in place. When deploying the system to facilities, supporting practices for roll-out approaches and testing of the facility integration were developed through trial and error. The first deployment of the system failed due to performance issues. It appeared that the pilot system was tested in an environment that did not match the real environment and the scope of the system was not fully realized in the beginning of the development. The importance of testing of the facility integration was emphasized as a critical factor in deployments.

*"The more successful the testing sessions are between the facility system and the ERP, the better everything will start off. In that sense the testing of the facility integration is absolutely the key"–AO5*

**Nature of an Integration Project.** Different integration projects were constantly being done while developing the system further. Some of these projects were done by a dedicated integration team of AO, without the need of the vendor to be involved. Moreover, if a similar integration project had already been done before, the next one was carried out more rapidly. Sometimes the vendor had to be involved to make changes to the system, because of the integration requirements. The duration of integration projects ranged from several weeks to years, depending on the nature of the project. However, sometimes a separate integration project was not established. In these projects, the need for integration was realized in later stages and that caused problems when allocating resources for carrying out the integration and testing. The integration requirements, especially the need of integration testing, were sometimes overestimated in these projects.

*"Now and then you underestimate things like the demands of system integration."* –AO5

## 4.2   EDN Partners

The organizations in EDN (others than AO) influenced integration with varying emphasis. In the context of this implementation, the following organizations had an impact on ERP system integration: *consultants, ERP vendor, business partners, standardization partners* and *suppliers of supporting software*.

**Consultants.** Because of the serious performance and scalability issues encountered, the middleware provider was involved in the beginning of the ERP system implementation to redesign the system architecture. The original 2-tier architecture was replaced with a middleware solution based on transaction processing monitors. This made the system architecture more scalable for a broader user base and enabled the integration of business functions. The relationship between the middleware provider and the vendor appeared to be crucial when redesigning the system architecture. The cooperation with the vendor was considered as challenging in the beginning, but after the initial conflicts, an improved system architecture was developed.

*"Practically, [the vendor] didn't have a clue of how to make it work [...] and when we looked at it, it seemed that the way of implementing the system and the use of object model was completely wrong."* –MP2

**ERP Vendor.** The vendor had the key role in ERP system integration. Because of the long-term relationship with AO, the vendor built many of the systems used in facilities and had the required knowledge on these systems when integrating systems. Furthermore, the vendor's knowledge on AO's business was proven to be a major facilitator in cooperation. Even though both AO and vendor had a rather positive viewpoint on their relationship, neither of the partners had always been satisfied with this relationship. AO had even considered of buying the source code of the system from the vendor, but according to one interviewee, *"it did not turn out to be a realistic option"*. The other interviewee considered the relationship as a *"forced marriage"*. Deploying the system to facilities was carried out in a close cooperation between AO and vendor.

*"We are in a close cooperation daily, we are making things together. [The relationship] is not a traditional customer-vendor."* –V6.
*"We've had the benefit of very skilled representatives from the vendor side, with a long history with [the system] and system integration. This is worth its weight in gold, and more."* – AO5

**Business Partners.** Because of the complexity of the supply chain, many third party companies were involved, including freight forwarders, harbor operators and warehouses. The system had been integrated with the systems of these parties. This was occasionally considered challenging. It was pointed out that a sudden need to integrate an external system with the ERP system can occur. Besides the supply chain partners, AO worked with customers more intensively. In the early phases of the project, a web interface was built to allow customers to view the certain information of the system. Customer integration projects with the most important customers were ongoing. These projects were often initiated by customers that wanted to improve their own business processes or made an update to their ERP system. This then called for appropriate actions by AO that tried to fulfill the integration needs of its customers and other value chain partners.

> "And later came – it was not originally specified as a requirement of the system – this transportation cost management system came there." –AO7

**Standardization Partners.** Standardization partners appeared to be another EDN group that had an impact on ERP system integration. AO has participated in e-business standardization efforts within the domain in order to ease the collaboration with business partners. Through these standards, messaging between the system and external systems was made easier.

> "[It] is a separate messaging standard which has been built for [our] industry. [Our company] is one of the companies developing that. There are also all our biggest competitors involved in that work." –AO9

**Suppliers of Supporting Software.** The representative of middleware provider estimated that vendor's choice for the base technologies of the system was slightly affected by database vendors and their technologies the vendor was initially familiar with. AO relied on the supplier's expertise in this matter and the project ended up in difficulties because of the non-scalable system architecture designed by the vendor. Consultants from the middleware provider company small in size, were not able to convince AO to choose their technology until later when architectural problems occurred.

> "You should never believe in the sales speeches of salesmen, the organization should have sangfroid to test the options." –MP1

### 4.3   System Level

On system level the *amount of ERP system customization, ERP system architecture, integrative systems' characteristics* and *complexity of the IT architecture* influenced ERP system integration.

**Amount of ERP System Customization.** By having a fully customized ERP, AO could have a total control over the system and its integration capabilities. AO was not affected, for example, by the version updates made by the ERP flagship organization, such as SAP. In addition, the control of development, being free of licensing costs and the advanced functionality provided through customization were highlighted as benefits. The vendor saw that in some situations, the new application logic could be directly built into the system instead of adding additional application layers. However, development of a customized system introduced some of the specific challenges, such as performance issues due to the non-scalable system architecture. Moreover, the development was expensive and there were no other parties driving the development as it is often the case with packaged ERP systems.

> *"[AO] couldn't have had a better system what they got when they made a glove to a hand [...] I have never seen such advanced functionality anywhere, you can just drag a shipping container and drop it to a ship" –V4*

**ERP System Architecture.** The system had to be flexible enough to enable integration of various different systems. Moreover, it had to enable the rearrangements as some of the logistics functionality previously provided by the system was replaced by external integrations. However, it appeared that replacing certain functionality in the system was not always straightforward, because of the system architecture. More modular architectural design that would better enable these modifications, was emphasized. Also, the system messaging between internal systems was not standardized, but instead, messages had a proprietary format made by the vendor. This has led to a situation, in which more intermediary was needed and also required the vendor to be involved in integration.

> *"[The system] has enabled many things that we have been doing over the years to increase our competitiveness and supported the organizational changes. We have been able to rearrange the services by fluently combining different machine lines and production pipelines according to how we want to arrange our business." –AO6*

**Characteristics of Integrative Systems.** Because of the heterogeneity of the facility systems, such as some of them even programmed in Cobol in 1970s, the system integration approach was different in each location due to varying functionality of the facility system in question. The system had to be modified based on the characteristics of the facility system in question. Different approaches for roll-outs were established to deploy the system.

> *"In many cases it will require big changes to [the system], depending on the facility. Some facilities don't require many changes [...] The ease of the roll-out may vary greatly between facilities." –S2*

**Complexity of the IT Architecture.** The IT architecture of AO was a complex one. Besides the two main ERP systems, it consisted of tens of facility systems, local ERP systems, integration platforms and many other internal and external systems. Besides the AO's attempt to reduce the complexity, some islands of technology were formed. The complexity of the IT architecture introduced difficult integration scenarios. For example, sending an invoice from one office to another involved the system, the global SAP ERP and a local SAP in the target location, and exchanging the information between these systems was problematic. The project that was started four years ago for internal invoicing was still ongoing.

> *"So we have [the system], then [one business area] has huge amount of different systems [...] We have a global SAP for finance purposes. Then we have a local SAP in some of our sites. And we're trying to get all these different systems to work together. It's a total headache. It's a mission impossible, I would say." –AO9*

## 4.4    Business Environment

The business environment had an effect on the other three groups, thus it had an indirect impact on integration. By defining the domain where AO operated, it also determined the EDN partners to collaborate with. *Economic situation* and *business process support of ERP products* were identified as factors that had impact on other groups but eventually they had an impact on integration.

**Economic Situation.** Because of changing business conditions, AO constantly had to cut down the development costs. It was suggested that business processes of AO could be developed further, for example through mobile applications that would provide interfaces to the users and business partners to access the system. However, economic situation postponed the development of these features.

> *"[Mobile interfaces] have a quite big price tag, so that when you have to save in costs, they are probably the first thing to drop out." –V6*

**Business Process Support of ERP Products.** During the time when AO made the decisions about the system, business process support of available ERP products in the market was not comprehensive. This was seen as the major driver that led to the decision to make a fully customized ERP system. The business process support of ERP products affected the amount of customization of the system which in turn affected ERP system integration.

> *"[Logistics] is quite complicated and SAP didn't manage this back then. I still feel that it wouldn't." –AO10*

## 4.5    Summary of Results

Figure 2 displays the four groups of factors that have influence on ERP system integration. Based on the ERP strategy of AO, the system was integrated with the packaged ERP system and was to be taken into use in any new facility in order to reach synergy benefits. When planning new features to the system, enterprise architecture was evaluated to investigate if the new functionality could be achieved through integration. Political agendas taking place in AO led to more fragmented IT architecture and additional integrations. Practices supporting integration were developed in order to

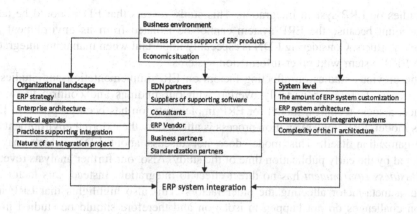

**Fig. 2.** Factors influencing ERP system integration.

enable smooth deployments to facilities. The nature of an integration project determined how easily the integration was carried out. Sometimes a separate project was not established because the integration requirements were not realized.

ERP system integration was affected by five EDN partners. Suppliers of supporting software slightly affected the decisions made on integration technologies. Consultants were needed to re-design the system architecture. AO's close relationship with the vendor as well as vendor's expertise have aided especially the internal integration. Business partners introduced additional systems to be integrated with and some of the integration requirements emerged directly from them. Standardization partners were involved when further enhancing the supply chain collaboration.

By having a fully customized system, some of the integration challenges that would emerge with a packaged ERP system could be bypassed. Sometimes integration introduced changes to the ERP system architecture, which had to enable the rearrangements. When deploying the system to a facility, the characteristics of the facility systems determined how easily the integration was carried out. The complexity of the IT architecture introduced challenging integration scenarios when trying to transfer the data between several different ERP systems.

Business environment had an indirect impact on integration by defining the domain of AO and the business partners and standardization partners to cooperate with. It also had an impact on the economic situation. Because of the cost cutting of AO, business process improvement through a mobile infrastructure was postponed. Business environment also defined the business process support of ERP products, which was the main reason for AO to build a customized ERP system.

# 5 Discussion

The analysis of the EDN of a global manufacturing enterprise highlights the socio-technical nature of the ERP system integration and the role and impact of different organizations involved in it. The role of EDN has not been often emphasized in the studies on ERP system integration. This study reveals that EDN should be taken into account because the ERP system cannot be isolated from its environment and business partners. Considering EDN is especially important when managing integration of the ERP system with other information systems.

The previous studies on affecting factors on ERP implementation and studies on ERP success factors are partially overlap with our findings and confirm them. For instance, a socio-technical model for ERP implementation has been proposed in [32]. In this model, ERP implementation process is affected by the external environment and the organization itself. This model does not discuss about EDN, which may be explained by the early publication time of the study. Also, our further analysis revealed that *Business environment* has no direct effect to integration. Instead, this factor represents a meta-factor affecting the other factors. This also highlights that ERP integration challenges do not happen in isolation and therefore should be studied in the context of EDN.

Although ERP success factors have been studied comprehensively, e.g. in [11, 33], they are often organizational and lack the EDN perspective. The relationship between the client (AO) and the vendor has been identified as a success factor in ERP implementation [33]. Our findings suggest its importance also in ERP system integration. In addition, our findings suggest that the vendor-consultant relationship can have a key role when solving integration issues. Moreover, it has been noted that enterprise application integration (EAI) success factors are similar to general ERP success factors – successful EAI needs to consider the factors on the levels of business, organization, technology, project as well as environmental factors [12, 34]. Hoverer, this classification does not either address the role of EDN. Besides the role of the vendor, our evidence suggests the important roles of consultants and business partners in ERP system integration. It means that further studies on ERP system integration should not be limited to understanding the relationships between the AO and the vendor only, because this perspective lacks the input from other partners involved in resolving integration issues.

As in all qualitative studies, the findings of this study cannot be easily generalized. The findings are related only to the specific case and the generalization of the findings of the study is theoretical [35], i.e. they generalize specific observations to theoretical concepts. With these concepts we can explain the events in the studied organization and we also strongly believe that these factors influencing ERP system integration are similar in other contexts as well. In future, we will study different EDNs and apply the results of this study in different contexts, e.g. in cases were a packaged ERP is adopted. Moreover, investigating how integration is governed in EDNs, especially how decision making on integration evolves in them and what is the role of enterprise architecture in integration governance are the topics of our future interests.

## 6   Conclusions

We have proposed empirically grounded factors that had an effect on ERP system integration in a large manufacturing enterprise. The factors are divided into four groups: *Business environment*, *Organizational landscape*, *ERP development network partners*, and *System level*. The findings reflect the nature of ERP system integration as socio-technical endeavor that involves interaction and collaboration between stakeholders. This perspective is often ignored by ERP integration studies that often focus on the adopting organization only. Through our findings, managers can better understand the nature of integration in the context of ERP development networks and guide their strategic decisions on integration issues.

**Acknowledgements.** This study was funded by Academy of Finland grant #259454.

# References

1. Beheshti, H.M.: What managers should know about ERP/ERP II. Manage. Res. News **29**(4), 184–193 (2006)
2. de Albuquerque, J., Simon, E.: Dealing with socio-technical complexity: towards a transdisciplinary approach to IS research. In: Proceedings of the European Conference on Information Systems (ECIS), 2007, pp. 1458–1468 (2007)
3. Law, C.C.H., Chen, C.C., Wu, B.J.P.: Managing the full ERP life-cycle: considerations of maintenance and support requirements and IT governance practice as integral elements of the formula for successful ERP adoption. Comput. Ind. **61**(3), 297–308 (2010)
4. Liang, H., Xue, Y.: Coping with ERP-related contextual issues in SMEs: a vendor's perspective. J. Strateg. Inf. Syst. **13**(4), 399–415 (2004)
5. IDG Consumer & SMB: 10 Biggest ERP Software Failures of 2011. http://www.pcworld.com/article/246647/10_biggest_erp_software_failures_of_2011.html
6. Lehmann, H., Gallupe, B.: Information systems for multinational enterprises - some factors at work in their design and implementation. J. Int. Manage. **11**(2), 163–186 (2005)
7. Xu, L.D.: Enterprise systems: state-of-the-art and future trends. IEEE Trans. Ind. Inform. **7**(4), 630–640 (2011)
8. Hsu, P.-F.: Integrating ERP and e-business: resource complementarity in business value creation. Decis. Support Syst. **56**, 334–347 (2013)
9. Hvolby, H.-H., Trienekens, J.H.: Challenges in business systems integration. Comput. Ind. **61**(9), 808–812 (2010)
10. Doedt, M., Steffen, B.: Requirement-driven evaluation of remote ERP-system solutions: a service-oriented perspective. In: 34th IEEE Software Engineering Workshop (SEW), 2011, pp. 57–66 (2011)
11. Momoh, A., Roy, R., Shehab, E.: Challenges in enterprise resource planning implementation: state-of-the-art. Bus. Process Manage. J. **16**(4), 537–565 (2010)
12. Chowanetz, M., Legner, C., Thiesse, F.: Integration: an omitted variable in information systems research. In: European Conference on Information Systems (ECIS) 2012 Proceedings (2012)
13. Gulledge, T.: What is integration? Ind. Manag. Data Syst. **106**(1), 5–20 (2006)
14. Kähkönen T., Smolander, K.: ERP integration - a systematic mapping study. In: 15th International Conference on Enterprise Information Systems (ICEIS) 2013 Proceedings (2013)
15. Corbin, J., Strauss, A.: Grounded theory research: procedures, canons, and evaluative criteria. Qual. Sociol. **13**(1), 3–21 (1990)
16. Linthicum, D.S.: Next generation application integration: from simple information to Web services. Addison-Wesley, Boston (2004)

17. Barki, H., Pinsonneault, A.: A model of organizational integration, implementation effort, and performance. Organ. Sci. **16**(2), 165–179 (2005)
18. Shafiei, F., Sundaram, D., Piramuthu, S.: Multi-enterprise collaborative decision support system. Expert Syst. Appl. **39**(9), 7637–7651 (2012)
19. Tao, Y.-H., Hong, T.-P., Sun, S.-I.: An XML implementation process model for enterprise applications. Comput. Ind. **55**(2), 181–196 (2004)
20. Watts, C.A., Mabert, V.A., Hartman, N.: Supply chain bolt-ons: investment and usage by manufacturers. Int. J. Oper. Prod. Manag. **28**(12), 1219–1243 (2008)
21. Møller, C.: ERP II: a conceptual framework for next-generation enterprise systems? J. Enterp. Inf. Manag. **18**(4), 483–497 (2005)
22. Skok, W., Legge, M.: Evaluating enterprise resource planning (ERP) systems using an interpretive approach. Knowl. Process Manage. **9**(2), 72–82 (2002)
23. Somers, T.M., Nelson, K.G.: A taxonomy of players and activities across the ERP project life cycle. Inf. Manage. **41**(3), 257–278 (2004)
24. Metrejean, E., Stocks, M.H.: The role of consultants in the implementation of enterprise resource planning systems. Acad. Inf. Manag. Sci. J. **14**(1), 1–25 (2011)
25. Sammon, D., Adam, F.: Decision Making in the ERP Community. In: European Conference on Information Systems (ECIS) 2002 Proceedings (2002)
26. Koch, C.: ERP - a moving target. Int. J. Bus. Inf. Syst. **2**(4), 426–443 (2007)
27. Seaman, C.B.: Qualitative methods in empirical studies of software engineering. IEEE Trans. Softw. Eng. **25**(4), 557–572 (1999)
28. Charmaz, K.: Constructing Grounded Theory. SAGE Publications, London (2006)
29. Welker, G.A., van der Vaart, T., van Donk, D.P.: The influence of business conditions on supply chain information-sharing mechanisms: a study among supply chain links of SMEs. Int. J. Prod. Econ. **113**(2), 706–720 (2008)
30. Strauss, A., Corbin, J.: Basics of Qualitative Research: Techniques and Procedures for Developing Grounded Theory, 3rd edn. SAGE Publications, Thousand Oaks (2008)
31. Urquhart, C., Lehmann, H., Myers, M.D.: Putting the 'theory' back into grounded theory: guidelines for grounded theory studies in information systems. Inf. Syst. J. **20**(4), 357–381 (2010)
32. Somers, T., Nelson, K., Ragowsky, A.: Enterprise Resource Planning (ERP) for the next millennium: development of an integrative framework and implications for research. In: AMCIS Proceedings (2000)
33. Ngai, E.W.T., Law, C.C.H., Wat, F.K.T.: Examining the critical success factors in the adoption of enterprise resource planning. Comput. Ind. **59**(6), 548–564 (2008)
34. Lam, W.: Investigating success factors in enterprise application integration: a case-driven analysis. Eur. J. Inf. Syst. **14**(2), 175–187 (2005)
35. Lee, A.S., Baskerville, R.L.: Generalizing generalizability in information systems research. Inf. Syst. Res. **14**(3), 221–243 (2003)

# Using Complex Correspondences for Integrating Relational Data Sources

Valéria Pequeno[1](✉), Helena Galhardas[2], and Vânia M. Ponte Vidal[3]

[1] INESC-ID, Taguspark, Oeiras, Portugal
vmp@inesc-id.pt
[2] Instituto Superior Técnico, Universidade de Lisboa and INESC-ID,
Taguspark, Oeiras, Portugal
helena.galhardas@tecnico.ulisboa.pt
[3] Universidade Federal do Ceará, Fortaleza, Brazil
vvidal@lia.ufc.br

**Abstract.** Data Integration (DI) is the problem of combining a set of heterogeneous, autonomous data sources and providing the user with a unified view of these data. Integrating data raises several challenges, since the designer usually encounters incompatible data models characterized by differences in structure and semantics. One of the hardest challenges is to define correspondences between schema elements (e.g., attributes) to determine how they relate to each other. Since most business data is currently stored in relational databases, here present a declarative and formal approach to specify 1-to-1, 1-m, and m-to-n correspondences between relational schema components. Differently from usual approaches, our (CAs) have semantics and can deal with outer-joins and data-metadata relationships. Finally, we demonstrate how to use the CAs to generate mapping expressions in the form of SQL queries, and we present some preliminary tests to verify the performance of the generated queries.

**Keywords:** Schema matching · Correspondence assertions · Data integration · Relational model

## 1 Introduction

A DI system aims at integrating a variety of data obtained from different data sources, usually autonomous and heterogeneous, and providing a unified view of these data, often using an integrated schema. The integrated schema makes a bridge between the data sources and the applications that access the DI system. Data in a DI system can be physically reconciled in a repository (*materialized data integration approach*), or can remain at data sources and is only consolidated when a query is posed to the DI system (*virtual data integration approach*). A data warehouse system [1] is a typical example of the first approach. As examples of the second approach, we can cite federated information systems [2] and mediator systems [3]. In the present work, both scenarios can be used, but in this paper we will focus on the materialized integration approach.

© Springer International Publishing Switzerland 2015
J. Cordeiro et al. (Eds.): ICEIS 2014, LNBIP 227, pp. 57–74, 2015.
DOI: 10.1007/978-3-319-22348-3_4

One of the hardest problems to solve in DI is to define mappings between the integrated schema (the target) and each data source schema, known as *the schema mapping problem*. It consists of two main tasks: *i) schema matching* to define/generate correspondences (a.k.a. matches) between schema elements (e.g., attributes, relation, XML tags, etc.); and *ii) schema mapping* to find data transformations that, given data instances of a source schema, obtain data instances of the target schema.

The result of schema matching is a set of correspondences that relate elements of a source schema to elements of the target schema, where an element can be a relation name or attribute in the relational model. These correspondences can be described using a Local-as-view (LAV), a Global-as-view (GAV), or a Global and Local-asview (GLAV) language. In summary, in a LAV approach, each data source is described as a view over the integrated schema. In a GAV approach, the integrated schema is expressed as a view over the data sources. Finally, the GLAV combines the expressive power of both GAV and LAV. Once the schema matching is performed, the correspondences are used to generate the schema mappings. For example, a schema mapping can be codified through an SQL query that transforms data from the source into data that can be stored in the target.

Extensive research on schema matching has been carried out in recent years [4,5]. The majority of the works on this subject identifies 1-1 correspondences between elements of two schemas. For example, a 1-1 correspondence can specify that element **title** in one schema matches element **film** in another schema, or that relation GENRE matches relation CATEGORY[1]. This kind of schema matching is known in the literature as *basic matching*. Good surveys can be found in [6,7].

While basic matching is common, it leaves out numerous correspondences of practical interest, in particular when we consider DI systems. Thus, more complex matches are necessary. A complex matching specifies 1:n, m:n, or n:1 correspondences between elements of two schemas. For example, it may specify that **totalPrice** corresponds to **unitPrice * quantity**; or that **name** matches *concatenate*(**firstName, lastName**), where *concatenate* is a function that applies to two strings and returns a concatenated string; or even that the average departmental salary **avgWage** corresponds to grouping the salaries (**salary**) of all employees (**emp**) by department (**dept**). Works in [8,9] are examples of approaches that deals with complex matches.

Some researchers go beyond dealing with complex matches and add semantics to the correspondences to improve the overall matching quality. In the Sect. 2, we explain more about complex matches and show a motivation example. The remainder of the paper is structured as follows. In Sect. 3, we present the necessary background in Correspondence Assertions (CAs), the formalism used in this work to specify correspondences between elements of schemas. In Sect. 4, we propose new CAs to deal with join operators and metadata. Section 5 shows how to

---

[1] We use **bold** to represent attribute names and UPPERCASE to represent relation names.

generate mapping expressions from CAs. Section 6 shows some preliminary tests to evaluate our approach. Section 7 describes the related work. Finally, Sect. 8 concludes and describes future work.

## 2 Motivating Example

Consider a motivating example with the source schemas $S_1$ and $S_2$ in Fig. 1, which contain information about movies. $S_1$ keeps a catalog of movies with information about different types of media (dvd, blue rays, etc.) in which the movies are available. The names of the relations and attributes are mostly self-explanatory. Some non-self-explanatory attributes in $S_1$ have the following meaning: **id** is the movie identifier, **year** is the year of a movie, **film** is the title of a movie, **number** is the tape identifier, **name** can be a producer or a director name, and **role** can be *producer* or *director*. FK1 and FK2 are foreign keys. We use the notation $FK(R{:}L, S{:}K)$ to denote a foreign key, named FK, where R and S are relation names and $L$ and $K$ are list of attributes from R and S, respectively, with the same length. FK1 is the foreign key of TAPE that refers to MOVIE and FK2 is the foreign key of MOVIEMAKERS that refers to MOVIE. $S_2$ stores general information about movies and the places (in different cities) where movies are being shown. We assume that $S_1$ can store older movies than $S_2$. Some non-self-explanatory attributes in $S_2$ have the following meaning: **rate** is the classification of the movie with regard the audience, **location** and **city** are, respectively, the cinema and the name of the city where the movie is shown, and **time** is the date when the movie is shown.

```
* Schema S₁                              * Schema M
MOVIE(id, film, year, summary)           MOVIE(title, genre, year, description)
TAPE(number, format, id)                 FILMMAKERS(movie, producer, director)
  FK1(TAPE, ⟨id⟩, MOVIE, ⟨id⟩)             FK4(FILMMAKERS, ⟨movie⟩, MOVIE, ⟨title⟩)
MOVIEMAKERS(id, name, role)              SCHEDULE(movie, cinema, startTime)
  FK2(MOVIEMAKERS, ⟨id⟩, MOVIE, ⟨id⟩)      FK5(SCHEDULE, ⟨movie⟩, MOVIE, ⟨title⟩)
* Schema S₂                              REMAKES(title, nvYear, ovYear)
FILM(id, title, year, rate)               FK6(REMAKES, ⟨title⟩, MOVIE, ⟨title⟩)
SHOWTIME(id, location, time, city)       RATING(rate, quantity)
  FK3(SHOWTIME, ⟨id⟩, FILM, ⟨id⟩)
```

**Fig. 1.** Example of source schemas and a integrated schema.

The integrated schema **M**, also shown in Fig. 1, provides a unified user view of movies currently shown in cinemas of Lisbon. It is populated by information from schemas $S_1$ and $S_2$. The relation MOVIE stores movies shown currently at a cinema. The relation FILMMAKERS keeps information about professionals of show businesses. The relation SCHEDULE contains information about the schedule of movies shown in Lisbon. The relation REMAKES keeps the years of movies for which there is at least one remake. The relation RATING stores the classification of movies with regard to suitability audience. Some non-self-explanatory attributes in **M** have the following meaning: **description** is the summary of a movie, **nvYear** is the year of the most recent version of a movie, **ovYear** is the year of the older versions of a movie, and **quantity** is the total of movies with the same rating.

Given the schemas $S_1$, $S_2$, and **M**, we can consider the correspondences between the source schemas $S_1$ and $S_2$, and the target schema **M**. As an example, we can state that **M**.SCHEDULE corresponds to $S_2$.SHOWTIME, because both relations store information regarding the same real world concept[2]. However, in this correspondence, it is not clear that **M**.SCHEDULE only keeps schedules about movies shown in Lisbon. The additional information: **M**.SCHEDULE *corresponds to* $S_2$.SHOWTIME *when* $S_2$.SHOWTIME.**city** = "*Lisbon*", specifies better the matching.

The works reported in [10–12] and [5](chap. 3) propose schema matching approaches that can specify correspondences to deal with situations as required in the example The reader can see more proposals to add semantics to schema matching in [8,10,12,13]. However, the following situations have not been fully covered yet:

1. *Correspondences Between Relations Involving Join Conditions Other than Equality of Attributes.* Consider the relation **M**.REMAKES that keeps a list of remakes with the years of the oldest versions. Knowing that $S_2$.FILM keeps current movies and $S_1$.MOVIE may contain older versions of the same movie, we want to indicate which of the current movies are remakes and store this information in **M**.REMAKES. The correspondence between these relations can be specified as: **M**.REMAKES *corresponds to* $S_2$.FILM *join* $S_1$.MOVIE *where* $S_2$.FILM.**title** = $S_1$.MOVIE.**film** *and* $S_2$.FILM.**year** > $S_1$.MOVIE.**year**. Usual schema matching approaches cannot specify this correspondence, because join conditions are not explicitly defined in schema matching. Moreover, join paths are normally automatically discovered in the schema mapping phase [14], and the algorithms used can only find equi-join conditions, so they cannot automatically discover the condition $S_2$.FILM.**year** > $S_1$.MOVIE.**year**. Hence, we need a schema matching approach that makes it possible to specify the join between relations and allows general join conditions containing operators different from equality.

2. *Correspondences Between Relations Involving Outer-joins (Full, Left, or Right).* We want to indicate how **M**.MOVIE is related to source schemas $S_1$ and $S_2$. **M**.MOVIE and $S_2$.FILM represent the same concept of the real world (i.e., both relations store current movies shown at some cinema). However, it is not enough to specify that **M**.MOVIE matches $S_2$.FILM, because there are attributes in $S_1$.MOVIE (namely, **category** and **summary**) that contain information required in the schema of **M**.MOVIE. Hence, we should specify that

---

[2] We use a path representation: an attribute **A** of a given relation R in a given database schema **D** is referred to as **D**.R.**A**. For simplicity, we omit the database schema when the context is clear.

**M**.MOVIE is related to both **S**$_1$.MOVIE and **S**$_2$.FILM. However, it is not correct we simply match **M**.MOVIE to **S**$_1$.MOVIE because **S**$_1$.MOVIE can store movies that are not being shown in a cinema anymore and **M**.MOVIE can store recent movies that are not available in dvds yet. In summary, we should specify that: **M**.MOVIE *corresponds to* **S**$_2$.FILM *left outer-join* **S**$_1$.MOVIE *on* **S**$_2$.FILM.**title** = **S**$_1$.MOVIE.**film** *and* **S**$_2$.FILM.**year** = **S**$_1$.MOVIE.**year**. Note that the condition **S**$_2$.FILM.**title** = **S**$_1$.MOVIE.**film** and **S**$_2$.FILM.**year** = **S**$_1$.MOVIE.**year** guarantees that we refer to a same movie stored in both **S**$_1$.MOVIE and **S**$_2$.FILM. Again, we cannot specify this type of correspondence since joins (and their variants) are not explicitly defined in current schema matching approaches.

3. *Correspondences Between Data and Metadata.* Consider the relations **S**$_1$.MOVIEMAKERS and **M**.FILMMAKERS. Both keep information about the relationship between a movie, a producer, and a director. We want to indicate that **M**.FILMMAKERS corresponds to **S**$_1$.MOVIEMAKERS since they represent the same concept in the real world. In addition, we want to specify the correspondences between the attributes of these relations. Knowing that **S**$_1$.MOVIEMAKERS.**name** can be a producer name or a director name, we would like to specify that **M**.FILMMAKERS.**producer** corresponds to **S**$_1$.MOVIEMAKERS.**name** when **S**$_1$.MOVIEMAKERS.**role** = "producer" and that **M**.FILMMAKERS.**director** corresponds to **S**$_1$.MOVIEMAKERS.**name** when **S**$_1$.MOVIEMAKERS.**role** = "director". However, we cannot specify these correspondences using traditional schema matching approaches, because these correspondences involve semantics not covered yet by these approaches. Actually, we can only specify that **M**.FILMMAKERS.**producer** matches to **S**$_1$.MOVIEMAKERS.**name** and **M**.FILMMAKERS.**director** matches to **S**$_1$.MOVIEMAKERS.**name**.

In order to deal with these situations, we propose to use a formalism based on CAs [10,15]. Using CAs, we can declaratively specify basic and complex matchings with semantics. We propose to adapt CAs to be able to express schema matching between relational schemas, as well as to extend this formalism with new types of CAs to deal with joins, outer-joins, and data-metadata relationships. Finally, we demonstrate how mapping expressions in the form of SQL queries can be generated from CAs.

## 3  Background

In this section, we present the basic terminology used in this paper. We also review the different classes of CAs, and adapt them to the Relational Data Model (RDM).

### 3.1  Basic Concept and Notation

We assume that the reader is familiar with the relational concepts. We denote a relation schema as $R(\mathcal{A}_1, \mathcal{A}_2, \ldots, \mathcal{A}_n)$, and a foreign key as $FK(R{:}L, S{:}K)$. We say that FK relates R and S.

A relational schema is a pair $S = (\mathcal{R}, \Omega)$, where $\mathcal{R}$ is a set of relation schemas and $\Omega$ is a set of relational constraints such that: (i) $\Omega$ has a unique primary key for each relation schema in $\mathcal{R}$; (ii) if $\Omega$ has a foreign key of the form $FK(R{:}L,$ $S{:}\,K)$, then $\Omega$ also has a constraint indicating that $K$ is the primary key of S. Given a relation schema $R(\mathcal{A}_1, \mathcal{A}_2, \ldots, \mathcal{A}_n)$ and a tuple variable $t$ over R, we use $t[\mathcal{A}_i]$ to denote the projection of $t$ over $\mathcal{A}_i$.

Let $S = (\mathcal{R}, \Omega)$ be a relational schema and R and T be relation names of relation schemas in $\mathcal{R}$. We denote $\varrho = FK_1 \bullet FK_2 \bullet \cdots \bullet FK_{n-1}$ a path from R to T iff there is a list $R_1, \ldots, R_n$ of relation schemas in $S$ such that $R_1 = R$, $R_n = T$, and $FK_i$ relates $R_i$ and $R_{i+1}$. We say that tuples of R reference tuples of T through $\varrho$.

## 3.2  Correspondence Assertions

We use Correspondence Assertions (CAs) in order to express schema matchings between schema elements. CAs are formal expressions of the general form $\psi$: $\mathcal{T} \leftarrow \mathcal{S}$, where $\psi$ is the name of the CA, $\mathcal{T}$ is an expression formed by elements of the target schema, and $\mathcal{S}$ is an expression formed by elements of a source schema. The symbol "$\leftarrow$" means "is matched from".

In accordance to [10], there are four types of CAs: Relation Correspondence Assertion (RCA), Attribute Correspondence Assertion (ACA), Summation Correspondence Assertion (SCA), and Grouping Correspondence Assertion (GCA). RCAs and SCAs specify the relationship between relations of distinct schemas, while ACAs and GCAs specify the relationship between attributes of relations of distinct schemas. We now shortly describe each type of CA, adapting them to the RDM. In the remainder of this Section, consider: $S_i = (\mathcal{R}_i, \Omega_i)$ be relational schemas for $1 \le i \le n$, with $R_i$ being relation names of relation schemas in $\mathcal{R}_i$.

**Definition 1.** *Let $\sigma$ be a selection over $R_2$. A Relation Correspondence Assertion RCA is an expression of one of the following forms:*

1. $\psi$: $S_1[R_1] \leftarrow S_2[R_2]$
2. $\psi$: $S_1[R_1] \leftarrow S_2[R_2\sigma]$
3. $\psi$: $S_1[R_1] \leftarrow S_2[R_2] - S_3[R_3]$

4. $\psi$: $S_1[R_1] \leftarrow \bigcup_{i=1}^{n} S_i[R_i]$
5. $\psi$: $S_1[R_1] \leftarrow \bigcap_{i=1}^{n} S_i[R_i]$    $\square$

In Definition 1, we say that $\psi$ matches $R_1$ and $R_i$, for $1 \le i \le n$. RCAs express the various kinds of semantic equivalent relationships. Two relations $R_1$ and $R_2$ are semantically equivalent if they represent the same real concept and there is a 1-to-1 correspondence between their instances. $\psi_1$, shown in Fig. 2, is an example of a RCA.

$\psi_1$ specifies that $M$.SCHEDULE is semantically equivalent to $S_2$.SHOWTIME when the condition $S_2$.SHOWTIME.**city** = "Lisbon" is satisfied. This means that only a subset of tuples of $S_2$.SHOWTIME, those that satisfy the condition are involved in the match.

Before we define an Attribute Correspondence Assertion (ACA), we need introduce the concept of *attribute expression*, as follows:

| $\psi_1$:**M**[SCHEDULE]←**S**$_2$[SHOWTIME(**city** = "Lisbon")] | RCA |
|---|---|
| $\psi_2$:**M**[SCHEDULE]•**movie**←**S**$_2$[SHOWTIME]•FK$_3$/**title** | ACA |
| $\psi_3$:**M**[RATING]⇐groupby(**S**$_2$[FILM] (**rate**)) | SCA |
| $\psi_4$:**M**[RATING] • **quantity**⇐ count(**S**$_2$[FILM] • **rate**) | GCA |

**Fig. 2.** Examples of correspondence assertions.

**Definition 2.** *Let* $R_2$ *and* T *be relation names in* $\mathcal{R}_2$*, with* $\mathcal{A}$ *being an attribute of* $R_2$ *and* $\mathcal{B}$ *an attribute of* T*. Let also* $\varrho$ *be a path from* $R_2$ *to* T*. An attribute expression* $\mathcal{E}$ *over* $R_2$ *is an expression with one of the following forms:*

*1.* $\mathbf{S}_2[R_2] \bullet \mathcal{A}$          *2.* $\mathbf{S}_2[R_2] \bullet \varrho/\mathcal{B}$.      □

**Definition 3.** *Let* $\mathcal{A}_i$ *be attributes of* $R_1$ *(for* $1 \leq i \leq n$*). Let also* $\mathcal{E}_j$*, for* $1 \leq j \leq m$*, be attribute expressions over* $R_2$*. An Attribute Correspondence Assertion (ACA) is an expression of one of the following forms:*

*1.* $\psi: \mathbf{S}_1[R_1] \bullet \mathcal{A}_1 \leftarrow \mathcal{E}_1$        *3.* $\psi: \mathbf{S}_1[R_1] \bullet \mathcal{A}_1 \leftarrow (\mathcal{E}_1, \mathbf{p}_1); \ldots; (\mathcal{E}_m; \mathbf{p}_m); v$
*2.* $\psi: \mathbf{S}_1[R_1] \bullet \mathcal{A}_1 \leftarrow \varphi(\mathcal{E}_1, \mathcal{E}_2, \ldots, \mathcal{E}_m)$    *4.* $\psi: \mathbf{S}_1[R_1](\mathcal{A}_1, \ldots, \mathcal{A}_n) \leftarrow (\mathcal{E}_1, \ldots, \mathcal{E}_n)$

*Where* $\varphi$ *is a function over attributes of* $R_2$*,* $\mathbf{p}_j$ *(for* $1 \leq j \leq m$*) are boolean conditions over attributes of* $R_2$*, and* $v$ *is a value. We say that* $\psi$ *matches* $R_1$ *and* $R_2$*.*      □

ACAs specify the relationship between the attributes of relations that are matched by a RCA. They allow to define 1:1, 1:n, n:1, or m:n relationships between attributes of relations of different schemas. For example see the ACA $\psi_2$ presented in Fig. 2. It specifies the correspondence between **M**.SCHEDULE.**movie** and **S**$_2$.FILM.**title** through a path from SHOWTIME to FILM.

**Definition 4.** *Let* $\sigma$ *be a selection over* $R_2$*. Let also* $\mathcal{A}'_i$ *attributes of* $R_2$ *(for* $1 \leq i \leq m$*). A Summation Correspondence Assertion (SCA) is an expression of one of the following forms:*

*1.* $\psi: \mathbf{S}_1[R_1] \Leftarrow groupby(\mathbf{S}_2[R_2](\mathcal{A}'_1, \mathcal{A}'_2, \ldots, \mathcal{A}'_m))$
*2.* $\psi: \mathbf{S}_1[R_1] \Leftarrow groupby(\mathbf{S}_2[R_2\sigma](\mathcal{A}'_1, \mathcal{A}'_2, \ldots, \mathcal{A}'_m))$
*3.* $\psi: \mathbf{S}_1[R_1] \Leftarrow normalise(\mathbf{S}_2[R_2](\mathcal{A}'_1, \mathcal{A}'_2, \ldots, \mathcal{A}'_m))$
*4.* $\psi: \mathbf{S}_1[R_1] \Leftarrow normalise(\mathbf{S}_2[R_2\sigma](\mathcal{A}'_1, \mathcal{A}'_2, \ldots, \mathcal{A}'_m))$      □

In Definition 4, we say that $\psi$ matches $R_1$ and $R_2$. SCAS specify 1:n, n:1, m:n relationships between relations with distinct schemas. Here we use the symbol "⇐" instead of "←" in order to emphasize that the correspondence is not 1:1 as is usual in the most part of schema matching approaches. SCAS are used to describe the summary of a relation whose tuples are related to the tuples of another relation by gathering them into logical groups. This means that a SCA has only the necessary information to indicate which grouping field is involved in the relationship and the process used to grouping the tuples. $\psi_3$ shown in Fig. 2 is a simple example of a SCA.

GCAs specify the relationship 1:1, 1:n, n:1, or m:n between attributes of relations that are matched by a SCA.

**Definition 5.** *Let $\mathcal{A}$ be an attribute of $R_1$. Let also $\mathcal{E}_i$, for $1 \leq i \leq m$, be attribute expressions over $R_2$. A Grouping Correspondence Assertion (GCA) is an expression of one of the following forms:*

1. $\psi\colon \mathsf{S}_1[R_1] \bullet \mathcal{A} \Leftarrow \mathcal{E}_1$
2. $\psi\colon \mathsf{S}_1[R_1] \bullet \mathcal{A} \Leftarrow \varphi(\mathcal{E}_1, \mathcal{E}_2, \ldots, \mathcal{E}_m)$
3. $\psi\colon\mathsf{S}_1[R_1]\bullet\mathcal{A}\Leftarrow(\mathcal{E}_1, \mathbf{p}_1); \ldots; (\mathcal{E}_m; \mathbf{p}_m); v$
4. $\psi\colon \mathsf{S}_1[R_1] \bullet \mathcal{A} \Leftarrow \gamma(\mathcal{E}_1)$.

5. $\psi\colon \mathsf{S}_1[R_1] \bullet \mathcal{A} \Leftarrow \gamma(\varphi(\mathcal{E}_1, \mathcal{E}_2, \ldots, \mathcal{E}_m))$
6. $\psi\colon \mathsf{S}_1[R_1] \bullet \mathcal{A} \Leftarrow \gamma(\mathcal{E}_1, \mathbf{p})$.
7. $\psi\colon \mathsf{S}_1[R_1]\bullet\mathcal{A} \Leftarrow \gamma(\varphi(\mathcal{E}_1, \mathcal{E}_2, \ldots, \mathcal{E}_m), \mathbf{p})$

*Where $\varphi$ is a function over attributes of $R_2$, $\mathbf{p}_j$ (for $1 \leq j \leq m$) are boolean conditions over attributes of $R_2$, $v$ is a value, and $\gamma$ is one of the aggregate functions: sum (summation), max (maximum), min (minimum), avg (average), or count. We say that $\psi$ matches $R_1$ and $R_2$.* □

Consider the relations $\mathsf{S}_2$.FILM and $\mathbf{M}$.RATING. $\psi_4$, represented in Fig. 2, specifies that $\mathbf{M}$.RATING.**quantity** corresponds to the counting of all distinct values of $\mathsf{S}_2$.FILM.**rate**.

**Definition 6.** *Let $\mathsf{S}_1, \mathsf{S}_2, \ldots, \mathsf{S}_n$ and $\mathsf{T}$ be relational schemas; $R_1$ be a relation schema of $\mathsf{T}$, and $R_2$ a relation schema of some $\mathsf{S}_i$, $1 \leq i \leq n$. Let also $\mathcal{E}_j$ (for $1 \leq j \leq m$) be expressions as defined in Definition 2. A schema matching between schemas $\mathsf{S}_1, \mathsf{S}_2, \ldots, \mathsf{S}_n$ and the schema $\mathsf{T}$ is a set $\mathcal{M}$ of CAs such that:*

1. *if $\mathcal{M}$ has an ACA $\psi$ such that $\psi$ matches $R_1$ and $R_2$, then $\mathcal{M}$ has a RCA $\psi'$ that matches $R_1$ and $R_2$.*
2. *if $\mathcal{M}$ has a GCA $\psi$ such that $\psi$ matches $R_1$ and $R_2$, then $\mathcal{M}$ has a SCA $\psi'$ that matches $R_1$ and $R_2$.*
3. *if $\mathcal{M}$ has a RCA $\psi$ such that $\psi$ matches $R_1$ and $R_2$, then $\mathcal{M}$ has an ACA $\psi'\colon \mathsf{S}_1[R_1](\mathcal{A}_1, \ldots, \mathcal{A}_n) \leftarrow (\mathcal{E}_1, \ldots, \mathcal{E}_n)$ that matches $R_1$ and $R_2$.* □

## 4   Specifying New CAs

In Sect. 1, we identified the following types of relationships between schemas elements that are not properly handled in current schema matching approaches: (1) matches involving explicit join conditions; (2) matches involving outer-joins; and (3) matches involving data-metadata. Join (and outer-join) relationships can express one-to-one or many-to-many correspondences between the relations involved. Matches involving data-metadata can express many-to-many correspondences between the relations involved. So, we extend our previous definitions of RCA and SCA in order to better specify these types of matchings. In the following text consider $\mathsf{S}_i$ relational schemas, $R_i$ relation schemes of $\mathsf{S}_i$ (for $1 \leq i \leq 3$), $\theta$ a join condition between $R_2$ and $R_3$, and $\mathcal{A}_j$ attributes of $R_2$ (for $1 \leq j \leq n$)

**Definition 7.** *A Relation Correspondence Assertion (RCA) is an expression of one of the following forms:*

1. *Expressions shown in Definition 1*
2. $\psi$: $\mathbf{S}_1[R_1] \leftarrow \mathbf{S}_2[R_2] \bowtie \mathbf{S}_3[R_3]\theta$
3. $\psi$: $\mathbf{S}_1[R_1] \leftarrow \mathbf{S}_2[R_2] \rightthreetimes\bowtie \mathbf{S}_3[R_3]\theta$
4. $\psi$: $\mathbf{S}_1[R_1] \leftarrow \mathbf{S}_2[R_2] \bowtie\mathclose{\subset} \mathbf{S}_3[R_3]\theta$
5. $\psi$: $\mathbf{S}_1[R_1] \leftarrow \mathbf{S}_2[R_2] \rightthreetimes\bowtie\mathclose{\subset} \mathbf{S}_3[R_3]\theta$     $\square$

**Definition 8.** *A Summation Correspondence Assertion (SCA) is an expression of one of the following forms:*

1. *Expressions shown in Definition 4*
2. $\psi$: $\mathbf{S}_1[R_1] \Leftarrow \mathbf{S}_2[R_2] \bowtie \mathbf{S}_3[R_3]\theta$
3. $\psi$: $\mathbf{S}_1[R_1] \Leftarrow \mathbf{S}_2[R_2] \rightthreetimes\bowtie \mathbf{S}_3[R_3]\theta$
4. $\psi$: $\mathbf{S}_1[R_1] \Leftarrow \mathbf{S}_2[R_2] \bowtie\mathclose{\subset} \mathbf{S}_3[R_3]\theta$
5. $\psi$: $\mathbf{S}_1[R_1] \Leftarrow \mathbf{S}_2[R_2] \rightthreetimes\bowtie\mathclose{\subset} \mathbf{S}_3[R_3]\theta$
6. $\psi$: $\mathbf{S}_1[R_1] \Leftarrow metadata(\mathbf{S}_2[R_2](A_1,\ldots,A_n))$   $\square$

Consider the three examples about join, outer-join, and data-metadata correspondences described in Sect. 1. The correspondence between **M**.REMAKES and both **S**$_1$.MOVIES and **S**$_2$.FILM can be specified by the SCA $\psi_5$ shown in Fig. 3. $\psi_5$ specifies that **M**.REMAKES corresponds to a join between **S**$_1$.MOVIES and **S**$_2$.FILM where the join condition: **S**$_2$.FILM.**title**= **S**$_1$.MOVIE.**film** and **S**$_2$.FILM.**year** > **S**$_1$.MOVIE.**year** is satisfied.

| |
|---|
| $\psi_5$:**M**[REMAKES] $\Leftarrow$**S**$_2$[FILM]$\bowtie$**S**$_1$[MOVIE]$\theta$, where $\theta$= (**S**$_2$[FILM].**title**=**S**$_1$[MOVIE].**film** and **S**$_2$[FILM].**year** > **S**$_1$[MOVIE].**year** |
| $\psi_6$:**M**[MOVIE]$\leftarrow$**S**$_2$[FILM]$\rightthreetimes\bowtie$**S**$_1$[MOVIE]$\theta'$, where $\theta'$ = (**S**$_2$[FILM].**title**=**S**$_1$[MOVIE].**film** and **S**$_2$[FILM].**year** = **S**$_1$[MOVIE].**year** |
| $\psi_7$:**M**[FILMMAKERS] $\Leftarrow$ *metadata* (**S**$_1$[MOVIEMAKERS] (**id**)) |

**Fig. 3.** Examples of CAs involving joins, outer-joins and data-metadata.

The correspondence between **M**.MOVIE and both **S**$_2$.FILM and **S**$_1$.MOVIE can be specified by the RCA $\psi_6$, shown in Fig. 3. $\psi_6$ specifies that **M**.MOVIE corresponds to a left outer-join between **S**$_2$.FILM and **S**$_1$.MOVIE.

The correspondence between **M**.FILMMAKERS and **S**$_1$.MOVIEMAKERS can be specified by the SCA $\psi_7$, shown in Fig. 3. $\psi_7$ specifies that **M**.FILMMAKERS corresponds to grouping **S**$_1$.MOVIEMAKERS by the attribute **id**, being that a data-metadata translation should be performed (i.e., some data should be converted into metadata).

Once the schema matching is finished, the CAs generated can be used, for example, to generate mapping expressions that convert data sources into data target. We propose that the mapping expressions are automatically generated in the form of SQL queries, which are used to load the relations (the materialized views) of the integrated schema.

## 5    From CAs to Mapping Expressions

In our proposal, the process to create queries to transform data from a schema to another one consists of three steps:

1. Indicate the source schemas and the integrated schema using a high-level data model. In our case, we use the RDM.
2. Define the CA that formally specify the relationships between the integrated schema and the source schemas.
3. Generate a set of queries based on the CAs generated in step 2, in order to populate the relations of the integrated schema.

In order to illustrate our approach, consider the integrated schema **M** and the sources schemas $S_1$ and $S_2$ shown in Fig. 1.

Now, we should define CAs between **M** and $S_1$, and CAs between **M** and $S_2$. In our work, the CAs are specified using a GAV approach rather than a LAV one. One of reasons for our choices was due to the GAV approach makes the query answering easier than LAV one, both in materialized and in virtual integration approaches.

The process to generate the CAs consists of the following steps:

1. To each relation $R^T$ of the target **T** do:
   (a) Identify the correspondences at a relation level (i.e., if there is a RCA or a SCA matching a target relation $R^T$ and some source relation $R^S$).
   (b) Identify the correspondences at an attribute level: (1) identify the ACAs between the attributes of $R^T$ and $R^S$ (if there is a RCA between $R^T$ and $R^S$); (2) identify the GCA between the attributes of $R^T$ and $R^S$ (if there is a SCA between $R^T$ and $R^S$).
   (c) Determine which RCA and SCA can be combined to form a single CA.

In the current work, CAS were manually specified. However, we can use traditional schema matching tools (e.g.,[8,9]) as a starting point to find basic matchings. Then these basic matchings can be enriched through our formalism (using the CAs).

Some examples of RCAs, ACAs, SCAs, and GCAs between elements of **M** and the source schemas $S_1$ and $S_2$ can be found in Figs. 3 and 4.

The final step in the process of creating queries to transform data from a schema to another is the generation of the queries. In our proposal, they are defined based on the definition of the schemas and the CAs. Here we use SQL syntax of MySQL, since MySQL is an open source database that allows to combine the information from many databases in a single query. However, our CAs can be used to generate queries in any SQL syntax or even other federating queries languages as SchemaSQL [16].

Let $\mathcal{M}$ be a set of CAs that defines a matching between the source schemas $S_1$, $S_2$ and the integrated schema **G**, that is, $\mathcal{M}$ satisfies the conditions stated in Definition 6. Algorithm 1 shows the procedure to automatically generate the statements of SQL queries from the CAs in $\mathcal{M}$.

| |
|---|
| $\psi_8$:**M**[MOVIE]•**title** ← **S**$_2$[FILM]• **title** |
| $\psi_9$:**M**[MOVIE]•**year** ← **S**$_2$[FILM]• **year** |
| $\psi_{10}$:**M**[MOVIE]•**genre** ← **S**$_1$[MOVIE]• **category** |
| $\psi_{11}$:**M**[MOVIE]•**description**←**S**$_1$[MOVIE]• **summary** |
| $\psi_{12}$:**M**[FILMMAKERS]•**producer**⇐(**S**$_1$[MOVIEMAKERS]• **name**, **S**$_1$[MOVIEMAKERS]• **role** = = "producer") |
| $\psi_{13}$:**M**[FILMMAKERS]•**director**⇐(**S**$_1$[MOVIEMAKERS]• **name**, **S**$_1$[MOVIEMAKERS]• **role** = = "director") |
| $\psi_{14}$:**M**[FILMMAKERS]• **movie** ⇐ **S**$_1$ [MOVIEMAKERS] • FK4/**film** |

**Fig. 4.** Examples of ACAs and GCAs.

The Algorithm 1 generates a set of SQL queries, one for each relation schema $R^T$ in the integrated schema. First it spans all ACAs and GCAs that relates attributes of $R^T$, and puts the correct value in lists **S**, **J**, and **LA**, in accordance to the type of the CA. **S** keeps the relation schemas that will be included in the FROM clause, **J** keeps the *join conditions* that will be included in the WHERE clause, and **LA** keeps the attributes that will be included in the SELECT clause. The procedure $G\_SQL\_ACA()$, shown in Algorithm 2, spans the ACAs, while the procedure $G\_SQL\_GCA()$, shown in Algorithm 3, spans the GCAs. After, the algorithm spans the RCAs and SCAs, of $R^T$, in order to create the SQL query to load $R^T$, using templates in Table 1. In accordance to type of CA besides **S**, **J**, and **LA**, other variables are needed to keep the *join conditions* that will be included in the ON clause ($\theta$), the relation schema that will be included in (inner, outer, left, or right) JOIN clause (**RJ**), and the grouping attributes that will be included in the GROUP BY clause (**G**). Due to space limitations, Algorithms 1, 2, and 3, as well as the Table 1, do not cover the whole set of CAs as defined in Definitions 3, 5, 7, and 8.

In Algorithms 2, we assumed that $\varphi()$ is a pre-defined SQL function or a user-defined function on SQL. In Algorithms 3, **JAux**, and **Aux** are lists used when it is necessary to create temporary tables in SQL. This occurs when the SQL query is created from a SCA of metadata. **JAux** stores the *joins* that will be included in the WHERE clause of the temporary table, while **Aux** keeps the relation schema that will be the alias of the temporary table.

In Table 1, $Att()$ is a function that returns the list of attribute names of a relation schema. We use the short word *outer join* to emulate a UNION of a LEFT JOIN and a RIGHT JOIN, since MySQL does not support directly full outer-joins.

The SQL queries generated by our algorithms can be used to compute the data target once, and to recompute them at pre-stablished times in order to maintain the target data up-to-date (this approach is named *rematerialization*). Generally, a more efficient approach is to periodically modify only part of the target data to reflect updates in data sources (this approach is named *incremental maintenance*). Rematerialization is adequate, for example, when the integrated schema is firstly populated, or in situations involving complex operations.

---

**Algorithm 1.** Generate the SQL query to load a integrated schema **G** from the sources.

---

**for all** relation schema $\mathbf{N} = \mathrm{R}^T$ in **G** do
    Let $\psi_R$ be a RCA or SCA of $\mathrm{R}^T$
    **if** $\psi_R$ is a RCA **then** G_SQL_ACA( $\mathrm{R}^T, \psi_R$)
    **else** G_SQL_GCA( $\mathrm{R}^T, \psi_R$)
    append $[\mathrm{R}^T]$ to **S**
    **switch** $\psi_R$ **do**
        **case** $\psi_R$: $\mathbf{G}[\mathrm{R}^T] \leftarrow \mathbf{S}[R]$
            **if J** = [ ] **then** use template T1
            **else** use template T3
        **case** $\psi_R$: $\mathbf{G}[\mathrm{R}^T] \leftarrow \mathbf{S}_1[R_1] \cup \mathbf{S}_2[R_2]$
            append $[R_2]$ to **RJ**
            $\theta$ keeps join conditions formed by primary key attributes of $R_1$ and $R_2$
            **if J** = [ ] **then** use template T7
            **else** use template T8
        **case** $\psi_R$: $\mathbf{G}[\mathrm{R}^T] \leftarrow \mathbf{S}_1[R_1] \bowtie \mathbf{S}_2[R_2]\theta$
            append $[R_2]$ to **RJ**
            **if J** = [ ] **then** use template T5
            **else** use template T6
        **case** $\psi_R$: $\mathbf{G}[\mathrm{R}^T] \Leftarrow metadata(\mathbf{S}[R](\mathcal{A}))$
            append $[\mathcal{A}]$ to **AL**
            **if J** = [ ] **then** use template T13
            **else** use template T4
        **case** $\psi_R$: $\mathbf{G}[\mathrm{R}^T] \Leftarrow normalise(\mathbf{S}[R](\mathcal{A}))$
            append $[\mathcal{A}]$ to **G**
            Use template T15
    **end switch**
**end for**

---

---

**Algorithm 2.** G_SQL_ACA().

---

**Input:** $\mathrm{R}^T$, $\psi_R$

Let $\mathbf{S}[R]$ be a source's relation in $\psi_R$
**for all** attribute $\mathcal{A}^T$ in $\mathrm{R}^T$ **do**
    **while** $\exists \psi_A / \psi_A$ is an ACA of $\mathcal{A}^T$ relating it to some atribute of $\mathbf{S}[R]$ **do**
        **if** $\psi_A$: $\mathbf{G}[\mathrm{R}^T] \bullet \mathcal{A}^T \leftarrow \mathbf{S}[R] \bullet \mathcal{A}_1$ **then** append $[\mathcal{A}_1]$ to **LA**
        **if** $\psi_A$: $\mathbf{G}[\mathrm{R}^T] \bullet \mathcal{A}^T \leftarrow \varphi(\mathbf{S}[R] \bullet \mathcal{A}_1, \mathbf{S}[R] \bullet \mathcal{A}_2, \ldots, \mathbf{S}[R] \bullet \mathcal{A}_m)$ **then** append
        $[\varphi(\mathcal{A}_1, \mathcal{A}_2, \ldots, \mathcal{A}_m)]$ to **LA**
    **end while**
**end for**

---

Figure 5 presents the SQL query to transform data from $\mathbf{S}_1$.MOVIE and $\mathbf{S}_2$.FILM to $\mathbf{M}$.MOVIE from the RCA $\psi_6$ and ACA $\psi_8, \psi_9, \psi_{10},$ and $\psi_{11}$. The "*select*" clause (in line 2) is derived based on ACAS $\psi_8, \psi_9$, $\psi_{10}$ and $\psi_{11}$. The "*from*" clause (in line 3) implements a join operation as specified by RCA $\psi_6$. The "*on*" clause (in line 4) is based on the join condition indicated in the end of $\psi_6$.

---

01. *insert into* **M**.MOVIE**(title,year,genre,description)**
02. *select* FILM.**title** *as* **title**, FILM.**year** *as* **year**, MOVIE.**category** *as* **genre**,MOVIE.**summary** *as* **description**
03. *from* $\mathbf{S}_2$.FILM *as* FILM *left join* $\mathbf{S}_1$.MOVIE *as* MOVIE *on* FILM.**title** = MOVIE.**film** *and* FILM.**year** = MOVIE.**year**;

**Fig. 5.** Query definition to populate **M**.MOVIE from $\mathbf{S}_2$.FILM and $\mathbf{S}_1$.MOVIE.

---

**Algorithm 3.** G_SQL_GCA( ).

---

Input: $R^T$, $\psi_R$

Let $S[R]$ be a source's relation in $\psi_R$
for all attribute $\mathcal{A}^T$ in $R^T$ do
  while $\exists \psi_A / \psi_A$ is an GCA of $\mathcal{A}^T$ relating it to some atribute of $S[R]$ do
    if $\psi_A$: $G[R^T] \bullet \mathcal{A}^T \leftarrow S[R] \bullet \mathcal{A}_1$ then append $[\mathcal{A}_1]$ to **LA**
    if $\psi_A$: $G[R^T] \bullet \mathcal{A}^T \leftarrow S[R] \bullet \varrho / \mathcal{B}_k$ then
      for all FK in $\varrho$ do
        Let $R_1$ and $R_2$ be relation schemas related by FK
        Let $[a_1, \ldots, a_n]$ and $[b_1, \ldots, b_n]$ be lists of key attributes of, respectively, $R_1$ and $R_2$
        append $[R_1, R_2]$ to **S**
        append $[a_1 = b_1, \ldots, a_n = b_n]$ to **J**
        append $[\mathcal{B}]$ to **LA**
      end for
    if $\psi_A$:$G[R^T] \bullet \mathcal{A}^T \leftarrow (S[R] \bullet \mathcal{A}_1, \mathbf{p}_1)$ and $\psi_R$ is of metadata then
      append $[\mathcal{A}_1]$ to **LA**
      append $[Temp\_R]$ to **Aux**
      append $[\mathbf{p}_1]$ to **JAux**
  end while
end for

---

**Table 1.** Templates to generate SQL Statements induced by RCAS and ACAS.

| | |
|---|---|
| T1 | *insert into* N (att[1], att[2], . . . , att[n]) *select* LA[1], LA[2], . . . , LA[n] *from* S[1] |
| | $\psi$: $\mathbf{S}_1[R_1] \leftarrow \mathbf{S}_2[R_2]$ |
| T5 | *insert into* N (att[1], att[2], . . . , att[n]) *select* LA[1], LA[2], . . . , LA[n] *from* S[1], S[2], . . . , S[m] *left join* RJ[1] *on* $\theta$ |
| | $\psi$: $\mathbf{S}_1[R_1] \leftarrow \mathbf{S}_2[R_2] \bowtie \mathbf{S}_3[R_3]\theta$ |
| T7 | *insert into* N (att[1], att[2], . . . , att[n]) *select* LA[1], LA[2], . . . , LA[n] *from* S[1] *outer join* RJ[1] *on* $\theta$ |
| | $\psi$: $\mathbf{S}_1[R_1] \leftarrow \mathbf{S}_2[R_2] \cup \mathbf{S}_3[R_3]$ <br> $\psi$: $\mathbf{S}_1[R_1] \leftarrow \mathbf{S}_2[R_2(\mathbf{p}_2)] \bowtie \mathbf{S}_3[R_3(\mathbf{p}_3)]\theta$ |
| T13 | *insert into* N (att[1], att[2], . . . , att[n]) *select* att[1], att[2], . . . , A TT[n] *from* (*select* LA[1], LA[2], . . . , LA[w] *from* S[1] *where* JAux[1] ) *as* Aux[1]) *outer join* (*select* LA[1], LA[2], . . . , LA[w] *from* S[1] *where* JAux[2] ) *as* Aux[2]) *on* (Aux[1].ID = Aux[2].ID) |
| | $\psi$: $\mathbf{S}_1[R_1] \Leftarrow metadata(\mathbf{S}_2[R_2](\mathcal{A}_1)$ |
| T15 | *insert into* N (att[1], att[2], . . . , att[n]) *select* LA[1], LA[2], . . . , LA[n] *from* S[1] *group by* G[1] |
| | $\psi$: $\mathbf{S}_1[R_1] \Leftarrow normalise(\mathbf{S}_2[R_2](\mathcal{A}_1))$ |

Figure 6 presents the definition of the query to transform data from $S_1$.MOVIEMAKERS to $M$.FILMMAKERS. For this query, we have to define a nested select statement to each case-base GCA that relates attributes of $S_1$.MOVIEMAKERS to attributes of $M$.FILMMAKERS. Each nested select statement must be joined through an outer-join in order to guarantee both: i) that duplicate tuples will be merged properly, and 2) not duplicate tuples will be stored in $M$.FILMMAKERS. Thus, the clauses *"from"* (line 3), *"outer join"* (line 7), and *"on"* (line 12) correctly implement the data-metadata relationship specified by the SCA $\psi_7$. The *"on"* clause (line 12) is based on the attribute indicated in $\psi_7$. The first nested select statement (lines 4 to 6) is defined based on the GCAS $\psi_{12}$ and $\psi_{14}$. The second nested select statement (lines 8 to 11) is similar to the first one, but now it is based on $\psi_{13}$ and $\psi_{14}$. The *"select"* clause in line 2 is based on the left-hand side of GCAs $\psi_{12}$, $\psi_{13}$ and $\psi_{14}$.

```
01. insert into M.FILMMAKERS(movie, producer, director)
02. select movie, producer, director
03. from
04. (select MOVIE.film as movie,MOVIEMAKERS.name as producer, MOVIEMAKERS.id as ID
05.      from S₁.MOVIEMAKERS as MOVIEMAKERS, S₁.MOVIE as MOVIE
06.      where MOVIEMAKERS.id=MOVIE.id and MOVIEMAKERS.role = 'producer') as T1_MOVIEMAKERS
07. outer join
08. (select MOVIE.film as movie,MOVIEMAKERS.name as director, MOVIEMAKERS.id as ID
09.      from S₁.MOVIEMAKERS as MOVIEMAKERS, S₁.MOVIE as MOVIE
10.      where MOVIEMAKERS.id=MOVIE.id
11.      and MOVIEMAKERS.role = 'director') as T2_MOVIEMAKERS
12.      on (T1_MOVIEMAKERS.ID = T2_MOVIEMAKERS.ID);
```

**Fig. 6.** Query definition to populate **M**.FILMMAKERS from **S**$_1$.MOVIEMAKERS.

# 6    Empirical Evaluation

We have performed some preliminary tests to verify that our approach is tractable for reasonably sized input.

## 6.1    Study Case Scenario

For our evaluation, we create a case study to simulate a situation close to the real world. We need to integrate information of three different sources: IES, FSP, and CDV to get a more complete information about Brazil's universities. IES contains data about Brazil's universities (name, city, state, etc.). It has a single relation (IES_2011) with 26 attributes and 2366 tuples[3]. FSP contains data about the ranking of the Brazil's universities (ranking, university, grade, etc.). It has two relations, but only one of them (RANKING, with 13 attributes and 191 tuples) was used in the evaluation[4]. CDV contains data about the living cost of some cities of Brazil. It has a single relation (LIVINGCOST) with 5 attributes and 84 tuples[5].

The integrated schema, named G, contains the necessary structure to keep the information required by the designer. It contains 8 relations with a total of 31 attributes and 8 foreign keys, as can be saw in the Fig. 7.

## 6.2    Method

We measure the performance of the data translation (i.e., the run time of the queries to load the schema G). For our tests, we have used a Macbook Pro/2.3GHz Intel Core (4GB of RAM and 499Gb of HD) running OSx 10.9.5. All databases were locally stored in this machine using the MySQL 5.6.

We first manually defined the CAs, with the aid of a tool implemented by us. For this case study, we defined 3 RCAs, 5 SCAs of normalize, 31 ACAs,

---

[3] IES data was extract from http://www.dados.gov.br/dataset/instituicoes-de-ensino-superior.

[4] FSP data was extract from http://ruf.folha.uol.com.br/2014/rankingdeuniversidades/.

[5] CDV data was extract from http://wwwcustodevida.com.br/brasil.

FSP_RANKING(**univ_id**, **census_year**, **ranking**, **grade**)
FK1(FSP_RANKING, ⟨univ_id⟩, UNIVERSITY, ⟨id⟩)
LIVINGCOST(**city_id**, **year**, **livingCost**, **state_id**)
FK3(LIVINGCOST, ⟨city_id⟩, CITY, ⟨city_id⟩)
FK4(LIVINGCOST, ⟨state_id⟩, STATE, ⟨ibge_id⟩)

UNIVERSITY_TYPE(**code**, **type**)
STATE(**ibge_id**, **state**, **s_mark**)
PLACE(**code**, **place**)
ORGANIZATION(**code**, **type**)
CITY(**city_id**, **city**, **state_id**)
FK2(CITY, ⟨state_id⟩, STATE, ⟨ibge_id⟩)

UNIVERSITY(**id**, **name**, **short_name**, **city_id**, **place_id**, **type_id**, **org_id**, **postalCode**, **address**, **telephone**, **contact**, **homepage**)
FK5(UNIVERSITY, ⟨place_id⟩, PLACE, ⟨code⟩)
FK6(UNIVERSITY, ⟨org_id⟩, ORGANIZATION, ⟨code⟩)
FK7(UNIVERSITY, ⟨city_id⟩, CITY, ⟨city_id⟩)
FK8(UNIVERSITY, ⟨type_id⟩, UNIVERSITY_TYPE, ⟨code⟩)

**Fig. 7.** The integrated schema G.

and 8 GCAs, being a total of 52 CAs. Using the Algorithm 1, we generate 8 SQL queries: 5 queries of group by, 2 simple *select-from* queries, and 1 more complex query that simulates the outer join operator. Some queries use stored functions defined to looks for the value of a primary key in a target relation based on the attribute value of a source relation.

For data translation test, we measured the time that MySQL took to load each target relation using the queries generated by the Algorithm 1. Due to the run time of SQL queries can change depending on internal and external factors, we ran each query by 50 times and took the average to each 10 executions. All tests were performed locally in a same machine and only the MySQL server and MySQLWorkbench were running at the time. The result of the test can be observed through the chart shown in Fig. 8.

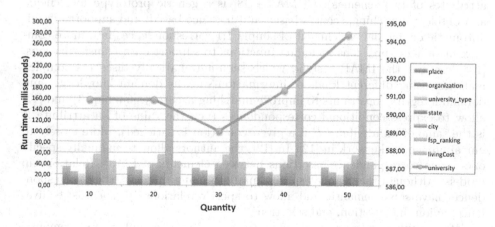

**Fig. 8.** Run time query by quantity of executions chart.

## 6.3   Discussion

We noted that the run time to most queries are more or less constant and below that 60 ms. It is not a surprise that the queries with higher execution time were those to load FSP_RANKING (about 200ms) and UNIVERSITY (about 590 ms), because both has more tuples to load than the others. Considering the number of tuples of the UNIVERSITY (more than 2000) and that the query generated is a bit complex (includes left-join, right-join, union all, and 5 stored functions), we believe that 590 ms is a good performance.

# 7   Related Work

Schema matching is an important step of the data integration process. Typically, 1:1 correspondences between two different schemas are manually defined using a GUI or are (semi-) automatically discovered using matchers (usually through heuristics). Each correspondence, in general, only specifies which elements refer to a same attribute or relation in the real world [17]. AgreementMaker [4], and OII Harmony [9] are some examples of tools for schema matching. Agreement-Maker [4] can match schemas and ontologies using schema information as well as instance-level data to generate the correspondences. OII Harmony [9] combines multiple matchers algorithms based on natural-language processing to identify correspondences between schemas.

Correspondences such as those defined/generated in [4,9] do not provide all necessary information for discovering expressions to transform data sources in data target (i.e., the mapping expressions), the next phase in the schema mapping process. Richer models for specifying correspondences between schemas were proposed by [8,11–13] and [5](chap. 3). These approaches allow to define one-to-one or many-to-one attribute correspondences (i.e., association between attributes of two schemas). COMA++ [8] is a generic prototype for schema and ontology matching, schema-based and instance-based, and support a semi-automatic or manual enrichment of simple 1:1 correspondences into more complex mapping expressions including functions to support data transformations. [13] describes the IMAP system, which semi-automatically discovers complex matches, using different kinds of information such as domain knowledge, and domain integrity constraints to improve matching accuracy. [5](chap. 3) and [11] allow to express conditional correspondences (i.e., the value of an attribute $A$ is the same of an attribute $B$ if a given condition is satisfied). More closely to our approach is the work in [12]. In [12], the authors allow to manually specify one-to-one correspondence assertions between elements of Entity Relationship models. Although they cannot specify many-to-many matches, their correspondences have some semantic and allow to specify relationships such as: equivalence, union, intersection, and selection.

[10] specify one-to-one and many-to-many basic, complex, and semantic matches between elements of object-relational schemas. They can specify most part of the correspondences specified in [12] and other more complex. For example, they can deal with aggregate functions, denormalisations, and grouping (i.e., *group by* in SQL). Joins and outer-joins are implicitly defined based on the

integrity constraints or match functions[6]. A distinguished feature of the approach proposed in [10] is that it allows to match, in the same correspondence,
relations and attributes of two or more schemas. Yet, the information they provide is not sufficient, since they do not explicitly enable the specification of join
paths and its variants, nor to deal with data-metadata relationships.

Data-metadata translations between elements of different relational schemas
have been studied extensively. SchemaSQL [16] and FIRA/FISQL [18] are the
most notable works on this subject. SchemaSQL [16] is a SQL-like metadata
query language that uses view statements to restructure one column of values of a relation into metadata in another one. FISQL [18] is a sucessor of
SchemaSQL and it is equivalent to the query algebra FIRA. Both SchemaSQL
and FIRA/FISQL were proposed to provide interoperability in relational multi-
database systems. Our SCA of metadata was based on the *promote metadata*
operator of FIRA.

# 8    Conclusions

This paper focused on present CAs that deal with 1:1 and m:n matchings between
schemas components, including correspondences involving aggregations, joins,
and metadata. We emphasize that, in our approach, the CAs can specify basic
and complex correspondences with semantics. Using CAs, we shown how SQL
queries can be automatically generated to populate relations (views) of a global
schema.

We presented some preliminary tests to evaluate the performance of the
queries generated from CAs. We intend to realize more tests to evaluate the
performance to different types of queries and other datasets.

We currently are working in as specifying complex correspondences between
relational schemas and (RDF). Some initial work was published in [19]. We intent
extend the initial proposal with the CAs presented here.

**Acknowledgements.** This work was partially supported by national funds through
FCT - Fundação para a Ciência e a Tecnologia, under the project PEst-OE/EEI/
LA0021/2013, DataStorm Research Line of Excellency funding (EXCL/EEI-ESS/
0257/2012) and the grant SFRH/BPD/76024/2011. We are especially grateful to Diego
Cardoso (UFC, Brazil) for the implementation of the algorithms.

# References

1. Kimball, R., Ross, M., Thornthwaite, W., Mundy, J., Becker, B.: The Data Warehouse Lifecycle Tookit, 2nd edn. Wiley, Indianapolis (2008)
2. Popfinger, C.: Enhanced Active Databases for Federated Information Systems.
PhD thesis, Heinrich Heine University Düsseldorf (2006)

---

[6] Match functions are functions that determine if two different instances represent the
same concept in the real world.

3. Langegger, A., Wöß, W., Blöchl, M.: A semantic web middleware for virtual data integration on the web. In: Bechhofer, S., Hauswirth, M., Hoffmann, J., Koubarakis, M. (eds.) ESWC 2008. LNCS, vol. 5021, pp. 493–507. Springer, Heidelberg (2008)
4. Cruz, I.F., Antonelli, F.P., Stroe, C.: Agreementmaker: efficient matching for large real-world schemas and ontologies. Proc. VLDB Endow. **2**(2), 1586–1589 (2009)
5. Bellahsene, Z., Bonifati, A., Rahm, E. (eds.): Schema Matching and Mapping. Data-Centric Systems and Applications. Springer, Heidelberg (2011)
6. Rahm, E., Bernstein, P.A.: A survey of approaches to automatic schema matching. VLDB J. **10**(4), 334–350 (2001)
7. Shvaiko, P., Euzenat, J.: A survey of schema-based matching approaches. In: Spaccapietra, S. (ed.) Journal on Data Semantics IV. LNCS, vol. 3730, pp. 146–171. Springer, Heidelberg (2005)
8. Massmann, S., Raunich, S., Aumueller, D., Arnold, P., Rahm, E.: Evolution of the COMA match system. In: The 6th Intl. Workshop on Ontology Matching. (2011)
9. Mork, P., Seligman, L., Rosenthal, A., Korb, J., Wolf, C.: The Harmony integration workbench. J. Data Semant. **11**, 65–93 (2008)
10. Pequeno, V.M., Pires, J.C.M.: Using perspective schemata to model the ETL process. In: ICMIS 2009, pp. 332–339. World Academy of Science, Engineering and Technology (2009)
11. Bohannon, P., Elnahrawy, E., Fan, W., Flaster, M.: Putting context into schema matching. In: VLDB, pp. 307–318 (2006)
12. Vidal, V.M.P., Lóscio, B.F.: Updating multiple databases through mediators. In: ICEIS 1999, pp. 163–170 (1999)
13. Dhamankar, R., Lee, Y., Doan, A., Halevy, A.Y., Domingos, P.: IMAP: Discovering complex mappings between database schemas. In: ACM SIGMOD, pp. 383–394 (2004)
14. Yan, L.L., Miller, R.J., Haas, L.M., Fagin, R.: Data-driven understanding and refinement of schema mappings. In: ACM SIGMOD, pp. 485–496. ACM (2001)
15. Pequeno, V.M., Aparício, J.N.: Using correspondence assertions to specify the semantics of views in an object-relational data warehouse. In: ICEIS 2005, pp. 219–225 (2005)
16. Lakshmanan, L., Sadri, F., Subramanian, I.: SchemaSQL - a language for interoperability in relational multi-database systems. In: VLDB, pp. 239–250. Morgan Kaufmann (1996)
17. Doan, A., Halevy, A., Ives, Z.: Principles of Data Integration. Morgan Kaufmann, Waltham (2012)
18. Wyss, C.M., Robertson, E.L.: Relational languages for metadata integration. ACM Trans. Database Syst. **30**, 624–660 (2005)
19. Pequeno, V.M., Vidal, V.M.P., Casanova, M.A., Neto, L.E.T., Galhardas, H.: Specifying complex correspondences between relational schemas and rdf models for generating customized R2RML mappings. In: IDEAS 2014, pp. 96–104. ACM (2014)

# Towards an Efficient and Distributed DBSCAN Algorithm Using MapReduce

Ticiana L. Coelho da Silva$^{(\boxtimes)}$, Antonio C. Araújo Neto, Regis Pires Magalhães,
Victor A.E. de Farias, José A.F. de Macêdo, and Javam C. Machado

Computing Science Department, Federal University of Ceara, Fortaleza, Brazil
{ticianalc,javam}@ufc.br,
{antonio,regispires,victorfarias,jose.macedo}@lia.ufc.br

**Abstract.** Clustering is a major data mining technique that groups a
set of objects in such a way that objects in the same group are more
similar to each other than to those in other groups. Among several types
of clustering, density-based clustering algorithms are more efficient in
detecting clusters with varied density and different shapes. One of the
most important density-based clustering algorithms is DBSCAN. Due to
the huge size of generated data by the widespread diffusion of wireless
technologies and the complexity of big data analysis, new scalable algorithms for efficiently processing such data are needed. In this chapter we
are particularly interested in using traffic data for finding congested areas
in a city. For this purpose, we developed a new distributed and efficient
strategy of DBSCAN algorithm that uses MapReduce to detect dense
areas based on the input parameters. We conducted experiments using
real traffic data of a brazilian city, Fortaleza, and compared our approach
with the centralized and the MapReduce-based approaches. Our preliminary results confirmed that our approach is scalable and more efficient
than the other ones. We also present an incremental version of DBSCAN
considering the MapReduce version of it.

**Keywords:** DBSCAN · MapReduce · Traffic data

## 1 Introduction

One of the most important density-based clustering algorithms known in literature is DBSCAN (Density-based Spatial Clustering of Application with Noise) [4].
Its advantages over other clustering techniques are that it groups data into clusters of arbitrary shape, it does not require a priori number of clusters, and it deals
with outliers in the data set. However, DBSCAN is more computationally expensive than other clustering algorithms, such as k-means, for example. Moreover,
DBSCAN does not scale when executed on large data sets in a single machine.
Recently, many researchers have been using cloud computing infrastructure in
order to solve scalability problems of some traditional centralized clustering algorithms [2]. Thus, the strategy to parallelize DBSCAN in shared-nothing computer
clusters is an adequate solution to solve such problems [9].

© Springer International Publishing Switzerland 2015
J. Cordeiro et al. (Eds.): ICEIS 2014, LNBIP 227, pp. 75–90, 2015.
DOI: 10.1007/978-3-319-22348-3_5

Clearly, the provisioning of an infrastructure for large scale processing requires software that can take advantage of the large amount of machines and mitigate the problem of communication between them. It has been increasing the amount of techniques to manage computer clusters, among which stands out the paradigm MapReduce [3] and its open source implementation Hadoop [15], used to manage large volumes of data across clusters of computers.

Hadoop framework is attractive because it provides a simple programming model that makes it easier for users to implement relatively sophisticated distributed programs. The MapReduce programming model is recommended for parallel processing of large data volumes in computational clusters [8]. It is also scalable and fault tolerant. The MapReduce platform divides a task into small activities and materializes its intermediate results locally. When a fault occurs in this process, only failed activities are re-executed.

This chapter is based on [10] which aims at identifying, in a large data set, traffic jam areas in a city using mobility data. In this sense, a parallel version of DBSCAN algorithm, based on the MapReduce paradigm, was proposed as a solution. Related works, such as [6] and [2] also use MapReduce to parallelize DBSCAN and they are explained on Sect. 3.

The main contributions of this work are: (1) Our partitioning strategy is less costly than the one proposed on [2]. In [2], the authors present a grid-based partitioning strategy. Our approach is traffic data aware and it partitions the data set with regard to one attribute (in our experiments we used the streets' name); (2) To gather clusters of different partitions, our merge strategy does not need data replication as [6] and [2]. Moreover, our approach guarantees the same result of the centralized DBSCAN; (3) We proved that our distributed DBSCAN algorithm is correct on Sect. 4; (4) An incremental and distributed version of DBSCAN.

The structure of this chapter is organized as follows. Section 2 introduces basic concepts needed to understand the solution of the problem. Section 3 presents our related work. Section 4 addresses the methodology and implementation of this work, that involves the solution of the problem. The discussion of the incremental version is presented in Sect. 5. The experiments are described in Sect. 6. Section 7 presents our conclusion.

## 2    Preliminary

### 2.1    MapReduce

The need for managing, processing, and analyzing efficiently large amounts of data is a key issue in the Big Data scenario. To address these problems, different solutions have been proposed, including the migration/building applications for cloud computing environments, and systems based on Distributed Hash Table (DHT) or structure of multidimensional arrays [12]. Among these solutions, there is the MapReduce paradigm [3], designed to support the distributed processing of large data sets on clusters of servers and its open source implementation Hadoop [15].

The MapReduce programming model is based on two primitives of functional programming: Map and Reduce. The MapReduce execution is carried out as follows: (i) The Map function takes a list of key-value pairs $(K_1, V_1)$ as input and a list of intermediate key-value pairs $(K_2, V_2)$ as output; (ii) the key-value pairs $(K_2, V_2)$ are defined according to the implementation of the Map function provided by the user and they are collected by a master node at the end of each Map task, then sorted by the key. The keys are divided among all the Reduce tasks. The key-value pairs that have the same key are assigned to the same Reduce task; (iii) The Reduce function receives as input all values $V_2$ from the same key $K_2$ and produces as output key-value pairs $(K_3, V_3)$ that represent the outcome of the MapReduce process. The reduce tasks run on one key at a time. The way in which values are combined is determined by the Reduce function code given by the user.

Hadoop is an open-source framework developed by the Apache Software Foundation that implements MapReduce, along with a distributed file system called HDFS (Hadoop Distributed File System). What makes MapReduce attractive is the opportunity to manage large-scale computations with fault tolerance. The developer only needs to implement two functions called Map and Reduce. Therefore, the system manages the parallel execution and coordinates the implementation of Map and Reduce tasks, being able to handle failures during execution.

## 2.2 DBSCAN

DBSCAN is a clustering algorithm widely used in the scientific community. Its main idea is to find clusters from each point that has at least a certain amount of neighbors ($minPoints$) within a specified range ($eps$), where $minPoints$ and $eps$ are input parameters. Finding values for both the parameters might be difficult, once it depends on the data and on the information one desires to discover. The following definitions are used in DBSCAN algorithm and they will be used in the Sect. 4:

- Card(A): cardinality of the set A.
- $N_{eps}(o)$: $p \in N_{eps}(o)$, if and only if the distance between $p$ and $o$ is less or equal than $eps$.
- Directly Density-Reachable (DDR): $o$ is DDR from $p$, if $o \in N_{eps}(p)$ and $Card(N_{eps}(p)) \geq minPoints$.
- Density-Reachable (DR): $o$ is DR from $p$, if there is a chain of points $\{p_1, ..., p_n\}$ where $p_1 = p$ and $p_n = o$, such as $p_{i+1}$ is DDR from $p_i$ and $\forall i \in \{1, ..., n-1\}$.
- Core Point: $o$ is a Core Point if $Card(N_{eps}(o)) \geq minPoints$.
- Border Point: $p$ is a Border Point if $Card(N_{eps}(p)) < minPoints$ and $p$ is DDR from a Core Point.
- Noise: $q$ is Noise if $Card(N_{eps}(q)) < minPoints$ and $q$ is not DDR from any Core Point.

DBSCAN finds for each point $o$, $N_{eps}(o)$ in the data. If $CardN_{eps}(o) \geq$ minPoints, a new cluster $C$ is created and it contains the points o and $N_{eps}(o)$. Then each point $q \in C$ that has not been visited is also checked. If $N_{eps}(q) \geq$ minPoints, each point $r \in N_{eps}(q)$ that is not in $C$ is added to $C$. These steps are repeated until no new point is added to $C$. The algorithm ends when all points from the data set are visited.

## 3   Related Work

P-DBSCAN [7] is a density-based clustering algorithm based on DBSCAN for analysis of places and events using a collection of geo-tagged photos. P-DBSCAN introduces two new concepts: density threshold and adaptive density, that is used for fast convergence towards high density regions. However P-DBSCAN does not have the advantages of the MapReduce model to process large data sets.

Another related work is GRIDBSCAN [14], that proposes a three-level clustering method. The first level selects appropriate grids so that the density is homogeneous in each grid. The second stage merges cells with similar densities and identifies the most suitable values of *eps* and *minPoints* in each grid that remain after merging. The third step of the proposed method executes the DBSCAN method with these identified parameters in the data set. However, GRIDBSCAN is not suitable for large amounts of data. Our proposed algorithm in this work is a distributed and parallel version of DBSCAN that uses MapReduce and is suitable for handling large amounts of data.

The paper [6] proposes an implementation of DBSCAN with a MapReduce of four stages using grid based partitioning.

The paper also presents a strategy for joining clusters that are in different partitions and contain the same points in their boundaries. Such points are replicated in the partitions and the discovery of clusters, that can be merged in a single cluster, is analyzed from them. Note that the number of replicated boundary points can affect the clustering efficiency, as such points not only increase the load of each compute node, but also increase the time to merge the results of different computational nodes.

Similar to the previous work, [2] proposes DBSCANMR that is a DBSCAN implementation using MapReduce and grid based partitioning. In [2], the partition of points spends a great deal of time and it is centralized.

The data set is partitioned in order to maintain the uniform load balancing across the compute nodes and to minimize the same points between partitions. Another disadvantage is the proposed strategy is sensitive to two input parameters. How to obtain the best values for those parameters is not explained in the paper. The DBSCAN algorithm runs on each compute node for each partition using a KD-tree index. The merge of clusters that are on distinct partitions is done when the same point belongs to such partitions and it is also tagged as a core point in any of the clusters. If it is detected that two clusters should merge, they are renamed to a single name. This process also occurs in [6].

This work has similar approach to the papers [6] and [2] because they consider the challenge of handling large amounts of data and use MapReduce to parallelize the DBSCAN algorithm. However, this chapter presents a data partitioning technique that is data aware, which means partitioning data according to their spatial extent. The partitioning technique proposed by [2] is centralized and spends much time for large amount of data as we could see on our experiments. Furthermore, unlike this work to merge clusters, [6] and [2] proposed approaches that require replication, which can affect the clustering efficiency. The cluster merging phase in this work checks if points previously considered as a noise point becomes a border or core point.

# 4    Methodology and Implementation

Mobility data has been fostered by the widespread diffusion of wireless technologies, such as call details records from mobile phones and GPS tracks from navigation devices, society-wide proxies of human moving behaviour. These data opens new opportunities for discovering the hidden patterns and models that characterize the trajectories humans follow during their daily activity. This research topic has recently attracted scientists from several fields, being not only a major intellectual challenge, but also a very important issue to domains such as urban planning, sustainable mobility, transportation engineering, public health, and economic forecasting [5].

The increasing popularity of mobility data has become the main source for evaluating the traffic situation to support drivers' decisions related to displacement in a city in real time. Traffic information in big cities can be collected from GPS devices or from traffic radars, or even gathered from tweets. This information can be used to complement the data generated by cameras and physical sensors in order to guide municipality actions in finding solutions to mobility problems. Through these data it is possible to analyze where the congested areas are within a city in order to discover which regions are more likely to have traffic jams. Such discovery may assist the search for effective reengineering traffic solutions in the context of smart cities. This is an application for our propose approach.

Normally the traffic data indicates the name of the street, the geographic position (latitude and longitude), the average speed of vehicles at the moment, among others. We address in this chapter the problem of discovering density areas, that may be represent a traffic jam. We also consider that frequent updates can happen in the data set. After insertions or deletions to the dynamic database, the clusters discovered by DBSCAN has to be updated. So we discuss how the incremental approach of DBSCAN [11] algorithm can be applied on our distributed approach.

In this section, we focus on the solution of finding density areas or clusters from raw traffic data on MapReduce. We formulate the problem as follows:

**Problem Statement.** Given a set of d-dimensional points on the traffic data set $DS = \{p_1, p_2, ..., p_n\}$ such that each point represents one vehicle with the average speed, the *eps* value, the minimum number of points required to form a cluster minPoints and a set of virtual machines $VM = \{vm_1, vm_2, ..., vm_n\}$ with a MapReduce program; find the density areas on the traffic data with respect to the given *eps* and *minPoints* values. In this chapter, we only consider two dimensions (latitude and longitude) for points. Furthermore, each point has the information about the street it belongs to.

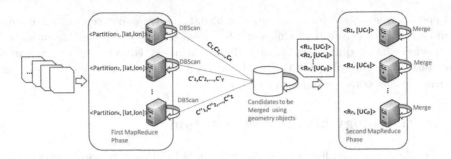

**Fig. 1.** The phases of distributed and parallel DBSCAN execution.

### 4.1 MapReduce Phases and Detection of Possible Merges

This section presents the implementation of the proposed solution to the problem. Hereafter, we explain the steps or phases to parallelize DBSCAN using the MapReduce programming model as we can see on Fig. 1.

– **Executing DBSCAN Distributedly.** This phase is a MapReduce process. Map and Reduce functions for this step are explained below.
  1. Map function. Each point from the data set is described as a pair $\langle key, value \rangle$, such that the key refers to the street and the value refers to a geographic location (latitude and longitude) where the data was collected. As we could see on Algorithm 1.
  2. Reduce function. It is presented on Algorithm 2. This function receives a list of values that have the same key, i.e. the points or geographical positions (latitude and longitude) that belongs to the same street. The DBSCAN algorithm is applied in this phase using the KD-tree index [1].

---

**Algorithm 1.** First MapReduce - Map.

    **Input**: Set of points of the data set $T$
1 **begin**
2     **for** $p \in T$ **do**
3         $createPair\langle p.street\ name, p.Lat,\ p.Lon \rangle$

---

The result is stored in a database. This means that the identifier of each cluster and the information about their points (such as latitude, longitude, if it is core point or noise) are saved.

– **Computing Candidate Clusters.** Since there are many crossroads between the streets in the city and the partitioning of data is based on the streets, it is necessary to discover what are the clusters of different streets that intersect each other or may be merged into a single cluster. For example, it is common in large cities have the same traffic jam happening on different streets that

---

**Algorithm 2.** First MapReduce - Reduce.

**Input**: Set $P$ of pairs $\langle k, v \rangle$ with same $k$, minPoints, eps
1 **begin**
2 | **DBSCAN(P, eps, minPoints)**
3 | Store results on database;

---

intersect to each other. In other words, two clusters may have points at a distance less than or equal to *eps* in such a way that if the data were processed by the same reduce or even if they were in the same partition, they would be grouped into a single cluster. Thus, the clusters are also stored as a geometric object in the database and only the pairs of objects that have distance at most *eps* will be considered in the next phase that is the merge phase. Tuples with pairs of candidate clusters for merge are passed with the same key to the next MapReduce. As we could see on Algorithm 3.

---

**Algorithm 3.** Find merge candidates clusters.

**Input**: Set $C$ of Clusters
**Output**: $V$ is a set of merge candidates clusters
1 **begin**
2 | **for** $C_i \in C$ **do**
3 | | Create its geometry $G_i$;
4 | **for** *all geometries* $G_i$ *and* $G_j$ *and* $i <> j$ **do**
5 | | **if** $Distance(G_i, G_j) \leq eps$ **then**
6 | | | $V \leftarrow \langle C_i, C_j \rangle$
7 | **return** $V$;

---

**Algorithm 4.** Second MapReduce - REDUCE.

**Input**: Set $V$ of pairs $\langle C_i, C_j \rangle$ of clusters candidates to merge
1 **begin**
2 | **for** $\langle C_i, C_j \rangle \in V$ **do**
3 | | **if** $CanMerge(C_i, C_j)$ **then**
4 | | | Rename $C_j$ to $C_i$ in V

---

– **Merging Clusters.** It is also described by a MapReduce process. Map and reduce functions for this phase are explained below.
  1. Map function. It is the identity function. It simply passes each key-value pair to the Reduce function.

2. Reduce function. It receives as key the lowest cluster identifier from all the clusters that are candidates to be merged into a single cluster. The value of that key corresponds to the other cluster identifiers that are merge candidates. Thereby, if two clusters must be merged into a single cluster, the information about points belonging to them are updated. The Algorithms 4 and 5 are executed in this phase.

Lines 2 to 5 from Algorithm 5, we check and update the neighbors of each point $p_i \in C_i$ and $p_j \in C_j$. This occurs because if $C_i$ and $C_j$ are merge clusters candidates, there are points in $C_i$ and $C_j$ that the distance between them is less or equal than $eps$. On the lines 6 to 11, the algorithm verifies if there is some point $p_i \in C_i$ and $p_j \in C_j$ that may have become core points. This phase is important, because $C_i$ and $C_j$ can merge if there is a core point $p_i \in C_i$ and another core point $p_j \in C_j$, such that $p_i$ is DDR from $p_j$ as we can see on lines 12 to 15 on the Algorithm 5. In the next section, we present a proof that validate our merge strategy.

This work considers the possibility that a noise point in a cluster may become a border or core point with the merge of clusters different of our related works. We do that on the line 16 of Algorithm 5 calling the procedure **updateNoisePoints()**. Considering that $p_i \in C_i$, $p_j \in C_j$ and $p_i \in N_{eps}(p_j)$, if $p_i$ or $p_j$ were noise points before the merge phase and it occurred an update on $N_{eps}(p_i)$ and $N_{eps}(p_j)$, $p_i$ or $p_j$ could not be more a noise point, but border point or core point. That is checked on the procedure **updateNoisePoints()**.

Our merge phase is efficient, because it does not consider replicated data as our related work. Next, we prove that our strategy merges clusters candidates correctly.

## 4.2   Validation of Merge Candidates

**Theorem 1.** *Let $C_1$ be a cluster of a partition $S_1$, $C_2$ be a cluster of a partition $S_2$, and $S_1 \cap S_2 = \emptyset$. Clusters $C_1$ and $C_2$ should merge if there are two points $p_1 \in C_1$ and $p_2 \in C_2$ that satisfy the following properties:*

- *$Distance(p_1, p_2) \leq eps$;*
- *$N_{eps}(p_1) \geq minPoints$ in $S_1 \cup S_2$;*
- *$N_{eps}(p_2) \geq minPoints$ in $S_1 \cup S_2$;*

*Proof.* First, we can conclude that there are at least two points $p_1 \in C_1$ and $p_2 \in C_2$ such that the distance between them is less than or equal to $eps$, otherwise it would be impossible for any points from $C_1$ and $C_2$ to be placed in the same cluster in the centralized execution of DBSCAN because they would never be Density-Reachable (DR). Moreover, such condition is necessary to allow the merge between two clusters. Still considering the points $p_1$ and $p_2$, we have the following possibilities:

1. $p_1$ and $p_2$ are core points in $C_1$ and $C_2$ respectively;
2. $p_1$ is core point in $C_1$ and $p_2$ is border point in $C_2$;

---

**Algorithm 5.** CanMerge.

---
Input: Clusters $C_i, C_j$ candidates to merge

```
 1  begin
 2      for p_i ∈ C_i do
 3          for p_j ∈ C_j do
 4              if ((p_i ∈ N_eps(p_j)) then
 5                  setAdjacent(p_i, p_j)

 6      for p_i ∈ C_i do
 7          if (Card(N_eps(p_i)) ≥ minPoints) then
 8              p_i.isCore ← true

 9      for p_j ∈ C_j do
10          if (Card(N_eps(p_j)) ≥ minPoints) then
11              p_j.isCore ← true

12      for p_i ∈ C_i do
13          for p_j ∈ C_j do
14              if (Adj(p_i, p_j) ∧ p_i.isCore ∧ p_j.isCore) then
15                  merge ← true
16              updateNoisePoints();

17      if (merge) then
18          for p_j ∈ C_j do
19              p_j.cluster ← i

20      return merge
```

---

3. $p_1$ is border point in $C_1$ and $p_2$ is core point in $C_2$;
4. $p_1$ and $p_2$ are border points in $C_1$ and $C_2$ respectively;

Analyzing the first case, where $p_1$ is a core point, by definition $Card(N_{eps}(p_1)) \geq minPoints$. Considering the partitions $S_1 \cup S_2$, we observe that $p_2 \in N_{eps}(p_1)$. When being visited during the execution of DBSCAN, the point $p_1$ would reach point $p_2$ directly by density. As $p_2$ is also a core point, all others points from $C_2$ could be density reachable from $p_1$. Thus, the points from clusters $C_1$ and $C_2$ would be in the same cluster. Similarly, we can state the same for point $p_2$, as it could reach by density all points from $C_1$ through point $p_1$. In this case, $C_1$ and $C_2$ will be merged.

The analysis is analogous in the second case, where only $p_1$ is a core point. Thus, when visiting $p_1$ its neighbors, particularly $p_2$, will be expanded. Considering the space $S_1 \cup S_2$, suppose that $N_{eps}(p_2) < minPoints$. So, the point $p_2$ is not expanded when visited and point $p_1$ will not reach the core point belonging to cluster $C_2$, that is a $p_2$ neighbor. In this case, $C_1$ and $C_2$ will not be merged.

Similarly one can analyze the third case and reach the same conclusion of the second case.

For the fourth and last case, consider that none of the two points $p_1$ and $p_2$ have more than or equal to $minPoints$ neighbors, i.e., $N_{eps}(p_1) < minPoints$ and $N_{eps}(p_2) < minPoints$ in $S_1 \cup S_2$. When visited, neither will be expanded, because they will be considered border points. In the case that only one of them has more than $minPoints$ neighbors in $S_1 \cup S_2$ (the previous case), we could see that such condition is not enough to merge the clusters. Therefore, the only case in which such clusters will merge is when $N_{eps}(p_1) \geq minPoints$ and $N_{eps}(p_2) \geq minPoints$ in $S_1 \cup S_2$ or in the first case ($p_1$ and $p_2$ are core points).

## 5 Incremental Version DBSCAN

Due to the high rate of updates in some data sets, the results of a data mining algorithm execution may change very often, and so the analisys. Also, when it comes to large volumes of data, it is infeasible to rerun the algorithm at every data set update.

Incremental data mining means applying data mining algorithms on incremental database, i.e., that changes with time. The goal of incremental data mining algorithms is to minimize the scanning and calculation effort for updated records [13].

Typically, updates are applied on the data set periodically. Thus, the clusters computed by the clustering algorithm have to be updated as well. Due to the very large size of the databases, it is highly desirable to perform these updates incrementally [11]. The paper [11] examines which part of an existing clustering is affected by an update of the database in a centralized way.

On this chapter we present how the algorithms for incremental updates of a clustering can be applied after insertions and deletions based on our distributed DBSCAN.

### 5.1 Insertions

Consider that we have the clusters derived from the original data set using our DBSCAN algorithm. Let $C$ be the clustering using DBSCAN, such that $C = \{S_0, ..., S_m, Out\}$ where $Out$ is called the set of outliers and $\forall i, i \in \{0, ..., m\}, S_i$ be a DBSCAN cluster.

For each new point inserted on the data set, a geometric object is stored on the database. We can imagine that each new point is a cluster $S'_i$, so $C' = \{S'_0, ..., S'_n\}$. We should compare the elements of $C$ and $C'$ in order to find possible merges between them, or if the new points just create new clusters and some outliers. Thus, we can apply the Computing candidate clusters and Merging clusters phases described on the Sect. 4.1 to find the merges between $C$ and $C'$ or to find the new clusters. For $S'_j \in C'$ that do not merge with any cluster or create a new cluster, $S'_j$ becomes an outlier on the whole data set.

Note that for incremental DBSCAN we just reuse only two phases of our proposed distributed and parallel DBSCAN. It is cheaper than executing DBSCAN from scratch for the updated data set.

## 5.2    Deletions

As well as insertions of new entries on the data set might happen, the deletion of old entries is also possible. Considering this, one can easily see that the deletion of some particular points or even of a subset of the data set might change the clustering result. For example, a core point might become a border point or a noise point and break a cluster into two. Similar cases are considered and presented on [11], where the authors proved the correctness of their strategy. When it comes to a distributed version of DBSCAN, the deletion of entries in the data set is a special case due to the phisycal distribution of the data across a computer cluster.

Considering a previous clustering processing, for each point in the data set, whether it belongs to a cluster or it is an outlier. As stated in [11], a point removal affects only a part of the data set, that belongs to the same cluster of the point to be removed. Thus, in a distributed scenario, each cluster would be assigned to a specific machine, and if the point to be removed belongs to a cluster $S_i$, the processing needs to be done only on the machine that contains this cluster. Such strategy allows multiple parallel point removals from multiple clusters with no interference between them. Furthermore, the processing on the machine is similar to the one proposed originally on [11], but with the benefits of executing it at the same time for several clusters.

## 6    Experimental Evaluation

The experimental evaluation was performed in a private cloud environment at the Federal University of Ceara. In total, 11 virtual machines running Ubuntu 12.04, each with 8GB of RAM and 4 CPU units, were deployed for this purpose. The Hadoop version used on each machine was 1.1.2 and the environment variables were set according to the Table 1. Each scenario was carried out 5 times and reported the average, maximum and minimum observed values of execution time.

The data sets used in the experiments were related to avenues from Fortaleza city in Brazil and the collected points were retrieved from a website that obtains the data from traffic radar. Each entry contains the avenue's name, the geographic position of vehicles (latitude and longitude), as well as its speed at a specific moment of time. In the context of the problem, what our approach identifies groups with high density of points from the data set that have low speeds. The results can be used to detect traffic jam areas in Fortaleza city.

The first test varied the *eps* value and kept the same amount of points in each street, i.e., of the original data set that corresponds to 246142 points. The *eps* values used were 100, 150, 200, 250, 300 and 350, while keeping the value of 50 to *minPoints*. As it was expected, the Fig. 2 shows that with the increase of *eps*, the processing time has also increased, because more points in the neighborhood of a core point could be expanded.

The Fig. 3 illustrates the variation of the number of points from the input data set related to the processing time. The number of points used was 246142,

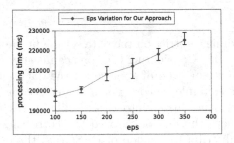

**Fig. 2.** eps variation.

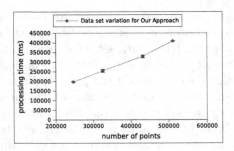

**Fig. 3.** Data set size variation.

**Table 1.** Hadoop configuration variables used in the experiments.

| Variable name | Value |
|---|---|
| hadoop.tmp.dir | /tmp/hadoop |
| fs.default.name | hdfs://master:54310 |
| mapred.job.tracker | master:54311 |
| mapreduce.task.timeout | 36000000 |
| mapred.child.java.opts | -Xmx8192m |
| mapred.reduce.tasks | 11 |
| dfs.replication | 5 |

324778, 431698 and 510952 points. As expected, when the number of points processed by DBSCAN is increased, the processing time also increases, showing that our solution is scalable.

The Table 2 presents a comparison of our approach execution time and centralized DBSCAN execution time. We varied the number of points that was 246142, 324778, 431698 and 510952 points for $eps = 100$ and $minPoints = 50$. In all cases, our approach found the same clusters that centralized DBSCAN on the data set, but spent less time to process as we expected.

The Figs. 4 and 5 show a comparison between our approach and DBSCANMR [2] that has the partitioning phase centralized, different of our approach. On the

**Table 2.** Comparing the execution time of our approach and centralized DBSCAN for eps=100 and minPoints = 50.

| Data set | Our Approach [ms] | Centralized [ms] |
|---|---|---|
| 246142 | 197263 | 1150187.6 |
| 324778 | 254447 | 2002369 |
| 431698 | 330431 | 3530966.6 |
| 510952 | 409154 | 4965999.6 |

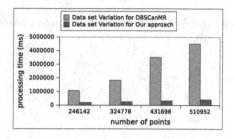

**Fig. 4.** Varing the data set size and comparing our approach with DBSCANMR.

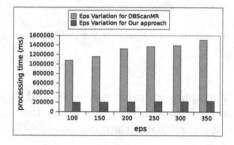

**Fig. 5.** Varing eps and comparing our approach with DBSCANMR.

both experiments, our solution spent less processing time than DBSCANMR, because DBSCANMR spends great cost to build the grid during the centralized partitioning phase.

Moreover, DBSCANMR strategy is sensitive to two input parameters that are the number of points that could be processed on memory and a percentage of points in each partition. For these two parameters, the paper does not present how they could be calculated and what are the best values. We did the experiments using the first one equals to 200000 and the second as 0,49.

We did not compare our approach with the other related work [6]. However, we believe that our approach presents better results than [6], because our merge strategy does not need data replication, that can affect the clustering efficiency for a large data set.

The Fig. 6 presents the points plotted for 246142 points of data set. Note that each color represents an avenue of Fortaleza. On the Fig. 7, we can see

**Fig. 6.** The data set with 246142 points plotted.

**Fig. 7.** Clusters found after run our approach for 246142 points (eps=100 and min-Points = 50).

the clusters found by our approach using $eps = 100$ and $minPoints = 50$. Each cluster found is represented by a different color on the Fig. 7. Note that the merge occurred where there are more than one avenue that crosses each other as we expected.

## 7 Conclusions

Clustering is a major data mining technique that groups a set of objects in such a way that objects in the same group are more similar to each other than to those in other groups. Among many types of clustering, density-based clustering algorithms are more efficient in detecting clusters with varied density and different shapes. One of the most important density-based clustering algorithms is the DBSCAN.

In this chapter we present a distributed DBSCAN algorithm using MapReduce to identify congested areas within a city using a large traffic data set. We also discuss an incremental version for DBSCAN using our distributed DBSCAN. This incremental version is cheaper than running the distributed DBSCAN from scratch.

Our approach is more efficient than DBSCAN-MR as confirmed by our experiments, while varying the data set size and the *eps* value. We also compare our approach to a centralized version of DBSCAN algorithm. Our approach found the same clusters as the centralized DBSCAN algorithm, moreover our approach spent less time to process, as expected.

# References

1. Bentley, J.L.: Multidimensional binary search trees used for associative searching. In: Communications of the ACM, vol. 18, pp. 509–517. ACM (1975)
2. Dai, B.-R., Lin, I.-C.: Efficient map/reduce-based dbscan algorithm with optimized data partition. In: 2012 IEEE 5th International Conference on Cloud Computing (CLOUD), pp. 59–66. IEEE (2012)
3. Dean, J., Ghemawat, S.: Mapreduce: simplified data processing on large clusters. Commun. ACM **51**(1), 107–113 (2008)
4. Ester, M., Kriegel, H.-P., Sander, J., Xu, X.: A density-based algorithm for discovering clusters in large spatial databases with noise. In: KDD, vol. 96, pp. 226–231 (1996)
5. Giannotti, F., Nanni, M., Pedreschi, D., Pinelli, F., Renso, C., Rinzivillo, S., Trasarti, R.: Unveiling the complexity of human mobility by querying and mining massive trajectory data. VLDB J. Int. J. Very Large Data Bases **20**(5), 695–719 (2011)
6. He, Y., Tan, H., Luo, W., Mao, H., Ma, D., Feng, S., Fan, J.: Mr-dbscan: an efficient parallel density-based clustering algorithm using mapreduce. In: 2011 IEEE 17th International Conference on Parallel and Distributed Systems (ICPADS), pp. 473–480. IEEE (2011)
7. Kisilevich, S., Mansmann, F., Keim, D.: P-dbscan: a density based clustering algorithm for exploration and analysis of attractive areas using collections of geo-tagged photos. In: Proceedings of the 1st International Conference and Exhibition on Computing for Geospatial Research & Application, p. 38. ACM (2010)
8. Lin, J., Dyer, C.: Data-intensive text processing with mapreduce. Synth. Lect. Hum. Lang. Technol. **3**(1), 1–177 (2010)
9. Pavlo, A., Paulson, E., Rasin, A., Abadi, D.J., DeWitt, D.J., Madden, S., Stonebraker, M.: A comparison of approaches to large-scale data analysis. In: Proceedings of the 2009 ACM SIGMOD International Conference on Management of data, SIGMOD 2009, pp. 165–178, New York, NY, USA. ACM (2009)
10. Coelho da Silva, T.L., Araujo, A.C.N., Magalhaes, R.P., de Farias, V.A.E., de Macêdo, J.A., Machado, J.C.: Efficient and distributed dbscan algorithm using mapreduce to detect density areas on traffic data. In: Proceedings of International Conference on Enterprise Informational Systems, ICEIS 2014
11. Ester, M., Kriegel, H.-P., Sander, J. and Wimmer, M., Xu, X.: Incremental clustering for mining in a data warehousing environment. In: The VLDB Journal – The International Journal on Very Large Data Bases (1998)
12. Sousa, F.R.C., Moreira, L.O., Macêdo, J.A.F., Machado, J.C.: Gerenciamento de dados em nuvem: Conceitos, sistemas e desafios. Simpsio Brasileiro de Banco de Dados. SBBD 2010, pp. 101–130 (2010)
13. Chakraborty, S., Nagwani, N.K.: Analysis and study of Incremental DBSCAN clustering algorithm. In: International Journal of Enterprise Computing and Business Systems 2011, pp. 101–130

14. Uncu, O., Gruver, W.A., Kotak, D.B., Sabaz, D., Alibhai, Z., Ng, C.: Gridbscan: grid density-based spatial clustering of applications with noise. In: IEEE International Conference on Systems, Man and Cybernetics, 2006. SMC 2006, vol. 4, pp. 2976–2981. IEEE (2006)
15. White, T.: Hadoop: the definitive guide. O'Reilly, Sebastopol (2012)

# Discovering Frequent Patterns on Agrometeorological Data with TrieMotif

Daniel Y.T. Chino[1]([✉]), Renata R.V. Goncalves[2], Luciana A.S. Romani[3],
Caetano Traina Jr.[1], and Agma J.M. Traina[1]

[1] Institute of Mathematics and Computer Science, University of São Paulo,
São Carlos, Brazil
{chinodyt,caetano,agma}@icmc.usp.br
[2] Cepagri-Unicamp, Campinas, Brazil
renata@cpa.unicamp.br
[3] Embrapa Agriculture Informatics, Campinas, Brazil
luciana.romani@embrapa.br

**Abstract.** The "food safety" issue has concerned governments from several countries. The accurate monitoring of agriculture have become important specially due to climate change impacts. In this context, the development of new technologies for monitoring are crucial. Finding previously unknown patterns that frequently occur on time series, known as motifs, is a core task to mine the collected data. In this work we present a method that allows a fast and accurate time series motif discovery. From the experiments we can see that our approach is able to efficiently find motifs even when the size of the time series goes longer. We also evaluated our method using real data time series extracted from remote sensing images regarding sugarcane crops. Our proposed method was able to find relevant patterns, as sugarcane cycles and other land covers inside the same area, which are really useful for data analysis.

**Keywords:** Time series · Frequent motif · Remote sensing image

## 1 Introduction

One of the issues being pursued by the database researchers is how to take advantage of the large volume of data daily generated by the plethora of sensors placed in many environments and systems. The information gathered by the sensors are usually stored in time series databases, being a rich source for decision making for the owners of such data. One of the main tasks when mining time series is to find the motifs present therein, that is, to find patterns that frequently occurs in time series. That is, the motifs provide key information to mine association rules aimed at spotting patterns indicating that some events frequently lead to others.

Existing applications involving time series, such as stock market analysis, are not yet able to record all the factors that govern the data stored in the time series, such as political and technological factors. On the contrary, climate variations nowadays have most of its governing factors being recorded, using sensing

© Springer International Publishing Switzerland 2015
J. Cordeiro et al. (Eds.): ICEIS 2014, LNBIP 227, pp. 91–107, 2015.
DOI: 10.1007/978-3-319-22348-3_6

equipments such as satellites and ground-based weather stations. However, the diversity of data available makes it hard to discover complex patterns that can support more robust analyzes. In this scenario, finding motifs has an even greater importance.

An example of time series, is the one extracted from remote sensing imagery containing Normalized Dierence Vegetation Index (NDVI) measurements. The NDVI time series present the vegetative strength of the plantation [14]. To follow the development of a crop is strategic for agribusiness practices in Brazil, since agriculture is the country's main asset. The accurate monitoring of agriculture in the whole world have become more and more important specially due to climate change impacts. The "food safety" issue has concerned governments from several countries and the development of new technologies for monitoring, as well as the proposition of mitigation and adaptation measures, are crucial. In this sense, remote sensing can be an important tool to improve the fast detection of changes in the land cover besides to aid at monitoring the crop cycle.

Since the volume of time series databases as well as the length of the series is growing at a very fast pace, it is mandatory to develop algorithms and methods that can deal with time series in the scenario of big data. In this paper we present the TrieMotif, a new method to extract motifs from time series and a new algorithm to index them in a trie data structure that performs well over large time series, which is up to 3 times faster than the state-of-the-art method. We evaluated TrieMotif over both synthetic and real data time series, obtaining very promising results.

This paper is organized as follows. Section 2 summarizes the main concepts used as basis to develop our work. Section 3 describes the TrieMotif algorithm and Sect. 4 discusses its evaluation. Section 5 shows the TrieMotif performance on real data obtained from remote sensing images. Section 6 concludes this paper.

## 2    Background and Related Works

A time series motif is a pattern that occur frequently. They were first defined in [11] and a generalized definition was given in [2]. In this section we recall these definitions and notations, as they will be used in this paper. First we begin with a definition of time series:

**Definition 1.** *Time Series:* A time series $T = t_1, \ldots, t_m$ is an ordered set of $m$ real-valued variables.

Since we want to find patterns that frequently occur along a time series, we will not work with the whole time series, we are aiming only at parts of a time series, which are called subsequences and are defined as follows.

**Definition 2.** *Subsequence:* Given a time series $T$ of length $m$, a subsequence $S_p$ of $T$ is a sampling of length $n < m$ of contiguous positions from $T$ beginning at position $p$, that is, $S_p = t_p, \ldots, t_{p+n-1}$ for $1 \leq p \leq m - n + 1$.

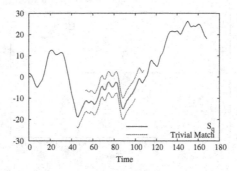

**Fig. 1.** The best matches of a subsequence $S_q$ are probably the trivial matches that occur right before or after $S_q$.

In order to find frequent patterns, we need to define a matching between patterns.

**Definition 3.** *Match:* Given a distance function $D(S_p, S_q)$ between two subsequences, a positive real number $R$ (*range*) and a time series $T$ containing a subsequence $S_p$ and a subsequence $S_q$, if $D(S_p, S_q) \leq R$ then $S_q$ is called a *matching* subsequence of $S_p$.

On subsequences of the same time series, the best matches are probably subsequences that are slightly shifted. Matching between two overlapped subsequences is called a trivial match. Figure 1 illustrates the idea of a trivial match. The trivial match is defined as follows:

**Definition 4.** *Trivial Match:* Given a time series $T$, containing a subsequence $S_p$ and a matching subsequence $S_q$, we say that $S_q$ is a *trivial match* to $S_p$ either if $p = q$ or if there is no subsequence $S_{q'}$ beginning at $q'$ such that $D(S_p, S_{q'}) > R$, and either $q < q' < p$ or $p < q' < q$. That is, if two subsequences overlaps, there must exist a subsequence between them that is not a match.

These definitions allow defining the problem of finding Frequent $K$-Motif. First, all subsequences are extracted using a sliding window. Then, since we are interested in patterns, each subsequence is z-normalized to have zero mean and one standard deviation [6]. The $K$-Motif is defined as follows.

**Definition 5.** *Frequent $K$-Motifs:* Given a time series $T$, a subsequence of length $n$ and a range $R$, the most significant motif in $T$ (*1-Motif*) is the subsequence $F^{\{1\}}$ that has the highest count of non-trivial matches. The $K^{th}$ most significant motif in $T$ (*K-Motif*) is the subsequence $F^{\{K\}}$ that has the highest count of non-trivial matches, and satisfies $D(F^{\{K\}}, F^{\{i\}}) > 2R$, for all $1 \leq i < K$.

The Nearest Neighbor motif was defined by Yankov et al. [17], and it represents the closest pair of subsequences. In our proposed work, we focus on the Frequent $K$-Motif problem and we will be referring to them as $K$-Motif. Since the $K$-Motifs are unknown patterns, a brute-force approach would compare every

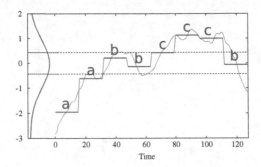

**Fig. 2.** A time series subsequence of size $n = 128$ is reduced to a PAA representation of size $w = 8$ and then is mapped to a string of $a = 3$ symbols *aabbcccb*.

subsequence with each other. It has quadratic computational cost on the time series size, since it requires $O(m^2)$ distance function evaluations.

An approach to reduce the complexity of this problem employs dimensionality reduction and discretization of the time series [11]. The SAX (Symbolic Aggregate approXimation) technique allows time series of size $n$ to be represented by strings of arbitrary size $w$ ($w < l$) [10]. For a given time series, SAX consists of the following steps. Firstly, the time series is z-normalized, so that the data follow normal distribution [4]. Next, the normalized time series is converted into the Piecewise Aggregate Approximation (PAA) representation, decreasing the time series dimensionality [5]. The time series is then replaced with $w$ values corresponding to the average of the respective segment. Thus, in the PAA representation, the time series is divided into $w$ continuous segments of equal length. Finally, the PAA representation is discretized into a string with an alphabet of size $a > 2$. Figure 2 shows an example of a time series subsequence of size $n = 128$ discretized using SAX with $w = 8$ and $a = 3$. It is also possible to compare two SAX time series using the MINDIST function. The MINDIST lower bounds the Euclidean distance [12], warranting no false dismissals [3].

Chiu et al. proposed a fast algorithm based on Random Projection [2]. Each time series subsequence is discretized using SAX. The discretized subsequences are mapped into a matrix, where each row points back to the original position of the subsequence on the time series. Then, the algorithm uses the random projection to compute a collision matrix, which counts the frequency of subsequence pairs. Through the collision matrix, the subsequences are checked on the original domain seeking for motifs. Although fast, the collision matrix is quadratic on the time series length, requiring a large amount of memory. Also using the SAX discretization, Li and Lin [8,9] proposed a variable length motif discovery based on grammar induction. Catalano et al. [1] proposed a method that works on the original domain of the data. The motifs are discovered in linear time and constant memory costs using random sampling. However, this approach can lead to poor performance for long time series with infrequent motifs [13].

Several works proposed to solve the motif discovery problem taking advantage of tree data structures. Udechukwu et al. proposed an algorithm that uses a suffix tree to find the Frequent Motif [15]. The time series are discretized considering the slopes between two consecutive measures. The symbols are chosen according to the angle between the line joining the two points and the time axis. Although this algorithm do not require to set the length of the motif, the algorithm is affected by noise. A suffix tree was also used to find motifs in multivariate time series [16]. Keogh et al. solved a problem similar to the motif discovery using a trie structure to find the most unusual subsequence in a time series [7].

The TrieMotif algorithm is up to 3 times faster and requires up to 10 times less memory than the current state of the art, the Random Projection approach, because TrieMotif selects only the candidates that are most probably a match to a motif. Using this approach, TrieMotif reduces the number of unnecessary distance calculations.

## 3   The TrieMotif Algorithm

In this section we present the TrieMotif algorithm. Since a motif is an unknown pattern, one of the problem of finding them is the need to compare every subsequence with every other. On this context, we intend to reduce the number of subsequence comparisons by discarding subsequences that are discrepant from each other. Let $S_q$ be a possible motif, matching subsequences might have values similar to $S_q$ and therefore they might be on a region near $S_q$, as shown in Fig. 3. The TrieMotif algorithm defines this area by setting an upper and a lower limit to $S_q$, this way, we only compare possible matching subsequences. The TrieMotif algorithm consists of three stages:

- First, all subsequences are extracted from the time series and converted into a symbolic representation;
- The subsequences are indexed using a Trie and a list of possible non trivial matches (candidates) are generated for each subsequence using the Trie index;
- The distances between the motif candidates on the original time series are calculated.

On the first stage, all subsequences $S_i$ of size $n$ are extracted using a sliding window and are z-normalized. These subsequences pass through a dimensionality reduction process to reduce the computational cost on the next stage. A subsequence of size $n$ can be represented as a sequence of size $w$, via the PAA algorithm. On the next step of this stage, subsequences are converted into a symbolic representation. This representation is obtained by dividing the interval of the subsequence values into $a$ equal size bins, where each bin receives a symbol. Each value in the subsequence is converted into the symbol of the corresponding bin. Figure 4 shows an example that converts a subsequence $S$ of size $m = 128$ and values between $[-2.83, 1.36]$ into a string of size $w = 8$ using an alphabet $a$ of 3 symbols. Initially the subsequence passes through a dimensionality reduction via PAA with $w = 8$. Then, assuming $a = 3$, three bins are

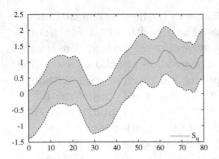

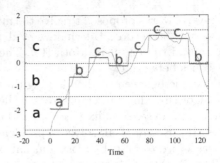

**Fig. 3.** Subsequences $S_i$ that satisfy $D(S_q, S_i) \leq R$ are possibly in the highlighted area.

**Fig. 4.** A time series subsequence of size $m = 128$ is converted into a string of $a = 3$ symbols and size $w = 8$.

created: $a = [-2.83, -1.43)$, $b = [-1.43, -0.03)$ and $c = [-0.03, 1.36]$. Notice, that we kept the zero mean and the standard deviation requirements. Finally, the symbolic representation of $S$ is $\hat{S} = abcbcccb$.

To find the top $K$-Motifs, the brute force algorithm calculates the distance of each subsequence $S_q$ to every other subsequence. Our proposal reduces the number of distance calculations by selecting only candidates $S_i$ that may be a match – the trivial matches are discarded on the next stage. To select the candidates we index all subsequences (already represented as a string) in a trie. For example, consider the subsequences $S_1$, $S_2$, $S_3$ and $S_4$, $w = 4$ and $a = 4$, as shown in Fig. 5. After processed in the first stage, they become $\hat{S}_1 = aabd$, $\hat{S}_2 = babd$, $\hat{S}_3 = abda$ and $\hat{S}_4 = dcca$ respectively. Figure 6(a) shows how the trie is built.

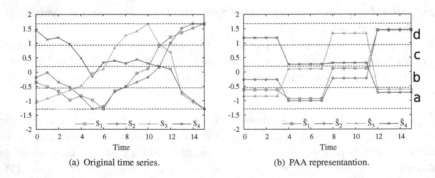

(a) Original time series.                    (b) PAA representantion.

**Fig. 5.** Symbolic conversion process of the subsequences $S_1$, $S_2$, $S_3$ and $S_4$ to the strings $\hat{S}_1 = aabd$, $\hat{S}_2 = babd$, $\hat{S}_3 = abda$ and $\hat{S}_4 = dcca$.

An exact search on the trie would return candidates faster, but some candidates $S_i$ that are a match could be discarded. If we search for candidates of $\hat{S}_1$, although $\hat{S}_2$ is probably a match, it would not be selected. To solve this problem, we modified the exact search on the trie to a range-like search. On the exact search, when the algorithm is processing the $j^{th}$ element of $\hat{S}_q$ ($\hat{S}_q[j]$), it only visits the path of the trie where $Node_{symbol} = \hat{S}_q[j]$. In our proposed approach, we associate numerical values to the symbols. For example, $A$ is equal to 1, $B$ is equal to 2, and so on. Therefore, we can take advantage of closer values to compute the similarity when comparing the symbols. On our modified search, the algorithm also visits paths where $|\hat{S}_q[j] - Node_{symbol}| \leq \delta$. That is, if $\hat{S}_q[j] = b$ and $\delta = 1$, then the algorithm visits the paths of $a$, $b$ and $c$ (one up or one down). As backtracking all possible paths might be computationally expensive, we exploit pruning of unwanted paths by indexing the elements of the strings in a non-sequential order. This approach is interesting, because time series measures over a short period tend to have similar values. For example, if in a given time there is a $b$ symbol, probably the next symbol might be $a$, $b$ or $c$ (even in large alphabets). Taking that into account, we interleave elements from the beginning and the end of the string, i.e., the first symbol, then the last symbol, then the second and so on.

Figure 6(a) shows how the modified search behave when searching for candidates to $\hat{S}_1$. On the first level, $\hat{S}_1[1] = A$ and the algorithm will visit the paths of the symbols $a$ and $b$. On the next level, $\hat{S}_1[4] = D$ and it will visit the paths of $c$ and $d$. This process is repeated until it reaches a leaf node. In this example, it will return the candidates $\hat{S}_1$ and $\hat{S}_2$, but $\hat{S}_3$ and $\hat{S}_4$ will not be checked. Figures 6(a) and 6(b) also show that changing the order of the elements can reduce the backtracking. If the subsequences were indexed using the sequential order, our modified search would also visit the path of $\hat{S}_3$ for at least one more level (marked in blue), while changing the order, this path is never visited.

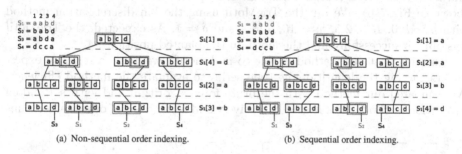

(a) Non-sequential order indexing.     (b) Sequential order indexing.

**Fig. 6.** By selecting candidates using our modified search, the algorithm backtracks only on nodes of the strings $\hat{S}_1$ and $\hat{S}_2$ paths. Creating the trie index using normal order increases the backtracking, since the algorithm visits part of the string $\hat{S}_3$ path (Color figure online).

On the last stage, after obtaining a list of candidates for each $S_q$, we calculate the distance between $S_q$ and $S_i$ on the original time series domain, discarding trivial matches of $S_q$. We also make sure that the $K$-Motifs satisfy Definition 5.

Algorithm 1 shows how to use the TrieMotif algorithm to locate the top $K$-Motifs. First, all subsequences $S_i$ are converted into a symbolic representation $\hat{S}_i$ and every $\hat{S}_i$ is indexed into a trie index. Through the Trie index, we can reduce the number of non-trivial match calculations by generating a set $C$ of the possible candidates for every $\hat{S}_i$. Then, we check on the original time series domain if the subsequences $C_j$ in $C$ satisfies $D(S_i, C_j) \leq R$ and it is not a trivial match. Since it is not possible to know the top K most frequent motifs before computing every subsequence, we store the motif on a list $(ListOfMotif)$. As the last step of the algorithm, it is needed to check if the top $K$-Motifs satisfies Definition 5. To do so, we sort $ListOfMotif$ by the decreasing number of non-trivial matches. Thus, the most frequent motifs appear at the list head. Thereafter we iterate through the sorted $ListOfMotif$ and whenever $F^{\{i\}}$ satisfies Definition 5, we insert $F^{\{i\}}$ in the result set $TopKMotif$, otherwise $F^{\{i\}}$ is discarded.

To improve the efficiency of the method, we also calculate every distance using the "early abandonment" approach. Note that, although we presented a method to symbolic represent time series subsequences, it is possible to use others symbolic representations, such as the SAX algorithm. In those cases, provided that the distance function is the Euclidean one, it is possible to take advantage of the low complexity of the $MINDIST$ and discard calculations on the original time series whenever $MINDIST(\hat{S}_q, \hat{S}_i) > R$, since the $MINDIST$ is a lower bound to the Euclidean distance.

## 4    Synthetic Data Analysis

To validate our method, we performed tests on a synthetic time series generated by random walk of size $m = 1,000$. We also embedded a motif of size 100 in four different positions of the time series. Figure 7(a) shows the planted motif and its variants. The motifs were planted on positions 32, 287, 568 and 875, as shown in Fig. 7(b). We ran the TrieMotif using the bin discretization method with $n = 100$, $R = 2.5$, $w = 16$, $a = 4$ and $\delta = 1$. As expected, the TrieMotif was able to successfully find the motif on the planted positions.

Knowing that our method is able to find motifs, we made a series of experiments varying the length of the time series to evaluate the method efficiency. We compared our method with the brute force algorithm and with a Random Projection method, since it used extensively and is the basis of others algorithms

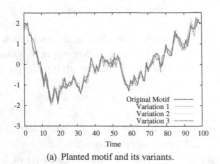

(a) Planted motif and its variants.

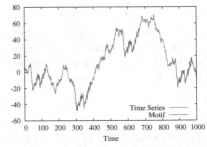

(b) A random walk time series with the implanted motif marked in blue.

**Fig. 7.** Planted motifs into a longer dataset for evaluation tests.

---

**Algorithm 1.** K-TrieMotif Algorithm.

---

**Input:** $T$, $n$, $R$, $w$, $a$, $\delta$, $K$

**Output:** List of the top $K$-Motif

1: $ListOfMotif \leftarrow \emptyset$
2: **for all** Subsequence $S_i$ with size $n$ of $T$ **do**
3:     $\hat{S}_i \leftarrow$ ConvertIntoSymbol($S_i$, $w$, $a$)
4:     Insert $\hat{S}_i$ in the Trie index
5: **end for**
6: **for all** Subsequence $\hat{S}_i$ of $T$ **do**
7:     $C \leftarrow$ GetCandidatesFromTrie($\hat{S}_i$, $\delta$)
8:     $MotifS \leftarrow \emptyset$
9:     **for all** $C_j \in C$ **do**
10:         **if** $NonTrivialMatch(S_i, C_j, R)$ **then**
11:             Add $C_j$ to $MotifS$
12:         **end if**
13:     **end for**
14:     Insert $MotifS$ in the $ListOfMotif$
15: **end for**
16: Sort $ListOfMotif$ by size in decreasing order
17: $TopKMotifs \leftarrow \emptyset$
18: $k \leftarrow 0$
19: **for all** $(F^{\{i\}} \in ListOfMotif)$ **and** $(k < K)$ **do**
20:     **if** $(Distance(F^{\{i\}}, F^{\{l\}}) \leq 2R)$, $\forall F^{\{l\}} \in TopKMotif$ **then**
21:         Discard $F^{\{i\}}$
22:     **else**
23:         Insert $F^{\{i\}}$ in $TopKMotif$
24:         $k{+}{+}$
25:     **end if**
26: **end for**
27: **return** $TopKMotif$

---

in the literature. We searched for motifs of size $n = 100$ and used the Euclidean distance. For both Random Projection and TrieMotif we used the same parameters for the discretization, $a = 4$ and $w = 16$. We ran the Random Projection with 100 iterations. For the TrieMotif, we used both bin and SAX representations with $\delta = 1$. We varied the time series length from $1,000$ to $100,000$. Each set of parameters were tested using 5 different seeds for the random walk. All tests were performed 5 times, totalizing 25 executions. The wall clock time and memory usage measurements were taken from these 25 runs of the algorithm. The presented values correspond to the average of the 25 executions. As it is too time consuming, the brute-force algorithm was not executed for time series with lengths above $40,000$. The experiments were performed in an HP server with 2 Intel Xeon 5600 quad-core processors with 96 GB of main memory, under CentOS Linux 6.2. All methods (TrieMotif, Random Projection and Brute-force) were implemented using the C++ programming language. The time spent comparison is shown in Fig. 8(a) and the memory usage is shown on Fig. 8(b).

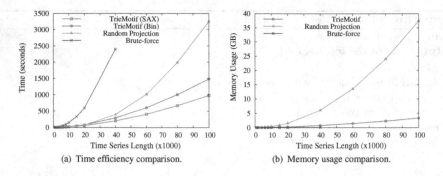

(a) Time efficiency comparison.

(b) Memory usage comparison.

**Fig. 8.** Comparison of the TrieMotif with brute force and random projection.

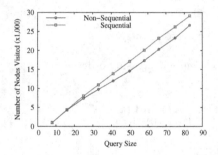

**Fig. 9.** Comparison of the number of visited nodes on the trie index using sequential and non-sequential order.

As expected, both Random Projection and TrieMotif performed better than the brute-force approach. For time series of length below 10, 000, both Random Projection and the TrieMotif had similar performance. However, as the time series length grows, the TrieMotif presented a increasingly better performance. This result is due to the fact that TrieMotif selects only the candidates that are probable matches for a motif, reducing the number of unnecessary distance calculations. TrieMotif also presents better performance using SAX because the interval of values is different for each symbol. The symbols corresponding to values near 0 are smaller and therefore, less candidates are selected. The TrieMotif also consumes less memory than the Random Projection, since the Random Projection algorithm needs at least $m^2$ memory for the collision matrix. From Fig. 8(b), we can see that the memory requirements of our method is significantly less demanding than Random Projection, requiring 10 times less memory than the state of the art (the Random Projection approach).

We also checked the differences between indexing the subsequences in sequential and non-sequential order. For this test we counted the number of nodes visited for each query on the trie index varying the query size. We executed the queries for every subsequence of the random walk time series. The presented values correspond to the average these executions. Figure 9 shows that the TrieMotif algorithm visited less nodes when using non-sequential order indexing.

## 5  Real Data Analysis

We also performed experiments using data from real applications. For this evaluation, we extracted time series from remote sensing images with two different spatial resolution. The spatial resolution of a remote sensing image specifies the size of the area that the pixel represents on the earth surface. On the first experiment, we extracted data from AVHRR/NOAA[1] images, a low spatial resolution image with a spatial resolution of 1 kilometer, i.e., each pixel represents an area of 1km x 1km on the ground. The AVHRR/NOAA images correspond to monthly measures of the Normalized Difference Vegetation Index (NDVI), which indicates the soil vegetative vigor represented in the pixels of the images and is strongly correlated with biomass. We used images of the São Paulo state, Brazil (Fig. 10), corresponding to the period between April 2001 and March 2010. From these images, we extracted 174,034 time series of size 108. Each time series corresponds to a geographical point in São Paulo state, excluding the coastal region.

**Fig. 10.** State of São Paulo, Brazil.

In order to find the motifs in the time series database, we submitted all the time series to the TrieMotif algorithm, generating a single index. The São Paulo state is one of the greatest producers of sugarcane in Brazil. In this work, we

---

[1] Advanced Very High Resolution Radiometer/National Oceanic and Atmospheric Administration.

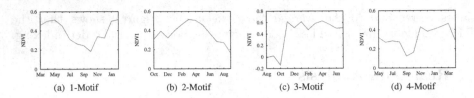

(a) 1-Motif          (b) 2-Motif          (c) 3-Motif          (d) 4-Motif

**Fig. 11.** Top 4-Motif for the São Paulo state area.

consider a complete sugarcane cycle of approximately one year, each starting in April and ending in March. We looked for the top 4-Motifs of size $n = 12$ (annual measures). We ran the TrieMotif algorithm using bin discretization with $R = 1.5$, $w = 4$, $a = 4$ and $\delta = 1$. The experiments were performed using the same computational infrastructure of the synthetic data.

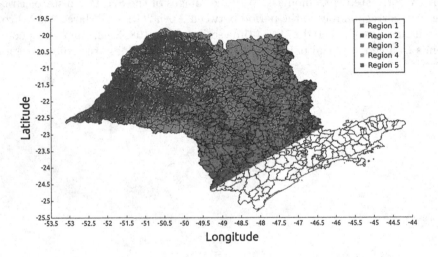

**Fig. 12.** The São Paulo state was divided into 5 regions of interest. Region 1 (purple) corresponds to water/cities, Region 2 and 3 (blue and green respectively) to a mixture of crops and grassland, Region 4 (yellow) is sugarcane crop and Region 5 (red) corresponds to forest. The black lines represent the political counties of the state. The south of the state is a forest nature federal reserve (Color figure online).

Figure 11 shows the top 4-Motifs for the São Paulo state. The plots are not z-normalized due to the experts restrictions for analyzing them. As expected, the two most frequent patterns (Figs. 11(a) and 11(b)) have a behavior similar to a sugarcane cycle, with high values of NDVI on April and low values on October. This behavior is due to the fact that sugarcane harvesting begins in April, when the NDVI slowly starts to decrease. On October, the harvest finishes and the soil remains exposed, when the NDVI has the lowest value. From October to March, the sugarcane grows and the NDVI increases again. This pattern

| Region | Color | # of Series | Represents |
|--------|-------|-------------|------------|
| 1 | Purple | 2,804 | Water and Cities |
| 2 | Blue | 55,815 | Grassland and |
| 3 | Green | 50,785 | Perennial Crops |
| 4 | Yellow | 48,301 | Sugarcane crops |
| 5 | Red | 16,329 | Forest |

**Fig. 13.** Number of time series in each region of interest.

was found on almost every area of the São Paulo state and according to the experts was not a coherent result. To overcome this problem, we divided the São Paulo state into 5 regions of interest as shown in Fig. 12. The regions were obtained through a clustering algorithm and the results were analyzed by experts in the agrometeorology and remote sensing fields. According to the experts, the region 1 found by the algorithm corresponds to water and urban areas, regions 2 and 3 correspond to a mixture of crops (excluding sugarcane) and grassland, region 4 corresponds to sugarcane crops and region 5 to forest. Figure 13 shows a summary of each region of interest and the number of time series in each region.

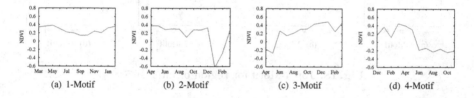

**Fig. 14.** Top 4-Motif for region of interest 1.

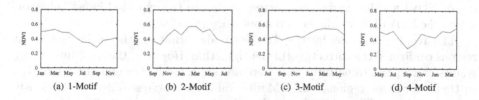

**Fig. 15.** Top 4-Motif for region of interest 2.

Figures 14, 15, 16, 17 and 18 show the top 4-Motif for each region of interest. Once again, the plots are not z-normalized due to the experts restrictions for analyzing them. The 1-Motif found on region 1 (Fig. 14(a)) has a pattern with low values and variation, which experts say correspond to urban regions. The other Motifs found in region 1 (Figs. 14(b), (c) and (d)) have a pattern that corresponds to water regions. Figures 15 and 16 show patterns with a higher value of NDVI

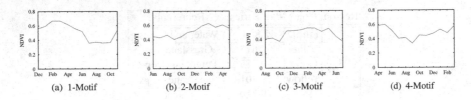

**Fig. 16.** Top 4-Motif for region of interest 3.

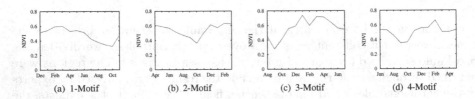

**Fig. 17.** Top 4-Motif for region of interest 4.

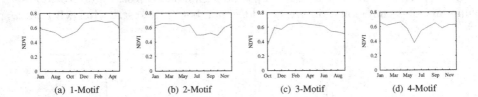

**Fig. 18.** Top 4-Motif for region of interest 5.

and with a high variation, which experts attribute to agricultural areas. The top 3-Motifs found on region 4 (see Figs. 17(a), (b) and (c)) is clearly recognized by agrometeorologists as a sugarcane cycle. Figure 18 shows a pattern with high values of NDVI and low variations, corresponding to the expected forest behavior, where the NDVI follows the local temperature variation.

The results obtained by the TrieMotif algorithm on the most prominent regions confirmed the correctness of the algorithm. However, the most interesting results correspond to patterns that were not expected by the experts. According to them, for some regions, the 4-Motifs found do not resemble the previously known patterns. The 4-Motifs found on both regions 2 and 3 (Figs. 15(d) and 16(d) respectively) indicates the presence of sugarcane and the 4-Motif found on region 4 (Fig. 17(d)) does not resemble a sugarcane cycle. This result indicates the need for a further inspection in the areas where these patterns occur.

On the second experiment, we used data extracted from MODIS[2] images. Each pixel in a MODIS image represents an area of 250 m x 250m, thus a higher spatial resolution. MODIS images correspond to biweekly NDVI measures. We used images of the São Paulo state, Brazil, corresponding to the period between

---

[2] Moderate-Resolution Imaging Spectroradiometer.

April 2004 and March 2005. Since MODIS images have a higher spatial resolution than AVHRR/NOAA images, they allow a better analysis of certain regions. We focused our analysis only on sugarcane crops regions and we extracted 40,133 time series of size 24. We ran the TrieMotif algorithm using bin discretization with $R = 1.5$, $w = 4$, $a = 4$ and $\delta = 1$. This time, we looked for the top 8-Motifs of size $n = 24$, annual measures for the MODIS images time series. The experiments were performed using the same computational infrastructure of the synthetic data.

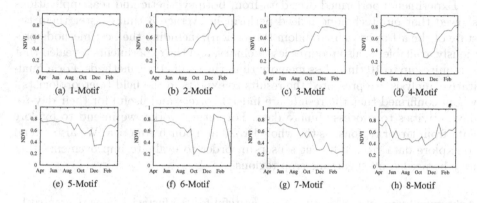

| (a) 1-Motif | (b) 2-Motif | (c) 3-Motif | (d) 4-Motif |
| (e) 5-Motif | (f) 6-Motif | (g) 7-Motif | (h) 8-Motif |

**Fig. 19.** Top 4-Motif for region of interest 1.

The results are shown on Fig. 19. As expected, the most frequent motif was a sugarcane cycle pattern (Fig. 19(a)) with high values of NDVI on April and low values on October. This time, the experts were also able to identify regions with different harvest periods (Figs. 19(b), (d) and (e)). And once again, they were able to spot regions with unexpected frequent patterns. Figure 19(f) shows a region where there was a problem with the sugarcane crop on March and Figs. 19(c), (g) and (h) show regions that might not be sugarcane regions.

## 6    Conclusions

Finding patterns in time series is highly relevant for applications where both the antecedent and the consequent events are recorded as time series. This is the case of climate and agrometeorological data, where it is known that the next state of the atmosphere depends in large amount of its previous state. Today, a large network of sensing devices, such as satellites recording both earth and solar activities, as well as ground-based whether monitoring stations keep track of climate evolution. However, the large amount of data and their diversity makes it hard to discover complex patterns able to support more robust analyzes. In this scenario, is very important to have powerful and fast algorithms to help analyzing that data.

In this paper we presented the TrieMotif, a technique that provides, in an integrated framework, an automated technique to extract frequent patterns in time series as $K$-Motifs. It reduces the resolution of the data, speeding up the sub-sequence comparison operations, indexes them in a trie structure and adopts heuristics commonly employed by the meteorologists to prune from the similarity search operations those branches that do not represent interesting answers. In this way, our technique is able to select only candidate subsequences that have high probability to match a motif, thus reducing the number of comparisons performed.

Experiments performed over data from both synthetic and real applications showed that our technique indeed perform in average 3 times faster them the state of the art approach (Random Projection), including the best methods previously available. It also requires less memory, and the experiments revealed that it requires up to 10 times less memory than the competitor methods. For a qualitative analysis, we presented the results to experts in the field (meteorologists), whom confirmed that the results are indeed correct and useful for their day-to-day activities to process climate data. For future works, we intend to explore data from larger regions, as the whole Brazil and South America. We also intend to explore data from different sensors in order to evaluate improvements that may be needed on sugarcane crop regions.

**Acknowledgements.** The authors are grateful for the financial support granted by FAPESP, CNPq, CAPES, SticAmsud and Embrapa Agricultural Informatics, Cepagri/Unicamp and Agritempo for data.

# References

1. Catalano, J., Armstrong, T., Oates, T.: Discovering patterns in real-valued time series. In: Fürnkranz, J., Scheffer, T., Spiliopoulou, M. (eds.) PKDD 2006. LNCS (LNAI), vol. 4213, pp. 462–469. Springer, Heidelberg (2006)
2. Chiu, B., Keogh, E., Lonardi, S.: Probabilistic discovery of time series motifs. In: Proceedings of the Ninth ACM SIGKDD International Conference on Knowledge Discovery and Data Mining, KDD 2003, pp. 493–498, New York, NY, USA. ACM (2003)
3. Faloutsos, C., Ranganathan, M., Manolopoulos, Y., Manolopoulos, Y.: Fast subsequence matching in time-series databases. In: Proceedings of the ACM SIGMOD International Conference on Management of Data, pp. 419–429. Minneapolis, USA (1994)
4. Goldin, D.Q., Kanellakis, P.C., Kanellakis, P.C.: On similarity queries for time-series data: Constraint specification and implementation. In: Proceedings of the 1st International Conference on Principles and Practice of Constraint Programming, pp. 137–153. Cassis, France (1995)
5. Keogh, E., Chakrabarti, K., Pazzani, M., Mehrotra, S.: Dimensionality reduction for fast similarity search in large time series databases. Knowl. Inf. Syst. **3**, 263–286 (2001)
6. Keogh, E., Kasetty, S.: On the need for time series data mining benchmarks: a survey and empirical demonstration. Data Min. Knowl. Disc. **7**, 349–371 (2003). Springer

7. Keogh, E., Lin, J., Lee, S.-H., Herle, H.: Finding the most unusual time series subsequence: algorithms and applications. Knowl. Inf. Syst. **11**(1), 1–27 (2007)
8. Li, Y., Lin, J.: Approximate variable-length time series motif discovery using grammar inference. In: Proceedings of the Tenth International Workshop on Multimedia Data Mining, MDMKDD 2010, pp. 10:1–10:9, New York, NY, USA. ACM (2010)
9. Li, Y., Lin, J., Oates, T.: Visualizing variable-length time series motifs. In: SDM, pp. 895–906. SIAM / Omnipress (2012)
10. Lin, J., Keogh, E., Lonardi, S., Chiu, B.: A symbolic representation of time series, with implications for streaming algorithms. In: Proceedings of the 8th ACM SIGMOD Workshop on Research Issues in Data Mining and Knowledge Discovery, DMKD 2003, pp. 2–11, New York, NY, USA. ACM (2003)
11. Lin, J., Keogh, E., Patel, P., Lonardi, S.: Finding motifs in time series. In: The 2nd Workshop on Temporal Data Mining, at the 8th ACM SIGKDD International Conference on Knowledge Discovery and Data Mining, International Conference on Knowledge Discovery and Data Mining, Edmonton, Alberta, Canada. ACM (2002)
12. Lin, J., Keogh, E.J., Wei, L., Lonardi, S.: Experiencing sax: a novel symbolic representation of time series. Data Min. Knowl. Disc. **15**, 107–144 (2007)
13. Mohammad, Y., Nishida, T.: Constrained motif discovery in time series. New Gener. Comput. **27**(4), 319–346 (2009)
14. Rouse, J.W., Haas, R.H., Schell, J.A., Deering, D.W.: Monitoring vegetation systems in the great plains with ERTS. In: Proceedings of the Third ERTS Symposium, Washington, DC, USA, pp. 309–317 (1973)
15. Udechukwu, A., Barker, K., Alhajj, R.: Discovering all frequent trends in time series. In: Proceedings of the winter international synposium on Information and communication technologies, WISICT 2004, pp. 1–6. Trinity College Dublin (2004)
16. Wang, L., Chng, E.S., Li, H.: A tree-construction search approach for multivariate time series motifs discovery. Pattern Recogn. Lett. **31**(9), 869–875 (2010)
17. Yankov, D., Keogh, E., Medina, J., Chiu, B., Zordan, V.: Detecting time series motifs under uniform scaling. In: Proceedings of the 13th ACM SIGKDD International Conference on Knowledge Discovery and Data Mining, KDD 2007, pp. 844–853. ACM, New York, NY, USA (2007)

# An Approach to the Discovery of Accurate and Expressive Fix-Time Prediction Models

Francesco Folino$^{(\boxtimes)}$, Massimo Guarascio, and Luigi Pontieri

ICAR-CNR, National Research Council of Italy,
via P. Bucci 41C, 87036 Rende, CS, Italy
{ffolino,guarascio,pontieri}@icar.cnr.it

**Abstract.** Predicting the fix time (i.e. the time needed to eventually solve a case) is a key task in an issue tracking system, which attracted the attention of data-mining researchers in recent years. Traditional approaches only try to forecast the overall fix time of a case when it is reported, without updating this preliminary estimate as long as the case evolves. Clearly, the actions performed on a case can help refine the prediction of its (remaining) fix time, by using Process Mining techniques, but typical issue tracking systems lack task-oriented descriptions of the resolution process, and store fine-grain records, just registering case attributes' updates. Moreover, no general approach has been proposed in the literature that fully supports the definition of high-quality derived data, which were yet proven capable to improve prediction accuracy considerably. A new fix-time prediction framework is presented here, along with an associated system, both based on the combination of two kinds of capabilities: *(i)* a series of modular and flexible data-transformation mechanisms, for producing an enhanced process-oriented log view, and *(ii)* several induction techniques, for extracting a prediction model from such a view. Preliminary results, performed on the logs of two real issue tracking scenarios, confirm the validity and practical usefulness of our proposal.

**Keywords:** Data mining · Prediction · Business process analysis · Bug tracking

## 1 Introduction

Issue tracking systems (a.k.a. "trouble/incident ticket" systems) are widely used in real collaboration environments, in order to manage, maintain and help resolve various issues arising within an organization or a community.

An important problem in such a context concerns the prediction of the fix time, i.e. the time needed to solve a case. Several data-mining works [1,9,10] recently approached this problem in the specific field of bug tracking systems, a popular sub-class of issue tracking systems, devoted to support the notification and fixing of bugs affecting some software artifact, within a software development/maintenance community.

© Springer International Publishing Switzerland 2015
J. Cordeiro et al. (Eds.): ICEIS 2014, LNBIP 227, pp. 108–128, 2015.
DOI: 10.1007/978-3-319-22348-3_7

The approaches proposed so far mainly try to induce discrete (i.e. classification-oriented) or continuous (i.e. regression-oriented) predictors from historical bug logs, by resorting to classical propositional prediction methods, and simply regards each bug case as a tuple, encoding all information available when the bug was initially reported, and labelled with a discrete or numerical (target) fix-time value. Therefore, all the data recorded along the life of a bug/issue case (e.g., changes made to properties like its priority, criticality, status, or assignee) are completely disregarded, despite they could turn useful for refining, at run-time, the prediction of (remaining) fix times.

The discovery of predictive (state-aware) process models [4,5,13] is a young line of research in the field of Process Mining. Unfortunately, the approaches developed in that field assume that log records be mapped to well-specified process tasks, which are, instead, hardly defined in real bug/issue systems, where the logs only store the sequence of changes made to a case's attributes. In fact, despite many systems support the design of workflows, these are rarely used in real applications. Moreover, different repositories tend to exhibit heterogeneous data schemes, even if developed over the same platform (e.g., Bugzilla).

In this work, we right attempt to overcome the limitations of current solutions by proposing a novel approach to the discovery of (state-aware) fix-time prediction models, out of low-level bug/issue logs, which can fully exploit all information stored in the form of both case attributes and attribute modification records. In order to reach a suitable abstraction level over case histories, a modular set of parametric data-transformation methods is defined, which allow to convert each case into a process trace (with update records abstracted into high-level activities), and to possibly enrich these traces with derived/aggregated data. In particular, the analyst is offered the possibility to effectively exploit textual descriptions, by summarizing them into a lower-dimensional concept space, with the help of SVD-based techniques. A high-quality process-oriented view of log data is so obtained, which can be analyzed with predictive process mining methods, to eventually induce a predictive process model, capable of supporting fix-time forecasts, at run-time, for future cases. The approach has been implemented into a system, provided with an integrated and extensible set of data-transformation and predictive learning tools, along with a series of functionalities for browsing, evaluating and analysing the discovered process models.

The remainder of the paper is organized as follows. After discussing relevant related works in Sect. 2, we introduce some basic concepts and notation in Sect. 3. Several core event manipulation methods and trace manipulation ones are presented in Sects. 4 and 5, respectively. Section 6 illustrates the whole approach to the discovery of predictive fix-time models, while Sect. 7 its current implementation. We finally discuss a series of tests in Sect. 8, and draw a few concluding remarks in Sect. 9.

## 2   Related Work

As mentioned above, previous fix-time prediction works focus on the case of bug tracking systems, and resort to classical learning methods, conceived for analyzing propositional data labelled with a discrete or numerical target.

Random-forest classifiers and linear regressors were trained in [9] and in [1], respectively, in order to predict bug lifetimes, using different bug attributes as input variables. Different standard classification algorithms were employed instead in [10] to the same purpose. Decision trees were also exploited in [7], in order to estimate how promptly a new bug report will receive attention. Standard linear regression was also used in [8] to predict whether a bug report will be triaged within a given amount of time.

As mentioned above, none of these approaches explored the possibly of improving such a preliminary estimate subsequently, as long as a case undergoes different treatments and modifications. The only (partial) exception is the work in [10], where some information gathered after the creation of a bug is used as well, but just for the special case of unconfirmed bugs, and till they were definitely accepted. Conversely, we want to exploit the rich amount of log data stored for bug/issue cases (across their entire life), in order to build a history-aware prediction model, capable of providing accurate run-time forecasts for the remaining fix time of new (unfinished) cases.

Predicting processing times is the goal of an emerging research stream in the field of Process Mining, which specifically addresses the induction of state-aware performance model out of historical log traces. In particular, the discovery of an annotated finite-state model (AFSM) was proposed in [13], where the states correspond to abstract representations of log traces, and store processing-time estimates. This learning approach was combined in [4,5] with a predictive clustering scheme, where the initial data values of each log trace are used as descriptive features for the clustering, and its associated processing times as target features. By reusing existing induction methods, each discovered cluster is then equipped with a distinct prediction model – precisely, an AFSM in [4], and classical regression models in [5].

Unfortunately, these Process Mining techniques rely on a process-oriented representation of system logs, where each event refers to a well-specified task; conversely, common bug tracking systems just register bug attribute updates, with no link to resolution tasks. In order to overcome this limitation, we want to help the analyst extract high-level activities out of bug/issue histories, by providing her/him with a set of data transformation methods, tailored to fine-grain attribute-update records, like those stored in typical bug/issue tracking systems.

The effectiveness of derived data in improving fix-time predictions was pointed out in [2], where a few summary statistics and derived properties were computed for certain Bugzilla repositories, in a pre-processing phase. We attempt to generalize such an approach, by devising an extensible set of data transformation and data aggregation/abstraction mechanisms, allowing to extract and evaluate such derived features from a generic bug/issue resolution trace.

# 3  Basic Concepts and Notation

We next illustrate the structure and main characteristics of issue/bug resolution logs, which are the source for extracting a process-oriented fix-time prediction model.

For the sake of concreteness, let us focus on the structure of bug repositories developed with *Bugzilla* (http://www.bugzilla.org), a general-purpose bug-tracking platform, devoted to support people in various bug-related tasks – e.g., keep track of bugs, communicate with colleagues, submit/review patches, and manage quality assurance (QA). We pinpoint that this choice does not limit the generality of our approach, since similar strategies take place in most real bug/issue -tracking applications.

Usually bug/issue resolution tasks are carried out in an unstructured fashion, without being enforced by a prescriptive process model. Such applications mainly looks like a repository, where an extensible set of attributes are kept for a case (concerning the resolution of a bug/issue), and possibly updated along the entire life of that case.

For example, in the Bugzilla repository of project *Eclipse* (also used in our tests), the main attributes associated with each bug $b$ are: the **status** and **resolution** of $b$; who entered $b$ into the system (**reporter**); the last solver $b$ was assigned to (**assignee**); the **component** and **product** affected by $b$; $b$'s **severity**'s and **priority**'s levels; a **milestone**; the list of users to be kept informed on $b$'s progress (**CC**); the lists of other bugs depending on $b$ (**dependsOn**), and of related documents (**seeAlso**).

Some attributes (e.g., **reporter**) are static, whereas others (e.g., **assignee**, **status**, **resolution**) may change while a case evolves. In particular, the **status** of a bug $b$ may take the following values: *unconfirmed* (i.e. $b$ was reported by an external user, and it must be confirmed by a project member), *new* (i.e. $b$ was opened/confirmed by a project member), *assigned, resolved* (i.e. a fix was made to $b$, but it needs to be validated), *verified* (i.e. a QA manager has validated the fix), *reopened* (if the last fix was insufficient), and *closed*. For a resolved bug $b$, the **resolution** field may take one of these values: *fixed, duplicate* (i.e. $b$ is a duplicate of another bug), *works-for-me* (i.e. $b$ has been judged unfounded), *invalid, won't-fix*.

In any Bugzilla repository, the whole history of a bug is stored as a list of update records, all sharing the same structure, which consists five predefined fields (in addition to a bug identifier): *who* (the person who made the update), *when* (a timestamp for the record), *what* (the attribute modified), *removed* (the former value of that attribute) and *added* (the newly assigned value).

Figure 1 reports, as an example, all the update records of a single Ecplise's bug.

*Traces and Associated Data.* The contents of a bug/issue tracking repository can be viewed as a set of *traces*, each storing the sequence of *events* recorded during a case. As explained above, each of these events concerns a modification to a case attribute, and takes the form of the records in Fig. 1.

| Who | When | What | Removed | Added |
|---|---|---|---|---|
| svihovec | 2012-06-20 10:12:27 EDT | CC | | margolis, svihovec |
| | | Target Milestone | --- | 0.8.1 Final |
| jinfahua | 2012-06-20 22:21:22 EDT | CC | | jinfahua, pfyu |
| | | Assignee | edt.ide.ui-inbox | songfan |
| pfyu | 2012-06-21 03:52:44 EDT | Attachment #217671 Flags | | review? |
| svihovec | 2012-06-21 11:09:34 EDT | CC | | jspadea, jvincens |
| pfyu | 2012-06-25 05:04:17 EDT | CC | | wxwu |
| jspadea | 2012-07-02 10:26:15 EDT | Assignee | songfan | jspadea |
| jspadea | 2012-07-02 15:21:21 EDT | Status | NEW | RESOLVED |
| | | Resolution | --- | FIXED |
| lasher | 2012-07-18 15:27:24 EDT | Attachment #218182 Flags | | iplog+ |
| mheitz | 2013-01-03 10:44:55 EST | Status | RESOLVED | CLOSED |

**Fig. 1.** Activity log for a single Bugzilla's bug (whose ID is omitted for brevity). Row groups gather "simultaneous" update records (sharing the same timestamp and executor).

Let $E$ be the universe of all possible events, and $\mathcal{T}$ be the universe of all possible traces defined over them. For any event $e \in E$, let $who(e)$, $when(e)$, $what(e)$, $removed(e)$, and $added(e)$ be the executor, the timestamp, the attribute modified, the former value and new value stored in $e$, respectively. In the case of Bugzilla repositories, each of these dimensions just corresponds to a label. This does not happen, however, in other issue tracking systems, where an event record can encode a change to multiple attributes, and gather different kinds of information on the organizational resource involved (e.g., her/his role, team, department, etc.). In such a case, the representation of log events can be generalized, by letting $who(e)$, $when(e)$, $what(e)$, $removed(e)$, and $added(e)$ take the form of a tuple (over some suitable attribute space).

For each trace $\tau \in \mathcal{T}$, let $len(\tau)$ be the number of events in $\tau$, $\tau[i]$ be the $i$-th event of $\tau$, for any $i = 1 \mathinner{..} len(\tau)$, and $\tau(i] \in \mathcal{T}$ be the *prefix* trace gathering the first $i$ events in $\tau$.

Prefix traces have the same form as fully unfolded ones, but only represent partial case histories. Indeed, the prefix traces of a case depicts the evolution of the case across its whole life. For example, the activity log of Fig. 1 (which just stores the history of one bug) will be represented as a trace $\tau_{ex}$ consisting of 12 events, one for each of the update records (i.e. rows of the table) in the figure; in particular, for the first event, it is $who(\tau_{ex}[1]) = svihovec$, $what(\tau_{ex}[1]) = \text{CC}$, $added(\tau_{ex}[1])) = \{margolis, svihovec\}$.

As mentioned above, typical tracking systems store several attributes for each case (e.g., `reporter`, `priority`, etc.), which may take different values during its life. Let $F_1, \ldots, F_n$ be all of the attributes defined for a bug. Then, for any (either partial of completed) trace $\tau$, let $data(\tau)$ be a tuple storing the updated values of these attributes associated with $\tau$ (i.e. the values taken by the corresponding case after the last event of $\tau$), and $data(\tau)[F_i]$ be the value taken by $F_i$ (for $i = 1 \mathinner{..} n$).

Finally, a *log* $L$ is a finite subset of $\mathcal{T}$, while the *prefix set* of $L$, denoted by $\mathcal{P}(L)$, is the set of all possible prefix traces that can be extracted from $L$.

*Fix-time Measurements and Models.* Let $\hat{\mu}_F : \mathcal{T} \to \mathbb{R}$ be an unknown function assigning a fix-time value to any (sub-)trace. The value of $\hat{\mu}_F$ is known over all $\mathcal{P}(L)$'s traces, for any given log $L$; indeed, for any trace $\tau$ and prefix $\tau(i]$, it is $\hat{\mu}_F(\tau(i]) = when(\tau[len(\tau)]) - when(\tau[i])$. For example, for the trace $\tau_{ex}(2]$ encoding the first 2 events in Fig. 1, it is $\hat{\mu}_F(\tau_{ex}(2]) = when(\tau[12]) - when(\tau[2]) = 197$ days.

A *Fix-time Prediction Model (FTPM)* is a model for estimating the remaining fix time of a case, based on its current trace. Learning such a model, which approximates the unknown function $\hat{\mu}_F$, is an induction task, where log $L$ plays as the training set, and the value $\hat{\mu}_F(\tau)$ of the target measure is known for each (prefix) trace $\tau \in \mathcal{P}(L)$.

# 4    Event Manipulation Operators

In the discovery of an *FTPM* model we want to consider both case histories (i.e. all sequences of update records) and case properties (e.g., the affected product, severity level, reporter). To this end, we will regard some of the actions performed on a case as a clue for the activities of an unknown (bug/issue resolution) process, in order to eventually exploit Process Mining techniques. In fact, simply defining such activities as all possible changes to the status of a case would lead to discarding relevant events, such as the (re-)assignment of the case to a solver, or the update of key properties (like its severity, criticality, or category). On the other hand, we do not either want to look at all attribute updates as resolution tasks, since many of them are hardly linked to fix times, and they may even produce a noise-like effect on the discovery of fix-time predictors.

## 4.1    Activity-Oriented Event Abstraction

An event abstraction function $\alpha$ is a function mapping each event $e \in E$ to an abstract representation $\alpha(e)$, which captures relevant facets of the action performed. In current process mining approaches, log events are usually abstracted into their associated tasks, possibly combined with other properties of them (e.g., their executors), under the assumption that the events correspond to the execution of work-items, according to a workflow-oriented view of the process analyzed.

In our framework, such a function $\alpha$ is intended to turn each issue/bug -tracking event into a high-level bug/issue-resolution activity, by mapping the former to a label that captures well its meaning. Since only attribute-update events are tracked, the analyst is allowed to define this function in terms of their fields (i.e. *who, when, what, added,* and *removed*).

The default instantiation of $\alpha$, denoted by $\overline{\alpha}$ and conceived for Bugzilla's records, is defined as follows (with $+$ denoting string concatenation):

$$\overline{\alpha}(e) = \begin{cases} what(e)+ \text{":="}+added(e), & \text{if } what(e) \in \{\texttt{status}, \texttt{resolution}\} \\ \text{"}\Delta\text{"}+what(e), & \text{otherwise} \end{cases} \tag{1}$$

This particular definition of $\alpha$ focuses on what attribute was modified, while abstracting any other event's field (namely, *who*, *when*, *removed*, and *added*); as an exception, the assigned value is included in the abstract representation when the update concerns the `status` or `resolution`, as such information, characterizing the state of a bug, can improve fix-time predictions. For example, for the first two events of trace $\tau_{ex}$ (gathering all the records in Fig. 1), it is $\overline{\alpha}(\tau_{ex}[1]) = \Delta CC$, and $\overline{\alpha}(\tau_{ex}[2]) = \Delta \texttt{TargetMilestone}$, while the activity label of the last event ($\tau_{ex}[12]$) is `status:=`*closed*.

Different event abstraction functions can be defined by the analyst, in order to focus on other facets of bug activities, or to change the level of detail, depending on the specific bug attributes (and associated domains) available in the application scenario at hand. For instance, with regard to the scenario of Sect. 3, one may refine the representation of severity-level changes by defining two distinct activity labels for them, say $\Delta Severity\text{-}Eclipse$ and $\Delta Severity\text{-}NotEclipse$, based on the presence of substring "eclipse" in the e-mail address of the person who made the change.

## 4.2   Macro-Events' Restructuring

In real bug tracking environments, multiple fields of a case are often modified in a single access session, and the corresponding activity records are all stored with the same timestamp, in a rather arbitrary order. For example, in our tests, we encountered many cases where the closure of the bug (i.e. an event of type `status:=`*closed*) preceded a "contemporaneous" change to the assignee (or a message dispatch).

Regarding each set of contemporaneous events as one *macro-event*, the analyst can define three kinds of data-manipulation rules, in order to rearrange them based on their fields: *(i)* a *predominance* rule, assigning different relevance levels to simultaneous events (with the ultimate aim of purging off less relevant ones); *(ii)* a set of *merging* rules, indicating when two or more contemporaneous events (with the same predominance level) must be merged together, and which activity label must be assigned to the resulting aggregated event; *(iii)* a set of *sort* rules, specifying an ordering relation over (non-purged and non-merged) simultaneous events.

Any combination of the above kinds of rules will be collectively regarded, hereinafter, as a *macro-event criterion*. The default instantiation of this criterion, tailored to Bugzilla's bugs, is summarized in Table 1, where each event is given a "predominance" level, only based on *what* attribute was updated in the event. Such levels acts as a sort of priority score in the selection of events (the lower the level, the greater the priority): an event is eventually kept only if there is no simultaneous event with a lower level than it. In particular, events involving a change to the `status` or `resolution` hide `assignee/priority/severity` updates, which, in their turn, hide changes to the `milestone` or `CC`.

A *merging* rule is defined in Table 1 only for 1-level simultaneous events, which states that, whenever the `status` and `resolution` of a bug are modified contemporarily, the respective events must be merged into a single macro-event, which is labelled with the concatenation of their associated activity labels. For example, this implies that the ninth and tenth events in Fig. 1 will be merged together, and labelled with the string "`state:=`*resolved* `+ resolution:=`*fixed*".

Also the default sort rule (shown in the table as an ordering relation $<$) only depends on the *what* field, and states that events involving attribute `milestone` must precede those concerning `CC`, and that `priority` (resp., `severity`) updates must precede `severity` (resp., `assignee`) ones. In this way, e.g., the first two events in Fig. 1 will be switched with one another.

**Table 1.** Default macro-event criterion: predominance, merging and sort rules over simultaneous events. No merging rules for levels 2 and 3, and no sort rules for level-1 events are defined.

| Predominance levels | | Merging rules | Sort rules |
|---|---|---|---|
| (lev.) | (bug attributes) | (macro-event activity label) | (ordering relation) |
| 1 | `status, resolution` | $\alpha(\langle \_, \_, \text{status}, \_, \_ \rangle) + \text{``+''}$ $+\, \alpha(\langle \_, \_, \text{resolution}, \_, \_ \rangle)$ | — |
| 2 | `priority, severity, assignee` | — | `priority<severity<assignee` |
| 3 | `milestone, CC` | — | `milestone<CC` |

*Example 1.* Let us apply all default log abstraction operators introduced above (i.e. the event abstraction function in Eq. 1 and the macro-event criterion of Table 1) to the bug trace $\tau_{ex}$ encoding the events in Fig. 1. For the sake of conciseness, we only consider events involving the attributes in Table 1. The resulting trace $\tau'_{ex}$ consists of 8 events, which are associated with the following activity labels, respectively: $l_1 = $"$\Delta$`milestone`", $l_2 = $"$\Delta$`CC`", $l_3 = $"$\Delta$`assignee`", $l_4 = $"$\Delta$`CC`", $l_5 = $"$\Delta$`CC`", $l_6 = $"$\Delta$`assignee`", $l_7 = $"`status:=`*resolved*`+resolution:=`*fixed*", $l_8 = $"`status` := *closed*", where $l_i$ denotes the activity label of $\tau'_{ex}[i]$, for $i \in \{1, \ldots, 8\}$. The respective timestamps (at 1-hour granularity) of these events are: $t_1 = t_2 = $(*2012-06-20 10EDT*), $t_3 = $(*2012-06-20 22EDT*), $t_4 = $(*2012-06-21 11EDT*), $t_5 = $(*2012-06-25 05EDT*), $t_6 = $(*2012-07-02 10EDT*), $t_7 = $(*2012-07-02 15EDT*), $t_8 = $(*2013-01-03 11EST*). ◁

# 5  Trace Manipulation Operators

By applying the event manipulation operators introduced in the previous section, each bug history can be turned into a "process trace", i.e. a sequence of resolution tasks. In order to profitably apply process-oriented prediction techniques, such a trace must be converted into some abstract state-oriented form, capturing somewhat the stage reached by the corresponding bug case along the resolution process. On the other hand, the accuracy of fix-time prediction can be empowered by taking advantage of context information stored for each case, in the form of native or derived trace attributes. These two issues are discussed in details next, in two separate subsections.

## 5.1    State-Oriented Trace Abstraction

For each trace $\tau$, a collection of relevant prefixes (i.e. sub-traces) $rp(\tau)$ is selected, in order to extract an abstract representation for the states traversed by the associated bug, during its life. Two strategies can be adopted to this end, named *event-oriented* and *block-oriented*. In the former strategy all possible $\tau$'s prefixes are considered, i.e. $rp(\tau) = \{\tau(i) \mid i = 1 \ldots len(\tau)\}$, whereas in the latter only prefixes ending with the last event of a "macro-activity" are selected, i.e. $rp(\tau) = \{ \tau(i) \mid 1 \leq i \leq len(\tau)$ and $when(\tau[j]) > when(\tau[i]) \; \forall j \in \{i+1,\ldots,len(\tau)\} \}$.

Independently of the selection strategy, each trace $\tau'$ in $rp(\tau)$ is turned into a tuple $state^{\alpha}(\tau')$, whose attributes are all the abstract activities produced by a given event abstraction function $\alpha$ (e.g., that in Eq. 1). The value taken by each of these activities, say $a$, is denoted by $state(\tau')^{\alpha}[a]$ and computed as follows:

$$state^{\alpha}(\tau')[a] = \mathrm{SUM}(\{ \; \delta(\tau'[i]) \mid \alpha(\tau'[i]) = a \text{ for } i = 1..len(\tau')\}) \qquad (2)$$

where $\delta$ is a function assigning an integer weight to each event, based on its properties; by default it is *(i)* $\delta(e) = |added(e)|$, if $e$ is not an aggregation of multiple simultaneous events (i.e. it corresponds to one raw update record) and $e$ involves a multivalued attribute (like CC, seeAlso), or *(ii)* $\delta(e) = 1$ otherwise.

Any prefix trace $\tau'$ is hence encoded by an integer vector in the space of the abstract activities extracted by $\alpha$, where each component accounts for all the occurrences, in $\tau'$, of the corresponding activity. Such a vector captures the state of a bug (at any step of its evolution) through a summarized view of its history.

*Example 2.* Let us consider the trace $\tau'_{ex}$ shown in Example 1. The unfolding of this trace gives rise to 8 distinct prefix sub-traces, denoted by $\tau'_{ex}(1)$, $\tau'_{ex}(2)$, $\ldots$, $\tau'_{ex}(8)$. Five abstract activities occur in these traces:

$a_1 =$ "$\Delta$milestone",

$a_2 =$ "$\Delta$CC",

$a_3 =$ "$\Delta$assignee",

$a_4 =$ "status:=*resolved*+resolution:=*fixed*",

$a_5 =$ "status :=*closed*".

As concerns trace abstractions, all components of $state^{\overline{\alpha}}(\tau'_{ex}(1))$ (i.e. the tuple encoding the state reached after the first step) are 0 but that associated with $a_1$ and $a_2$, which are $state^{\overline{\alpha}}(\tau'_{ex}(1))[a_1] = 1$, and $state^{\overline{\alpha}}(\tau'_{ex}(1))[a_2] = 2$. If using the event-oriented strategy, the above traces will generate 8 state tuples:

$state^{\overline{\alpha}}(\tau'_{ex}(1)) = \langle 1,2,0,0,0 \rangle$, $state^{\overline{\alpha}}(\tau'_{ex}(2)) = \langle 1,2,1,0,0 \rangle$,
$state^{\overline{\alpha}}(\tau'_{ex}(3)) = \langle 1,4,1,0,0 \rangle$, $state^{\overline{\alpha}}(\tau'_{ex}(4)) = \langle 1,5,1,0,0 \rangle$,
$state^{\overline{\alpha}}(\tau'_{ex}(5)) = \langle 1,5,2,0,0 \rangle$, $state^{\overline{\alpha}}(\tau'_{ex}(6)) = \langle 1,5,2,1,0 \rangle$,
$state^{\overline{\alpha}}(\tau'_{ex}(7)) = \langle 1,5,2,1,1 \rangle$. $\qquad\qquad\qquad\qquad\qquad\qquad\quad \triangleleft$

Such a state-oriented representation of a log $L$ will be eventually exploited to induce a fix-time prediction model (i.e. a $FTPM$) for $L$, as explained in the next section.

## 5.2    Insertion of Additional Trace Attributes

In order to possibly improve the accuracy of discovered prediction models, we want to give the analyst the possibility to inject additional attributes, accounting for the context where resolution tasks took place.

More specifically, our framework is meant to supports different kinds of operators for inserting additional data into bug traces, or for transforming a given (raw or derived) bugs/events attribute, and making it more expressive: *(i) indicators' derivation* operators, *(ii) attribute enrichment* operators, and *(iii) attribute summarization* operators.

*Indicators' Derivation.* The first kind of operators is essentially meant to compute some statistics over some suitable trace collection. In fact, the insertion of such additional data was already considered in previous bug analysis works [8,9]. We defined five standard indicator derivation operators, which allow for automatically inserting the following fields into each given trace $\tau$, respectively: *(i)* a workload measure indicating the overall number of cases currently opened in the system globally, and several variants of it, computed over specific groups of cases (e.g., all bugs regarding the same product version, component or OS as $\tau$); *(ii)* an analogous collection of counters for the cases fixed in the past year (globally, and for the version/component/OS associated with $\tau$); *(iii)* a "reputation" coefficient, computed for the reporter of $\tau$ as in [2]; *(iv)* the average fix time for various groups of related cases (e.g., all bugs concerning the same project or reporter as $\tau$) and closed in the past year; *(v)* several seasonality dimensions (such as, week-day, month, and year) derived from the date of the last event in $\tau$.

*Attribute Enrichment.* This class of operators is meant to extend the values of an attribute with correlated information, extracted from the same repository. As a standard attribute enrichment mechanism, we consider the possibility of replacing users' identifiers (possibly appearing, e.g., in *who* fields of bug history records, or in certain bug attributes) with their respective e-mail addresses — actually, no further information on people is available in many real bug repositories. To implement such an operator, a greedy matching procedure was developed, which founds on comparing any user ID with all the email addresses appearing in various attributes of the bugs.

*Clustering-based Attribute Summarization.* These operators aim at reducing the dimensionality of an attribute by partitioning its domain into classes. In particular, in order to get an effective level of abstraction over a trace attribute, say $F$, we considered the problem of finding a partition of $F$'s domain exhibiting high correlation with fix-time measurements, based on a given aggregation hierarchy $H$ over $F$. Let $dom(F)$ be the domain of $F$, and $h \in \mathbb{N}$ be the height (i.e. the number of levels) of $H$. Let also $H(i)$ be the *i-th* level of $H$ (for $i = 0, l \ldots, h$), and $values(H, i)$ be the values forming that aggregation level. Each level of $H$ corresponds to a partition of $dom(F)$, with a distinguished aggregation degree;

in particular, level 0 ($H$'s leaves) just encodes the raw values in $dom(F)$ without any aggregation, and level $h$ just consists of one node ($H$'s root). Such a hierarchy may be already available for the attribute (this is the case of email addresses and software products, which follow an implicit meronomical and taxonomical scheme, respectively), or it can be computed automatically through clustering methods. Let $C_H$ be a cut of the given hierarchy $H$, and $values(C_H)$ be the associated nodes, i.e. the set of aggregated $F$'s values identified by $C_H$. Any such a cut can be associated with a loss measure, denoted by $Loss(C_H)$, w.r.t. the target metrics $\mu_F$, as follows:

$$Loss(C_H) = \frac{\sum_{\tau \in \mathcal{P}(L)} [\hat{\mu}_F(\tau[len(\tau)]) - \tilde{\mu}_F(\tau, C_H)]^2}{|\mathcal{P}(L)|}$$

where $\tilde{\mu}_F(\tau, C_H)$ is average performance value over all trace prefixes owning a value of $F$ that was assigned to the same $C_H$'s node as $\tau$. An optimal cut of $H$ is one minimizing this loss measure, among all those satisfying a user-defined property. A greedy procedure has been implemented in our framework for computing such a cut, based on a maximal constraint on cut's size (i.e. number of nodes in the cut).

*Text-oriented Attribute Summarization.* In many real application scenarios, bug/issue handling systems store free-text contents for each case, ranging from notes to messages. In particular, in the case of Bugzilla's bug repositories, a *summary* field is kept for each bug case, providing a short description of the problem occurred. Let us assume that the textual contents of any bug $\tau$ are stored into a vector $text(\tau)$, encoding a bag-of-word representation for the concatenation of all $\tau$'s free-text fields, based on classic vector-space model and TF-IDF weights. Clearly, such a textual description can hold important information on the nature and characteristics of a bug, and it can help improve the estimation of its fix time, as pointed out in [6]. However, as the vocabulary used in such descriptions may be rather large and sparse, extending the attributes of each trace with a mere bag-of-word view of its text contents will hardly improve the accuracy of fix-time predictions; indeed, such an overly detailed representation might even confuse the learner and lead to overfitting and imprecise models.

In order to face this issue, we introduced a further kind of text-oriented attribute-summarization operators, meant to grasp a concise high-level representation of text contents. The standard implementation of this operator class relies on computing a low-rank approximation of the term-by-bug matrix, based on Singular Value Decomposition (SVD) techniques [12]. The mapping of cases to the underlying concept space (i.e., the $U$ matrix in the $U \times \Sigma \times V^T$ factorization of the term-by-bug matrix) is used to build a low-dimensional (and more abstract) representation of text contents. Such summarized "latent-semantics" vectors will be used to complement the attributes of each trace, so obtaining a richer description of the corresponding bug/issue case.

# 6 *FTPM* Discovery Algorithm

This section is meant to offer a summarized view of our whole approach to the discovery of a Fix-time Prediction Model (*FTPM*), based on a given set of raw bug records.

The approach is illustrated in Fig. 2 as a meta-algorithm, named FTPM Discovery, encoding the main steps of our (process-oriented) data-transformation methodology, and the eventual application of a predictive induction method to the transformed log.

The algorithm takes as input a bug/issue tracking repository, storing a collection of records (like those at the beginning of Sect. 3), and some parameters regarding the application of data-manipulation operators. In order to apply the abstraction operators introduced in Sect. 4, these data are first turned into a set of traces (i.e. a log).

Based on a given *filtering* criterion $\Phi$, function filterEvents possibly removes uninteresting events (e.g., outliers or noisy data), which may confuse the learner.

Function handleMacroEvents allows us to apply a given *macro-event* criterion $\Gamma$ (like that described in Table 1) to rearrange each group of simultaneous log events according to the associated *predominance, reordering* and/or *merging* rules.

Steps 4 and 5 are meant to possibly associate each trace $\tau$ with additional "derived" data, to complement the original contents of $data(\tau)$ with context information.

---

**Input:** Collection $B$ of bug/issue records, filtering criterion $\Phi$, a macro-event criterion $\Gamma$, event abstraction function $\alpha$, and prefix selection strategy $S \in$ {BLOCK, EVENT}
**Output:** An $FTPM$ (Fix-time Prediction Model) for $B$
**Method:** Perform the following steps:
  1 Convert $B$ into a log $L$ of traces;
  2 $L := $ filterEvents($L, \phi$);
  3 $L := $ handleMacroEvents($L, \Gamma$);
  4 $L := $ deriveTraceAttributes($L$);
  5 $L := $ refineTraceAttributes($L$);
  6 **if** $S = $ BLOCK **then**
  7    $RS := \{\tau(i)) \mid \tau \in L, 1 \leq i \leq len(\tau),$ and
      $when(\tau[j]) > when(\tau[i]) \ \forall j \in \mathbb{N} \text{ s.t. } i < j \leq len(\tau)\}$;
  8 **else**
  9    $RS := \{\tau(i)) \mid \tau \in L, \text{ and } 1 \leq i \leq len(\tau)\}$;
  10 **end if**
  11 $M := $ mineFTPM($RS, \alpha$);
  12 **return** $M$.

---

**Fig. 2.** Meta-algorithm FTPM Discovery.

Basically, function `deriveTraceAttributes` is devoted to insert new trace attributes, with the help of *indicators' derivation* operators and of *attribute enrichment* operators like those defined in the previous section.

Conversely, function `refineTraceAttributes` is meant to transform a number of (raw or derived) cases'/events' attributes, and eventually them into more expressive ones, by way of *attribute-summarization* operators.

Steps 6–10 are simply meant to extract a set $RS$ of relevant (sub-)traces out of $\mathcal{P}(L)$, based on the chosen event selection strategy $S$. $RS$ is then used by function `mineFTPM` as a training set, in order to eventually induce an $FTPM$. To this end, as explained in Sect. 4, each trace $\tau \in RS$ is converted into a tuple labelled with the fix-time measurement $\mu_F(\tau)$, and encoding both the representation of $\tau$'s state (w.r.t. the given event abstraction function $\alpha$), and its associated (augmented) data tuple $data(\tau)$. More precisely, $data(\tau)$ and $state^\alpha(\tau)$ are used as descriptive/input attributes, while regarding the actual remaining-time value $\mu_F(\tau')$ as the target of prediction.

At this point, various learning methods (including those mentioned in Sect. 2) can be used to induce a regression or classification model. Different solutions for carrying out this task have been implemented in our prototype system, as described next.

# 7    The Implemented System

A prototype system was developed to fully implement the approach above, and support the discovery and analysis of $FTPM$s. The system allows the analyst to flexibly and modularly apply all the data-processing operators presented in this work, in an interactive and iterative way, as well as to define and store (in a reusable form) new variants of them, according to a template-based paradigm.

The conceptual architecture of the system is shown in Fig. 3. System's functionalities are organized in three layers, which concern respectively: the storage, handling and manipulation of log data (*Data Management and Processing*), the implementation of core data mining techniques (*Data Mining*), and the handling and evaluation the prediction and clustering models found with these techniques (*Models' Management*).

The *Log Repository Gateway* module supports the importation of historical data stored in a remote bug/issue tracking repository. Its current implementation allows for connecting to the web interface of any Bugzilla repository, and converting the histories of selected bugs into bug traces. The imported log, possibly cleaned according to suitable filtering rules, is stored in the *Event Log* archive.

The *Event Manipulation* and *Trace Manipulation* modules provide various data-transformation mechanisms (possibly already stored in the form of *Event/ Trace Transformation Rules*), in order to produce enhanced views of the log, which are more suitable for fix time prediction. More specifically, the first module is responsible for manipulating groups of simultaneous events according to a desired macro-event criterion (sub-module *Macro-events' manipulation*), as discussed in Sect. 4, and for extracting high-level activity labels from event prop-

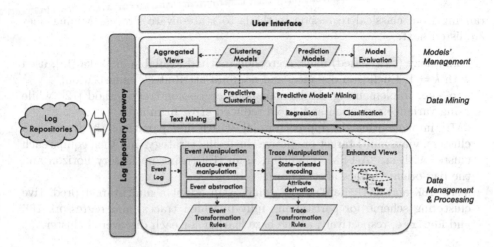

**Fig. 3.** Logical architecture of the implemented system.

erties (sub-module *Event abstraction*). On the other hand, the *Trace Manipulation* module allows to build a state-oriented abstraction for each selected trace (sub-module *State-oriented encoding*), while possibly enriching each trace with additional (derived and/or summarized) attributes (sub-module *Attribute derivation*), as explained in Sect. 5.2. In particular, one can extract high-level trace attributes capturing the semantics of text case fields, based on an SVD analysis of the term-by-case matrix. This task leverages the *Text Mining* module (from the *Data Mining* layer), implementing core text processing functionalities (including tokenization, stemming, TF-IDF encoding), and SVD calculations.

Each "refined" log view, obtained with of the above described functionalities. can be used as input for module *Predictive Models' Mining*. To this end, the abstracted traces are delivered to either the *Regression* or *Classification* sub-module, depending on which learning task was chosen by the user. Preliminary to the induction of a prediction model, the traces can be possibly partitioned into groups by one of the predictive clustering methods implemented by the *Predictive Clustering* module, which will also produce a set of decision rules for discriminating among the discovered clusters. In this case, each cluster will be eventually equipped with a distinct fix-time predictor.

All clustering and predictive models discovered can be explored and stored for subsequent analyses. The *Models' Management* layer also supports the evaluation of prediction models via several accuracy metrics (e.g., *rmse, mae, precision, recall*). Moreover, the *Aggregated views* module can compute aggregate statistics and graphics, concerning the distribution of any trace attribute in any trace cluster (like that in Fig. 4).

*Regression Algorithms.* Several alternative learning methods are currently implemented in our system, which support the induction of a *FTPM*, from a propositional training set like that described in the previous section. These methods, ranging from classical regression methods to state-aware Process Mining ones are listed next:

- IBK, a lazy (case-based) naïve regression method available in Weka [12], used with $k = 1$, Euclidean distance, and nominal attributes's binarization;
- RepTree, implementing the homonymous regression-tree method [12], while using variance reduction and 4-fold reduced-error pruning;
- CATP, implementing the approach in [4], which first partitions the traces into clusters, via a multi-target predictive clustering strategy, and then equips each cluster with an "A-FSM" predictor, as in [13] (using no history horizon and the bag-oriented trace abstraction);
- AATP-IBK and AATP-RepTree [5], which still adopt a multi-target predictive clustering scheme for partitioning fully-unfolded traces, and regressors IBK and RepTree, respectively, as the base learner for each discovered cluster.

*Classification Algorithms.* Like in previous bug analysis works, the analyst can also induce a classification model for the prediction of (discrete) fix times, after defining a set of a-priori classes in terms of fix-time ranges (possibly with the help of automated binning tools). To this end, a number of existing classifier-induction algorithms can be exploited, including popular decision-tree learning algorithm *J*48 (with 3-fold reduced error pruning), and the Random Forest Algorithm [3] (with size 10).

## 8    Experimental Evaluation

We performed a series of tests with our prototype system against two real datasets: a log from project *Eclipse*'s Bugzilla repository, and a collection of traces from a problem management system *BPI Challenge* [11]. In all tests, FTPM Discovery was used to find different numeric fix-time predictors, by varying the underlying regression algorithm, combined with the event-based prefix selection strategy (i.e. $S = $ EVENT).

The accuracy of the discovered models was evaluated with the standard error metrics *root mean squared error (rmse)* and *mean absolute error (mae)* — both computed via 10-fold cross validation, and normalized by the average fix time (i.e. 59 and 179 days for bug cases and problem management cases, respectively), for ease of interpretation.

### 8.1    Experiments on Bug Logs of Project Eclipse

A sample of 3906 bug records (gathered from January 2012 to March 2013) was turned into a set of bug trace like those described in Sect. 3. The length of full bug traces ranged from 2 to 27, while bug fix time ranged from one day (i.e., a bug is opened and closed in the same day) to 420 days, with an average of about 59 days.

*Log Manipulation Steps and Enhanced Log Views.* In order to put this log into a more suitable for prediction, we applied some of the log manipulation mechanisms defined in our framework. Five views of the original log, named $L_0, \ldots, L_4$, were produced by incrementally applying the basic event abstraction function $\overline{\alpha}$ in Eq. 1 and all the data-processing functions appearing in algorithm FTPM Discovery (cf. Figure 2).

- The basic "abstracted" view $L_0$ was obtained by only applying the event abstraction function $\overline{\alpha}$ to the selected bug traces;
- A "cleaned" view $L_1$, consisting of 2283 traces, was produced making $L_0$ undergo a specific instantiation of function filterEvents, removing the following data: *(i)* bugs never fixed, *(ii)* "trivial" bug cases (i.e. all bugs opened and closed in the same day), and *(iii)* trace attributes (e.g., version, whiteboard, and milestone) featuring many missing values, and bug/event fields (e.g. summary) containing long texts.
- View $L_2$ was produced by restructuring the simultaneous events in $L_1$ with the default implementation of function hanldeMacroEvents (based on the rules of Table 1).
- View $L_3$ was obtained by applying all the derivation mechanisms described in Sect. 5. As a result, each trace is equipped with the new attributes: week-day, month, and year; indicators workload, workload_version, workload_component, workload_OS (i.e. the number of bugs open in the system in general, an for the same product version, component and operating system, resp.); reporter_avgFT, project_avgFT (average fix-time for all past years' bugs with the same reporter or project, resp.); coefficient reporter_reputation [2].
- View $L_4$ was obtained by the built-in implementation of abstractTrace-Attributes, applied to $L_3$. In particular, all people identifiers in the reporter bug attribute were replaced with a number of reporters' groups representing different organizational units (namely, {*oracle, ibm.us, ibm.no_us, vmware, other*}), and extracted semi-automatically from e-mail addresses. A similar approach was used to produce a binary abstraction (namely {*eclipse, not_eclipse*}) of attribute assignee, and an aggregate representation of both product and component. Each bug was finally equipped with a series of attributes encoding a low-dimensional representation of its textual contents, computed with the help of the SVD-based technique described before.

*Prediction Results.* Table 2 reports the normalized *rmse* and *mae* errors obtained, with different regression methods available in our system, on the five log views described above. Two different learning setting were considered to this end: using bug history information (originally registered in terms of attribute-update events), and neglecting it. Note that the latter setting is intended to provide the reader with a sort of baseline, mimicking the approach followed by previous fix-time prediction works.

In general, it is easily seen that results obtained in the "no bug history" setting — where only the initial data of reported bugs are used as input variables

**Table 2.** Regression results on Eclipse bugs. Rows correspond to different *FTPM* induction methods, tested in two learning settings: without and with bug history events. Columns $L_0, \ldots, L_4$ correspond to different views of original data, obtained with our log manipulation operators.

| Predictors | | rmse | | | | | mae | | | | |
|---|---|---|---|---|---|---|---|---|---|---|---|
| Setting | Methods | $L_0$ | $L_1$ | $L_2$ | $L_3$ | $L_4$ | $L_0$ | $L_1$ | $L_2$ | $L_3$ | $L_4$ |
| No Bug History (Baseline) | IBK | 1.051 | 1.051 | 1.050 | 1.092 | 1.093 | 0.569 | 0.569 | 0.561 | 0.583 | 0.584 |
| | RepTree | 0.973 | 0.973 | 0.970 | 0.966 | 0.925 | 0.562 | 0.562 | 0.552 | 0.547 | 0.546 |
| | **Avg (no history)** | **0.973** | **0.973** | **0.970** | **0.966** | **0.925** | **0.562** | **0.562** | **0.552** | **0.547** | **0.546** |
| History-aware | CATP | 0.967 | 0.873 | 0.880 | 0.737 | 0.640 | 0.510 | 0.467 | 0.440 | 0.380 | 0.316 |
| | IBK | 0.983 | 0.823 | 0.807 | 0.793 | 0.803 | 0.430 | 0.360 | 0.360 | 0.347 | 0.345 |
| | AATP-IBK | 1.003 | 1.007 | 0.827 | 0.800 | 0.710 | 0.437 | 0.473 | 0.367 | 0.353 | 0.305 |
| | RepTree | 1.013 | 0.883 | 0.907 | 0.910 | 0.773 | 0.533 | 0.473 | 0.473 | 0.477 | 0.351 |
| | AATP-RepTree | 0.970 | 0.930 | 0.887 | 0.783 | 0.657 | 0.510 | 0.530 | 0.437 | 0.390 | 0.306 |
| | **Avg (history-aware)** | **0.987** | **0.903** | **0.862** | **0.8059** | **0.717** | **0.484** | **0.461** | **0.415** | **0.389** | **0.325** |

for the prediction — are rather poor, if compared to the average ones obtained in the "history-aware" setting. Indeed, the errors measured in the former setting are rather high, no matter which inductive method (i.e. IBK or RepTree) is used, and which pre-processing operations are applied to the original logs. Interestingly, this result substantiates our claim that exploiting bug activity information helps improve the precision of fix-time forecasts.

On the other hand, in the second setting, both *rmse* and *mae* errors tend to decrease when using more refined log views. In particular, substantial reductions were obtained with the progressive introduction of macro-event manipulations (view $L_2$), and of derived and abstracted data (views $L_3$ and $L_4$, respectively).

Very good results are obtained (in the history-aware setting) when using some kind of predictive clustering method, be it single-target (RepTree) or multi-target (CATP, AATP-RepTree and AATP-IBK). However, trace-centered clustering approaches (namely, CATP, AATP-RepTree, AATP-IBK achieve better results than RepTree, which considers all possible trace prefixes for the clustering. The benefit of using a clustering procedure is quite evident in the case of IBK, which generally gets worse achievements than any other approach, presumably due to its inability to fully exploit derived data. Indeed, still focusing on the history-aware setting, we note that IBK gets more precise when embedded in the predictive clustering scheme of AATP-IBK.

## 8.2    Experiments on the Problem Management Log

The analyzed log comes from a problem handling system (named *VINST*), offered by Volvo IT Belgium as a benchmark dataset [11] for 2013 BPI Challenge.

The main attributes of each problem resolution case $p$ are: $p$'s impact (i.e., medium, low, high); the product affected by $p$; the support team currently solving $p$, and the associated functional division and organization line;

**Table 3.** Regression results on the VINST problem management system's logs. Rows and columns still correspond to different $FTPM$ induction methods and different log views, respectively.

| Predictors | | rmse | | mae | |
|---|---|---|---|---|---|
| *Setting* | *Methods* | $L_0'$ | $L_1'$ | $L_0'$ | $L_1'$ |
| No Bug History (Baseline) | IBK | 0.924 | 0.818 | 0.499 | 0.363 |
| | RepTree | 0.937 | 0.539 | 0.523 | 0.245 |
| | **Avg (no history)** | **0.931** | **0.679** | **0.511** | **0.304** |
| History-aware | CATP | 0.930 | 0.563 | 0.542 | 0.278 |
| | IBK | 0.916 | 0.802 | 0.466 | 0.357 |
| | AATP-IBK | 0.914 | 0.613 | 0.465 | 0.242 |
| | RepTree | 0.888 | 0.508 | 0.470 | 0.235 |
| | AATP-RepTree | 0.887 | 0.467 | 0.466 | 0.205 |
| | **Avg (history-aware)** | **0.907** | **0.591** | **0.482** | **0.265** |

the country where the support team is located (organization country); the resource currently operating on $p$ and its nationality (resource country); the status and substatus of $p$. More specifically, the status of a problem may take the following values: *accepted, queued, completed,* and *closed.* Attribute substatus gives finer grain information on the resolution stage reached by a problem, and can be: *assigned, awaiting_assignment, cancelled, in_progress, wait* (i.e. information from third parts is needed to correctly diagnose the issue), *unmatched,* and *closed.* With respect to the formalization of Sect. 3, for any event $e$, *what*$(e)$ takes the form of a pair ⟨status, substatus⟩ (i.e. both case attributes are modified contemporaneously), while *added*$(e)$ (resp., *removed*$(e)$) stores the new (resp., old) values associated with these attributes.

*Log Manipulation Steps and Enhanced Log Views.* A sample of 1487 issue records (from January 2006 to May 2012) was turned into a set of traces, with lengths ranging from 3 to 37, and fix times ranging from 1 to 2255 days (179 days in the average).

By applying only a subset of our log manipulation operators, we generated two (slightly) refined views of the original log, named $L_0'$ and $L_1'$, as follows:

- View $L_0'$ was obtained by only applying, to the selected problem traces, a basic event abstraction function, just amounting to extracting a combination of the values assigned to attributes status and substatus;
- View $L_1'$ was produced by equipping each trace with several attributes derived from its starting time: the global workload indicator (i.e. the number of problems open at that time), and the starting week-day, month and year. Each trace was also enriched with an attribute firstOrg, indicating which organization line was initially chosen to work on it. Neither filtering nor macro-events restructuring was employed to generate this view.

*Prediction Results.* Table 3 shows the normalized *rmse* and *mae* errors obtained, with different regression methods, on the two log views described above, still considering two learning settings: with and without information on the past history of a case.

Similarly to the bug tracking scenario, a neat decrease in both error measures is achieved when working with the more refined log view $L'_1$ (w.r.t. $L'_0$), even though this latter was obtained by just using very simple log manipulation operators. Moreover, the performances of baseline predictors seem to get improved when exploiting information on past case history ("history-aware" setting) and/or some kind of predictive clustering method (compare `AATP-RepTree` and `AATP-IBK` to `RepTree` and `IBK`, respectively).

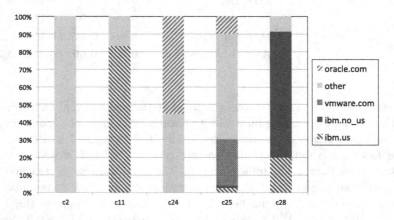

**Fig. 4.** Aggregated statistics for some trace clusters found (with `AATP-IBK`) on the Eclipse log.

**Table 4.** Clusters found on the bug scenario (left) and the problem management scenario (right).

| id | condition |
|---|---|
| $c_2$ | Reporter_avgFT > 137.4 days ∧ workload > 600 ∧ Component ∈ {*Data, LuaTools, Graphiti, MQTT, documentation, Editor, General, Define, Photran, Scout, Report, runtime, RDT, Website*} |
| $c_{11}$ | 54.46 days < Reporter_avgFT ≤ 117.9 days ∧ Component ∈ {*IDE, Deployment, EDT, spdy, JavaGen, documentation, runtime*} |
| $c_{25}$ | 16.57 days< Reporter_measure ≤ 54.47 days ∧ Component ∈ {*Search, Extra, Model, …*} ∧ Product ∈ {*Data, JDT, EclipseLink, STEM, Jubula, Platform, Linux, Orbit, WTP, OSEE, MDT, PTP, Virgo, JSDT, Orion*} |

| id | condition |
|---|---|
| $c_1$ | product ∈ {*PROD659, PROD476, PROD289, …*} ∧ year > 2011 ∧ workload > 437 |
| $c_6$ | product ∈ {*PROD378, PROD660, PROD473, …*} ∧ year > 2011 |
| $c_8$ | product ∈ {*PROD276, PROD277, PROD372, …*} ∧ firstOrg ∈ {*Line C, Line B, Line V2, Line G4*} ∧ year > 2011 ∧ workload > 219 |
| $c_{12}$ | product ∈ {*PROD659, PROD793, PROD597, PROD96, PROD671, PROD231, PROD637, PROD209, PROD13, PROD812, PROD813, PROD153*} ∧ 2010 < year ≤ 2011 ∧ workload > 587 |
| $c_{28}$ | year ≤ 2010 ∧ workload ≤ 11 |

## 8.3 Qualitative Results: Discovered Clusters and Aggregate Statistics

Table 4 shows the classification rules associated with some of the (about 30) clusters discovered, on each of the application scenarios, when using our approach with AATP-IBK as base regressor. Beside supporting accurate cluster-based predictions, these rules offer a readable and interesting description of different context-dependent execution variants discovered for both issue resolution processes. In particular, in the case of Ecplise's bugs, most of the discovered variants mainly depend on the reporter-based average fix time, on the component/product affected, and on the workload indicator. Conversely, the variants discovered for the problem management scenario are mainly linked to the product, the workload and the year when the problem was reported.

Figure 4 shows a chart for the distribution of certain reporters' groups (computed over attribute `reported` with one of ours attribute summarization procedures) in some of the clusters discovered (namely, $c_2$, $c_{11}$, $c_{24}$, $c_{25}$, $c_{28}$).

## 9 Conclusions

We proposed a framework and an associated system for predicting issue/bug resolution times, which fully exploit case attributes' change logs. A rich collection of flexible data-transformation methods allows the analyst to produce high-quality process-oriented logs, and eventually reuse regression/classification to discover a state-based prediction model. Encouraging results obtained on real logs empirically proved the validity of our approach, and the interestingness of discovered models.

As to future work, we plan to extend our approach as to deal with a wider variety of target measures, ranging from Quality of Services measures to process-centric Key Performance Indicators. We will also investigate the application of our methods to the logs of other kinds of data-centric and lowly-structured collaboration environments.

## References

1. Anbalagan, P., Vouk, M.: On predicting the time taken to correct bug reports in open source projects. In Proceedings of International Conference on Software Maintenance (ICSM 2009), pp. 523–526 (2009)
2. Bhattacharya, P., Neamtiu, I.: Bug-fix time prediction models: can we do better? In: Proceedings of 8th International Conference on Mining Software Repositories (MSR 2011), pp. 207–210 (2011)
3. Breiman, L.: Random forests. Mach. Learn. 45(1), 5–32 (2001)
4. Folino, F., Guarascio, M., Pontieri, L.: Discovering context-aware models for predicting business process performances. In: Proceedings of 20th Intlernational Conference on Cooperative Information Systems (CoopIS 2012), pp. 287–304 (2012)

5. Folino, F., Guarascio, M., Pontieri, L.: A data-adaptive trace abstraction approach to the prediction of business process performances. In: Proceedings of 15th International Conference on Enterprise Information Systems (ICEIS 2013), pp. 56–65 (2013)
6. Folino, F., Guarascio, M., Pontieri, L.: Discovering high-level performance models for ticket resolution processes. In: Proceedings of 21st International Conference on Cooperative Information Systems (CoopIS 2013), pp. 275–282 (2013)
7. Giger, E., Pinzger, M., Gall, H.: Predicting the fix time of bugs. In: Proceedings of 2nd International Workshop on Recommendation Systems for Software Engineering (RSSE 2010), pp. 52–56 (2010)
8. Hooimeijer, P., Weimer, W.: Modeling bug report quality. In: Proceedings of 22nd IEEE/ACM International Conference on Automated Software Engineering (ASE 2007), pp. 34–43 (2007)
9. Marks, L., Zou, Y., Hassan, A.E.: Studying the fix-time for bugs in large open source projects. In: Proceedings of 7th Intlernational Conference on Predictive Models in Software Engineering (Promise 2011), pp. 11:1–11:8 (2011)
10. Panjer, L.: Predicting eclipse bug lifetimes. In: Proceedings of 4th International Workshop on Mining Software Repositories (MSR 2007), p. 29 (2007)
11. Steeman, W.B.P.I.: Challenge : closed problems. Ghent University (2013). doi:10.4121/uuid:c2c3b154-ab26-4b31-a0e8-8f2350ddac11
12. Tan, P.-N., Steinbach, M., Kumar, V.: Introduction to Data Mining. Addison-Wesley Longman, Boston (2005)
13. van der Aalst, W.M.P., Schonenberg, M.H., Song, M.: Time prediction based on process mining. Inf. Syst. **36**(2), 450–475 (2011)

# Artificial Intelligence and Decision Support Systems

# Solving the Unrelated Parallel Machine Scheduling Problem with Setup Times by Efficient Algorithms Based on Iterated Local Search

Matheus N. Haddad[1][(✉)], Luciano P. Cota[1],
Marcone J.F. Souza[1], and Nelson Maculan[2]

[1] Departamento de Computação, Universidade Federal de Ouro Preto,
Ouro Preto, MG 35.400-000, Brazil
{mathaddad,lucianoufop}@gmail.com, marcone@iceb.ufop.br
[2] Programa de Engenharia de Sistemas e Computação,
Universidade Federal Do Rio de Janeiro, Rio de Janeiro, RJ 21941-972, Brazil
maculan@cos.ufrj.br

**Abstract.** The *Unrelated Parallel Machine Scheduling Problem with Setup Times* (UMPSPST) is a problem that belongs to the $\mathcal{NP}$-Hard class and it is frequently found in many practical situations, like in textile and chemical industries. The objective in UMPSPST is to schedule jobs in machines in order to achieve the maximum completion time, known as *makespan*. In an attempt to solve this problem, it is proposed two algorithms: the AIV and the HIVP. Both algorithms are based on *Iterated Local Search* (ILS) and *Variable Neighborhood Descent* (VND). The difference between AIV and HIVP is that the first one generates a greedy initial solution, while the second applies a partially greedy procedure to construct the initial solution and it includes the *Path Relinking* (PR) technique. Neighborhoods based on swaps and multiple insertions are investigated in the developed algorithms. AIV and HIVP were tested on benchmark test problems from literature and statistical analysis of the computational results showed the superiority of them, outperforming the previously best known solutions for UMPSPST.

**Keywords:** Unrelated parallel machine scheduling · Iterated local search · Random Variable Neighborhood Descent · Makespan

## 1 Introduction

This paper deals with the *Unrelated Parallel Machine Scheduling Problem with Setup Times* (UMPSPST), which can be formally defined as follows. Let $N = \{1, ..., n\}$ be a set of jobs and let $M = \{1, ..., m\}$ be a set of unrelated machines. The UMPSPST consists of scheduling $n$ jobs on $m$ machines, satisfying the following characteristics: (i) Each job $j \in N$ must be processed exactly once by only one machine $k \in M$. (ii) Each job $j \in N$ has a processing time $p_{jk}$ which

© Springer International Publishing Switzerland 2015
J. Cordeiro et al. (Eds.): ICEIS 2014, LNBIP 227, pp. 131–148, 2015.
DOI: 10.1007/978-3-319-22348-3_8

depends on the machine $k \in M$ where it will be allocated. (iii) There are setup times $S_{ijk}$, between jobs, where $k$ represents the machine on which jobs $i$ and $j$ are processed, in this order. (iv) There is a setup time to process the first job, represented by $S_{0jk}$. The objective is to minimize the maximum completion time of the schedule, the so-called *makespan* or also denoted by $C_{\max}$. Because of such characteristics, UPMSPST is defined as $R_M \mid S_{ijk} \mid C_{\max}$ [1]. In this representation, $R_M$ represents the unrelated machines, $S_{ijk}$ the setup times and $C_{\max}$ the *makespan*.

Figure 1 illustrates a schedule for a test problem composed by two machines and seven jobs. In Table 1 are presented the processing times of these jobs in both machines. The setup times of these jobs in these machines are showed in Table 2.

**Table 1.** Processing times in machines M1 and M2.

|   | M1 | M2 |
|---|----|----|
| 1 | 20 | 4  |
| 2 | 25 | 21 |
| 3 | 28 | 14 |
| 4 | 17 | 32 |
| 5 | 43 | 38 |
| 6 | 9  | 23 |
| 7 | 58 | 52 |

**Table 2.** Setup times in machines M1 and M2.

| M1 | 1 | 2 | 3 | 4 | 5 | 6 | 7 | M2 | 1 | 2 | 3 | 4 | 5 | 6 | 7 |
|----|---|---|---|---|---|---|---|----|---|---|---|---|----|----|---|
| 1 | 0 | 1 | 8 | 1 | 3 | 9 | 6 | 1 | 0 | 4 | 6 | 5 | 10 | 3 | 2 |
| 2 | 4 | 0 | 7 | 3 | 7 | 8 | 4 | 2 | 1 | 0 | 6 | 2 | 7 | 7 | 5 |
| 3 | 7 | 3 | 0 | 2 | 3 | 5 | 3 | 3 | 2 | 6 | 0 | 6 | 8 | 1 | 4 |
| 4 | 3 | 8 | 3 | 0 | 5 | 2 | 2 | 4 | 5 | 7 | 1 | 0 | 12 | 10 | 6 |
| 5 | 8 | 3 | 7 | 9 | 0 | 5 | 7 | 5 | 7 | 9 | 5 | 7 | 0 | 4 | 8 |
| 6 | 8 | 8 | 1 | 2 | 2 | 0 | 9 | 6 | 9 | 3 | 5 | 4 | 9 | 0 | 3 |
| 7 | 1 | 4 | 5 | 2 | 3 | 5 | 0 | 7 | 3 | 2 | 6 | 1 | 5 | 6 | 0 |

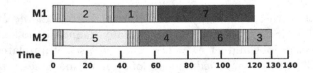

**Fig. 1.** An example of a possible schedule.

It can be observed that in machine M1 the jobs 2, 1 and 7 are allocated in this order. In machine M2 the schedule of the jobs 5, 4, 6 and 3, in this order, is also perceived by this figure. The cross-hatched areas of the figure represent the setup times between jobs and the numbered areas the processing times. On the line below the schedule there is the timeline, in which the times 120 and 130 represent the completion times of each machine.

As the job 6 is allocated to machine M2 its processing time $p_{62}$ will be 23. Its predecessor and its successor are the jobs 4 and 3, respectively. So, in this example, are computed the times $S_{462} = 5$ and $S_{632} = 5$. Thus, it can be calculated the completion time of machine M1 as $S_{021} + p_{21} + S_{211} + p_{11} + S_{171} + p_{71} = 120$. Equivalently it is also calculated the completion time of machine M2 as $S_{052} + p_{52} + S_{542} + p_{42} + S_{462} + p_{62} + S_{632} + p_{32} = 130$. After the calculation of the completion times of machines M1 and M2, it can be concluded that the machine M2 is the bottleneck machine. In other words, M2 is the machine that has the highest completion time, the *makespan*.

The UPMSPST appears in many practical situations, like in textile and chemical industries [2]. On the other hand, the UPMSPST is in $\mathcal{NP}$-Hard class, as it is a generalization of the *Parallel Machine Scheduling Problem with Identical Machines and without Setup Times* [3,4]. The theoretical and practical importance instigate the study of the UPMSPST. Under these circumstances, finding the optimal solution for UPMSPST using exact methods can be computationally infeasible for large-sized problems. Thus, metaheuristics and local search heuristics are usually developed to find good near optimal solutions.

In order to find these near optimal solutions for the UPMSPST, this paper proposes two algorithms based on *Iterated Local Search* – ILS [5] and *Variable Neighborhood Descent* – VND [6]. The first algorithm is called AIV, it starts from an initial solution constructed on a greedy way by the *Adaptive Shortest Processing Time* – ASPT rule. Then, this initial solution is refined by ILS, using as local search the Random VND procedure. In this procedure, here called RVND, there is no fixed sequence of neighborhoods, because they are sorted on each application of the local search. In [7] the authors showed the effectiveness of RVND over the conventional VND. The second algorithm named HIVP is an endeavour to upgrade AIV, constructing the solution by a partially greedy procedure and including the *Path Relinking* – PR technique.

Both algorithms were tested using benchmark instances from [8] and the computational results showed that they are able to produce better solutions than the ones found in literature, with lower variability and setting new upper bounds for the majority of instances.

The rest of this paper is structured as follows. Firstly, works that inspired the development of this paper are described. Then, the methodology used for the deployment of this paper is presented. The computational results are shown on sequence. Finally, this paper is concluded and possible proposals to be explored are described.

## 2    Literature Review

In literature are found several works that seek to address the UPMSPST and similar problems. These approaches were inspirations for the development of this paper.

In [9] propose the development of seven heuristics with the objective of minimizing the weighted mean completion time. In [10], a problem with common due dates is addressed and four heuristics are implemented for minimizing the total weighted tardiness. In [11] aim to minimize the total weighted tardiness, considering dynamic releases of jobs and dynamic availability of machines and they used four dispatching rules in order to generate initial solutions and a *Tabu Search* as the basis for the development of six search algorithms. This problem is also addressed in [2], where a *Branch-and-Price* algorithm is developed.

More recent references are found when dealing with the UPMSPST. In [12] created a *Three-phase Partitioning Heuristic*, called PH. In [13] it is proposed a *Metaheuristic for Randomized Priority Search* (Meta-RaPS). In [14] bet in Tabu Search for solving the UPMSPST. In [15] implement the *Ant Colony Optimization* (ACO), considering its application to problems wherein the ratio of jobs to machines is large. In [16] it is implemented a *Restricted Simulated Annealing* (RSA), which aims to reduce the computational effort by only performing movements that the algorithm consider effective. In [17] is defined and proved a set of proprieties for the UPMSPST and also implemented an *Genetic Algorithm* and a *Simulated Annealing* using these proprieties. A hybridization that joins the *Multistart* algorithm, the VND and a mathematical programming model is made in [18]. In [19] solve the UPMSPST using *Genetic Algorithms*, with two sets of parameters, yielding two algorithms, GA1 and GA2. In [19], the authors created and provided test problems for the UPMSPST [8]. Also in [8] are presented the best known solutions to the UPMSPST so far.

## 3    Methodology

### 3.1    Representation and Evaluation of a Solution

To represent a solution $s$ it is used a vector $v$ of $m$ positions, with each position representing a machine. In addition, each machine is associated with a list of jobs allocated to it. The order of the jobs in this list represents the sequence of execution.

The evaluation of a solution $s$ is done by calculating the processing time of the machine that will be the last to conclude the execution of its jobs. In other words, the evaluation value is the *makespan*.

### 3.2    Proposed Algorithms

In this section two algorithms, AIV and HIVP, are proposed for solving UPM-SPST. The details of operation of these algorithms are described below.

**The AIV Algorithm.** The first proposed algorithm, named AIV, combines the heuristic procedures *Iterated Local Search* (ILS) and *Random Variable Neighborhood Descent* (RVND). The main structure of AIV is based on ILS, using the RVND procedure to perform the local searches.

The pseudo-code of AIV is presented in Algorithm 1.

The Algorithm 1 has only two input parameters: (1) *timesLevel*, which represents the number of times in each level of perturbation; (2) *executionTime*, the time in milliseconds that limits the execution of the algorithm.

First of all, AIV begins initializing the variable that controls the time limit, *currentTime* (line 1). Next, it initializes three empty solutions: the current solution $s$, the modified solution $s'$ and the solution that will store the best solution found *bestSol* (line 2).

In line 3 a new solution is created based on the *Adaptive Shortest Processing Time* (ASPT) rule (see Subsect. 3.3). Then, this new solution passes through local searches at line 4, using the RVND module (see Subsect. 3.6).

---

**Algorithm 1:** AIV.

---

    **input** : *timesLevel, executionTime*
1  *currentTime* ← 0;
2  Solution s, s', bestSol;
3  s ← ASPT () ;                                        /* see subsection 3.3 */
4  s ← RVND (s) ;                                  /* see subsection 3.6 */
5  bestSol ← s;
6  level ← 1;
7  Update *currentTime*;
8  **while** *currentTime* < *executionTime* **do**
9      s' ← s;
10     times ← 0;
11     maxPerturb ← level + 1;
12     **while** times < timesLevel  **do**
13         perturb ← 0;
14         s' ← s;
15         **while** perturb < maxPerturb **do**
16            perturb ++;
17            s' ← perturbation (s') ;           /* see subsection 3.8 */
18         **end**
19         s' ← RVND (s') ;                  /* see subsection 3.6 */
20         **if** $f$(s') < $f$(s) **then**
21            s ← s';
22            updateBest (s, bestSol) ;
23            times ← 0;
24         **end**
25         times ++;
26         Update *currentTime*;
27     **end**
28     level ++;
29     **if** level ≥ *4* **then**
30         level ← 1;
31     **end**
32  **end**
33  **return** bestSol;

---

---

**Algorithm 2: HIVP.**

```
Input    : timesLevel, executionTime
Output   : bestSol
1  currentTime ← 0;
2  Solution s, s', bestSol;
3  elite ← {};
4  s ← CPG_HBSS () ;                                  /* see subsection 3.4 */
5  s ← RVND(s) ;                                       /* see subsection 3.6 */
6  bestSol ← s;
7  elite ← elite ∪ {bestSol};
8  level ← 1;
9  Update currentTime;
10 while currentTime ≤ executionTime do
11 │   s' ← s;
12 │   times ← 0;
13 │   maxPerturb ← level + 1;
14 │   while times < timesLevel do
15 │   │   perturb ← 0;
16 │   │   s' ← s;
17 │   │   while perturb < maxPerturb do
18 │   │   │   perturb ++;
19 │   │   │   s' ← perturbation (s') ;               /* see subsection 3.8 */
20 │   │   end
21 │   │   s' ← RVND(s') ;                            /* see subsection 3.6 */
22 │   │   elite ← update (s');
23 │   │   pr ← random (0,1) ;
24 │   │   if pr ≤ 0.05 e |elite| ≥ 5 then
25 │   │   │   el ← random (1,5) ;
26 │   │   │   s' ← PR (elite [el], s') ;             /* see subsection 3.7 */
27 │   │   end
28 │   │   if f(s') < f(s) then
29 │   │   │   s ← s';
30 │   │   │   times ← 0;
31 │   │   │   updateBest (s, bestSol) ;
32 │   │   │   elite ← update (s) ;
33 │   │   end
34 │   │   times ++;
35 │   │   Update currentTime;
36 │   end
37 │   level ++;
38 │   if level ≥ 4 then
39 │   │   level ← 1;
40 │   end
41 end
42 return bestSol ;
```

In the next step, the current best known solution, $bestSol$, is updated (line 5) and the level of perturbations is set to 1 (line 6).

After all these steps, the execution time is recalculated in line 7.

The iterative process of ILS is situated in lines 8 to 32 and it finishes when the time limit is exceeded. A copy of the current solution to the modified solution is made in line 9.

In lines 10 and 11 the variable that controls the number of times in each level of perturbation ($times$) is initialized, as well as the variable that limits the maximum number of perturbations ($maxPerturb$). The following loop is responsible to control the number of times in each level of perturbation (lines 12–27).

The next loop, lines 15 to 18, executes the perturbations (line 17) in the modified solution (see Subsect. 3.8). The number of times this loop is executed depends on the level of perturbation. With the perturbations accomplished, the new solution obtained is evaluated and the RVND procedure is applied in this new solution until a local optimum is reached, in relation to all neighborhoods adopted in RVND.

In lines (20–24) it is verified if the changes made in the current solution were good enough to continue the search from it. When the time is up, in *bestSol* will be stored the best solution found by AIV.

Each module of AIV will be detailed afterwards.

**The HIVP Algorithm.** The second proposed algorithm, HIVP, is an attempt to improve the AIV algorithm, differing only by two procedures: the construction of the initial solution and the incorporation of an intensification/diversification technique, the Path Relinking – PR [20]. The Algorithm 2 presents the pseudo-code of HIVP.

Since HIVP is an upgrade of AIV, only the different lines will be described next. The elite set is initialized at line 3. At line 4 the solution $s$ receives a solution generated by the partially greedy procedure $CPG_{HBSS}$ (see Subsect. 3.4). Following, $s$ passes through local searches using the RVND procedure (see Subsect. 3.6) and *bestSol* receives the resulting solution from RVND. This solution is inserted in the elite set (line 7). In the iterative loop of HIVP, after the application of the RVND in the modified solution (line 21) the elite set is updated and a random real number between 0 and 1 is generated (lines 22 and 23). If this number is less than or equal to 0.05 and the elite set is full (with 5 solutions) it is performed an intensification/diversification of the search using the PR technique - lines 23 to 27 (see Subsect. 3.7). The modified solution and a random solution from the elite set are the input parameters of PR. If the modified solution is considered an improvement (line 28), then the elite set is updated at line 32.

### 3.3 ASPT: The Adaptive Shortest Processing Time Rule

The *Adaptive Shortest Processing Time* (ASPT) rule is an extension of the *Shortest Processing Time* rule [21].

In ASPT, firstly, it is created a set $N = \{1, ..., n\}$ containing all jobs and a set $M = \{1, ..., m\}$ that contains all machines.

From the set $N$, the jobs are classified according to an evaluation function $g_k$. This function is responsible to obtain the completion time of the machine $k$. Given a *Candidate List* (CL) of jobs, it is evaluated, based on the $g_k$ function, the insertion of each of these jobs in all positions of all machines. The aim is to obtain in which position of what machine that the candidate job will produce the lowest completion time, that is, the $g_{min}$.

If the machine with the lowest completion time has not allocated any job yet, its new completion time will be the sum of the processing time of the job to be inserted with the initial setup time for such job.

If this machine has some job, its new completion time will be the previous completion time plus the processing time of the job to be inserted and the setup times involved, if it has sequenced jobs before or after.

This allocation process ends when all jobs are assigned to some machine, thus producing a feasible solution, $s$. This solution is returned by the heuristic. The algorithm is said to be adaptive because the choice of a job to be inserted depends on the preexisting allocation.

### 3.4    $CPG_{HBSS}$: The Partially Greedy Procedure

The $CPG_{HBSS}$ procedure is a partially greedy constructive method which also uses the evaluation function $g_k$ to classify the jobs. The same Candidate List (CL) created in ASPT is generated here. Notwithstanding, instead of deterministically choosing the job that produces the $g_{min}$, the $CPG_{HBSS}$ procedure chooses a candidate in the CL based on the *Heuristic-Biased Stochastic Sampling* (HBSS) [22]. The jobs in the CL are chosen according to a probability arising from a *bias* function.

In Table 3 are presented the following *bias* functions: Random, Logarithmic, Polynomial of degree 2, Polynomial of degree 3, Polynomial of degree 4 and Exponential. The first column shows the index of the candidates. In each cell of the table there is the probability of the candidate $i$ be chosen using the respective *bias* function. For example, if the *bias* function selected is the Exponential, the fifth element of the CL will have 1.2 % chance of being chosen.

The *bias* function chosen in this work was the Exponential, this choice was made based on empirical tests. With the *bias* function selected, it can be explained how the $CPG_{HBSS}$ procedure constructs a solution.

Initially, as in ASPT, all the jobs and machines are stored in the sets $N$ and $M$, respectively. Then, all jobs are inserted in the CL.

While there are jobs in the CL: firstly, jobs are classified according to the $g_k$ function (see Subsect. 3.3), analyzing their inclusion at the last position of a machine and creating a list named *Rank*. *Rank* is composed by combinations of $(j, k)$, with $j \in LC$ and $k \in M$, ordered according to the value calculated by the $g_k$ function.

A probability according to the Exponential *bias* function values, as presented in Table 3, is associated to each pair in *Rank*. Secondly, the Wheel Selection method is performed, in order to select which job will be inserted in the partial

Table 3. Table containing *bias* functions. Source: [22].

|      | $Rand$ | $Log$ | $Linear$ | $Poly^2$ | $Poly^3$ | $Poly^4$ | Exp   |
|------|--------|-------|----------|----------|----------|----------|-------|
| 1    | 0.033  | 0.109 | 0.250    | 0.620    | 0.832    | 0.924    | 0.632 |
| 2    | 0.033  | 0.069 | 0.125    | 0.155    | 0.104    | 0.058    | 0.233 |
| 3    | 0.033  | 0.055 | 0.083    | 0.069    | 0.031    | 0.011    | 0.086 |
| 4    | 0.033  | 0.047 | 0.063    | 0.039    | 0.013    | 0.004    | 0.031 |
| 5    | 0.033  | 0.042 | 0.050    | 0.025    | 0.007    | 0.001    | 0.012 |
| 6-30 | 0.033  | 0.678 | 0.429    | 0.092    | 0.013    | 0.002    | 0.006 |

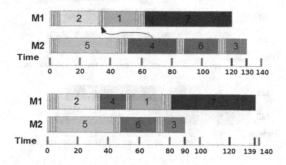

**Fig. 2.** Example of a multiple insertion movement.

solution. Then, the selected job is removed from $LC$ and all pairs containing this job are removed from $Rank$. This loop is executed until all jobs are inserted in the solution, generating a feasible solution.

### 3.5 Neighborhood Structures

Three neighborhood structures are used to explore the solution space. These structures are based on swap and multiple insertion movements of the jobs.

**Multiple Insertion.** The Multiple Insertion (MI) movement consists in reallocating a job from a position and inserting it on any position of the entire schedule, including the machine that it was previously allocated. The MI movement belongs to the $N^{MI}(.)$ neighborhood. To exemplify this movement, Fig. 2 illustrates the transfer of the job 4 from the second position of machine $M2$ to the second position of machine $M1$.

**Swap in the Same Machine.** The Swap in the Same Machine (SSM) movement, as the name suggests, is done by swapping the positions of two jobs presented in the same machine. The SSM movement belongs to the $N^{SSM}(.)$ neighborhood. Figure 3 shows the swap of jobs 5 and 6 in machine $M2$.

**Swap Between Different Machines.** The Swap Between Different Machines (SDM), which belongs to the $N^{SDM}(.)$ neighborhood, consists in swapping two jobs that are allocated in different machines. This movement can be better exemplified by Fig. 4, where the swap of the jobs 7 ($M1$) and 5 ($M2$) is perceived.

### 3.6 RVND: The Random Variable Neighborhood Descent Procedure

The *Random Variable Neighborhood Descent* – RVND procedure [7,23] is a variant of the VND procedure [6].

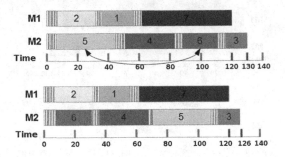

**Fig. 3.** Example of a swap in the same machine movement.

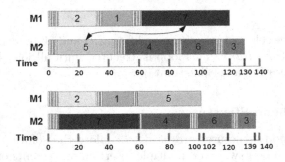

**Fig. 4.** Example of a swap between different machines movement.

Each neighborhood of the set $\{N^{MI}, N^{SSM}, N^{SDM}\}$ described in Sect. 3.5 defines one local search. Unlike VND, the RVND explores the solution space using these three neighborhoods in a random order each time the procedure is triggered. The RVND is finished when it is found on a local optimum with relation to the three considered neighborhoods.

Following are described the local searches procedures used in RVND.

$FI^1_{MI}$: **Local Search with Multiple Insertion.** The first local search uses multiple insertions movements ($N^{MI}(.)$ neighborhood) with the *First Improvement* strategy. In this search, each job of each machine is inserted in all positions of all machines.

The selection of the jobs to be removed respects the allocation order in the machines. That is, initially, the first job is selected to be removed, then the second job until all jobs from a machine are chosen. The machines that will have their jobs removed are selected based on their completion times. The search starts with machines with higher completion times to machines with lower completion times.

By contrast, the insertions are made from machines with lower completion times to machines with higher completion times. The jobs are inserted starting from the first position and stopping at the last position.

The movement is accepted if the completion times of the machines involved are reduced. If the completion time of a machine is reduced and the completion time of another machine is added, the movement is also accepted. However, in this case, it is only accepted if the value of reduced time is greater than the value of time increased.

It is noteworthy that even in the absence of improvement in the value of *makespan*, the movement can be accepted. Upon such acceptance of a movement, the search is restarted and only ends when it is found a local optimum, that is, when there is no movement that can be accepted in the neighborhood of multiple insertion.

$FI_{SMD}$: **Local Search with Swaps Between Different Machines.** The second local search makes swap movements between different machines, exploring the $N^{SMD}(.)$ neighborhood. For each pair of existing machines every possible swap of jobs between them are analyzed.

Exchanges are made from machines that have higher completion times to machines with lower completion times. The acceptance criteria are the same as those applied in the first local search. If there are reductions in completion times on two machines involved, then the movement is accepted. If the reduced value of the completion time of a machine is larger than the completion time plus another machine, the movement is also accepted. Once a movement is accepted, the search stops.

$BI_{SSM}$: **Local Search with Swaps on the Same Machine.** The third local search examines the $N^{SSM}(.)$ neighborhood and uses the strategy *Best Improvement*.

The machines are ordered from the machine that has the highest value of completion time to the machine that has the lowest value of completion time.

For each machine, starting from the first, all possible swaps involving pairs of jobs are investigated. The best movement is accepted if the completion time of the machine is reduced and, in this case, the local search is repeated from this solution; otherwise, the next machine is analyzed.

This local search only ends when no improvements is found in 30 % of the machines.

## 3.7   Path Relinking

The Path Relinking – PR [20] technique makes a balance between intensification and diversification of the search. Its objective is to explore existing paths between high quality solutions. These high quality solutions are stored in an elite set.

In order to a solution $s'$ enter in this elite set, one of the following conditions must be satisfied: (i) be better than the best solution of the elite set, in terms of the *makespan* value; (ii) be better (lower *makespan*) than the worst solution of the elite set and differentiate itself from all solutions of the elite set at least by 10 %. The diversity criterion, when comparing two solutions, is the percentage of jobs allocated in different positions.

The *Backward Path Relinking* (BkPR) strategy is used. According [20] BkPR usually outperforms forward path relinking. Thus, a path is constructed from a base solution to a guide solution, being the best solution as the base solution and the worst solution as the guide solution. In this work, this strategy is applied over the following solutions: (1) a solution chosen randomly in the elite set; (2) the solution returned by the RVND local searches.

The attribute chosen for building the path is the position of a job. Initially, the jobs positions of the guide solution are inserted in a list named $\Phi$. In each iteration is analyzed the insertion, in the base solution, of an attribute that belongs to the guide solution. Following, the other copy of this job is removed from the base solution. Moreover, if the machine that receives this job has another different job at the same position, then this job is relocated to another position that has not set its attribute from the guide solution yet.

With all attributes from guide solution analyzed, it is included to base solution the attribute which produces the lower cost. This cost is given by the sum of all completion times of all machines in base solution. After the insertion of an attribute, to this new base solution is applied the $FI^2_{MI}$ local search, defined next. It is important to highlight that once an attribute is inserted in base solution, this attribute can not be changed.

Following, the selected attribute is removed from $\Phi$. These steps are repeated until $\Phi$ is empty. At the end of the algorithm the base solution will have the same scheduling as the guide solution and the best solution found during this procedure is returned.

$FI^2_{MI}$: **Local Search with Multiple Insertion.** As the local search $FI^1_{MI}$, the local search $FI^2_{MI}$ also explores the $N^{MI}(.)$ neighborhood with the *First Improvement* strategy. But it differs by two characteristics: (i) the only acceptance criterion is the improvement of the *makespan*; (ii) when an improvement occurs, the method is stopped and the new solution is returned.

### 3.8 Perturbations

A perturbation is characterized by applying an insertion movement in a local optimum, but this movement differs when inserting the job in another machine. The job will be inserted into its best position, that is, in the position that will produce the lowest completion time. Doing so, sub parts of the problem are optimized after each perturbation. The machines and the job involved are chosen randomly.

In both AIV and HIVP, the number of perturbations applied to a solution is controlled by the level of perturbation. A level $l$ of perturbation consists in the application of $l + 1$ insertion movements. The maximum level allowed for the perturbations is set to 3.

If *timeslevel* perturbed solutions are generated without an improvement in the current solution the perturbation level is increased. If an improvement of the current solution is found, the level of perturbation is set to its lowest level ($l = 1$).

## 3.9   Efficient Evaluation of the Objective Function

The evaluation of an entire solution after every movement, multiple insertion or swap, demands a large computational effort. Aiming to avoid this situation, it was created a procedure that evaluates only the processing and setup times involved in the movements. In this way, in order to obtain the new completion time of each machine it is necessary few additions and subtractions.

Taking the example of the multiple insertion movement illustrated in Fig. 2, the new completion time of machine M2 is obtained by subtracting from its previous value the processing time of job 4 $p_{42}$ and also subtracting the setup times involved, $S_{542}$ and $S_{462}$. The setup time $S_{562}$ also needs to be added to the completion time of machine M2. In machine M1, the processing time of job 4 $p_{41}$ and the setup times $S_{241}$ and $S_{411}$ are included in the new completion time. Then, the new completion time of machine M1 is $M1 = 120 - 4 + 3 + 17 + 3 = 139$ and the new completion time of machine M2 is $M2 = 130 - 7 - 32 - 5 + 4 = 90$. Although the given example is for the multiple insertion movement, it is trivial to apply the same procedure for a swap movement.

# 4   Computational Results

Using a set of 360 test problems from [8] the computational tests were performed. This set of test problems involves combinations of 50, 100 and 150 jobs with 10, 15 and 20 machines. There are 40 instances for each combination of jobs and machines. The best known solutions for each of these test problems are also provided in [8].

AIV was developed in C++ language and HIVP was developed in Java language. All experiments were executed in a computer with *Intel Core i5 3.0 GHz* processor, 8 GB of RAM memory and in *Ubuntu 12.04* operational system.

The parameters used in both AIV and HIVP are: (i) the number of iterations on each level of perturbation: *timeslevel* = 15; (ii) the stop criterion: $Time_{max}$, which is the maximum time of execution, in milliseconds, obtained by Eq. 1. In this equation, $m$ represents the number of machines, $n$ the number of jobs and $t$ is a parameter that was tested with three values for each instance: 10, 30 and 50. It is observed that the stop criterion, with these values of $t$, was the same adopted in [19].

$$Time_{max} = n \times (m/2) \times t \ \ ms \tag{1}$$

With the objective to verify the variability of final solutions produced by the algorithms it was used the metric given by Eq. 2. This metric is used to compare algorithms. For each algorithm *Alg* applied to a test problem $i$ is calculated the *Relative Percentage Deviation* $RPD_i$ of the solution found $\bar{f}_i^{Alg}$ in relation to the best known solution $f_i^*$.

In this paper, the algorithms AIV and HIVP were executed 30 times, for each instance and for each value of $t$, calculating the *Average Relative Percentage Deviation* $RPD_i^{avg}$ of the $RPD_i$ values found. In [19] the algorithms were executed 5 times for each instance and for each value of $t$.

$$RPD_i = \frac{\bar{f}_i^{Alg} - f_i^*}{f_i^*} \tag{2}$$

**Table 4.** Average Relative Percentage Deviation of the algorithms AIV, HIVP and GA2 with $t = 10/30/50$.

| Set of Instances | AIV[a] | HIVP[a] | GA2[b] |
|---|---|---|---|
| 50 x 10 | 3.69/1.83/1.30 | **2.27/0.25/-0.44** | 7.79/6.92/6.49 |
| 50 x 15 | 1.52/-0.77/-1.33 | **-0.6/-2.78/-3.47** | 12.25/8.92/9.20 |
| 50 x 20 | 5.26/2.01/1.65 | **-2.14/-4.06/-4.68** | 11.08/8.04/9.57 |
| 100 x 10 | 5.06/2.93/2.00 | **4.45/2.04/1.23** | 15.72/6.76/5.54 |
| 100 x 15 | **1.80/-0.40/-1.29** | 2.17/-0.64/-1.78 | 22.15/8.36/7.32 |
| 100 x 20 | **0.52/-1.64/-2.89** | 0.58/-2.44/-3.92 | 22.02/9.79/8.59 |
| 150 x 10 | **3.77/1.99/1.07** | 4.21/2.15/**0.98** | 18.40/5.75/5.28 |
| 150 x 15 | **1.83/-0.24/-1.04** | 3.37/0.42/-0.44 | 24.89/8.09/6.80 |
| 150 x 20 | **-1.04/-3.10/-4.00** | 1.22/-2.19/-3.39 | 22.63/9.53/7.40 |
| $RPD^{avg}$ | 2.49/0.29/-0.50 | **1.72/-0.8/-1.77** | 17.44/8.02/7.35 |

[a]Executed on Intel Core i5 3.0 GHz, 8 GB of RAM, 30 runs for each instance
[b]Executed on Intel Core 2 Duo 2.4 GHz, 2 GB of RAM, 5 runs for each instance

In Table 4 are presented, for each set of instances, the $RPD_i^{avg}$ values obtained for each value of $t = 10, 30, 50$ by AIV and HIVP, and also it contains the $RPD_i^{avg}$ values obtained by GA2, a genetic algorithm developed in [19]. To our knowledge, the results reported in the literature for this set of test problems are only presented in [19] and the best algorithm tested by the authors was GA2.

There are three values of $RPD_i^{avg}$ separated by a '/' for each set of instances in the table. Each separation represents test results with different values of $t$, 10/30/50. If a negative value is found, it means that the reached result outperformed the best value found in [19] on their experiments.

The best values of $RPD^{avg}$ are highlighted in bold. It is remarkable that HIVP is the algorithm that found the best results. Not only it improved the majority of best known solutions, but also it won in 63 % of the sets of instances. The algorithm AIV found the best results in 37 % of the remainder sets of instances.

A table with all results found by both algorithms and also the previous best known values for the UPMSPST can be found in http://www.decom.ufop.br/prof/marcone/projects/upmsp/Experiments_UPMSPST_AIV_HIVP.ods

The box plot, Fig. 5, contains all $RPD^{avg}$ values for each algorithm. It is notable that 100 % of the $RPD$ values encountered by both AIV and HIVP

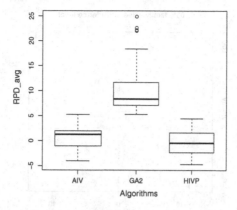

**Fig. 5.** Box plot showing the $RPD^{avg}$ of the algorithms.

**Table 5.** Results from Tukey HSD test.

| Algorithms | diff | lwr | upr | p |
|---|---|---|---|---|
| GA2-AIV | 10.077407 | 7.495481 | 12.659333 | 0.0000000 |
| HIVP-AIV | -1.041481 | -3.623408 | 1.540445 | 0.6018344 |
| HIVP-GA2 | -11.118889 | -13.700815 | -8.536963 | 0.0000000 |

outperformed the ones obtained by GA2 algorithm. By the way, it is observed that 75 % of solutions found by the developed algorithms are near the best known solutions. Besides, more than 50 % of solutions found by the HIVP algorithm are better than the best known so far. With AIV this percentage drops to 25 %.

The results were submitted to the Shapiro-Wilk test [24] to verify if the sample satisfies the normality test, so that it can be decided which test to use for analyzing statistical differences between all algorithms. The Shapiro-Wilk returned, with significance level of 5 %, $W = 0.9261$ and $p = 0.2692$. As $p = 0.2692 > 0.05$ then it can be concluded with 95 % of confidence level that the sample are taken from a normal distribution.

Thus, in order to verify if exist statistical differences between the $RPD$ values, it was applied an analysis of variance (ANOVA) [25]. This analysis returned, with 95 % of confidence level and $threshold = 0.05$, that $p = 2 \times 10^{-16}$. As $p < threshold$, it is possible to ensure that exist statistical differences between the $RPD$ values.

A Tukey HSD test, with 95 % of confidence level and $threshold = 0.05$, was used for checking where are these differences. Table 5 contains the differences in the average values of $RPD$ (diff), the lower end point (lwr), the upper end point (upr) and the $p$-value ($p$) for each pair of algorithms.

The $p$-value shows that when comparing AIV to GA2 there is a statistical difference between them, because it was less than the $threshold$. The same conclusion can be achieved when comparing HIVP to GA2. However, when AIV is

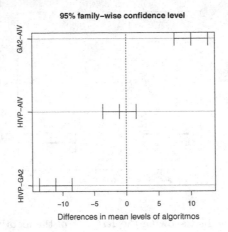

**Fig. 6.** Graphical results from Tukey HSD test.

compared to HIVP they are not statistically different from each other, since the *p-value* was greater than the *threshold*.

By plotting the results from the Tukey HSD test (Fig. 6) it is more noticeable that HIVP and AIV are statistically different from GA2, as their graphs do not pass through zero. Comparing algorithms HIVP and AIV it can be perceived that they are not statistically different from each other, because the graph passes through zero. Thus, with a statistical basis it can be concluded, within the considered instances, that AIV and HIVP are the best algorithms on obtaining solutions for UPMSPST.

## 5   Conclusions

This paper studied the *Unrelated Parallel Machine Scheduling Problem with Setup Times* (UPMSPST), aiming to the minimization of the maximum completion time of the schedule, the *makespan*.

In order to solve the UPMSPST it was proposed two algorithms based on *Iterated Local Search* (ILS) and *Variable Neighborhood Descent* (VND). The first algorithm was named AIV and it implements the *Adaptive Shortest Processing Time* (ASPT) rule to create an initial solution. The *Random Variable Neighborhood Descent* (RVND) procedure was used to perform the local searches, randomly exploring the solution space with insertions and swap movements. A perturbation in AIV is an application of an insertion movement. The second algorithm, called HIVP, is an attempt to upgrade AIV, constructing the solution using a partially greedy procedure and incorporating the *Path Relinking* (PR) technique in order to intensify and diversify the search.

The two developed algorithms were applied to instances taken from literature and the results were compared the genetic algorithm GA2, developed in [19]. Statistical analysis of the computational results showed that AIV and HIVP are able to produce 100 % of better solutions than GA2. HIVP and AIV were also able to generate new upper bounds for these test problems. Although HIVP seems to be better than AIV, statistically this was not proved. Nevertheless, it can be concluded that both AIV and HIVP are two efficient algorithms when dealing with the UPMSPST.

For future works it is proposed the application of both algorithms on the entire set of test problems available in [8]. An improvement that will be studied is an incorporation of a Mixed Integer Programming (MIP) model to AIV or HIVP for solving related sub problems.

**Acknowledgements.** The authors thank the Brazilian agencies FAPEMIG and CNPq, and the Universidade Federal de Ouro Preto (UFOP) for the financial support on the development of this work.

# References

1. Graham, R., Lawler, E., Lenstra, J., Kan, A.: Optimization and approximation in deterministic sequencing and scheduling: a survey. Ann. Discret. Math. **5**, 287–326 (1979)
2. Lopes, M.J.P., de Carvalho, J.M.: A branch-and-price algorithm for scheduling parallel machines with sequence dependent setup times. Eur. J. Oper. Res. **176**, 1508–1527 (2007)
3. Karp, R.M.: Reducibility among combinatorial problems. Complex. Comput. Comput. **40**, 85–103 (1972)
4. Garey, M., Johnson, D.: Computers and Intractability: A Guide to the Theory of Np-Completeness., vol. 174. WH Freeman & Co., San Francisco (1979)
5. Lourenço, H.R., Martin, O., Stützle, T.: Iterated local search. In: Glover, F., Kochenberger, G. (eds.) Handbook of Metaheuristics. International Series in Operations Research and Management Science, vol. 57, pp. 321–353. Kluwer Academic Publishers, Norwell (2003)
6. Mladenovic, N., Hansen, P.: Variable neighborhood search. Comput. Oper. Res. **24**, 1097–1100 (1997)
7. Souza, M., Coelho, I., Ribas, S., Santos, H., Merschmann, L.: A hybrid heuristic algorithm for the open-pit-mining operational planning problem. Eur. J. Oper. Res. **207**, 1041–1051 (2010)
8. de Optimización Aplicada, S.: A web site that includes benchmark problem data sets and solutions for scheduling problems (2011). http://soa.iti.es/problem-instances
9. Weng, M.X., Lu, J., Ren, H.: Unrelated parallel machine scheduling with setup consideration and a total weighted completion time objective. Int. J. Prod. Econ. **70**, 215–226 (2001)
10. Kim, D.W., Na, D.G., Chen, F.F.: Unrelated parallel machine scheduling with setup times and a total weighted tardiness objective. Robot. Comput. Integr. Manuf. **19**, 173–181 (2003)
11. Logendran, R., McDonell, B., Smucker, B.: Scheduling unrelated parallel machines with sequence-dependent setups. Comput. Oper. Res. **34**, 3420–3438 (2007)
12. Al-Salem, A.: Scheduling to minimize makespan on unrelated parallel machines with sequence dependent setup times. Eng. J. Univ. Qatar **17**, 177–187 (2004)

13. Rabadi, G., Moraga, R.J., Al-Salem, A.: Heuristics for the unrelated parallel machine scheduling problem with setup times. J. Intell. Manuf. **17**, 85–97 (2006)
14. Helal, M., Rabadi, G., Al-Salem, A.: A tabu search algorithm to minimize the makespan for the unrelated parallel machines scheduling problem with setup times. Int. J. Oper. Res. **3**, 182–192 (2006)
15. Arnaout, J., Rabadi, G., Musa, R.: A two-stage ant colony optimization algorithm to minimize the makespan on unrelated parallel machines with sequence-dependent setup times. J. Intell. Manuf. **21**, 693–701 (2010)
16. Ying, K.C., Lee, Z.J., Lin, S.W.: Makespan minimisation for scheduling unrelated parallel machines with setup times. J. Intell. Manuf. **23**, 1795–1803 (2012)
17. Chang, P., Chen, S.: Integrating dominance properties with genetic algorithms for parallel machine scheduling problems with setup times. Appl. Soft Comput. **11**, 1263–1274 (2011)
18. Fleszar, K., Charalambous, C., Hindi, K.: A variable neighborhood descent heuristic for the problem of makespan minimisation on unrelated parallel machines with setup times. J. Intell. Manuf. **23**, 1949–1958 (2011). doi:10.1007/s10845-011-0522-8
19. Vallada, E., Ruiz, R.: A genetic algorithm for the unrelated parallel machine scheduling problem with sequence dependent setup times. Eur. J. Oper. Res. **211**, 612–622 (2011)
20. Resende, M.G.C., Ribeiro, C.C.: GRASP: greedy randomized adaptive search procedures. In: Burke, E.K., Kendall, G. (eds.) Search Methodologies, 2nd edn, pp. 287–312. Springer, New York (2013)
21. Baker, K.R.: Introduction to Sequencing and Scheduling. John Wiley & Sons, New York (1974)
22. Bresina, J.L.: Heusistic-biased stochastic sampling. In: Proceedings of the Thirteenth National Conference on Artificial intelligence, vol. 1, pp. 271–278 (1996)
23. Subramanian, A., Drummond, L., Bentes, C., Ochi, L., Farias, R.: A parallel heuristic for the vehicle routing problem with simultaneous pickup and delivery. Comput. Oper. Res. **37**, 1899–1911 (2010)
24. Shapiro, S.S., Wilk, M.B.: An analysis of variance test for normality (complete samples). Biometrika **52**, 591–611 (1965)
25. Montgomery, D.: Design and Analysis of Experiments, 5th edn. John Wiley & Sons, New York (2007)

# Using Data Mining for Prediction of Hospital Length of Stay: An Application of the CRISP-DM Methodology

Nuno Caetano[1], Paulo Cortez[2](✉), and Raul M.S. Laureano[3]

[1] HFAR - Hospital Das Foras Armadas, Azinhaga Ulmeiros, 1620-060
Lisboa, Portugal
nmcaetano@gmail.com

[2] ALGORITMI Research Centre, Department of Information Systems,
University of Minho, 4800-058 Guimarães, Portugal
pcortez@dsi.uminho.pt

[3] Business Research Unit (UNIDE-IUL), Instituto Universitário de Lisboa
(ISCTE-IUL), Av. Das Forças Armadas, 1629-026 Lisboa, Portugal
raul.laureano@iscte.pt

**Abstract.** Hospitals are nowadays collecting vast amounts of data related with patient records. All this data hold valuable knowledge that can be used to improve hospital decision making. Data mining techniques aim precisely at the extraction of useful knowledge from raw data. This work describes an implementation of a medical data mining project approach based on the CRISP-DM methodology. Recent real-world data, from 2000 to 2013, were collected from a Portuguese hospital and related with inpatient hospitalization. The goal was to predict generic hospital Length Of Stay based on indicators that are commonly available at the hospitalization process (e.g., gender, age, episode type, medical specialty). At the data preparation stage, the data were cleaned and variables were selected and transformed, leading to 14 inputs. Next, at the modeling stage, a regression approach was adopted, where six learning methods were compared: Average Prediction, Multiple Regression, Decision Tree, Artificial Neural Network ensemble, Support Vector Machine and Random Forest. The best learning model was obtained by the Random Forest method, which presents a high quality coefficient of determination value (0.81). This model was then opened by using a sensitivity analysis procedure that revealed three influential input attributes: the hospital episode type, the physical service where the patient is hospitalized and the associated medical specialty. Such extracted knowledge confirmed that the obtained predictive model is credible and with potential value for supporting decisions of hospital managers.

**Keywords:** Medical data mining · Hospitalization process · Length of stay · CRISP-DM · Regression · Random forest

© Springer International Publishing Switzerland 2015
J. Cordeiro et al. (Eds.): ICEIS 2014, LNBIP 227, pp. 149–166, 2015.
DOI: 10.1007/978-3-319-22348-3_9

# 1    Introduction

In recent decades, hospitals have been collecting large amounts of data into their clinical information systems. All this data hold valuable knowledge and therefore there is an increasing potential of the use of Data Mining (DM) [1], to facilitate the extraction of useful knowledge and support clinical decision making, in what is known as medical data mining [2]. There are several successful medical data mining applications, such as the prediction of mortality [3] and degree of organ failure [4] at Intensive Care Units, and the segmentation of tissue from magnetic resonance imaging [5], among others.

This work focuses on the prediction of the Length Of Stay (LOS), defined in terms of the inpatient days, which are computed by subtracting the day of admission from the day of discharge. Extreme LOS values are known as prolonged LOS and are responsible for a major share in the hospitalization total days and costs. The use of data-driven models for predicting LOS is of value for hospital management. For example, with an accurate estimate of the patients LOS, the hospital can better plan the management of available beds, leading to a more efficient use of resources by providing a higher average occupancy and less waste of hospital resources [6,7].

DM aims at the extraction of useful knowledge from raw data [1]. With the growth of the field of DM, several DM methodologies were proposed to systematize the discovery of knowledge from data, including the tool neutral and popular Cross-Industry Standard Process for Data Mining (CRISP-DM) [8], which is adopted in this work. The methodology is composed of six stages: business understanding, data understanding, data preparation, modeling, evaluation and implementation.

This study describes the adopted DM approach under the first five stages of CRISP-DM, given that implementation is left for future work. The main goal was to predict generic LOS (for all hospital services) under a regression approach using past patterns existing in the hospitalization process, based on a DM techniques. The data is related with a Portuguese hospital, based on recent data collected from the hospitalization process between 2000 and 2013, including a total of 26462 records from 15253 patients. At the preprocessing stage, the data were cleaned and attributes were selected, leading to 14 inputs and the LOS target. During the modeling stage, six regression methods were tested and compared: Average Prediction (AP), Multiple Regression (MR), Decision Tree (DT) and state-of-the-art regression methods [9], including an Artificial Neural Network (ANN) ensemble, Support Vector Machine (SVM) and Random Forest (RF). The predictive models were compared using a cross-validation procedure with three popular regression metrics: coefficient of determination ($R^2$), Mean Absolute Error (MAE) and Root Mean Squared Error (RMSE). Moreover, the best predictive model (RF) was opened using a sensitivity analysis procedure [10] that allows ranking the input attributes and also measuring the average effect of a particular input in the predictive response.

This work is organized as follows. Firstly, the relevant related work is presented (Sect. 2). Then, the adopted DM approach is detailed in terms of the CRISP-DM methodology first five phases (Sect. 3). Finally, closing conclusions are drawn (Sect. 4).

## 2    Related Work

Nowadays, hospital managers are pressured to accomplish several goals, such as providing better health care, increasing the number of available beds for new admissions and reduce surgical waiting lists. Under this context, LOS is used worldwide as a highly relevant measure to analyze the hospital resources consumption and to monitor hospital performance [7]. Given the importance of LOS, a large number of studies have adopted a data-driven approach for modeling LOS. In the next few paragraphs, we present some examples of related studies.

In 1998, Merom et al. [11] estimated the rate of inappropriate hospital days (failure of established criteria for admission) and the identification of the variables associated with this impropriety. During such study, 1369 patients from 24 hospitals were analyzed under a multiple regression model. Several attributes were used in their analysis: occupation, group age, gender, inappropriate days, government, another hospital entity, another diagnosis, origin, admission diagnosis and period of stay.

In 2007, Abelha et al. [12] evaluated LOS of patients submitted to a non-cardiac surgery and admitted to a surgical Intensive Care Unit (ICU) between October 2004 and July 2005. The attributes used to categorize patients were: age, gender, body mass index, physical status, type and magnitude of surgery, type and duration of anesthesia, temperature on admission, LOS in the ICU and in hospital mortality in the ICU and hospital. A simple linear regression model was adopted and from the results it was found that the average LOS was $4.22\pm8.76$ days.

In 2010, Oliveira et al. [13], proposed to evaluate factors associated with higher mortality and prolonged LOS in ICUs. The study included 401 patients consecutively admitted to the ICU, within a six-month period. The collected attributes were: gender, age, diagnosis, personal history, APACHE II score, mechanical ventilation days, endotracheal reintubation, tracheostomy, LOS in the ICU, ICU discharge or death. In terms of results, the average LOS in the ICU was $8.2\pm10.8$ days. The study concluded that factors such as APACHE II, reintubation and tracheostomy were associated with higher mortality and prolonged LOS in the ICU.

Also in 2010, Karla et al. [14] studied the temporal trends of the workflow in the internal medicine service of an University Hospital. The data analyzed were obtained in that service for three different time periods spanning through 13 years. The most relevant data features data were: date of admission, date of departure or death, gender, age, residence code, financial entity and primary diagnosis. Their results have confirmed several changes in LOS behavior through time (e.g., the number of admissions in the internal medicine service statistically increased from 1991 to 2004).

More recently, Freitas et al. [15] analyzed in 2012 LOS outliers based on inpatient episodes of Portuguese public hospitals belonging to the national health system, with data collected between 2000 and 2009. The variables used for analysis were: age, distance from residence to hospital, year of discharge, comorbidities, A-DRG complexity, readmission, admission and DRG type, discharge status and hospital type. In the analysis they used logistic regression models to examine the association of each variable with the time of admissions outliers, and model with all variables to calculate the adjusted odds ratios and respective confidence intervals (95 %). In terms of results, nine million inpatient episodes were analyzed, of which 3.9 % were considered high LOS outliers. They concluded that age, type of admission and hospital type attributes were significantly associated with high LOS outliers.

In the same year (2012), Azari et al. [6] explored a classification approach to predict LOS. The main attributes of their analysis were: specialty services, days elapsed since the first act of the year, primary condition group (generalized code for the principal diagnosis) and Charlson index (diagnostic code) and LOS. The LOS was divided in three different classification groups: one to two days, greater than two and less than seven days, and longer or equal to seven days. The study concluded that the performance of classification techniques could be improved by incorporating a clustering step during the training stage.

Also in 2012, Castillo [7] developed a statistical model to predict the LOS in Mexican public hospitals. The following attributes were used: age, gender, occupation, education level, previous visits, origin, surgical first diagnosis, diagnosis, surgical procedure, number of surgical procedures and ward. The best predictive model was given by a probabilistic model based on a cluster analysis.

Finally, Sheikh-Nia in 2012 [16] used a sequential ensemble of classification algorithms to predict LOS of patients in the next year, based on the patient previous medical history. The main attributes considered were: age at first claim, gender, provider, year, medical specialty, number of days from the first record, primary condition group, Charlson index and LOS. The results showed that all of the independent classifiers exceeded the baseline by a factor of 1.78 for the ANN, 1.20 for K-Nearest Neighbor and 1.17 for DT.

Instead of predicting LOS in specialized medical services, as in UCI [12,13] or internal medicine [14], in this work we predict generic LOS, for all hospital services (e.g., internal medicine, general surgery, pneumology), which is a more challenging task. Also, as a case study, we only analyze data from one hospital. Nevertheless, we approach a much larger dataset (with 26462 records collected from 2000 to 2013), when compared with the datasets used by some of the mentioned works (e.g., Merom et al. [11] included data from 1369 patients and Oliveira et al. [13] analyzed only 401 records). In addition, the attributes that we adopt (described in Sect. 3) were defined by a hospital expert's medical panel and are commonly available at the hospitalization process. Most of the proposed attributes (e.g., gender, age, episode type, medical specialty) were also adopted by the literature (as shown in Sect. 3.3). Moreover, in contrast with several literature works [6,7,16], we do not perform a classification task, which requires defining *a priori* which are the interesting LOS class intervals. Instead, we adopt the more informative pure regression approach, which predicts the actual number of LOS days and not classes.

# 3   CRISP-DM Methodology

In this section, we describe the main procedures and decisions performed when following the first five phases of the CRISP-DM methodology for LOS prediction of a Portuguese hospital, namely: business understanding (Sect. 3.1), data understanding (Sect. 3.2), data preparation (Sect. 3.3), modeling (Sect. 3.4) and evaluation (Sect. 3.5).

## 3.1   Business Understanding

The prediction of LOS is inserted within the wider problem of hospital admission scheduling, where there is a pressure to increase the availability of beds for new patients. In this particular Hospital, most patients come from the emergency department and from the region of Lisbon. The goal was set in terms of predicting LOS using regression models, thus favoring predictions that are closer to the target values. As a baseline business objective (to determine if there is success), we defined a coefficient of determination with a minimum value of $R^2 = 0.6$, which often corresponds to a reasonable regression.

In terms of software, we adopted open source tools, using structured query language (SQL) to extract data from the hospital database and the **R** tool for the data analysis (http://www.r-project-org). In particular, we adopt the **rminer** package [17], for applying the DM regression models (i.e., AP, MR, DT, ANN, SVM and RF) and sensitive analysis methods.

## 3.2   Data Understanding

The data was collected between October 2000 and March 2013. During this period, a total of 26462 inpatient episodes were stored, related with 15253 patients and associated with the distinct hospital medical specialties.

The selection of relevant data attributes for LOS prediction was performed by an expert medical panel. The panel was composed with 9 physicians from different medical specialties (e.g., internal medicine, general surgery, gynecology). The panel presented a total of 28 attributes that were considered related with LOS and that were analyzed in the data preparation phase (Table 1). The first seven rows of Table 1 are related with the patient's characteristics while the remaining rows are related with the inpatient clinical process. The description column of the table contains in brackets the attribute type (date, nominal, ordinal or numeric), as found in the original hospital database.

## 3.3   Data Preparation

In this phase, a substantial effort was performed using a semi-automated approach to preprocess the data. In particular, the **R** tool was adopted to perform an exploratory data analysis (e.g., histograms and box plots) and preprocess the original dataset. The processing involved the operations of cleaning, discarding redundant attributes, handling missing values and attribute transformations.

**Table 1.** List of attributes related with LOS prediction (attributes used by the regression models are in **bold**.

| Name | Description (attribute type) |
|---|---|
| **Patient Characteristics:** | |
| **Sex** | Patient gender (nominal) |
| Date of Birth | Date of birth (date) |
| **Age** | Age at the time of admission (numeric) |
| Country | Residence country (nominal) |
| Residence | Place of residence (nominal) |
| **Education** | Educational attainment (ordinal) |
| **Marital Status** | Marital status (nominal) |
| **Inpatient clinical process:** | |
| Initial Diagnosis | Initial diagnosis description (ordinal) |
| **Episode Type** | Patient type of episode (nominal) |
| **Inpatient Service** | Physical inpatient service (nominal) |
| **Medical Specialty** | Patient medical specialty (nominal) |
| **Origin Episode Type** | Origin episode type of hospitalization (nominal) |
| Admission Request Date | Date for hospitalization admission request (date) |
| Admission Date | Hospital admission date (date) |
| Admission Year | Hospital admission year (ordinal) |
| **Admission Month** | Hospital admission month (ordinal) |
| **Admission Day** | Hospital admission day of week (ordinal) |
| **Admission Hour** | Hospital admission hour (date) |
| **Main Procedure** | Main procedure description (nominal) |
| **Main Diagnosis** | Main diagnosis description (ordinal) |
| Physician ID | Identification of the physician responsible for the internment (nominal) |
| Discharge Destination | Patient destination after hospital discharge (nominal) |
| Discharge Date | Hospital discharge date (date) |
| Discharge Hour | Hospital discharge hour (date) |
| GDH | Homogeneous group diagnosis code (numeric) |
| Treatment | Clinic codification for procedures, treatments and diseases (ordinal) |
| GCD | Great diagnostic category (ordinal) |
| **Previous Admissions** | Number of previous patient admissions (numeric) |
| **Target attribute:** | |
| **LOS** | Length Of Stay (numeric) |

During the exploratory data analysis step, a few outliers were first detected and then confirmed by the Physicians. The respective records were cleaned: one LOS with 2294, an age of 207 and 29 entries related with a virtual medical specialty, used only for testing the functionalities of the hospital database. After cleaning, the database contained 26431 records.

Then, fourteen attributes from Table 1 were discarded in the variable selection analysis step: Date of Birth (reason: reflected in Age); Country (99 % patients were from Portugal); Residence (30 % of missing values, very large number of nominal levels); Admission Request Date (48 % of missing values, reflected in Admission Date); Admission Date (reflected in Admission Month, Day, Hour and LOS); admission year (not considered relevant); Physician ID (19 % of missing values and large number of 156 nominal levels); Initial Diagnosis (63 % of missing values); and attributes not known at the patient's hospital admission process (i.e., GDH, GCD, Treatment, Discharge Destination, Date and Hour). The remaining 14 attributes (**bold** in Table 1) were used as input variables of the regression models (Sect. 3.4). As shown in Table 2, all input attributes proposed in this study (except for Marital Status) were also used in previous works, which is a clear indication that the selected attributes (**bold** in Table 1) can have a potential predictive LOS value. In particular, there are three input variables (gender, age and main diagnosis) that were used in five or more studies.

Next, missing values were replaced by using the hotdeck method [18], which substitutes a missing value by the value found in the most similar case. In particular, the **rminer** package uses a 1-nearest neighbor applied over all attributes with full values to find the closest example [17]. The following attributes were affected by this operation: Education (11771 missing values), Marital Status (10046 values), Main Procedure (19407 values) and Main Diagnosis (19268 values).

**Table 2.** List of input attributes proposed in this work and that were also used in the literature.

| Attribute Name | Previous LOS studies that adopted this attribute |
| --- | --- |
| Sex | [7, 11–14, 16] |
| Age | [7, 12–16] |
| Education | [7] |
| Episode Type | [7, 15] |
| Inpatient Service | [7] |
| Medical Specialty | [6, 16] |
| Origin Episode Type | [11] |
| Admission Month | [14] |
| Admission Day | [14] |
| Admission Hour | [14] |
| Main Procedure | [7, 12] |
| Main Diagnosis | [6, 7, 11, 13, 14, 16] |
| Previous Admissions | [7] |

Finally, several attributes were transformed, to facilitate the modeling stage. To reduce skewness and improve symmetry of the underlying variable distribution, the logarithm transform $y=\ln(x+1)$ was applied to the Previous Admissions and LOS variables. This is a popular transformation that often improves regression results for right-skewed variables [19]. Also, the Admission Hour variable was standardized to include only 24 levels. Moreover, the values of nominal attributes with a large number of levels were recoded/standardized to reduce the number of levels: Education (transformed from 14 to 6 levels), Main Procedure (from hundreds of values to 16 levels) and Main Diagnosis (from hundreds to 19 levels). Finally, using medical knowledge, we transformed the Age numeric attribute into 5 ordinal classes: A - lower than 15 years; B - between 15 and 44; C - between 45 and 64; D - between 65 and 84; and E - equal or higher than 85.

## 3.4   Modeling

Due to its importance, in the last decades, several methods have been proposed for regression, such as DT, ANN, SVM and RF [9]. In this phase, we tested six regression methods, as implemented in the **rminer** package [17]: AP, MR, DT, ANN, SVM and RF.

The AP is a naive model that consists in predicting the same average LOS ($\bar{y}$, as found in the training set) and is used as baseline method for the comparison.

The DT is a branching structure that represents a set of rules, distinguishing values in a hierarchical form.

The MR is a classical statistical model defined by the equation:

$$\hat{y} = \beta_0 + \sum_{i=1}^{I} \beta_i x_i \tag{1}$$

where $\beta_0, \dots, \beta_i$ are the set of parameters to be adjusted, usually by applying an ordinary least squares (OLS) algorithm.

ANN is based in the popular multilayer perceptron, with one hidden layer of $H$ hidden nodes and logistic activation functions, while the output node uses the linear function. Since ANN training is not optimal, the final solution is dependent of the choice of starting weights. To solve this issue, **rminer** first trains $N_r$ different networks and then uses an ensemble of these networks such that the final output is set in terms of the average of the distinct $N_r$ individual predictions.

The SVM model performs a nonlinear transformation to the input space by adopting the popular Gaussian kernel. SVM regression is achieved under the commonly used $\epsilon$-insensitive loss function. Under this setup, the SVM performance is affected by three parameters: $\gamma$ – Gaussian kernel parameter; $\epsilon$ and $C$ – a trade-off between fitting the errors and the flatness of the mapping. Finally, RF is an ensemble of $T$ unpruned DT, where each tree is based on a random feature selection with up to $m$ features from bootstrap training samples. The RF predictions are built by averaging the outputs of $T$ trees. RF is a substantial modification of bagging (fit of several models to bootstrap samples of training data) and on many problems RF performance is similar to boosting, while being more simpler to train and tune [9].

The **rminer** package full implementation details can be found in [17]. Under this package, before fitting the MR, ANN and SVM models, the input data is first standardized to a zero mean and one standard deviation [9]. Except for the hyperparameters of the most complex methods (ANN, SVM and RF), **rminer** adopts the default parameters of the learning algorithms, such as: MR and ANN – BFGS algorithm, as implemented in **nnet** package; DT - CART algorithm, as implemented in the **rpart** package; SVM - sequential minimal optimization algorithm, as implemented in the **kernlab** package; and RF - Breiman's random forest algorithm, as implemented in the **randomForest** package.

In this work, we set $N_r = 3$ for the ANN ensemble. Also, heuristics were adopted to set two of the three SVM hyperparameters [17]: $C = 3$ (for standardized data) and $\epsilon = 3\sigma_y\sqrt{\log(N)/N}$, where $\sigma_y$ denotes the standard deviation of the predictions given by a 3-nearest neighbor and $N$ is the dataset size. For RF, we adopted the default $T = 500$ value. For the most complex methods, **rminer** uses grid search to select the best hyperparameter values: $H$ for ANN, $\gamma$ for SVM and $m$ for RF. In this work, the grid method searches ten values for each hyperparameter ($H \in \{0,1,...,9\}$; $\gamma \in \{2^{-15}, 2^{-13}, ..., 2^3\}$; and $m \in \{1, 2, ..., 10\}$). During the grid search, the absolute error is measured over a validation set (with 33 % of the training data). The configuration that corresponds to the lowest validation error is selected. Finally, the selected model is retrained with all training data.

The method used for estimating the predictive performance of a model was a 5-fold cross-validation, which divides the data into 5 partitions of equal size. In each 5-fold iteration, a given subset is used as test set (to measure predictive capability) and the remaining data is used for training (to fit the model). To assure statistical robustness, 20 runs of this 5-fold procedure were applied to all methods. For demonstration purposes, we present here a portion of the R/rminer code used to test the RF model:

```
library(rminer) # load the library
# read the data:
d=read.table("data.csv",header=T,sep=",")
# execute 20 runs of 5-fold using RF:
M=mining(LOS~.,data=d,Runs=20, method=c("kfold",5),
         model="randomforest", search="heuristic10")
# save the results into a file:
savemining(M,"rf.results")
```

### 3.5 Evaluation

To evaluate the predictions, three regression metrics were selected, the coefficient of determination ($R^2$), Mean Absolute Error (MAE) and Root Mean Squared Error (RMSE), which can be computed as [20]:

$$R^2 = 1 - \frac{\sum_{i=1}^{N} (y_i - \hat{y}_i)^2}{\sum_{i=1}^{N} (y_i - \overline{y}_j)^2}$$
$$MAE = 1/N \times \sum_{i=1}^{N} |y_i - \hat{y}_i| \qquad (2)$$
$$RMSE = \sqrt{\sum_{i=1}^{N} (y_i - \hat{y}_i)^2 / N}$$

where $N$ denotes the number of predictions (test set size), $y_i$ is the target value for example $i$, $\overline{y}_i$ is the average of the target values in the test set and $\hat{y}_i$ is the predicted value for example $i$.

$R^2$ is a popular regression metric that is scale independent, the higher the better, with the ideal model presenting a value of 1.0. The lower the RMSE and MAE values, the better the predictions. When compared with MAE, RMSE is more sensitive to extreme errors. The Regression Error Characteristic (REC) curve is useful to compare several regression methods in a single graph [21]. The REC curve plots the error tolerance on the x-axis versus the percentage of points predicted within the tolerance on the y-axis.

Table 3 presents the regression predictive results, in terms of the average of the 20 runs of the 5-fold cross-validation evaluation scheme. From Table 3, it is clear that the best results were obtained by the RF model, which outperforms other DM models for all three error metrics. A pairwise t-student statistical test, with a 95 % confidence level, was applied, confirming that the differences are significant (i.e., p-value<0.05) when comparing RF with other methods. We emphasize that a very good $R^2$ value was achieved (0.813), much higher than the minimum success value of 0.6 set in Sect. 3.1.

**Table 3.** Predictive results (average of 20 runs, as measured over test data; best values in **bold**).

| Method | Metrics | | |
|--------|---------|------|------|
|        | $R^2$   | MAE  | RMSE |
| AP     | 0.000   | 0.861 | 1.085 |
| MR     | 0.641   | 0.446 | 0.650 |
| DT     | 0.622   | 0.415 | 0.667 |
| ANN    | 0.736   | 0.340 | 0.558 |
| SVM    | 0.745   | 0.296 | 0.547 |
| RF     | **0.813***  | **0.224*** | **0.469*** |

[*] statistically significant under a pairwise comparison with other methods.

The REC analysis, shown in Fig. 1, also confirms the RF as the best predictive model, presenting always a higher accuracy ($y$-axis) for any admitted absolute tolerance value ($x$-axis). For instance, for a tolerance of 0.5 (at the logarithm transform scale), the RF correctly predicts 85.4 % of the test set examples. The REC results are further complemented in Table 4, which compares the accuracy

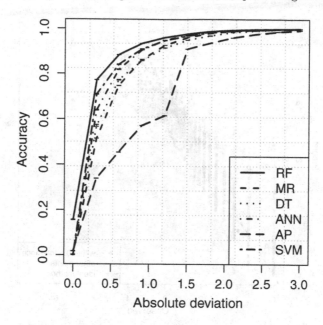

**Fig. 1.** REC curves for all tested models.

**Table 4.** RF vs SVM accuracy for some absolute deviation values (average of 20 runs, best values in **bold**).

| Absolute Deviation | SVM Accuracy | RF Accuracy |
|---|---|---|
| 0.0 | 0.0 % | **15.6%** |
| 0.1 | 50.1 % | **61.3%** |
| 0.2 | 63.3 % | **70.9%** |
| 0.3 | 70.9 % | **77.2%** |
| 0.4 | 76.3 % | **81.8%** |
| 0.5 | 80.6 % | **85.4%** |
| 0.6 | 84.0 % | **88.2%** |
| 0.7 | 86.7 % | **90.3%** |
| 0.8 | 89.0 % | **91.9%** |
| 0.9 | 80.8 % | **93.3%** |
| 1.0 | 92.3 % | **94.4%** |

of the best two models (RF and SVM) for eleven absolute deviation values within the range [0,1]. The table confirms the superiority of the RF model, which always presents higher accuracy values, with a difference that ranges from 2.1 % points (for a tolerance of 1.0) to 15.6 (for a tolerance of 0.0).

The quality of the predictions for the RF model can also be seen on Fig. 2, which plots the observed ($x$-axis) versus the predicted values ($y$-axis). In the

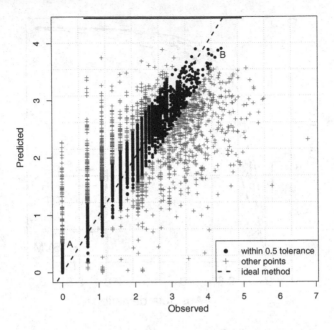

**Fig. 2.** Observed versus predicted RF values.

plot, values within the 0.5 tolerance are shown with solid circles (85.4 % of the examples), values outside the tolerance range are plotted with the + symbol and the diagonal dashed line denotes the performance of the ideal prediction method. It should be noted that the observed (target) values do not cover the full space of LOS values, as shown in Fig. 2. This is an interesting property of this problem domain that probably explains the improved performance of RF when compared with other methods, since ensemble methods (such as RF) tend to be useful when the sample data does not cover the tuple space properly. The large diversity of learners (i.e., $T$=500 unpruned trees) can minimize this issue, since each learner can specialize into a distinct region of the input space.

It should be noted that the presented predicted results were computed over the logarithm transform scale (see Sect. 3.3). In Fig. 2 and within a 0.5 tolerance (solid circles), the predictions are above the origin point (point A, $x$=0) and below the right upper observed values (point B, $x$=4.2). This means that at the normal scale ($x'$, using the inverse of the logarithm transform), the RF model error is capable of correctly predicting 85.4 % of the examples with a real maximum error that ranges from 0.7 days (point A, $x'$ = 0) to 26.0 days (point B, $x'$ = 65.7 days).

When compared with DT and MR, the ANN, SVM and RF data-driven models are difficult to be interpreted by humans. Yet, sensitivity analysis and visualization techniques can be used to open these complex models [10]. The procedure works by analyzing the responses of a model when a given input is varied though its domain. By analyzing the sensitivity response changes, it

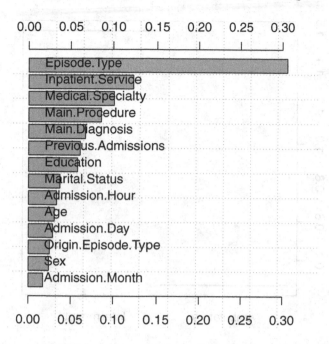

**Fig. 3.** Input importance bar plot for the RF model.

is possible to measure input relevance (higher changes denote a more relevant input) and average impact of an input in the model. The former can be shown using an input importance bar plot and the latter by plotting a Variable Effect Characteristic (VEC) line curve or segments.

To extract explanatory knowledge from the RF model and open the black-box, we applied the Data-Based Sensitivity Analysis (DSA) method, as implemented in the *Importance* function of the **rminer** package. DSA has the advantage of being a fast method that can measure the overall influence of a particular input, including its iterations with other inputs (Cortez and Embrechts, 2013). The DSA algorithm was executed over the RF model fit with all data. The obtained sensitivity responses were first used to rank the RF inputs, according to their relevancy in the predictive model (Fig. 3). Then, the average effects of the most relevant inputs were analyzed using VEC line segments (Figs. 4, 5 and 6).

The input importance bar plot (Fig. 3) ranks the Episode Type (30.1 % impact) as the most relevant attribute, followed by Inpatient Service (12.3 %) and Medical Specialty (10.1 %). Overall, the bar plot shows a much greater influence of the inpatient clinical process attributes (e.g., Episode Type, Medical Specialty, Previous Admissions) when compared with the patients' characteristics (e.g., Education, Sex). This is an interesting outcome for hospital managers. In the next paragraphs, we detail the particular influence of the top three inputs by analyzing their VEC line segments.

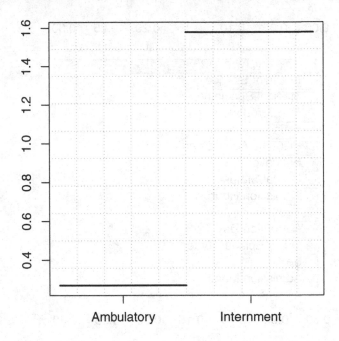

**Fig. 4.** VEC line segments, showing the average influence of the Episode Type (x-axis) on the RF model output (y-axis).

Figure 4 shows the global influence of the most relevant input (Episode Type), which is a nominal attribute with two classes. The VEC line segments clearly confirm that the ambulatory type (scheduled admission, typically involving a 1 day LOS) is related with an average lower LOS (0.1 in the logarithm transform scale, 0.1 days in the normal scale) when compared with the internment type (1.58 in the logarithm scale, 3.9 days).

Next, we analyze the average influence of the Inpatient service (Fig. 5). The greatest LOS is associated with five services: medicine, average LOS of 1.45, corresponding to 3.3 days at the normal scale; orthopedics, average of 1.39, corresponding to 3.0 days; specialties, average of 1.37, corresponding to 2.9 days; surgery, average of 1.36, corresponding to 2.9 days; and pneumology, average of 1.32, corresponding to 2.7 days.

Finally, we analyze the third most relevant attribute, the Medical Specialty (Fig. 6). The internal medicine is related with the highest average LOS (1.64, corresponding to 4.2 days). The second highest average LOS (1.50, corresponding to 3.5 days) is related with orthopedics. Two Medical Specialty values are ranked third in terms of their average effect on LOS: general surgery and urology, both related with an average LOS of 1.40, corresponding to 3.1 days.

These results were shown to hospital specialists and a positive feedback was obtained, confirming meaningful and interesting effects between these attributes and the average expected LOS. Moreover, we would like to stress that the top four relevant attributes were also in agreement with several literature works

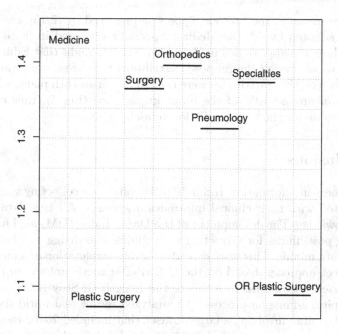

**Fig. 5.** VEC line segments, showing the average influence of the Inpatient service ($x$-axis) on the RF model output ($y$-axis).

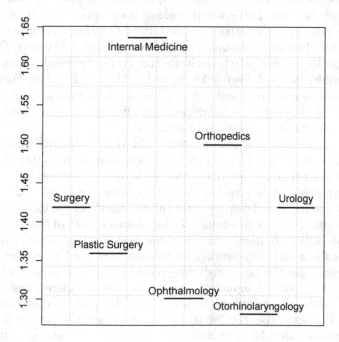

**Fig. 6.** VEC line segments, showing the average influence of the Medical specialty ($x$-axis) on the RF model output ($y$-axis).

(Table 2). For instance, the Episode Type was proposed by [7,15], the Inpatient Service was adopted by [7], the Medical Specialty was used in [6,16], and the Main Procedure was approached in [7,12]. We also highlight that Education and Marital Status are two of the proposed attributes that are scarcely adopted by the literature. Yet, these attributes were ranked at 7th and 8th place, with a total contribution of around 10 % of the input importance (Fig. 3), thus confirming their added value for the LOS prediction model.

## 4    Conclusions

Due to advances in Information Technology, hospitals are collecting vast amounts of data related with their clinical information systems. All this data can hold valuable knowledge. The development of the Data Mining (DM) field has created new exciting possibilities for extracting such clinical knowledge, in what is known as medical data mining. This work describes an implementation of a medical data mining project approach based on the CRISP-DM methodology. In particular, a DM approach was applied to estimate the Length Of Stay (LOS) of patients at their hospital admission process. We analyzed recent real-world data from a Portuguese hospital, involving a large dataset that included 26462 records (from 15253 patients) and an initial set of 28 attributes (as defined by a medical panel).

The DM approach was guided by the popular CRISP-DM methodology, under a regression approach. After the data preparation phase of CRISP-DM, a cleaned dataset (without outliers and missing data) was achieved, with a total of 26431 records, 14 input attributes and the LOS target. During the modeling phase, six distinct regression models were explored: Average Prediction (AP), Multiple Regression (MR), Decision Tree (DT), Artificial Neural Network (ANN) ensemble, Support Vector Machine (SVM) and Random Forest (RF). These models were compared and tested under a robust evaluation scheme that used 20 runs of a 5-fold cross-validation. Finally, at the evaluation phase of CRISP-DM, the obtained results were analyzed.

The best prediction performance was achieved by the RF model, which presents a very good coefficient of determination value of $R^2 = 0.81$ and that is 21 % points higher than the minimum threshold of $R^2 = 0.60$ set in the business understanding phase. A Regression Error Characteristic (REC) curve analysis revealed that the RF model can correctly predict 85.4 % of the examples under a tolerance deviation that ranges from 0.7 (for observed LOS of 0 days) to 26 days (for observed LOS of 66 days). At the same evaluation phase of CRISP-DM, sensitivity analysis and visualization techniques were used to extract explanatory knowledge from the best predictive model (RF). The sensitivity analysis revealed a high impact of inpatient clinical process attributes, instead of the patient's characteristics. In effect, the top three influential input attributes were: the hospital Episode Type, the Inpatient Service where the patient is hospitalized and the associated Medical Specialty. Moreover, the average influence of each of these input attributes in the prediction model has been detailed by using a Variable Effect Characteristic (VEC) analysis. Such analysis has confirmed that several input values associated with high LOS, such as: 'internment" (for Episode Type), "medicine" (for Inpatient Service) and "internal medicine" (for Medical Specialty).

The obtained DM predictive and explanatory knowledge results were considered credible by the hospital specialists and are valuable for hospital managers. By having access to better estimates of the LOS that is more likely to occur in the future and which factors affect such estimates, hospital managers can make more informed decisions. Such informed decisions can lead to a better planning of the hospital resources, resulting in a better hospital management performance, with an increase in the number of available beds for new admissions and reduction of surgical waiting lists.

In the future, we intend to address the implementation phase of CRISP-DM by testing the obtained data-driven model in a real-environment (e.g., by designing a friendly interface to query the RF model). After some time, this would allow us to obtain additional feedback from the hospital managers and also enrich the datasets by gathering more examples. The proposed approach has also the potential to predict well LOS using data from other hospitals, since we address generic LOS and use 14 variables that are easily available at the hospitalization process.

**Acknowledgments.** We wish to thank the physicians that participated in this study for their valuable feedback. Also, we would like to thank the anonymous reviewers for their helpful suggestions. The work of P. Cortez has been supported by FCT – Fundação para a Ciência e Tecnologia within the Project Scope: PEst-OE/EEI/UI0319/2014.

# References

1. Fayyad, U., Piatetsky-Shapiro, G., Smyth, P.: Advances in Knowledge Discovery and Data Mining. MIT Press, Cambridge (1996)
2. Cios, K., Moore, G.: Uniqueness of Medical Data Mining. Artificial Intelligence in Medicine 26(1–2), 1–24 (2002)
3. Silva, Á., Cortez, P., Santos, M.F., Gomes, L., Neves, J.: Mortality assessment in intensive care units via adverse events using artificial neural networks. Artif. Intell. Med. 36(3), 223–234 (2006)
4. Silva, Á., Cortez, P., Santos, M.F., Gomes, L., Neves, J.: Rating organ failure via adverse events using data mining in the intensive care unit. Artif. Intell. Med. 43(3), 179–193 (2008)
5. Chiusano, G., Stagliano, A., Basso, C., Verri, A.: Unsupervised tissue segmentation from dynamic contrast-enhanced magnetic resonance imaging. Artif. Intell. Med. 61(1), 53–61 (2014)
6. Azari, A., Janeja, V.P., Mohseni, A.: Predicting hospital length of stay (phlos): a multi-tiered data mining approach. In: 2012 IEEE 12th International Conference on Data Mining Workshops (ICDMW), pp. 17–24. IEEE (2012)
7. Castillo, M.G.: Modelling patient length of stay in public hospitals in Mexico. PhD thesis, University of Southampton (2012)
8. Clifton, C., Thuraisingham, B.: Emerging standards for data mining. Comput. Stan. Interfaces 23(3), 187–193 (2001)

9. Hastie, T., Tibshirani, R., Friedman, J.: The Elements of Statistical Learning: Data Mining, Inference, and Prediction, 2nd edn. Springer, New york (2008)
10. Cortez, P., Embrechts, M.J.: Using sensitivity analysis and visualization techniques to open black box data mining models. Information Sciences 225, 1–17 (2013)
11. Merom, D., Shohat, T., Harari, G., Oren, M., Green, M.S.: Factors associated with inappropriate hospitalization days in internal medicine wards in israel: a cross-national survey. Int. J. Qual. Health Care 10(2), 155–162 (1998)
12. Abelha, F., Maia, P., Landeiro, N., Neves, A., Barros, H.: Determinants of outcome in patients admitted to a surgical intensive care unit. Arq. Med. 21(5–6), 135–143 (2007)
13. Oliveira, A., Dias, O., Mello, M., Arajo, S., Dragosavac, D., Nucci, A., Falcão, A.: Fatores associados à maior mortalidade e tempo de internação prolongado em uma unidade de terapia intensiva de adultos. Rev. Bras. de Terapia Intensiva 22(3), 250–256 (2010)
14. Kalra, A.D., Fisher, R.S., Axelrod, P.: Decreased length of stay and cumulative hospitalized days despite increased patient admissions and readmissions in an area of urban poverty. J. Gen. Intern. Med. 25(9), 930–935 (2010)
15. Freitas, A., Silva-Costa, T., Lopes, F., Garcia-Lema, I., Teixeira-Pinto, A., Brazdil, P., Costa-Pereira, A.: Factors influencing hospital high length of stay outliers. BMC Health Serv. Res. 12(265), 1–10 (2012)
16. Sheikh-Nia, S.: An Investigation of Standard and Ensemble Based Classification Techniques for the Prediction of Hospitalization Duration. University of Guelph, Ontario, Canada, Thesis for Master Science Degree (2012)
17. Cortez, P.: Data mining with neural networks and support vector machines using the R/rminer Tool. In: Perner, P. (ed.) ICDM 2010. LNCS, vol. 6171, pp. 572–583. Springer, Heidelberg (2010)
18. Brown, M., Kros, J.: Data mining and the impact of missing data. Ind. Manage. Data Syst. 103(8), 611–621 (2003)
19. Menard, S.: Applied logistic regression analysis, vol. 106. Sage, Thousand Oaks (2002)
20. Witten, I.H., Frank, E., Hall, M.: Data Mining: Practical Machine Learning Tools and Techniques, 3rd edn. Morgan Kaufmann, San Franscico (2011)
21. Bi, J., Bennett, K.: Regression error characteristic curves. In: Fawcett, T., Mishra, N. (eds.) Proceedings of 20th International Conference on Machine Learning (ICML). AAAI Press, Washington DC, USA (2003)

# Applying Artificial Immune Systems for Deploying Router Nodes in Wireless Networks in the Presence of Obstacles

Pedro Henrique Gouvêa Coelho[✉], Jorge Luís Machado do Amaral,
José Franco Machado do Amaral, Luciane Fernanda de Arruda Barreira,
and Adriano Valladão de Barros

State University of Rio de Janeiro, FEN/DETEL,
Rua São Francisco Xavier, 524, Sala 5001E, Maracanã, Rio de Janeiro,
RJ 20550-900, Brazil
{phcoelho,jamaral,franco}@uerj.br,
{lucianebarreira,adriano_vbarros}@yahoo.com.br

**Abstract.** This work deals with the deploying of router nodes using artificial immune systems techniques, particularly for industrial applications of wireless sensor networks. Possible scenarios include configurations with sensors blocked by obstacles. These nodes make possible the transmission of data from sensors to the gateway in order to meet criteria especially those that lead to a low degree of failure and reducing the number of retransmissions by the routers. These criteria can be set individually or in groups, associated with weights. Router nodes deploying is accomplished in two phases, the first uses immune networks concepts and the second employs potential fields ideas for deploying the routers in such way that critical sensors attract them while obstacles and other routers repel them. A large number of case studies were considered from which some representative ones were selected to illustrate the method, for different configurations in the presence of obstacles.

**Keywords:** Artificial immune systems · Node positioning and wireless sensor networks

## 1 Introduction

Data transmission in wireless technology has grown dramatically in society. The wireless technology has taken over the world and the field of industrial automation is no exception. Main advantages are reduced installation time of devices, no need of cabling structure, cost saving projects, infrastructure savings, device configuration flexibility, cost savings in installation, flexibility in changing the existing architectures, possibility of installing sensors in hard-to-access locations and others.

Safety, reliability, availability, robustness and performance are of paramount importance in the area of industrial automation. The network cannot be sensitive to interference nor stop operation because of an equipment failure, nor can have high latency in data transmission and ensure that information is not misplaced [1, 3].

© Springer International Publishing Switzerland 2015
J. Cordeiro et al. (Eds.): ICEIS 2014, LNBIP 227, pp. 167–183, 2015.
DOI: 10.1007/978-3-319-22348-3_10

In industrial automation environment, data transmission in a wireless network faces the problem of interference generated by other electrical equipment, such as walkie-talkies, other wireless communication networks and electrical equipment, moving obstacles (trucks, cranes, etc.) and fixed ones(buildings, pipelines, tanks, etc.). In an attempt to minimize these effects, frequency scattering techniques and mesh or tree topologies are used, in which a message can be transmitted from one node to another with the aid of other nodes, which act as intermediate routers, directing messages to other nodes until it reaches its final destination. This allows the network to get a longer range and to be nearly fault tolerant, because if an intermediate node fails or cannot receive a message, that message could be routed to another node. However, a mesh network also requires careful placement of these intermediate nodes, since they are responsible for doing the forwarding of the data generated by the sensor nodes in the network to the gateway directly or indirectly, through hops. Those intermediate nodes are responsible for meeting the criteria of safety, reliability and robustness of the network and are also of paramount importance in the forwarding of data transmission. They could leave part or all the network dead, if they display any fault [7]. Most solutions to the routers placement solve this problem with optimization algorithms that minimize the number of intermediate router nodes to meet the criteria for coverage, network connectivity and longevity of the network and data fidelity [8, 9].

This work proposes to solve this problem using Artificial Immune Networks, based on the human immune system. The algorithms based on immune networks have very desirable characteristics in the solution of this problem, among which we can mention: scalability, self-organization, learning ability and continuous treatment of noisy data [10].

The present work is divided into four sections. Section 2 discusses briefly artificial immune systems. Section 3 presents the application of artificial immune systems to the node positioning problem and Sect. 4 discusses case studies results including obstacles and conclusions.

## 2  Immune Systems Foundations

Artificial immune systems (AISs) are models based on natural immune systems which protect the human body from a large number of pathogens or antigens [13]. Due to these characteristics the AISs are potentially suitable for solving problems related to computer security and they inherit from natural immune systems the properties of uniqueness, distributed sensing, learning and memory efficiency. In fact, the immune system is unique to each individual. The detectors used by the immune system are small, efficient and highly distributed and are not subject to centralized control. Moreover, it is not necessary that every pathogen is fully detected, because the immune system is more flexible, there is a compromise between the resources used in the protection and breadth in coverage.

Anomaly detection is another important feature, since it allows the immune system to detect and respond to pathogens (agents that cause diseases) for which they have not previously been found. The immune system is able to learn the structures of pathogens and remember these structures so that future responses to these agents are faster. In summary, these features make the immune system scalable, robust and flexible. The immune system uses distributed detection to distinguish the elements of the organism itself, the self, and foreign to the body, the non-self. The detection of the non-self is a difficult task because its number, of the order of $10^{16}$, is much superior to the number of self-patterns, around $10^6$, taking place in a highly distributed environment. It should be also noted that all these actions occur while the living organism must continue in operation and the available resources are scarce.

Cells that perform the detection or recognition of pathogens in the acquired or adaptive immune system are called lymphocytes that recognize pathogens joining them. The antigens are detected when a molecular bond is established between the pathogens and the receptors present on the surface of lymphocytes. A given receiver will not be able to join all antigens. A lymphocyte has approximately 100,000 receptors on its surface which however have the same structure, and therefore can only join with structurally related epitopes (the site on an antigen at which a specific antibody becomes attached). Such epitopes define a similarity subset of epitopes which lymphocytes can detect.

The number of receivers that can join the pathogens defines the affinity of a lymphocyte to a certain antigen. Lymphocytes can only be activated by an antigen if their affinities exceed a certain threshold. As this threshold increases, the number of epitopes types capable of activating a lymphocyte decreases, i.e., the similarity subset becomes smaller. A receiver may be obtained by randomly recombining possible elements (from the memory of the immune system), producing a large number of possible combinations indicating a wide range in the structure of the receptors. Although it is possible to generate approximately $10^{15}$ receptor types, the number present at a given instant of time is much smaller, in the range of $10^8$ to $10^{12}$ [12]. The detection is approximate, since it is a difficult task to evolve structures that are complementary to receptor epitopes for which the organism has never encountered before. If an exact complementarity was needed, the chance of a random lymphocyte epitope join a random would be very small. An important consequence of that approximate detection is that one single lymphocyte is capable of detecting a subset of epitopes, which implies that a smaller number of lymphocytes is required for protection against a wide variety of possible antigens.

## 2.1 Metaphors of the Immune System

The main algorithms that implement the artificial immune systems were developed from metaphors of the immune system: the mechanism of negative selection, the theory of immune network and the clonal selection principle.

The function of the negative selection mechanism is to provide tolerance to self-cells, namely those belonging to the organism. Thus, the immune system gains the ability to detect unknown antigens and not react to the body's own cells. During the generation of T-cells, which are cells produced in the bone marrow, receptors are generated by a pseudo-random process of genetic arrangement. Later on, they undergo a maturation mechanism in the thymus, called negative selection, in which T cells that react to body proteins are destroyed. Thus, only cells that do not connect to the body proteins can leave the thymus. The T cells, known as mature cells, circulate in the body for immune functions and to protect it against antigens.

The theory of immune system network considers several important aspects like the combination of antibodies with the antigens for the early elimination of the antigens. Each antibody has its own antigenic determinant, called idiotope. In this context, Jerne [14] proposed the Immune Network Theory to describe the activity of lymphocytes in an alternative way. According to Jerne [14], the antibodies and lymphocytes do not act alone, but the immune system keeps a network of B cells for antigen recognition. These cells can stimulate and inhibit each other in various ways, leading to stabilization of the network. Two B cells are connected if they share an affinity above a certain threshold and the strength of this connection is directly proportional to the affinity they share.

The clonal selection principle describes the basic features of an immune response to an antigenic stimulus, and ensures that only cells that recognize the antigen are selected to proliferate. The daughter cells are copies or clones of their parents and are subject to a process of mutation with high rates, called somatic hypermutation. In the clonal selection the removal of daughter cells are performed, and these cells have receptors that respond to the body's own proteins as well as the most suitable mature cell proliferation, i.e., those with a greater affinity to the antigens [5].

## 3   Router Nodes Positioning

Router Nodes positioning has been addressed in the literature by several researchers. Cannons et al. [4] proposed an algorithm for positioning router nodes and determine which router will relay the information from each sensor. Gersho and Gray [6] proposed one to promote the reliability of wireless sensors communication network, minimizing the average probability of sensor transmission error. Shi et al. [11] proposed a positioning algorithm of multi-router nodes to minimize energy consumption for data transmission in mobile ad hoc network (MANET - Mobile Ad Hoc Network). The problem was modeled as an optimization clustering problem. The suggested algorithm to solve the problem uses heuristic methods based on the k-means algorithm. Costa and Amaral [2] described an approach for router nodes placement based on genetic algorithm which minimizes the number of nodes required for network routers, decreasing the amount critical nodes for all involved devices and the number of hops of the transmitted messages.

The use of wireless sensor network in industrial automation is still a matter of concern with respect to the data reliability and security by users. Thus, an appropriate node positioning is of paramount importance for the wireless network to meet safety, reliability and efficiency criteria.

Positioning of nodes is a difficult task, because one should take into account all the obstacles and interference present in an industrial environment. The gateway as well as the sensors generally have a fixed position near the control room. But the placement of router nodes, which are responsible for routing the data, generated by the sensors network to the gateway directly or indirectly, is determined by the characteristics of the network.

The main characteristics of wireless sensor networks for industrial automation differ from traditional ones by the following aspects: The maximum number of sensors in a traditional wireless network is on the order of millions while automation wireless networks is on the order of tens to hundreds; The network reliability and latency are essential and fundamental factors for network wireless automation. To determine the number of router nodes and define the position in the network, some important aspects in industrial automation should be considered. It should be guaranteed:

(1) Redundant paths so that the system be node fault-tolerant;
(2) Full connectivity between nodes, both sensors and routers, so that each node of the network can be connected to all the others exploring the collaborative role of routers;
(3) Node energy efficiency such that no node is overwhelmed with many relaying information from the sensors;
(4) Low-latency system for better efficiency in response time;
(5) Combined attributes for industrial processes to avoid accidents due to, for example, high monitored process temperature;
(6) Self-organization ability, i.e. the ability of the network to reorganize the retransmission of data paths when a new sensor is added to the network or when a sensor stops working due to lack of power or a problem in wireless communication channel.

All these factors must be met, always taking into consideration the prime factor security: the fault tolerance. In the end of the router nodes placement, the network of wireless sensors applied to industrial automation should be robust, reliable, scalable and self-organizing.

The positioning of router nodes in industrial wireless sensor networks is a complex and critical task to the network operation. It is through the final position of routers that one can determine how reliable, safe, affordable and robust the network is.

In the application of immune systems to router nodes positioning reported in this work, B cells that make up the immune network will be composed by a set of sensor nodes and a set of router nodes. The sensor nodes are located in places where the plant instrumentation is required. These nodes have fixed coordinates, i.e. they cannot be moved. For security to be guaranteed it is necessary to have redundant paths between these nodes and the gateway. The set of router nodes will be added to allow redundant paths. The position of these nodes will be changed during the process of obtaining the final network. The stimulation of the B cells, corresponding to the set of routers, is defined by the affinity degree among B cells in the training of the network. In this work, the role of the antigen is viewed more broadly as the entity that stimulates B cells. Thus, the function of the antigen takes into consideration possible missing paths to critical sensors, the number of times that a router is used and its proximity to sensors. The modeling of B cells affinity is the weighted sum of the three criteria that the positioning of each router will answer. The criteria are: fault degree of each router, number of times each router is used depending on the path and number of sensor nodes neighboring to each router.

### 3.1   The Proposed Router Nodes Algorithm

In the proposed algorithm, process dynamics can be divided into two processes: network pruning and cloning, and node mutation of the network routers.

In the pruning process, $n_p$ router nodes that during a certain time failed to become useful to the network will be removed from it. The cloning process is responsible for generating $n_c$ clones of router nodes that were over stimulated. The clones may suffer mutations of two kinds:

(i)   Hypermutation – for positioning new elements in the network which are inversely proportional to the degree of stimulation of the router node selected;
(ii)  Net Mutation – for positioning the new information into the network in order to assure the new clones are neighbors of the selected clone [16].

After the inclusion of the new router nodes, a stop condition is performed. If the condition is not met, all routers undergo an action of repulsive forces, generated by obstacles and routers for other nodes, followed by attractive forces created by critical sensor nodes. Those critical nodes are the ones that do not meet the minimum number of paths necessary to reach the gateway. The actions of repelling potential fields have the function of driving them away from obstacles, to allow direct line of sight for the router network nodes to increase the reliability of transmission and also increase the distance among the routers to increase network coverage. On the other hand, the attractive potential fields attract routers to critical sensors, easing the formation of redundant paths among sensors and the gateway. After the action of potential fields, from the new positioning of routers, a new network is established and the procedure continues until the stopping criterion is met.

The algorithm proposed in this work deals with a procedure based on artificial immune networks, which solves the problem of positioning the router nodes so that every sensor device is able to communicate with the gateway directly and or indirectly by redundant paths.

Figure 1 shows the main modules of the algorithm. The first module is called immune network, and the second, is called potential fields (i.e. positioning module) containing elements used in positioning sensor networks using potential fields [15].

The immune network module performs an algorithm that can be described by the following steps:

– Creation: Creation of an initial set of B cells to form a network.
– Evaluation: Determination of the B cells affinity to calculate their stimulation.
– Pruning: Performs the resource management and remove cells that are without resources from the network.
– Selection: Selects the most stimulated B cells to be cloned.
– Cloning: Generates a set of clones from the most stimulated B cells.
– Mutation: Does the mutation of cloned cells.

In the stage of creation, an initial set of routers is randomly generated to initiate the process of obtaining the network, and the user can specify how many routers to place it initially.

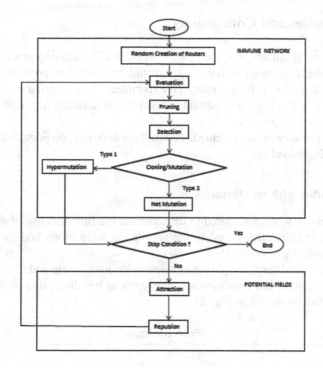

**Fig. 1.** The proposed algorithm.

In the evaluation phase, a network which is represented by a graph is formed with sensor nodes and router nodes. From this graph, values of several variables are obtained that will be used to calculate the affinity. Examples of such variables are the number of paths that exist between each sensor and the gateway, the number of times that a router is used on the formed paths, etc.

It should be stressed that the affinity value is calculated for each router and comprises three parts. The first part provides the degree of fault of each network router - this affinity is the most important of all. It defines the value or importance each router has in the network configuration. This is done as follows: a router is removed from the network, and the number of paths that remain active for the sensors send information for the gateway is evaluated. If the number of active paths remaining after the node removal is small, the router node needs another nearby router to reduce their degree of fault.

Furthermore, if the node suffers battery discharge or hardware problems, other paths to relay information should be guaranteed until the problem is solved.

The second part relates to the number of times that each router is used in paths that relay the information from the sensors to the gateway. The greater the number of times it is used, more important is that router.

The third part relates the number of sensor nodes neighboring to each router – one can say that the more sensor nodes neighbors, the greater the likelihood that it will become part of the way that the sensor needs to transmit your message to the gateway.

## 4   Case Studies and Conclusions

Case studies were simulated in a 1 × 1 square scenario. The cloning procedure considered that only the router with higher affinity would be selected to produce three clones in each generation. For each case study 10 experiments were carried out that demonstrated the algorithm's ability to create at least two redundant paths to get the information from any sensor to the gateway.

Two set of results will be presented. The first set does not consider obstacles which are treated in the second set.

### 4.1   Case Studies with no Obstacles

Two configurations were considered to demonstrate the functionality of the proposed algorithm. The configurations used in the simulation were motivated by oil and gas refinery automation applications.

The first one called PosA consists of five network nodes, where node 1 is the gateway and nodes 2, 3, 4 and 5 are fixed sensors. The gateway has direct line of sight with all the network nodes as shown in Fig. 2.

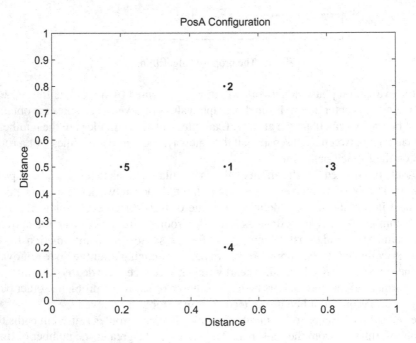

**Fig. 2.**   Sensors and gateway for PosA configuration. Node 1 is the gateway and nodes 2 to 5 are the sensors.

The second one (PosB) considers a network with nine nodes, where node one is the gateway and the others are fixed sensors. As in configuration PosA, PosB has direct line of sight with all the network nodes as shown in Fig. 3. For both configurations it will be considered that there is no connectivity among them, i.e. the distance between them will be greater than their operating range.

For the case study simulations considered, the goal is to get any two paths for each sensor to transmit the monitored sensor data to the gateway node. The operating range for both cases is 0.2, i.e. for both configurations there is no connectivity between any sensor and the gateway.

Table 1 describes the parameters used in the case study 1. After completion of ten experiments, the best network configuration can be seen in Fig. 4, and the consolidations of the tests are shown in Table 2.

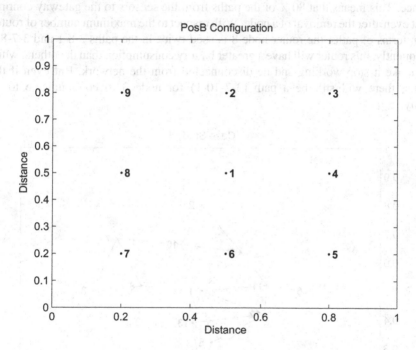

**Fig. 3.** Sensors and gateway for PosB configuration. Node 1 is the gateway and nodes 2 to 9 are the sensors.

**Table 1.** Case study 1. PosA configuration parameters.

| Simulation Parameters | Values | Method |
|---|---|---|
| No. of generations | 50 | – |
| Initial no. of routers | 10 | – |
| Mutation operator as indicated in Fig. 1 | – | Hypermutation (Type 1) |
| Affinity | – | Fault degree |

**Table 2.** Network performance for case study 1. PosA configuration.

| Network | Min. | Average | Max. | Standard deviation |
|---|---|---|---|---|
| Number of nodes | 13 | 13.7 | 15 | 0.67 |
| Number of routers | 8 | 8.7 | 10 | 0.67 |
| Number of critical sensors | 0 | 0 | 0 | – |
| Number a router is used | 1 | 2.1 | 3 | 0.57 |

Figure 4 also shows that one of the paths from sensor node 3 to the gateway shows three jumps (3-7-8-1) i.e. the information had to be relayed by two routers to reach the gateway node. Regarding the degree of fault, all eight routers have 20 % degree of fault tolerance. This means that 80 % of the paths from the sensors to the gateway continue to exist even after the removal of a node. With respect to the maximum number of routers used in terms of paths, the router node 8 is used twice in the paths 3-8-1 and 3-7-8-1. Consequently, this router will have a greater battery consumption than the others, which could make it stop working and be disconnected from the network. But even if that happens, there will still be a path (3-7-10-1) for node 3 to communicate to the gateway.

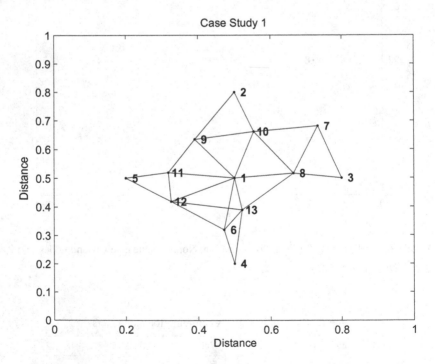

**Fig. 4.** Best router nodes positioning for case study 1 in PosA configuration. Node 1 is the gateway, nodes 2 to 5 are the sensors, and nodes 6 to 13 are the router nodes.

**Table 3.** Case study 2. PosB configuration parameters.

| Simulation Parameters | Values | Method |
|---|---|---|
| No. of generations | 15 | – |
| Initial no. of routers | 3 | – |
| Mutation Operator (as indicated in Fig. 1) | | Net mutation (Type 2) |
| Affinity | – | Fault degree, number of times a router is used and number of neighbor sensors |

Case study 2 considers configuration PosB for the sensors and gateway. Table 3 shows the parameters used in the case study 2 simulations. The goal is still obtain at least two paths for each sensor and gateway but now the affinity criteria consider fault degree, number of times a router is used and number of neighbor sensors. After ten experiments the best network configuration is shown in Fig. 5 and the network performance is seen in Table 4. Table 4 indicates that even using a low number of initial routers the algorithm was able to reach a positioning result meeting the goals and avoided again critical nodes.

Figure 5 also shows that node 3 in the path 3-15-17-13-1 features four hops to the gateway. That means that the information sent by these devices will be delayed when received by the gateway node, since it will need to be relayed through three intermediate nodes. Regarding to the degree of fault, the intermediate node 22 has 22 % degree of fault, and all the other routers have an index less than 22 %. Thus if node 22 is lost for device failure or end of battery, it results that information sent by sensor 5 will not reach the gateway. Regarding to the maximum number of routers used in terms of paths, router nodes 10 and 13 are used three times in the paths 3-15-17-13-1, 3-26-13-1, 4-13-1, 9 -18-12-10-1, 9-24-10-1 and 2-11-10-1.That means that these devices will have their lifetime reduced because their high levels of retransmission. As far as the number of sensors to neighboring routers is concerned, routers 15, 19, 22 and 26 can relay the data sent by two sensors, and the sensors are also used with relays. This makes these sensors and routers consume more power, and as a result, battery runs out sooner.

**Table 4.** Network performance for case study 2. PosB configuration.

| Network | Min. | Average | Max. | Standard deviation |
|---|---|---|---|---|
| Number of nodes | 23 | 25.3 | 28 | 1.49 |
| Number of routers | 14 | 16.3 | 19 | 1.49 |
| Number of critical sensors | 0 | 0 | 0 | – |
| Number a router is used | 3 | 3.7 | 5 | 0.67 |

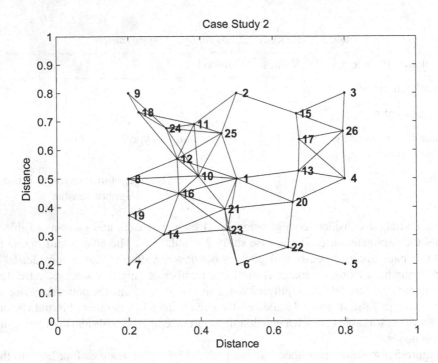

**Fig. 5.** Best router nodes positioning for case study 2 in PosB configuration. Node 1 is the gateway, nodes 2 to 9 are the sensors, and nodes 9 to 26 are the router nodes.

## 4.2 Case Studies with Obstacles

Two configurations with obstacles were considered to illustrate the proposed router nodes positioning algorithm in environments with obstacles.

The first configuration (PosC) comprises two circular obstacles with a radius of 0.1, and five nodes, in which node 1 is the gateway and the others are sensor nodes. Initially, the gateway has not direct line of sight with sensor nodes 3 and 5 and is not connected, i.e. out of range, to any of the network nodes, as depicted in Fig. 6.

The second configuration (PosD) has eight obstacles: three circular ones have radius of 0.05, another circular one has radius 0.15 and four rectangular obstacles with different sizes. Besides, the gateway is node 1 and nodes 2 to 8 are the seven sensor nodes. Initially, the gateway has not direct line of sight to any of the sensor nodes and is not connected to any network node as it is out range to the other nodes. Moreover, sensor nodes have also not a direct line of sight with each other and are also not connected as they are out of range with each other too. Figure 7 shows the PosD configuration.

In this section, case studies 3 and 4 are considered using the configurations PosC and PosD.

For case study 3, the network configuration is cross shaped, the operating range of the network nodes is 0.2 and the positioning procedure lead to two disjoint paths for the sensors send data to the gateway.

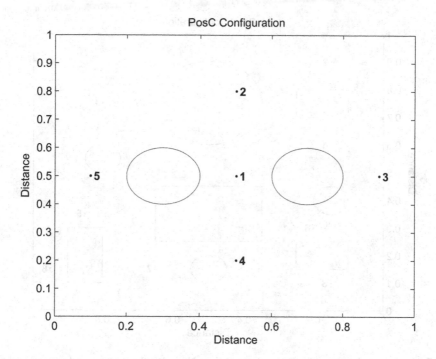

**Fig. 6.** Sensors and gateway for PosC configuration. Node 1 is the gateway and nodes 2 to 5 are the sensors.

Case study 4 uses configuration PosD and considers the same operating range as in the case study 3, 0.2, and now three disjoint paths are required.

Tables 5 and 7 show the used parameters for case studies 3 and 4 respectively.

**Table 5.** Case study 3. PosC configuration parameters.

| Simulation Parameters | Values | Method |
|---|---|---|
| No. of generations | 30 | – |
| Initial no. of routers | 10 | – |
| Mutation Operator (as indicated in Fig. 1) | | Net mutation (Type 2) |
| Affinity | – | Fault degree, number of times a router is used and number of neighbor sensors |

**Table 6.** Network performance for case study 3. PosC configuration.

| Network | Min. | Average | Max. | Standard deviation |
|---|---|---|---|---|
| Number of nodes | 19 | 19.9 | 22 | 0.99 |
| Number of routers | 14 | 14.9 | 17 | 0.99 |
| Number of critical sensors | 0 | 0 | 0 | – |
| Number a router is used | 2 | 2 | 2 | 0 |

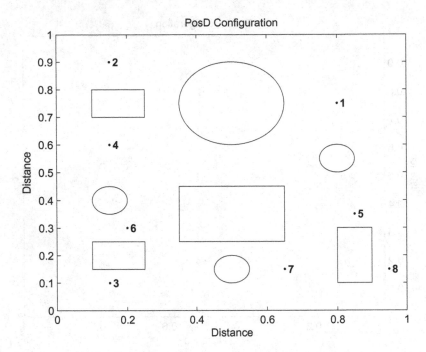

**Fig. 7.** Sensors and gateway for PosD configuration. Node 1 is the gateway and nodes 2 to 8 are the sensors.

**Table 7.** Case study 4. PosD configuration parameters.

| Simulation Parameters | Values | Method |
|---|---|---|
| No. of generations | 100 | – |
| Initial no. of routers | 10 | – |
| Mutation Operator (as indicated in Fig. 1) | | Net mutation (Type 2) |
| Affinity | – | Fault degree, number of times a router is used and number of neighbor sensors |

Figure 8 shows the best configuration obtained from the 10 experiments. Table 6 shows the network performance for case study 3.

It can be seen in Fig. 8 that the sensor nodes 3 and 5 in the paths 3-16-17-20-1, 3-19-7-10-1, 5-13-11-18-1 and 5-12-14-15-1 show four jumps to the gateway. This means the data sent by these devices suffer a delay when received by the gateway, since it will need to be relayed through three intermediate nodes. With respect to the degree of fault, the intermediate nodes 7, 10, 11, 12, 13, 14, 16, 17 and 19 have a 30 % degree of fault, and the other router nodes have an index lower than 30 %. So 70 % of the paths from the sensors to the gateway, continue to exist even after the removal of a node.

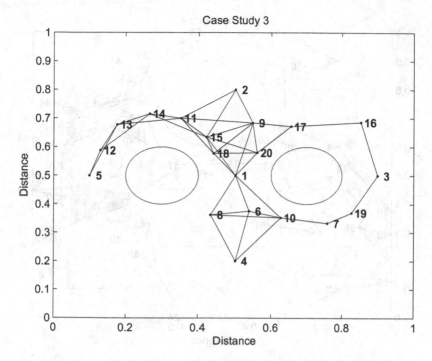

**Fig. 8.** Best router nodes positioning for case study 3 in PosC configuration. Node 1 is the gateway, nodes 2 to 5 are the sensors, and nodes 6 to 20 are the router nodes.

Figure 9 shows the best configuration out of ten experiments for case study 4 and Table 8 shows the network performance for case study 4.

Figure 9 indicates that for sensor nodes 3 and 6, the paths 3-20-22-24-7-40-63-53-36-1, 3-50-49-61-4-52-15-56-39-1 and 6-58-61-4-60-31-15-37-26-1 show nine hops to the gateway. This means that the data sent by these devices suffer a delay in the gateway, since it will need to be relayed by eight intermediate nodes. With respect to the degree of fault, the router node 32 have 21 % degree of fault, and the other router nodes have an index lower than 21 %. This means that 79 % of the paths from the sensors are still present even after a node removal.

**Table 8.** Network performance for case study 4. PosD configuration.

| Network | Min. | Average | Max. | Standard deviation |
|---|---|---|---|---|
| Number of nodes | 59 | 60.50 | 63 | 1,18 |
| Number of routers | 51 | 52.50 | 55 | 1.18 |
| Number of critical sensors | 0 | 0 | 0 | – |
| Number a router is used | 5 | 5,4 | 8 | 0.97 |

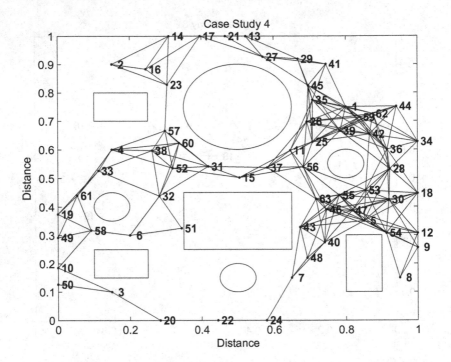

**Fig. 9.** Best router nodes positioning for case study 4 in PosD configuration. Node 1 is the gateway, nodes 2 to 8 are the sensors, and nodes 9 to 63 are the router nodes.

This work proposed a positioning algorithm for router nodes in wireless network using immune systems techniques. The algorithm creates redundant paths to the data collected by the sensors to be sent to the gateway by any two or more paths, meeting the criteria of degree of failure, the number of retransmission by routers and number of sensors to neighboring routers. The algorithm allows each criterion is enabled at a time or that they be combined with weights. The affinity function, which works as an objective function, is multi-objective, so several other objectives could be jointly considered.

## References

1. Zheng, J., Lee, M.J.: A comprehensive performance study of IEEE 802.15.4. Sensor Network Operations, Chapter 4, pp. 218–237. IEEE Press, Wiley InterScience (2006)
2. Costa, M.S., Amaral, J. L.M.: A tool for node positioning analysis in wireless networks for industrial automation. In: XVIII Automation Brazilian Congress. Bonito, pp. 1521–1527, in portuguese (2010)
3. Moyne, J.R., Tilbury, D.M.: The emergence of industrial control, diagnostics, and safety data. Proc. IEEE **95**(1), 29–47 (2007)
4. Cannons, J., Milstein, L.B., Zeger, K.: An algorithm for wireless relay placement. IEEE Trans. Wirel. Commun. **8**(11), 5564–5574 (2006)

5. Coelho, P.H.G., Amaral, J.L.M., Amaral, J.F.M., Barreira, L.F.A., Barros, A.V.: Deploying nodes for industrial wireless networks by artificial immune systems techniques. In: 15th International Conference on Enterprise Information Systems, Angers, France (2013)
6. Gersho, A., Gray, R.M.: Vector quantization and signal compression. Kluwer Academic Publishers, Norwell (1992)
7. Hoffert, J., Klues, K., Orjih, O.: Configuring the IEEE 802.15.4 MAC Layer for Single-sink Wireless Sensor Network Applications, Technical report (2007). http://www.dre.vanderbilt.edu/~jhoffert/802_15_4_Eval_Report.pdf
8. Youssef, W., Younis, M.: Intelligent gateways placement for reduced data latency in wireless sensor networks. In: ICC 2007 International Conference on Communications, Glasgow, pp. 3805–3810 (2007)
9. Molina, G., Alba, E., Talbi, E.G.: Optimal sensor network layout using multi objective metaheuristics. J. Univers. Computer Sci. 15(15), 2549–2565 (2008)
10. Coelho, P.H.G., Amaral, J.L.M., Amaral, J.F.M.: Node positioning in industrial plants wireless networks. In: WES 2012 International Conference on Communications, Rio Grande, R.S., in Portuguese (2012)
11. Shi, Y., Jia, F., Hai-Tao, Y.: An improved router placement algorithm base on energy efficient strategy for wireless network. In: ISECS International Colloquium on Computing, Communication, Control and Management (CCCM 2009), pp. 421–423 (2009)
12. Silva, L.N.C.: Immune Engineering: Development and Application of Computational Tools Inspired by Artificial Immune Systems, Ph. D. thesis, State University of Campinas, Campinas, in Portuguese (2001)
13. Amaral, J.L.M.: Artificial Immune Systems Applied to Fault Detection, Ph. D. thesis, Pontifical Catholic University of Rio de Janeiro, Rio de Janeiro, in Portuguese (2006)
14. Jerne, N.K.: Towards a Network Theory of the Immune System. Ann. Immunol. (Inst. Pasteur) 125C, 373–389 (1974)
15. Howard, A., Mataric, M.J., Sukhatme, G.S.: Mobile sensor network deployment using potential fields: a distributed, scalable solution to the area coverage problem heuristics. In: Asama, H., Arai, T., Fukuda, T., Hasegawa, T. (eds.) DARS 2002, 6th International Symposium on Distributed Autonomous Robotics Systems, vol. 2002, pp. 299–308. Springer, Japan (2002)
16. Poduri, S., Pattem, S., Krishnamachari, B., Sukhatme, G.: Controlled Deployments of Sensor Networks. In Press (2006)

# Information Systems Analysis
# and Specification

# Performance Evaluation of Aspect-Oriented Programming Weavers

Michel S. Soares[1][✉], Marcelo A. Maia[2], and Rodrigo F.G. Silva[2]

[1] Computing Department, Federal University of Sergipe, São Cristóvão, Brazil
mics.soares@gmail.com
[2] Computing Faculty, Federal University of Uberlândia, Uberlândia, Brazil

**Abstract.** Aspect-oriented programming (AOP) was proposed with the purpose of improving software modularization by treating crosscutting concerns. Since its introduction, there is no consensus about the impact on performance of the use of AOP techniques to deal with crosscutting concerns. This article explores further the evaluation of performance by proposing a systematic literature review to find out how performance is affected by the introduction of aspects. Then, an experiment is performed to find results about the performance of AOP and weavers. This experiment showed the assessment of several versions of an application. According to this study, the difference concerning resource consumption through variation of weavers can be considered irrelevant considering web applications.

**Keywords:** Aspect-oriented programming · Systematic literature review · Crosscuting concerns · Performance · MVC framework

## 1 Introduction

Aspect Oriented Programming (AOP) [1] was proposed as an attempt to deal with crosscutting concerns aiming to improve modularization. AOP has gained importance since its introduction to implement crosscutting concerns, with varying degree of success [2–5]. Within AOP, crosscutting concerns are implemented as aspects and are further weaved into code. The way aspects are weaved into code may affect performance as the weaving process introduces new code to the original programs.

The impact on performance, caused by AOP techniques, has motivated previous works in scientific literature. Liu [6] showed that the aspect-oriented approach does not have significant effect on performance, and that in some cases, aspect-oriented software even outperform the non-aspect one. Additionally, introduction of a large number of join points does not have significant effect on performance. Remko [7] assessed the performance effects between programs created by a weaver and a hand-coded version. This work came to the conclusion that simple advices give no real performance penalties, but the more sophisticated advices are, the slower they become. Kirsten [8] compared the four leading

© Springer International Publishing Switzerland 2015
J. Cordeiro et al. (Eds.): ICEIS 2014, LNBIP 227, pp. 187–203, 2015.
DOI: 10.1007/978-3-319-22348-3_11

AOP tools at the time (2004) and, when it comes to performance, he postulated that, in general, code with aspects performs similarly to that of a purely object-oriented solution, where the crosscutting code is scattered throughout the system.

The use of AOP to implement crosscutting concerns and its impact on performance is the motivation for this study. First, a systematic literature review is performed. The goal of this systematic review is to understand the extent of the impact of AOP on the performance of software systems, if there is an impact. The purpose of the experiment described following the review is to find results about performance and aspect-oriented implementations. Considering the fact that AOP techniques add additional complexity in software in order to treat cross-cutting concerns, this addition can generate an overhead in software execution, leading to impact on performance.

Considered factors or independent variables for evaluating performance in AOP software include the weaver, the type of weaving, the type of advice, the number of join points, the size measured in lines of code, and the number of classes to be loaded in the load-time weaving process. In order to evaluate the impact of AOP techniques on performance, this article proposes the evaluation of a major factor that may impact these techniques: the type of weaving. The factors *number of lines of code*, *types of advices*, *number of joinpoints* and *number of classes* to be loaded during load-time weaving will be considered in future research. Therefore, the hypotheses of this article is that changing the weaving process sensitize the outcomes.

## 2 Protocol for Systematic Review

The main question that motivated the systematic literature review [9] we conducted in this paper is: *Does the use of aspect-oriented techniques to implement crosscutting concerns impact software performance ?* A derived research question is *"If the impact exists, how meaningful is it ?"*. The answer to both questions could help developers to reason about the feasibility of the use of AOP techniques to handle crosscutting concerns on architectures where performance is itself a concern. The systematic review started by searching in a number of software engineering conferences and journals. The search was performed considering publications in the past 6 years. The chosen conferences were: AOSD (International Conference on Aspect-Oriented Software Development) and ICSE (International Conference on Software Engineering). The chosen journals were: JSS (Journal of Systems and Software), IST (Information and Software Technology), SCP (Science of Computer Programming), TSE IEEE (IEEE Transactions on Software Engineering), TOSEM (ACM Transactions on Software Engineering Methodology). ENTCS (Electronic Notes in Theoretical Computer Science), which can be considered a series, was also included.

The search string was ("Aspect-oriented programming" AND "performance"). The search has retrieved 338 papers. From these 338 papers, a subselection has been made with the purpose of separating those relating AOP with

**Table 1.** Search results and selected papers.

| Publication | Retrieved papers | Relevant papers | Selected papers | Data source |
|---|---|---|---|---|
| JSS | 38 | 2 | 1 | ScienceDirect |
| IST | 32 | 10 | 5 | ScienceDirect |
| SCP | 32 | 2 | 1 | ScienceDirect |
| TSE | 1 | 1 | 1 | IEEExplorer |
| TOSEM | 21 | 3 | 1 | ACM Digital Library |
| ENTCS | 26 | 3 | 1 | ScienceDirect |
| AOSD | 127 | 9 | 3 | ACM Digital Library |
| ICSE | 61 | 2 | 2 | ACM Digital Library |
| Total | 338 | 32 | 15 | |

**Table 2.** Selected papers.

| | Venue/year | Reference |
|---|---|---|
| 1 | ICSE/07 | [10] |
| 2 | SCP/08 | [11] |
| 3 | IST/09 | [12] |
| 4 | ENTCS/09 | [13] |
| 5 | IST/09 | [14] |
| 6 | ICSE/09 | [15] |
| 7 | AOSD/09 | [16] |
| 8 | JSS/10 | [17] |
| 9 | ACM/10 | [18] |
| 10 | IST/10 | [19] |
| 11 | AOSD/10 | [20] |
| 12 | IST/10 | [21] |
| 13 | AOSD/10 | [22] |
| 14 | IEEE/12 | [4] |
| 15 | IST/12 | [23] |

any performance metrics. In a first step, 32 papers were selected and classified as relevant. For the first selection, the title, the keywords and the abstract were read. If the subject was pertinent to AOP and performance, the introduction and the conclusion were read as well. In case of doubt about the relevance of the paper, specific keywords were searched in the paper, such as *aspect, crosscutting* and *performance*. There were also relevant papers which used other terms, including *cost, payload* and *overhead* when considering assessment of performance of some AOP technique, and in those cases, they were selected too.

In a second step, of the 32 relevant papers, only those ones which assess the performance of implementation of some crosscutting concern were selected to be fully read. As a result, 15 papers were selected in total. Several types of concerns have been classified by the papers as crosscutting concerns, even though some of them were domain specific. However, papers which had crosscutting concerns implemented through some AOP technique but which did not consider any assessment of the used technique(s), or this assessment was incomplete, were discarded. The summary of the filtering process can be seen in Table 1 and the final selection of papers is presented in Table 2.

## 3   Systematic Review Results

All 15 selected papers were fully read for the evaluation. The selected papers were evaluated based on two sets of criteria: Application Type and Performance.

### 3.1   Application Type Criteria

The first set of criteria concerns about Application Type and encompass the following metrics: number of assessed studies, lines of code (size, in LOCs), original programming language (Original PL), aspect programming language (Aspect PL) and application domain.

The application type is related to the type of application of the case studies or experiments which have been assessed by the papers. The following types were retrieved from the papers: Middleware, Web Service, Embedded, Platform, System or Application, Language or Extension (Language) and Framework. Cases where their case studies were described as Monitoring Systems were classified as System or Application. Papers which did not mention the application type of their experiments have been classified under the closest definition of these ones already mentioned. The number of assessed studies indicates only those studies that were implemented by some AOP technique and were assessed by some kind of metric.

The application domain includes: e-commerce, industrial application, Office, Bank and Generic. Cases where there is no specific domain, for example a toolkit or a language extension, were classified as Generic. Some papers, mostly in application type, did not mention the application domain and were also classified by proximity.

The summary of studies is presented in Table 3. Cases where no metric was presented or in which it was not possible to identify were classified as not available (NA).

### 3.2   Performance Criteria

The second set of criteria concerns *Performance*. Four metrics were extracted from the papers: weaving type, implemented crosscutting concerns, used performance method, and performance overhead.

**Table 3.** Summary of studies.

| Type | Article | Studies | Size | Original PL | Aspect PL | Domain |
|---|---|---|---|---|---|---|
| Middleware | [17] | 2 | NA | | AspectJ | Generic |
| | [15] | 3 | 12.7KLOC, 113Kb, 190Kb | Java | FlexSync | Industrial |
| Embedded | [13] | 1 | NA | | ObjectTeams, Java | |
| | [23] | 2 | NA | GPL | NA | |
| System or Application | [21] | 1 | NA | | JBoss AOP | Generic |
| | [14] | | | | AspectJ | Office |
| | [16] | 1 | 46KLOC | Java | Java, AspectJ | Generic |
| | [11] | 1 | NA | | KALA | Bank |
| | [10] | | | | AspectJ, JBoss AOP | Industrial |
| | [4] | 3 | 1.6KLOC, 13.9KLOC, 51.6KLOC | C++ | AspectC++ | |
| Language | [20] | 1 | 118KLOC | JavaScript | AspectScript | Generic |
| | [18] | 2 | | Java | NA | Industrial |
| Framework | [22] | 1 | NA | Java | Compatible with AspectJ | Generic |
| Platform | [12] | | | | NA | NA | E-commerce |
| Web Service | [19] | | | Java | AspectJ | |

The weaving type indicates the type of weaving performed by the studies in the papers. Two main kinds were considered: *Compile-time* and *Runtime weaving*.

Several kinds of crosscutting concerns were retrieved from the papers. There were cases where the crosscutting concerns were domain specific. Papers which treated only one concern in the study prevailed, but there were cases where more than one concern was considered, one of them domain specific [4].

The performance methods retrieved were the measurements of running or execution time (ext), business operations per second (bos), average memory overhead (avmo), CPU usage (cpu), qualitative observation of the overall execution (obs), parsing time (pat), and average number of method calls per second (met). Some papers presented more than one assessed variable. In these cases, when there was performance reduction, the considered measurements were based on the worst case. Some cases related the performance overhead as negligible (negl).

The results of the performance assessment performed by the papers are presented in Table 4. In the Performance Overhead column, the "+" and the "−" signs means decrease and increase in performance, respectively. If a sign is followed by negl, it means that the paper reported a degradation or gain in performance, but this result is negligible according to the authors.

Table 4. Performance analysis of studies.

| Weaving | Article | Crosscutting concerns | Performance Method | Performance overhead |
|---|---|---|---|---|
| Run-time | [17] | Stylistic | ext, avmo | ext: -negl, avmo: +1.03x to 1.1x |
| | [15] | Synchronization | bos | negl |
| | [13] | Maintainability, Extensibility and Reusability | ext | -2x for 100 instances |
| | [21] | Reconfigurability | ext, cpu, avmo | ext: +1.1x to 1.22x, cpu: +NA, avmo: +NA |
| | [14] | Monitoring | Qualitative Observation | not observable |
| | [16] | Security | pat | +up to 1.16x |
| | [20] | Expressiveness | met, cpu | met: +up to 16.1x, cpu: negl |
| | [11] | Transaction Management | NA | + NA |
| Compile-time | [4] | Caching, CheckFwArgs, Excepter, Singleton, Tracing, CadTrace, FwErrs, FetTypeChkr, Timer, UnitCvrt, ViewCache, ErcTracing, QueryConfig, QueryPolicy | ext, avmo | ext: + up to 1.18x, avmo: + up to 1.15x |
| | [22] | Comunication between threads | ext | + factor up to 31.08x |
| | [19] | Device adaptation | ext | negl |
| Compile-time / runtime | [10] | Constraint validation | ext | + varies according to approach |
| Domain Specific | [18] | Cache | met | +1.015x |
| NA | [23] | Safety | NA | + NA |
| | [12] | Security | ext | + varies according to approach |

## 3.3 On the Target Applications

From the first set of criteria, related to *Application type*, it is possible to conclude that most papers, 10 out of 15, assessed only one study or experiment. However, only four of them showed the LOC or size of their assessed studies. The two studies that have evaluated more systems, evaluated three small-scale systems (at most 50KLOC or 190 Kb). The larger evaluated system had 118KLOC. One hypothesis for such lack of large scale studies is that AOP is not extensively adopted such as OOP or procedural programming. Therefore, the low adoption from the community restricts the availability of large systems for experimentation.

The prevailing application type was *System* or *Application*. That is reasonable to expect because in general this kind of applications are more frequent and more accessible. The prevailing application domain was *Industrial applications* followed by applications with no specific domain, hereby classified as Generic. We can observe that there is reasonable variability in terms of *Application Type* and *Application domain*. We could observe that in Middleware software the overhead was negligible. In the category *System* or *Application*, there is a tendency of more impact in the performance.

The LOC seems not to influence because the larger studies systems had negligible impact on execution time and CPU performance. The Application Domain also seems not to influence the performance because of the high variation in the results. The application domain did not present a clear influence in performance. The *Industrial* domain, which has the larger number of studies, had also presented negligible and positive impact in performance.

Finally, concerning the implemented crosscutting concerns in the applications, there was no prevailing concern in the studies, and surprisingly, none of the studies implemented common concerns such as Logging or Exception Handling. This can be an indicative that the studied cases were not representative in terms of typical aspect-oriented software.

## 3.4   On the Used Programming Languages

The prevailing original programming language was Java with 11 out of 15 studies and the prevailing aspect programming language was AspectJ with 6 out of 15 studies. JBoss AOP was present only in two cases, and Spring AOP was not used in any of them. Considering the impact of the programming language in performance, we can observe that the original programming language that has significant number of studies is Java, but there was no clear indication that Java is an influence factor. In the same way, AspectJ, which is the prevailing aspect language, has shown no direct influence on the performance because it presented either negligible or positive impact in performance. Although only two studies were carried out with JBoss AOP, both studies have shown a positive impact in performance.

## 3.5   On the Type of Weaving

From the second set of criteria, it is possible to conclude that run-time is the most common weaving type process presented by papers in the experiments. One of the reasons for this choice, instead of compile-time weaving, is the fact that runtime weaving allows aspects to be added to the base program dynamically, which is better for a context-aware adaptation of the applications [13]. Some papers not only used the runtime weaving process but also extended it to adequate the process to their studies. Also concerning the weaving process, the papers in general postulated that runtime weaving requires more effort at runtime, impacting on performance, but no proofs about this assumption were found in this research.

### 3.6   On the Experimental Setting of Reviewed Papers

Papers assessed their experiments in different ways, but the prevailing performance metric was measurement of execution time (ext). The performance overhead varied according to a set of variables such as the used approach, implemented concern, the aspect programming language, weaving type process and the used aspect weaver.

The workload is strongly influenced by the target application, which defines several other sub-factors: the kind of join points, pointcuts and advices, the ratio of occurrence of AOP constructs and the other non-AOP constructs, the requirement of the application for specific type of weaving. Considering the space for combination of levels for these factors, it is challenging (if not impossible) to find a real world application (or a set of them) that can have all the possible levels. Therefore, an alternative could be the design of a synthetic application that could be use as a benchmark for performance evaluation of AOP techniques. This benchmark would need to be meaningful to mimic real world scenarios and would need to be comprehensive to guarantee that all important factors and their respective levels would be considered.

## 4   Experimental Settings

In order to produce further evidences on the impact of the type of weavers in the performance of AOP programs, we decided to conduct our own experiment. This section explains the conditions of the experiment and how the experiment was executed. The section is organized as follows. In Subsect. 4.1 the environment in which the experiment was performed is explained. Subsection 4.2 shows the versions of the case study. Subsection 4.3 explains about the scenario of the experiment. Subsection 4.4 shows the plan of the experiment designed for executing the tests.

### 4.1   Environment

The original software in which the experiment was performed is a web application system called SIGE. Designed in 2011, it has the purpose of automating the management of information of academic and administrative units at Federal University of Uberlândia. The System was developed in Java. SIGE uses two frameworks, Struts (version 2.3.3) and Spring (version 3.0.0). SIGE also access a DB2 database.

The crosscutting concern implemented by AOP is Logging, responsible for logging some methods in service and DAO layers of the system for purposes of auditing. In order to perform the experiment, a copy of the last version of SIGE was produced and named as version V0. Version V0 has as size 297.915 LOC, considering files of the following extensions: java, jsp, js, html, xml and css. From version V0, other versions were built. This work adopted the same idea of inheritance from Object Orientation for extended versions. Each extended versions preserve the same properties of the parents and override the interested properties so the proposed factors could be measured and analyzed.

Three weaving processes were considered regarding AOP. These are compile-time weaving, load-time weaving, and runtime weaving. The class responsible for implementing the Logging aspect is the AspectProfiler class. The adopted style for enabling AOP into the class was the AspectJ annotation Style, provided by the Spring AOP AspectJ support. Each method is composed of an advice annotation where a *pointcut* expression is used to match the join points, which is a method execution for all expressions. Despite the fact that AspectJ has several definitions for join points, those used in the AspectProfiler class always represent a method execution because of the Spring AOP framework restriction which limits join points to be only method executions. This kind of join point was adopted as default in order to enable comparisons among the different considered weavers. This class was the only class used to implement the Logging aspect and had its content varied in versions, according to the purpose of each version. Each phase of the experiment explains how this content was modified for its purposes.

Two types of invocations were considered to perform the experiment, internal and external invocations. External invocations are generated by the JMeter[1] tool while internal invocations are generated by a JUnit class, which are explained in details in Sect. 4.4.

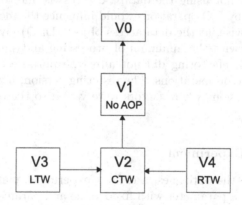

**Fig. 1.** Versions for the case study.

Concerning system settings, all tests were executed under the same hardware and software conditions. The hardware was composed of one notebook with Intel Core i5-2410M 2.30 GHz processor and 4 GB of RAM memory running Ubuntu 12.04 LTS operational system. The used Java version was 1.7.0. Before all test measurements, memory and swap conditions were verified through Ubuntu System Monitor and were always under 55 % and 2 % respectively. The running processes during applications were, besides regular Ubuntu processes, Eclipse, System Monitor, LibreOffice calc, VisualVM and, in specific stages, JMeter.

---

[1] https://jmeter.apache.org/.

Despite the fact that only 4 assessed versions of the experiment access the database, a running DB2 database was necessary for the application context to run. The version of the running DB2 database was 9.7. Network was disabled during tests in order to avoid CPU interruptions.

## 4.2   Versions

Figure 1 shows the design of proposed versions. The image is divided into versions that will be compared to each other. It contains the original version (version V0), one version with no AOP involved (version V1) and three other versions weaved by three different weaving processes, which are compile-time weaving (CTW), load-time weaving (LTW) and runtime weaving (RTW), respectively versions V2, V3 and V4.

## 4.3   Scenario

The chosen scenario for the experiment was the user authentication scenario. This scenario was chosen because it is composed of several method calls in different system layers and it does not present complex business rules.

The scenario was refactored so that the invocations do not access the database. The reason for not using the database access is due to the fact that the resources consumed by I/O operations would influence the measurements of the logging aspect. Likewise, at the data access object (DAO) layer, all methods of the scenario returns with the minimum of processing and simulate a successful authentication. This refactoring did not alter the purpose of the methods or the scenario sequence of operations. The resulting version, named V1, was used to build all other versions where factors were varied so the outcomes could be measured.

## 4.4   Plan of the Experiment

In order to measure the outcomes, a default experiment plan was made. This plan is composed by a parameter with fixed value and parameters with variable values, which are set in each system version. The parameter with fixed value is the number of test executions, which defines how many times the test is executed to generate outcomes data and was set to 15.

One of the parameters with variable value is the *loopCount* variable, present in the JUnit test class for internal invocations and configured in the JMeter experiment plan for external invocations. The loop count defines how many times each internal invocations or HTTP request is executed on the scenario in a test. It was initially set to 10.000. The criteria to choose is because this number should be high enough to emphasize the small impact on performance caused by some interested factor, but low enough to allow the assessment of the set of invocations in an acceptable time. From a set of considered options, which were 1, 10, 100, 1.000, 10.000 and 100.000, the number 10.000 was the best choice for versions with disabled database and which used internal invocations as default measuring method.

CPU, memory and time were measured in two forms, depending on the type of invocation. For internal invocations, the execution of each test is launched through Eclipse. A breakpoint is set at the beginning of test execution in JUnit test class, where the start method of StopWatch is invoked and starts time counting. This breakpoint is necessary for the process inspection through VisualVM tool. When the JUnit running thread stops at the breakpoint, VisualVM is configured to inspect only memory and CPU in the application process. After these steps, breakpoint is released, the process run and the current aspect mechanism perform over the scenario method executions. After the end of the process execution, StopWatch class calculate the elapsed time in milliseconds and shows it at Eclipse console while VisualVM generates the real time report of memory and CPU history. CPU and memory are manually retrieved and, the highest values of the graphics, respectively, in percentage and megabytes (MB), were always considered.

For external invocations, no breakpoint is necessary for VisualVM to inspect CPU and memory. After the launch of tomcat through Eclipse debug, VisualVM is capable of inspecting the running process of tomcat before the beginning of the invocations. After configuring VisualVM to inspect CPU and memory on tomcat process, the JMeter experiment plan is invoked. After the execution of the test, JMeter report provides the time report while CPU and memory are retrieved manually, as done for the internal invocations.

## 5  Design of the Experiment

The experiment plan was run in each phase with the proper parameters. This Section explains the design of the experiment, showing the phases, their details and purposes.

### 5.1  Versions of the Software

The purpose of this phase is the generation of versions containing different weaving processes and serves as template to be used for building the other versions. In this Section the building process of versions V1, V2, V3 and V4 is presented.

**Version V1.** The purpose of this version is to establish baselines of values related to the dependent variables to be compared with values obtained in other phases of the experiment.

**Version V2.** From version V1, version V2 was built. This version has the purpose of assessing the impact on performance by adopting the **compile-time weaving process**, provided by the AspectJ weaver. The results of this phase are compared to the results of version V1, this way it is possible to assess if the weaver AspectJ sensitizes the dependent variables through the compile-time weaving process. In this version all log generation messages were removed from the scenario methods. The weaver was provided by the plugin of the AspectJ Development Eclipse Tools. This plugin, when enabled, forces the project to re-compile, thus injecting the aspect code bytecodes to the classes at compile time.

The following parameters were set:

- Weaver: AspectJ compile-time weaver;
- Number of advices: 6;
- Type of advices: 2 before, 2 around, 2 after, having log messages invoked only on before advices;
- PointCut Expressions: interception of all methods present in service and DAO packages.

**Version V3.** From version V2, version V3 was built. This version has the purpose of assessing the impact on performance by adopting the **load-time weaving process**, provided by the AspectJ weaver. Like in version V2, the results of this phase are compared to the results of version V1 in order to verify if this weaver, using this weaving process, sensitizes the dependent variables. In this version, the AspectJ plugin, which is responsible for compiling the aspects, was disabled and the weaving type paremeter was overridden to the load-time weaving process. The load-time weaving process is used in the context of Spring Framework. AspectJ is responsible for weaving aspects into the application's class files as they are being loaded into JVM. From an aop.xml file created in META-INF folder, which was added to the build path of the project, with the necessary configuration to weave aspects of AspectProfiler class into the project classes, this file specifies the loading of two classes to the JVM, and one DAO class containing the methods of the scenario.

**Version V4.** From version V2, version V4 was built. This version has the purpose of assess the impact on performance by adopting the **runtime weaving process**, provided by the Spring AOP framework. Like in versions V3 and V2, the results of this phase are compared to the results of version V1 in order to verify if this weaver, using this weaving process, sensitizes the dependent variables. In this version, the AspectJ capability provided by the AspectJ plugin was disabled and the weaver overridden to Spring AOP.

This phase has the purpose of analyzing AOP together with two layers which impacts performance significantly, which are the chain of mechanisms present in the front end controller provided by the MVC framework, in this case Struts 2, and the access to the database, here represented by DB2.

Previous tests reported that the time spent to assess each external invocation of this version varied between 6000 and 7000 ms. The time consumed to assess the initial value for the loop count parameter, which is 10.000, would be impracticable, which addresses the loop count value to be overridden to a new value, for less. Besides this difficulty on measuring time, the maximum values of CPU and memory are manually selected on the chosen profiling tool, which is in this case VisualVM, and the higher this value, the higher the difficulty to select these maximums. However, in terms of assessing the impact on performance, the lower this value, the less the impact on performance would be noticed, which addressed this number to be 50.

# 6    Results

This Section presents the results of versions for each region of the map of versions for the proposed factors, as follows.

The weaver factor was varied in versions of the software. The values of the measures are shown in box plot graphs and grouped by dependent variable. In Figs. 2, 3 and 4 graphs are represented containing the consumption of time, CPU and memory for versions V1, V2, V3 and V4 respectively.

Results of versions V2, V3 and V4 were compared with results of version V1. Table 5 shows this comparison to the averages of the dependent variables.

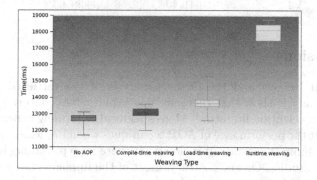

**Fig. 2.** Time consumption for versions V1, V2, V3 and V4.

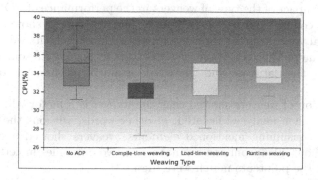

**Fig. 3.** CPU consumption for versions V1, V2, V3 and V4.

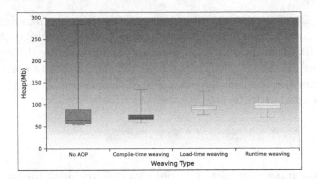

**Fig. 4.** Memory consumption for versions V1, V2, V3 and V4.

**Table 5.** Comparison between averages of dependent variables of versions V2, V3 and V4 with V1.

| Compared to V1 | Time(%) | CPU(%) | Memory(%) |
|---|---|---|---|
| V2 | +3, 41 | −8, 5 | +3, 24 |
| V3 | +7, 32 | −4, 56 | +30, 69 |
| V4 | +41, 40 | −2, 58 | +39, 93 |

## 7   Conclusions

The systematic review and the further analysis of the retrieved papers presented in this article show that there are few experiments concerning AOP and performance in scientific literature. More specifically, too few experiments were reported about the performance of AOP techniques when implementing crosscutting concerns. From the results, it is clear that there is no prevailing implemented concern in the studies. On the contrary, most of the implemented concerns were domain specific. Most papers postulated that runtime weaving requires more effort at run-time, impacting on performance. In order to produce further evidences on the impact of the type of weavers in the performance of AOP programs, we decided to conduct our own experiment. The experiment showed the assessment of several versions of an application, where measurements were made with and without the presence of heavy system layers in terms of resource consumption which are the database and the whole chain of mechanisms of the MVC framework.

The variation of weavers showed that the weaver is a factor which sensitizes performance. When analyzed isolated, in other words, without the presence of the resources consuming mentioned elements, weavers showed a performance variation of about 40 % from one to another in two outcomes in certain circumstances where the pointcuts match were high.

Results of this experiment have shown that, in general, in applications which have database calls and/or MVC frameworks, the impact on performance caused by AOP solely could be considered to be negligible. However, this impact could be meaningful for applications without these layers and where AOP would be widely used. According to this study, the difference concerning resource consumption through variation of weavers can be considered irrelevant considering common web applications, but nothing can be confirmed about embedded applications where resource consumption might be limited.

The analyzed crosscutting concern was Logging. However, the focus of the analysis was on the AOP interception mechanism of each tool and not in the AOP implementation of the crosscutting concern itself. The implementation through AOP of crosscutting concerns by frameworks such as Spring could be more studied and compared to manual implementations with regard to performance. Future works could also study the performance of AOP techniques for embedded applications, where hardware conditions are limited.

Threats to validity were considered as follows. The considered outcomes were measured through three different tools. Time outcome was provided by Stop-Watch class on internal invocations and displayed at Eclipse console, and by JMeter on external invocations, displayed on a summarized report. CPU and memory, however, were not provided directly by any tool. Differently from time, which could be measured in absolute values, CPU and memory varies during the tests. As VisualVM did not provide the average of each one in a time shift, the used metric for obtaining these values was a manually selection of the maximum values of the graphs generated by VisualVM for each one. Measurements where the maximum values were far higher from the average values represent a threat to validity, once that these top points could not represent the real behaviour of the outcomes related to the application. Besides, mistakes on manual selection could have influenced wrong results.

The external invocations generated by JMeter were configured to be sequential. Despite the fact that on real production environments calls to the application generate multiple threads working simultaneously, sequential calls were more proper for this experiment because they do not require a possible extra effort to be scheduled. Besides, in order to achieve a possible impact on performance, the number of calls needed to be high in most cases, considering that the impact provoked by AOP instrumentation was discrete. This high number of calls would not be supported by the web container in case these calls were generated by multiple threads simultaneously. This restriction addressed the experiment to be based on sequence calls only.

**Acknowledgements.** The authors would like to thank CAPES (www.capes.gov.br), CNPq grant 475519/2012-4, CNPq Grant 445500/2014-0, FAPEMIG Grant APQ-01589-11, and FAPEMIG grant APQ-2086/2011 for the financial support.

# References

1. Kiczales, G., Lamping, J., Mendhekar, A., Maeda, C., Lopes, C., Loingtier, J.-M., Irwin, J.: Aspect-oriented programming. In: Akşit, M., Matsuoka, S. (eds.) ECOOP 1997. LNCS, vol. 1241, pp. 220–242. Springer, Heidelberg (1997)

2. Ali, M.S., Ali, M., Babar, L., Chen, K.-J., Stol, A.: A systematic review of comparative evidence of aspect-oriented programming. Inf. Softw. Technol. **52**, 871–887 (2010)
3. Przybylek, A.: Impact of aspect-oriented programming on software modularity. In: Proceedings of the 15th European Conference on Software Maintenance and Reengineering, pp. 369–372 (2011)
4. Mortensen, M., Ghosh, S., Bieman, J.: Aspect-oriented refactoring of legacy applications: an evaluation. IEEE Trans. Softw. Eng. **38**(1), 118–140 (2012)
5. França, J.M.S., Soares, M.S.: A systematic review on evaluation of aspect oriented programming using software metrics. In: ICEIS 2012 - Proceedings of the 14th International Conference on Enterprise Information Systems, vol. 2, pp. 77–83 (2012)
6. Liu, W.-L., Lung, C.-H., Ajila, S.: Impact of aspect-oriented programming on software performance: a case study of leader/followers and half-sync/half-async architectures. In: Proceedings of the 2011 IEEE 35th Annual Computer Software and Applications Conference, COMPSAC 2011, pp. 662–667 (2011)
7. Bijker, R.: Performance effects of Aspect Oriented Programming. Twente University, Technical report, Enchede, The Netherlands (2005)
8. Kirsten, M.: AOP@Work: AOP tools comparison, Part 1: Language mechanisms, Technical report, IBM Developer Works (2005). http://www-128.ibm.com/developerworks/java/library/j-aopwork1/
9. Kitchenham, B.: Procedures for Performing Systematic Reviews, Keele university. Technical report tr/se-0401, Department of Computer Science, Keele University, UK (2004)
10. Froihofer, L., Glos, G., Osrael, J., Goeschka, K.M.: Overview and evaluation of constraint validation approaches in java. In: Proceedings of the 29th International Conference on Software Engineering, ICSE 2007, pp. 313–322, Washington (2007)
11. Fabry, J., Tanter, É., D'Hondt, T.: KALA: kernel aspect language for advanced transactions. Sci. Comput. Program. **71**(3), 165–180 (2008)
12. Georg, G., Ray, I., Anastasakis, K., Bordbar, B., Toahchoodee, M., Houmb, S.H.: An aspect-oriented methodology for designing secure applications. Inf. Softw. Technol. **51**(5), 846–864 (2009)
13. Hundt, C., Glesner, S.: Optimizing aspectual execution mechanisms for embedded applications. Electron. Notes Theor. Comput. Sci. **238**(2), 35–45 (2009)
14. Ganesan, D., Keuler, T., Nishimura, Y.: Architecture compliance checking at runtime. Inf. Softw. Technol. **51**(11), 1586–1600 (2009)
15. Zhang, C.: FlexSync: an aspect-oriented approach to java synchronization. In: Proceedings of the 31st International Conference on Software Engineering, ICSE 2009, pp. 375–385, Washington (2009)
16. Cannon, B., Wohlstadter, E.: Enforcing security for desktop clients using authority aspects. In: Proceedings of the 8th ACM International Conference on Aspect-Oriented Software Development, AOSD 2009, pp. 255–266. New York (2009)
17. Malek, S., Krishnan, H.R., Srinivasan, J.: Enhancing middleware support for architecture-based development through compositional weaving of styles. J. Syst. Softw. **83**(12), 2513–2527 (2010)
18. Dyer, R., Rajan, H.: Supporting dynamic aspect-oriented features. ACM Trans. Softw. Eng. Methodol. **20**(2), 1–34 (2010)
19. Ortiz, G., Prado, A.G.D.: Improving device-aware web services and their mobile clients through an aspect-oriented model-driven approach. Inf. Softw. Technol. **52**(10), 1080–1093 (2010)

20. Toledo, R., Leger, P., Tanter, E.: AspectScript: expressive aspects for the web. In: Proceedings of the 9th International Conference on Aspect-Oriented Software Development, AOSD 2010, pp. 13–24 (2010)
21. Janik, A., Zielinski, K.: AAOP-based dynamically reconfigurable monitoring system. Inf. Softw. Technol. **52**(4), 380–396 (2010)
22. Ansaloni, D., Binder, W., Villazón, A., Moret, P.: Parallel dynamic analysis on multicores with aspect-oriented programming. In: Proceedings of the 9th International Conference on Aspect-Oriented Software Development, AOSD 2010, pp. 1–12 (2010)
23. de Roo, A., Sozer, H., Aksit, M.: Verification and analysis of domain-specific models of physical characteristics in embedded control software. Inf. Softw. Technol. **54**(12), 1432–1453 (2012)

# ABOR: An Automatic Framework for Buffer Overflow Removal in C/C++ Programs

Sun Ding[1(⊠)], Hee Beng Kuan Tan[1], and Hongyu Zhang[2]

[1] School of Electrical and Electronic Engineering,
Nanyang Technological University, Singapore city, Singapore
{ding0037, ibktan}@ntu.edu.sg
[2] School of Software, Tsinghua University, Beijing, China
hongyu@tsinghua.edu.cn

**Abstract.** Buffer overflow vulnerability is one of the commonly found significant security vulnerabilities. This vulnerability may occur if a program does not sufficiently prevent input from exceeding intended size and accessing unintended memory locations. Researchers have put effort in different directions to address this vulnerability. How, authorized reports and data showed that as more sophisticated attack vectors are being discovered, efforts on a single direction are not sufficient to resolve this critical issue well. In this paper, we characterize buffer overflow vulnerability in four patterns and propose ABOR, a framework to remove buffer overflow vulnerabilities from source code automatically. It only patches identified code segments, which means it is an optimized solution that eliminates buffer overflows at the maximum while adds runtime overhead at the minimum. We have implemented the proposed approach and evaluated ABOR over a set of real world C/C++ applications. The results prove ABOR's effectiveness in practice.

**Keywords:** Buffer overflow · Static analysis · Automatic bug fixing · Security vulnerability

## 1 Introduction

Buffer overflow in C/C++ is still ranked as one of the major security vulnerabilities [1], though it has been 20 years since this vulnerability was first exploited. This problem has never been fully resolved and has caused enormous losses due to information leakage or customer dissatisfaction [1].

To mitigate the threats of buffer overflow attacks, a number of approaches have been proposed. Existing approaches and tools focus mainly on three directions [2]:

- Prevent buffer overflow attacks by creating a run-time environment, like a sandbox, so that taint input could not directly affect certain key memory locations;
- Detect buffer overflows in programs by applying program analysis techniques to analyze source code;
- Transform the original program by adding additional verification code or external annotations.

© Springer International Publishing Switzerland 2015
J. Cordeiro et al. (Eds.): ICEIS 2014, LNBIP 227, pp. 204–221, 2015.
DOI: 10.1007/978-3-319-22348-3_12

For approaches in the first direction, as modern programs are becoming more complex, it is difficult to develop a universal run-time defense [2]. For approaches in the second direction, even if buffer overflow vulnerabilities are detected, the vulnerable programs are still being used until new patches are released. For the third direction, though it is well-motivated to add extra validation to guard critical variables and operations, the existing approaches will add considerable runtime overhead. For example, a recent novel approach that adds extra bounds checking for every pointer may increase the runtime overhead by 67 % on average [3].

We noticed though none of the existing methods can resolve the problem fully, they share many commonalities and also have differences. In this paper, we first integrate existing methods and characterize buffer overflow vulnerability in the form of four patterns. We then propose a framework—ABOR that combines detection and removal techniques together to improve the state-of-the-art. ABOR iteratively detects and removes buffer overflows in a path-sensitive manner, until all the detected vulnerabilities are eliminated. Unlike the related methods [3–6], ABOR only patches identified code segments; thus it can eliminate buffer overflows while keeping a minimum runtime overhead.

We have evaluated the proposed approach on a set of benchmarks and three industrial C/C++ applications. The results show that the proposed approach is effective. First it can remove all the detected buffer overflow vulnerabilities in the studied subjects. Second we also compare ABOR with methods that focus on buffer overflow removal. On average, it removes 58.28 % more vulnerabilities than methods that apply a straight-forward "search and replace" strategy; it inserted 72.06 % fewer predicates than a customized bounds checker.

The contribution of the paper is as following:

- The proposed approach integrates and extends existing techniques to remove buffer overflows automatically in a path-sensitive manner.
- The proposed approach guarantees a high removal accuracy while could keep a low runtime overhead.
- The proposed approach contains an exhaustive lookup table that covers most of the common buffer overflow vulnerabilities.

The paper is organized as follows. Section 2 provides background on buffer overflows vulnerability. Section 3 covers the proposed approach that detects buffer overflows and removes detected vulnerability automatically. Section 4 evaluates the proposed approach and Sect. 5 reviews the related techniques that mitigate buffer overflow attacks. Section 6 concludes the paper.

## 2 Background

In this section, we give background information about buffer overflow vulnerability and attack. We also introduce a collection of rules for preventing such attacks.

Buffer overflow based attacks usually share a lot in common: they occur anytime when a program fails to prevent input from exceeding intended buffer size(s) and accessing critical memory locations. The attacker usually starts with the following attempts [1, 7]: they first exploit a memory location in the code segment that stores operations accessing memory without proper boundary protection. For example, a piece of code allows writing arbitrary length of user input to memory. Then they Locate a desired memory location in data segment that stores (a) an important local variable or (b) an address that is about to be loaded into the CPU's Extended instruction Counter (EIP register).

Attackers attempt to calculate the distance between the above two memory locations. Once such locations and distance are discovered, attackers construct a piece of data of length $(x1 + x2)$. The first x1 bytes of data can be any characters and is used to fill in the gap between the exploited location and the desired location. The second $x2$ bytes of data is the attacking code which could be (a) an operation overwriting a local variable, (b) a piece of shell script hijacking the system or (c) a handle redirecting to a malicious procedure.

Therefore, to prevent buffer overflow attack, it is necessary to ensure buffer writing operations are accessible only after proper validations.

Figure 1 shows an example of one buffer overflow vulnerability. For the sample procedure _encode, node s1 uses the C string function *strcpy* to copy a bulk of data to a destination buffer. Such a function call is vulnerable because *strcpy* does not have any built-in mechanism that prevents over-sized data from being written to the destination buffer. And before node s1, there is no explicit validation to constraint the relationship between the pvpbuf's size and req_bytes's length. At node14, the variable req_bytes is defined as an array length of 1024 and it receives a bulk of data size of 1024 from user input via the command-line. Along the path (n9, n10, n11, n12, n13, n14, n15, n16, s1), the variable *pvpbuf* is defined as an array size of *c2*. However there is no validation to

**Fig. 1.** A sample code with exploited buffer overflow vulnerability.

ensure *c2* is larger than 1024, in order to prevent pvpbuf being overwritten. Therefore the system running this procedure *_encode* becomes vulnerable due to the existence of (n9, n10, n11, n12, n13, n14, n15, n16, s1).

## 3  The Proposed Approach

In this paper, we propose Automatic Buffer Overflow Repairing (ABOR), a framework that integrates and extends existing techniques to resolve the buffer overflow vulnerabilities in a given program automatically. Figure 2 demonstrates the overall structure of the framework. ABOR consists of two modules: vulnerability detection and vulnerability removal. ABOR works in an iterative way: once the vulnerability detection module captures a vulnerable code segment, the segment is fed to the removal module; the fixed segment will be patched back to the original program. ABOR repeats the above procedure until the program is buffer-overflow-free. In this section, we introduce the two modules of ABOR in detail.

### 3.1  Buffer Overflow Patterns

We first review some basic definitions of static analysis [8, 9]. A control flow graph (**CFG**) for a procedure is a graph that visually presents the control flow among program statements. A **path** is one single trace of executing a sequential of program statements. A variable in a program is called an **input variable** if it is not defined in the program solely from constants and variables. An abstract syntax tree (**AST**) is a tree structure that represents the abstract syntax of source code written in a particular programming language. We call a program operation that may cause potential buffer overflows as a buffer overflow sensitive sink (**bo-sensitive sink**). In this paper, we shorten the name "bo-sensitive sink" to **sink**. The node that contains a sink is called a sink node.

There are many methods to protect sinks from being exploited [10–14]. One general way is to add extra protection constraints to protect sinks [2]. After a careful review, we collect a list of common sinks and the corresponding protection constraints. We characterize them in a form of four patterns:

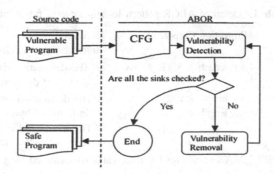

**Fig. 2.** Overview of ABOR.

(1) **Pattern#1:** A statement is a bo-sensitive sink when it defines or updates a destination buffer with an input from either (1) a C stream input function which is declared in < *stdio.h* >, or (2) a C ++ input[a] function inherited from the base class *istream*. The protection constraint shall ensure the length of the destination buffer is not smaller than the input data.

(2) **Pattern#2:** A statement that copies/moves the content a block of memory to another block of memory is a bo-sensitive sink. The protection constraint shall ensure that the copied/moved data is not larger than the length of the destination memory block.

(3) **Pattern#3:** A statement is a bo-sensitive sink when it calls a C stream output function when (1) this function is declared in < *stdio.h* > ; or (2) this function contains a format string that mismatches its corresponding output data; or (3) the function's output is data dependent on its parameters [12]. The protection constraint shall ensure that:

- the output data should not contain any string derived from the prototype [15]: *%[flags][width][.precision][length]specifier;*
- or all the character "%" in the output data has been encoded in a backslash escape style, such as "\%".

(4) **Pattern#4:** A statement other than the above cases but referencing a pointer or array is a bo-sensitive sink. Before accessing this statement, there should be a protection constraint to do boundary checking for this pointer or array.

We use the above four patterns as a guideline to construct the buffer overflow detection and removal modules of ABOR. In order to specify these cases clearly, we use metadata to describe them exhaustively at the AST level. The metadata is maintained in Table 1 (Here we only show a fragment of Table 1; the full table is presented on our website). Each row in Table 1 stands for a concrete buffer overflow case. The column *Sink* lists the AST structure of sinks. The column *Protection Constraint* specifies the AST structure of the constraint which could prevent the sinks being exploited. Additionally, in order to concrete the protection constraints ABOR needs to substitute in constants, local variables, expressions, and also two more critical data structures: the length of a buffer and the index of a buffer.

**Table 1.** Detail of ABOR pattern lookup table (a fragment).

| Pattern | Sink | Protection Constraint | Required Intermediate Variable |
|---|---|---|---|
| 1 | gets(dst) | dst_length ≥ SIZE_MAX[a] | /*The destination buffer dst's length (bytes).*/ dst_length |
| 2 | memcpy (dst, src, t) | dst_length ≥ t; src_length ≥ t; | //The destination buffer dst's length, in terms of bytes. dst_length, //The source buffer src's length, in terms of bytes. src_length |

[a]SIZE_MAX stands for the max value of unsigned long

In C/C++, there is no universal way to retrieve a buffer's length and index easily. To resolve this, ABOR creates intermediate variables to represent them. In Table 1, the last column *Required Intermediate Variable* records the required intermediate variables for each constraint.

## 3.2  Buffer Overflow Detection

Among the existing detection methods, approaches working in a path sensitive manner offer higher accuracy because they target at modeling the runtime behavior for each execution path: for each path, path sensitive approaches eventually generate a path constraint to reflect the relationship between the external input and target buffer, and the path's vulnerability is verified through validating the generated path constraint.

In the current implementation of ABOR, we modified a recent buffer overflow detection method called Marple [16] and integrated it into ABOR. We chose Marple mainly because it detects buffer overflows in a path sensitive manner, which offers high precision.

Marple maintained a lookup table to store the common bo-sensitive sinks' syntax structure. For each recognized bo-sensitive sink node and the path passing through the sink node, Marple generates an initial constraint, called query and backward propagates the query along the path. The constraint will be updated through symbolic execution when encountering nodes that could affect the data flow information related to the constraint. Once the constraint is updated, Marple tries to validate it by invoking its theorem prover. If it is proved the constraint is unsatisfiable, Marple concludes this path buffer-overflow-vulnerable. Figure 3 demonstrates how ABOR integrates and extends Marple:

(1)  ABOR replaces Marple's lookup table with Table 1. We enforce Marple to search for the syntax structures listed in the column Sink of Table 1. Additionally, Marple will raise a query based on the column Protection Constraint.

(2)  ABOR uses a depth-first search to traverse a given procedure's control flow graph: each branch will be traversed once. If a bo-sensitive sink is found, the

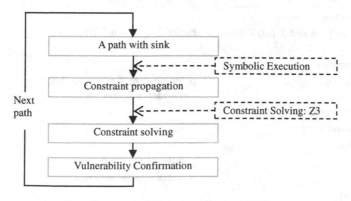

**Fig. 3.** Vulnerability detection in ABOR.

segment starting from the sink back to the procedure entry will be constructed to be a set of paths and each path will be fed to Marple for processing.

(3) ABOR replaces Marple's constraint solver with Z3 (Z3, 2013), a latest SMT solver from Microsoft with strong solvability.

(4) If one path is identified vulnerable, ABOR records the sub-path that causes the vulnerability or infeasibility [16]. Later, paths containing any of such sub-paths will not be examined.

(5) We follow the way Marple handles loop structures: we treat a loop structure as a unit and try to compute each loop's impact on the propagating constraint, if and only if such impact is linear.

We illustrate the above procedure with an example. In Table 4, s1 is a sink node. Therefore, Marple raises a constraint as $pvpbuf\_length \geq req\_bytes\_length$. It propagates backward along the paths that pass through s1 and tries to evaluate the constraint.

For example, along the path (n1, n2, n3, n4, n5, n6, n7, n9, n10, n11, n12, n9, n13, n14, n15, n16, s1), the constraint is updated at node n13 and becomes $c2 \geq 1024$. The variable $c2$ is affected by the loop [n9, n10, n11, n12, n9]. The variable $c2$ is used in the loop, and it is data dependent on the input–ADDRSIZE. There exists a counterexample to violate the constraint $c2 \geq 1024$. So this path is identified as being vulnerable. The method introduced in Sect. 3.3 will be used to remove this vulnerability.

### 3.3    Buffer Overflow Removal

The removal module takes an identified vulnerable path, analyzes the sink's AST and picks the corresponding constraint to protect the sink. The main challenge is to concrete the selected protection constraint into valid C ++ code.

ABOR propagates backward along the given path to enable the intermediate variables simulating their semantics. It maintains Table 2 to assist this propagation.

**Table 2.** Update intermediate variable during propagation.

| Syntax Structure | Update Operation |
| --- | --- |
| Buffer definition | |
| •buffer = new *wildcard* T [n]; T buffer [n]; | buffer_length = n * sizeof(T); |
| Buffer referencing | |
| •T * p = buffer; | p_length = buffer_length; && p_index = buffer_index; |
| Array index subscription | |
| •buffer[i] = *wildcard* | buffer_index = i; |
| Pointer arithmetic | |
| •p ++; p–; | p_index ++; p_index–; |
| •p = p+n; | p_index = p_index +n; |
| Free memory | |
| •free (p); delete [] p; | p_length = 0; p_index = NULL; |

In Table 2, the column *Syntax Structure* stands for the AST structure ABOR searches for during the propagation. The column *Update Operation* stands for how ABOR updates the corresponding intermediate variables.

The algorithm *removeVul* shown in Table 3 shows the workflow of ABOR's removal module. This algorithm takes an identified vulnerable path pth and its control flow graph $G$ as parameters. It inserts defensive code into $G$ to remove the vulnerability. The defensive code includes statements to update intermediate variables and a predicate to protect the sink. After this, *removeVul* concretes the protection constraint by substituting required local variables, expressions, constants and intermediate variables. The protection constraint is used to construct a predicate node. This predicate node wraps the sink node to provide protections. At last, *removeVul* converts the modified control flow graph back to source code. Therefore, the vulnerability caused by the sink has been removed by ABOR.

Table 4 presents a full example of using ABOR. The vulnerable program is in the left side column. The procedure of ABOR is as follows:

**Table 3.** Vulnerability removal in ABOR.

| Input: | $G$:  the CFG of a procedure;<br>*pth*: the identified vulnerable path<br>*sink*: the sink node |
|---|---|
| Global<br>     Variables: | $\delta$:  based on Table 1, $\delta$ is the protection constraint for the sink<br>$\{v\}$: based on Table 1, $\{v\}$ is the set of required intermediate variables<br>$G'$:  the CFG with the inserted defensive code |
| Output: | SrcFile': the converted program |

Algorithm *removeVul* ( $G$ , *pth* , *s* )
begin
1.   $\delta$ =NULL; $\{v\}$=$\varnothing$; $G'$=$G$;
2.   CFGNode cur_node = NULL; //the current traversed CFGNode
3.   <$\delta$, $\{v\}$> = LookupT1(*sink*); //this sub-procedure lookups in Table 1 and gets the metadata
4.   **for** (cur_node := **From** *sink* **To** *pth*'s entry node) **do**
       // update intermediate variables
5.    **for each** *v* in $\{v\}$ **do**
6.       Insert a CFGNode into $G'$ as the its Entry Node's   immediate post-dominator, to declare *v*
          and  initialize *v*=0;
7.       **if** ( LookupT2(cur_node , *v* ) ==TRUE) **then**
8.          /*this sub-procedure lookups in Table 2 to check   whether the current CFG Node
             contains AST matching the Syntax Structures in Table 2*/
             Insert a CFGNode into $G'$ as cur_node's immediate post- dominator, to perform the
             corresponding update operation in Table 2;
9.       **endIf**
10.   **endFor**
11.   **endFor**
12.   Concrete $\delta$ with required local variables, expressions, constants and intermediate variables in $\{v\}$;
13.   Use $\delta$ as condition to construct a predicate and insert this predicate node into $G'$ as *sink's*
       immediate dominator's immediate post-dominator;
14.   Place *sink* and the rest part of G' on the predicate's TRUE branch;
15.   Add an exception-handling node on the predicate's FALSE branch and link this FALSE branch to
       G's exit node.
16.   $G'$ $\rightarrow$ SrcFile' // convert $G'$ back to source code
End

**Table 4.** An example of applying ABOR.

| Vulnerable path | Sink | Pattern | Protection Constraint |
|---|---|---|---|
| (n1,n2,n3,n4,n5,n6,n7, n9,n10,n12,n13,n14,n15, n16,s1) | /*s1*/ strcpy(pvpbuf, req_bytes) | Pattern 1 | length(pvpbuf)≥length(req_bytes) |
| **Vulnerable Program** | **Repaired Program** | | |

| Vulnerable Program | Repaired Program |
|---|---|
| #define min_size 10; <br> #define max_size 1024; <br> /*addr is an existing array with the size of ADDRSIZE, <br> n2 and n16 are two basic blocks that are not related to pvpbuf and req_bytes*/ <br> int _encode (bool bslashmode, char *addr, int ADDRSIZE){ <br><br> /*n1*/  do{ <br> /*n2*/    BLOCK1; <br> /*n3*/  }while(...); <br><br> /*n4*/  int c1=0; int c2=0; <br> /*n5*/  int PSBUFSIZE= max_size; <br> /*n6*/  int *pvpbuf; <br> /*n7*/  if (bslashmode == TRUE){ <br> /*n8*/    pvpbuf = <br>             new int [PSBUFSIZE]; <br>         }else{ <br> /*n9*/    while(c1<ADDRSIZE){ <br> /*n10*/      if(addr[c1]!='#') <br> /*n11*/        c2++; <br> /*n12*/      c1++; <br>         } <br> /*n13*/  pvpbuf = new int [c2]; <br>         } <br> /*n14*/ char req_bytes[1024]; <br> /*n15*/ scanf("%1024s", req_bytes); <br> /*n16*/ BLOCK2; <br> /*s1*/  strcpy(pvpbuf,req_bytes); <br> }//END _encode | #define min_size 10; <br> #define max_size 1024; <br> /*addr is an existing array with the size of ADDRSIZE, <br> n2 and n16 are two basic blocks that are not related to pvpbuf and req_bytes*/ <br><br> int _encode (bool bslashmode, char *addr, int ADDRSIZE){ <br> /*p1*/  **int pvpbuf_temp0_size=0;** <br>         **int req_bytes0_size=0;** <br> /*n1*/  do{ <br> /*n2*/    BLOCK1; <br> /*n3*/  }while(...); <br> /*n4*/  int c1=0; int c2=0; <br> /*n5*/  int PSBUFSIZE= max_size; <br> /*n6*/  int *pvpbuf; <br> /*n7*/  if (bslashmode == TRUE){ <br> /*n8*/    pvpbuf = new int [PSBUFSIZE]; <br> /*p2*/  **pvpbuf_temp0_size=PSBUFSIZE;** <br>         }else{ <br> /*n9*/    while(c1<ADDRSIZE){ <br> /*n10*/      if(addr[c1]!='#') <br> /*n11*/        c2++; <br> /*n12*/      c1++; <br>         } <br> /*n13*/  pvpbuf = new int [c2]; <br> /*p3*/  **pvpbuf_temp0_size=c2;** <br>         } <br> /*n14*/ char req_bytes[1024]; <br> /*p4*/  **req_bytes_temp0_size=1024;** <br> /*n15*/ scanf("%1024s", req_bytes); <br> /*n16*/ BLOCK2; <br> /*p5* **if(pvpbuf_temp0_size >= req_bytes_temp0_size)** <br> /*s1*/    **strcpy(pvpbuf,req_bytes);** <br>         **else** <br> /*p6*/  **cerr<<"Attempt to cause buffer overflow** <br>             **reject";** <br> }//END _encode |

(1) ABOR's buffer overflow detection module finds that the path (n1, n2, n3, n4, n5, n6, n7, n9, n10, n11, n12, n13, n14, n15, n16, s1) is vulnerable. The path will be passed to *removeVul*.

(2) *removeVul* traverses the sink node s1's AST and determines that the first pattern shall be applied. The constraint is to validate that the length of *pvpbuf* is larger than or equal to the length of *req_bytes*.

(3) ABOR inserts one node p1 into the CFG and creates two intermediate variables with an initial value of 0: *pvpbuf_temp0_size* for the length of *pvpbuf* and *req_bytes_temp0_size* for the length of *req_bytes*. ABOR inserts another three

nodes p2, p3, and p4 into CFG, to manipulate the two intermediate variables to track the lengths of *pvpbuf* and *req_bytes*.

(4) ABOR constructs the protection constraint as *pvpbuf_temp0_size* ≥ *req_bytes_ temp0_size* and transforms the original program by wrapping statement s1 with statements p5, and p6.

(5) At last, ABOR converts the modified CFG back to source code, which is listed in the right side column of Table 4. Therefore, the vulnerability has been removed.

# 4   Evaluation

## 4.1   Experiment Design

We have implemented the proposed approach as a prototype system based on the CodeSurfer infrastructure [20]. The prototype has two parts: Program Analyzer and ABOR. The Program Analyzer receives C/C++ programs as input and utilizes Code-Surfer to build an inline inter-procedural CFG. This CFG is then sent to the ABOR for the vulnerability detection and removal.

Nine systems are selected to evaluate ABOR's performance: (a) six benchmark programs from Buffer Overflow Benchmark [17] and BugBench [18] are selected for the evaluation, namely Polymorph, Ncompress, Gzip, Bc, Wu-ftdp and Sendmail; and (b) three industrial C/C++ applications, namely RouterCore, PathFinder, and RFID-Scan, are selected. This is to further evaluate the effectiveness of the proposed approach on real-world programs.

For each system, we first run ABOR and then manually validate the results. The experiments are carried out on a desktop computer with Intel Duo E6750 2-core processor, 2.66 GHz, 4 GB memory and Windows XP system.

## 4.2   Experimental Results

### 4.2.1   System Performance

We evaluate ABOR's performance in terms of removal accuracy and time cost.

**Removal Accuracy.** For benchmark systems, the experimental results are shown in Table 5(a). A false negative case occurs if we manually find that the proposed method

**Table 5(a).**  Vulnerabilities removed by ABOR in benchmarks.

| System | KLOC | #Reported | #Repaired | #FP | #FN |
|---|---|---|---|---|---|
| Polymorph-0.4.0 | 1.7 | 15 | 15 | 0 | 0 |
| Ncompress-4.2.4 | 2.0 | 38 | 38 | 0 | 0 |
| Gzip-1.2.4 | 8.2 | 38 | 38 | 0 | 0 |
| Bc-1.06 | 17.7 | 245 | 245 | 0 | 0 |
| Wu- ftdp-2.6.2 | 0.4 | 13 | 13 | 0 | 0 |
| Sendmail-8.7.5 | 0.7 | 21 | 21 | 0 | 0 |
| Total | 30.7 | 370 | 370 | 0 | 0 |

**Table 5(b).** Vulnerabilities removed by ABOR in industrial programs.

| System | KLOC | #Detected | #Repaired | #Manual | #FP | #FN | ErrorRate(%) |
|---|---|---|---|---|---|---|---|
| RouterC ∼ | 137.15 | 217 | 217 | 309 | 3 | 41 | 14.23 |
| Pathfinder | 104.23 | 79 | 79 | 103 | 1 | 25 | 25.24 |
| RFIDscan | 219.36 | 312 | 312 | 406 | 2 | 96 | 24.13 |
| Total | 460.74 | 608 | 608 | 818 | 6 | 162 | 20.53 |

failed to remove one buffer overflow vulnerability. A false positive case occurs if we manually find the proposed method patched a piece of code that is actually buffer overflow free. We calculate the error rate of the proposed method by dividing the total number of vulnerabilities by the sum of the number of false positives and false negatives. The column *KLOC* stands for thousands of lines of code. The column *#Reported* records the real reported number of vulnerabilities while column *#Repaired* records the number of vulnerabilities removed by ABOR. The columns *#FP* and *#FN* stand for the numbers of false positives and false negatives respectively. For all the systems, the total number of reported buffer overflow vulnerabilities is 370. Therefore, ABOR can correctly remove all the vulnerabilities reported in previous work [17, 18].

For industrial programs, the results are shown in Table 5(b). The columns *KLOC*, *#Repaired*, *#FN* and *#FP* have the same meaning with Table 5(a). Additionally, the column *#Detected* stands for the number of detected vulnerabilities; and the column *#Manual* stands for the number of vulnerabilities discovered from manual investigations. The manual investigation double checked the detection result and analyzed the reason behind the cases that ABOR failed to proceed. As shown in Table 5(b), our approach detects 608 buffer overflow vulnerabilities and can successfully remove all of them. The results confirm the effectiveness of the proposed approach in removing buffer overflow vulnerabilities. However, due to implementation limitations, ABOR's detection modules didn't capture all the buffer overflow vulnerabilities in the industrial programs. On average, the error rate of our proposed method is 20.53 %, which consists of 19.80 % false negative cases and 0.73 % false positive cases. The details of the error cases are discussed in Sect. 4.2.3.

**Time Cost.** We measured the time performance of the proposed approach on both benchmarks and industrial programs. Table 6 records the time spent on processing each program individually. ABOR is scalable to process large programs. The time cost over the entire 9 systems is 4480 s, which is nearly 75 min. It is also discovered that a large amount of time is spent on vulnerability detection, which is 77.77 % of the total time. The vulnerability removal process is relatively lightweight, which costs only 22.23 % of the total time.

#### 4.2.2   Comparison

There are another two types of commonly used removal methods [2], which are "search & replace" and "bounds checker".

**Search and Replace.** The first category of methods replaces those common vulnerable C string functions with safe versions. If a program contains a large number of C string

**Table 6.** The time performance of ABOR.

| System | Total time (ms) | Detection time | | Removal time | |
|---|---|---|---|---|---|
| | | Time(ms) | % | Time (ms) | % |
| Polymorph | 95.25 | 81.91 | 85.99 | 13.34 | 14.01 |
| Ncompress | 214.32 | 160.81 | 75.03 | 53.51 | 24.98 |
| Gzip | 3698.16 | 2388.71 | 64.59 | 1309.45 | 35.41 |
| Bc | 149469.60 | 132026.90 | 88.33 | 17442.66 | 11.67 |
| Wu- ftdp | 221.13 | 185.33 | 83.81 | 35.80 | 16.19 |
| Sendmail | 134.82 | 103.76 | 76.96 | 31.06 | 23.04 |
| Routercore | 2446656.17 | 1781649.13 | 72.82 | 665007.07 | 27.18 |
| Pathfinder | 654987.43 | 564359.17 | 86.16 | 90628.22 | 13.84 |
| RFIDscan | 1224366.67 | 1003880.72 | 81.99 | 220485.98 | 18.01 |
| Total | 4479843.55 | 3484836.44 | 77.77 | 995007.09 | 22.23 |

functions, this category of methods can achieve a good effect. Additionally, they are straight-forward for implementation [19]. But as the fast development of attacking techniques based on buffer overflows [2], the "search and replace", methods will miss many buffer overflows in real code.

Bounds checker: The second category of methods chases high precision by inserting effective validation before every memory access. In practice, they are usually used by mission-critical systems [2, 3]. However, they normally bring in high runtime overhead as a number of inserted validations are redundant.

ABOR is the method that only patches identified detected vulnerable code segment in a path-sensitive way. So it guarantees the removal precision while it can keep a low runtime overhead. Using the same benchmarks and industrial programs, we compare ABOR with the other two main categories of removal methods.

First, we compare ABOR with the "search and replace" category. In Fig. 4(a), we compare ABOR with a recent "search and replace" method from Hafiz and Johnson [6]. It maintains a static database that stores common C/C++ vulnerable functions with their safe versions.

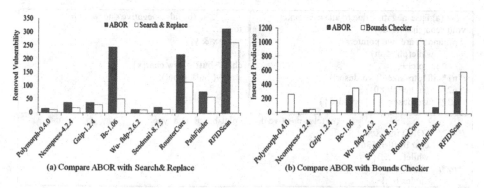

(a) Compare ABOR with Search& Replace          (b) Compare ABOR with Bounds Checker

**Fig. 4.** Compare ABOR with existing methods.

Figure 4(a) represents the histograms on the number of removed buffer overflows. It contains a pair of bars for each test case. The shadowed ones are for ABOR while the while bars are for the applied "search and replace" method. The Longer bars are better as they represent the higher removal precision. For the entire 9 systems, in total, the "search and replace" method removes 570 vulnerabilities while ABOR removes 978 vulnerabilities (41.72 % more). This is mainly because (1) many vulnerable codes are not covered by the static database of the "search and replace" method; (2) even after using a safe version of certain C/C++ functions, the vulnerabilities are not removed due to improper function parameters.

Second, we compare ABOR with the bounds checker" category. At the current stage, we implemented a customized bounds checker following a novel approach from Nagarakatte et al. [3]. It will insert predicates to protect every suspicious sink.

Figure 4(b) represents the histograms on the number of inserted predicates. As with more inserted predicates, runtime overhead will increase. Figure 4(b) contains a pair of bars for each test case. The shadowed ones are for ABOR while the white ones are for the applied bounds checker. Shorter bars are better as they represent the fewer number of inserted predicates. For the entire 9 systems, in total, the applied bounds checker inserts 3500 predicates. ABOR only patches confirmed sinks so it only inserts 978 predicates, which are 72.05 % less than the applied bounds checker.

Last but not least, though detection of buffer overflow is not a new research, till now, no approaches can detect buffer overflow with full coverage and precision. As the proposed approach uses these approaches, it is also limited by the accuracy of these approaches.

### 4.2.3    Discussion

It is also found that ABOR caused some false positive and false negative cases when processing the industrial programs. We further investigate these error cases and found the errors are mainly caused by implementation limitations. We categorize them into three types:

*Error 1* - inaccuracy from alias analysis: it is difficult to implement a comprehensive alias analysis (CodeSurfer, [20]). Table 7(a) shows a false-negative example from

**Table 7.** Examples of errors from processing the industrial programs.

| (a) false-negative due to aliased pointer | (b) false-negative due to loop |
|---|---|
| void send(char mode){<br>// ptr and slt are two pointers<br>    while(ptr < slt)<br>        ptr++;<br>/*n1*/ if(*ptr<sizeof(worduser)){<br>/*n2*/    cin.get(slt,80) ;<br>/*n3*/    worduser[*ptr] =mode; }} | for(......){<br>    x= x & y;<br>}<br>char * buff = new char[x];<br>strcpy( buff, input); |
| (c) false-positive due to plat-based data type | |
| /*n1*/  WORD index=0;<br>        char buff[65536];<br>        while(......){<br>/*n2*/    buff[index] = cin.get();<br>        index++;} | |

RouterCore that is caused by inaccurate pointer analysis. In the loop, pointer *ptr* is incremented by one in each iteration until it equals to the address of pointer *slt*. So after the loop, *ptr* and *slt* are actually aliased. However, currently we cannot detect such alias relationship. The node n2 could overwrite the value of *\*ptr*. Though node n1 does the boundary checking, it no longer protects node n3.

*Error 2*- inaccuracy from loop structure. So far only variables that are linearly updated within an iteration are handled by ABOR. Table 7(b) shows an example found in RouterCore. The variable $x$ is non-linearly updated by using a bitwise operation. Therefore the corresponding constraint, which compares the size between buff and input, is beyond the solvability of our current implementation.

*Error 3*- platform-based data types: the industrial programs PathFinder and RFIDScan both involve external data types of Microsoft Windows SDK (e.g., WORD, DWORD, DWORD_PTR, etc.). This requires extra implementations to interpret them. Additionally the value ranges of these data types specify implicit constraints. Table 7(c) shows a false-positive case from PathFinder. In this example, although accessing the buffer element via index at node n2 has no protection, there will be no buffer overflow vulnerability because index ranges only from 0 to 65535.

We summarize the error analysis in Table 8. In the future, further engineering effort is required to address these implementation difficulties.

# 5 Related Work

We reviewed the recent techniques in addressing the buffer overflow vulnerability. We categorize them into three types: buffer overflow detection, runtime defense and vulnerability removal.

## 5.1 Buffer Overflow Detection

Buffer overflow vulnerability could be effectively detected by well-organized program analysis. The analysis could be performed either on source code or binary code. The current detection methods can be classified into path-sensitive approaches and non-path-sensitive approaches.

Path-sensitive approaches analyze given paths and generate path constraints according to the properties that ensure the paths are not exploitable for any buffer overflow attack. The path constraints are extracted using symbolic evaluation through

**Table 8.** Accuracy and error analysis.

| System | Total error | E1 | | E2 | | E3 | |
|---|---|---|---|---|---|---|---|
| | | # | % | # | % | # | % |
| Routercore | 44 | 23 | 52.27 | 10 | 22.73 | 11 | 25.00 |
| Pathfinder | 26 | 16 | 61.54 | 0 | 0 | 10 | 38.47 |
| RFIDscan | 98 | 31 | 31.63 | 22 | 22.45 | 45 | 45.92 |
| Total | 168 | 70 | 41.67 | 32 | 19.05 | 66 | 39.29 |

either forward or backward propagation. A theorem prover or customized constraint solver is instrumented to evaluate the constraints. If a constraint is determined as unsolvable, the path is concluded as vulnerable. These methods pursue soundness and precision but usually include heavy overhead due to the use of symbolic evaluation. Typical examples include ARCHER [21], Marple [16], etc.

Non-path-sensitive approaches try to avoid complex analysis. They usually rely on general data flow analysis. These methods compute the environment, which is a mapping of program variables to values at those suspected locations. The environment captures all the possible values at a location $L$. Therefore, if any values are found to violate the buffer boundary at $L$, a buffer overflow vulnerability is detected. Choosing proper locations and making safe approximation requires heuristics and sacrifices precision. However, such a design gains more scalable performance, which is highly essential when dealing with large-scale applications. Typical examples include the from Larochelle and Evans [22], CSSV [23], etc.

## 5.2 Run-Time Defense

This type of approaches adopt run-time defense to prevent exploiting potential vulnerabilities of any installed programs. These approaches aim to provide an extra protection regardless of what the source program is. Normally such protections are implemented using three different kinds of techniques: code instrumentation, infrastructure modification, and network assistance.

The first aspect is to simulate a run-time environment partially, execute the suspicious program in the virtual environment and check whether malicious actions have taken place. Examples include StakeGuard and RAD [24], which are tools that create virtual variables to simulate function's return address. Suspicious code will be redirected to act over the virtual variables first.

The second aspect is to modify the underlying mechanism to eliminate the root of attacks: Xu et al. [25] proposed a method to split stack and store data and control information separately; Ozdoganoglu et al. [26] proposed to implement a non-executable stack. More details and corresponding tools of run-time defense could be found in recent surveys [2, 27].

The third aspect is to do a taint analysis for the input data from any the untrusted network source. This analysis compares network data with vulnerability signatures of the recorded attacks, or inspects payload for shell code for detecting and preventing exploitation. TaintCheck [28], proposed by Newsome and Song, tracks the propagation of tainted data that comes from un-trusted network sources. If a vulnerability signature is found, the attack is detected. Similar approaches include PASAN from Smirnov and Chiueh [29], and Vigilante from Costa et al. [30].

## 5.3 Attack Prevention Through Auto Patching

The last category aims to removal the vulnerability from the source code. The objective is to add defensive code to wrap sink nodes so that no taint data could access the sinks directly. There are three strategies to design defensive code and insert them: search and replace, bounds checker, and detect and transform [2].

The first strategy is to search common vulnerable C string functions and I/O operations and replaces the found operations with a safe version. For example, vulnerable functions *strcpy* and *strcat* could be replaced as *strncpy* and *strncat* or *strlcpy* and *strlcat* [19], or even with a customized version. Munawar and Ralph [6] proposed a reliable approach to replace *strcpy* and *strcat* with a customized version based on heuristics. This strategy is straight-forward and easy to implement. However, it misses many complex situations.

The second strategy is aiming to insert effective validation before each memory access to perform an extra bounds checking. A typical design is to add validation before each pointer operation, named "pointer-based approach". These approaches track the base and bound information for every pointer and validate each pointer manipulation operation against the tracked information. Examples include CCured, MSCC, SafeC, and Softbound [3]. These approaches are designed to provide high precision. However, as nearly every pointer operation will be wrapped with additional checking, the code may grow large and the runtime performance could be downgraded.

The third strategy is to locate the vulnerability first and then transform the vulnerable code segment into a safe version. Comparing with the second strategy, this helps reduce the size of added code without compromising the removal precision. Relatively few efforts have been put in this direction. Lin et al. [11] proposed to slice the code based on a taint analysis, and then detect the buffer overflow vulnerability over each slice. The detected vulnerable slice will be inserted in additional code for vulnerability removal. However, their approach is based on path-insensitive information only. Wang et al. [10] proposed a method to add extra protection constraints to protect sink nodes. The method called model checker to verify the satisfiability of the inserted protection constraints. If the constraint fails to hold, that sink node will be recorded vulnerable, and the corresponding constraints will be left to protect the sink node. However, this method is path-insensitive.

ABOR follows the third strategy and pushes the state-of-the-art one step ahead. It first detects the buffer overflows based on path sensitive information and then only add defensive code to repair the vulnerable code segment. Therefore, it adds limited code and has a low runtime overhead.

# 6 Conclusions

In this paper, we have presented an approach to remove buffer overflow vulnerabilities in C/C++ programs automatically. We first characterize buffer overflow vulnerability in the form of four patterns. We then integrate and extend existing techniques to propose a framework—ABOR that removes buffer overflow vulnerability automatically: ABOR iteratively detects and removes buffer overflows in a path-sensitive manner, until all the detected vulnerabilities are eliminated. Additionally, ABOR only patches vulnerable code segment. Therefore, it keeps a lightweight runtime overhead. Using a set of benchmark programs and three industrial programs written in C/C++, we experimentally show that the proposed approach is effective and scalable for removing all the detected buffer overflow vulnerabilities.

In the future, we will improve our approach and tool to minimize the number of wrongly detected cases. We will also integrate ABOR into existing testing frameworks, such as CUnit, GoogleTest, to further demonstrate its practicality.

**Acknowledgements.** The authors thank the Jiangsu Celestvision from China for assisting this study and providing their internal programs for our experiment.

# References

1. US-CERT (2014). http://www.us-cert.gov/
2. Younan, Y., Joosen, W., Piessens, F.: Runtime countermeasures for code injection attacks against C and C ++ programs. ACM Comput. Surv. **44**, 1–28 (2012)
3. Nagarakatte, S., Zhao, J., Martin, M.M.K., Zdancewic, S.: SoftBound: highly compatible and complete spatial memory safety for C. In: Proceedings of the 2009 ACM SIGPLAN Conference on Programming Language Design and Implementation, pp. 245–258. ACM, Dublin, Ireland (2009)
4. Criswell, J., Lenharth, A., Dhurjati, D., Adve, V.: Secure virtual architecture: a safe execution environment for commodity operating systems. SIGOPS Oper. Syst. Rev. **41**, 351–366 (2007)
5. Dhurjati, D., Adve, V.: Backwards-compatible array bounds checking for C with very low overhead. In: Proceedings of the 28th international conference on Software engineering, pp. 162–171. ACM, Shanghai, China (2006)
6. Hafiz, M., Johnson, R.E.: Security-oriented program transformations. In: Proceedings of the 5th Annual Workshop on Cyber Security and Information Intelligence Research: Cyber Security and Information Intelligence Challenges and Strategies, pp. 1–4. ACM, Oak Ridge, Tennessee (2009)
7. Vallentin, M.: On the Evolution of Buffer Overflows. Addison-Wesley Longman Publishing Co., Boston (2007)
8. Sinha, S., Harrold, M.J., Rothermel, G.: Interprocedural control dependence. ACM Trans. Softw. Eng. Methodol. **10**, 209–254 (2001)
9. en.wikipedia.org/wiki/Abstract_syntax_tree
10. Lei, W., Qiang, Z., Pengchao, Z.: Automated detection of code vulnerabilities based on program analysis and model checking. In: Eighth IEEE International Working Conference on Source Code Analysis and Manipulation 2008, pp. 165–173 (2008)
11. Lin, Z., Jiang, X., Xu, D., Mao, B., Xie, L.: AutoPaG: towards automated software patch generation with source code root cause identification and repair. In: Proceedings of the 2nd ACM symposium on Information, Computer and Communications Security, pp. 329–340. ACM, Singapore (2007)
12. Lhee, K.-S., Chapin, S.J.: Buffer overflow and format string overflow vulnerabilities. Softw. Pract. Exper. **33**, 423–460 (2003)
13. Necula, G.C., Condit, J., Harren, M., McPeak, S., Weimer, W.: CCured: type-safe retrofitting of legacy software. ACM Trans. Program. Lang. Syst. **27**, 477–526 (2005)
14. Kundu, A., Bertino, E.: A new class of buffer overflow attacks. In: Proceedings of the 2011 31st International Conference on Distributed Computing Systems, pp. 730–739. IEEE Computer Society (2011)

15. C ++ Ref (2014). http://www.cplusplus.com/reference/
16. Le, W., Soffa, M.L.: Marple: a demand-driven path-sensitive buffer overflow detector. In: Proceedings of the 16th ACM SIGSOFT International Symposium on Foundations of Software Engineering, pp. 272–282. ACM, Atlanta, Georgia (2008)
17. Zitser, M., Lippmann, R., Leek, T.: Testing static analysis tools using exploitable buffer overflows from open source code. SIGSOFT Softw. Eng. Notes **29**, 97–106 (2004)
18. Lu, S., Li, Z., Qin, F., Tan, L., Zhou, P., Zhou, Y.: Bugbench: benchmarks for evaluating bug detection tools. In: Workshop on the Evaluation of Software Defect Detection Tools. (2005)
19. Miller, T.C., Raadt, T.D.: Strlcpy and strlcat: consistent, safe, string copy and concatenation. In: Proceedings of the Annual Conference on USENIX Annual Technical Conference, pp. 41–41. USENIX Association, Monterey, California (1999)
20. GrammaTech (2014). http://www.grammatech.com/products/codesurfer
21. Xie, Y., Chou, A., Engler, D.: ARCHER: using symbolic, path-sensitive analysis to detect memory access errors. In: ESEC/FSE-11: Proceedings of the 9th European Software Engineering Conference Held Jointly with 11th ACM SIGSOFT International Symposium On Foundations Of Software Engineering, pp. 327–336. ACM, (2004)
22. Larochelle, D., Evans, D.: Statically detecting likely buffer overflow vulnerabilities. In: Proceedings of the 10th Conference on USENIX Security Symposium, vol. 10, pp. 14–14. USENIX Association, Washington, D.C. (2001)
23. Dor, N., Rodeh, M., Sagiv, M.: CSSV: towards a realistic tool for statically detecting all buffer overflows in C. In: PLDI 2003: Proceedings of the ACM SIGPLAN 2003 Conference on Programming Language Design and Implementation, pp. 155–167. ACM, (2003)
24. Wilander, J., Kamkar, M.: A comparison of publicly available tools for dynamic buffer overflow prevention. In: Network and Distributed System Security Symposium (NDSS), pp. 149–162 (2003)
25. Xu, J., Kalbarczyk, Z., Patel, S., Ravishankar, I.: Architecture support for defending against buffer overflow attacks. In: Second Workshop on Evaluating and Architecting System Dependability, pp. 55–62 (2002)
26. Ozdoganoglu, H., Vijaykumar, T.N., Brodley, C.E., Kuperman, B.A., Jalote, A.: SmashGuard: a hardware solution to prevent security attacks on the function return address. IEEE Trans. Comput. **55**, 1271–1285 (2006)
27. Padmanabhuni, B., Tan, H.: Techniques for Defending from Buffer Overflow Vulnerability Security Exploits. Internet Computing, IEEE PP, 1–1 (2011)
28. Newsome, J., Song, D.: Dynamic taint analysis for automatic detection, analysis, and signature generation of exploits on commodity software. In: Proceedings of the Network and Distributed System Security Symposium (2005)
29. Smirnov, A., Tzi-cker, C.: Automatic patch generation for buffer overflow attacks. In: Third International Symposium on Information Assurance and Security, IAS 2007, pp. 165–170 (2007)
30. Costa, M., Crowcroft, J., Castro, M., Rowstron, A., Zhou, L., Zhang, L., Barham, P.: Vigilante: end-to-end containment of internet worm epidemics. ACM Trans. Comput. Syst. **26**, 1–68 (2008)
31. Automatic Buffer Overflow Repairing (2014). http://sunshine-nanyang.com/index.html

# ValueApping: An Analysis Method to Identify Value-Adding Mobile Enterprise Apps in Business Processes

Eva Hoos[1(✉)], Christoph Gröger[1], Stefan Kramer[2], and Bernhard Mitschang[1]

[1] Graduate School of Excellence Advanced Manufacturing Engineering (GSaME),
University of Stuttgart, Universitätsstraße 38, 70569 Stuttgart, Germany
Eva.Hoos@gsame.uni-stuttgart.de
[2] Daimler AG, 71034 Böblingen, Germany

**Abstract.** Mobile enterprise apps provide novel possibilities for the optimization and redesign of business processes, e.g., by the elimination of paper-based data acquisitioning or ubiquitous access to up-to-date information. To leverage these business potentials, a critical success factor is the identification and evaluation of value-adding MEAs based on an analysis of the business process. For this purpose, we present ValueApping, a systematic analysis method to identify usage scenarios for value-adding mobile enterprise apps in business processes and to analyze their business benefits. We describe the different analysis steps and corresponding analysis artifacts of ValueApping and discuss the results of a case-oriented evaluation in the automotive industry.

**Keywords:** Business processes · Analysis framework · Mobile application

## 1 Introduction

As Apple released the first iPhone in 2007, the success story of mobile applications running on smartphones and tablets, so called mobile apps, began. In 2014, there will be over 138 Billion app downloads [1]. Nowadays, the majority of target users are consumers, but there is an increasing focus on mobile technology in enterprises. Mobile apps used in business are called mobile enterprise apps (MEA) and they are one of the top ten strategic technology trends for enterprises in 2014 [2]. The unique features of MEAs like intuitive touchscreen-based handling, anywhere and anytime usage as well as sensor capabilities enable a large spectrum of opportunities for new business models and novel business processes. The employment of MEAs can lead to higher productivity, higher employee satisfaction, integration of mobile process activities, elimination of paper-based data acquisitioning and ubiquitous information access [3].

Typically, the introduction of MEAs is realized in a technology-driven manner, which means MEAs are developed because it is technically feasible and fancy. However, a benefit from a business point of view cannot be guaranteed. In order to realize the business value of MEAs, the enterprise has to establish a mobile strategy. Thereby, a critical success factor is the business-driven identification and evaluation of value-adding MEAs

© Springer International Publishing Switzerland 2015
J. Cordeiro et al. (Eds.): ICEIS 2014, LNBIP 227, pp. 222–243, 2015.
DOI: 10.1007/978-3-319-22348-3_13

based on a comprehensive analysis of the business process to be optimized. The goal is to identify process activities suited for MEAs and the derivation of corresponding usage scenarios. This includes the analysis of business benefits of desired MEAs and their communication with the corporate management and the employees [4].

A key problem in the identification of value-adding MEAs is that the spectrum of new fields of application enabled by mobile apps in business is not yet well-understood, especially the conceptual differences compared to existing mobile IT systems like laptops have not been analyzed sufficiently. Furthermore, there is a methodological lack to systematically identify value-adding MEA usage scenarios. Previous methodologies consider mobile applications in general but do not focus on mobile apps and their unique features specifically [5–7]. Moreover, there is no clear picture of the business benefits of mobile app usage as these benefits comprise monetary and non-monetary factors [8].

To address these problems, we present *ValueApping*, an analysis method to identify value-adding MEA usage scenarios in business processes. It contains a criteria catalogue which combines technological and business-oriented aspects of mobile app usage and comprises several systematic analysis steps. By applying this method, it can be decided, which type of IT technology fits best to support a particular process activity. Moreover, ValueApping enables the analysis of the business benefits of a MEA usage scenario for a certain process activity.

The remainder of this paper is structured as follows: Sect. 2 characterizes mobile enterprise apps in general. Section 3 gives an overview of ValueApping including addressed requirements, analysis steps and the underlying analysis artifacts. Section 3 details on the analysis artifacts whereas the analysis steps are described in Sect. 4. An evaluation of ValueApping is presented in Sect. 5 based on a case-oriented application in the automotive industry. Section 6 reviews related work. Finally, Sect. 7 concludes the paper and highlights future work.

This paper represents a significantly revised and extended version of our work presented in [9]. In particular, we extend our method by several components for a business benefit analysis. Furthermore, we investigate the special characteristics of mobile enterprise apps compared to traditional mobile enterprise applications.

## 2 Mobile Enterprise Apps

In this section, MEAs are defined and characterized based on the term "mobile apps". According to [10], mobile apps are applications running on smart mobile touch-based devices (SMTD) such as smartphones and tablets. Thereby, applications comprise all types of executable programs as well as browser-based web applications. MEAs are mobile apps used in business, whereas we specifically focus on mobile apps for employees. MEAs differ from traditional mobile applications running on mobile devices such as laptops, PDAs and mobile phones by the technical capabilities of SMTDs as well as the way they are developed, distributed and consumed which is known as the mobile ecosystem. Thereby, several technical and organizational challenges have to be addressed to leverage MEAs. These aspects are explained in the following.

## 2.1  Mobile Devices and Technical Capabilities

Originally, there were two different types of mobile devices [11]: *Mobile PCs* such as laptops and *mobile handhelds* such as mobile phones and PDAs. Mobile PCs have similar capabilities as desktop PCs. In contrast, mobile handhelds are highly portable, always-on and they are equipped with various sensors, but they have limited resources such as computing power. The evolution of mobile technology lead to the combination of these two device types into smart mobile touch-based devices (SMTD) such as smartphones and tablets [12–15] as shown in Fig. 1. SMTDs are more and more replacing mobile handhelds and due to their increasing technical capabilities they are becoming an alternative to mobile PCs [14], as well. In contrast to mobile PCs, SMTDs are characterized by a unique feature set [10, 13–17] comprising anywhere and anytime usage, intuitive touch-based interaction as well as various device sensors like a GPS receiver. In the following, these features are discussed in detail.

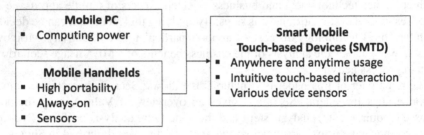

**Fig. 1.**  Evolution of mobile devices.

Due to mobile networks, SMTDs allow for *anywhere and anytime usage*. This enables employees to access the enterprise back-end whenever it is required. Besides, the small and handy form factor of SMTDs leads to a higher portability. Moreover, SMTDs have no long boot process, because they are designed to be always on. This increases the reachability and working ability of the user.

Due to their touchscreen handling and multi-modal input capabilities, SMTDs enable an *intuitive touch-based interaction* using touch events and gestures [18]. This is more appropriate in mobile environments than the usage of mouse and keyboard. Due to the small screen size, the interaction design has to be tailored towards the functionality relevant for the task. We call this a task-oriented design. Moreover, the new interaction paradigm enables people who are generally uncomfortable with computers to interact with SMTDs without prior training [19]. In addition, sensors enable further input capabilities as described in the following.

SMTD are equipped with *various device sensors* including camera, GPS receiver, and accelerometer. They can be used for interaction as well as context sensing and enrichment. Regarding context sensing, sensors can be used for taking a photo, for voice recording, and for positioning. Furthermore, sensors can be used for interaction using voice commands or motion gestures. The camera can also be used for sensing the environment and in augmented reality application.

## 2.2 Mobile Ecosystems and Challenges to Leverage Mobile Enterprise Apps

Generally, mobile apps are part of complex mobile ecosystems which define the way apps are developed and distributed. A mobile ecosystem consists of the SMTD as a hardware component, the mobile operating system, native apps running on the operating system as well as a storefront and supplementary online services [20]. Google's Android, Apple's iOS, and Microsoft's Windows 8 are the three major mobile ecosystems competing nowadays. Each defines software development kits and user interaction guidelines as well as app store concepts to distributed mobile apps.

The unique features of SMTDs as well as the preexistence of mobile ecosystems lead to five core challenges to leverage MEAs according to [10]:

- *MEA Portfolio*: Systematic identification of usage scenarios for MEAs in business processes to derive value-adding MEAs and define a corresponding MEA portfolio.
- *MEA Development*: The development of MEAs is challenged by the requirements of high usability and restricted computing resources as well as limited network capacities [4]. In particular, a task-oriented interaction design is a critical success factor for usability. Moreover, the coexistence of different mobile ecosystems requires cross-platform development approaches.
- *MEA Infrastructure:* In order to distribute and manage MEAs, enterprises have to design company-internal app stores oriented towards apps store for consumers. Moreover, a unified device management is necessary, e.g., to define policies and control operating system updates across various types of SMTDs and mobile operating systems.
- *MEA Security and Privacy*: The use of MEAs poses new risks on privacy and security. Business-critical information has to be secured even in case of loss of SMTDs [21]. Moreover, personal data and context data on SMTDs have to be protected to avoid employee tracking.
- *MEA IT Architecture:* The use of MEAs on top of existing back-end IT systems requires an adaption and extension of the IT architecture especially with respect to the design of lightweight and context-aware back-end services.

With ValueApping, we address the MEA portfolio challenge by providing a systematic analysis method to derive value-adding MEA usage scenarios in business processes.

## 3 Requirements and Overview of ValueApping

In this section, we first define the requirements of an analysis method to identify value-adding MEA usage scenarios. Then, we give an overview of ValueApping and its parts.

### 3.1 Requirements

In order to identify value-adding MEA usage scenarios in business processes, for each process activity, the type of IT technology which fits best has to be selected. The technologies range from PCs as stationary IT technology and laptops as mobile PCs to SMTDs such as smartphones and tablets as a basis for MEAs.

The corresponding decision making process is complex, because there are several issues and requirements to consider. On the basis of shortcomings of existing analysis approaches (see Sect. 7), we identified the following three major requirements $R_i$ our method has to address:

*Potential of mobile technology (R1):* A central question is whether there is a business benefit of using mobile technology. Generally, mobile technology can have two different effects on business processes [7]:

- Supporting existing mobility given by the process
- Enabling novel mobility in processes where none existed before

However, not every employment of mobile technology leads to an improvement of the business processes in terms of efficiency and effectiveness. Hence, activities that profit from one of the two effects have to be identified systematically.

*Types of mobile devices (R2):* There are a lot of different devices for mobile technology such as laptops, smartphones, tablets, PDAs, and mobile phones differing in hardware and software characteristics. In this work, we are considering the following types of mobile devices as described in Sect. 2.1:

- Mobile PCs like laptops
- Smart mobile touch-based devices like smartphones and tablets

*Holistic Point of View (R3).* The combination of business-oriented and technology-oriented aspects avoids a purely technology-driven introduction of mobile technology. The latter typically focuses on porting existing back-end applications on mobile apps without a detailed business analysis. Besides, business aspects do not only refer to the mobility of process activities but further contextual factors like the elimination of manual data acquisition. In addition, not only aspects of the process activity but also infrastructural and organizational issues of the enterprise, e.g., the availability of a mobile network, have to be considered.

## 3.2 Overview of ValueApping

The purpose of ValueApping is to systematically analyze process activities with respect to their improvement potential using mobile technology in order to support enterprises in the decision which IT technology fits best. At this, ValueApping incorporates the above requirements and takes a holistic view on both technological and business-related aspects (R3), differentiates between SMTDs and mobile PCs (R1) and investigates both the support of existing mobility and the enablement of novel mobility in the process (R2). Process improvements can be determined according to the goal dimensions time, quality, and flexibility. The major result is a portfolio of analyzed process activities which are categorized according to the IT technology which fits best. On this basis, a business benefit radar chart for each process activity suited for SMTD support is derived. The radar chart represents the business benefits of a corresponding MEA usage scenario for the activity according to the goal dimen-sions. This provides a starting point to define corresponding MEA development projects and IT investments.

ValueApping is made up of two major parts, namely analysis steps and analysis artifacts (see Fig. 2). The analysis steps are executed in a sequence and create different analysis artifacts as input and output. Thereby, we distinguish between four groups of analysis artifacts, namely

- the criteria catalogue and criteria values,
- the app potential as a metric,
- the app management portfolio, and
- the business benefit radar chart.

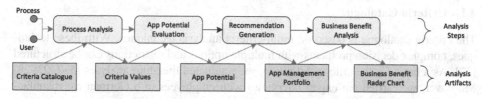

**Fig. 2.** Overview of ValueApping.

The *criteria catalogue* reflects the different aspects for the usage of mobile technology in enterprises. The *app potential* is a metric to operationalize the improvement potential of each activity with respect to MEA. This means, the higher the app potential the more the activity can be improved using a MEA. The *app management portfolio* enables the classification and ranking of the activities according to the IT technology which fits best. The *business benefit radar chart* is based on a *business benefit breakdown structure*. It indicates on which goal dimensions the usage of a MEA has a positive impact for a particular process activity. The chart enables a comparison with other activities according to the goal dimensions and constitutes a graphical representation to easily communicate potential benefits.

ValueApping comprises four analysis steps, namely

- process analysis,
- app potential evaluation,
- recommendation generation, and
- business benefit analysis.

The two *starting points* represent different application variants of the method. The user point of view enables employees to validate improvement suggestions for selected activities across different processes. The process point of view considers improvements of an entire process including all activities.

*Process analysis* refers to a procedure to determine the value of each criterion in the criteria catalog. The input is the criteria catalogue and the output comprises a criteria value for each analyzed criterion. These values represent in turn the input for the *evaluation of the app potential*. The latter defines a procedure to calculate the app potential for each activity as a metric. Then, *recommendation generation* reveals the app management portfolio according to the app potential of each activity. On this basis, recommendations are deduced according to the IT technology which fits best for each activity in the portfolio. At last, the *business benefit analysis* step reveals the business benefits of corresponding MEAs for all process activities which are suited for SMTD support according to the app management portfolio.

# 4    Analysis Artifacts

This section describes the analysis artifacts, namely the criteria catalogue, the app potential, the app management portfolio, as well as the business benefit breakdown structure and radar chart.

## 4.1    Criteria Catalogue

The criteria catalogue is based on multi-criteria analysis techniques. With these techniques, complex decision problems with multiple options and restrictions can be structured [22]. As a basis for the criteria definition, we conducted literature analyses [5–7, 23–28] Moreover, we carried out expert interviews with employees of a German car manufacturer to refine the identified criteria.

The criteria catalogue reflects the different aspects of mobile app usage in enterprises including the requirements R1, R2, and R3. The criteria are grouped into four categories: *mobility, process, technology requirement,* and *corporate conditions*. Each criterion has predefined ordinal values following a qualitative approach. In addition, some criteria are complemented by indicators to ease the determination of their value. Table 1 shows the structure of the criteria catalogue. In the following, an overview of the different categories and the corresponding criteria is given.

**Mobility of the Activity.** This category includes two criteria: *task* and *actor*. These criteria consider the aspects given in R1. The criterion *task* is based on the definition of mobile processes given in [5] and has the predefined values of *high, medium* and *low*. The indicators are a stationary workplace, the uncertainty of the execution space, moving actor or multiple execution places. The uncertainty of the execution space emerges if the execution space is unknown at the start of the process or it differs in multiple instances of the process. For example, the value of the criterion *task* is *high*, if there is a high uncertainty of the execution space, a moving actor or multiple execution spaces. The value is *low* if the task is executed on a stationary workspace. This criterion investigates whether mobile technology can be employed to support existing mobility in the process. In contrast, the criterion *actor* considers if there is a benefit by enabling the location independent execution of a stationary activity. Therefore, the cross-process mobility of the actor is investigated on the basis of the definition of mobile workers given in [7]. The predefined values of the criterion *actor* are *high, medium* and *low*. The indicators are stationary workspace, mobile workforce, and frequent business trips. For example, the value is *high* if the actor is part of a mobile workforce, rarely at his stationary workspace or often on business trips.

**Process.** The category *process* considers aspects given by the process itself. This comprises, on the one hand, the effects of the improvement of the activity on the entire process and, on the other hand, the improvement potential of the underlying information

**Table 1.** Criteria catalogue.

| |
| --- |
| Mobility of the activity |
|     *Actor:* Mobility of the actor |
|     *Task:* Mobility of the task |
| Process |
|   Relevance |
|     *Frequency:* Number of execution |
|     *Acuteness:* Importance of performing the task immediately |
|   Current Information System |
|     *Digitalization:* Potential of digitalization |
|     *Devices:* Possibilities to replace other devices with mobile touch-based devices |
|     *Usability:* Improvements of usability through mobile touch-based devices |
|     *Sensors:* Enrichment of the application through the use of sensors |
| Technology Requirements |
|   Performance |
|     *Data Volume Transmit:* Amount of data which have to be transmitted |
|     *Date Volume Receive:* Amount of data which have to be received |
|     *Computing Power:* Amount of computing power the application requires |
|     *Presentation:* Data representation on a small screen |
|     *Type of Input:* Structure of data input |
|   Software Quality |
|     *Availability:* Availability requirements of the application |
|     *Security:* Security requirements of the application |
| Corporate Conditions |
|   Individual |
|     *User:* Acceptance of the user |
|     *Management:* Support of management to introduce mobile apps |
|   Organizational |
|     *Mobile Devices:* Existence of mobile touch-based devices |
|     *Guidelines:* Guidelines limiting the usage of mobile touch-based devices |
|   Infrastructural |
|     *Data Communication:* Availability of mobile networks |

system. Therefore, the category is divided into two subcategories: *relevance* and *current information system*. The category *relevance* contains the criteria *frequency* and *acuteness*. Based on these criteria, the impact on the process by improving the respective activity is analyzed. The criterion *frequency* refers to the frequency of execution of an activity. Thereby, it is not differentiated if the activity is executed multiple times in one process instance or if multiple process instance lead to frequent activity executions as the potential impact of the activity is higher the more often it is executed in general. The predefined values are *often*, *regularly*, and *rarely*. There are no concrete numbers as these depend on industry-specific process conditions. The subcategory *current information system* considers the improvement potential regarding the current information system. The criteria are *digitalization*, *existence of devices*, *usability* and *sensors*. For instance, the criterion *sensors* investigates if the use of sensors has the potential to improve the activity, e.g., by taking photo of a situation instead of describing it textually.

**Technology Requirements.** The category *technology requirements* analyzes technological aspects of the application used in the activity. They are deduced from [23–25, 28]. The category is divided into *performance* aspects and *software quality* aspects. The *performance* subcategory contains the following criteria: *Data Volume of send* and *receive*, *computing power*, *presentation* and *type of input*. With these criteria, the required performance can be matched with the different types of mobile technology. For instance, the criterion *presentation* refers to the characteristics of small screens. It is investigated if it is possible to present the data on small screens. Indicators are type of the data, e.g., text or picture, and number of data sets. The subcategory *software quality* refers to non-functional properties and contains the criteria *availability* and *security*. Security is one of the biggest barriers to introduce mobile technology in enterprises [10]. In this paper, *security* refers to data security which can be divided into confidentiality, integrity, authenticity, non-repudiation. The predefined values are *high*, *medium* and *low*. For the determination, the risks of violating each aspect have to be considered.

**Corporate Conditions.** The category *corporate conditions* combines general organizational and technological conditions for the use of mobile technology in the enterprise. Thereby, aspects of mobile readiness as well as the context of the usage have to be considered [29]. Thus, the subcategories are *individual*, *organizational* and *infrastructural*. Individual considers the *user* and the *management* and their readiness to use and accept MEAs. For instance, the criterion *user* estimates if the users have a general affinity for mobile devices. Indicators are technical interests of the user and whether he already uses SMTDs. The predefined values are *high*, *medium* and *low*. If the value is *high*, then the possibility that the user would use the devices is high. The subcategory *organizational* refers to organizational aspects of the enterprises and includes the criteria *mobile devices* and *guidelines*. The criterion *mobile devices* investigates if the actor already employs mobile devices that he can reuse for other applications. Guidelines may prescribe, for instance, that in some restricted company areas mobile device are not allowed. *Infrastructural* contains one criterion, *data communication*. It represents the availability of mobile networks.

### 4.2   App Potential

The app potential is a metric representing the improvement potentials for a process activity when supported by a MEA. The app potential has two dimensions, *mobilization potential* and *app capability*.

The *mobilization potential* refers to the aspect whether a mobile execution of the activity is beneficial: the higher the mobilization potential, the higher the advantages of using mobile technology in general. The *app capability* refers to the question, whether the application supporting the activity is suited to be realized as an application on SMTDs.

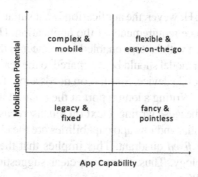

**Fig. 3.** App management portfolio.

In order to determine the app potential, the criteria of the catalogue are mapped to the two dimensions of the app potential. The numerical calculation is then based on scored and weighted criteria values as explained in Sect. 5.2.

The app potential metric enables the ranking and prioritization of process activities in a portfolio (see Sect. 4.3) and makes them comparable regarding their improvement potential using MEAs.

## 4.3 App Management Portfolio

The app management portfolio is based on portfolio analysis concepts. The latter are typically used for evaluating, selecting and managing research and development projects in order to make strategic choices [30–32]. We adapted these concepts to the evaluation and selection of process activities regarding mobile technology. The app management portfolio groups the process activities into four categories according to their mobilization potential and their app capability. The goal is to define action recommendations for each category. These recommendations focus on the type of IT technology which fits best for each category. The four categories are *flexible & easy-on-the-go*, *complex & mobile*, *legacy & fixed*, and *fancy & pointless*. The resulting portfolio is shown in Fig. 3. The higher the app potential of an activity, the more it is positioned further up on the right of the portfolio.

Activities in the *flexible & easy-on-the-go* category have a high mobilization potential and a high app capability. That is, process improvements are high when using apps for this activity. It is highly recommended to deduce a corresponding usage scenario for a mobile app. For instance, if a mobile worker needs current information of an enterprise backend system or has to record information on-the-go, these activities may be in the *flexible & easy-on-the-go* category. A corresponding app could not only provide mobile access but easily enrich the information by sensor data, e.g., photos, location, voice or video as provided by most smartphones. The recorded information can be transmitted directly to the backend instead of describing the situation textually on paper and transferring it manually.

The *complex & mobile* category is characterized by a high mobilization potential and a low app capability. That is, activities in that category can be improved, if their applications run on mobile devices. However, the application is not suitable for running on SMTDs due to, e.g., high performance requirements of the application. Hence, the actors of these activities should be equipped with laptops enabled to connect to the enterprise IT backend. For example, if a simulation model should be compared to the real world, the employee has to go to this area with his mobile device. Simulation needs a lot of computing power, hence a notebook might be suited. Writing a long report at the point of action is another example for a notebook application because writing a text on touchscreens is not appropriate.

Low mobilization potential and low app capabilities are the characteristics of activities positioned in the *legacy & fixed* quadrant. This implies that there are no improvements when using mobile technology. Thus, there is a clear suggestion to refer to traditional stationary technology like PCs.

The *fancy & pointless* category has low mobilization potential and high app capabilities. That is, it is possible to create an app for this application but the app does not add value, because the execution of the activity is not improved. For instance, an engineer might use an app for mobile product data management without having mobile tasks. Technology-driven approaches are in danger of producing apps for this type of process activities. Activities in this category should be supported by stationary IT technology although it is technologically possible to employ apps.

The boundaries of the quadrants can be varied according to the enterprise strategy. By default, boundaries are based on half of the maximum values for mobilization potential and app capability revealing quadrats of equal size. The numerical calculation of these values is described in Sect. 5.3 and the categorization of activities in the portfolio is detailed in Sect. 5.4.

### 4.4 Business Benefit Breakdown Structure and Business Benefit Radar Chart

The *business benefit breakdown structure* offers a mechanism to analyze the business benefits of MEA usage for a certain process activity. The structure is based on the three goal dimensions of process improvement, namely flexibility, time, and quality. For each dimension, we identified major business benefits which can be achieved by the usage of a MEA in a particular activity, e.g., a reduction of reaction times in the time dimension. It has to be remarked that we do not consider the cost dimension, because a profound cost analysis requires additional investment calculations regarding the use of information systems in organizations [33]. However, the benefits can be used as basis for a traditional cost-benefit analysis.

The benefits were identified on the basis of both a comprehensive literature study [26, 34–36] and a case-oriented investigation of mobile apps in the engineering domain presented in [37]. To determine, whether a certain benefit can be realized for an activity, we mapped related criteria of the criteria catalogue to each benefit. In the following, we give an overview of the business benefit breakdown structure with major benefits according to the three goal dimensions. Related criteria for each benefit are written in brackets.

**Flexibility.** In the context of ValueApping, flexibility means that the execution of the activity can be modified or adapted at process runtime.

- *Location Independent Task Execution* (→ actor): Due to the anywhere and anytime characteristics, the actor is not restricted to perform the task in a specific place and is enabled to perform his work even on-the-go. Hence, this is determined by the criterion *actor*.
- *Task Scheduling* (→ mobility of the task, availability): Different circumstances can necessitate a rescheduling of a task during mobile work. For example, a service engineer may receive an urgent service request while being at the customer. When he is able to access the required information relevant for the new task in the back-end system, he can reschedule his work immediately and reprioritize his tasks. Therefore, the corresponding criteria are *availability* and *task*.

**Quality.** Quality refers to the data quality in the process. A higher quality refers to fewer input errors as well as more precise information representation [38].

- *Reduction of Input Errors* (→ digitalization, usability): Due to digitalization, media breaks can be avoided, because the data are entered directly into the IT system. The corresponding criterion is digitalization. In addition, the intuitive touch-based inter-action and targeted functionality of MEAs can avoid errors during activity execution in general. This benefit can be realized if the usability of the existing IT system is low. Thus, the corresponding criterion is *usability*.
- *Contextualization and Enrichment of Information* (→ sensor): Device sensors can be used to record data, which was not available before such as taking a photo or deter-mining the geographic location of the user. This enables an informational enrichment by multimedia data as well as the additional contextualization of input data. The relevant criterion for this benefit is *sensor*.
- *Access to Real Time Data* (→ availability): Due to the mobile connection to the back-end system, the user can access current data and base his decision on up-to-date information. This is determined by the criterion *availability*.

**Time.** Time refers to the reduction of the entire lead time of the process. That is, the time from the start of the first activity until the end of the last activity of the process.

- *Reduction of Activity Execution Time* (→ sensor, usability): Due to a higher usability and the sensor-based contextualization, the human computer interaction can be improved. For example, taking a picture is faster than describing a situation textually. Moreover, due to their strictly task-oriented user interface, MEAs only provide the functionality which is actually necessary to perform an activity in contrast to complex multi-functioned desktop applications. This leads to a faster execution of the activity, especially for untrained employees. Hence, the corresponding criteria are *sensor* and *usability*.
- *Reduction of Waiting Time* (→ actor, availability): MEAs increase the reachability and working ability of employees as described in Sect. 2.1. This is important, if the start of an activity depends on receiving an event from a back-end system. With a MEA the actor receives the notification of the event immediately and waiting times between process activities can be reduced. This benefit is determined by the criteria *actor* and *availability*.

- *Elimination of Activities* (→ digitalization, sensor): One of the main optimization potentials of MEAs is the elimination of activities for paper-based data acquisitioning through digitalization. In addition, due to the integration of multiple IT functions in one mobile device, further data processing activities can be eliminated, e.g., due to the integrated camera, it is not necessary to use a separate camera and transfer the data from the camera to the IT system. The corresponding criteria are *sensor* and *digitalization*.

On the basis of the benefit breakdown structure, the *business benefit radar chart* (see Fig. 4) aggregates the benefits for each analyzed activity according to the goal dimensions time, quality, and flexibility in a graphical manner. At this, the chart does not represent a detailed quantified statement but an indicator for the achievable benefits and can be used to relatively compare particular MEA usage scenarios of different process activities. The value for each dimension ranges between 0 and 1 and represents the proportion of achievable benefits compared to the maximum. The calculation of the values is detailed in Sect. 5.4.

# 5   Analysis Steps

In this section, the analysis steps of ValueApping are explained, namely process analysis, evaluation of app potential, recommendation generation and business benefit analysis.

## 5.1   Process Analysis

The process analysis refers to the application of the criteria catalogue and the determination of the criteria values for a given process activity. It comprises four analysis activities, one for each category of criteria. The entire procedure for process analysis is shown in Fig. 5.

The input for the activity *analysis of mobility* depends on the application variants. In the user-driven approach, the input is one activity whereas in the process-driven approach the input is the entire process. Then, each activity is analyzed by determining the values of the criteria from the category *mobility of activity*. To minimize the effort, there is a condition for early termination after the analysis of mobility: If no mobility is detected, then the analysis of the activity is terminated because mobility is the prerequisite for the use of mobile devices. No mobility is given, if the values of the criteria *actor* and *task* are both *low*.

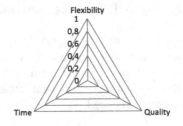

**Fig. 4.**   Business benefit radar chart.

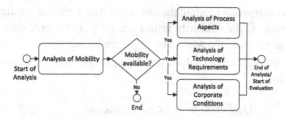

**Fig. 5.** Procedure and activities for process analysis.

After this step, the activities for the *analysis of process aspects*, the *analysis of technology requirements* and the *analysis of corporate conditions* follow. Thereby, these activities are executed in parallel. The advantages of dividing the process analysis into four sub analyses are that the entire procedure is clearly structured and the results can be reused. For example, if two activities are executed in the same environment, the corporate conditions have to be analyzed only once and the results are used for both activities.

## 5.2    App Potential Evaluation

In order to evaluate the app potential, the criteria and their values have to be mapped to the dimensions of the app potential as explained in Sect. 4.2. For this purpose, the influence of the criteria on the dimensions has to be examined. For example, the criterion *task* in the category *mobility of the activity* has an influence on the mobilization potential due to the fact that a mobile task would benefit from mobilization. Hence, the criterion *task* is assigned to the dimension *mobilization potential* $(D_{MobPot})$. In contrast, the criterion *computing power* is assigned to the dimension app capability $(D_{AppCap})$, because this differentiates laptops from SMTDs.

The next step is to specify the concrete influence of a criterion value on the dimension it belongs to. Therefore, a scoring function $s\left(C = k_c\right)$ maps the ordinal value $k_c$ of a criterion $C$ to a numerical value. The scoring function is based on a scoring matrix as shown in Table 2. For example, if the criterion *actor* has the value *high*, then $s\left(Actor = high\right) = 3$ and in case the value is *low* it is $s\left(Actor = low\right) = 1$.

**Table 2.**  Excerpt of the scoring matrix.

| Score | 3 | 2 | 1 |
|---|---|---|---|
| Task | High | Medium | Low |
| Actor | High | Medium | Low |
| Frequency | Often | Regularly | Rarely |
| ... | .... | | |

In addition, the influence of individual criteria on the app potential can be adapted by weighting each scored criterion $C$ with weight $w_c$ as in $s\left(C = k_c\right) * w_c$. The weighting enables enterprises to adapt the impact of the criteria according to their mobile strategy. For example, if data security issues are very important, such as with product data for manufacturing cars, the weight $w_{security}$ can be increased.

On this basis, the numerical values for the app potential of a process activity are calculated as follows:

$$AppPotential = \left(x_{AppCap}, x_{MobPot}\right)$$

*with*

$$x_j = \sum_{C \in D_j} s\left(C = k_c\right) * w_c$$

### 5.3 Recommendation Generation

The step recommendation generation positions the activities in the app management portfolio and defines action recommendations for each portfolio category (see Sect. 4.3). Process activities are positioned according to their values for app capability and mobilization potential. For example, activities with the app potential (0,0) belong to the category *legacy & fixed*. The higher the app potential of an activity, the more it is positioned further up on the right of the portfolio.

Using this portfolio, the stakeholders can decide which activities should be supported by apps and prioritize corresponding development projects. Hence, the enterprise gets a structured overview about the app potential across various processes.

### 5.4 Business Benefit Analysis

In this step, the business benefits of MEA usage scenarios for activities located in the *flexible & easy-on-the-go* quadrant in the portfolio are analyzed based on the business benefit breakdown structure and the criteria (see Sect. 4.4): if one of the scored criteria values related to a benefit is larger than zero, we assume that this benefit is likely to be realized with the corresponding MEA. For example, the benefit *reduction of execution time* has the corresponding criteria *sensor* and *usability*. Hence, this benefit will occur if the value of the criterion *sensor* is *yes* or the value of the criterion *usability* is *medium* or *high*. For the business benefit radar chart, all scored criteria values for all benefits are then aggregated for each goal dimension. The calculation of the value $v_i$ for each goal dimension $GD_i$ is defined as follows:

$$v_i = \frac{\sum_{C \in GD_i} s\left(C = k_c\right)}{\sum_{C \in GD_i} \max s\left(C = k_c\right)}$$

*with* $i \in \{flexibility, time, quality\}$ *and* $0 \leq v_i \leq 1$

It is important to remark that the value of $v_i$ does not denote the absolute quantified improvement of a goal dimension but enables a relative comparison of different MEA usage scenarios for certain process activities. For instance, $v_{quality} = 0,5$ does not represent an improvement of the process quality by 50 % but, compared to another MEA usage scenario with $v_{quality} = 0,25$, the first has a higher impact on the quality dimension.

# 6  Case-Oriented Evaluation in the Automotive Industry

As an initial evaluation, we applied ValueApping in a real case at a large German car manufacturer. At this, we used the method to analyze a concrete process in the engineering domain. In the following, we briefly describe the process and the analysis procedure and discuss major results.

## 6.1  Modification Approval Process

The modification approval process is part of the car development process. During the development of a car, a lot of change requests arise. For instance, the design of the seat is changed or another breaking system should be used. However, single changes have impacts on the whole car. For instance, it has to be checked whether the new seat design fits the car's interior. The modification approval ensures that the product data in the product data management (PDM) system is in a consistent state despite modifications. In general, a faster execution of the process is desirable to reduce development times.

For our analysis, a process description is needed. Therefore, we conducted interviews with the organizational owners of the process to get a high level overview of the process and deduce a simple process model. The process model is shown in Fig. 6. It consists of six sequential activities. The process starts if product data is modified. Product data comprises both product geometry representation in terms of computer-aided-design models and the product structure in form of a bill of materials. When the modification is done, the engineer has to create a modification document including all relevant changes. Once the document is checked into the PDM system, the process starts. Then, the system forwards the document to various persons with different responsibilities following a pre-determined order. At first, the responsible person for this component, the creator himself or his boss, has to perform the *check modification record* activity. This includes checking the document for correctness and completeness. After that, the activity *verify packaging* is performed by the packaging manager. A package is a higher level component built from multiple parts. For example, the worker checks if there is an installation space collision, e.g., whether the new engine fits in the engine compartment. After that, the design validator performs the activity *verify design* to ensure data quality. Then, the activity *verify and approve modification* has to be executed by the technically responsible persons. First, the team lead has to give his approval and then the department leader approves as well. If the document received all required approvals, the documentarian performs the activity *create entries in PDM*. With that, the modification is completely documented in the PDM and the modification approval process finishes.

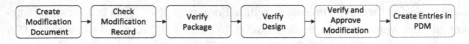

**Fig. 6.** Process model of the modification approval process.

This simple modelling is sufficient for our analysis, because all other important aspects for mobile IT support, e.g., location and roles, are covered in the criteria catalogue. Yet, for further stages like the development of suitable apps for the process, the process model has to be extended by other process characteristics such as location, actors, business domains and resources [39, 40].

### 6.2 Method Application and Results

On the basis of the process model described above, we applied ValueApping in the process-driven approach in order to analyze the entire process. Thereby, we conducted interviews with process experts to determine the criteria values.

On this basis, we investigated the mobility of each activity according to the procedure described in Fig. 5. To this end, the criteria *task* and *actor* were used. We observed that all tasks have a low mobility. The reason is that they are all executed at the actor's stationary workspace. However, during the evaluation of the criterion *actor*, two groups of activities were identified. One group has actors with a low mobility and the other one has actors with a high mobility. The activities *create modification record document*, *check document*, *verify packaging*, *verify design*, and *create entries in PDM* have actors with a low mobility because they are most of their working time at their stationary workspaces. In contrast, the activities *check record* and *verify and approve modification* have actors who are rarely at their workplaces. Thus, according to the termination condition, we further analyzed only the activities from group two, *check record* and *verify and approve modification*, and skip process analysis for group one.

Our analysis results of these activities revealed that the values of the sub–categories *process*, *performance,* and *individual* have a positive influence on the app potential of these activities, because the process is very important, so enhancement is beneficial for the enterprise and the performance requirements make it possible to run the application on SMTDs. In addition, employees and the corporate management welcome the usage of SMTDs. However, security requirements are a big challenge. Product data are highly sensitive and no unauthorized person should be able to access them.

After performing the app potential evaluation (see Fig. 7), two activities were positioned in the category *flexible & easy-on-the-go,* namely *check record* and *verify and approve modification.* For these activities, an app usage scenario was defined as a basis for the development of a concrete app within the car manufacturer, called ApprovalApp. The other activities *create entries in PDM*, *check package*, *check design*, and *create modification* cannot be improved through mobile technology due to a low mobilization potential.

The business benefit analysis for the ApprovalApp usage scenario revealed the following benefits:

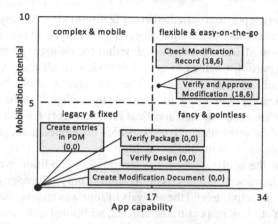

**Fig. 7.** App management portfolio of the modification approval process.

- Location-independent task execution
- Reduction of waiting time
- Access to real time data

The resulting business benefit radar chart (see Fig. 8) reveals that the ApprovalApp improves flexibility, time, and quality of the modification approval process. Many actors of the *verify and approve modification* activity are senior managers. Hence, they are rarely at their stationary workplaces, most of the time they are on business trips and meetings. With the ApprovalApp, they are informed immediately if a new approval task occurs and they can perform the task right on-the-go. Furthermore, the decision can be made on the basis on up-to-date product data.

## 6.3 Discussion

We discussed both the procedure of applying ValueApping as well as the concrete results for the modification approval process with experts on mobile technology within the industry partner and summarize major results in the following.

It was underlined that the strict structure and the systematic procedure of analysis steps make the results of ValueApping comprehensible and transparent. Moreover, it

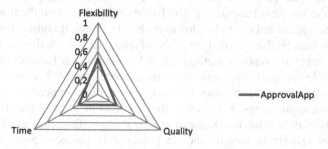

**Fig. 8.** Benefit radar chart of the ApprovalApp.

was emphasized that the portfolio-oriented visualization enables an easy communication and representation of the analysis results especially for corporate management. Before, various ideas for new MEAs were discussed within the industry partner without clear prioritization. The portfolio helped to get an overview of all analyzed activities and corresponding possibilities for new apps. This provided a sound basis for decision making and prioritization of investments in mobile technology. On the one hand, potential users could be convinced that their app ideas in the category *fancy & pointless* should not be realized. On the other hand, IT responsibles developed a deeper understanding for a business-driven view on mobile technology.

With respect to the analysis steps, the termination condition was recognized as helpful because it decreased the analysis effort significantly. The approval modification process comprised six activities and the analysis of four was terminated using the termination condition. Yet, with respect to the criteria, additional indicators revealed to be helpful in order to precisely determine the value of each criterion. At this, more fine-grained values for some criteria like security and data volume would be helpful, too.

Considering the usage of MEAs in the modification approval process, the need for supporting the activities *check record* and *verify and approve modification* through a MEA was recognized by the industry partner. It was stated that an app has the potential to reduce execution times and enhance flexibility of the process significantly as highlighted by the business benefit radar chart.

# 7 Related Work

In this section, we give an overview of work related to our approach. A further qualitative evaluation of ValueApping based on a comparison with similar approaches can be found in our previous work [9]. For the discussion of related work, we differentiate three groups of work with respect to mobile technology in business processes.

The first group comprises work on the general potential and impact as well as the basic conditions for the use of mobile technology in business processes [26, 29, 34, 41]. These works discuss different high level aspects of mobile technology in enterprises such as benefits of mobilizing processes, transformational impact of mobile technology and mobile enterprise readiness. Yet, they do not address issues of a methodology to systematically realize the benefits of mobile technology.

The second group comprises concepts which are similar to our ValueApping method. Gumpp and Pousttchi propose a framework to evaluate mobile applications according to their potential business benefits [7]. The framework is based on the theory of informational added values and its application to mobile business. It constitutes a high level approach and misses the detailed analysis of processes to derive concrete usage scenarios. Gruhn et al. present a method called Mobile Process Landscaping to choose a suitable mobile application to enhance business processes [5]. The authors make use of typical return on investment concepts to analyze mobility in processes and evaluate different mobile applications. Yet, they neither incorporate technological aspects, e.g., the complexity of data input, nor do they focus on the specific characteristics of MEAs. Scherz defines criteria to identify mobile potential in business processes during a condition-analysis as part of a classical system analysis [6]. These criteria are divided into four categories, namely actor, process classification, data and information system as well as devices. Yet, mobile apps are not addressed specifically.

The third group of work considers the usage of mobile apps in enterprises [10, 42, 43]. They point out that apps have a great potential to improve business processes, suggest general application areas for apps and discuss selected app-oriented aspects, e.g., technical requirements for the IT back-end. Yet, they do not focus on an analysis methodology to identify concrete usage scenarios.

## 8 Conclusions and Future Work

In this work, we presented ValueApping, an analysis method to identify value-adding usage scenarios for mobile enterprise apps in order to improve business processes. ValueApping helps stakeholders to decide which type of IT technology fits best for a given process activity. It is based on a comprehensive criteria catalog to systematically analyze business processes and reveals an app management portfolio, which categorizes process activities according to their improvement potential using MEAs Furthermore, the business benefits of the resulting app usage scenarios are evaluated and represented in a graphical manner.

ValueApping can not only be employed to identify usage scenarios for one process. It can also be used to get a general view on mobile potentials of several processes in an enterprise in order to identify cross-process synergies and prioritize company-wide investments. On this basis, ValueApping enables both a systematic prioritization of IT investments in mobile technology and a transparent IT portfolio management as part of a mobile enterprise strategy.

Our future work comprises two aspects. On the one hand, we plan to implement ValueApping as a software tool to ease the application of the method, especially the determination of the criteria values. On the other hand, we want to extend ValueApping in order to apply it at the business modelling stage and determine usage scenarios for mobile enterprise apps during the initial design of a new business process.

**Acknowlegements.** The authors would like to thank the German Research Foundation (DFG) for financial support of this project as part of the Graduate School of Excellence advanced Manufacturing Engineering (GSaME) at the University of Stuttgart.

## References

1. Gartner Inc.: Gartner Says Mobile App Stores Will See Annual Downloads Reach 102 Billion in 2013. http://www.gartner.com/newsroom/id/2592315
2. Gartner Inc.: Gartner Identifies the Top 10 Strategic Technology Trends for 2014. http://www.gartner.com/newsroom/id/2603623
3. Stieglitz, S., Brockmann, T.: Mobile enterprise. HMD Prax. der Wirtschaftsinformatik **49**, 6–14 (2012)
4. Stieglitz, S., Brockmann, T.: Increasing organizational performance by transforming into a mobile enterprise. MIS Q. Executive **11**, 189–201 (2012)

5. Gruhn, V., Köhler, A., Klawes, R.: Modeling and analysis of mobile business processes. J. Enterp. Inf. Managementscher **20**, 657–676 (2007)
6. Scherz, M.: Mobile Business. Schaffung eines Bewusstseins für mobile Potenziale im Geschäftsprozesskontext. VDM Verlag, Munich (2008). Dr. Müller
7. Gumpp, A., Pousttchi, K.: The "Mobility-M"-framework for application of mobile technology in business processes. In: Proceedings of 35th GI-Jahrestagung, pp. 523–527 (2005)
8. Pousttchi, K., Becker, F.: Gestaltung mobil-integrierter Geschäftsprozesse. In: Meinhardt, S., Reich, S. (eds.) Mobile Computing. Dpunkt.verlag, Heidelberg (2012)
9. Hoos, E., Gröger, C., Kramer, S., Mitschang, B.: Improving business processes through mobile apps - an analysis framework to identify value-added app usage scenarios. In: Proceedings of the 16th International Conference on Enterprise Information Systems (ICEIS). SciTePress (2014)
10. Gröger, C., Silcher, S., Westkämper, E., Mitschang, B.: Leveraging apps in manufacturing. Framework App. Technol. Enterp. **7**, 664–669 (2013). Procedia CIRP
11. Coulouris, G.F.: Distributed Systems. Concepts and Design. Addison-Wesley, Boston (2012)
12. Kornak, A., Teutloff, J., Welin-Berger, M.: Enterprise Guide to Gaining Business value from Mobile Technologies. Wiley, Hoboken (2004)
13. Abolfazli, S., Sanaei, Z., Gani, A., Xia, F., Yang, L.T.: Rich mobile applications: genesis, taxonomy, and open issues. J. Network Comput. Appl. **40**, 345–362 (2014)
14. Pitt, L., Berthon, P., Robson, K.: Deciding when to use tablets for business applications. MIS Q. Executive **10**, 133–139 (2011)
15. Pitt, L.F., Parent, M., Junglas, I., Chan, A., Spyropoulou, S.: Integrating the smartphone into a sound environmental information systems strategy: principles, practices and a research agenda. J. Strateg. Inf. Syst. **20**, 27–37 (2011)
16. Andersson, B., Henningsson, S.: Accentuated factors of handheld computing. In: Pooley, R., Coady, J., Schneider, C., Linger, H., Barry, C., Lang, M. (eds.) Information Systems Development, pp. 293–304. Springer, New York (2013)
17. Sammer, T., Brechbühl, H., Back, A.: The new enterprise mobility: seizing the opportunities and challenges in corporate mobile IT. In: Proceedings of the 19th Americas Conference on Information Systems (2013)
18. Bragdon, A., Nelson, E., Li, Y., Hinckley, K.: Experimental analysis of touch-screen gesture designs in mobile environments. In: Tan, D., Fitzpatrick, G., Gutwin, C., Begole, B., Kellogg, W.A. (eds.) Proceedings of the 9th SIGCHI Conference on Human Factors in Computing Systems, p. 403
19. Häikiö, J., Wallin, A., Isomursu, M., Ailisto, H., Matinmikko, T., Huomo, T.: Touch-based user interface for elderly users. In: Cheok, A. D., Chittaro, L. (eds.) Proceedings of the 9th International Conference on Human Computer Interaction with Mobile Devices and Services, pp. 289–296
20. Kenney, M., Pon, B.: Structuring the smartphone industry: is the mobile internet OS platform the key? J. Ind. Competition Trade **11**, 239–261 (2011)
21. Oberheide, J., Jahanian, F.: When mobile is harder than fixed (and Vice Versa): demystifying security challenges in mobile environments. In: Proceedings of the 11th Workshop on Mobile Computing Systems and Applications, pp. 43–48. ACM, New York, NY, USA (2010)
22. Cansando, F., Vasconcelos, A., Santos, G.: Using multi-criteria analysis to evaluate enterprise architecture scenarios. In: Proceedings of 14th International Conference on Enterprise Information Systems (ICEIS), pp. 232–237 (2012)
23. Forman, G., Zahorjan, J.: The challenges of mobile computing. Computer **27**, 38–47 (1994)

24. Krogstie, J.: Requirement engineering for mobile information systems. In: Proceedings of the Seventh International Workshop on Requirements Engineering: Foundations for Software Quality (REFSQ 2001) (2001)
25. Murugesan, S., Venkatakrishnan, B.: Addressing the challenges of Web applications on mobile handheld devices. In: Proceedings of the International Conference on Mobile Business, pp. 199–205. IEEE Computer Society, Los Alamitos, Calif (2005)
26. Nah, F.F.-H., Siau, K., Sheng, H.: The value of mobile applications: a utility company study. Commun. ACM **48**, 85–90 (2005)
27. Sarker, S., Wells, J.D.: Understanding mobile handheld device use and adoption. Commun. ACM **46**, 35–40 (2003)
28. Wasserman, A.I.: Software engineering issues for mobile application development. In: Proceedings of the FSE/SDP Workshop on Future of Software Engineering Research, pp. 397–400. ACM, New York, NY, USA (2010)
29. Basole, R.: Mobilizing the enterprise: a conceptual model of transformational value and enterprise readiness. In: 26th ASEM National Conference Proceedings (2005)
30. Bohanec, M., Rajkovič, V., Semolić, B., Pogačnik, A.: Knowledge-based portfolio analysis for project evaluation. Inf. Manage. **28**, 293–302 (1995)
31. Mikkola, J.H.: Portfolio management of R&D projects: implications for innovation management. Technovation **21**, 423–435 (2001)
32. Killen, C.P., Hunt, R.A., Kleinschmidt, E.J.: Project portfolio management for product innovation. Int. J. Q. Reliab. Manage. **25**, 24–38 (2008)
33. Ward, J., Peppard, J.: Strategic planning for information systems. J. Wiley, Chichester (2002)
34. Basole, R.C.: The value and impact of mobile information and communication technologies. In: Proceedings of the IFAC Symposium on Analysis, Modeling and Evaluation of Human-Machine Systems, pp. 1–7 (2004)
35. der Heijden, H., van, Valiente, P.: The value of mobility for business process performance: evidence from sweden and the netherlands. In: Proceeding of European Conference on Information Systems, p. 34 (2002)
36. Picoto, W.N., Palma-dos-Reis, A., Bélanger, F.: How does mobile business create value for firms? In: 2010 Ninth International Conference on Mobile Business and 2010 Ninth Global Mobility Roundtable (ICMB-GMR), pp. 9–16
37. Hoos, E., Gröger, C., Mitschang, B.: Mobile apps in engineering: a process-driven analysis of business potentials and technical challenges. In: Proceedings of 9th CIRP Conference on Intelligent Computation in Manufacturing Engineering (to be published)
38. Schmelzer, H.J., Sesselmann, W.: Geschäftsprozessmanagement in der Praxis. Kunden zufrieden stellen - Produktivität steigern - Wert erhöhen. Hanser, Carl, München (2010)
39. Gao, S., Krogstie, J.: Capturing process knowledge for multi-channel information systems: a case study. Int. J. Inf. Syst. Model. Design (IJISMD) **3**, 78–98 (2012)
40. Gopalakrishnan, S., Krogstie, J., Sindre, G.: Capturing location in process models comparing small adaptations of mainstream notation. Int. J. Inf. Syst. Model. Design **3**, 24–45 (2012)
41. Gebauer, J., Shaw, M.J.: Success factors and impacts of mobile business applications: results from a mobile e-procurement study. Int. J. Electron. Commer. **8**, 19–41 (2004)
42. Lunani, M.: Enterprise Mobile Apps (2011)
43. Clevenger, N.C.: iPad in the Enterprise. Developing and deploying business applications. Wiley, Indianapolis (2011)

# An Overview on Aspect-Oriented Requirements Engineering Area

Paulo Afonso Parreira Júnior[1,2(✉)] and Rosângela Dellosso Penteado[1]

[1] Departament of Computer Science,
Federal University of São Carlos, São Carlos, Brazil
paulojunior@jatai.ufg.br, rosangela@dc.ufscar.br
[2] Computer Science Course, Federal University of Goiás, Jataí, Goiás, Brazil

**Abstract.** Background: Aspect-Oriented Requirements Engineering (AORE) is a research field that aims to provide appropriate strategies for identification, modularization and composition of crosscutting concerns (also called early-aspects). Several AORE approaches have been developed recently, with different features, strengths and limitations. Goals: the aim of this paper is threefold: (i) cataloguing existing AORE approaches based on the activities encompassed by them; (ii) describing what types of techniques have been used by these approaches for "Concern Identification and Classification" – a bottleneck activity; and (iii) identifying which are the most used means of publication of AORE-based studies and how it has been the progress of these studies over the years. Results: we have selected and analyzed 60 (sixty) papers and among them, we identified 38 (thirty-eight) AORE distinct approaches. Some interesting results are: (i) few approaches lead to "Conflict Identification and Resolution", an activity responsible for discovering and treating the mutual influence between different concerns existing in a software; (ii) there is a lack of evaluation studies about already existing AORE approaches; (iii) the most productive research institutions on AORE in the world are located in Lancaster (UK) and Nova Lisboa (Portugal); among other.

**Keywords:** Systematic mapping · Concern identification and classification · Aspect-oriented requirements engineering · Crosscutting concerns · Early-Aspects

## 1 Introduction

The Requirements Engineering (RE) encompasses activities related to the elicitation and analysis of information about the software: its requirements. Each sub-activity (or task) performed during requirements elicitation will result in a document with the textual description of all the software requirements. This document is then analyzed and requirements are structured in individual units, such as viewpoints, goals, use cases, scenarios. This is done in order to promote the Separation of Concerns - SoC [1], *i.e.*, the identification and modularization of pieces of the software that are relevant for a particular purpose.

In the context of RE, a "concern" can be understood as a set of one or more software requirements for a given purpose. For example, a security concern can

© Springer International Publishing Switzerland 2015
J. Cordeiro et al. (Eds.): ICEIS 2014, LNBIP 227, pp. 244–264, 2015.
DOI: 10.1007/978-3-319-22348-3_14

encompass several requirements related to the following goal: "ensuring that software is secure".

In an ideal scenario of software development, each concern should be allocated in a specific module, which achieves its goals. When it occurs, the software is called well-modularized, because all their concerns are clearly separated [2]. However, there are some types of concerns, for which, this allocation is not possible, only using traditional software engineering abstractions, such as viewpoints, goals, use cases, scenarios, among others. These concerns are called "crosscutting concerns" or "early aspects" and are defined as software requirements that are spread and tangled within other requirements. Some examples of common crosscutting concerns include: Persistence, Security, Caching, and Synchronization. The existence of crosscutting concerns can lead to lack of modularization and make harder the software maintenance and evolution activities.

Aspect-Oriented Requirements Engineering (AORE) is a research field that provides the most appropriate strategies for identification, modularization and composition of crosscutting concerns. A concern, in the context of AORE, encapsulates one or more requirements specified by stakeholders, and a crosscutting concern is a concern whose requirements cut across requirements of other software concerns. For example, a security concern may contain a requirement related to "encryption" and another one related to "checking access permissions". In addition, this set of security requirements can affect other software requirements, such as the requirement of sending registration information to a customer, which is related to another software concern. Hence, the security concern is called "crosscutting concern".

Several AORE approaches have been proposed recently, although with different features, strengths and limitations. However, there are few studies in the literature that describe: (i) the amount of studies produced about this subject; (ii) the location of these studies and in what time they were produced; (iii) which are the main AORE activities explored by researchers; among others.

This paper shows the planning and execution of a Systematic Mapping (SM) [3, 4], conducted with a focus on AORE, aiming to catalogue, identify and classify approaches related to this subject. A SM can be understood as a wider review of primary studies available in the literature, in order to identify the amount and types of studies about a particular subject. It also may indicate the evolution of the published studies about this subject over the years [3].

In this SM, we have selected and analyzed 60 (sixty) papers and among them, we identified 38 (thirty-eight) AORE distinct approaches. Some interesting results are: (i) few approaches lead to "Conflict Identification and Resolution", an activity responsible for discovering and treating the mutual influence between different concerns existing in a software; (ii) the most of sixty studies consist of presenting new AORE approaches or extensions of previous approaches - therefore, there is a lack of evaluation studies on already existing approaches; (iii) few studies have been published in journals, what can be a consequence of the item (ii); (iv) the most productive research institutions on AORE in the world are located in Lancaster (UK) and Nova Lisboa (Portugal); among other.

The obtained results in this SM can help other researchers to conduct further studies from this work, proposing new methods/techniques/tools for AORE as well as comparing their proposals with the catalogue present in this paper. The remainder of this paper is organized as follows: Sect. 2 presents an overview about Aspect-Oriented Requirements Engineering; Sect. 3 illustrates the planning of the Systematic Mapping, along with the research questions for which we have found answers in this work. In Sect. 4, the answers to the research questions are given and discussed. In Sect. 5, some threats to validity are discussed and, finally, Sect. 6 presents the final remarks and proposals for future works.

## 2 Background

The SoC principle is based on the identification and modularization of pieces of the software relating to a particular concept, goal or purpose [1]. Several traditional approaches for software development, such as Object-Orientation, were created based on this principle; however, some broad scope concerns (*e.g.*, security, synchronization, and logging) are not easy to be modularized and maintained separately during the development of software. When these concerns are not appropriately modularized, the software can contain tangled and scattered representations, making its understanding and evolution harder.

An effective approach for RE must take into account the SoC principle and the need to satisfy broad scope concerns [5]. AORE emerges as an attempt to encompass this goal through the usage of specific strategies to modularize concerns that are difficult to be isolated in individual modules (crosscutting concerns). The concern identification on requirements level allows software engineers to think about them in an isolation way from the beginning of software development, hence facilitating the creation/usage of strategies to modularization.

Figure 1 shows a generic process for AORE, proposed by Chitchyan et al. [6], which was developed based on other approaches available in the literature [5, 7–9]. The rounded-corner rectangles represent the process activities.

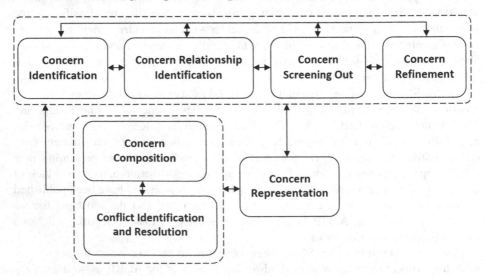

**Fig. 1.** A generic process for AORE (Chitchyan et al. [6]).

From an initial available set of requirements, the activity "Concern Identification" identifies and classifies software concerns as basis or crosscutting ones. The software engineer knows the influences and constraints imposed by crosscutting concerns on other software concerns, through the activity "Concern Relationship Identification". The activity "Concern Screening Out" aid software engineers to identify if there is repetition in the list of identified concerns and decide which of these concerns are relevant to the software. The activity "Concern Refinement" happens when there is a need to change the set of already identified concern and relationships.

During the activity "Concern Representation", the concerns are then represented in a particular template. This template can vary according to the used AORE approach, *e.g.*, it can be a text, a use case model, viewpoints, among others. For example, the approach developed by Rashid et al. [8, 10] represents base concerns using viewpoints; in the Baniassad and Clarke's approach [7, 11] it is defined themes as a new concept for representation of base and crosscutting concerns. Still in the "Concern Representation" activity, the software engineer can identify the need for refinement, for example, for addition/removal concerns and/or relationships. Therefore, he/she can return to the previous activities (Fig. 1). Finally, the base and crosscutting concerns represented in a specific template must be composed and then analysed to identify conflicts between them. These tasks are performed in the "Concern Composition" and "Conflict Identification and Resolution" activities. Then, identified conflicts are solved by the software engineers with the help of stakeholders.

In general, the activities described in the process presented in Fig. 1 are aggregated into four major activities, namely: "Concern Identification and Classification", "Concern Representation", "Concern Composition" and "Conflict Identification and Resolution". These activities are used as a basis for cataloguing the AORE approaches (Sect. 4).

## 3  Systematic Mapping Planning

Kitchenham et al. [4] argue that a systematic review should be carried out following the steps of planning, execution and documentation of the review and these steps can be used in the context of a Systematic Mapping (SM). This section shows the planning and strategy of execution of the SM performed in this work, according to the model of Kitchenham et al. Further, a discussion about the results of this SM is presented in Sect. 4.

### 3.1  Research Questions

The SM conducted aims to answer the questions presented in Table 1. The first column shows the code of the research question, which will be referenced throughout this text, and the second one, shows its description.

The goal of the **question Q1** is discovering the AORE approaches existing in the literature and what activities they encompass. This question is important for at least two reasons, it allows to: (i) catalogue existing approaches based on the activities encompassed by them; and (ii) indicate the approaches that deal with concern identification and classification - which will facilitate obtaining data to answer the question Q3.

**Table 1.** Research questions for the SM.

| # | Description |
|---|---|
| Q1 | What are the AORE approaches available in the literature and which activities they cover? |
| Q2 | What are the types of studies (Validation Study, Evaluation Study, Original Solution, Adapted Solution, Philosophical Study, Opinion Papers and Experience Papers) that have been proposed regarding the approaches identified in Question Q1? |
| Q3 | What are the types of techniques that have been used by the approaches listed in Question Q1 for concern identification and classification? |
| Q4 | Which are the events (conferences, workshops, among others), journals, book chapters, among others, where the approaches listed in Question Q1 have been published and when this happened? |

The **question Q2** classifies the studies analysed in the SM based on the type of study conducted by the authors: "Validation Study", "Evaluation Study", "Original Solution", "Adapted Solution", "Philosophical Study", "Opinion Papers" and "Experience Papers". This classification was initially defined by Wieringa et al. [13] and is used to guide the development of SMs proposed by Kai et al. [3]. An adaptation of the original classification is presented in Table 2.

**Table 2.** Classification of the types of studies (adapted from Wieringa et al., [13]).

| Classification | Description |
|---|---|
| Validation Study | It presents an evaluation of a proposed approach in simulated environments (laboratories), through controlled experiments, case studies or proof of concept. |
| Evaluation Study | It presents a practical evaluation of a proposed approach, through experiments on real industrial environment. This type of study, in general, is conducted on more mature approaches, whose strengths have been evaluated by means of "validation studies". |
| Original Solution | It presents the description of an original solution to a given problem. The potential benefits and applicability of the proposed solution are presented by small examples and good arguments by the authors of the study. |
| Adapted Solution | It presents a description of a solution to a given problem, but it is an adaptation of an existing solution. An adaptation may be considered as a supplementary solution or a solution that minimize certain limitations of the original approach. Similarly, the type of study "original solution", the potential benefits and applicability of the proposed solution are shown by small examples and good argumentation from the authors of the study. |
| Philosophical Study | It delineates a new way to look at existing approaches and structures them in the form of a taxonomy, conceptual framework or catalogue. |
| Opinion Papers | This type of study expresses the personal opinion of a (some) researcher(s) about the benefits and/or limitations of a particular approach or how the approach should be used. |
| Experience Papers | It consists in testimonials expressed by professionals/researches about how the approaches can be used in practice. It is the personal experience of the author(s) from the usage of a particular approach. |

It is important to highlight few points regarding the classification presented in Table 2:

- This work adapts the classification proposed by Wieringa et al. in the following way: the category "proposed solution" [13] was subdivided into "original solution" and "adapted solution". This adaptation let we know which approaches are new and which ones are extensions of existing approaches;
- In the context of this paper, a study is classified as an "adapted solution" when it comes to an extension of an existing AORE approach. For example, a study that describes the development of a computational support for an approach proposed in another study. However, studies that show solutions non-based on AORE approaches are considered original solutions, because the extensions made in the original approach, generally, are more significant. For example, a study that presents an approach for concern identification and classification based on use cases, which is a traditional approach for software development, is classified as "original solution"; and
- A study can be classified in more than one class described in Table 2. For example, a study may provide an original solution to a problem while presenting a description of a controlled experiment for evaluating this approach ("validation study").

Regarding to the **question Q3**, some studies [2, 14] describe that concern identification and classification activity is a bottleneck in the AORE process. While this activity serves as a basis for execution of the other activities, it is important to know: (i) what types of techniques have been used for concern identification and classification; (ii) what are the strengths and limitations of these techniques; and (iii) which of them has been more used.

Finally, the **question Q4** was proposed in order to know which are the most used means of publication of AORE-based studies and how it has been the progress of these studies over the years.

To answer these questions, it is necessary to conduct an investigation in the literature aiming to recovery primary studies, as full papers, experience reports, among others. Kitchenham et al. [4] describe certain criteria to lead to an appropriate selection of primary studies, they are: population, intervention and outcomes.

The population refers to the group of studies that will be observed. In this work, the population consists of publications (full papers published in conference proceedings, journals, among others) with a focus on Aspect-Oriented Requirements Engineering. The intervention refers to what will be observed in SM. In this case, all type of AORE approaches, techniques, methods and tools was observed. The outcomes refer to the expected results at the end of the SM. In this case, the expected results are: (i) a catalogue of AORE approaches available in the literature; (ii) the classification of the main AORE activities encompassed by the identified approaches; (iii) a catalogue of the main techniques used for concerns identification and classification; and (iv) the presentation of the evolution of the publications related to AORE over the years, as well as vehicles in which they have been published.

## 3.2    Search String and Keywords

The keywords used in the search string to obtain the primary studies of this SM are: "requirements engineering", "approach", "aspect-oriented", "aspect orientation", "tool", "method" and "technique". Based on this set of keywords, the search string was generated: *((approach OR approaches OR technique OR techniques OR tool OR tools OR method OR methods) AND ("aspect-orientation" OR "aspect-oriented") AND ("requirements engineering")).*

Some studies that were not retrieved by the search engines used in this SM were manually added to the repository of the studies. These works were mainly obtained from references found in publications considered relevant for this work.

## 3.3    Criteria for Inclusion of the Sources and Method
for the Search of Primary Studies

The *IEEE Xplorer* (*ieeexplore.ieee*.org) and *Scopus* (www.scopus.com) search sources of primary studies were select based on the following criteria: (i) the source must index publications in the field of Computer Science; (ii) the source should allow searches to studies published in conference proceedings and journals via web; and (iii) the source must provide advanced search engines, using the keywords and filters. The method used to search for primary studies was the search engines available for these sources. Beside, a manual review of the references from studies returned by these sources was performed to obtain publications that were not retrieved by the search engines and that are relevant for this SM.

## 3.4    Criteria for Inclusion of Primary Studies, Quality Criteria
and Methods for Evaluation of Primary Studies

The **inclusion and exclusion criteria** for primary studies are presented in Table 3.

**Quality Criteria:** as a way to assess the quality of selected primary studies, we have considered only publications that present a complete and detailed description of the

**Table 3.** Inclusion and exclusion criteria for the primary studies.

| Inclusion (I) and Exclusion (E) Criteria |
| --- |
| (I1) The text of the study is written in English. |
| (I2) The complete version of the text of the study is available on web. |
| (I3) The study treats to the usage, adaptation, and/or creation of AORE approaches. |
| (E1) The study text is written in another language, not in English. |
| (E2) The complete version of the study text *is not* available on web. |
| (E3) The study *does not* treat to the usage, adaptation, and/or creation of AORE approaches. |
| (E4) The study is a duplicated version of another study. |
| (E5) The study is an older version of another study. |
| (E6) The study is a short paper or a poster up to 2 pages. |

proposed approach. Thus, short papers and posters up to two pages were not considered. Moreover, only the newer versions of studies were analysed.

**The Evaluation Method:** consists in selecting primary studies according to the inclusion criteria described in Table 3 and the quality criteria, as previously comment. This protocol was applied for each study obtained from the research method described in Sect. 3.3 and the selected papers were stored for later analysis.

### 3.5   Data Extraction from the Selected Primary Studies

The data extraction from the selected primary studies for this SM was performed in four steps.

**Step 1.** One of the researchers has applied the research method to identify potential primary studies. Based on the preliminary identified studies, a researcher read the title, the abstract and the keywords of the publication, applying the criteria described in Table 3. It was recovered 217 studies: 162 coming from the source Scopus and 55 from the *IEEE Xplorer*; 112 of these studies were accepted and then, completely analyzed in the second step of this SM.

The other ones were considered duplicated (48) or rejected (57). Duplicated studies are those ones that consist of exactly the same publication, without any extension. This occurs because the source Scopus can also index publications available in other sources, such as IEEE, among others. Fifty-seven studies were rejected mainly due to the exclusion criteria E3 (the study does not treat to the usage, adaptation, and/or creation of AORE approaches.). Examples of rejected studies are those that propose the usage of aspect orientation to create tools for requirements management. In this case, the meaning of keyword "requirements engineering" was not directly related to AORE.

**Step 2.** In this step, the same researcher who has completed Step 1 also has read the full text of the 112 accepted studies. The criteria described in Table 3 were reapplied, as well as the quality criteria (Sect. 3.4). Several studies were rejected because they were short papers (exclusion criterion E6) without enough information for answering the research questions of this work.

The classification of the primary studies after finishing Step 2 can be seen in Fig. 2. It can be noticed that some duplicated studies were identified yet. This occurred because the researcher has not detected this situation, while performing Step 1. The obtained results reinforces that Systematic Mapping must be done at stages, as well as by more than one researcher [3, 4].

Due to the manual insertion of some relevant studies referenced in the selected papers of the Step 1, the amount of studies has increased in 14 (fourteen). It is important to mention these studies also were submitted to the same set of inclusion and quality criteria already discussed in the paper.

**Step 3.** The results of the Step 2 were reviewed by another researcher involved in this study, so that any disagreements were discussed and resolved. There was not need to change the previously selected set of studies, but the interaction between the researchers was important for the next step (Step 4), as it will be explained below.

**Step 4.** Finally, the resulting set of primary studies was used to extract the information required to answer the questions listed at the beginning of this study (Table 1). In this step, the collaboration between the researches was important to reduce the interpretation errors about some data extracted to the studies. The results of this step are presented in detail in Sect. 4.

## 4 Results

In this section, answers to the research questions for this SM (Table 1) are presented. The data needed to answer the **question Q1** are in Table 4; there are 38 approaches identified and analysed in this SM. The columns 1 and 2 show the code of the approach, used to identify it in other parts of this paper, the name of the approach and the reference of the study(ies) that present(s) it, respectively.

If there is not a specific name for an approach, we have used the title of the study in which this approach was presented. Then, the reader can find, at any time, what are the AORE approaches analysed in this SM and which studies are related to them. Columns 3, 4, 5 and 6 of Table 4 describe which AORE activities, as discussed in Sect. 2, are encompassed by the identified approaches.

It is possible to notice that many approaches include the concern identification and classification, representation and composition activities. However, there is a lack of approaches related to the "Conflict Identification and Resolution" activity. Other interesting points are that only 16 % of the analysed approaches (7, 8, 13, 15, 18 and 23) are complete, *i.e.*, include all activities related to AORE and 55 % of them encompass just one or two activities. This provides indications that conducting studies on a specific AORE activity or a small subset of activities can be an interesting strategy of research instead of trying to develop approaches that deal with all activities. A final point to be emphasized with respect to Table 4 is that not every 60 studies analysed in this SM are referenced in this table. This occurs because some studies are related to the usage and/or comparison of some AORE approaches, *i.e.*, they did not develop or extend any approach.

In order to answer the **question Q2**, Fig. 3 presents the classification of primary studies analysed in this SM according to the classes described in Table 2.

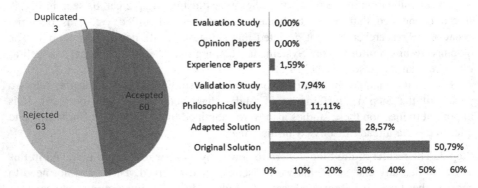

**Fig. 2.** Classification of the studies.

**Fig. 3.** Classification of Primary Studies.

**Table 4.** AORE approaches.

| # | Approach | AORE Activities | | | |
|---|---|---|---|---|---|
| | | CIC | CR | CC | CIR |
| 1 | An approach for crosscutting concern identification at requirements level using NLP [16–18] | X | | | |
| 2 | ACE - Aspect Clustering Engine [19] | X | | | |
| 3 | AWC - Aspect Weaving Connector [20] | | X | X | |
| 4 | RDL - Requirements Description Language [21, 22] | | | X | |
| 5 | ASSD - Aspects Specification for the Space Domain [23] | X | X | | |
| 6 | A semi-automatic strategy to identify crosscutting concerns in PL-AOVgraph requirement models [24] | X | | | |
| 7 | EA-Miner [24, 25] | X | X | X | X |
| 8 | NFR/AUC [26, 27] | X | X | X | X |
| 9 | DERAF [28] | | X | X | |
| 10 | An evolutionary model of requirements correctness with early aspects [29] | X | X | X | |
| 11 | AORE/XML [30] | X | X | X | |
| 12 | Theme [7, 11] | X | X | X | |
| 13 | AspOrAs [31, 32] | X | X | X | X |
| 14 | EA-Analyzer [33] | | | | X |
| 15 | AORE with Arcade [8, 10] | X | X | X | X |
| 16 | PROBE [34] | | | | X |
| 17 | MAST - Modeling Aspectual Scenarios with Theme [35] | X | X | X | |
| 18 | Integrating Problem Frames with Aspects [36] | X | X | X | X |
| 19 | Interaction Analysis in Aspect-Oriented Models [37] | | | | X |
| 20 | Isolating and relating concerns in requirements using latent semantic analysis [38] | X | | | |
| 21 | ADORA [39] | | X | | |
| 22 | Multi-ComBO [40] | | | X | X |
| 23 | Multi-Dimensional Separation of Concerns in Requirements Engineering [5] | X | X | X | X |
| 24 | Concern Interaction Graph (CIG) [41, 42] | | | | X |
| 25 | On the discovery of candidate aspects in software requirements [43] | X | | | |
| 26 | Promoting the software evolution in AOSD with early aspects: Architecture-oriented model-based pointcuts [44] | | X | X | |
| 27 | RCT - Requirements Composition Table [45] | X | X | X | |
| 28 | AOZCL [46] | | X | | |
| 29 | Scenario Modeling with Aspects [15] | X | X | X | |
| 30 | VisualAORE [47] | | X | | |
| 31 | Aspectual i* Model [48] | X | X | | |
| 32 | AO-ADL [49] | | X | | |
| 33 | AoUCM-to-RAM [50, 51] | | X | X | |

*(Continued)*

**Table 4.** *(Continued)*

| # | Approach | AORE Activities | | | |
|---|----------|-----|-----|-----|-----|
| | | CIC | CR | CC | CIR |
| 34 | Using tagging to identify and organize concerns during pre-requirements analysis [52] | X | | | |
| 35 | VGraph - From Goals to Aspects [9] | | X | X | X |
| 36 | AORA - Aspect-Oriented Requirements Analysis [53] | X | X | X | |
| 37 | AoURN - Aspect-oriented User Requirements Notation [54] | X | X | X | |
| 38 | RAM - Reusable Aspect Models [55] | | X | X | |
| | Amount of approaches for each AORE activity | 22 | 26 | 22 | 12 |

Subtitle: CIC – Concern Identification and Classification; CR – Concern Representation; CC – Concern Composition; CDR– Conflict Identification and Resolution.

Seventy nine percent of the studies were classified as an "Original Solution" or an "Adapted Solution" and there were few validation studies and none evaluation studies. This fact calls our attention, because many approaches are being used/adapted without having been submitted to evaluation studies. In addition, new approaches are being proposed without knowing the real accuracy of the existing approaches.

Another evidence about the previously affirmation is presented in Table 5, that presents: (i) the code of the AORE approach; (ii) the year of the first publication of this approach; (iii) the years of publication corresponding to adaptations of this approach; (iv) the references of the approaches used as basis for development of this approach; and (v) the references of the studies that evaluate this approach.

**Table 5.** Evolution of the AORE approaches.

| # | Proposal | Evolutions | Based on | Performed Evaluations | # | Proposal | Evolutions | Based on | Performed Evaluations |
|---|----------|-----------|----------|----------------------|---|----------|-----------|----------|----------------------|
| 1 | 2008 | 2011 | 12 | - | 20 | 2006 | - | 12 | |
| 2 | 2007 | - | 20 | - | 21 | 2007 | - | - | - |
| 3 | 2007 | - | - | - | 22 | 2008 | - | 36 | |
| 4 | 2007 | 2008 | - | [22] | 23 | 2005 | - | - | [2] |
| 5 | 2008 | - | 36 | - | 24 | 2009 | - | 29 | - |
| 6 | 2013 | - | 35 | - | 25 | 2009 | - | - | - |
| 7 | 2005 | 2006 | - | [14] | 26 | 2009 | - | - | - |
| 8 | 2009 | 2010 | - | - | 27 | 2012 | - | - | [22] |
| 9 | 2007 | - | - | - | 28 | 2007 | - | - | - |
| 10 | 2007 | - | - | - | 29 | 2004 | - | - | - |
| 11 | 2006 | - | - | [2] | 30 | 2010 | - | - | [47] |
| 12 | 2004 | 2005 | - | [14] | 31 | 2010 | - | - | - |
| 13 | 2005 | 2008 | - | - | 32 | 2007 | - | - | - |
| 14 | 2009 | - | - | - | 33 | 2007 | 2011 | 37; 38 | - |
| 15 | 2002 | 2003 | - | [2, 22] | 34 | 2009 | - | - | - |
| 16 | 2004 | - | - | - | 35 | 2004 | - | - | [2, 22] |
| 17 | 2010 | - | 12; 29 | - | 36 | 2003 | - | - | - |
| 18 | 2009 | - | - | - | 37 | 2010 | - | - | [54] |
| 19 | 2006 | - | - | - | 38 | 2009 | - | - | - |

Approximately 74 % of the approaches (28 of 38) were not evaluated through case studies, controlled experiments, among others, performed in a laboratory or an industrial environment. In addition, many approaches (55 %: 2, 3, 5, 6, 9, 10, 14, 16, 17, 18, 19, 21, 22, 23, 24, 25, 26, 28, 31, 32 and 34) have been proposed and then they have not been adapted, evaluated or used as a basis for other approaches anymore. In other hand, some approaches that have been evaluated, adapted and/or used as a basis for other approaches are: 4, 7, 11, 12, 15, 20, 23, 27, 29, 30, 35, 36, 37 and 38. The approaches 15 [8, 10] and 35 [9] have been evaluated in more than one experimental study. The approaches 12 [7, 11] and 29 [15] were used as basis for, at least, two other approaches.

With regard to the **question Q3**, Table 6 presents the name and description of five concern identification and classification techniques and the approaches that use them. Some experimental studies [2, 14] describe that concern identification and classification activity is a bottleneck in the AORE process. Then, knowing the techniques used in this activity can help professionals and researchers to obtain better strategies to perform this activity.

As can be seen the most used technique in different approaches is "Manual Analysis of the Requirements Document by the Software Engineers with the Aid of Guidelines". Despite being limited to large scale software, this technique has promising benefits, such as minimizing the dependence of users' experience during the application of the approach.

This is an indication that this technique has significant benefits for the concern identification and classification and should be studied more carefully. Another important point to notice is that few approaches (7, 23 and 27) use more than one technique for concern identification and classification. This fact can be an interest research field, because the usage of combined techniques can lead to higher accuracy of AORE approaches.

Finally, to answer the **question Q4**, two bubble charts were built and they are presented, respectively, in Figs. 4 and 5. Regarding to these figures, it is important to comment that:

(i)   the distribution of the published studies on conference proceedings is in Y-axis of the graph of the Fig. 4;
(ii)  the distribution of the published studies on journals, books and other vehicles of scientific publication is in Y-axis of the graph of the Fig. 5. Aiming to simplify the visualization of these graphs, only the initials of the events/journals was used to identify them; and
(iii) the amount of publications per event, journal or book and the year in which they occurred are presented in X-axis of the graphs of Figs. 4 and 5.

It may be notice that most publications (eleven) comes from the Workshop in Aspect-Oriented Requirements Engineering and Architecture Design (EA). This makes sense, because this is an event dedicated to publishing works related to AORE. Another event that has a relevant amount of publications related to AORE (eight) is the International Requirements Engineering (RE), a good and well-known conference in the RE field.

Another important point to be observed in Figs. 4 and 5 is the evolution of AORE publications over the years. It is possible to notice that there was a great amount of publications between 2007 and 2009. In this period, the scientific community have published 52 % of all studies published from 2002 to 2013. Finally, we also can observe that most of studies have been published in conference proceedings and only eight studies (13 %) were published in journals.

This indication is consistent to what we have said about the lack of evaluation studies on the existing approaches. Since the approaches are not mature enough, *i.e.*, the evidences of the robustness and accuracy of such approaches are fragile, publishing them in good journals may be a hard task.

Beside the answers for the questions of Table 1, we aimed to know what are the major research institutions and countries involved with AORE. This information is important because it can help to improve: (i) the dissemination of the work carried out by research groups; and (ii) the cooperation between different research institutions, interested in the same area, *i.e.*, AORE.

Regarding the distribution of studies among research institutions, the graph of Fig. 6 presents the name of the research institution and the percentage of studies published by this institution. Lancaster University (UK) and University of Nova

Lisboa (Portugal) are the most productive research institutions on AORE in the world, with a total of 18.5 % and 21 % of the studies published on this area, respectively. All other research institutions, with only one published study, were grouped in the category "Other ones".

Once the institutions located in Lancaster and Nova Lisboa have published the most of studies related to AORE, countries that had the greatest amount of published studies in this area were Portugal and the UK, as can be seen in the graph of Fig. 7 (besides the University of Nova Lisboa, Polytechnic Institute of Beja also had publications on AORE and is located in Portugal). In third place is Brazil, with 13.6 % of the amount of published studies on AORE. The main universities in Brazil responsible for these publications are Federal University of Rio Grande do Norte and Federal University of Rio de Janeiro (Fig. 6). All other countries, with only one published study, were grouped in the category "Other ones".

Another relevant point that can be raised from this SM, but that was not systematized through research questions, is the identification of the main researchers involved with AORE in the world. The graph in Fig. 8 presents the word cloud (generated by Word Cloud Generator tool, available at: http://www.jasondavies.com/wordcloud/#) generated from the names of the authors of the studies analyzed in this SM. From this graph is possible to identify the main researchers involved with AORE as João Araújo (University of Nova Lisboa), Ana Moreira (University of Nova Lisboa), Awais Rashid (Lancaster University), among others. This information is important because it can serve as a "control" for performing other secondary studies, such as Systematic Mappings or Systematic Reviews. A control can be used to judge whether the search string allows recovering relevant studies or not.

**Table 6.** Techniques for concern identification and classification.

| Concern Identification and Classification Technique | Description |
|---|---|
| Natural Language Processing (NLP) | It is based on NLP techniques such as part-of-speech, lemmatization (approach 7), among others to find keywords of the text of requirements document that are related to with some kind of concern. According to the analyzed studies, this technique was not good for identification of implicit concerns, *i.e.*, concern that are not explicitly described in the text of the requirements document. |
| Approaches that use this technique: 1, 7 and 23. | |
| Probabilistic Models and Clustering | It is based on statistical models, such as (Latent Semantic Analysis - approach 20) and clustering techniques such as the use of tags (approach 34) to find concern candidates. As this is a technique based on statistical analysis, it does not usually bring good results when the requirements document is small, *i.e.*, when the sample is small. |
| Approaches that use this technique: 2, 20, 25 and 34. | |
| Manual Analysis of Requirements Document by Software Engineers | In this type of technique, the software engineer performs a manual inspection in the requirements document trying to discover the software concern. As limitations, we have: (i) the results obtained with this technique are strongly dependent on the experience of those who apply it; and (ii) this technique is error-prone, difficult to replicate its application and has high cost of execution when requirements documents of large software are used. |
| Approaches that use this technique: 10, 13, 15 and 17. | |
| Manual Analysis of Requirements Document by Software Engineers with the Aid of Guidelines | It is similar to the technique of manual analysis, but differs by the fact that users of this technique have guidelines that can assist them during the process of concern identification. One type of guidelines quite common is non-functional requirements catalogs, such as proposed by Chung and Leite [57]. This type of technique can minimizing the dependence of the user experience that applies it, however, it remains costly to be performed on large software. In addition, it takes a certain user experience to understand and follow the guidelines. |
| Approaches that use this technique: 5, 7, 8, 11, 23, 27, 29, 31, 36 and 37. | |
| Software Visualization | It is based on visualization techniques to help the user identify the software concerns. A type of well-known visualization if "Action Views", proposed by Baniassad and Clarke (approach - 12). A limitation of this technique is that for building the visualizations, usually, the user must perform a manual inspection from the requirements document, *i.e.*, it suffer the same problems of technical based on manual analysis of requirements document, cited above. |
| Approaches that use this technique: 6, 18, 12 and 27. | |

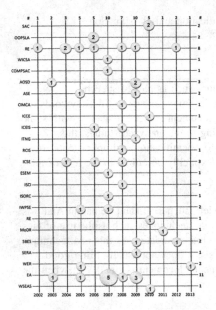

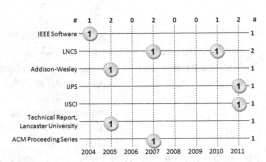

**Fig. 4.** Distribution of the published studies on conference proceedings.

**Fig. 5.** Distribution of the published studies on journals and books.

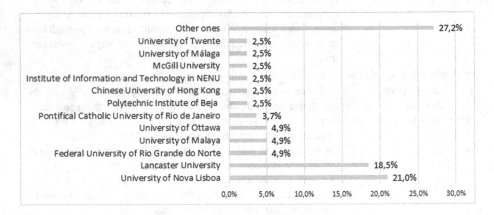

**Fig. 6.** Distribution of the studies regarding to research institutions.

## 5  Threats to Validity

**Primary Studies Selection.** Aiming at ensuring an unbiased selection process, we defined research questions and devised inclusion and exclusion criteria we believe are detailed enough to provide an assessment of how the final set of primary studies was obtained. However, we cannot rule out threats from a quality assessment perspective, we simply selected studies without assigning any scores. In addition, we wanted to be

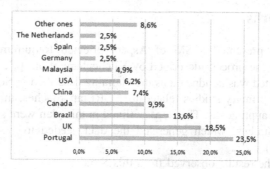

**Fig. 7.** Distribution of the studies regarding to the country where the research institutions are located.

**Fig. 8.** Word cloud derived from the names of the authors of the studies analyzed.

as inclusive as possible, thus no limits were placed on date of publication and we avoided imposing many restrictions on primary study selection since we wanted a broad overview of the research area.

**Missing Important Primary Studies.** The search for primary studies was conducted in two well-known search engines (*Scopus* and *IEEE Xplorer*), even though it is rather possible we have missed some relevant primary studies. Nevertheless, this threat was mitigated by selecting search engines which have been regarded as the most relevant scientific sources [56] and therefore prone to contain the majority of the important studies.

**Reviewers' Reliability.** All the reviewers of this study are researchers in the software engineering, focused on the aspect-oriented development, requirements engineering and aspect mining. Therefore, we are not aware of any bias we may have introduced during the analyses.

**Data Extraction.** Another threat for this review refers to how the data were extracted from the digital libraries, since not all the information was obvious to answer the questions and some data had to be interpreted. Therefore, in order to ensure the validity, multiple sources of data were analysed, *i.e.* papers, technical reports, white papers. Furthermore, in the event of a disagreement between the two primary reviewers, a third reviewer acted as an arbitrator to ensure full agreement was reached.

## 6 Final Remarks

In this paper, we presented a SM of Aspect-Oriented Requirements Engineering (AORE), based on the process described by Kitchenham et al., [4].

The SM presented was conducted as the planning described in Sect. 3. Through an examination of 60 primary studies related to AORE approaches, this review has presented 38 different approaches. The steps outlined in this plan were sufficient to obtain relevant primary studies, which generated the data needed to answer the research questions (Table 1).

Summarizing the results observed from this SM:

1. We have identified 38 (thirty-eight) distinct AORE approaches;
2. The most of identified approaches are related to concern identification and classification, representation and composition activities; we have notice there is a lack of studies based on conflicts detection and resolution;
3. The most studies analysed in this SM consist of presenting either new AORE approaches or adaptation of existing approaches; this indicates that more evaluation studies, based on these existing approaches, need to be performed to verify the real accuracy of them;
4. We have identified five different types of techniques for concern identification and classification, which are used by the AORE approaches: "Natural Language Processing (NLP)", "Probabilistic Models and Clustering", "Manual Analysis of Requirements Document by Software Engineers", "Manual Analysis of Requirements Document by Software Engineers with the Aid of Guidelines" and "Software Visualization". The most used technique is the "Manual Analysis of Requirements Document by Software Engineers with the Aid of Guidelines". Despite being limited to large software, it has promising benefits, such as minimizing the dependence users' experience during the application of the approach;
5. It was notice that most of the studies has been published in conference proceedings, which reinforces the idea that many approaches have been proposed, but few of them are mature enough to be published in journals; and
6. Finally, data show that the most productive research institutions on AORE in the world are Lancaster University and University of Nova Lisboa, located in UK and Portugal, respectively.

Researchers can use this SM as a base for advancing the field, while practitioners can use it to identify approaches that are well-suited to their needs. With the results obtained through this SM, it was possible to develop a set of comparison criteria for AORE approaches, based on common features and variability of the approaches analysed in this SM [58]. Such criteria were then applied on six of the main AORE approaches: 7, 11, 12, 15, 23 and 29. The results can serve as a guide so that users can choose the approach that best meets their needs, and to facilitate the conduct of research in AORE. The main future directions that emerged from this mapping are the need for empirical, comparative evaluations and the opportunity for developing combined AORE approaches.

# References

1. Dijkstra, E.W.: A Discipline of Programming. Pearson Prentice Hall, Englewood Cliffs. p. 217. ISBN: 978-0132158718, 1976
2. Sampaio, A., Greenwood, P., Garcia, A.F., Rashid, A.A.: Comparative study of aspect-oriented requirements engineering approaches. In: 1st International Symposium on Empirical Software Engineering and Measurement, pp. 166–175 (2007)
3. Kai, P., Robert, F., Shadid, M., Michael, M.: Systematic mapping studies in software engineering. In: 12th International Conference on Evaluation and Assessment in Software Engineering Proceedings, Swinton, UK, pp. 68–77 (2008)
4. Kitchenham, B., Charters, S.: Guidelines for performing systematic literature reviews in software engineering. Technical Report. Keele University and Durham University (2007)
5. Moreira, A., Rashid, A., Araújo, J.: Multi-dimensional separation of concerns in requirements engineering. In: Proceedings of the 13th International Conference on Requirements Engineering (RE), pp. 285–296 (2005)
6. Chitchyan, R., Sampaio, A., Rashid, A., Rayson, P.: A tool suite for aspect-oriented requirements engineering. In International Workshop on Early Aspects. ACM, pp. 19–26 (2006)
7. Baniassad, E., Clarke, S.: Theme: an approach for aspect-oriented analysis and design. In: 26th International Conference on Software Engineering (ICSE 2004) (2004)
8. Rashid, A., Sawyer, P., Moreira, A., Araújo, J.: Early aspects: a model for aspect-oriented requirements engineering. In: International Conference on Requirements Engineering (RE) (2002)
9. Yijun, Y., Leite, J.C.S.P., Mylopoulos, J.: From goals to aspects: discovering aspects from requirements goal models. In: International Conference on Requirements Engineering (RE) (2004)
10. Rashid, A., Moreira, A., Araújo, J.: Modularisation and composition of aspectual requirements. In: 2nd International Conference on Aspect-Oriented Software Development (AOSD 2003). ACM (2003)
11. Clarke, S., Baniassad, E.: Aspect-Oriented Analysis and Design: The Theme Approach. Addison-Wesley, New York (2005)
12. Kitchenham, B., et al.: Systematic literature reviews in software engineering – a tertiary study. Inf. Softw. Technol. 52, 792–805 (2010)
13. Wieringa, R., Maiden, N.A.M., Mead, N.R., Rolland, C.: Requirements engineering paper classification and evaluation criteria: a proposal and a discussion. Requirements Eng. 11(1), 102–107 (2006)
14. Herrera, J., et al.: Revealing crosscutting concerns in textual requirements documents: an exploratory study with industry systems. In: 26th Brazilian Symposium on Software Engineering, pp. 111–120 (2012)
15. Whittle, J., Araújo, J.: Scenario modeling with aspects. IEEE Softw. 151(4), 157–172 (2004)
16. Ali, B.S., Kasirun, Z.M.D.: An approach for crosscutting concern identification at requirements level using NLP. Int. J. Phy. Sci. 6(11), 2718–2730 (2011)
17. Ali, B.S., Kasirun, Z.M.: 3CI: a tool for crosscutting concern identification. In: Proceedings of the International Conference on Computational Intelligence for Modeling Control and Automation, Vienna, Austria, pp. 351–355 (2008a)
18. Ali, B.S., Kasirun, Z.M.: Developing tool for crosscutting concern identification using NLP. In: Proceedings of the International Symposium on Information Technology, Kuala Lumpur, Malaysia (2008b)

19. Duan, C., Cleland-Huang, J.: A clustering technique for early detection of dominant and recessive crosscutting concerns. In: Proceedings of the International Conference on Software Engineering, Minneapolis, MN (2007)

20. Lau, Y., Zhao, W., Peng, X., Tang, S.: A connector-centric approach to aspect-oriented software evolution. In: Proceedings of the International Computer Software and Applications Conference, Beijing, China, pp. 391–396 (2007)

21. Weston, N., Chitchyan, R., Rashid, A.: A formal approach to semantic composition of aspect-oriented requirements. In: Proceedings of the 16th IEEE International Requirements Engineering Conference, Catalunya, Spain, pp. 173–182 (2008)

22. Chitchyan, R., et al.: Semantic vs. syntactic compositions in aspect-oriented requirements engineering: An empirical study. In: Proceedings of the 8th International Conference on AOSD, Virginia, USA, pp. 149–160 (2009)

23. Agostinho, S., et al.: A Metadata-driven approach for aspect-oriented requirements analysis. In: Proceedings of the 10th International Conference on Enterprise Information Systems, Barcelona, Spain, pp. 129–136 (2008)

24. Medeiros, M., Silva, L., Medeiros, A.L.: A semi-automatic strategy to identify crosscutting concerns in PL-AOVgraph requirement models. In: Proceedings of the Workshop on Requirements Engineering, Rio de Janeiro, Rio de Janeiro, pp. 46–59 (2013)

25. Sampaio, A., Chitchyan, R., Rashid, A., Rayson, P.: EA-Miner: a tool for automating aspect-oriented requirements identification. In: Proceedings of the International Conference Automated Software Engineering, California, USA, pp. 353–355 (2005)

26. Monteiro, M.P., Fernandes, J.M.: Towards a catalogue of refactorings and code smells for aspectj. In: Rashid, A., Akşit, M. (eds.) Transactions on Aspect-Oriented Software Development I. LNCS, vol. 3880, pp. 214–258. Springer, Heidelberg (2006). Zheng, X., Liu, X., Liu, S.: Use case and non-functional scenario template-based approach to identify aspects. In: Proceedings of the 2nd International Conference on Computer Engineering and Applications, Bali Island, Indonesia, pp. 89–93 (2010).

27. Liu, X., Liu, S., Zheng, X.: Adapting the NFR framework to aspectual use-case driven approach. In: Proceedings of the 7th International Conference on Software Engineering Research, Management and Applications, Hainan Island, China, pp. 209–214 (2009)

28. Wehrmeister, M.A., Freitas, E.P., Pereira, C.E., Wagner, F.R.: An aspect-oriented approach for dealing with non-functional requirements in a model-driven development of distributed embedded real-time systems. In: Proceedings of the 10th International Symposium on Object and Component-Oriented Real-Time Distributed Computing, Orlando, Florida, USA, pp. 428–432 (2008)

29. Araújo, J., Zowghi, D., Moreira, A.: An evolutionary model of requirements correctness with early aspects. In: Proceedings of the 9th International Workshop on Principles of Software Evolution, Dubrovnik, Croatia, pp. 67–70 (2007)

30. Soeiro, E., Brito, I.S., Moreira, A.: An XML-based language for specification and composition of aspectual concerns. In: Proceedings of the 8th International Conference on Enterprise Information Systems, Paphos, Cyprus (2006)

31. Ribeiro, J.C., Araújo, J.: AspOrAS: a requirements agile approach based on scenarios and aspects. In: Proceedings of the 2nd International Conference on Research Challenges in Information Science, Marrakech, Morocco, pp. 313–323 (2008)

32. Araújo, J., Ribeiro, J.C.: Towards an aspect-oriented agile requirements approach. In: Proceedings of the International Workshop on Principles of Software Evolution, Lisbon, Portugal, pp. 140–143 (2005)

33. Sardinha, A., Chitchyan, R., Weston, N., Greenwood, P., Rashid, A.: EA-Analyzer: automating conflict detection in aspect-oriented requirements. In: Proceedings of the 24th

International Conference on Automated Software Engineering, Auckland, New Zealand, pp. 530–534 (2009)

34. Katz, S., Rashid, A.: From aspectual requirements to proof obligations for aspect-oriented systems. In: Proceedings of the IEEE International Conference on Requirements Engineering, Kyoto, Japan, pp. 48–57 (2004)

35. Penim, A.S., Araújo, J.: Identifying and modeling aspectual scenarios with theme and MATA. In: Proceedings of the ACM Symposium on Applied Computing, Switzerland, pp. 287–291 (20100

36. Marques, G., Araújo, J., Lencastre, M.: Integrating problem frames with aspects. In: Proceedings of the 23rd Brazilian Symposium on Software Engineering, Fortaleza/CE, pp. 196–206 (2009)

37. Mehner, K., Monga, M., Taentzer, G.: Interaction analysis in aspect-oriented models. In: Proceedings of the 14th IEEE International Conference Requirements Engineering, Minnesota, USA, pp. 69–78 (2006)

38. Kit, L.K., Man, C.K., Baniassad, E.: Isolating and relating concerns in requirements using latent semantic analysis. ACM SIGPLAN Not. 41(10), 383–396 (2006)

39. Meier, S., Reinhard, T., Stoiber, R., Glinz, M.: Modeling and evolving crosscutting concerns in ADORA. In: Proceedings of the International Conference on Software Engineering, Minneapolis, MN (2007)

40. Marques, A., Moreira, A., Araújo, J.: Multi-dimensional composition by objective. In: Proceedings of the International Conference on Software Engineering, Leipzig, Germany, pp. 19–25 (2008)

41. Mussbacher, G., Amyot, D.: On modeling interactions of early aspects with goals. In: Proceedings of the Workshop on Aspect-Oriented Requirements Engineering and Architecture Design, Charlottesville, VA, USA, pp. 14–19 (2009)

42. Mussbacher, G., Whittle, J., Amyot, D.: Semantic-based interaction detection in aspect-oriented scenarios. In: Proceedings of the IEEE International Conference on Requirements Engineering, Georgia, USA, pp. 203–212 (2009)

43. Hamza, H.S., Darwish, D.: On the discovery of candidate aspects in software requirements. In: Proceedings of the 6th International Conference on Information Technology: New Generations, Las Vegas, USA, pp. 819–824 (2009)

44. Pinto, M., Fuentes, L., Valenzuela, J.A., Pires, P.F., Delicato, F.C.: Promoting the software evolution in AOSD with early aspects: Architecture-oriented model-based pointcuts. In: Proceedings of the Workshop on Aspect-Oriented Requirements Engineering and Architecture Design, Charlottesville, VA, USA, pp. 31–37 (2009)

45. Chernak, Y.: Requirements composition table explained. In: Proceedings of the 20th IEEE International Requirements Engineering Conference, Chicago, Illinois, USA, pp. 273–278 (2012)

46. de Paula, V., Batista, T.: Revisiting a formal framework for modeling aspects in the design phase. In: Proceedings of the International Conference on Software Engineering, Minneapolis, MN (2007)

47. Oliveira, A.R., Araújo, J., Amaral, V.: The VisualAORE DSL. In: Proceedings of the 5th International Workshop on Requirements Engineering Visualization, Sydney, Australia, pp. 11–19 (2010)

48. Alencar, F., et al.: Towards modular i* models. In: ACM Symposium on Applied Computing, pp. 292–297 (2010)

49. Pinto, M., Gamez, N., Fuentes, L.: Towards the architectural definition of the health watcher system with AO-ADL. In: Proceedings of the Workshop in Aspect-Oriented Requirements Engineering and Architecture Design, Minneapolis (2007)

50. Mussbacher, G., Kienzle, J., Amyot, D.: Transformation of aspect-oriented requirements specifications for reactive systems into aspect-oriented design specifications. In: Proceedings of the Model-Driven Requirements Engineering Workshop, Trento, Italy, pp. 39–47 (2011)
51. Mussbacher, G., Amyot, D., Weiss, M.: Visualizing aspect-oriented requirements scenarios with use case maps. In: Proceedings of the First International Workshop on Visualization in Requirements Engineering (2007)
52. Ossher, H., et al.: C. Using tagging to identify and organize concerns during pre-requirements analysis. In: Proceedings of the Aspect-Oriented Requirements Engineering and Architecture Design, Charlottesville, VA, USA, pp. 25–30 (2009)
53. Brito, I., Moreira, A.: Towards a composition process for aspect-oriented requirements. In: Proceedings of the Early Aspects Workshop at AOSD, Massachusetts, USA (2003)
54. Mussbacher, G., Amyot, D., Araújo, J., Moreira, A.: requirements modeling with the aspect-oriented user requirements notation (AoURN): a case study. In: Katz, S., Mezini, M., Kienzle, J. (eds.) Transactions on Aspect-Oriented Software Development VII. LNCS, vol. 6210, pp. 23–68. Springer, Heidelberg (2010)
55. Kienzle, J., Abed, W.A., Klein, J.: Aspect-oriented multi-view modeling. In: Proceedings of the 8th International Conference on AOSD, New York, USA, pp. 87–98 (2009)
56. Dyba, T., Dingsoyr, T., Hanssen, G.K.: Applying systematic reviews to diverse study types. In: Proceedings of the International Symposium on Empirical Software Engineering and Measurement, Washington, DC, USA (2007)
57. Chung, L., Leite, J.S.P.: Non-Functional Requirements in Software Engineering, p. 441. Springer, Heidelberg (2000)
58. Parreira Júnior, P.A., Penteado, R.A.D.: Criteria for comparison of aspect-oriented requirements engineering approaches. In: Brazilian Symposium on Software Engineering Brasília/DF, Brazil, 2013 (in Portuguese)

# SpecQua: Towards a Framework for Requirements Specifications with Increased Quality

Alberto Rodrigues da Silva[✉]

Instituto Superior Técnico, Universidade de Lisboa and INESC-ID, Lisbon, Portugal
alberto.silva@tecnico.ulisboa.pt

**Abstract.** Requirements specifications describe multiple technical concerns of a system and are used throughout the project life-cycle to help sharing a system's common understanding among multiple stakeholders. The interest to support the definition and the management of system requirements specifications (SRSs) is evident by the diversity of many generic and RE-specific tools. However, little work has been done in what concerns the quality of SRSs. Indeed, most recommended practices are mainly focused on human-intensive tasks, mainly dependent on domain experts, and so, these practices tend to be time-consuming, error-prone and unproductive. This paper proposes and discusses an innovative approach to mitigate this status, and defends that with proper tool support – such as the SpecQua framework discussed in the paper –, we can increase the overall quality of SRSs as well as we can increase the productivity associated to traditional tasks of RE such as documentation and validation.

**Keywords:** Requirements specification · Quality of requirements specification · Requirements validation

## 1 Introduction

Requirements Engineering (RE) intends to provide a shared vision and understanding of the system to be developed between business and technical stakeholders [1–3]. The adverse consequences of disregarding the importance of the early activities covered by RE are well-known [4, 5]. System requirements specification, software requirements specification or just requirements specifications (SRS) is a document that describes multiple technical concerns of a software system [1–3]. An SRS is used throughout different stages of the project life-cycle to help sharing the system vision among the main stakeholders, as well as to facilitate communication and the overall project management and system development processes. For achieving an effective communication, everyone should be able to communicate by means of a common language, and natural language provides the foundations for such language. Natural language is flexible, universal, and humans are proficient at using it to communicate with each other. Natural language has minimal adoption resistance as a requirements documentation technique [1, 3]. However, although natural language is the most common and preferred form of requirements representation [6], it also exhibits some intrinsic characteristics that often present themselves as the root cause of many requirements quality problems, such as incorrectness, inconsistency, incompleteness

© Springer International Publishing Switzerland 2015
J. Cordeiro et al. (Eds.): ICEIS 2014, LNBIP 227, pp. 265–281, 2015.
DOI: 10.1007/978-3-319-22348-3_15

and ambiguousness [1, 3]. From these causes, in this paper we emphasize inconsistency and incompleteness because avoiding – or at least mitigating – them requires significant human effort due to the large amount of information to process when combined with inadequate tool support, namely to perform the typical requirements linguistic analysis. On the other hand, although ambiguity and incorrectness – by definition – cannot be fixed without human validation [7], we consider that the tasks required to minimize the effects of both inconsistency and incompleteness (and also ambiguity at some extent) can be automated if requirements are expressed in a suitable language, and if adequate tool support is provided.

In our recent research we consider the RSLingo approach [9–11] as a starting point for this challenge. RSLingo is an approach for the formal specification of software requirements that uses lightweight Natural Language Processing (NLP) techniques [8] to translate informal requirements – originally stated in unconstrained natural language by business stakeholders – into a formal representation provided by a language specifically designed for RE. Unlike other RE approaches, which use languages that typically pose some difficulties to business stakeholders (namely graphical modeling languages such as UML or SysML, whose target audience are engineers), RSLingo encourages business stakeholders to actively contribute to the RE process in a collaborative manner by directly authoring requirements in natural language. To achieve this goal, RSLingo provides (1) the RSL-PL language for defining linguistic patterns that frequently occur in requirements specifications written in natural language, (2) the RSL-RSL language that covers most RE concerns, in order to enable the formal specification of requirements, and (3) an information extraction mechanism that, based on the linguistic patterns defined in RSL-PL, translates the captured information into a formal requirements specification encoded in RSL-IL [10]. However, RSLingo does not provide yet any guarantees that the RSL-IL specifications have the required quality. Therefore, *the main contribute of this research is to propose and discuss that, with proper tool support and an intermediate representation language such as RSL-IL, we can increase the overall quality of SRSs as well as the productivity associated to documentation and validation tasks.* To the best of our knowledge, and apart from our own research on this issue [12], no further works have been proposed before in relation to this complex approach and the way we support automatic validation of SRSs as well as we have discussed the subject of modularity, dependencies and combinatorial effects at requirements level [13].

The structure of this paper is as follows. Section 2 introduces the background underlying this research. Section 3 overviews the SpecQua framework. Section 4 introduces some more technical details of the SpecQua with the purpose to show and discuss the practicability of the proposed approach. Section 5 discusses some experiments that are being implemented in the context of the SpecQua, in particular related to consistency, completeness and unambiguousness. Finally, Sect. 6 presents the conclusion and ideas for future work.

# 2    Background

This section briefly introduces the definition for SRS's quality attributes, overviews requirements specification languages, introduces some considerations on requirements validation, and briefly introduces the RSLingo approach.

## 2.1    SRS's Quality Attributes

Writing good requirements is a human-intensive and error prone task. Hooks summarize the most common problems in that respect [14]: making bad assumptions, writing implementation (How) instead of requirements (What), describing operations instead of writing requirements, using incorrect terms, using incorrect sentence structure or bad grammar, missing requirements, and over-specifying. To achieve quality SRSs must embody several characteristics. For example, the popular "IEEE Recommended Practice for Software Requirements Specifications" states that a good-quality SRS should be [7]: correct, unambiguous, complete, consistent, prioritized, verifiable, modifiable, and traceable. From all of them, we briefly discuss those that are most relevant for the scope of this paper.

**Complete.**  A SRS is considered *complete* if it fulfills the following conditions: (1) Everything that the system is supposed to do is included in the SRS; this can lead us to a never ending cycle of requirements gathering; (2) Syntatic structures filled, e.g.: all pages numbered; all figures and tables numbered, named, and referenced; all terms defined; all units of measure provided; and all referenced material present; and (3) No sections or items marked with "To Be Determined" (TBD) or equivalent sentences. Completeness is probably the most difficult quality attribute to guarantee. In spite that some elements are easy to detect and correct (e.g., empty sections, TBD references), but one never knows when the actual requirements are enough to fully describe the system under consideration. To achieve completeness, reviews of the SRS by customer or users are essential. Prototypes also help raise awareness of new requirements and help us better understand poorly or abstractly defined requirements.

**Consistent.**  A SRS is *consistent* if no requirements described in it conflict among themselves. Disagreements among requirements must be resolved before development can proceed. One may not know which (if any) is consistent until some research is done. When modifying the requirements, inconsistencies can slip in undetected if only the specific change is reviewed and not any related requirements.

**Unambiguous.**  A SRS is *unambiguous* if every requirement stated there has only one possible interpretation. The SRS should be unambiguous both to those who create it and to those who use it. However, these groups of users often do not have the same background and therefore do not tend to describe software requirements the same way. Ambiguity is a very complex phenomenon because natural language is inherently ambiguous (a simple word can have multiple meanings) and most of the times this ambiguity is unintentionally introduced. The most recommended solution to minimize ambiguity is the use of formal or semi-formal specification languages rather than or in complement to natural languages. Also, the use of checklists and scenario-based reading are common recommendations [15].

## 2.2 Requirements Specification Languages

Traditionally, the requirements documentation activity has consisted in creating a natural language description of the application domain, as well as a prescription of what the system should do and constraints on its behavior [16]. However, this form of specification is both ambiguous and, in many cases, hard to verify because of the lack of a standard computer-processable representation [17].

Apparently, the usage of formal methods could overcome these problems. However, this would only address part of the problem, as we still need to take care while interpreting the natural language requirements to create a formal specification, given that in general engineers often misinterpret natural language specifications during the design phase. The same occurs with the attempt to directly create formal requirements specifications, especially when the real requirements are not discovered and validated at first by the business stakeholders [18]. Thus, the usage of such formal languages entails an additional misinterpretation level due to the typically complex syntax and mathematical background of formal method languages [17]. Given that formal methods are expensive to apply – because they require specialized training and are time-consuming [2] –, creating formal requirements specifications might have a negative impact.

In the attempt of getting the best from both worlds – the familiarity of natural language and the rigorousness of formal language –, one can document requirements with controlled natural languages, which are languages engineered to resemble natural language. However, these languages are only able to play the role of natural language to a certain extend: while they are easy to read, they are hard to write without specialized tools [19, 20].

Finally, there are graphical approaches, such as UML and SysML for traditional RE modeling, and i*, KAOS and Tropos notation for Goal-Oriented RE [1]. However, these graphical languages are less expressive than natural language and cannot be regarded as a common language to communicate requirements, because business stakeholders still require training to understand them. Also, despite being "easier to understand" than formal method languages, these graphical modeling languages are regarded as less powerful in terms of analytical capabilities because they often lack tool support to enforce the implicit semantics of their modeling elements, or might even intentionally leave some unspecified parts of the language itself to ease its implementation by tool vendors, in which case they are considered as semi-formal. Some authors even argue that the simplicity of these languages comes precisely from this lack of semantic enforcement: it is easy to create models because "anything goes" [5].

Furthermore, the usage of graphical languages might cause another problem when the modeler includes too much detail in the diagram, cluttering it and thus affecting its readability. Therefore, despite the existence of such graphical approaches, textual natural language specifications are still regarded by many as the most suitable, fast, and preferred manner to initiate the requirements development process of the envisioned software system.

## 2.3    Tools and Interoperability Formats

Regarding the documentation and management of requirements there are two main approaches depending on the respective tool support. On one hand, the approach based on *generic tools (usually office applications and suites, word processors, or just text editors)* such as MS-Word, MS-Excel, OpenOffice or GoogleDocs. This is the most popular approach and many times the solution for simple projects: these tools are ubiquitous and everyone knows how to use them; they are flexible and good enough for most documentation needs. However, these tools do not provide specific features, particularly in what concerns the validation and management of requirements. On the other hand, *RE-specific tools* – such as Doors, RequisitePro, ProR, CaliberRM or Visure Requirements –, allow to define each requirement as a set of attributes, can establish link requirements with each other, and offer analysis and reporting features. Additionally, some tools allow for concurrent editing and change tracking, and to establish links between textual requirements and visual models represented in languages such as UML, SysML or BPMN. Depending on these approaches there are different formats to support requirements interoperability between tools. The common formats provided by generic tools are TXT (plain text) and RTF (rich text format) while RE-specific tools provide XML-based formats such as XMI (usual in UML CASE tools) and ReqIF (Requirements Interchange Format).

## 2.4    Requirements Validation

There is not a consensus in the literature about the use of the terms "verification" and "validation" in the context of RE. However, in this paper we adopt the term as suggested by Pohl and Robertsons, who define *requirements validation* as checking requirements with the purpose of detecting errors such as inconsistencies, ambiguities, and ignored standards. These authors recommend the use of the term "verification" to denote the formal (mathematical) proof of properties of a model, related to properties of concurrent systems, such as safety or absence of deadlocks [1, 2]. Considering the premises regarding the current practices of the requirements documentation and validation activities – such as inspections, walkthroughs, checklists, or using scenarios and prototypes [1–3] –, we consider that the quality of a SRS still strongly depends on the expertise of whoever is performing this activity. Given that most RE activities are still manually performed and involve a large amount of information, to produce a high quality requirements specification one requires an experienced requirements engineer with a vast skills set. However, to avoid large discrepancies in the results of the RE process, we advocate that the quality of requirements specifications and the productivity of the requirements documentation activity can be increased through the formalization of requirements. The computer-processable requirements specifications that are obtained through such a formalization process enable the automation of some manual validations thus relieving requirements engineers from the burden of manually handling a large amount of information to identify requirements quality problems. Additionally, the degree of formalization achieved can be employed to generate complementary artefacts to better support RE tasks, such as requirements validation.

## 2.5    The RSLingo Approach

RSLingo is an approach for the formal specification of software requirements that uses lightweight Natural Language Processing (NLP) techniques to (partially) translate informal requirements – originally stated by business stakeholders in unconstrained natural language – into a formal representation provided by a language specifically designed for RE [9].

The name RSLingo stems from the paronomasia on "RSL" and "Lingo". On one hand, "RSL" (Requirements Specification Language) emphasizes the purpose of formally specifying requirements. The language that serves this purpose is RSL-IL, in which "IL" stands for Intermediate Language [10]. On the other hand, "Lingo" expresses that its design has roots in natural language, which are encoded in linguistic patterns used during by the information extraction process [8, 21] that automates the linguistic analysis of SRSs written in natural language. The language designed for encoding these RE-specific linguistic patterns is RSL-PL, in which "PL" stands for Pattern Language [11]. These linguistic patterns are used by lightweight NLP techniques and, when combined with general-purpose linguistic resources (e.g., VerbNet (http://verbs.colorado.edu/~mpalmer/projects/verbnet.html) and WordNet, (http://wordnet.princeton.edu)), enable the extraction of relevant information from the textual representations of requirements. Finally, the extracted information with these lightweight NLP techniques is formally specified in RSL-IL notation through predefined transformations from RSL-PL into RSL-IL. Upon a match of a requirement's textual representation with one of the RSL-PL linguistic patterns, a transformation should become active. This transformation takes into consideration the semantic roles of each word within the linguistic pattern, and drives the mapping between RSL-PL and RSL-IL.

RSL-IL provides several constructs that are logically arranged into viewpoints according to the specific RE concerns they address [10]. These viewpoints are organized according to two abstraction levels: business and system levels.

To properly understand and document the business context of the system, the business level of the RSL-IL supports the following business-related concerns, namely: (1) the concepts that belong to the business jargon; (2) the people and organizations that can influence or will be affected by the system; and (3) the objectives of business stakeholders regarding the value that the system will bring. Considering these concerns, business level requirements comprise respectively the following viewpoints: Terminology, Stakeholders, and Goals.

On the other hand, at the system level, the RSL-IL supports the specification of both static and dynamic concerns regarding the system, namely: (1) the logical decomposition of a complex system into several system elements, each with their own capabilities and characteristics, thus providing a suitable approach to organize and allocate requirements; (2) the requirements that express the desired features of the system, and also the constraints and quality attributes; (3) the data structures aligned with the business jargon, their relations, and a logical description of their attributes; and (4) the actors, functions, event-based state transitions, and use cases that further detail the aforementioned requirements. Considering these concerns, the System Level comprises the following viewpoints: Architectural; Requirements; Structural; and Behavioral, respectively.

# 3  SpecQua Framework – General Overview

Figure 1 illustrates the context diagram of the SpecQua framework and in particular shows the actors that might interact with it, namely: users (such as requirements engineers and business analysts), and tool superusers and administrators; and third-party tools that directly or indirectly interact with SpecQua. SpecQua provides several import and export features to guarantee the maximum interoperability with third-party tools, namely with commercial or open-source RE-specific tools and also general-purpose text-based authoring tools.

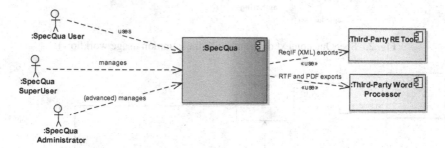

**Fig. 1.** SpecQua context diagram.

Figure 2 shows the common usage workflow supported by the SpecQua framework. This starts (1) by importing a set of requirements specifications produced in the context of third-party tools, namely by importing from one of the following formats: RSL-IL plain text, NL (natural language) plain text, or ReqIF. Then, users might (2) author the requirements directly in the SpecQua tool and (3) run a selected number of tests to automatically validate the quality of the involved requirements. Finally, if the requirements have the intended quality, (4) the requirements can be exported to third-party tools in formats such as ReqIF, RTF or PDF, and this process can iterate as many cycles as needed.

The key concepts underlying the SpecQua tool are depicted in Fig. 3 in a simplified way. There are two levels of abstraction in this domain model: project-level and generic-level. The concepts defined at *generic-level* are managed by users with most responsibility (i.e., by the SpecQua SuperUsers), and involve the definition of GenericSpecifications and Tests. *GenericSpecification* consists in a set of requirements (following the ReqIF terminology) that are defined in a project-independent way, so that they can be reused throughout different projects with minor changes. *Test* is a type of automatic validation that can be defined and run against one or more requirement specifications (see below for more information about Tests).

On the other hand, at *project-level*, there are common concepts to support the management of different projects, assign them to different users, with different permissions, and so on. At this level, any user can create a project, invite other users to participate in that project, and then start to import from third-party tools or author requirement

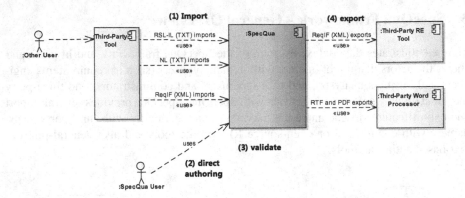

**Fig. 2.** SpecQua context diagram (with the common usage workflow).

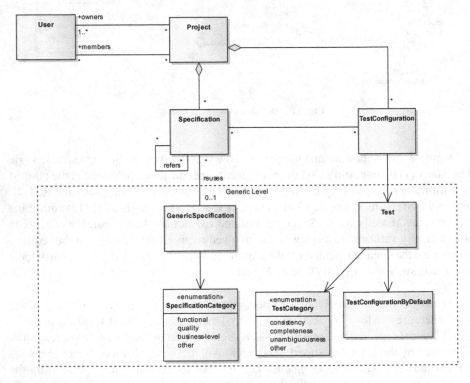

**Fig. 3.** SpecQua domain model.

*Specifications* directly. Users can also establish relationships between specifications and reuse (by copy and customization) GenericSpecifications previously defined. Users may select and configure the relevant tests (via *TestConfiguration*) in order to automatically validate their specifications. If these specifications have the required quality they can be exported to third-party tools or some kind of SRS report can be produced automatically.

Figure 4 suggests the general operation of the validation process with its main input, outputs, and supporting resources. The major input is the `Specifications` files that are the SRS defined in the RSL-IL concrete syntax (or the alternative formats, such as NL or structured ReqIF). The validation outputs are the `Parsing Log` file and the `TestRun Reports` file with the errors and warnings detected by the tool during its execution, respectively during the `Parsing` and the `Validation` processes. Additionally, there are some supporting resources used to better extend and support the tool at run-time, namely: `Tests`, `TestConfiguration`, and `Lexical Resources`.

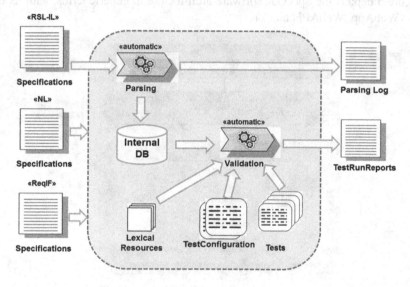

**Fig. 4.** Overview of the validation process.

`Tests` are directly implemented in a given programming language and have additional metadata such as name, description and quality category. (Figure 9 gives an example of such test directly implemented in C#.) `TestConfiguration` is a resource used to support the validation in a flexible way. For example, this resource allow requirements engineers to configure the level of completeness needed for their purpose, in a project basis. This means that different projects may have different needs regarding completeness for their specifications. Finally, `Lexical Resources` are public domain resources (such as WordNet or VerbNet) that support some tests, mostly those related with linguistic issues.

## 4   SpecQua Framework – More Details

The proposed high-level approach has to be implemented by a concrete software tool to offer a real interest and utility. Due to that we have implemented the SpecQua Framework with the purpose to show and discuss the practicability of this approach.

The SpecQua has the following objectives. First, provide SRS's quality reports: for a given RSL-IL specification, the system should be able to provide results for quality tests applied to that specification. Second, easily add and configure new quality tests: it should be easy to develop and add new quality tests in order to extend the tool; additionally it should be easy to configure those tests. Third, provide a Web collaborative workspace: the tool should be accessible via a Web browser and should provide the means for multiple users to work together while specifying, analyzing and validating RSL-IL specifications. (A preliminary prototype is available at http://specqua.apphb.com).

Figure 5 depicts the SpecQua software architecture in generic terms, with its main blocks: WebApp, WebAPI and Core.

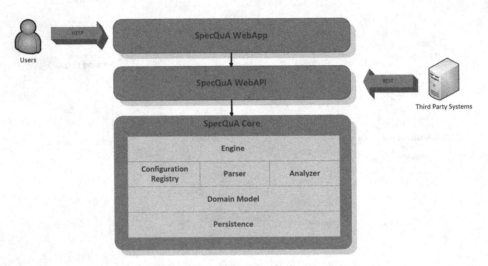

**Fig. 5.** SpecQua architecture.

**SpecQua WebApp.** The WebApp layer corresponds to how users interact with the tool. In a 3-tier layer architecture this corresponds to the presentation layer, although this is more than a simple frontend: the WebApp is a Web-based independent application with its own logic that connects to SpecQua Core via its API.

**SpecQua WebAPI.** This intermediate layer serves as the Application Programming Interface (API) that exposes all the relevant functions that Core provides to the outside. Besides serving as a proxy between WebApp and Core, the API can still be accessed from other clients that do not intend to use the main frontend but still want to take advantage of SpecQua analyses or data resources.

**SpecQua Core.** This layer is the kernel of the SpecQua tool and this is where all the action takes place. A key feature for the system SpecQua is the ease to add new tests and this is implemented using two advanced programming techniques (i.e., dependency injection and reflection) which combined make it possible to associate new quality tests to the tool with minimal effort. At system startup, and based on referenced assemblies, all classes that implement a specific interface become available to the system as new quality tests, and are logically grouped into analyses. Currently, this grouping of testing analysis is performed using a configuration file as exemplified in Fig. 6.

```xml
<?xml version="1.0"?>
<analyses>
  <analysis id="completeness" name="Completeness" descrip-
tion="Completeness">
    <test id="comp-test-1"                type=" Spec-
QuA.Core.Tests.Completeness.ViewpointsElementsAndAttributesNotEmptyTes
t, SpecQuA.Core" />
    <test id="comp-test-2" type=" Spec-
QuA.Core.Tests.Completeness.StakeholdersAsGlossaryTermsTest, Spec-
QuA.Core" />
  </analysis>
  <analysis id="consistency" name="Consistency" descrip-
tion="Consistency">
    <test id="cons-test-1"                type=" Spec-
QuA.Core.Tests.Consistency.NoSynonmsAreReferencedOnSpecificationTest,
SpecQuA.Core" />
    <test id="cons-test-2"                type=" Spec-
QuA.Core.Tests.Consistency.SynsetPropertyMustMatchExternalLexicalDatab
aseTest, SpecQuA.Core"/>
  </analysis>
  <analysis id="prioritization" name="Prioritization" descrip-
tion="Prioritization">
    <test id="pri-test-1"                type=" Spec-
QuA.Core.Tests.Prioritization.SpecificationHasPrioritiesCorrectlyDistr
ibutedTest, SpecQuA.Core"/>
  </analysis>
</analyses>
```

**Fig. 6.** Example of a SpecQuA's test configuration file.

Each test is independent from each other and may have its own particular configuration. This configuration is defined in XML format and has no restriction on the schema level: it is up for those who develop the test (i.e., the SpecQua superuser), to define the schema and interpret it in the respective test. Each test may or may not have a default configuration.

Additionally, the SpecQua Core has the Parser component which is responsible to parse the input RSL-IL text and map it to the Domain Model (in the internal database). This parsing is done by ANTLR (http://www.antlr.org/) using a grammar specific for the RSL-IL language. With this grammar, ANTLR generates a parser and a lexer that can be used to validate the syntax and the semantic of a given input. If the input does not have errors, then the result is a representation of the domain model entities that can be tested. This grammar has some similarities with the BNF notation as expressed in Fig. 7. (Other parsers to different import formats might be developed in the future.)

## 5    Discussion

Despite having a simple user-interface, a lot is done in the background when carrying out the analysis of a specification. In this case, when the user wants to validate the

```
public specification returns [ProjectSpecification Specification]
  : spec = projectDef { $$Specification = $spec.specification; };

projectDef returns [ProjectSpecification specification]
  : { $specification = new ProjectSpecification(); }
    LPAR PROJECT (retAtt=attribute {CollectAttribute($specification, $retAtt.att.Key, ... ;})*
    (LPAR gloss = glossary { $specification.Glossary = $gloss.glossary ;} RPAR)?
      (LPAR stk = stakeholders {$specification.Stakeholders = $stk.stakeholders;} RPAR)?
      (LPAR gls = goals {$specification.Goals = $gls.goals;} RPAR)?
      (LPAR system {} RPAR)?
    RPAR;
  ...
```

**Fig. 7.** An excerpt from the RSL-IL grammar for ANTLR.

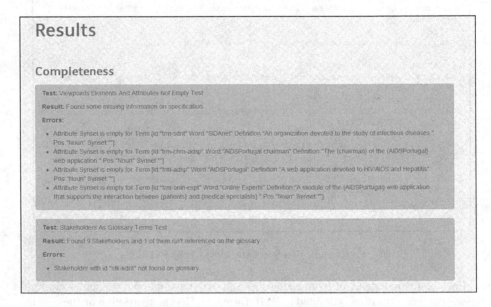

**Fig. 8.** Excerpt of a report test for the AIDSPortal example.

specification, it is parsed with the specific ANTLR grammar. If any syntactic or semantic error is detected in the specification, the user is alerted and the process stops. However, if the specification is successfully parsed, the tests can be selected and configured and are run against the specification. Finally, a report is shown to the user such as the example shown in Fig. 8. In the following subsections we introduce and discuss some tests that are being implemented in the context of the SpecQua framework.

### 5.1 Consistency Validation

The consistency validation enforces that the information model underlying the RSL-IL specification is well-formed, or consistent in accordance with the RSL-IL metamodel, which involves, for example, the following concrete validations.

**Consistent Attribute Values.** SpecQua verifies whether the value assigned to a given attribute is valid based on the semantics of its RSL-IL construct. For instance, SpecQua can systematically enforce that every *id* attribute follows the predefined prefix of each RSL-IL construct. Also, SpecQua can also provide a short mnemonic for the *id* attribute based on the word attribute of the related Term, which is more meaningful than just a numeric sequence.

The combination of the specific prefix with this mnemonic allows one to better understand when two RSL-IL constructs of different types refer to the same underlying concept (e.g., they describe different concerns about the same business notion).

**Consistent Numeric Sequences.** There are several attributes in RSL-IL constructs that follow a certain numeric sequence. For instance, SpecQua checks the *order* attribute of each Sentence within a given Requirement. Also, SpecQua verifies the values assigned to the *label* attributes of a given UseCase's Steps. In all these cases, SpecQua must ensure that each construct was assigned a unique numeric value of that sequence, and that all the assigned numbers follow a monotonic increasing sequence without gaps.

**Referential Integrity.** SpecQua must check and enforce that those relationships between different RSL-IL constructs are properly defined in terms of the values (i.e., references) assigned to the attributes that support the establishment of such relationships. The most obvious case is given by the strong dependency of most RSL-IL constructs on a Term that unambiguously defines the semantics of the underlying concept. Thus, SpecQua must check whether all RSL-IL constructs that depend on the Terminology viewpoint effectively provide a valid reference for a previously defined Term through its *id*. That is the example of the test shown in Fig. 9 that checks if all Stakeholders are referenced as Terms defined in the glossary.

Another important aspect of this validation is also to support for the resolution of Term references based on their *acronym* or *word* values, instead of only relying on the value of its *id* attribute.

Although we are illustrating this sort of validations mostly based on the Terminology viewpoint, there are similar cases in other RSL-IL viewpoints. For instance, this problem is similar to the validation performed regarding the *source* attribute of a given Goal, which should be resolved to a well-defined Stakeholder.

## 5.2   Completeness Validation

The completeness validation is based on the test's configuration resource that enables the definition of the level of completeness required for each RSL-IL specification. This level of completeness varies on a project basis or even, for the same project, along the timeline according the needs of the project team. We consider three levels of completeness:

**Completeness at Model Level.** At the macro level, one can define which viewpoints are required for considering a concrete RSL-IL specification to be complete. For example, during the initial stage of a project lifecycle, one may only require the Terminology, Stakeholders, and Goals viewpoints to consider the specification as being complete. On the other hand, if the project is running in a more advanced stage

```
namespace ReSQuA.Core.Tests.Completeness
{
    public class StakeholdersAsGlossaryTermsTest : AbstractTest
    {
        private int stkMissed;
        private int stkCount;

        protected override void InnerExecute(ProjectSpecification specification, ConfigurationNode configuration)   {
            stkMissed = 0; stkCount = 0;

            foreach (var stakeholder in specification.Stakeholders.GetAll())  {
                VerifyStakeholder(stakeholder, specification);
            }

            CurrentReport.Success = (stkMissed == 0);

            if (!CurrentReport.Success) {
                CurrentReport.Message = string.Format("Found {0} Stakeholders and {1} of them {2} referenced on the glossary.",
                    stkCount, stkMissed, (stkMissed == 1) ? "isn't" : "aren't");
            }
        }

        private void VerifyStakeholder(Stakeholder stakeholder, ProjectSpecification specification) {
            if (stakeholder == null) throw new ArgumentException("The provided argument isn't a stakeholder.");

            stkCount++;
            Term stkTerm = specification.Glossary.GetTerm(stakeholder.Role);

            if (stkTerm == null)  {
                stkMissed++;
                CurrentReport.Errors.Add(string.Format("Stakeholder with id \"{0}\" not found on glossary.", stakeholder.Id));
            }

            foreach (var child in stakeholder.GetChildElements())    {
                VerifyStakeholder(child as Stakeholder, specification);
            }
        }
    }
}
```

Fig. 9. An excerpt of a concrete Test.

(for instance, after a couple of iterations), the remaining System Level viewpoints should be also considered in order to provide a complete requirements specification.

**Completeness at Viewpoint Level.** For each viewpoint one can define which constructs are mandatory or optional. For example, for the Behavioral viewpoint one might only consider as being relevant the existence of the Function construct (and not of Event) in order to consider that viewpoint as being complete.

**Completeness at Construct Level.** For each construct (e.g., Term, Stakeholder, Goal, Entity, Use Case) one can define which attributes are mandatory or optional. For example, for the Goal construct one can define the criticality as a mandatory attribute and the source (a reference for the Stakeholder responsible for that goal) as an optional attribute. Still at construct level, we can enforce that the names of some of these constructs (e.g., the names of actors and entities) should be defined as a unique term in the Terminology viewpoint.

### 5.3   Unambiguousness Validation

While in a formal specification (such as in RSL-IL) inconsistencies and incompleteness can be automatically detected, ambiguities deal directly with the meaning of those specifications, thus they are hard to be detected by automatic processes. Consequently, ambiguity tends to be detected mostly by human intervention, for example through analysis and inspection of the specification and through the use of prototypes. However, regarding this semantic level, still some automatic validation can be applied to reduce ambiguity, such as those discussed below.

**Semantic Analysis.** First, based on general-purpose linguistic resources that encode world knowledge, SpecQua can further verify the semantic validity of relations established between RSL-IL constructs, especially those strongly related with the natural language representation of concepts. For instance, an advanced validation feature consists in using WordNet to check whether the value of the word attribute of synonym Terms are indeed synonyms of the word attribute's value of the primary Term to which they are associated. Second, the information encoded within WordNet can be used to cross-check whether the Term associated with a given Stakeholder (through its role attribute) is aligned with the classification provided by the StakeholderType enumeration based on the *lexname* attribute of the WordNet synset referred by the *synset* attribute's value of that Term. Third, and still regarding the relations between different Stakeholders, SpecQua must verify the semantics of the hierarchical composition of these RSL-IL constructs. For instance, it does not make sense to specify that a Stakeholder whose type is "group.organizational" is MemberOf of another Stakeholder whose type is "individual.person". This means that the hierarchical Stakeholders composition must follow the implicitly semantics entailed in the values of the StakeholderType enumeration, which are ordered from broader groups to more specific entities. Fourth, SpecQua can determine whether the relation between a given RSL-IL construct and a Term is semantically valid based on the *pos* attribute of that Term and the semantics of the other RSL-IL construct. For instance, it does not make sense to associate an Entity with a Term whose part-of-speech (provided by either its *pos* or *synset* attributes) classifies the Term as a *verb*, instead of a *noun*. Fifth, another example consists in checking whether nouns associated with the agent thematic relation (e.g., the subject of natural language sentences in the active voice) are defined as Actors and, if so, whether they can be traced back to the respective Stakeholders via a shared Term.

**Terminology Normalization.** The RSL-IL glossary (i.e., its Terminology viewpoint) formally defined the terms associated with the main concepts used throughout the requirements specification. There are different types of relations that can be established between terms, i.e. relations of type *synonym*, *antonym*, and *hyponym*. One motivation for using these relations is to reduce the number of redundant Terms employed within the RSL-IL specification, by providing a unique Term for each concept. So, it is important to avoid the definition of two or more synonym Terms by clearly stating which one of them should be classified as the *primary* Term, and the other(s) as *secondary* Term(s). Based on this information, SpecQua can perform a systematic normalization of Terms through a common find and replace process and, consequently, reduce the requirements specification's ambiguity.

## 6 Conclusions

RE comprises several tasks including requirements elicitation, analysis and negotiation, documentation and validation. We recognize that natural language is the most common and popular form to document SRSs. However, natural language exhibits several limitations, in particular those related with requirements specification quality such as incorrectness, inconsistency, incompleteness and ambiguousness.

This research extends the RSLingo approach by considering that requirements are represented in RSL-IL, automatically extracted from natural language specifications or authored directly by their users. This paper proposes a generic approach to automatically validate these specifications and describes the SpecQua framework that shows the practicability and utility of this proposal. The flexibility of SpecQua and the initial cases studies developed so far allows us to preliminary conclude that this approach helps to mitigate some of the mentioned limitations, in particular in what respect inconsistency, incompleteness and ambiguousness.

For future work we plan to implement SpecQua in a more extensive way, in particular with features related with the support of a collaborative environment, allowing end-users to author and validate directly their requirements [22], eventually with different representations beyond natural language, RSL-IL and ReqIF. Several import and export features would also be relevant in order to promote tools interoperability as discussed in the paper. Finally, we still intend to explore the integration of requirements specifications with testing [23] and model-driven engineering approaches [24–26] to still increase the quality and productivity of Software Engineering in general terms.

**Acknowledgements.** This work was partially supported by national funds through FCT – Fundação para a Ciência e a Tecnologia, under the project PEst-OE/EEI/LA0021/2013 and DataStorm Research Line of Excellency funding (EXCL/EEI-ESS/0257/2012). Particular thanks to my students David Ferreira and Joao Marques for their strong participation and involvement in this research.

## References

1. Pohl, K.: Requirements Engineering Fundamentals, Principles, and Techniques, 1st edn. Springer, Heidelberg (2010)
2. Sommerville, I., Sawyer, P.: Requirements Engineering: A Good Practice Guide. Wiley, New York (1997)
3. Robertson, S., Robertson, J.: Mastering the Requirements Process, 2nd edn. Addison-Wesley, Boston (2006)
4. Emam, K., Koru, A.: A replicated survey of IT software project failures. IEEE Softw. **25**(5), 84–90 (2008)
5. Davis, A.M.: Just Enough Requirements Management: Where Software Development Meets Marketing, 1st edn. Dorset House Publishing, New York (2005)

6. Kovitz, B.: Practical Software Requirements: Manual of Content and Style. Manning, Greenwich (1998)
7. IEEE Computer Society, 1998. IEEE Recommended Practice for Software Requirements Specifications. IEEE Std 830-1998
8. Bird, S., Klein, E., Loper, E.: Natural Language Processing with Python. O'Reilly Media, Sebastopol (2009)
9. Ferreira, D., Silva, A.R.: RSLingo: an information extraction approach toward formal requirements specifications. In: Proceedings of the 2nd Int. Workshop on Model-Driven Requirements Engineering (MoDRE 2012), IEEE CS (2012)
10. Ferreira, D., Silva, A.R.: RSL-IL: An interlingua for formally documenting requirements. In: Proceedings of the of Third IEEE International Workshop on Model-Driven Requirements Engineering (MoDRE 2013), IEEE CS (2013)
11. Ferreira, D., Silva, A.R.: RSL-PL: A linguistic pattern language for documenting software requirements. In: Proceedings of the of Third International Workshop on Requirements Patterns (RePa 2013), IEEE CS (2013)
12. Silva, A.R.: Quality of requirements specifications: a framework for automatic validation of requirements In: Proceedings of ICEIS 2014 Conference, 2014, SCITEPRESS (2014)
13. Silva, A.R., et al.: Towards a system requirements specification template that minimizes combinatorial effects. In: Proceedings of QUATIC 2014 Conference, IEEE CS (2014)
14. Hooks I.: Writing good requirements. In: Proceedings of the Third International Symposium of the INCOSE, vol. 2 (1993)
15. Kamsties, E., Berry, D.M., Paech, B.: Detecting ambiguities in requirements documents using inspections. In: Proceedings of the First Workshop on Inspection in Software Engineering (2001)
16. van Lamsweerde, A.: From Worlds to Machines. In: Nuseibeh, B., Zave, P. (eds.) A Tribute to Michael Jackson. Lulu Press (2009)
17. Foster, H., Krolnik, A., Lacey, D.: Assertion-based Design. Springer, Heidelberg (2004)
18. Young, R., 2003. The Requirements Engineering Handbook. Artech Print on Demand
19. Fuchs, N.E., Kaljurand, K., Kuhn, T.: Attempto controlled english for knowledge representation. In: Baroglio, C., Bonatti, P.A., Małuszyński, J., Marchiori, M., Polleres, A., Schaffert, S. (eds.) Reasoning Web. LNCS, vol. 5224, pp. 104–124. Springer, Heidelberg (2008)
20. Kuhn, T.: Controlled English for Knowledge Representation. Ph.D. thesis, Faculty of Economics, Business Administration and Information Technology of the University of Zurich (2010)
21. Cunningham, H.: Information extraction, automatic. Encyclopedia of Language and Linguistics, 2nd edn. Elsevier, Amsterdam (2006)
22. Ferreira, D., Silva, A.R.: Wiki supported collaborative requirements engineering. In: Proceedings of the 4th International Symposium on Wikis. ACM (2008)
23. Moreira, R., Paiva, A.C.R., Memon, A.: A pattern-based approach for GUI modeling and testing. In: IEEE 24th International Symposium on Software Reliability Engineering (ISSRE), IEEE CS (2013)
24. Silva, A.R., et al.: Integration of RE and MDE paradigms: the ProjectIT approach and tools. IET Softw. J. 1(6), 294–314 (2007)
25. Savic, D., et al.: Use case specification at different levels of abstraction. In: Proceedings of QUATIC 2012 Conference, 2012, IEEE CS (2012)
26. Ribeiro, A., Silva, A.R.: XIS-Mobile: a DSL for mobile applications. In: Proceedings of SAC 2014 Conference, ACM (2014)

# Software Agents and Internet Computing

# Analyzing Virtual Organizations' Formation Risk in P2P SON Environments

Rafael Giordano Vieira, Omir Correia Alves Junior, and Adriano Fiorese[✉]

Department of Computer Science, Santa Catarina State University, Joinville, Brazil
{rafaelgiordano12,omalves,adriano.fiorese}@gmail.com

**Abstract.** Virtual Organizations (VOs) have emerged as a powerful enterprising strategy to leverage the activities of Small and Medium sized Enterprises, by providing a way of sharing their costs and benefits when attending to particular demands. Along with their numerous advantages, VOs also pose several challenges, including additional risks that need to be considered to ensure its correct operation. Proper risk analysis provides more solid means for managers to evaluate and further decide about the most suitable VO composition for a given business. Therefore, this paper aims to develop a mathematical method that analyzes and measures the risk in a set of partners, synthesized in the form of Service Providers, which will compose a VO in a P2P SON environment. By means of validation of the proposed method, a set of simulations were carried out and the results are presented in this paper.

**Keywords:** Virtual organization · Risk analysis · P2P SON

## 1 Introduction

The fundamental developments in network technologies, particularly the advent of Peer-to-Peer Service Overlay Networks (P2P SON) [1,2], provided an advantageous environment for companies make their services available to the user community at large. The joining of the SON and P2P fields offers a high potential for handling services, by creating dynamic and adaptive value chain networks across multiple Service Providers (SPs). Moreover, a wide range of services can be made available, as well as an environment where price and quality can be competitive differentials [3].

The P2P SON concept applies to a broad range of network architectures. This paper deals particularly with the Virtual Organization (VO) type of network. A VO is a temporary and dynamic strategic alliance of autonomous, heterogeneous and usually geographically dispersed companies created to attend very particular business opportunities [4,5]. In this sense, the P2P SON acts as infrastructure that provides an environment for VO formation and, additionally, enhances benefits to SPs, e.g., sharing costs, bandwidth and others [6].

Although the mentioned advantages of using P2P SON can improve the VO formation process, the natural VO networked structure faces additional

© Springer International Publishing Switzerland 2015
J. Cordeiro et al. (Eds.): ICEIS 2014, LNBIP 227, pp. 285–301, 2015.
DOI: 10.1007/978-3-319-22348-3_16

risks than other general forms of organization. These additional risks come, in part, from the increasing sharing of responsibilities among companies and their dynamic nature of relationships [7]. The problem is that there is a lack of more systematic and integrated methods to handle the several dimensions of risk, which includes both intra-organizational and inter-organizational aspects of the VO. Since the analysis of these risks is key to ensure the VO's proper operation, it should be complemented with the risk analysis support methods that can provide more agility and transparency when creating new VOs [8].

In a previous work, it was designed a three-layer architecture for services management in P2P SONs, named OMAN [6]. The OMAN offers an efficient search and selection process of most suitable SPs in a multi-provider environment. Authors also presented results of SP selection by using a geographical location criteria [2]. However, the VO risk aspects in the context of P2P SONs were not addressed.

This paper presents an exploratory work, which complements the proposals of [2] and [8], and looks for answering how SPs can be properly selected when considering risks. This work consists in adding an additional risk management level in the search and selection process and conceiving a new risk analysis method, named MARTP (Multi criteria Risk Analysis Method applied to P2P Service Overlay Networks). In the proposed method, the SPs are two-stage evaluated, both individually and collectively. The goal of the method is to measure the level of risk and identify which SPs are most risky for the VO formation. This will allow decision-makers to decide wisely about which SPs should be effectively discarded for a given business collaboration opportunity, and additionally, the identified risks can be managed and hence mitigated throughout the VO formation process.

The remainder of this paper is organized as follows: Sect. 2 addresses the problem of SPs search and selection in P2P SONs and contextualizes it within the VO risk analysis proposal. Section 3 describes the proposed method for VO risk analysis. Section 4 presents the set of experiments conducted to evaluate the proposed method and also presents the final results. Finally, Sect. 5 concludes the paper and outlines some future work.

## 2    General Background

### 2.1    Service Provider Integration

As cited in Sect. 1, different SPs can be grouped in a given VO in order to accomplish a mutual goal, the so-called collaboration opportunity. These SPs might range from non-governmental organizations to autonomous software entities, by sharing costs, benefits and risks, acting as they were one single enterprise [5]. Regarding to the classical main phases of a VO life cycle (creation, operation, evolution and dissolution phases) [9], this paper focuses on the creation (or formation) phase, which is seen in Fig. 1. Within the creation phase, this analysis is carried out during the *Partner's Search and Selection* step (left circle).

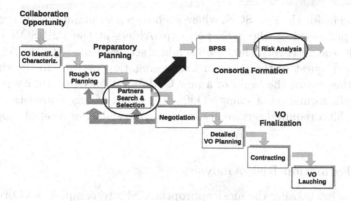

**Fig. 1.** Framework for the VO formation process. extended from [9].

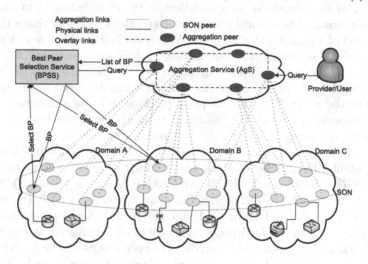

**Fig. 2.** BPSS model [2].

The process of collaboration among the SPs in a VO is accomplished through interactions between their business processes, which are usually supported by a network infrastructure. Particularly, this work addresses the use of P2P SON to organize all the SPs committed with the eventual VO formation. A P2P SON is an infrastructure designed to provide services and, in the context of this work, it can be seen as a breeding environment for the creation of VOs [10]. It is also considered that the SP's search and selection procedures are performed by a service management architecture developed in [6], particularly through its BPSS module, which aims to select one SP from the set of SPs that fulfill a required service according a particular metric.

Figure 2 details the BPSS module. P2P SON, shown as the elliptic curve, is created covering domains (clouds in Fig. 2) that contain SPs. Every peer in the P2P SON runs service(s) from the corresponding SPs. The AgS is created in a higher level inside the P2P SON, where each AgS peer maintains an aggregation of services published by the SON peers (providers at the P2P SON level). In order to select a SP (peer), the BPSS sends a service request to the AgS, which forwards the request to the peers in the aggregation overlay. In the context of this work, this means the begin of a new Collaboration Opportunity (CO) that will trigger the formation of a new VO [9]. The result of this request is a list of all SPs that fulfill a required service according a particular, or a set of, application metrics.

## 2.2   VO Formation Risk Analysis

The problem in choosing the most appropriate SPs to compose a VO is critical. The concept of risk can be handled at a number of perspectives. [11] provides an overview of risk definition, as a variation in the distribution of possible outcomes, their probabilities, and their subjective values. [12] associates risk with the likelihood of an unfavorable outcome. When applied on this research context, the risk can then be viewed as a composition of three basic elements: the general environment where it can happens; its occurrence probability; and the scope of its impact in the case of its occurrence [13]. Specifically, a risk is characterized by the potential of an SP – that in principle is able to be a member of a VO – to do not perform correctly its assigned task regarding the associated CO's requirements and hence hazarding the VO success.

In the literature review, a number of risk analysis methods has been identified as potentially suitable for VOs, namely FMEA (Failure mode and effects analysis), FTA (Fault Tree Analysis), AHP/ANP (Analytic Hierarchy/Network Process), ETA (Event Tree Analysis), Bayesian Networks, CNEA (Causal Network Event Analysis) and Ishikawa Diagram [13–17]. Some requirements can be pointed out for the tackled problem: events can be treated as independent from each other; the deterministic relation between events can be known; events analysis can be both qualitative and quantitative; a risk can be globally quantified after a succession of events. Regarding these requirements, ETA and AHP techniques were selected to be used and combined in the proposed method.

In that same reasoning line, there is a number of works related VO's sources of risk and its analysis. In [7,18], thirteen KPIs were identified as general risk sources in VOs, further identifying the importance of each one. In [19], the problem of risk mitigation in VO was discussed, and four processes were identified to improve the level of VOs performance reliability. In [20] two sources of risks were specified (external and internal), and risk occurrence likelihood in the life span of a VO was calculated based on them. [21,22] considered the fuzzy characteristics and the project organization mode of VOs to propose Multi Strategy Multi Choice (MSMC) risk programming models.

In addition, [23] presented a competence model to support efficiently the process of partner's selection, which works in the context of Service-Oriented Virtual Organization Breeding Environments. When dealing with SP as the type of partners, the same authors have proposed a hybrid DEA-Fuzzy method for analyzing the risk in the process of VO partners search and selection [24]. The method is strongly based in the concept of SPs importance and efficiency within the VO, where aspects like SPs historical performance and relative efficiency are considered in the analysis and therefore in the calculation performed.

All the reviewed works in the literature have proposed contributions to isolated elements of the whole tackled problem of this research. Nevertheless, none have somehow formalized how the proposed KPIs should be used nor provided means to quantity VO partners risks before the VO formation. Moreover, it was not identified proposals that specify a method or procedure that aims to systematize the process of risk qualification/quantification involved in the SPs' Search and Selection for the VO formation, while focusing in the SP type of partner. Therefore, this paper presents as a contribution a way to specify KPIs together with a mathematical method that enable measuring the risk in the VO formation.

The way the risk is represented should be aligned with the organization goals so that the most important ones can be determined for further and more proper management. Identifying risk sources is the first and most important step in risk management [13]. Therefore, there are four main sources of risks regarding VOs that were considered the most critical ones: *trust, communication, collaboration* and *commitment* [7]. In this work they are modeled as KPIs and their values are calculated and provided by the methodology developed in [8]:

- **Trust.** SPs who are going to compose a VO do not necessarily have prior knowledge about each other before starting collaborating. Thus, trust is crucial to bear in mind, which in turn involves commitment in doing the planned tasks. When trust among providers is not enough established there is a hesitation to share risks and so the VO can be jeopardized;
- **Communication.** Communication among VO's SPs is a key factor for its proper operation. They should provide correct information about parts, products and services, collaborating in solving conflicts, sharing practices, etc. However, this can be complicated by the fact SPs are heterogeneous, independent, geographically dispersed and usually have distinct working cultures. The insufficient communication can put a VO on risk;
- **Collaboration.** Collaboration is characterized when the sharing of risks, costs and benefits of doing business are agreed and fairly distributed among partners. However, when a collaboration agreement is not clearly defined, i.e., when there is no clear definition of its main objectives, the VO risk increases;
- **Commitment.** Commitment is related to the attitude of VO members with each other, i.e., it considers the contributions and agreements made by and among them for a business. This is important as partners have complementary skills and so it is important they feed the whole environment with the right and timely information. The VO risk gets higher when partners fail in that attitude.

# 3   The Proposed Method

## 3.1   MARTP Overview

The devised method for risk analysis is generally presented in Fig. 3. It starts having as input a pre-selected and ranked list of most adequate SPs (through BPSS simulation) registered in a P2P SON environment. The main goal of the proposed risk analysis method is to add another support dimension for decision-making, identifying and measuring how risky is each of those SP candidates involved in the VO formation process. In this work, considering VO reference theoretical foundations [5], the so-called VO Manager is seen as the main decision-maker.

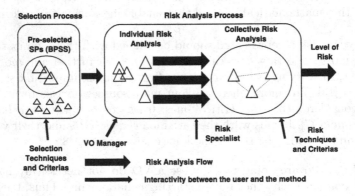

Fig. 3. Overview of MARTP.

The method splits the problem into two stages. In the first stage, it starts measuring the risks individually, for each possible SP, and after and based on that, collectively, for the entire SP team for the given VO. In this context, the VO manager has the following role: to quantify the level of importance of each SP in the VOs before creating it. There is also a risk specialist, who is in charge of auditing the SPs historical KPI metrics. The risk techniques and criteria are applied to assess the risk according to the VO manager guidelines.

## 3.2   MARTP Architecture

The MARTP method itself is illustrated in Fig. 4. It divides the problem into two phases: the first phase does the individual risk analysis applying the Event Tree Analysis (ETA) method for that. The second phase does the risk analysis taking the group of SPs as a whole into account, applying the Analytic Hierarchy Process (AHP) method [14,15].

**Individual Risk Analysis.** In the first phase of MARTP, it is performed an individual risk analysis for pre-selected SPs. ETA is particularly suitable for risk analysis of systems where there are interactions between several types of

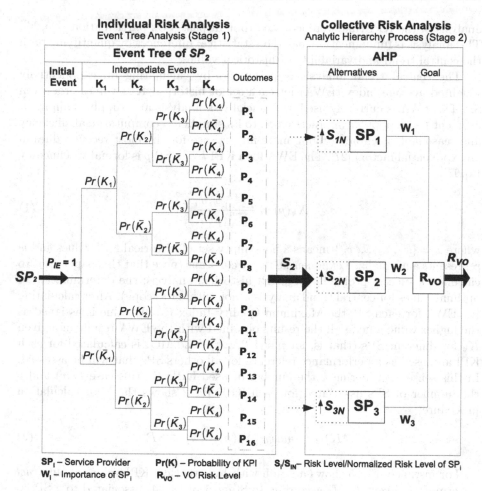

**Fig. 4.** MARTP architecture.

probabilistic events, whether dependent or independent [14]. It uses a visual representation based on a logical binary tree structure, known as Event Tree (ET), as shown in Stage 1 of Fig. 4.

An ET is a probability tree, which provides two possible conditions: success and failure. It also has three basic components: initial event; intermediary events; and outcomes. The initial event begins the ET creation process. In this work, it corresponds to one pre-selected SP, and the assigned probability ($P_{IE}$) is always 1 (or 100 %) in the beginning [14]. Next step consists in specifying the (four) intermediary events, which are represented by the (four) KPIs: *trust*, *communication*, *collaboration* and *commitment*.

These events are used to quantify the effectiveness of a particular SP, i.e., if it is able or not to compose a VO, and to generate an ET by assigning success and failure probabilities to each of them as shown in Stage 1 of Fig. 4. The criterion to assign the KPI success probability to each SP takes the historical values analysis of the KPI that were assigned to it in past VOs participations [25, 26]. This analysis is fundamentally based on statistical inferences by quantifying both the central trend and variability of historical values.

The central trend analysis is performed by calculating an exponentially weighted average index (EWA) for each set of historical KPI values of a given SP. The EWA is currently used in financial risk analysis and supply chain management being popular in practice due to its simplicity, computational efficiency and reasonable accuracy (giving more importance for the most recent values in an exponential factor) [27]. The EWA for a KPI $k$ of a SP $p$ is formally defined by Eq. 1:

$$\bar{X}_k(p) = \frac{\sum_{i=1}^{n} x_i w_i}{\sum_{i=1}^{n} w_i} \tag{1}$$

where $x = \{x_1, x_2, ..., x_n\}$ means a non-empty set of historical KPI values and $w$ represents a normalized exponential decay constant (note that this paper aims to calculate a success probability by KPI historical analysis; the determination of optimal values for central trend analysis is not within its scope). After calculating the EWA for each SP, the Maximum Quality Index (MQI) value is assigned as the higher value among all the results obtained with the EWA results of a given $K_k$ for different SPs (that is, for $p = 1, 2, ...n$). The MQI is calculated for each KPI and used as a performance reference for all others SPs that will be assessed. In this sense, considering $k$ the number of used KPIs (in this case *four*) and $p$ the number of SPs associated for each KPI, Eq. 2 shows the MQI calculation procedure:

$$MQI_k = max_k \left( \bar{X}_k(p) \right) \quad \forall p \in SP \tag{2}$$

For instance, Fig. 5 shows a graph with hypothetical KPI values about *trust* (intermediate event $KPI_1$ according to Stage 1 of Fig. 4) associated to a SP.

The value of the MQI (left circle in Fig. 5) assigned for this KPI would have been set up as 6.7 (this value is the highest EWA value calculated for SPs using the KPI trust). Nevertheless, it is obvious that, when taking into account only the highest MQI value, a few KPIs will reach an acceptable success probability. For this reason, a variability metric is well-suited in this scope. The metric used is the standard deviation (SD) of MQI. Therefore, the acceptable interval will range not only values above 6.7, but also includes the SD interval, which are 2.4 (right circle in Fig. 5). So, the acceptable range turn to $6.7 - 2.4 = 4.3$.

The values assigned to each KPI can vary from 0 to 10 and are associated with a probability success rate which varies from 0 to 1, respectively. Assuming that each SP has participated in $n_{PA}$ past VOs and since that $n_R$ represents the number of SP's previous participation in VOs where its KPIs values are higher than $MQI_k - SD_k$ (those values with an * in Fig. 5), Eq. 3 calculates the KPI success probability for the current participation.

$$Pr\left( K_k \right) = \frac{n_R}{n_{PA}} \tag{3}$$

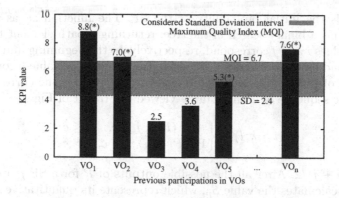

**Fig. 5.** Trust KPI historical values for a given SP.

The failure rate for a given KPI is represented as $Pr\left(\bar{K}_k\right)$ by the following equation:

$$Pr\left(\bar{K}_k\right) = 1 - Pr\left(K_k\right) \tag{4}$$

According to Fig. 4, the success and failure probability rates are calculated for all KPIs that compose the ET of an SP, which are presented by the four intermediate (and independent from each other) events $K_{1:4}$ that populate the ET. Event $K_2$, for instance, would be related to KPI communication, with success and failure values of $Pr(K_2) = 0.90$ and $Pr\left(\bar{K}_2\right) = 0.10$, respectively.

After assigning all probabilities for all ET branches, it is necessary to identify if the SPs are minimally qualified to compose a VO. For this, a calculation is performed to obtain the final probabilities for all event combinations composing the ET. They are determined for each of the $2^{|K|}$ branches of ET and are got by multiplying the probabilities of events that compose each path. Following, it is applied the Harmonic Weighted Average (HWA) calculation over the set of results obtained in the ET, in order to obtain the level of risk for each SP.

The presented concepts can be formalized as follows:

Let $SP = \{SP_1, SP_2, ..., SP_n\}$ be a set of $n$ SPs previously selected, where each element in this set is associated with a different type of service activity that is being requested in a CO. Let $K = \{K_1, K_2, ..., K_m\}$ be a set of $m$ KPIs associated to a $SP_n$, and $Pr\left(K_k\right)$ the probability function associated with each event $K_k$ (as defined in Eq. 3). ETA events occur independently, i.e., where the occurrence of an event does not affect the occurrence of the other.

Now consider $P = \{P_1, P_2, ..., P_{2^{|K|}}\}$ as a set of all possible outcomes from the $2^{|K|}$ ET events combinations. The procedure for obtaining this set was performed using a Binary Search Tree (BST) [28], which travels $2^{|K|}$ different paths and assigns a value to each element of $P$, as shown in Eq. 5:

$$P = \bigcup_{k=1}^{2^{|K|}} \left[ P_{IE} * \prod_{l=1}^{|K|} \omega(i, j, k, l) \right] \tag{5}$$

where $P_{IE}$ is the initial probability of the SP. The function $\omega$, as shown in Eq. 6, performs a binary search in the tree, returning a path element from each iteration. Values $i$ and $j$ correspond, respectively, to the beginning and ending of the search, and have $i = 0$ and $j = 2^{|K|}$ as initial values. The value $k$ corresponds to the index of the sought element (an element of $P$) and $l$, the current level of the tree. The sequence of events can be viewed in Stage 1 of Fig. 4.

$$\omega\,(i, j, k, l) = \begin{cases} Pr\,(K_l)\,; j = c, & k \leq c \\ 1 - Pr\,(K_l)\,; i = c, & k > c \end{cases} \tag{6}$$

where $c = (i + j)/2$. After all the possible outputs of $P$ for a SP $p$ are defined, the method calculates the value $S_p$, which represents its quantitative risk level, as formalized in Eq. 7. The procedure for calculating the $S_p$ takes into account performing a Harmonic Weighted Average (HWA) over all elements of $P$. The HWA comprises a particular type of average where the weights follow a sequence of harmonic numbers (i.e., the sequence harmonically converges to zero at each new number).

$$S_p = \sum_{j=1}^{k} \left(\frac{1}{j}\right) P_j \tag{7}$$

Therefore, from the set of $S_p$ obtained results (i.e., the risk of each partner), the proposed method will be able to measure and analyze the SP's risk collectively.

**Collective Risk Analysis.** The second phase of the MARTP method aggregates the results provided by the first phase (that is, the risk level of each pre-selected SPs) to calculate the VO success probability as a whole (if the VO formation can succeed or not). To perform this, it is used the Analytic Hierarchy Process (AHP) [15], as seen in Stage 2 of Fig. 4. The AHP method arranges the problems resolution in a hierarchy, starting from the more general element (usually the goal) to the most specific elements (often alternatives). In this paper, the problem to be solved using AHP is specified by two components: the goal and the alternatives. The goal of AHP is to determine the overall VO risk. The alternatives consist in the individual risk levels for each SP ($S_p$) obtained through the individual risk analysis (Stage 1 of Fig. 4).

The first step to perform the AHP evaluation consists in defining a normalized level of risk $S_{pN}$ for each SP $p$. The normalization procedure is necessary as a way to enable the collective risk analysis step. The level of risk of each SP ($S_p$) is normalized in a scale that varies from 0 to 1 as seen in Eq. 8:

$$S_{pN} = \frac{S_p}{|S|max(S)} \tag{8}$$

where $max(S)$ represent the highest value of $S$ and $|S|$ the number of elements in $S$.

After normalizing the risk level of each SP, it is applied a correspondent weight $W_p$, which determines the degree of importance of each $SP_p$ regarding the VO. In this work, the degree of importance of each SP is determined by an external entity named VO Manager [5], which is seen as the main decision maker. Therefore, the VO Manager plays a key role in the process of evaluating the VOs since he will inform which SPs have greater or lesser importance, so prioritizing some specific SPs in relation to the other ones.

For example, given a VO in the formation process, composed by three SPs (as illustrated in Fig. 4), each SP will have a level of importance (weight). The importance of each SP can be classified as follows: $[0.0; 0.25]$: very low; $[0.25; 0.50]$: relatively low; $[0.50; 0.75]$: relatively high; $[0.75; 1.00]$: very high. In this sense, the VO manager can change the weights $W_p$ according to the degree of importance that is assigned to each $SP_p$. This feature increase the robustness of the method when compared to other techniques, by determining collectively the influence that each SP has within the VO and the level of risk of each one will impact overall VO risk level.

Accordingly, let be $W_1, W_2, ..., W_n$ the weight of each alternative $S_{1N}, S_{2N}, \cdots, S_{pN}$ associated the goal. The overall goal, i.e., to measure the VO risk level, is represented by $R_{VO}$, whose simplified calculation procedure is shown in Eq. 9:

$$R_{VO} = 1 - \sum_{i=1}^{p} W_i S_{iN} \qquad (9)$$

From the calculation presented in Eq. 9, is obtained the overall level of risk in the VO formation, considering the importance of each SP in the process.

## 4   Evaluation Framework

This section presents results of the MARTP method evaluation. A computational simulation is conducted based on the preliminary results of [2] and [24] researches, in order to add the risk analysis context and also analyze the impact in the process of selecting SPs. Next subsections present the results obtained.

### 4.1   Computational Prototype

The developed computational prototype was split into two modules: BPSS (Best Peer Selection Service) [2] and DFRA (Decision Framework for Risk Analysis). The first module implements the BPSS model developed by [2,6] (view Sect. 2.1) using the PeerFactSim.KOM discrete event simulator [29] to support the creation of the P2P SON infrastructure and additionally make available the process for SPs search and selection. On the other hand, the DFRA module focuses specifically on the risk analysis method simulation. This model was integrated with BPSS in order to group the pre-selected SPs into a new potential VOs and to perform a MARTP evaluation (see Fig. 3).

Regarding technical system specifications, the prototype was built and the tests were developed in a computer Intel Core i5 3.1GHz, 4.0GB of RAM and Linux Mint 14.1 64-bit distribution.

## 4.2 Simulations Setup

The initial configuration for the risk scenario follows the same rules used for the SP's selection. The data was taken from the CAIDA project and MaxMind GeoIP database [30]. The SPs are represented by a set of pre-selected SON peers whose identifiers (IPs addresses) belong to five geographical domains, corresponding to the five countries (Portugal, Spain, France, Italy and Germany). They are also equally distributed between the five domains.

Taking into account the data setup for the risk analysis, the KPIs values assigned to each SP follows a linear distribution (varying from 0 to 1) during the simulation. The linear distribution strategy for generating the KPIs values is primarily used because companies are often very variable and the implementation of the four chosen KPIs (trust, communication, collaboration and commitment) in real scenarios depends on the culture and working methods currently applied by the involved organizations. In the same way, it is also considered that each SP has participated at 10 previous VOs (in average) when it was selected.

## 4.3 Results

The results presented in this section aims to present a comparative analysis of the proposed MARTP method that analyses risk of SPs to form a VO with: (a) the selection process proposed by [2]; and (b) the DEA-Fuzzy risk analysis method proposed by [24]. The main goal of this comparison is to verify which of the three procedures present a more critical analysis regarding the risk level of sets of "preformed VOs" (i.e., a set of grouped SPs). The overall procedures for obtaining the selection and risk results are divided into two different phases as follows:

- The first phase basically performs the process of SP's search and selection through the BPSS model [2]. In this paper, the process for VO formation will take into account a set of three distinct SPs that will provide the following services: VPN ($SP_1$), Billing ($SP_2$) and Video-Streaming ($SP_3$). For this reason, the BPSS model should be used three-times in order to provide the three different SPs, each of them providing its particular service.
- The second phase take emphasis on the risk analysis process (MARTP). Thus, this phase uses as input the three SPs acquired at the first phase ($SP_1$, $SP_2$ and $SP_3$) to group them into a consortia to measure the risk of their collaboration in composing a new VO. It is worth to mention that the MARTP and the DEA-Fuzzy risk analysis methods uses the same criteria (KPIs), thus enabling the comparison of the results.

The results comprise four test cases, where each one present a different distribution in the absolute importance of $SP_1$, $SP_2$ and $SP_3$ (that compose a potential VO), as specified in Table 1. It means that there will be evaluated from cases where both the three SPs have little importance in the VO to cases where both the three SPs have great importance at all.

**Table 1.** Level of importance assigned for each SP in the four test cases.

|  | $SP_1$ | $SP_2$ | $SP_3$ |
|---|---|---|---|
| Test case 1 (Fig. 6(a)) | 0.30 | 0.30 | 0.30 |
| Test case 2 (Fig. 6(b)) | 0.50 | 0.50 | 0.50 |
| Test case 3 (Fig. 6(c)) | 0.70 | 0.70 | 0.70 |
| Test case 4 (Fig. 6(d)) | 0.30 | 0.50 | 0.70 |

The process of comparison between the level of risk of preformed VOs without risk analysis (i.e., only grouping the three SPs acquired in the first phase into a consortia) and with risk analysis (analyzing the risk of the previous formed consortia with the MARTP and the DEA-Fuzzy methods) is depicted in Figs. 6(a) – (d). The simulation comprises 11 sets of individual scenarios divided into clusters that range [50, 300] SPs. For each of the eleven scenarios (50 SPs, 75 SPs, $\cdots$, 300 SPs), the first and second phase early mentioned are performed 100 times, which will result in eleven 3-bar clusters, which one varying from 0 to 100. This scale is represented by the vertical axis and shows, in percentage, the average level of risk of the simulated VOs when: not using any method of risk analysis (just selection), using the MARTP method and using the DEA-Fuzzy method.

It is worth mentioning that the selected SPs in the first phase (i.e., without risk analysis), will always form VOs since there is no criteria to prevent their formation beyond those for selection. In this case, the risk level regarding the first-bar cluster in the results figures will be always assigned to zero. On the other hand, there is a significant increase on the risk percentage in the analyzed VOs under the methods that consider the risk analysis as the formation decision criterion (MARTP and DEA-*Fuzzy*) for all the four simulated test cases. In this sense, it can be pointed out that both methods behave like a VO formation filter, regardless of whether pre-selected SPs have been rated as the best or the worst according to a particular selection criteria.

Considering average results (and based on a confidence interval of 95 %), the greatest increase in the level of risk of the analyzed VOs when using the MARTP method was 77.54 %, and for the DEA-*Fuzzy* method, 98.81 %. On the other hand, the smallest increase when adding the MARTP method was 41.22 %, and for the DEA-*Fuzzy* method, 8.03 %.

Taking into account the comparison between the two methods of risk analysis, one can notice a reasonable difference in their VO's level of risk distribution (in average), which can be seen in the Figs. 6(a) and (c). Although analyzing the

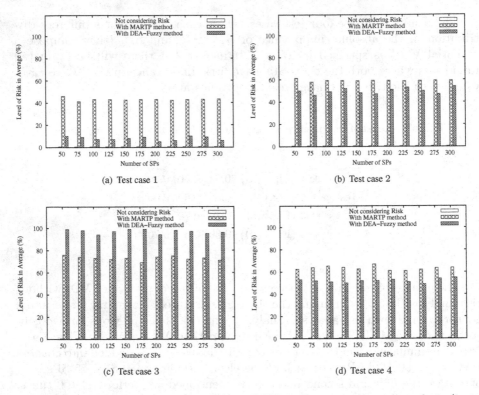

**Fig. 6.** Distribution in the number of formed VOs when not using risk analysis (just selection), MARTP method and the DEA-Fuzzy method [24].

risk in a similar way (i.e., the more importance have the SPs, the more risky is the VO) the DEA-Fuzzy method presented a very higher and lower VO's level of risk distribution when compared with the MARTP method (41.22 % and 77.54 % for MARTP, versus 8.03 % and 98.81 % for DEA-Fuzzy method) while in the Figs. 6(b) and (d) there were a similar occurrence of these distributions (59.76 % and 62.69 % versus 49.04 % and 50.54 %).

The main factor that contributes to this result is related to the bicriterial facet of the proposed method (MARTP), which takes into account a more critical and balanced analysis regarding its stages of individual and collective risk analysis. This means that MARTP avoids the small oscillations in the calculation of each step that generates large variations in the distribution of VO's level of risk in [24]. It means that the performance of a given SP has more equal – or similar – importance in relation to their relative importance within the VO, what is desirable to ensure the consistency of the proposed method in different kinds of scenarios. In the work presented in [24], these minor variations in the degree of importance of each SP led to huge variation in the distribution of risk (standing near from 0 % or near from 100 %), as shown in Figs. 6(a) and (c).

In this sense, one can conclude that the risk analysis compared methods may favour a greater or lesser critical evaluation, where both the individual SP's performance and its importance in the VO plays a decisive role in the final outcome to calculate the final VO level of risk. Therefore, it should be taken great prevention and control by the VO Manager and risk specialists when evaluating the importance as well as the competence of each SP in order to provide confidence in the future operation of the VO, which is the next step further the VO formation.

## 5   Conclusions

This paper addressed some issues related to VO risk identification and measurement. Overall, risk analysis has become a key element in VO planning since small errors can lead them to impairment as a whole. Therefore, it is proposed a new method to perform a risk analysis in a set of Service Providers (SPs) that are going to compose a Virtual Organization (VO).

The presented method, named MARTP, is composed of two stages. The first stage performs an individual risk analysis for all pre-selected SPs, by basing it on ETA analysis. Having as input the results from the first stage, the second stage calculates and analyzes the global risk considering all SPs together. It applies AHP method to accomplish that.

Most of the works in the literature review have approached the problem of selecting partners via an analysis focused on members competences and capabilities. This work extended this vision incorporating an additional dimension of decision, which is risk. Therefore, besides considering these two dimensions, this work qualifies and quantifies the risk of each possible VO, suggesting to decision-makers a measurable rank of the less risky compositions.

The risk measurement is also based on four chosen KPIs (trust, communication, collaboration and commitment) that seem appropriate regarding the technical literature. Moreover, these indicators are combined with real geographical data in a simulation environment. The performed simulations involved sets of pre-selected SPs (taken in [2]) in order to explore the comparison between the proposed method and the method previously proposed by [24], evaluating which of the two methods presents more criticality in the process of analyzing the risk in VOs.

The achieved results seem promising about the suitability of the method regarding its purpose. There were found that the proposed method may be more or less critical for the assessment of an SP to be part of a VO, where this analysis is equally dependent on both the individual SPs' performance and their importance in the VO, unlike [24]. This particular feature enhances the consistency of the proposed method when dealing with different kind of scenarios, which is very common in VOs. The VO Manager plays a key role in the evaluation since it informs which SPs have greater or lesser importance in the VO.

Likewise, the presented method contributes to a more concrete way to express, measure, assess and deal with the risks in VO forming, both individually and collectively, while focusing only on SPs. Nevertheless, the use of the method in the process of risk analysis provides an evaluation with a lower level of subjectivity, discarding SPs or not, before composing a VO, according to the established criteria. Future work includes testing the method in near-real scenarios as well as extending the evaluation to an expert panel, in order to improve its quality.

# References

1. Duan, Z., Zhang, Z.L., Hou, Y.T.: Service overlay networks: SLAs, QoS, and bandwidth provisioning. IEEE/ACM Trans. Netw. **11**, 870–883 (2003)
2. Fiorese, A., Simões, P., Boavida, F.: Peer selection in P2P service overlays using geographical location criteria. In: Murgante, B., Gervasi, O., Misra, S., Nedjah, N., Rocha, A.M.A.C., Taniar, D., Apduhan, B.O. (eds.) ICCSA 2012, Part II. LNCS, vol. 7334, pp. 234–248. Springer, Heidelberg (2012)
3. Zhou, S., Hogan, M., Ardon, S., Portman, M., Hu, T., Wongrujira, K., Seneviratne, A.: Alasa: when service overlay networks meet peer-to-peer networks. In: Proceedings of the 11th Asia-Pacific Conference on Communications (APCC 2005), pp. 1053–1057, Perth, Australia (2005)
4. Mowshowitz, A.: Virtual organization. Commun. ACM **40**, 30–37 (1997)
5. Camarinha-Matos, L.M., Afsarmanesh, H.: On reference models for collaborative networked organizations. Int. J. Prod. Res. **46**, 2453–2469 (2008)
6. Fiorese, A., Simões, P., Boavida, F.: OMAN – a management architecture for P2P service overlay networks. In: Stiller, B., De Turck, F. (eds.) AIMS 2010. LNCS, vol. 6155, pp. 14–25. Springer, Heidelberg (2010)
7. Alawamleh, M., Popplewell, K.: Risk sources identification in virtual organisation. In: Popplewell, K., Harding, J., Raul, P., Chalmeta, R. (eds.) Enterprise Interoperability IV, pp. 265–277. Springer, London (2010)
8. Junior, O.C.A., Rabelo, R.J.: A KPI model for logistics partners' search and suggestion to create virtual organisations. Int. J. Netw. Virtual Organ. **12**, 149–177 (2013)
9. Camarinha-Matos, L.M., Afsarmanesh, H.: Collaborative networks: a new scientific discipline. J. Intell. Manuf. **16**, 439–452 (2005)
10. Afsarmanesh, H., Camarinha-Matos, L.M.: A framework for management of virtual organization breeding environments. In: Proceedings of the 6th Working Conference on Virtual Enterprises (PRO-VE 2005), pp. 35–48, Valencia, Spain (2005)
11. March, J.G., Shapira, Z.: Managerial perspectives on risk and risk taking. Manage. Sci. **33**, 1404–1418 (1987)
12. Moskowitz, H., Bunn, D.: Decision and risk analysis. Eur. J. Oper. Res. **28**, 247–260 (1987)
13. Vose, D.: Risk Analysis: A Quantitative Guide. John Wiley & Sons, New Jersey (2008)
14. Ericson, C.A.: Hazard Analysis Techniques for System Safety. John Wiley & Sons, New York (2005)
15. Saaty, T.L.: Decision making - the analytic hierarchy and network processes (AHP/ANP). J. Syst. Sci. Syst. Eng. **13**, 1–35 (2004)
16. Rychlik, I.: Probability and Risk Analysis: An Introduction for Engineers. Springer-Verlag, Berlin (2006)
17. Rhee, S.J., Ishii, K.: Using cost based fmea to enhance reliability and serviceability. Adv. Eng. Inf. **17**, 179–188 (2003)

18. Alawamleh, M., Popplewell, K.: Analysing virtual organisation risk sources: an analytical network process approach. Int. J. Netw. Virtual Organ. **10**, 18–39 (2012)
19. Grabowski, M., Roberts, K.H.: Risk mitigation in virtual organizations. J. Comput. Mediate. Commun. **3**, 704–721 (1998)
20. Li, Y., Liao, X.: Decision support for risk analysis on dynamic alliance. Decis. Support Syst. **42**, 2043–2059 (2007)
21. Min, H., Xue-Jing, W., Lu, F., Xing-Wei, W.: Multi-strategies risk programming for virtual enterprise based on ant colony algorithm. In: Proceedings of the 1st International Conference on Industrial Engineering and Engineering Management, pp. 407–411, Singapore (2007)
22. Fei, L., Zhixue, L.: A fuzzy comprehensive evaluation for risk of virtual enterprise. In: Proceedings of the 10th International Conference on Internet Technology and Applications, pp. 1–4, Corfu, Greece (2010)
23. Paszkiewicz, Z., Picard, W.: Modelling competences for partner selection in service-oriented virtual organization breeding environments (2011). CoRR abs/1111.5502
24. Lemos, F.S.B.d., Vieira, R. G., Fiorese, A., Junior, O.C.A.: A hybrid dea-fuzzy method for risk assessment in virtual organizations. In: Proceedings of the 11th International FLINS Conference on Decision Making and Soft Computing (2014)
25. Pidduck, A.B.: Issues in supplier partner selection. J. Enterp. Inf. Manage. **19**, 262–276 (2006)
26. Goranson, H.T.: The Agile Virtual Enterprise Cases, Metrics, Tools. Quorum Books, Westport (1999)
27. Montgomery, D.C., Runger, G.C.: Applied Statistics and Probability for Engineers. John Wiley & Sons, New Jersey (2011)
28. Bentley, J.L.: Multidimensional binary search trees used for associative searching. Commun. ACM **18**, 509–517 (1975)
29. Stingl, D., Gross, C., Ruckert, J., Nobach, L., Kovacevic, A., Steinmetz, R.: PeerfactSim.KOM: a simulation framework for peer-to-peer systems. In: Proceedings of the 13th International Conference on High Performance Computing and Simulation (HPCS 2011), pp. 577–584, Istanbul, Turkey (2011)
30. Caida: Macroscopic topology project (2013). http://www.caida.org/analysis/topology/macroscopic/

# CRAWLER-LD: A Multilevel Metadata Focused Crawler Framework for Linked Data

Raphael do Vale A. Gomes[1(✉)], Marco A. Casanova[1],
Giseli Rabello Lopes[1], and Luiz André P. Paes Leme[2]

[1] Departamento de Informática, PUC-Rio, Rio de Janeiro, Brazil
{rgomes, casanova, grlopes}@inf.puc-rio.br
[2] Instituto de Computação, UFF, Niterói, Brazil
lapaesleme@ic.uff.br

**Abstract.** The Linked Data best practices recommend to publish a new tripleset using well-known ontologies and to interlink the new tripleset with other triplesets. However, both are difficult tasks. This paper describes CRAWLER-LD, a metadata crawler that helps selecting ontologies and triplesets to be used, respectively, in the publication and the interlinking processes. The publisher of the new tripleset first selects a set $T$ of terms that describe the application domain of interest. Then, he submits $T$ to CRAWLER-LD, which searches for triplesets whose vocabularies include terms direct or transitively related to those in $T$. CRAWLER-LD returns a list of ontologies to be used for publishing the new tripleset, as well as a list of triplesets that the new tripleset can be interlinked with. CRAWLER-LD focuses on specific metadata properties, including subclass of, and returns only metadata, hence the classification "metadata focused crawler".

**Keywords:** Focused crawler · Tripleset recommendation · Linked data

## 1 Introduction

The Linked Data best practices [1] recommend publishers of triplesets to use well-known ontologies in the triplification process and to interlink the new tripleset with other triplesets. However, despite the fact that extensive lists of open ontologies and triplesets are available, such as DataHub,[1] most publishers typically do not adopt ontologies already in use and link their triplesets only with popular ones, such as DBpedia[2] and Geonames.[3] Indeed, according to [2–4], linkage to popular triplesets is favored for two main reasons: the difficulty of finding related open triplesets; and the strenuous task of discovering instance mappings between different triplesets.

This paper describes CRAWLER-LD, a crawler that addresses the problem of recommending vocabulary terms and triplesets to assist publishers in the publication and the interlinking processes. Unlike typical Linked Data crawlers, the proposed crawler then focuses on metadata with specific purposes, illustrated in what follows.

---

[1] http://datahub.io.
[2] http://dbpedia.org.
[3] http://www.geonames.org.

© Springer International Publishing Switzerland 2015
J. Cordeiro et al. (Eds.): ICEIS 2014, LNBIP 227, pp. 302–319, 2015.
DOI: 10.1007/978-3-319-22348-3_17

In a typical scenario, the publisher of a tripleset first selects a set $T$ of terms that describe an application domain. Alternatively, he could use a database summarization technique [5] to automatically extract $T$ from a set of triplesets. Then, the publisher submits $T$ to CRAWLER-LD, which will search for triplesets whose vocabularies include terms direct or transitively related to those in $T$. The crawler returns a list of vocabulary terms, as well as provenance data indicating how the output was generated. For example, if the publisher selects the term "Music" from WordNet, the crawler might return "Hit music" from BBC Music. Lastly, the publisher inspects the list of triplesets and terms returned, with respect to his tripleset, to select the most relevant vocabularies for triplification and the best triplesets to use in the interlinking process, possibly with the help of recommender tools. We stress that the crawler was designed to help recommender tools for Linked Data, not to replace them.

This paper is organized as follows. Section 2 presents related work. Section 3 summarizes background information about the technology used. Section 4 briefly explains how the crawler works with the help of an example. Section 5 details the crawling process. Section 6 describes experiments that assess the usefulness of the crawler. Finally, Sect. 7 presents the conclusions and future work.

## 2  Related Work

We first compare CRAWLER-LD with Linked Data crawlers. Fionda et al. [6] present a language, called NAUTILOD, which allows browsing through nodes of a Linked Data graph. They introduced a tool, called *swget* (semantic web get), which evaluates expressions of the language. An example would be: "find me information about Rome, starting with its definition in DBpedia and looking in DBpedia, Freebase and the New York Times databases".

```
swget < dbp:Rome > (< owl:sameAs >)* -saveGraph
-domains {dbpedia.org,rdf.freebase.com,data.nytimes.com}
```

LDSpider [7] is another example of a Linked Data crawler. Similarly to the crawler proposed in this paper, LDSpider starts with a set of URIs as a guide to parse Linked Data. Ding et al. [8] present the tool created by Swoogle to discover new triplesets. The authors describe a way of ranking Web objects in three granularities: Web documents (Web pages with embedded RDF data), terms and RDF Graphs (triplesets). Each of these objects has a specific ranking strategy.

The Linked Data crawlers just described have some degree of relationship with the proposed crawler, though none has exactly the same goals. As explained in the introduction, the proposed crawler focuses on finding metadata that are useful to design new triplesets. Furthermore, rather than just dereferencing URIs, it also adopts *crawling queries* to improve recall, as explained in Sect. 5.1.

We now comment on how the proposed crawler relates to recommender tools for Linked Data. Some generic recommender tools use keywords as input. Nikolov et al. [2, 3] use keywords to search for relevant resources, using the label property of the resources. Indeed, a label is a property used to provide a human-readable version of the name of the resource.[4] A label value may be inaccurate, in another language or simply be a synonymous of the desired word. There is no compromise with the schema and its relationships. Therefore, the risk of finding an irrelevant resource is high. Martínez-Romero et al. [4] propose an approach for the automatic recommendation of ontologies based on three points: (1) how well the ontology matches the set of keywords; (2) the semantic density of the ontology found; and (3) the popularity of the tripleset on the Web 2.0. They also match a set of keywords to resource label values, in a complex process.

CRAWLER-LD may be used as a component of a recommender tool, such as those just described, to locate: (1) appropriate ontologies during the triplification of a database; (2) triplesets to interlink with a given tripleset. We stress that the crawler was not designed to be a full recommender tool, but rather to be a component of one such system.

## 3   Background

The Linked Data principles advocate the use of RDF [9], RDF Schema [10] and other technologies to standardize resource description.

RDF describes resources and their relationships through *triples* of the form $(s, p, o)$, where: $s$ is the *subject* of the triple, which is an RDF URI reference or a blank node; $p$ is the *predicate* or *property* of the triple, which is an RDF URI reference and specifies how $s$ and $o$ are related; and $o$ is the *object*, which is an RDF URI reference, a literal or a blank node. A triple $(s, p, o)$ may also be denoted as "$<s> <p> <o>$".

A *tripleset* is just a set of triples. In this paper will use *dataset* and *tripleset* interchangeably.

RDF Schema is a semantic extension of RDF to cover the description of classes and properties of resources. OWL [11] in turn extends RDF Schema to allow richer descriptions of schemas and ontologies, including cardinality and other features.

RDF Schema and OWL define the following predicates that we will use in the rest of the paper:

- `rdfs:subClassOf` indicates that the subject of the triple defines a subclass of the class defined by the object of the triple
- `owl:sameAs` indicates that the subject denotes the same concept as the object
- `owl:equivalentClass` indicates that both the subject and the object are classes and denote the same concept
- `rdf:type` indicates that the subject is an instance of the object

For example, the triple

```
<dbpedia:Sweden > < rdf:type > < dbpedia:Country > .
```

indicates that the resource Sweden is an instance of the class Country.

Triplesets are typically available on the Web as SPARQL endpoints [12] or as file dumps (large files containing all the data from a tripleset, or small files containing only the relevant data for a defined term). A third option is through URL dereferencing,

---

[4] http://www.w3.org/TR/rdf-schema/#ch_label

which means that the resource contains description data about itself so it is possible to discover more data simply by reading the resource content.

More than just a query language similar to SQL, SPARQL is a protocol: it defines the query interface (HTTP), how requests should be made (POST or GET) and how the data should be returned (via a standard XML). Thus, an agent can perform queries on a dataset and acquire knowledge to create new queries and so on.

Finally, VoID [13] is an ontology used to define metadata about triplesets. A VoID document is a good source of information about a tripleset, such as the classes and properties it uses, the size of the tripleset, etc.

Let $d$ be a tripleset and $V$ be a set of VoID metadata descriptions. The classes and properties used in $d$ can be extracted from tripleset partitions defined by the properties void:classPartition and void:propertyPartition that occur in $V$. *Class partitions* describe sets of triples related to subjects of a particular class. *Property partitions* describe sets of triples that use a particular predicate. These partitions are described by the properties void:class and void:property respectively. The set of vocabulary terms used in $d$ can be generated by the union of all values of the properties void:class and void:property. In some cases, the VoID description of a tripleset does not define partitions, but it specifies a list of namespaces of the vocabularies used by the tripleset with the void:vocabulary predicate. One can enrich the set of vocabulary terms used in $d$ with such a list.

# 4  Use Case

Consider a user who wants to publish as Linked Data a relational database $d$ storing music data (artists, records, songs, etc.). The crawler proposed in this paper will help the user to publish $d$ as follows.

First, the user has to define an initial set $T$ of terms to describe the application domain of $d$. Suppose that he selects just one term dbpedia:Music, taken from DBpedia.

The user will then invoke the crawler, passing $T$ as input. The crawler will query the DataHub catalogue of Linked Data triplesets to crawl triplesets searching for new terms that are direct or transitively related to dbpedia:Music. The crawler focuses on finding new terms that are defined as subclasses of the class dbpedia:Music, or that are related to dbpedia:Music by owl:sameAs or owl:equivalent-Class properties. The crawler will also count the number of instances of the classes found.

The crawler will return: (1) the list of terms found, indicating their provenance - how the terms are direct or transitively related to dbpedia:Music and in which triplesets they were found; and (2) for each class found, an estimation of the number of instances in each tripleset visited.

The user may take advantage of the results the crawler returned in two ways. He may manually analyze the data and decide: (1) which of the probed ontologies found he will adopt to triplify the relational database; and (2) to which triplesets the crawler located he will link the tripleset he is constructing. Alternatively, he may submit the results of the crawler to separate tools that will automatically recommend ontologies to be adopted in the triplification process, as well as triplesets to be used in the linkage process [14, 15].

For example, suppose that the crawler finds two subclasses, `opencyc:Love_Song` and `opencyc:Hit_Song`, of `wordnet:synset-music-noun-1` in the ontology `opencyc:Music`. Suppose also that the crawler finds large numbers of instances of these subclasses in two triplesets, `musicBrainz` and `bbcMusic`. The user might then decide that `opencyc:Music` is a good choice to adopt in the triplification process and that `musicBrainz` and `bbcMusic` are good choices for the linkage process.

## 5    A Metadata Focused Crawler

### 5.1    Processors

The crawler works with catalogues that use the CKAN framework (such DataHub) to identify SPARQL endpoints and RDF dumps, and the user can also manually add new datasets. It receives as input a set of terms $T$, called the *initial crawling terms*. Such terms are typically selected from generic ontologies, such as WordNet,[5] DBpedia and Schema.org,[6] albeit this is not a requirement for the crawling process. Given $T$, the crawler uses a list $C$ of *processors*, in successive *stages* (see Sect. 5.2), to extract new terms from the triplesets listed in the catalogues.

The tool is engineered as a framework, whose pseudo-code is listed in Appendix 1. It passes each *crawling term $t$* to each processor in $C$. The processor annotates the provenance of its crawled data and returns a list of terms to be crawled in the next stage, after filtering, based on parameters specified by the user (see Sect. 5.2). Currently, the crawler includes three processors, described in the rest of this section.

*Dereference Processor.* The first processor is responsible for extracting information of the resource itself. It tries to find new resources using the properties `owl:sameAs`, `owl:equivalentClass` and `rdfs:subclassOf` (see Sect. 3). For each such property, the processor applies a SPARQL query to extract new information. The following template illustrates how each query works, where p is one of the above properties and t is the crawling term itself; the values assigned to the variable ?item are resources that to be crawled in a next stage.

```
SELECT distinct ?item
WHERE {< t > p ?item}
```

[5] http://wordnet.princeton.edu/.

[6] http://schema.org.

Given that `owl:sameAs` and `owl:equivalentClass` are reflexive, the processor also applies SPARQL queries generated by a new code template, with the subject and object inverted:

```
SELECT distinct ?item
WHERE {?item p < t>}
```

***Property Processor.*** This processor is responsible for crawling other datasets. It uses a special SPARQL query, which runs over each dataset discovered in DataHub and manually as described Sect. 5.1. The motivation is to extract information that is not directly related to the resources already processed. Given the crawling term $R$ that will be processed by CRAWLER-LD and a dataset $D$ that uses $R$ to describe a fraction of its data. While a conventional crawling algorithm is not able to find $D$ since $R$ does not have any reference to $D$, CRAWLER-LD, on the other hand, traverses all datasets available and is able to find the relationship between $D$ and $R$.

The processor uses the following SPARQL template, where t is the resourced being crawled:

```
SELECT distinct ?property ?item
WHERE {
{?item owl:sameAs < t>.}
UNION { < t > owl:sameAs ?item.}
UNION {?item owl:equivalentClass < t>.}
UNION { < t > owl:equivalentClass ?item.}
UNION {?item rdfs:subClassOf < t>.}
?item ?property < t>. }
```

Note that, for each term t to be crawled, the template inverts the role of t (for the details, see lines 7 and 9 of the code in Appendix (1), when the predicate is `owl:sameAs` and `owl:equivalentClass`, since these predicates are reflexive. However, the crawler does not invert the role of t, when the predicate is `rdfs:subClassOf`, since this predicate is not reflexive.

For example, in the specific case of the crawling property `rdfs:subClassOf`, suppose that $C$ and $C'$ are classes defined in triplesets $S$ and $S'$, respectively, and assume that $C'$ is declared as a subclass of $C$ through a triple of the form

$$(C', \text{rdfs:subClassOf}, C)$$

Triples such as this are more likely to be included in the tripleset where the more specific class $C'$ is defined than in the tripleset where the more generic class $C$ is defined. Hence, after finding a class $C$, the crawler has to search for subclasses of $C$ in all triplesets it has access using the template above.

Another case occurs when the relationship between $C$ and $C'$ is defined in a third ontology $S''$. Similarly to the previous example, we need a subclass query over $S''$ to discover that $C'$ is a subclass of $C$. $S''$ is obtained by dereferencing the URI of $C'$. In most cases the returned tripleset is the complete ontology where $C'$ is defined, while in some other cases only a fragment of the ontology where $C'$ is defined is returned.

*Instance Counter Processor.* The last processor extracts information about the quantity of instances available in each dataset for each crawling term. It runs queries over all datasets, using the same principle as the property processor. To reduce the bandwidth, the processor uses grouping functions to query datasets:

```
SELECT distinct (count(?instance) AS ?item)
WHERE {?instance rdf:type < %s > . }
```

Unfortunately, grouping functions are only available in SPARQL version 1.1 [16] and above. Therefore, the processor also crawls the remaining datasets using the following query, which spend more bandwidth:

```
SELECT distinct ?item
WHERE {?item rdf:type < %s > . }
```

## 5.2   Crawling Stages

The crawler simulates a breath-first search for new terms. Stage 0 contains the initial set of terms. The set of terms of each new stage is computed from those of the previous stage, as described in Sect. 5.1.

The *crawling frontier* is the set of terms found which have not yet been processed. To avoid circular references, we used a hash map that indicates which terms have already been processed.

Since the number of terms may grow exponentially from one stage to the next, we prune the search by limiting:

- The number of stages of the breath-first search
- The maximum number of terms probed
- The maximum number of terms probed in each tripleset, for each term in the crawling frontier
- The maximum number of terms probed for each term in the crawling frontier

For each new term found, the processors create a list that indicates the provenance of the term: how the term is direct or transitively related to an initial term and in which tripleset(s) it was found. That is, the crawler identifies the sequence of relationships it traversed to reach a term, such as in the following example:

```
wordnet:synset-music-noun-1 - > owl:sameAs ->
opencyc:Music - > rdfs:subClassOf ->
opencyc:LoveSong - > instance ->
500 instances.
```

# 6  Tests and Results

## 6.1  Organization of the Experiments

We evaluated the crawler over triplesets described in DataHub. The tool was able to recover 1,042 triplesets with SPARQL endpoints. However, despite this number, it could run queries on just over 35 % of the triplesets due to errors in the query parser or simply because the servers were not available.

To create the initial crawling terms, we used three generic ontologies, WordNet, DBpedia and Schema.org, as well as ontologies specific to the application domain in question.

Table 1. Namespace abbreviation.

| Abbreviation | Namespace |
|---|---|
| akt | http://www.aktors.org/ontology/portal# |
| bbcMusic | http://linkeddata.uriburner.com/about/id/entity/http://www.bbc.co.uk/music/ |
| dbpedia | http://dbpedia.org/resource/ or http://dbpedia.org/ontology/ |
| dbtune | http://dbtune.org/ |
| freebase | http://freebase.com/ |
| freedesktop | http://freedesktop.org/standards/xesam/1.0/core# |
| lastfm | http://linkeddata.uriburner.com/about/id/entity/ http://www.last.fm/music/ |
| mo | http://purl.org/ontology/mo/ |
| musicBrainz | http://dbtune.org/musicbrainz/ |
| nerdeurocom | http://nerd.eurecom.fr/ontology# |
| opencyc | http://sw.opencyc.org/2009/04/07/concept/en/ |
| schema | http://schema.org/ |
| twitter | http://linkeddata.uriburner.com/about/id/entity/http://twitter.com/ |
| umbel | http://umbel.org/ |
| wordnet | http://wordnet.rkbexplorer.com/id/ |
| yago | http://www.yago-knowledge/resource/ |

WordNet is a lexical database that presents different meanings for the same word. For example, the word "music" is given two different meanings, denoted by two distinct terms: wordnet:synset-music-noun-1 means "an artistic form of auditory communication incorporating instrumental or vocal tones in a structured and continuous manner", while wordnet:synset-music-noun-2 means "any agreeable (pleasing and harmonious) sounds; "he fell asleep to the music of the wind chimes"".

DBpedia is the triplified version of the Wikipedia database. The triplification process is automatically accomplished and the current English version already has 2.5 million classified items.

Schema.org is the most recent ontology of all three. It focuses on HTML semantics and was created by Google, Bing and Yahoo. Therefore, Schema.org is now used by many triplesets.[7] Schema.org is also developing other ways to increase the search results by creating a mapping with other ontologies, such as DBpedia and WordNet.

In the examples that follow, we use the abbreviations shown in Table 1.

## 6.2  Results

The experiments involved two domains, Music and Publications, and used the following parameters:

- Number of stages: 2
- Maximum number of terms probed: 40
- Maximum number of terms probed for each term in the crawling frontier: 20
- Maximum number of terms probed in each tripleset, for each term in the crawling frontier: 10

Music Domain.  We chose Music as the first domain to evaluate the crawler and elected three ontologies, DBpedia, WordNet and Music Ontology,[8] to select the initial crawling terms. The Music Ontology is a widely accepted ontology that describes music, albums, artists, shows and some specific subjects.

The initial crawling terms were:

| | |
|---|---|
| mo:MusicArtist | dbpedia:Album |
| mo:MusicalWork | dbpedia:MusicalArtist |
| mo:Composition | dbpedia:Single |
| dbpedia:MusicalWork | wordnet:synset-music-noun-1 |
| dbpedia:Song | |

In what follows, we will first comment on the results obtained in Stage 1, for each initial term. Then, we will proceed to discuss how the new terms obtained in Stage 1 were processed in Stage 2.

Table 2(a) shows the results of Stage 1 for mo:MusicalArtist. On Stage 2, for each of the terms mo:MusicGroup and mo:SoloMusicArtist, the crawler obtained different results: while mo:MusicGroup recovered over 1.5 million instances over three datasets, mo:SoloMusicArtist did not find any new result.

Table 2(b) shows the results of Stage 1 for mo:MusicalWork. Note that the crawler found a variety of instances from multiple databases. On Stage 2, when processing mo:Movement, the crawler did not find any new instance or class.

Table 2(c) shows the results of Stage 1 for the first DBpedia term, dbpedia:MusicalWork. The crawler found 5 subclasses from DBpedia and over a million instances in 13 datasets, with 8 being DBpedia in different languages (such as French, Japanese, Greek and others), which was only possible because it focused on metadata.

---

[7] http://schema.rdfs.org/mappings.html.

[8] http://musicontology.com/

**Table 2.** Related terms.

| Related terms | |
| --- | --- |
| Query type | Description |
| **(a)** Related terms for `mo:MusicArtist` | |
| subclass | `mo:MusicGroup, mo:SoloMusicArtist` |
| instance | 2,647,957 instances from over four datasets |
| **(b)** Related terms for `mo:MusicalWork` | |
| subclass | `mo:Movement` |
| instance | 1,166,365 instances found in multiple databases |
| **(c)** Related terms for `dbpedia:MusicalWork` | |
| subclass | `dbpedia:Album, dbpedia:Song, dbpedia:Single, dbpedia:Opera, dbpedia:ArtistDiscography` |
| instance | 939,480 instances from 13 datasets |
| **(d)** Related terms for `dbpedia:Song` | |
| equivalentclass | `schema:MusicRecording` |
| subclass | `dbpedia:EurovisionSongContestEntry` |
| instance | 35,702 instances from 9 datasets |
| **(e)** Related terms for `dbpedia:Album` | |
| equivalentclass | `schema:MusicAlbum` |
| instance | 871,348 instances from 13 datasets |
| **(f)** Related terms for `dbpedia:MusicalArtist` | |
| instance | 424,152 instances from 19 datasets |
| **(g)** Related terms for `dbpedia:Single` | |
| instance | 305,041 instances from 10 datasets |

Crawlers that use text fields [2] can only retrieve data in the same language as that of initial terms.

The first three terms, `dbpedia:Album`, `dbpedia:Song` and `dbpedia:Single`, will be analyzed in the next paragraphs since they are also in the initial set of terms.

On Stage 2, the processing of `dbpedia:Opera` returned no results and the processing of `dbpedia:ArtistDiscography` returned 48,784 instances, but no new term.

Table 2(d) shows the results of Stage 1 for `dbpedia:Song`. The crawler was able to find a relationship with other generic dataset (Schema.org) and also found a variety of resources from DBpedia in different languages.

On Stage 2, when processing `dbpedia:EurovisionSongContestEntry`, the crawler found 7,807 instances from 7 datasets. The other resource probed on the Stage 2 was `schema:MusicRecording`, which returned 38,464 instances and no new crawling terms.

Table 2(e) shows the results of Stage 1 for `dbpedia:Album`. The processing of this term also found `schema:MusicAlbum` and a large number of instances. On

Stage 2, the tool was able to find 662,409 instances of schema:MusicAlbum, but no new resource.

Table 2(f) shows the results of Stage 1 for dbpedia:MusicalArtist. The tool was not able to find any new related resource, but it found a large number of datasets that have instances of this class.

Table 2(g) shows the results of Stage 1 for dbpedia:Single. The tool found more than 300 thousand instances from triplesets in many languages.

The last term probed in Stage 1 was wordnet:synset-music-noun-1. The crawler found a *sameAs* relationship with an analogue term from another publisher: http://www.w3.org/2006/03/wn/wn20/instances/synset-music-noun-1.

Finally, we remark that, when we selected the terms to evaluate, we expected to find relationships between DBpedia and the Music Ontology, which did not happen. In addition, we found much better results using terms from DBpedia than from the Music Ontology, which is specific to the domain in question. The definition of links between the Music Ontology and DBpedia could increase the popularity of the former. For example, if the term mo:MusicArtist were related to the term dbpedia:MusicalArtist, crawlers such as ours would be able to identify the relationship. Also, matching or recommendation tools would benefit from such relationship.

***Publications Domain.*** For the second domain, we focused on two ontologies, Schema.org and Aktors,[9] which is commonly used by publications databases. We selected the following terms:

```
schema:TechArticle
schema:ScholarlyArticle
akt:Article-Reference
akt:Article-In-A-Composite-Publication
akt:Book, akt:Thesis-Reference akt:Periodical-Publication
akt:Lecturer-In-Academia
akt:Journal
```

The results were quite simple. Both ontologies (Schema.org and Aktors) returned a small number of instances, but with no complex structure. A quick analysis showed that almost all triplesets were obtained from popular publications databases (such as DBLP, IEEE and ACM) by the same provider (RKBExplorer), which used the Aktors ontology. In addition, the Aktors ontology is not linked to other ontologies, which lead to an almost independent cluster in the Linked Data cloud.

***Processing Times.*** Table 3 shows the processing time for each experiment. In general, the time spent to process each term was direct related to the number of terms found (some exceptions apply due to bandwidth issues). The experiment was performed on a virtual machine hosted by Microsoft Azure[10] with 56 GB and two AMD Opteron™ 4171 processors.

---

[9] http://www.aktors.org

[10] http://azure.microsoft.com/

Table 3 shows that the minimum time was 4 min, when no new terms were found, but the maximum time depended on the number of new terms in the crawling frontier and how the network (and the endpoints) responded.

Finally, we observe that the processing time can be optimized, provided that: (1) the endpoints queries have lower latency; (2) the available bandwidth is stable across the entire test; (3) cache features are used.

**Table 3.** Performance evaluation.

| Term | Proc. time (minutes) |
| --- | --- |
| *Music domain* | |
| mo:MusicArtist | 11 |
| mo:MusicalWork | 8 |
| mo:Composition | 4 |
| dbpedia:MusicalWork | 22 |
| dbpedia:Song | 11 |
| dbpedia:Album | 8 |
| dbpedia:MusicalArtist | 4 |
| dbpedia:Single | 4 |
| wordnet:synset-music-noun-1 | 11 |
| *Publications domain* | |
| schema:TechArticle | 4 |
| schema:ScholarlyArticle | 4 |
| akt:Article-Reference | 4 |
| akt:Article-In-A-Composite-Publication | 8 |
| akt:Book | 5 |
| akt:Thesis-Reference | 5 |
| akt:Periodical-Publication | 4 |
| akt:Lecturer-In-Academia | 5 |
| akt:Journal | 4 |

**Table 4.** Number of terms found using *swget*.

| Term | Subclass | SameAs | Equivalentclass | Type |
| --- | --- | --- | --- | --- |
| mo:MusicArtist | 6 | 0 | 0 | 0 |
| mo:MusicalWork | 8 | 0 | 0 | 0 |
| dbpedia:MusicalWork | 21 | 0 | 0 | 0 |
| dbpedia:Song | 7 | 0 | 1 | 0 |
| dbpedia:Album | 6 | 0 | 1 | 0 |
| dbpedia:MusicalArtist | 10 | 0 | 0 | 0 |
| dbpedia:Single | 6 | 0 | 0 | 0 |

## 6.3   A Comparison with *Swget*

We opted for a direct comparison between CRAWLER-LD and *swget* for three reasons. First, there is no benchmark available to test Linked Data crawlers such as ours and it is nearly impossible to manually produce one such (extensive) benchmark. Second, *swget* is the most recent crawler available online. Third, it was fairly simple to setup an experiment for *swget* similar to that described in Sect. 6.2 for the Music domain.

Briefly, the experiment with *swget* was executed as follows. Based on the examples available at the *swget* Web site, we created the following template to run queries (where t' is the term to be probed and q' the current crawling property):

t' -p < q' > < 2-2>

The above query means "given a term t', find all resources related to it using the predicate q', expanding two levels recursively.

Then, we collected all terms *swget* found from the same initial terms of the Music domain used in Sect. 6.2, specifying which crawled property *swget* should follow. Table 4 shows the number of terms *swget* found, for each term and crawling property.

Based on the experiments with *swget* and CRAWLER-LD, we compiled a list of terms shown in Appendix 2. Then, we manually inspected the terms and marked those that pertain to the Music domain and those that *swget* and CRAWLER-LD found.

The results can be summarized by computing the precision, recall and balanced F-measure $(F_1)$ [17] obtained by *swget* and CRAWLER-LD for the list of terms thus obtained:

- *swget*: Precision = 29.17 % Recall = 100 % $F_1$ = 45.16 %
- CRAWLER-LD: Precision = 100 % Recall = 78.57 % $F_1$ = 88.00 %

These results should be interpreted as follows. *Swget* achieved a much lower precision since it finds more generic and more specific terms at the same time, while CRAWLER-LD only searches for the more specific terms. This feature creates undesirable results for the purposes of focusing on an application domain. For example, using rdfs:subClassOf as predicate and dbpedia:MusicalWork as object, *swget* returned dbpedia:Work, a superclass at the first level. At the next stage, *swget* then found resources such as dbpedia:Software and dbpedia:Film, each of them subclasses of dbpedia:Work, but unrelated to the Music domain.

*Swget* achieved a larger recall value. However, *Swget* found only two related resources that CRAWLER-LD could not find. The basic reason is that the crawling resources were subclasses of domain resources, which implied that CRAWLER-LD could not reach the resources, while *swget* was able to.

Analyzing the overall quality of the crawlers using balanced F-measure, CRAWLER-LD outperformed *swget*, obtaining an F1 result almost twice as large as that of *swget*. Thus, in this experiment, CRAWLER-LD was able to find a better balance between recall and precision values than *swget*.

*Swget* was also unable to identify the same number of instances as CRAWLER-LD. While CRAWLER-LD searched a large number of datasets, *swget* tried to obtain data only by reading the resource's content, which does not describes instances from any other dataset. This behavior should not be regarded as defect of *swget*, though, but a consequence of working with a general-purpose crawler, rather than a metadata focused crawler, such as CRAWLER-LD.

## 6.4    Lessons Learned

In this section, we highlight the main lessons learned from the results of our experiments. We first enumerate some aspects that may influence the crawling results, such as the settings of the parameters and the availability of sufficient information about the crawled triplesets.

*Parameter Setting.* Since, in our crawler, the set of terms of each new stage is computed from that of the previous stage, the number of terms may grow exponentially. We defined some parameters to prune the search. Hence, the user must adequately set such parameters to obtain results in reasonable time, without losing essential information.

*Choosing the Initial Crawling Terms.* In the Music domain experiments, we started with terms from three different triplesets, DBpedia, WordNet and Music Ontology, the first two being more generic than the last one. It seems that the resources defined in the Music Ontology are not interlinked (directly or indirectly) with the more popular triplesets. This limitation is related to the fact that some triplesets do not adequately follow the Linked Data principles, in the sense that they do not interlink their resources with resources defined in other relevant triplesets.

*Ontologies Describing the Domain of Interest.* Our crawler proved to return more useful when there are relationships among the metadata. In the experiments using the publications domain, our crawler returned a simplified result because all triplesets related to the initial crawling terms used the same ontology to describe their resources. In general, the larger the number of triplesets in the domain, the more useful the results of our crawler will be.

*Reducing the Number of Request.* Our crawler demands a high number of requests for each dataset, and creating ways to reduce this number would improve the performance. Our approach, primarily implemented on *property processor,* combines all queries inside one using the *UNION* clause and processing the result set locally.

We now highlight some improvements obtained by our metadata focused crawler, when compared to traditional crawlers.

*Discovering Relationships Between Resources of Two Triplesets Described in a Third One.* Using our crawler, we can find cases in which a relationship between two resources $r$ and $r'$, respectively defined in triplesets $d$ and $d'$, was described in another tripleset $d''$. This happens, for example, when the ontologies used by $d$ and $d'$ are only stored in a different dataset $d''$. In these cases, it is necessary to crawl all triplesets, other than $d$ and $d'$, to find the relationship between $r$ and $r'$. A traditional crawler following links from $d$ would not find any link between $r$ and $r'$ because it is only declared in $d''$.

*Crawling with SPARQL Queries.* Our crawler returns richer metadata than a traditional crawler since it uses SPARQL queries, executed over all triplesets. In particular, our crawler discovers not only the links between resources, but also the number of instances related to the crawling terms.

*Identifying Resources in Different Languages and Alphabets.* Our crawler was able to identify resources in different languages, even in different alphabets, through the *sameAs* and *seeAlso* queries.

*Performing Simple Deductions.* Using the provenance lists the crawler generates, one may perform simple deductions, using the transitivity of the subclass property, perhaps combined with the *sameAs* relationship. For example, suppose that the crawler discovered that `opencyc:Hit_music` is a subclass of `opencyc:Music`, which in turn has a *sameAs* relationship with `wordnet:synset-music-noun-1`. Then, one may deduce that `opencyc:Hit_music` is a subclass of `wordnet:synset-music-noun-1`.

## 7    Conclusions and Future Work

This paper presented CRAWLER-LD, a metadata focused crawler for Linked Data. The crawler works in stages, starting with a small set $T_0$ of generic RDF terms and creating a new set of terms $T_{i+1}$ by enriching $T_i$ with related terms. The tool is engineered as a framework that currently includes three processors, implementing different crawling strategies.

In general, the metadata focused crawler introduced in this paper helps simplify the triplification and the interlinking processes, thereby contributing to the dissemination of Linked Data. Indeed, the results of the crawler may be used: to recommend ontologies to be adopted in the triplification process; and to recommend triplesets to be used in the linkage process.

Finally, the overall crawling process is open to several improvements. For example, we may use summarization techniques to automatically select the initial set of terms. We could also use some sort of caching system to improve overall performance.

**Acknowledgements.**    A This work was partly funded by CNPq, under grants 160326/2012-5, 303332/2013-1 and 57128/2009-9, by FAPERJ, under grants E-26/170028/2008, E-26/103.070/2011 and E-26/101.382/2014, and by CAPES. Microsoft Azure for Research program was also valuable providing capable machines for experimentations.

# Appendix 1: Framework Pseudo-Code

*CRAWLER-LD(maxLevels, maxTerms, maxFromTerm, maxFromSet; T, C, PR; Q, P, D)*

*CRAWLER-LD(maxLevels, maxTerms, maxFromTerm, maxFromSet; T, C, PR; Q, P, D)*

**Parameters:**  *maxLevels*  - maximum number of levels of the breath-first search
                 *maxTerms*   - maximum number of terms probed
                 *maxFromTerm* - maximum number of new terms probed from each term
                 *maxFromSet*  - maximum number of terms probed from a tripleset, for each term

**input:**  T  - a set of input terms
            C  - a list of catalogues of triplesets
            PR - a list of processors

**output:**  Q  - a queue with the terms that were crawled
             P  - a provenance list for the terms in Q
             D  - a provenance list of the triplesets with terms in Q

```
begin   Q, P, D := empty;
        #levels, #terms := 0;
        nextLevel := T;
        while #levels < maxLevels and #terms < maxTerms do
        begin
                #levels := #levels + 1;
                currentLevel := nextLevel;      /* currentLevel and nextLevel are queues of terms */
                nextLevel := empty;
                for each t from currentLevel do
                begin
                        terms += terms;
                        if ( #terms > maxTerms ) then exit;
                        add t to Q;
                        resourcesForEachDataset := (dataset,resourceList) := empty
                        for each p from PR do
                        begin
                        /* use t on the processor p and save the results for each dataset */
                        call (dataset,resultList) := p(t,P,D)
                        add p to resourceForEachDataset
                        end
                        /* limiting results phase */
                        resourcesFromTerm := empty
                        for each dataset d from resourcesForEachDataset
                        begin
                        resultList := results from dataset D on term t;
                        truncate resultList to contain just the first maxFromSet terms;
                        resourcesFromTerm := concatenate(resultList, resourcesFromTerm);
                        end
                        truncate resourcesFromTerm to contain just the first maxFromTerm terms;
                        nextLevel := concatenate(resourcesFromTerm, nextLevel);
                end /* t loop */
        end /* level loop */
        return Q, P, D;
end /* algorithm */
```

# Appendix 2: A Comparison Between Swget and CRAWLER-LD for the Music Domain

| Terms retrieved by *swget* or CRAWLER-LD | MV | SW | RC |
|---|---|---|---|
| (Terms retrieved by *swget*) | | | |
| dbpedia:MusicalWork | - | - | - |
| 1 | dbpedia:Song | Y | Y | Y |
| 2 | dbpedia:Single | Y | Y | Y |
| 3 | dbpedia:Album | Y | Y | Y |
| 4 | dbpedia:Work | N | Y | N |
| 5 | dbpedia:ArtistDiscography | Y | Y | Y |
| 6 | dbpedia:Opera | Y | Y | Y |
| 7 | dbpedia:EurovisionSongContestEntry | Y | Y | Y |
| 8 | owl:Thing | N | Y | N |
| 9 | dbpedia:Software | N | Y | N |
| 10 | dbpedia:RadioProgram | N | Y | N |
| 11 | dbpedia:Cartoon | N | Y | N |
| 12 | dbpedia:TelevisionSeason | N | Y | N |
| 13 | dbpedia:Film | N | Y | N |
| 14 | dbpedia:Website | N | Y | N |
| 15 | dbpedia:CollectionOfValuables | N | Y | N |
| 16 | dbpedia:WrittenWork | N | Y | N |
| 17 | dbpedia:Musical | Y | Y | N |
| 18 | dbpedia:Artwork | N | Y | N |
| 19 | dbpedia:LineOfFashion | N | Y | N |
| 20 | dbpedia:TelevisionShow | N | Y | N |
| 21 | dbpedia:TelevisionEpisode | N | Y | N |
| dbpedia:MusicalArtist | - | - | - |
| 22 | dbpedia:Artist | N | Y | N |
| 23 | schema:MusicGroup | Y | Y | N |
| 24 | dbpedia:Sculptor | N | Y | N |
| 25 | dbpedia:Painter | N | Y | N |
| 26 | dbpedia:Actor | N | Y | N |
| 27 | dbpedia:ComicsCreator | N | Y | N |
| 28 | dbpedia:Comedian | N | Y | N |
| 29 | dbpedia:FashionDesigner | N | Y | N |
| 30 | dbpedia:Writer | N | Y | N |
| 31 | dbpedia:Person | N | Y | N |
| dbpedia:Song | - | - | - |
| 32 | schema:MusicRecording | Y | Y | Y |
| 33 | dbpedia:MusicalWork | Y | Y | N |
| dbpedia:Album | - | - | - |
| 34 | schema:MusicAlbum | Y | Y | Y |
| dbpedia:Single | - | - | - |
| (No new term retrieved *swget*) | | | |
| mo:MusicArtist | - | - | - |
| 35 | mo:SoloMusicArtist | Y | Y | Y |
| 36 | foaf:Agent | N | Y | N |
| 37 | mo:MusicGroup | Y | Y | Y |
| 38 | foaf:Person | N | Y | N |
| 39 | foaf:Organization | N | Y | N |
| 40 | foaf:Group | N | Y | N |

| mo:MusicalWork | - | - | - |
|---|---|---|---|
| 41 | mo:Movement | Y | Y | Y |
| 42 | frbr:Work | N | Y | N |
| 43 | frbr:ScholarlyWork | N | Y | N |
| 44 | frbr:ClassicalWork | N | Y | N |
| 45 | frbr:LegalWork | N | Y | N |
| 46 | frbr:LiteraryWork | N | Y | N |
| 47 | frbr:Endeavour | N | Y | N |
| 48 | wordnet:Work~2 | N | Y | N |
| mo:Composition | - | - | - |
| (No term retrieved) | | | |
| (Terms retrieved only by CRAWLER-LD) | | | |
| (No term retrieved) | | | |

*Notes:*

- Column Headers / Values:
  "MV" ("Manual Validation"):
  o Y = term relevant for the Music domain
  o N = term not relevant for the Music domain
  "SW" ("Retrieved by *swget*") and
  "RC" ("Retrieved by CRAWLER-LD"):
  o Y = term retrieved by *swget* or CRAWLER-LD
  o N = term not retrieved by *swget* or CRAWLER-LD

- Terms retrieved by *swget* or CRAWLER-LD:
  Retrieved terms: 48
  Relevant terms that were retrieved (identified by "Y" in column "MV"): 14

- Terms retrieved by *swget*:
  Retrieved terms: 48
  Relevant terms that were retrieved (identified by rows with the pattern (Y,Y,-)): 14
  Precision = 14 / 48 = 0.2917
  Recall = 14 / 14 = 1.0
  $F_1$-Measure = 2 * ((0.2917*1.0) / (0.2917+1.0))
  = 0.4516

- Terms retrieved by CRAWLER-LD:
  Retrieved terms: 11
  Relevant terms that were retrieved (identified by rows with the pattern (Y,-,Y)): 11
  Precision = 11 / 11 = 1.0
  Recall = 11 / 14 = 0.7857
  $F_1$-Measure = 2 * ((1.0*0.7857) / (1.0+0.7857))
  = 0.8800

# References

1. Bizer, C., Heath, T., Berners-Lee, T.: Linked data - the story so far, Int'l. J. Seman. Web Info. Sys. **5**(3), 1–22 (2009)
2. Nikolov, A., d'Aquin, M.: Identifying relevant sources for data linking using a semantic web index. In: Proceedings Workshop on Linked Data on the Web. vol. 813 of CEUR Workshop Proceedings, CEUR-WS.org (2011)
3. Nikolov, A., d'Aquin, M., Motta, E.: What should I link to? identifying relevant sources and classes for data linking. In: Proceedings Joint Int'l Semantic Technology Conference, pp. 284–299 (2012)
4. Romero, M.M., Vázquez -Naya, J.M., Munteanu, C.R., Pereira, J., Pazos, A.: An approach for the automatic recommendation of ontologies using collaborative knowledge. In: Setchi, R., Jordanov, I., Howlett, R.J., Jain, L.C. (eds.) KES 2010, Part II. LNCS, vol. 6277, pp. 74–81. Springer, Heidelberg (2010)
5. Saint-Paul, R., Raschia, G., Mouaddib, N.: General purpose database summarization. In: Proceedings 31st Int'l Conference on Very Large Data Bases. VLDB Endowment, pp. 733–744 (2005)
6. Fionda, V., Gutierrez, C., Pirró, G.: Semantic navigation on the web of data: specification of routes, web fragments and actions. In: Proceedings of the 21st Int'l Conference on World Wide Web, pp. 281–290 (2012)
7. Isele, R., Harth, A., Umbrich, J., Bizer, C.: LDspider: an open-source crawling framework for the web of linked data. In: Proceedings Int'l Semantic Web Conference (Posters), Shanghai, China (2010)
8. Ding, L., Pan, R., Finin, T.W., Joshi, A., Peng, Y., Kolari, P.: Finding and ranking knowledge on the semantic web. In: Gil, Y., Motta, E., Benjamins, V., Musen, M.A. (eds.) ISWC 2005. LNCS, vol. 3729, pp. 156–170. Springer, Heidelberg (2005)
9. Manola, F., Miller, E.: RDF Primer, W3C Recommendation 10 February 2014 (2004)
10. Brickley, D., Guha, R.V. (eds.): RDF vocabulary description language 1.0: RDF schema. In: W3C Recommendation 10 February 2004 (2004)
11. W3C OWL Working Group: OWL 2 Web Ontology Language Document Overview (Second Edition). W3C Recommendation 11 December 2012
12. Prud'hommeaux, E., Seaborne, A.: SPARQL Query Language for RDF, W3C Recommendation 15 January 2009
13. Alexander, K., Cyganiak, R., Hausenblas, M., Zhao, J.: Describing linked datasets - on the design and usage of void, the 'vocabulary of interlinked datasets'. In: Proceedings Workshop on Linked Da-ta on the Web (LDOW 2009), Madrid, Spain (2009)
14. Leme, L.A.P., Lopes, G.R., Nunes, B.P., Casanova, M.A., Dietze, S.: Identifying candidate datasets for data interlinking. In: Daniel, F., Dolog, P., Li, Q. (eds.) ICWE 2013. LNCS, vol. 7977, pp. 354–366. Springer, Heidelberg (2013)
15. Lopes, G.R., Leme, L.A.P.P., Nunes, B.P., Casanova, M.A., Dietze, S.: Recommending tripleset interlinking through a social network approach. In: Proceedings 14th International Conference on Web Information System Engineering, Nanjing, China (October 13–15, 2013), pp. 149–161 (2013)
16. Garlik, S.H., Seaborne, A., Prud'hommeaux, E.: SPARQL 1.1 query language. World Wide Web Consortium (2013)
17. Manning, C.D., Raghavan, P., Schütze, H.: Introduction to Information Retrieval. Cambridge University Press, New York (2008)

# A Framework Reactive and Proactive for Pervasive Homecare Environments

Alencar Machado[1,2]([⊠]), Daniel Lichtnow[2], Ana Marilza Pernas[4],
Amel Bouzeghoub[5], Iara Augustin[3], Leandro Krug Wives[1],
and José Palazzo Moreira de Oliveira[1]

[1] Instituto de Informática, Universidade Federal do Rio Grande do Sul,
Porto Alegre, Brazil
`alencar.machado@ufsm.br`, `{wives,palazzo}@inf.ufrgs.br`
[2] Colégio Politécnico, Universidade Federal de Santa Maria, Santa Maria, Brazil
`dlichtnow@politecnico.ufsm.br`
[3] PPGI, Universidade Federal de Santa Maria, Santa Maria, Brazil
`august@inf.ufsm.br`
[4] Centro de Desenvolvimento Tecnológico, Universidade Federal de Pelotas,
Pelotas, Brazil
`marilza@inf.ufpel.br`
[5] Télécom SudParis, UMR CNRS 5157 SAMOVAR, Evry, France
`amel.bouzeghoub@telecom-sudparis.eu`

**Abstract.** Smart environments are spaces that interact with users taking into account their needs and preferences. Systems that manage these environments need to manipulate the context for interacting in a suitable way with users. One big challenge for creating a smart environment is to deal with context dynamicity. Ideally, these computer-supported environments must detect relevant events to forecast future situations and to act proactively to mitigate or eliminate situations related to specific user's needs. This paper proposes a framework for providing extensible, reactive and proactive behavior in Smart Environment systems. The focus of the present work is related to a specific class of Smart Environments: an Ambient Assisted Living. In this sense we define a framework and illustrate practical aspects of the use of framework by describing a home-care scenario in which the system observes the behavior of the user, as the time goes by, and detects relevant situations and acts reactively and proactively for preserving user health condition.

**Keywords:** Proactive · Reactive · Situation · Context · Event · Ambient intelligence

## 1 Introduction

Ambient Intelligence (AmI) aims to support people in their needs and to prevent user's behaviors [1]. Fields such as Ambient Assisted Living (AAL) [2] and Smart Homes [3] are emerging as Smart Environment focused on specific characteristics of the user.

These systems must (a) manage heterogeneous sources (sensors and appliances) to provide high level information such as situations; (b) process events for detecting

© Springer International Publishing Switzerland 2015
J. Cordeiro et al. (Eds.): ICEIS 2014, LNBIP 227, pp. 320–338, 2015.
DOI: 10.1007/978-3-319-22348-3_18

situations in the environment; (c) make predictions of unwanted situations and to react in advance; (d) determine the policy of actions to consume appropriate services for adapting the environment ahead the situation envisaged; (e) have expansive capacities to manipulate different situations. However, an Ambient Intelligence system does not incorporate reactive and proactive behavior in an adequate way.

Thus, taking into account these challenges, this paper focuses on how to process events to detect and predict future unwanted situations. In this sense, we argue that for fulfilling user needs, AmI systems should be reactive and proactive. Therefore, these systems must be aware of the user's current situation and foresee future situations. The system must make decisions in advance, taking into account evidences that demonstrate the possibility of an unwanted situation happening in the future.

In our approach, the user and his/her actions are monitored through sensors that capture environmental data. This data is used to characterize the user context, using entities for obtaining a semantic characterization that determines the state of the environment. In the proposed approach, the state of the environment is called "situation". Thus, when a situation is detected, if necessary, it is possible to act reactively and proactively on the environment, using capabilities (services) provided by electronically controlled devices, seeking to adapt automatically the environment according to the detected situation.

In our approach the actions of the system are achieved by using functionalities implemented by Web services embedded in physical objects such as mobile phones, televisions and radios. The use case of this work focuses on unwanted situations involving the lives of elderly people at home. In this context, systems that foresee and handle unwanted situations proactively can assist caregivers of users who do not have physical or cognitive conditions for managing their own health, because it is necessary to act before an unwanted situation occurs.

As first concept proof, the approach was applied to a specific case-based application for managing medicines. In this case, citizens self-manage their health, and an application assists this activity. Over time, the citizens are affected by cognitive decline, when they become unable to manager their medications and the system must adapt itself to assist caregivers. The aim is to analyze the user behavior for predicting the need of some early actions to aid them to take their medications at the right time, preventing a decrease in their health condition.

This paper is organized as follows. Section 2 discusses background and related work. Section 3 presents the proposed reactive and proactive approach. In Sects. 4 and 5, presents the case study developed. Finally, in Sect. 6, we present and discuss our conclusions and future works.

## 2  Background and Related Work

Ambient intelligence systems need to know the world around users they monitor and, in order to perform actions, they need to interact with users through the devices that surround them [4]. Therefore, intelligence systems must be context-aware and proactive, automatically adapted to changes in the environment and considering user needs, without requiring their personal attention.

Regarding to context-aware systems, the concept of *context* is not new. Among the large number of existing definition in the literature, we adopt the definition of Ye, Dobson and McKeever [5], in which context is seen as *"the environment in which the system operates"*. It's different from the most adopted definition of Dey [6]: *"context is the situation of an entity in an environment"*. In the present work, the context of an environment is thus represented by a set of entities that surround or interact with the user, and their semantic relations.

As the time goes by, different entities or interactions may be active. In this sense, we need to verify the current contextual state of the user and act upon it or on its changes. For that, we define the concept of *situation*, since it is used by us to characterize the state of the user environment. For instance, Ye, Stevenson and Dobson [7] define *situation* as *"the abstraction of the events occurring in the real world that are derived from the context and hypotheses about how the observed context relates to factors of interest"*.

In this sense, applications that deal with situations are called situation-aware. Awareness implies vigilance in observing or alertness in drawing inference from a previous experience, so something is aware only if it is able to observe some objects and design conclusions through previous observations [8]. Observations could be made by services provided through devices, such as sensors. Therefore, by these observations, it is possible to detected events that change the state of the environment, characterizing thus a situation.

Another important concept is the notion of *event*. According to Etzion and Niblet [9], *"an event is an occurrence within a particular system or domain, it is something that has happened, or is contemplated as having happened in that domain"*. Events can be modeled as raw or derived. Derived events are higher-level events in the semantic hierarchy. It normally corresponds to a pattern of observation. Raw events are produced by some entity of context (e.g., sensors). Events can change the state of the environment, therefore producing new situations.

Works such as SOPRANO [10], PERSONA [11], among others, aim at modeling context, events and situations in middleware systems to provide a platform of health services in Ambient Assisted Living (AAL). They propose conceptual models to transform homes into AAL environments, modeling their context and services [12]. SOPRANO, for instance, has the intention of recognizing facts, objects, and people surrounding users allowing systems to act more appropriately and providing support to daily activities. However, in these works, the system is reactive, since it only acts after the evidence that an unwanted situation has occurred. They are not able to provide proactive actions to mitigate or eliminate undesired situations in advance.

The term proactive computing was first described by Tennehouse [13], who proposed the following principles for proactive systems: *"they should be closely connected with their surrounding world; they should also deliver results to humans before the user action; and they must operate autonomously"*.

The characteristics proposed by Tennehouse turn systems essentially reactive. In this sense, proactive computing overlaps with the term of autonomic computing [14]. An autonomic system is one that reacts to events that already happened. Our approach follows the proactivity definition of Engel and Etzion [15] who describe proactively in computing systems as *"the ability to mitigate or eliminate undesired future situations, identifying and taking advantage of future opportunities by applying prediction and automated decision making technologies*". Thus, the aim of the system actions is to prevent future unwanted situations. One example is the work of Fu and Xu [16] where event correlations are used for predicting future failures in networked computing systems.

The current vision of proactive behavior is listed as the next phase in the evolution of complex event processing [9]. Thus, Engel and Etzion [15] present the Proactive Event-Driven Computing. They propose an extension of the event processing conceptual model and include more two types of agents to the architecture of proactive event-driven applications: *predictive* and *proactive*.

Proactive systems apply prediction methods for predicting future information and decision making. Boytsov and Zaslavsky [17], for instance, analyze and compare prediction methods in order to identify their benefits and shortcomings. Among these methods, they describe Bayesian networks as an appropriate approach for predictive models. Similarly, Nazerfard and Cook [18] present a sequence-based activity prediction approach that uses Bayesian networks in a two-step process to predict both activities and their corresponding features.

Lotfi et al. [19] seek to make prediction of abnormal behavior of elderly with partial dementia. They use sensor data for identifying anomalous sensor behaviors to predict the future values of the possible data for each sensor. The predicted values are used to inform a caregiver in the case of anomalous behavior of sensors in the near future.

Analyzing the facts presented above, we identify that works related to smart environments propose strictly reactive systems. We have seen some researches describing proactive behavior to anticipate user's actions, but reacting only after a situation has happened, such as, systems for handling situations of agitations for elderly patients who take actions to anticipate actions of the caregivers. They, however, do not seek to identify this situation in advance to avoid it happening. Besides, in general these proposals do not address or include extensibility technologies, i.e., are not able to handle different situations in the course of time.

## 3  A Reactive and Proactive Approach

Our approach differs from other works because we present a new reactive and proactive approach that is more appropriate to attend the proper demands of AAL systems. Besides, it provides extensibility for residential smart environments. The approach is explained taking into account the recent history of self-management of a citizen's health, where the system triggers reactive and proactive actions.

The extensibility aspect of our approach is related to the concept of pervasive applications, and is based in a work named Situation as a Service (SIaaS) [20], which is described in the next section. In the present work, we have added temporal aspects, prediction and decision making techniques in order to prevent the existence of unwanted situations in future (Sect. 3.2).

### 3.1   Situation as a Service

In our approach, pervasive applications are installed in a middleware named SItuation as a Service (SIaaS). Pervasive applications (appPerv) are software applications developed by companies specialized in specific fields, such as health, surveillance, energy. This feature allows to attend the requirement 'ready to use', plug-and-play style. Designers of appPerv must implement in a conceptual model that corresponds to specific situations of the environment that are relevant to the appPerv. They also must inform the appPerv context of interest, generating instances of a particular type (e.g., Patient, Sensor) and make the linking semantics among them (as *hasSensor*).

Therefore, the pervasive application informs the SIaaS middleware about the situations that are important and should be managed for the detection and prediction of situations, as well as a set of contextual information necessary for decision making. In this work, we are interested in a specific domain: home-care health support. Thus, users could extend the capabilities of the middleware buying a complete solution for managing chronic diseases or only one pervasive application for managing the schedules of their medicines. For example, the pervasive applications described by Machado et al. [20] perform reactive actions (consumption of services) when a patient's agitation situation becomes true.

The SIaaS manages the environment and provides the context of interest, as well as the situation of interest for pervasive applications, so it is possible to trigger the more appropriate action when a situation is detected. It is presented in Fig. 1.

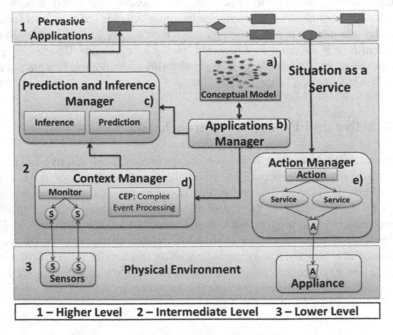

**Fig. 1.** Levels of the architecture.

The SIaaS is a Service-Oriented Architecture (SOA) with complex event processing that is implemented in three levels: Lower, Intermediate, and Upper. The Lower Level (3) corresponds to the physical environment (i.e., sensors and appliances).

The Intermediate Level (2) contains the middleware for providing a stable and secure environment for pervasive applications. The Applications Manager Subsystem installs applications and obtains the context and situation of interest. After this, Applications Manager Subsystem subscribes the situation of interest in Subsystem to Manager Prediction and Inference, also subscribes the context of interest of the installed application in Subsystem to Manager Context.

The Subsystem to Manager Context has two modules: the Monitor Module and the Complex Event Processing Module. The Monitor Module generates instances of events and manages raw data from sensors. Each time an event arises, Complex Event Processing Module sends the event to the Complex Event Processing Module. After the Complex Event Processing Module uses the pattern informed in the event description, it processes the flow of events to determine if some received events are relevant. If it is the case, the Complex Event Processing Module notifies the Prediction and Inference Managing Subsystem. The Prediction and Inference Managing Subsystem is composed of two models that are activated at the same time: Inference and Prediction. The Module of Inference processes the rules to detect the current situation, and the Module of Prediction processes the influence model (Sect. 3.4) to determine the probability of a situation happening in the future. If a situation happens or could happen in the environment, the application assigned to the situation is started. At this moment, the pervasive application chooses the most relevant action to manipulate the situation and sends a request to the Manager Action Subsystem to execute the action. The Manager Action Subsystem needs to select the services with the most appropriate functionalities of appliances, according to the detected situation.

The Upper Level (1) offers a stable computing environment for pervasive applications.

## 3.2 Proactive Model

A pervasive application has interest in specific situations that involve users and what happens in their living environment. The pervasive application contains the knowledge of what kind of reactive and proactive actions (two business processes) should be taken when an unwanted situation happens. The SIaaS middleware monitors the events that could generate a situation of interest for any pervasive application, and notifies it whenever such situation becomes true.

These events occur in time windows and are related to situations. These situations are described by pervasive applications that specify their situations of interest and subscribe their situations in the middleware. Taking into account examples from the health domain, we consider a scenario where the aim is to monitor medicine administration. Thus, the pervasive application declares to the middleware its interest in the event "medicine X is not administrated", and also provides how this event can be detected through of model (Sect. 3.4). For instance, if it is detected during consecutive days, it may result in health problems for the patient, i.e., an unwanted situation.

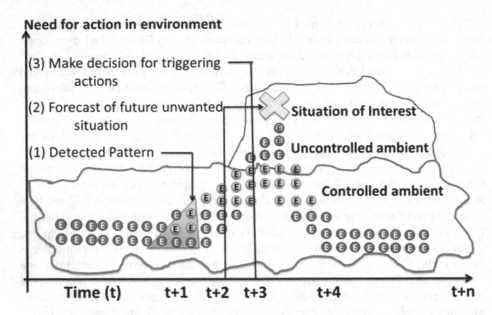

**Fig. 2.** Environmental states.

The SIaaS must avoid such unwanted situations (e.g., the patient *forgot to take* his medicine and became sicker). For this purpose, the SIaaS initially learns a predictive model using data provided by the pervasive application. The pervasive application data consists of patient's behavior patterns (proactive model and data) that will be managed by the SIaaS. After the learning stage, the SIaaS can predict situations through events detected in real-time and is able to perform proactive actions, avoiding the occurrence of unwanted situation. Consequently, the reactive actions requested by the pervasive applications will not be executed, because the events (e.g., patient *forgot to take* his medicine) that would determine the situation will not occur. In this sense, the SIaaS acts proactively to prevent an unwanted situation.

As depicted in Fig. 2, the environment may be in two states: controlled or uncontrolled. An event stream, predefined as normal (pattern that is not interest of the middleware), characterizes a controlled environment where reactive actions are helpful. However, if the events are being detected outside this predefined state (interest pattern of the middleware), it could characterize that the environment will become uncontrolled, thus increasing the dependency on proactive actions being performed by the SIaaS.

In the environment, event streams are constantly monitored through data made available by sensors. Still, evaluating the events flow of Fig. 2, at *t+1* a pattern of events (provided by the pervasive application) is detected (1) by the Context Manager. This subsystem uses a prediction algorithm to determinate the probability of an unwanted situation becoming true in the user living environment. The Context Manager has *t+2* times to make the prediction, having enough time to take corrective actions. After identifying the probability of the occurrence of a situation in *t+2* (2), the

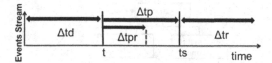

**Fig. 3.** Sliding Windows

Inference Manager processes the respective rules to determinate if the rate of probability is relevant. If it is positive, the Proactive Actions Manager must be activated in $t$ $+3$ (3) to trigger proactive actions. This module is responsible for choosing the most appropriate policy to consume appropriate services corresponding to environmental devices and health care providers.

All these actions are taken in order to conduct the environment towards a normal state and to avoid future unwanted situations. The goal is to return to the initial streams of events, thereby characterizing the consistency of the environment.

### 3.3    Sliding Windows

In the present approach, we consider that it is necessary to analyze a sequence of events for learning and detecting patterns aiming to predict situations. Besides, we consider that this sequence of events occurs in a period of time, referenced as Sliding Window, i.e., a valid space of time where situations are predicted or detected and the relevant decisions are taken. The Sliding Windows model used in our approach is adapted from Salfner, Lenk and Malek [21]. In this model, a sliding can be sized or timed. A sized sliding window (SSW) has a specific size that corresponds to the number of events of a given pattern of interest. For instance, it is possible to use a SSW with the last hundred events that match specific selection criteria. A timed sliding window (TSW) has a finite time frame where events of interest are monitored. In this work, only $\Delta td$ is modeled as these two possibilities, the remainders are windows of time, because they are used to model the window in future for an unwanted situation.

Figure 3 presents a sliding window associated with a real time proactive behavior. At time $t$ (current time), the possibility of occurrence of a situation can be predicted with some time in advance. This period of time is called prediction time ($\Delta tpr$) and is based on the events currently detected in the environment. Situations are predicted in $\Delta tpr$, which uses a size or time sliding window ($\Delta td$) that corresponds to the event stream monitored by the system. These timed or sized windows ($\Delta td$) are used to perform prediction. We assume that proactive actions are valid for some period of time, named period of proactivity ($\Delta tp$). In this time window, triggered actions can change predicted situations, which are expected to occur in the reaction time ($\Delta tr$). If $\Delta tpr >$ $\Delta tp$ then there will not be enough time for all proactive actions to be triggered before the predicted situation (i.e., an unwanted situation) becoming true. Thus, $\Delta tr$ is the maximum time the system has to react, since $\Delta tr$ is the time estimated to the situation to occur. Then, $\Delta tr$ is the period where reactive actions, related to a specific unwanted situation, are triggered.

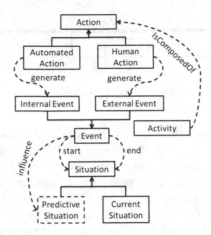

**Fig. 4.** Conceptual model.

### 3.4    Event and Situation Model

In this work, the semantic relations $\{R\}$ that form the context are represented by triples ⟨*Es, p, Eo*⟩ where the subject *Es* and the object *Eo* represent instances of entities of the environment, which could belong to the same domain or not. Similarly, as formalized by Ye, Stevenson and Dobson [7], *p* represents a context predicate that encapsulates two entities of context in a relation. For instance, in the relation ⟨John, *hasSensor*, RFID⟩ John and RFID represent entities. Subjects and objects can also be represented by variables in reasoning rules. For example, in the following triple, ⟨*x, hasSensor, y*⟩, *x* represents any entity instantiated in the user domain and *y* represents any entity instantiated in the sensor domain. In this example, any pair of values of User and Sensor, related by the relationship *hasSensor*, can validate this context predicate.

Figure 4 depicts the conceptual model of our approach. The Activity entity represents daily activities performed by the citizen in his home, like breakfasting, watching television, taking medicine or doing exercises. The activities are made up of human actions, for instance the activity to take medicine is composed by picking up a glass with water and taking the drug, represented by the semantic relations presented below (1).

⟨John, catch, glass⟩ ∧ ⟨glass, has,
water⟩ ∧ ⟨John, obtain, drug⟩ ∧
⟨John, take, drug⟩ ⇒
⟨John, took, medicine⟩

Besides human actions, we also take into account automated actions taken by the system. For instance, the system may notify the citizen through an audible warning using some device (we consider that automated actions are actions performed by devices). Thus, actions are carried out by an agent (human or device) in order to achieve a goal. When an action either achieves or not its goal, it can generate events.

In our approach, we adopt internal and external events, which are defined in the theory of Situation Calculus [22]. An external event is generated externally by human actions or by interacting with pervasive applications. In addition, external events can be generated by changing a user device or by changing the network connection used by a device. Internal events are generated internally by the system and are represented by assertions that can be given by an axiom. An internal event could be generated by an automated action, the detection of successive state variable changes, or by the modification of one specific state variable. Thus, as more human actions are transferred to automated actions, more extensible the system becomes. Events are represented by the following syntax (2).

$$Event : (name, \ type, \ time, \ \{R\}, \ p) \tag{2}$$

An event has a *name* and is characterized by a *type* (internal or external), a time (timestamp) within Δ*td* windows and a set of contextual semantic relations {*R*}. When the event is not produced by a single entity (e.g., raw data sensor), it may also have a detection pattern (*p*). Events can be linked to one or more contexts; for instance, a pattern that defines that an event must be detected if a specific sequence of events happens within a given sliding window of time or size involving the "user" in his/her living room. In this work, events can determine the evidence of the beginning and the ending of a situation. Thus, events change the state of the environment and characterize a new situation. The current situation is represented by the following syntax (3).

$$Cs : (name, \ Ie, \ \{a\}, \ Fe) \tag{3}$$

As shown in (2), the current situation (*Cs*) has a *name* and a set of *events* that characterize its beginning (*Ie*) and ending (*Fe*), and the *time* attribute of these events that characterize the valid time window of this situation, which will always be in Δ*tr*. In addition, the current situation has a set of triggered reactive actions {*a*} that were detected during a valid time for handling the current situation. For instance, below we present how to represent an event (*Ie*) that initiates the "unmedicated" situation (4), its corresponding final event (*Fe*) and the actions to be performed in this situation.

| name | unmedicated |
|---|---|
| Ie | ‹John, shouldTake, Drug X› ∧ ‹Medicine X, timeToAdminister, 10h› ∧ ‹currentTime, equals, 10:30› ⇒‹John, notTake, medicine› <br> ⇒‹John, isSituationOf, {unmedicated}› |
| {a} | ‹System, trigger, audibleWarning› ‹System, trigger, visualWarning› ‹System, notify, Caregiver› |
| Fe | ‹John, catch, glass› ∧ ‹glass, has, water› ∧ ‹John, obtain, drug› ∧‹John, take, drug› ∧ ‹John, onClick, appPerv› ⇒ ‹John, take, medicine› ⇒‹John, isSituationOf, {medicated}› |

The event evaluation can lead the system to find out that an unwanted situation has a probability of happening in the future. In (5) we show that a Predictive Situation (*Ps*) is characterized by a set of *events*; a set of patterns (*p*), which describes some form of correlation among events that shape this situation, the probability value (*pr*) of its occurrence in a context in the future; and a timestamp (*time*) during which it may occur within Δ*tr*.

$$Ps : (name, \{event\}, \{p\}, pr, time) \tag{5}$$

Figure 5 presents the influence model. The model is a set of events modeled by a pattern that determine a correlation model among the events. For example, the detection of the event "E3" influences event "E1", and the detection of the event "E4" influences "E1", and "E1" influences the arise of predictive situation. In this model, a situation is always a left node and their parents are always events.

## 4  Case Study Scenarios

This case study aims to demonstrate the use of our approach in a scenario where the necessity of a mechanism that acts in proactive way is emphasized. The scenario is related to the aforementioned self-administration of medicines by patients in their homes. The aim is to identify when patients are no longer able to control their own medication.

In this sense, we are considering that patients, in general, will take their medicine in a stipulated period of time or after an action system (e.g., using functionalities (services) of devices of the environment to remember the patient about the medication). However, some patients can have cognitive decline over time, compromising the self-management of their health condition, thus needing help to take the medication at the correct time. In this scenario, the situation known as "*unmedicated*" becomes habitual, and reactive/proactive actions are necessary to control this situation, considering the recent history of self-management of citizen's health, thus assisting the patient to take his medicine in the best possible way. We considered a pervasive application deployed in the SIaaS to help patients in the described scenario. For the implementation, we have used the monitoring component Esper [23], the Bayesian tool Netica [24], which provided an API that we used to create the Bayesian network that was inserted into the Context Manager. In addition Jess [25] was used to build Java software process able to perform inference rules in the Inference Manager module.

For the case study, the following fictitious scenario was considered for describing the approach supported by the decision making process implemented by the pervasive application. Imagine 'Ms. Smith', a 70 years old citizen who has some aging associated

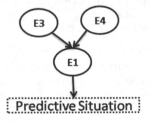

**Fig. 5.**  Influence model.

diseases such as diabetes, hypertension and lightweight dementia. Ms. Smith's home is an intelligent environment managed by a SIaaS middleware, where a number of pervasive applications are installed. An example is the *pervasive application for managing medications (appPervMed)*.

Ms. Smith initially controls the medication herself. However, as any ordinary person, sometimes, to be involved in some particular activity, she forgets to take or takes her medicines late, which puts her in an *"unmedicated"* situation. In these cases, the *appPervMed* requests to the SIaaS middleware to trigger an audible or visual warning through devices located near Ms. Smith. Whenever a warning reaches her attention, she can interact with the system through a smart phone or smart TV to report explicitly that she took her medication. After that interaction, the system will close (finish) the *"unmedicated"* situation.

After some stipulated time, if Ms. Smith does not take her medication, the system sends a warning to her caregiver. It warns her caregiver that Ms. Smith had not taken her medicine, thus placing the responsibility of interacting with the SIaaS on the caregiver. Once the caregiver gives her the medicine, and informs the system about that, the *appPervMed* will know that Ms. Smith took the medicine and will determine the end of the *"unmedicated"* situation.

Eventually, the caregiver himself may forget or may be not close to any device that could warn him about the moment that Ms. Smith must be medicated. Thus, the event "medicine X not taken" is detected, corresponding again to the beginning of the situation of *"Ms. Smith is unmedicated"*. Audible and visual warnings are generated in different moments in the environment, and, after some parameterized time, the caregiver is warned. The *appPervMed* waits for a notification that Ms. Smith took the medication by the caregiver. If it is not notified in a specific period, the *appPervMed* triggers a warning directly to the healthcare provider (consuming a specific Web service), placing the responsibility on the healthcare provider to make Ms. Smith taking her medicine, and, once taken, it ends the situation.

As explained, alerting the caregiver is an exception. However, after some time, if Ms. Smith takes her medicine only after a system warning to her caregiver and if this behavior becomes more usual, this behavior may indicate a cognitive decline of Ms. Smith.

Thus, it is necessary to identify (in a proactive way) when the cognitive impairment happens, because if this identification does not happens fast, the treatment will be harmed by the administration of drugs in wrong times. This moment may characterize the end of the patient's ability to medicate her-self, requiring the caregiver to this function. Therefore, the system must adapt itself and assist the caregiver in his task of assisting Ms. Smith.

## 5    Applying the Approach to the Case Study

The scenario described before shows that a pervasive application must react to an event (Ms. Smith did not take her medication) that characterize the unmedicated situation and also must forecast some situation (e.g., Ms. Smith will not take her medication without her caregiver help) and be proactive.

In this paper, the pervasive application has two business processes for taking decision (reactive and proactive). Next, following our approach, we show how a pervasive application should work either reactively and proactively.

### 5.1  Reactive Behavior

The events related to this case study that are relevant to the *appPervMed* are described here, as proposed in Sect. 3.4. For performing this task we used the Semantic Web Rule Language (SWRL), using the already defined semantic relations {R} and triplets in the form ⟨Es, p, Eo⟩, as presented in Sect. 3.4.

The Fig. 6 presents the reactive decision making process where the appPervMed is selected when Ms. Smith does not took her medicine and always it is initiate because event "ea1" is detected. The patterns to detect events were modeled as *Esper* statements. The variables were replaced to the values used in the scenario to provide an easier interpretation.

Event name: ea1; description: Not took the medicine; typed: Internal

```
{R}:⟨Ms. Smith, needToTake, Drug X⟩ ∧
⟨Drug X, timeToAdminister, 10h⟩ ∧
⟨currentTime, is, 10:15⟩ ⇒⟨Ms. Smith, notTaken, medicine⟩
Pattern   SELECT e FROM PATTERN[every e=Event(name ='ea1') ->
          (timer:at(*/15,10:00,*,*,*) and not Event(name ='ea2'))]
```

In this rule, timer:at is an expression of a specific time that turns true. The syntax is timer:at (minutes, hours, days of month, months, days of week, seconds) [23].

Event name: ea2; description: Took medicine; typed: External

```
{R}: ⟨Ms. Smith, medicationTime, Drug X⟩ ∧
⟨doorMedicineChest,  wasOpenedBy,  Ms.  Smith⟩  ∧  ⟨Ms.  Smith,
pressedOKButton, appPervMed⟩⇒⟨ Ms. Smith, took, medicine⟩
Pattern: SELECT e From e=Event(name='ea2')
```

Event name: ea3; description: Took medicine after some action; typed: External

```
{R}: the same semantic relations of ea2
Pattern   SELECT e FROM PATTERN[
          every e=Event(name ='ea3')-> (Event(name ='ea1') ->
          (Event(name = 'a1') or Event(name = 'a2') or
          Event(name = 'a3') or Event(name = 'a4')))]
```

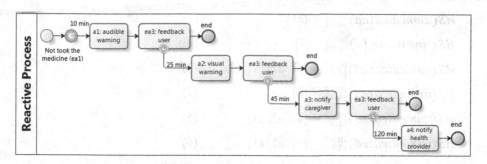

**Fig. 6.** Proactive and reactive network.

Event name: a1; description: Audible warning after 10 min of ea1; typed: Internal

```
{R}: <appPervMed, trigger, audibleService>
Pattern   SELECT e FROM PATTERN[every e=Event(name='a1')->
          (timer:at(*/25,10:00,*,*,*) and Event(name ='ea1'))]
```

The events "a2", "a3" and "a4" are modeled the same way and are not describe here. As presented above, if event *ea2* is detected, Ms. Smith is in the situation of "*medicated*". Therefore, the *appPervMed* is not started because the situation "*unmedicated*" did not happen. The internal and external events and relevant actions that determine each situation are presented below:

**Current Situation of Interest**

| name = unmedicated; | name = medicated; |
|---|---|
| Ie = ea1 | Ie = ea2 |
| {a} = a1, a2, a3, a4 | {a} = - |
| Fe = ea3 | Fe = ea1 |

If Ms. Smith does not take the medicine (event *ea1* was detected) the "*unmedicated*" situation is initiated and *appPervMed* chooses the reactive action to be triggered. After the detection of the event *ea1*, *appPervMed* waits for 10 min and, if an event *ea2* was not detected, it will trigger an audible warning (*a1*). After the audible warning, the application needs to wait for a feedback. If this feedback is not received, *appPervMed* triggers a2 to produce some visual warning. Thus, *appPervMed* terminate its execution when the resulting feedback is ea3 (i.e., took medicine after some action).

## 5.2   Proactive Behavior

This section presents the proactive behavior of the SIaaS, showing how it would prevent Ms. Smith from entering in an "*unmedicated*" situation. Initially, it makes a historical analysis of the situations generated by the events detected that are relevant for *appPervMed*.

Below, we present a historical situation (HS) that has happened and the reactive actions triggered for manipulating this situation.

$$HS(unmedicated)_{10:23}^{10:15} = \{a1\} \qquad (1)$$

$$HS(\ medicated\ )_{10:00}^{10:00} = \{-\} \qquad (2)$$

$$HS(unmedicated)_{10:33}^{10:15} = \{a1, a2\} \qquad (3)$$

$$HS(unmedicated)_{10:33}^{10:15} = \{a1, a2\} \qquad (4)$$

$$HS(unmedicated)_{11:03}^{10:15} = \{a1, a2, a3\} \qquad (5)$$

$$HS(unmedicated)_{11:03}^{10:15} = \{a1, a2, a3\} \qquad (6)$$

$$... \qquad (n)$$

$$HS(unmedicated)_{11:03}^{10:15} = \{a1, a2, a3\} \qquad (n+1)$$

This representation is based in a notation proposed by Wasserkrug, Gal and Etzion [26], which shows the initial and final time of the situation. In this case, curly brackets represent the actions triggered during the period of time when the situation was valid. For instance, the first event *ea1* was detected at 10:15 (1), and the situation was finalized when the event *ea3* was detected at 10:23 and the action *a1* was triggered. In (2), Ms. Smith took the medicine on the right time (10:00), so, no reactive action was triggered.

This historical data of behavioral management of medicines by Ms. Smith shows the sequence of actions that were needed to handle the unwanted *"unmedicated"* situation. This HS is used to generate the Conditional Probability Table (CPT) for each node event of the Bayesian network. In this case study, the generation of the CPT must be sensible to a cognitive decline, so the Bayesian network cannot be established with all the stored history of that situation. In order to identify a cognitive decline, the system needs to build a valid sliding window with an event stream of $\Delta td$ (which was described in Sect. 3.3) that corresponds to the current behavior of Ms. Smith. Therefore, the *appPervMed* will register in the Module Monitor (Esper) of the Context Manager only the patterns that correspond to the sliding window used to calculate the network CPT represented in (7).

```
select e from pattern [every e=Event].win:length(45)
where e.name='ea1' or e.name='a1' or name='a2' or name='a3'
or name='a4'
```

In the previous pattern, which was deployed in Esper, we have defined a sliding window of $\Delta td$ corresponding to the last 45 times in which Ms. Smith had not taken her medicine (event *ea1*), as well as the actions that were detected after that situation had happened. In this pattern, if Ms. Smith should take a medication once a day, this window would correspond to 45 days. Thus, the value of the probabilistic predictive situation always will be set to a percentage that corresponds to 45 days. In this sense, we avoid network scalability problems related to the excessive number of events (since they are modeled as nodes in the network), and detect cognitive declines with periods less than 45 days. This pattern generates the sequence of events that constantly updates the Bayesian network and the values of the probability of the event that determines the beginning of unwanted situations of this kind.

As Fig. 7 shows, event *ea1* is the cause of the "*unmedicated*" situation. This event, as well as events *a1*, *a2*, *a3*, *a4*, also influences event *ea3*. Besides, *ea2* and *ea3* influence the fact of Ms. Smith being medicated or not. The probability of Ms. Smith not taking her medicine at the correct time is 63.4%, according to the simulated behavior. Based on this data, the SIaaS will update the probability attribute of the corresponding predictive situation for this case, as shown below:

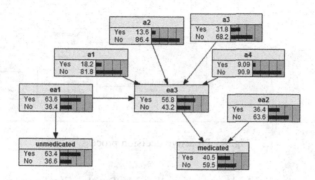

**Fig. 7.** appPervMed Bayesian network.

Predictive Situation name = unmedicated;
{event} = {ea1, ea3, a1, a2, a3, a4};
{p} = ea1; pr = 63.4%; time = ea1.drug.timeTakeDrug;

The value of *time* is extracted by navigating through the event *ea1* and following to the entity of context drug and attribute time to take the medicine (timeTakeDrug) this entity of context. The *appPervMed* thus registers the following rule (8) that shows the relevance of the prediction value.

```
IF ‹unmedicated.pr, greatherThan,60%›
    ⇒‹Ms. Smith, isUnmedicatedIn, ea1.drug.timeTakeDrug›
```

This rule demonstrates that the "*unmedicated*" situation could happen the next time that Ms. Smith needs to take the medicine, activating the proactive decision making process of the *appPervMed*.

Figure 8 presents how the pervasive application uses the Bayesian network to identify, among the triggered actions, which one had the greatest influence for *ea3* to be detected and ending the "*unmedicated*" situation of Ms. Smith. It gives more relevance to the actions that were followed by *ea3* (i.e., took medicine after some action). If there is a sequence of actions triggered after the detection of an unwanted situation (corresponding by *ea1*), the *appPervMed* will chose the last action as being responsible for the ending of the unwanted situation (i.e., *ea3* detected).

Figure 7 shows that the action *a3* (notify the caregiver) was the most successful action at this moment, thus the appPervMed request for middleware trigger the action *a3*, thus the polity will change from "notify caregiver after *45 min of ea1*" to "*notify caregiver BEFORE 5 min of ps.time (ea1.drug.timeTakeDrug)*". Thus, the SIaaS will

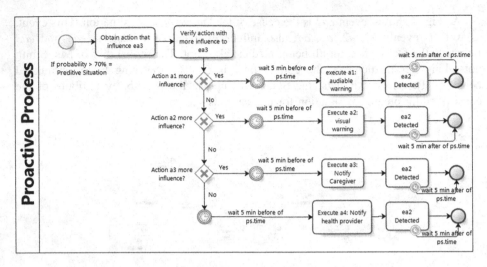

**Fig. 8.** Proactive decision process.

warn the caregiver that he/she has to ensure that Ms. Smith will take the medicine at the right time. In this case, the *appPervMed* will not be triggered to perform a reactive action, because event *ea*1 will not happen. This behavior causes more events of type *ea*2 to be detected since Ms. Smith starts taking her medicine at the right time, so consequently the situation "*unmedicated*" will not happen and the probability of the Bayesian Network for being medicated (*ea*2) increases.

We assume that there is a parameterized value with the criteria of policy selection actions to update the triggering order of proactive actions after this rule being updated. This will avoid that an action, after being identified as most effective, be always chosen as a proactive action that should be executed forever. This calibration is necessary because, in this case study, we are monitoring the behavior of a person, and this behavior may change over time. In the example given, Ms. Smith could not respond to the warnings of the SIaaS for some period of time because she was unmotivated with the treatment, so the warnings to the caregiver would effectively make her taking her medicine. However, if she did not show cognitive decline, she could return to her self-health management without requiring the notification of the caregiver. Therefore, there is a need for policies that trigger proactive actions to be updated. So, the SIaaS will again generate warnings to Ms. Smith.

## 6    Conclusions

Most of the research efforts in situation awareness for AAL are generally related to the detection of situations and the immediate reaction for these situations. In this sense, we have demonstrated the necessity of mechanisms to act reactivity in order to avoid unwanted situations in AAL.

In addition, we consider that for an Ambient Intelligence application to act pro-actively it must have learning capabilities. Therefore, these applications must understand and learn from the events that happened, predicting situations of interest and making decisions in advance related to the user needs. Thus, we consider the use of a Bayesian Network for identifying when it is necessary to act in a changed way.

In this paper, we presented an approach for enabling smart environments with extensible, reactive and proactive characteristics, more specifically in AAL. The extensible principles are related to an enrichment of pervasive applications, where different situations and contexts can be managed by the middleware over the time.

We introduce reactive and proactive principals related to a situation. Reactive actions are selected if the situation is occurring at the present moment and proactive actions are triggered if a situation is predicted in the nearby future.

The main contributions of our approach are: (i) a method for supporting extensibility in systems to Ambient Assisted Living by including experts experience while modeling pervasive applications; (ii) an approach for handling reactive and proactive behaviors; and (iii) a model of sliding windows for modeling time in complex event processing.

The next steps of this research include; (i) testing the situation prediction over a real world automated environment; (ii) improving aspects related to the prediction model; and (iii) adapting the predictive model for taking decisions in a dynamic Bayesian network.

# References

1. Sadri, F.: Ambient intelligence: a survey. ACM Comput. **43**(4), 1–66 (2011)
2. Jara, A.J., Zamora, M.A., Skarmeta, A.F.G.: An internet of things based personal device for diabetes therapy management in ambient assisted living (AAL). Pers. Ubiquit. Comput. **15** (4), 431–440 (2011)
3. Chan, M., Esteve, D., Escriba, C., Campo, E.: A review of smart homes—present state and future challenges. Comp. Comput. Methods Programs Biomed. **91**(1), 55–81 (2008)
4. Augusto, J.C., Nakashima, H., Aghajan, H.: Ambient intelligence and smart environments: a state of the art. In: Handbook of Ambient Intelligence and Smart Environments: Part 1. Springer, New York, pp. 3–31 (2009)
5. Ye, J., Dobson, S., McKeever, S.: Situation identification techniques in pervasive computing: a review. Pervasive Mobile Comput. **8**(1), 36–66 (2011)
6. Dey, A., Abowd, G.: The context toolkit: aiding the development of context-enabled applications. In: Proceedings of the SIGCHI Conference on Human Factors in Computing Systems, Pittsburgh, Pennsylvania, US, pp. 434–441 (1999)
7. Ye, J., Stevenson, G., Dobson, S.: A top-level ontology for smart environments. Pervasive Mobile Comput. **7**(3), 359–378 (2011)
8. Kokar, M.M., Matheus, C.J., Baclawski, K.: Ontology-based situation awareness. J. Inf. Fusion **10**(1), 83–98 (2009)
9. Etzion, O., Niblett, P.: Event Processing in Action. Manning Publications Co, Stamford (2010)

10. Sixsmith, A., Meuller, S., Lull, F., Klein, M., Bierhoff, I., Delaney, S., Savage, R.: SOPRANO – an ambient assisted living system for supporting older people at home. In: Mokhtari, M., Khalil, I., Bauchet, J., Zhang, D., Nugent, C. (eds.) ICOST 2009. LNCS, vol. 5597, pp. 233–236. Springer, Heidelberg (2009)

11. Tazari, M.R., Furfari, F., Lazaro, R.J.P., Ferro, E.: The persona service platform for AAL spaces. In: Nakashima, H., et al. (eds.) Handbook of Ambient Intelligence and Smart Environments, pp. 1171–1199. Springer, Heidelberg (2010)

12. Paganelli, F., Giuli, D.: An ontology-based system for context-aware and configurable services to support home-based continuous care. IEEE Trans. Inf Technol. Biomed. 15(2), 324–333 (2011)

13. Tennenhouse, D.L.: Proactive computing. Commun. ACM 43(5), 43–50 (2000)

14. Want, R., Pering, T., Tennenhouse, D.L.: Comparing autonomic and proactive computing. IBM Syst. J. (IBMSJ) 42(1), 129–135 (2003)

15. Engel, Y., Etzion, O.: Towards proactive event-driven computing. In: Proceedings of the 5th ACM International Conference on Distributed Event-based System, pp. 125–136 (2011)

16. Fu, S., Xu, C.: Quantifying event correlations for proactive failure management. Networked Comput. Syst. J. Parallel Distrib. Comput. 70(11), 1100–1109 (2010)

17. Boytsov, A., Zaslavsky, A.: Context prediction in pervasive computing systems: achievements and challenges. In: Supporting Real Time Decision Making, ser. Annals of Information Systems, Springer, vol. 13, pp. 35–63 (2011)

18. Nazerfard, E., Cook, D.J.: Bayesian networks structure learning for activity prediction in smart homes. In: 8th International Conference Onintelligent Environments (IE), pp. 50–56 (2012)

19. Lotfi, A., Langensiepen, C., Mahmoud, S.M., Akhlaghinia, M.J.: Smart homes for the elderly dementia sufferers: identification and prediction of abnormal behavior. J. Ambient Intell. Humanized Comput. 3(3), 205–218 (2012)

20. Machado, A., Pernas, A.M., Augustin, I., Thom, L.H., Krug, L., Palazzo, M., de Oliveira: Situation-awareness as a key for proactive actions in ambient assisted living. In: Proceedings of the 15th International Conference on Enterprise Information, pp. 418–426 (2013)

21. Salfner, F., Lenk, M., Malek, M.: A survey of online failure prediction methods. ACM Comput. Surv. 42(3), 10–42 (2010)

22. Mccarthy, J.: Actions and other events in situation calculus. In: Proceedings of the 8th International Conference on Principles of Knowledge Representation and Reasoning. Morgan Kaufmann Publishers, Toulouse, pp. 615–628 (2002)

23. Esper: Complex Event Processing. Espertech event stream intelligence (2010)

24. Netica (2013). https://www.norsys.com/netica.html

25. Friedman-Hill, E.: Jess in Action: Java Rule-based Systems. Manning Publications Company, Greenwich (2003)

26. Wasserkrug, S., Gal, A., Etzion, O.: A model for reasoning with uncertain rules in event composition systems. In: Proceedings of the 21st Annual Conference on Uncertainty in Artificial Intelligence, pp. 599–606 (2005)

# Human-Computer Interaction

# Designing an IDTV Application in a Situated Scenario: A Participatory Approach Based on Patterns

Samuel B. Buchdid[✉], Roberto Pereira, and Maria Cecília Calani Baranauskas

Institute of Computing, University of Campinas (UNICAMP), Av. Albert Einstein N1251,
Campinas, SP 13083-852, Brazil
{buchdid,rpereira,cecilia}@ic.unicamp.br

**Abstract.** Interactive Digital TV (iDTV) applications suffer with problems that are inherent to the technology and their social aspects. In addition, theoretical and practical references for designing iDTV applications are not easily found. In this sense, designing for iDTV has become an increasingly complex activity. In this paper, we propose three participatory practices for supporting a situated design and evaluation of iDTV applications. The practices were articulated in a situated design process conducted inside a Brazilian TV company. The approach favored the participation of important stakeholders, supporting different design activities: from design ideas to the creation and evaluation of an interactive prototype. The results suggest the practices' usefulness for supporting design activities, indicate the benefits of a situated and participatory approach for iDTV applications, and may inspire researchers and designers in other contexts.

**Keywords:** Socially aware computing · Organizational semiotics · Design patterns · Participatory design · HCI · iDTV

## 1 Introduction

In the last years, the amount and diversity of technical devices have increased both inside and outside people's homes (e.g., tools, mobiles, cars, airports), being increasingly interconnected (e.g., through bluetooth, wireless LAN, 4G) [15]. Systems are not working in isolation, but in plural environments, bringing different people together as citizens and members of global communities [29]. As Bannon [2] suggests, in this scenario, there are problems that go beyond the relationship between users and technologies, requiring more than a man-machine approach and ergonomic fixes to make useful and meaningful design.

Therefore, designing interactive systems is becoming a more complex task, not only in the technical sense, but also in the social one [15]. However, Winograd [37] highlights that the majority of techniques, concepts, methods and skills to make design for a new and complex scenario are foreign of the computer science mainstream. In this sense, it is necessary to look at the technology comprehensively within the situated context in which it is embedded, incorporating knowledge of several stakeholders, areas, subjects and theories [19].

© Springer International Publishing Switzerland 2015
J. Cordeiro et al. (Eds.): ICEIS 2014, LNBIP 227, pp. 341–360, 2015.
DOI: 10.1007/978-3-319-22348-3_19

Within this scenario, the emergency of the Interactive Digital TV (iDTV) (which includes digital transmission, receiver processing capability and interactivity channel) opens up a variety of possibilities for new services for TV [28]. However, as Bernhaupt et al. [6] argue, with new devices connected to TV, watching it has become an increasingly complicated activity.

In fact, the iDTV has technical issues as well as social characteristics that influence directly their use and acceptance. For instance: the interaction limited by the remote control, the lack of custom of people to interact with television, the high amount and diversity of users, the usual presence of other viewers in the same physical space, to cite a few [20]. As Cesar et al. [11] assert, the TV is a highly social and pervasive technology — characteristics that make it a challenging and interesting field to investigate, but that usually are not receiving attention from current works. Furthermore, Kunert [20] highlights that every emergent technology suffers from a lack of references, processes and artifacts for supporting its design. Therefore, new simple techniques and artifacts that fit the broadcasters' production chain and explore the challenge of designing applications within the broadcasters' context are welcome.

Despite not abundant, some literature has proposed ways to support the design of iDTV applications. Chorianopoulos [12] analyzed works on media and studies about television and everyday life, proposing design principles to support user interactivity during leisure pursuits in domestic settings. Piccolo et al. [27] proposed recommendations to help designers with accessibility issues for iDTV applications. Kunert [20] proposed a collection of pattern for the iDTV focused in usability issues. Solano et al. [30] presented a set of guidelines that should be considered in iDTV applications for preventing frequent usability problems.

Focused on the users' aspects, Rice and Alm [28] proposed methodologies and interactive practices influenced by the Participatory Design (PD) to design solutions for supporting elderly people to interact with iDTV. Bernhaupt et al. [6], in turn, used the Cultural Probes Method to conduct ethnographic studies in order to understand users' media behavior and expectations, indicating trends concerned with personalization, privacy, security and communication.

Focusing on the broadcaster company's aspects, some works have adapted traditional methodologies for software development [18] and Agile Methods [35] to the companies' production chain. The adapted methodologies encompass the entire software development process (e.g., requirement analysis, project, implementation, testing and support); although robust in terms of the technical process of software development, end users are usually not considered in the process.

Shedding light on this scenario, we draw on Socially Aware Computing (SAC) [3, 5], Organizational Semiotics theory [22], Participatory Design [24], and Design Patterns for iDTV applications [20] to propose three situated and participatory practices for supporting designers to create and evaluate iDTV applications: (i) the Participatory Pattern Cards; (ii) the Pattern-guided Braindrawing; and (iii) the Participatory Situated Evaluation.

In this paper, we present the three practices and the theories underlying them, and discuss the results obtained from their usage in the practical context of a Brazilian broadcasting company. The practices were planned to facilitate the participation of professionals from the TV domain that are not familiar with iDTV applications design.

A group of 9 persons, with different profiles, participated in design workshops for creating an iDTV application for one of the company's programs. The results suggest both the practices' usefulness for supporting design activities and the benefits of situated and participatory design for iDTV applications, indicating the viability of conducting the practices in industrial settings.

The paper is organized as follows: the Sect. 2 introduces the theories and methodologies that ground our work. Section 3 describes the new practices created for supporting a situated and participatory design of iDTV applications. Section 4 presents the case study in which the techniques were applied, and Sect. 5 presents and discusses the findings from the case study analysis. Finally, Sect. 6 presents our final considerations and directions for future research.

### 1.1  Software Development Vs TV Content Processes

TV Companies have teams with well-defined roles (e.g., director, designer, producer and engineer) and tasks (e.g., pre-production, production and transmission) that work in a synchronized way to produce the television content [7]. For example, while the production teams produce television content, engineers provide infrastructure for broadcasting the TV content to viewers. A software development process has also well-defined steps and roles. Pressman [16] argues that the main steps depend on different process models (e.g., Cascade Model, Agile Methods) and should encompass from requirements analysis and design to development and testing of the system. These steps are supported by designers, developers, testers, and analysts among other professionals.

With iDTV and the need to produce interactive content, the production process of television content gains new roles and new needs toward the software production. However, the broadcasting companies are not ready for this new component into their production chains. In addition, Veiga [35] argues that designing iDTV applications is hardly supported by existing methodologies (e.g., Cascade Model) because it is different from designing traditional software systems (e.g., desktop, web). There is a distance between a production process of television content and conventional software development process. In this sense, the application of iDTV must be created on the optics of the two process models, and the opportunity arises to develop a new model specific process model for developing iDTV applications, from inspirations in both process models. In this work we draw on the SAC approach that seeks to understand the needs of the production chain from TV Company, and brings theoretical references from software engineering, but also seeks to bring the end user's needs for the artifact to be designed.

## 2  Theoretical and Methodological Foundation

Organizational Semiotics (OS) and Participatory Design (PD) are two disciplines which represent the philosophical basis for the design approach considered in this work. Design patterns for iDTV add to this theoretical basis contributing to shaping the design product.

OS proposes a comprehensive study of organizations at different levels of formalization (informal, formal, and technical), and their interdependencies. OS understands that all organized behavior is effected through the communication and interpretation of signs by people, individually and in groups [22, 32]. In this sense, the OS supports the understanding of the context in which the technical system is/will be inserted and the main forces that direct or indirectly act on it. If an information system is to be built for an organization, the understanding of organizational functions from the informal to the technical level is essential [22].

The PD, originated in the 70's in Norway, had the goal of giving to workers the rights to participate in design decisions regarding the use of new technologies in the workplace [24]. In this sense, PD proposes conditions for user participation during the design process of software systems. PD makes use of simple practices that use fewer resources (e.g., pen and paper), and considers that everyone involved in a design situation is capable of contributing, regardless of his/her role, hierarchical level, and socio-economic conditions. Two examples of participatory practices are Brainwriting [34] and Braindrawing [24]. Both practices are examples of cyclical brainstorming conducted to generate ideas and perspectives from various participants for the system to be built. While Brainwriting was created to generate ideas for system features, Braindrawing was proposed for generating graphical ideas for the User Interface (UI).

Drawing on OS and PD, the Socially Aware Computing (SAC) proposes to understand the design cycle by working on the informal, formal and technical issues in a systematic way; moreover, it recognizes the value of participatory practices to understand the situated character of design.

## 2.1 Socially Aware Computing

The Socially Aware Computing (SAC) is a socially motivated approach to design [3] that supports the understanding of the organization, the solution to be designed, and the context in which the solution will be inserted, so that it can effectively meet the socio-technical needs of a particular group or organization.

Considering the Semiotic Onion (see "SAC's Meta-Model" detail in Fig. 1), SAC understands design as a process that must go through the informal, formal and technical layers cyclically — see the dashed cycle. According to Baranauskas [5], the design process should be understood as a movement that starts in the society (outside of the semiotic onion) and progresses through the informal and formal layers in order to build the technical system. Once (an increment of) the technical system is projected, the movement returns impacting on formal and informal layers alike, including the people for whom the system was designed, the environment in which it is/will be inserted, and the society in general. SAC is an iterative and incremental process. Therefore, each iteration favors the problem clarification, knowledge-building, and the design and evaluation of the proposed solution.

For understanding the organization's situational context and the system inside it, SAC uses concepts and techniques inspired by PD and OS. More than the end user, SAC considers and involves key stakeholders and heterogeneous groups of people who may influence and/or may be influenced by the problem being discussed and/or the solution to be designed.

The practices conducted in SAC are held throughout the design process within Semio-participatory Workshops (SpW). According to Baranauskas [4], each SpW has

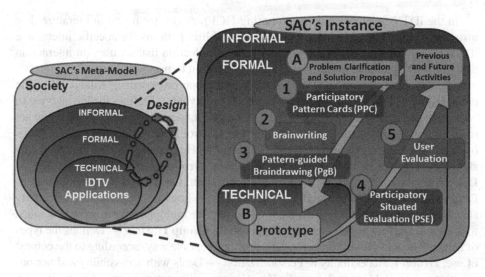

**Fig. 1.** Design process.

well-defined goals and rules within the design process, such as: (i) socialization and personal introductions of the participants. (ii) explanations about the SpW to be conducted, its concepts and objectives. (iii) the role of the SpW in a whole design process (in the cases where there are more than one SpW to be conducted). (iv) a well-defined schedule for activities. (v) artifacts and methods created/adapted to be articulated with the practices, and so on.

SAC has been used to support design in several different contexts, being applied in design scenarios of high diversity of users (e.g., skills, knowledge, age, gender, special needs, literacy, intentions, values, beliefs) and to create different design products in both academic and industrial environments [25]. Specifically for the iDTV context, SAC has being used to support the consideration of stakeholders' values and culture during the design process [26], for proposing requirements and recommendations to iDTV applications [27], and to physical interaction devices [23].

## 2.2 Design Patterns for IDTV

Design patterns were originally proposed to capture the essence of successful solutions to recurring problems of architectural projects in a given context [1]. In addition to their use in the original field of architecture, design patterns have been used in other fields, such as Software Engineering [17] and Human-Computer Interaction (HCI) [8], and within different contexts, such as Ubiquitous Computing [13] and iDTV [20].

For new technologies, Kunert [20] and Chung et al. [13] argue that design patterns present advantages: (i) they are distributed within a hierarchical structure, which makes it easier to locate and differentiate between patterns of different granularity; (ii) they are proposed in a simple language; and (iii) they incorporate references that may indicate other forms of design guidance.

In the iDTV field, few studies proposing HCI patterns are found in literature. For instance, Sousa et al. [31] identified a list of usability patterns for specific interactive iDTV tasks, and Kunert [20] proposed a pattern collection that focuses on interaction design for iDTV applications, paying special attention to usability issues.

The pattern collection used in this work is the one proposed by Kunert [20]. The patterns are divided into 10 groups: **Group A**: Page Layout — Defines the layout types to be used in the application; **Group B**: Navigation — Defines what types of navigation are to be used in the application; **Group C**: Remote Control Keys — Defines the main keys of the remote control; **Group D**: Basic Functions — Highlights the basic functions that should be considered in the design of interaction; **Group E**: Content Presentation — Determines the basic elements that form an application; **Group F**: User Participation — Describes the interaction of specific tasks; and the way how the approval for connectivity should be handled; **Group G**: Text Input — Defines the multiple ways to input text, when to use each, and how to use them in an application; **Group H**: Help — Defines the types of help and how to provide them for users in an appropriate way, according to the context of use; **Group I**: Accessibility & Personalization — Deals with accessibility and personalization issues; and **Group J**: Specific User Groups — Illustrates patterns for specific user groups (e.g., children). Each of the 10 groups describes and illustrates first-level problems that are divided into new design problems of second and third levels. On the second level, there are 35 interaction problems; for each one, there is a corresponding pattern.

There is not a strict order when choosing patterns, however, Kunert [20] suggests choosing the layout and navigation patterns before the other patterns, because this initial decision directly influences the remaining ones.

## 3   The Proposed Participatory Practices

Drawing on the design patterns and the participatory design techniques, we proposed three practices for supporting design activities in a situated context: (i) Participatory Pattern Cards; (ii) Pattern-guided Braindrawing; and (iii) Participatory Situated Evaluation. These practices were articulated with other design activities in an instantiation of Baranauskas' SAC design process [3, 5] in order to favor the situated and participatory design of iDTV applications — see Fig. 1.

The "A" detail in Fig. 1 suggests that the problem domain must be clarified and a solution proposal must be discussed in a participatory way before engaging in further design activities. When the problem is clarified and a solution is proposed, three participatory practices ("1", "2" and "3" details) support the production of the first version of the prototype ("B" detail); one participatory practice supports the inspection of the designed prototype ("4" detail), and one extra evaluation may be conducted with prospective end-users ("5" detail). These activities contribute to build and evaluate a prototype for the application, offering useful information for further iterations of the process (e.g., the codification stage, the design of new functionalities, redesign).

The **Participatory Pattern Cards** (PPC) ("1" detail in Fig. 1) was conceived to support discussions about design patterns for the iDTV, and the identification and selection of the patterns suitable for the application being designed. For this practice, we created 34 cards based on Kunert's Design Patterns [20] for the iDTV. Table 1 presents a description for the practice.

**Table 1.** Description of the PPC practice.

| Participatory Pattern Cards (PPC) | |
|---|---|
| **Materials (input)** | 1. A set of 34 cards representing Kunert's collection of patterns [20]: the cards are organized in 5 predefined groups (e.g., patterns for the application's layout; patterns for the text input mode); <br> 2. All the material produced in previous activities (e.g., a brief description of the design problem, a general description of a solution proposal, a list of requirements). |
| **Methodology** | 1. Cards overview: participants are introduced to the Pattern Cards, their different types and usage examples; <br> 2. Selection of patterns: for each card group, participants should individually select the cards that would potentially be used in the application. <br> 3. Consensus: a brainstorming section where the participants present the selected patterns and discuss the pros and cons of each one in order to decide the ones they will adopt; <br> 4. Justification for the choices: once a consensus was reached, participants must justify their choices based on the project's scope and requirements. |
| **Results (output)** | 1. A subset of patterns that will potentially be used for the application. <br> As byproducts, the practice: i) brings participants closer to the iDTV domain; ii) draws attention to the limited resources and technology that will be provided for the system to be designed; and iii) may inspire design ideas for future projects. |

Figure 2 illustrates an example of a Pattern Card created for the practice. Each card has the following sections: (i) group, reference and name of the pattern, (ii) an example of the pattern being used in a given situation; (iii) a brief description of the problem; (iv) forces (advantages and disadvantages) that act directly and indirectly on the problem to be solved; and (v) the solution to the problem.

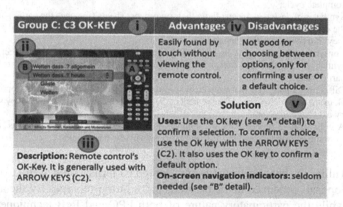

**Fig. 2.** Example of a pattern card created from Kunert's collection [20] of patterns.

The PPC practice is useful to clarify the constraints and potentials of iDTV technology and to choose design patterns in a participatory way, contributing to the construction of a shared knowledge among the participants.

The **Brainwriting** ("2" detail in Fig. 1) is a silent and written generation of ideas by a group in which participants are asked to write ideas on a paper sheet during a pre-defined time (e.g., 60 s). Once this time was elapsed, each participant gives his/her paper sheet with ideas to other participant and receives another paper sheet to continue the ideas written on it. This process is repeated several times until a predefined criterion is satisfied — e.g., the fixed time has run out; each paper sheet passed by all the participants [36]. On the one hand, Brainwritting is a good method for producing different ideas in a parallel way, allowing the participation of all without inhibition from other participants. On the other hand, it focuses on the question/problem being discussed rather than on the person discussing it [34], avoiding conflicts between the participants.

The **Pattern-guided Braindrawing** (PgB) ("3" detail in Fig. 1) is an adapted version of Braindrawing that aims to generate ideas for the UI of the application being designed, taking into account the Design Patterns for iDTV. Table 2 presents a description for the technique.

**Table 2.** Description of the PgB practice.

| Pattern-guided Braindrawing (PgB) |
|---|
| **Materials (input)** — Paper sheets for drawing, colored pens, chronometer. |
| **Methodology** — 1. Situating: participants are arranged in a circle; the design problem and the results from the previous activities (e.g., requirements, PPC) are briefly reviewed; <br> 2. Generation of design elements: keeping visible the design patterns selected in the PPC and a list of requirements for the application, participants start drawing the application's interface on a paper sheet. After a pre-defined time (e.g., 60 seconds), participants stop drawing, move the paper sheet to the colleague seated on their right side, and receive a paper sheet from a colleague seated on their left side, continuing to draw on the received paper sheet. This step repeats until all participants contributed with ideas to all the paper sheets at last once, i.e., a complete cycle; <br> 3. Synthesis of design elements: From their own paper sheets (the ones the participants initiated the drawing), participants highlight the design elements that appeared in their draws and that they find relevant for the application. <br> 4. Consensus: Based on the highlighted design elements from each paper sheet, the group synthesizes the ideas and consolidates a final proposal that may include elements from all the participants; |
| **Results (output)** — 1. Different UI proposals that were created in the participatory activity: each proposal presents elements drawn by different participants, differing from each other because they were started by a different person; <br> 2. A collaborative proposal for the application's UI, guided by design patterns, and created from the consolidation of the different proposals by the participants. |

The PgB allies the benefits from PD and Design Patterns, being useful to materialize ideas and proposals produced in the previous steps into prototypes for the application. Therefore, while the participatory nature of both PPC and PgB techniques motivate participants to generate design ideas that rely on the perspectives of different stakeholders, the use of Design Patterns informs these ideas and guides their materialization.

A picture of a television device and a screenshot of the TV program may be used as background of the paper sheets used in PgB. This contributes to bring reality to the participants during the activity, situating them according to the device's physical limitations, the program layout and content. Example of this template is reported in Buchdid et al. [10].

The third practice created was the **Participatory Situated Evaluation** (PSE) ("4" detail in Fig. 1). The PSE is an adapted version of Thinking Aloud method [21] that aims to bring together all participants for the evaluation of an iterative application — Table 3 presents a description for the practice. This practice is useful to promote a collective analysis and discussion about the produced prototype; to identify shared doubts and difficulties, as well as ideas for improving the application. It avoids the prevalence of individual opinions, favoring the collective discussion and making sense about the application being evaluated, and optimizing the time spent by the participants during the activity.

**Table 3.** Description of the PSE practice.

| Participatory Situated Evaluation (PSE) | |
|---|---|
| **Materials (input)** | Laptop, interactive prototype, video camera, and software to record users interacting with the prototypes. |
| **Methodology** | 1. Situating: participants are arranged in a circle; the interactive prototype is introduced to the participants and the evaluation activity is explained; participants can either conduct pre-defined tasks (e.g., voting in a pool) or explore the application in a free way; |
| | 2. Interacting with the prototype: a participant is invited to interact with the prototype; using the Thinking Aloud method [21], the participant speaks aloud for the group while interacts with the prototype, reporting his/her thoughts (e.g., general impressions about the prototype, intentions, goals, difficulties, questions, reasoning). The other participants can talk to each other and to the person who is interacting with the prototype, speaking their thoughts alike. |
| | 3. Consensus: based on the doubts, ideas, feelings and difficulties found during the activity, the participants elaborate a list of problems and suggestions for improving the application. |
| **Results (output)** | 1. A mapping of the interaction and interface problems identified through the activity; |
| | 2. Suggestions of improvements presented in the group's suggestion list. |

**User Evaluation** ("5" detail in Fig. 1) proposal: the Thinking Aloud technique [21] can be used to capture users' impressions and opinions. The participants' interaction, voices and facial expressions can be recorded, and participants may be invited to answer an evaluation questionnaire, providing their overall impressions about the prototype. The activity and data usage should be conducted in accordance to ethical principles in academic research.

# 4   The Case Study

The case study was conducted in a real context of a television broadcasting company, named EPTV (Portuguese acronym for "Pioneer Broadcasting Television Stations"). EPTV is affiliate of a large Brazilian broadcasting company. Currently, EPTV programming reaches more than 10 million citizens living in a microregion of about 300 cities [14].

"*Terra da Gente*" (TdG, "Our Land", in English) is one of several programs produced by EPTV. The program explores local diversity in flora and fauna, cooking, traditional music, and sport fishing. Currently, the program runs weekly and is structured in 4 blocks of 8 to 10 min each. It counts on a team of editors, writers, producers, designers, technicians, engineers and journalists, among other staff members. In addition to the television program, the TdG team also produces a printed magazine and maintains a web portal. Both the magazine and the web portal serve as complementary sources of material for the TdG audience [33].

The activities reported in this paper were conducted from January to July, 2013, and involved 3 researchers from Computer Science and 6 participants playing different roles at EPTV:

- **TdG Chief Editor:** is the person who coordinates the production team (e.g., editors, content producers and journalists) of the television program and the web portal.
- **Designer:** is the responsible for the graphic art of the TV program as well as of the web portal, and who will be responsible for the graphic art of the iDTV application.
- **Operational and Technological Development Manager**: is the person who coordinates the department of new technologies for content production.
- **Supervisor of Development and Projects**: is the person who coordinates the staff in the identification and implementation of new technologies for content production and transmission.
- **Engineer on Technological and Operational Development**: is the engineer of infrastructure, and content production and distribution.
- **Technical on Technological and Operational Development**: is the person responsible for the implementation, support and maintenance of production systems and content distribution.
- **Researchers (3 people):** are researchers in Human-Computer Interaction and the responsible for preparing and conducting the workshops. One of them is expert in the SAC approach and other is an expert in iDTV technologies.

All the participants, except for the researchers, work in the television industry. The participants (P1, P2...P9) collaborated in the workshops proposed to the problem clarification, problem solving, requirement prospecting, as well as the creation of prototypes for the application and their evaluation, within a SAC approach.

Regarding the familiarity of participants with iDTV applications, from the 9 participants, 2 are experts; 2 are users of applications; 5 participants had already used/seen iDTV applications. Regarding the frequency which the participants watch the TdG program, 5 participants have been watching the TdG program, but not very often: 1 participant watches the program every week, 1 participant watches the program in average twice a month, and 2 participants watch at least once a month.

### 4.1   Designing an Application for TdG

This section presents the main activities conducted to create the first prototype of an iDTV application for the TdG program. Before these activities, participants had collaborated for the problem understanding, and for the clarification, analysis and organization of requirements for the application to be designed — as proposed by the SAC approach, and that are out of scope of this paper ("A" detail in Fig. 1). The materials produced by the previous activities were used as input for the design activities presented in this paper, and were reported in Buchdid et al. [9].

Before the beginning of each activity, the results obtained from the previous activities were presented and discussed briefly, and the techniques to be used, as well as their methodologies and purposes were introduced to the participants. For instance, before the PPC activity, examples of different existing iDTV applications, and the patterns from Kunert [20], were briefly presented and discussed with the participants.

The **PPC** activity was the first participatory practice conducted to design the application prototype ("1" detail in Fig. 1). Its input were the documentation produced in the problem clarification activities, the participant's knowledge about the project, and Pattern Cards based on the Kunert's patterns [20].

Originally classified into 10 different categories (from "A" to "J"), the patterns were grouped into 5 major groups in order to facilitate the participants' understanding: 1. Layout (Group A); 2. Navigation (Group B); 3. Operation (Groups C, D and G); 4. Content presentation (Groups E and F); and 5. Help, accessibility and personalization (Groups H and I). Patterns such as "B3 Video Multi-Screen" and "J1 Children" were not considered because they were out of the projects' scope.

The dynamic for this practice followed the description presented in Table 1. While each group of pattern was presented and discussed, participants were asked to select the ones that would potentially be used in the application — see "A" detail in Fig. 3. This practice lasted 90 min and was important to generate discussion and ideas to the application; they also led to a shared knowledge about iDTV potentialities and limitations among the participants.

**Fig. 3.** Participatory activities in a situated context.

Guided by the discussions and the results identified in the PPC practice, the **Brain-writing** ("2" detail in Fig. 1) was used to identify what the participants wanted in the application and what they thought the application should have/be. The dynamic for this activity is similar to the PgB presented in Table 2: each participant received a paper sheet with the following sentence: "I would like that the *"Terra da Gente"* application had...."; the participants should write their initial ideas and, after a pre-defined time (e.g., 60 s), they should exchange the paper sheets and continue to write on the ideas initiated by the other participants. After each paper had passed by all the participants and returned to the one who started writing the idea, participants should highlight the concepts that appeared in their paper sheet, and expose them to the group for discussion. The group reached a consensus creating a list of the main features that should appear in application — see "B" detail in Fig. 3. This activity took 90 min.

The **PgB** practice was conducted based on the ideas generated during the Brainwriting and took into account the patterns selected in the PPC (see "3" detail in Fig. 1). The dynamic for this activity is presented in Table 2: each participant received a template in a paper sheet, and they were asked to explore the initial call for the application, the layout and other specific content that they would like to see in the application. Participants started drawing the application interface, exchanging their paper sheets periodically and continuing to draw on the paper sheets of the other participants until they received their paper sheet back — see "C" detail in Fig. 3. This activity generated several ideas for the iDTV application that were consolidated by the team in a final proposal. This activity lasted 30 min.

Based on the results obtained from these activities, the first prototype for the application was built ("B" detail in Fig. 1) by a researcher who has experience in the development of iDTV applications. The *Balsamiq®* tool was used to create the UI and the *CogTool®* was used to model the tasks and to create an interactive prototype. The Pattern Cards were used again in order to inspect whether the application was in accordance with the design patterns, guiding the layout definition (e.g., font, elements size and position, visual arrangement of these elements) and interaction mechanisms (e.g., remote control's keys that were used).

The **PSE** was conducted in order to evaluate the produced prototype — "4" detail in Fig. 1. The activity was conducted according to the structure presented in Table 3. The interactive prototype was presented to the participants, and one of them explored the application using the "Thinking Aloud" technique — see "D" detail in Fig. 3. The other participants observed the interaction, took notes, and were able to ask, suggest and discuss with the evaluator at any time. Both the user interaction and the group dynamic were recorded, providing interesting information about the general perception of the participants and possible features to be redesigned before programming the final application. This practice lasted 50 min and, after concluded, participants answered a questionnaire evaluating the prototype.

Finally, a **User Evaluation** was conducted in order to evaluate the prototype with prospective representatives from the target audience that did not participate in design activities — "5" detail in Fig. 1. This activity was important to serve as a parameter to the PSE evaluation, assessing whether the prototype made sense to a more diverse audience. For this activity, 10 participants explored the prototype: 3 participants are 21–30 years old, 5 are 31–40 years old, 1 is 41–50 years old, and 1 participant is over 60 years old. Regarding their formal education, from the 10 participants: 1 has high school, 3 have bachelor's degree, 2 has specialization course, 3 have master's degree and 1 participant has a doctor's degree. None participant had previous experience using iDTV applications; 8 participants were aware of them, but had never seen any application; and 2 participants had seen them before. Furthermore, from the 10 participants, 6 have been watching the TdG program, but not often; 3 participants watch once a month; and 1 participant do not watch TdG.

# 5  Results and Discussion

In this section, we present and discuss the main results from the practices we proposed in this paper to create the interactive prototype for the TdG TV program.

## 5.1  Results of Design Practices

During **the PPC practice**, the participants selected 20 patterns that could be used in the application design. At least one pattern from each group of patterns was considered by the participants. Table 4 presents some of the patterns selected by the participants. The "Groups" column presents the general group of the selected pattern; the "Patterns" column presents the name of the pattern; the "PPC" column indicates whether the pattern was selected during the PPC practice; the "Explanation" column explains the reason why the pattern was selected; and the "PgB" column indicated whether the pattern was identified in the prototype produced in the Brain-Drawing practice.

**Table 4.**  List of Patterns used in the activities.

| Groups | Patterns | PPC | Explanation | PgB |
|---|---|---|---|---|
| Operation | C3 Ok-key | ✔ | It must be the main method of interaction together with arrow keys | ✔ |
| | C4 Colour keys | ✔ | To be used in case of voting and multiple-choice question | ✔ |
| | C5 Number keys | | Would not be used due to the difficulty of use | |
| | C6 Special keys | | Hard to find on remote control | ✔ |
| | D1 Initial call to action | ✔ | An unobtrusive call that does not disturb who does not want to use the application | ✔ |
| | ... | ... | ... | .. |
| | G3 Mobile phone keyboard | ✔ | Must not occupy much space on the screen. It will only be used in case of text input | |
| Help and cia | H1 On-Screen instruction | | It is not necessary because the application is simple | ✔ |
| | H2 Help section | ✔ | Help only in the Option menu | ✔ |
| | I1 Accessibility | ✔ | Universal Design | |
| | I2 Personalisation | | It is very sophisticated to this kind of application | |

For instance, the pattern "C3 Ok-key" was selected to be "*the main interaction method together with arrow keys*" in the PPC practice, and was identified in the prototype produced in the PgB. The pattern "C6 Special keys", in turn, was not selected in the PPC, but appeared in the prototype created by the participants: It can be partially explained by the fact that the participants got more used to the patterns and may have perceived the need/benefits of patterns they did not select during the PPC. Therefore, this is both an indication that the PPC does not narrow the participants' views during the creation of prototypes, and an evidence that the PgB facilitates the revision of the selected patterns during the creation of prototypes.

From **the Brainwritting practice**, 11 concepts were created to be included in the application: 1. Gallery/Making of: pictures from the TV program and information about the backstage; 2. Localization/Mapp: geographic coordinates of the place in which the TV program was recorded; additional information about roads, flights, trains, etc.

3. Recipe/Ingredients: it presents the ingredients of the recipe that will be prepared during the TV program. 4. Information/Curiosity: offers information and curiosities about the fauna and flora existing in the place where the TV program was recorded. 5. Evaluation Pool: a pool that allows users to answer whether they liked the program they are watching. 6. Quiz: a question-answer based-game about subjects directly related to the TV program content. 7. Fishing Game: a ludic game intended to keep users' attention through a virtual fishing while they watch the TV program (e.g., a little fish will appear on the screen and the user must select a different key to fish it). 8. Fisherman Story: a specific Quiz that allow users to answer whether a given story is true or false. 9. Abstract: a summary of the current TV program. 10. Prospection Pool: a pool that allows users to vote in the subjected that will be presented in the next program. 11. Chat: asynchronous communication on the TV program.

The first 6 concepts were selected to be used in the **PgB** activity. In addition, the participants were invited to explore ideas to application's trigger (Pattern: "DI Initial Call to Action") in the same activity. The other concepts were not considered because they were similar to a selected concept (e.g., Fisherman Story is similar to the Quiz), because they were considered uninteresting (e.g., Summary), or because they would require high attention and cognitive effort to be used (e.g., Chat).

All the six selected concepts appeared in the individual prototypes created by the participants of the PgB practice as well as in the final prototype consolidated by the participants. For instance, the "Gallery/Making of" concept appeared in 7 individual prototypes (see the column "Frequency" in Table 5), and was represented in 4 different forms (column "Forms"). The 9 individual prototypes also represented the "Localization/Mapp" concept in 4 different forms. Furthermore, the "Fishing Game" appeared 3 times even not being one of the chosen concepts; indicating that the activity favored the appearance of different and diverse ideas.

**Table 5.** List of concepts represented in the individual prototypes.

| Concept | Frequency | Forms |
|---|---|---|
| Gallery/Making Of | 7 | 4 |
| Localization/Mapp | 9 | 4 |
| Recipe/Ingredients | 7 | 4 |
| Information/Curiosities | 7 | 4 |
| Evaluation Pool | 5 | 3 |
| Quiz | 5 | 3 |
| Application's Trigger | 6 | 6 |
| Fishing Game | 3 | 3 |

The individual prototypes generated in the PgB were consolidated into a final prototype that, in turn, was used as the basis for creating an interactive prototype for the TdG iDTV application. The six concepts cited previously, as well as the patterns presented in Table 4, and general ideas elaborated by the participants were reflected in the interactive prototype. In fact, the design patterns selected in the PPC practice were reflected in both the final prototype produced by the participants and the interactive prototype created by the researcher. For instance, the patterns "C4 Colour keys" and "H2 Help section" were selected in the PPC activity and were considered in the individual proto-types — see Table 4, and were also considered in the interactive prototype — see details "C4" and "H2" in Fig. 4.

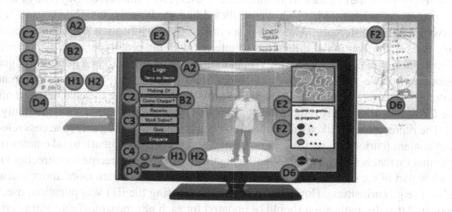

**Fig. 4.**  Patterns highlighted on the mockups from the PgB and on the final prototype.

## 5.2  Evaluation

*Results of the PSE Practice.* During the PSE we identified that users could leave the application at any moment/any level of interaction; however, the evaluation indicated that it could cause interaction problems, such as the user accidentally leaving the appli-cation while trying to see a picture from the backstage. The participants recommended disabling the "Exit" functions when the user enters in a second level menu/function. Furthermore, the "Help" function also should be applied only to the general application (not in specific sub-menus), because the application is very easy to use and the button could disturb the user in specific activities.

Other useful feedbacks were obtained from the PSE practice, such as the suggestion to use numbers in the pool's options in order to facilitate the selection, and not confuse users with other application's functions that use colors key; and the recommendation to not deploy the "Quiz" and the "Pool" features simultaneously in the application in order to not overload users with similar features.

The participant who explored the interactive prototype in the PSE practice was clearly pleased for not having difficulties while using it, highlighting the simplicity and consis-tency of the interactive prototype. Using his words: *"(…) if even me was able to under-stand and use the prototype, then it means the prototype is very intuitive."* [laughs] — he had never used an iDTV application before.

The participants' responses to the evaluation questionnaire also indicated a positive opinion about the interactive prototype. From the 9 participants who answered the ques-tionnaire, 7 (78 %) responded they really liked the prototype, and 2 (22 %) answered that they liked moderately. No indifferent or negative response was provided, indicating that the prototype met the participants' expectations

***Results of the* Test *with Prospective Users*.** The test with representatives from the audience reinforced a favorable opinion about the interactive prototype. The 10 prospective users were able to understand and explore the prototype, indicating its simplicity. From their responses to the evaluation questionnaire, 5 users (50 %) answered they really liked the prototype, 4 users (40 %) answered they liked moderately, and 1 users (10 %) answered with indifference. Although users reported the application was intuitive and easy to use, they had initial difficulties to interact with the prototype, in parts because of their lack of experience with iDTV applications. After a few interactions, users got more comfortable with the application and started to explore it, visiting its different features. However, when some users felt lost, they tried to change the channel, turn off the TV device, tried many remote key options or visited parts of application randomly.

The representatives liked the application because they would be able to access relevant content (curiosities, recipes, game fishing and exclusive content); to take notes of information that is difficult to annotate during the TV show (e.g., recipe and directions); to view part of the content they missed in the TV Show; iv) to learn more about a new subject (e.g., curiosities). However, to continue accessing the iDTV application, users answered that the application should be updated for each new program (e.g., extra curiosities, new games, and different recipes).

Although we need to test the application with a higher number of users in order to have data with statistical relevance, obtaining 90 % of positive responses is a good indication given that they did not participate in design activities and had no prior contact with iDTV applications.

***Preliminary Evaluation of the Design Process*.** The process has shown strong aspects in different situations. One of them, participants with different roles in EPTV showed themselves comfortable at all times of the process to expose their ideas and desires. While some participants want more interactivity and functionality, other participants, with responsibilities on the product itself (the TV program content), wanted an aesthetically simple application that does not influence on the television content. Accordingly, when conflicts emerged from the participants, the participatory activities guided by the Organizational Semiotics artifacts were important for achieving a cohesive and uniform decision from the whole group.

Other point that deserves consideration in this project is its situated context. The conduction of participatory practices in a situated context contributed to understand different forces related to the project and the organization in which it was being conducted. In each new practice, it was possible to clarify tensions between the participants, the context in which the EPTV operates, the high importance of the TdG program for EPTV organization, the relation between the affiliate and its headquarter and, mainly, the role that the application might play in the TV program. Participants have different views and understandings regarding the competition (for the user attention) between the interactive application and the TV program, and different opinions about what the application should offer to users and the way it should be offered. Such complex context would be difficult to capture and understand in a non-situated design approach, and such conflicts would be hard to deal with if participatory practices were not part of the methodology.

Furthermore, the four workshops conducted at EPTV took about 12 h. It means that all the process, from the problem clarification to the prototype evaluation, took them less than two days of work. It is clear that a great effort from the researchers was needed in order to summarize, analyze and prepare the practices as well as to prepare the presentations and build the interactive prototype. Indeed, this effort is expected because a lot of work must be done in parallel to the practices organization and conduction. Therefore, this experience shows that it is possible, viable and worth the time used to make participatory design in a situated context.

## 5.3 Discussion

During the participatory practices, the constructive nature of the process allowed to see how different viewpoints were conciliated, different proposals were consolidated, a shared understanding about the problem domain and the application was created, and how the discussions were materialized into a solution proposal. Ideas and concepts that were discussed when the project started could be perceived during the practices and were reflected in the final prototype.

The interactive prototype reflected the results from both PPC and PgB practices, allowing the participants to interact with the prototype of the application they co-created. The examples of existing applications presented to the participants were useful to illustrate different solutions regarding the patterns, inspiring the design of the new application and avoiding design decisions that would not satisfy them. The PPC practice was especially useful to: (i) present the constraints, limitations and challenges of designing for iDTV; and (ii) introduce participants to design patterns for iDTV, which may support their design decisions.

The PgB, in turn, was useful for supporting a pattern-guided construction of UI proposals for the application from the material produced in the previous activities. This practice is especially important because it favored the consideration of Design Patterns in the prototype design, and because it allowed all the participants to expose their ideas and to influence the prototype being designed, avoiding the dominance of a single viewpoint. For instance, the "Pool" and the "Quiz" were concepts that emerged from the Brainwritting and were materialized during the PgB practice, but were strongly discussed among the participants because some of them did not approve these features. However, after listening pros and cons of keeping/removing these concepts from the project's scope, the participants decided to keep both concepts in the final prototype.

Regarding the prototype evaluation, the PSE was important to foment discussions on the design decisions. Furthermore, the feedback from prospective users was important to verify decisions made with outsiders: people who did not participate in the design process (e.g., how to present the recipe: only the ingredients should be included? The preparation mode should also be displayed?).

The practices reported in this paper demonstrate that it is possible to conduct situated and participatory design in industrial settings. There is usually a myth that these practices are expensive and difficult to be conducted. In fact, in less than 4 h a prototype was built from the documentation produced in the previous practices and from the discussion between the participants — including the time spent to present examples of existing applications and the lecture for presenting the patterns. Some of the participants had a vague idea about how to design iDTV applications and none of them had designed this kind of application before.

The experience at EPTV also indicated that a situated and participatory design contributes to the development of solutions that are in accordance to both the people directly involved in design practices and the prospective end users of the designed solution. On the one hand, the participatory evaluation indicated that the participants approved the interactive prototype they co-designed; it was expected because of the participatory and situated nature of the process conducted. On the other hand, the evaluation with representatives from the target audience reinforced the positive results, indicating that the application was understood and well accepted by users that were not present in design activities and that had never experienced an iDTV application before.

These results suggest that a situated and participatory design perspective favors the ideas of solutions that make sense to the interested parties, reflecting an understanding about the problem domain and its complex social context.

# 6   Conclusions

Designing iDTV applications is a complex activity due to several factors including the ecosystem of media that compete and cooperate with the TV. In addition, the production chains of the broadcasters are still not prepared to the design of iDTV applications. This paper proposed three different practices and presented activities for supporting a situated and participatory design of iDTV applications; a case study situated in real scenario of a TV organization illustrated the proposal in action.

The results obtained from the case study indicated the benefits of using the practices for supporting the involved parties to understand the situated context that the iDTV application will be inserted, and to design an application that reflects that understanding. The results suggested that the interactive prototype designed was widely accepted by both the participants and prospective end users, pointing out the situated and participatory process as a viable and useful perspective for designing iDTV applications.

Although the results so far are very positive, the prototype still needs to be broadcasted as an iDTV application in *Terra da Gente* TV show. Thus, further work involves the next steps of implementing and testing the final application and releasing it for use by the TV program viewers. We also intend to conduct further studies within the perspective of the Socially Aware Computing, to investigate the potential impact of the practices presented in this paper to the TV staff and iDTV end users.

**Acknowledgements.** This research is partially funded by CNPq (#165430/2013-3) and FAPESP (#2013/02821-1). The authors thank the EPTV team and the participants who collaborated and authorized the use of the documentation of the project in this paper. This paper is an extended and revised version of a paper previously published at ICEIS 2014: "Playing Cards and Drawing with Patterns: Situated and Participatory Practices for Designing iDTV Applications" [10]. We thank the Editors for the invitation.

# References

1. Alexander, C.: The Timeless Way of Building, 1st edn. Oxford University Press, Oxford (1979)
2. Bannon, L.: Reimagining HCI: toward a more human-centered perspective. Interactions 18(4), 50–57 (2011)
3. Baranauskas, M.C.C.: Socially aware computing. In: ICECE 2009, VI International Conference on Engineering and Computer Education, pp. 1–5 (2009)
4. Baranauskas, M.C.C.: O Modelo semio-participativo de design. In: Baranauskas, M.C.C.; Martins, M. C.; Valente, J. A. (Org.). Codesign De Redes Digitais - Tecnologia e Educação a Serviço da Inclusão. 103edn., vol. 1, pp. 38–66. Penso, Porto Alegre (2013)
5. Baranauskas, M.C.C.: Social Awareness in HCI. ACM Interact. 21(4), 66–69 (2014)
6. Bernhaupt, R., Weiss, A., Pirker, M., Wilfinger, D., Tscheligi, T.: Ethnographic insights on security, privacy, and personalization aspects of user interaction in interactive TV. In: EuroiTV 2010, 8th international interactive conference on Interactive TV and Video, pp. 187–196. ACM Press, New York (2010)
7. Bonasio, V.: Televisão Manual de Produção & Direção. Editora Leitura, Minas Gerais (2002)
8. Borchers, J.: A Pattern Approach to Interaction Design. Wiley, England (2001)
9. Buchdid, S.B., Pereira, R., Baranauskas, M.C.: Creating an iDTV application from inside a TV company: a situated and participatory approach. In: Liu, K., Gulliver, S.R., Li, W., Yu, C. (eds.) ICISO 2014. IFIP AICT, vol. 426, pp. 63–73. Springer, Heidelberg (2014)
10. Buchdid, S.B., Pereira, R., Baranauskas, M.C.C.: Playing cards and drawing with patterns: situated and participatory practices for designing iDTV applications. In: ICEIS 2014, 16th International Conference on Enterprise Information Systems, pp. 14–27. SciTePress, Lisboa (2014)
11. Cesar, P., Chorianopoulos, K., Jensen, J.F.: Social television and user interaction. Mag. Comput. Entertainment 6(1), 1–10 (2008)
12. Chorianopoulos, K.: Interactive TV design that blends seamlessly with everyday life. In: Stephanidis, C., Pieper, M. (eds.) ERCIM Ws UI4ALL 2006. LNCS, vol. 4397, pp. 43–57. Springer, Heidelberg (2007)
13. Chung, E.S., Hong, J.I., Lin, J., Prabaker, M.K., Landay, J.A., Liu, A.L.: Development and evaluation of emerging design patterns for ubiquitous computing. In: DIS 2004, 5th Conference on Designing Interactive Systems: Processes, Practices, Methods, and Techniques, pp. 233–242. ACM Press, New York (2004)
14. EPTV Portal. http://www.viaeptv.com
15. Fallman, D.: The new good: exploring the potential of philosophy of technology to contribute to human-computer interaction. In: CHI 2011, Annual Conference on Human Factors in Computing Systems, pp. 1051–1060. ACM Press, New York (2011)
16. Pressman, R.S.: Software Engineering - A Practitionar's Approach, 5th edn. McGraw-Hill International Edition, New York (2001)
17. Gamma, E., Helm, R., Johnson, R., Vlissides, J.: Design Patterns: Elements of Reusable Object-Oriented Software. Addison-Wesley, Boston (1995)
18. Gawlinski, M.: Interactive Television Production. Editora Focal Press, Oxford (2003)
19. Harrison, S., Tatar, D., Sengers, P.: The three paradigms of HCI. In: Alt.CHI 2007 Annual Conference on Human Factors in Computing System, pp. 1–18. ACM Press, New York (2007)
20. Kunert, T.: User-Centered Interaction Design Patterns for Interactive Digital Television Applications, 1st edn. Springer, New York (2009)
21. Lewis, C.H.: Using the "Thinking Aloud" Method In Cognitive Interface Design. IBM Research Report RC-9265, Yorktown Heights, NY (1982)

22. Liu, K.: Semiotics in Information Systems Engineering, 1st edn. Cambridge University Press, Cambridge (2000)
23. Miranda, L.C., Hornung, H., Baranauskas, M.C.C.: Adjustable interactive rings for iDTV. IEEE Trans. Consum. Electron. **56**, 1988–1996 (2010)
24. Müller, M.J., Haslwanter, J.H., Dayton, T.: Participatory practices in the software lifecycle. In: Helander, M.G., Landauer, T.K., Prabhu, P.V. (eds.) Handbook of Human-Computer Interaction, 2nd edn, pp. 255–297. Elsevier, Amsterdam (1997)
25. Pereira, R.: Key pedagogic thinkers: Maria Cecília Calani Baranauskas. J. Pedagogic Dev. **3**(1), 18–19 (2013). UK
26. Pereira, R., Buchdid, S.B., Baranauskas, M.C.C.: Keeping values in mind: artifacts for a value-oriented and culturally informed design. In: ICEIS 2012, 14th International Conference on Enterprise Information Systems, pp. 25–34. SciTePress, Lisboa (2012)
27. Piccolo, L.S.G., Melo, A.M., Baranauskas, M.C.C.: Accessibility and interactive TV: design recommendations for the brazilian scenario. In: Baranauskas, C., Abascal, J., Barbosa, S.D.J. (eds.) INTERACT 2007. LNCS, vol. 4662, pp. 361–374. Springer, Heidelberg (2007)
28. Rice, M., Alm, N.: Designing new interfaces for digital interactive television usable by older adults. Comput. Entertainment (CIE) – Soc. Telev. User Interact. **6**(1), 1–20 (2008). Article 6
29. Sellen, A., Rogers, Y., Harper, R., Rodden, T.: Reflecting human values in the digital age. Commun. ACM **52**(3), 58–66 (2009)
30. Solano, A.F., Chanchí, G.E., Collazos, C.A., Arciniegas, J.L., Rusu, C.A.: Diseñando interfaces graficas usables de aplicaciones en entornos de televisión digital interactiva. In: IHC + CLIHC 2011, 10th Brazilian Symposium on Human Factors in Computing Systems and the 5th Latin American Conference on Human-Computer Interaction, pp. 366–375. ACM Press, New York (2011)
31. Sousa, K., Mendonça, H., Furtado, E.: Applying a multi-criteria approach for the selection of usability patterns in the development of DTV applications. In: IHC 2006, 7th Brazilian symposium on Human factors in computing systems, pp. 91–100. ACM Press, New York (2006)
32. Stamper, R., Liu, K., Hafkamp, M., Ades, A.: Understanding the roles of signs and norms in organisations: a semiotic approach to information system design. J. Behav. Inf. Technol. **19**(1), 15–27 (2000)
33. Terra da Gente Portal. http://www.terradagente.com.br
34. VanGundy, A.B.: Brainwriting for new product ideas: an alternative to brainstorming. J. Consum. Mark. **1**(2), 67–74 (1983)
35. Veiga, E.G.: Modelo de Processo de Desenvolvimento de Programas para TV Digital e Interativa. 141 f. Masters' dissertation - Computer Networks, University of Salvador (2006)
36. Wilson, C.: Brainstorming and Beyond: a User-Centered Design Method, 1st edn. Elsevier Science, Burlington (2013)
37. Winograd, T.: The design of interaction. In: Beyond Calculation: The Next Fifty Years of Computing, pp. 149–161. Copernicus/Springer, Secaucus/New York (1997)

# Video Stream Transmodality

Pierre-Olivier Rocher[1]($\boxtimes$), Christophe Gravier[1], Julien Subercaze[1],
and Marius Preda[2]

[1] Laboratoire Télécom Claude Chappe, Télécom Saint-Etienne,
Université Jean Monnet, 42000 Saint-Etienne, France
{pierre-olivier.rocher,christophe.gravier,
julien.subercaze}@telecom-st-etienne.fr
http://satin-ppl.telecom-st-etienne.fr/
[2] Département ARTEMIS/GRIN, Télécom SudParis, 91000 Evry, France
marius.preda@telecom-sudparis.eu

**Abstract.** *Transmodality* is the partitioning of an image into regions
that are expected to present a better entropy using different coding
schemes, depending on their structural density, at constant bandwidth.
In this paper we present the *transmodality* of video stream. Our contribution is a transmoder module that includes various different optimized
video codecs and implements the concept of *transmodality* on a set of
video streams. We evaluate our proposal in the context of cloud gaming, using an optimized remote rendering chain and several games. A per
game adaptation allows an optimal refinement of video encoding parameters, including both quantization and modality parameters. Our algorithm shows comprehensive results by saving up to 2 % of bandwidth for
the same PSNR in comparison with the state-of-the-art video encoding
baselines.

**Keywords:** Video encoding · Vectorization · Modality · Cloud gaming

## 1 Introduction

Video communication accords for one of the highest development slope among
various Internet applications for the last few years. It is forecasted to be one
of the main bandwidth consumer with respect to future applications. Different
kinds of applications are using video compression: live TV, online newspapers,
social networks... Over the last few years, new applications have emerged and
one of the most important one is probably the cloud gaming. All cloud gaming
solutions like Gaikai[1] or OnLive [2] are based on remote rendering; such a system
is generally based on two parts. On the server side, the game is rendered and
the current picture is compressed using a state-of-the-art video encoder like
MPEG-4 AVC (a.k.a. H.264), then streamed to the clients. Currently, for all

---

[1] http://www.gaikai.com/.
[2] http://www.onlive.com/.

© Springer International Publishing Switzerland 2015
J. Cordeiro et al. (Eds.): ICEIS 2014, LNBIP 227, pp. 361–378, 2015.
DOI: 10.1007/978-3-319-22348-3_20

previously described applications, the compression engine handles each image as an atomic element, regardless if the image contains more or less homogeneous regions. Adaptive encoding schemes bring new features, both in size and quality term, but the video is still processed as a pixel set. Some regions of the picture will be encoded with different parameters, but using the same global encoding scheme. Criteria used in the adaptative encoding scheme are most often related to objective metrics, like network bandwidth or latency. Recent studies highlight the importance of subjective approaches, they seemed to be an interesting alternative for controlling the adaptation process.

The intuition behind this work is to go one step beyond by defining an adaptive region-based encoding algorithm using fundamentally different encoding schemes. The encoding scheme should be chosen independently for each region, depending on its structure and heterogeneity. In this paper we propose several video coding systems to encode one video stream. More, proposed encoding solution uses important areas (from the user's viewpoint) in addition to a structure and heterogeneity analysis. Proposed modifications will ensure that the video stream is optimally compacted.

The remainder of this paper is organized as follows: Sect. 2 presents a review of background literature. Section 3 details the concept of transmodality. Section 4 presents our video encoding system from a global perspective to detailed components. Section 5 is dedicated to comparative testing and Sect. 6 concludes the paper and draws perspectives.

## 2    Related Work

This section investigates existing work in the broad field of video encoding. While a complete state-of-the-art on video coding is out of scope of this paper, we aim at focusing only on relevant results in this part. We present two major encoding methods relevant to our approach: matrix-based and the one based on graphics primitives. We also present their applications to image and video coding. The initiated reader may skip this section.

### 2.1    Image

We can consider that there are two ways to store and manipulate a digital picture. The first one is a matrix-based representation while the second one is based on graphics primitives. Nowadays, both solutions coexist but each representation brings specific advantages and flaws.

The matrix-based method is widely used for storing and sharing pictures. This image representation, also known as raster or bitmap, is based on the pixel definition. The most common encoders are BMP, PNG, and JPEG. Under this method, images are represented as 2D-matrices. This is a very convenient way for storing and even compressing pictures and pixel-based compression algorithms are proved to be quite efficient. Although, its major drawback is decrease quality while zooming into the parts of the picture. Even if the picture is uncompressed, the original pixel element will eventually outsize the corresponding pixel in the screen space. At this point, the picture quality will strongly suffer from this limitation.

The second competing method does not use the pixel as the atomic element but instead makes use of graphic primitives in addition to color profiles. Each graphic primitive is a mathematical objet: it can be a point, a line or a polygon, and is defined by a formal definition. These graphic primitives are a kind of skeleton for the picture on which corresponding color profiles will be applied. This representation then uses a set of graphic primitives and their associated color profiles to build an image. However, for complex fitting more powerfull objects like splines, Bezier curves or even Non Uniform Rational Basis Spline (NURBS) can be used. Each graphic primitive is positioned in a reference system and bears specific attributes like its color, shape or thickness. Due to its nature, the picture is first rendered and displayed in a second time. i.e. every point is computed using the formal definition to which it belongs. The result of this computation is what is being displayed on the users device. The very main advantage of this representation is the independence from the rendered image size. Performance in size term is to mitigate since its mainly related on the picture content itself: it can be greatly reduced, or largely more important. When a picture or a video is live recorded or streamed, the raster format is used. Meantime, graphic primitives formats (EPS, SVG) are more and more used in the numeric world: due to the increase of terminal heterogeneity in our daily lives (IPTV, smartphones, tablets...) multimedia content is now often included in web pages. These vector formats will insure that whatever the screen size, display picture quality is maximal.

Building a raster representation of a vector picture is a trivial task, but the reverse process (often called vectorization) is not obvious [1]. References on this subject can be found [2–4], but proposed solutions are quite basic and are most often limited to black and white pictures processing. Some approaches to handle color exist but they cannot bear with photo realistic pictures (natural shots). Another important limitation to overcome is the vectorization required process time which is mainly picture content related. In subsequent sections, we distinguish codec types based on pixel and vector: the first one is related to a raster representation while the second one denotes the vector representation.

## 2.2   Videos

This subsection presents state-of-the-art video encoders (based on the MPEG-4 AVC video encoding standard). Our main focus is on literature aiming to use several encoders to process a single video, but also on existing adaptive solutions. The first paragraph is a reminder on how a modern video encoder is working.

To compress a video, it is first splitted into a so called Group Of Pictures (GOP), which is basically made of three different types of pictures called $I$, $P$ and $B$. An I picture is a reference picture also known as a key frame. P pictures are predicted using a past referenced picture. B pictures are bi-predicted, using both past and future P pictures (depending on the standard definition). Main steps of such encoders are prediction, transformation, quantization and entropy coding. In the encoder scheme the main step responsible of data compression is quantization. In order to control the final bitrate, the user can tune the quantization factor, called $Qp$ in most common implementations. Various strategies can be applied to control this parameter throughout the encoding process, like constant $Qp$ or constant bitrate (therefore with a non-constant $Qp$). A little $Qp$ value will ensure a good video quality. Furthermore usually, when $Qp = 0$ the compression is lossless. Resulting entropy coded data, and necessary decoding information like prediction mode, motion vectors, quantization factor form the encoded video stream.

In [5,6] some macroblocks are encoded in a parametric manner, using an Auto Regressive (AR) process [7]. Selection of these macroblocks is done using a particular edge detection. Some moving textures can be modeled as a spatio-temporal AR process, which is in fact a tridimensional basis model version. In their system, I pictures are H.264 encoded, while P pictures are encoded using the proposed method. The process is based on $16 \times 16$ macroblock size (owing to H.264). macroblocks are then categorized in two sets: with or without edges, where macroblocks without edges are processed with the proposed solution. The quality assessment was done using the Mean Opinion Score (MOS) system since the reconstruction scheme is statistically built. No information within the video like spatial resolution, frames per second or even related enconding time are exploited. In [8] authors offer to simply delete some macroblocks during the encoding process and to rebuild them by synthesis methods at the decoding stage. The method chosen to regenerate missing parts is the spatio-temporal patch searching. The system is running with an I-P-B scheme. Some tests have been conducted with QCIF videos, at 30 FPS using different $Qp$. Experimental results show a bitrate reduction with a quite similar image quality (although no objective metrics were used). In [9] the encoding process is based on both a traditional bloc coding and on a model coding. For such appraoch, they use a long-term temporal redundancy. Object detection related part is based on region of interest (ROI) algorithms, these ROIs are detected using principal component analysis (PCA). ROI areas are then segmented using graph-cut algorithms [10]. Finally a resultant area analysis is done, aiming to regroup some of them for whole optimization. A tracking algorithm is used for following ROIs in futures images. Theses ROIs areas, defined by a rectangle and an angle are finally compressed using an active appearance model, which is statistically based.

Jointly to this research, work on adaptive video coding is largely present. One can discern two major trends: the first needs several versions of a same video; the second is based on a single version, which is adapted in realtime. The first solution is covered by the Scalable Video Coding (SVC), but also by the upcoming MPEG-DASH standard. Several recent articles can be found about the second adaptive way. An other wide used solution is to produce as many videos as screen sizes, like Netflix (each video is in 120 different copies). In [11] real time adaptation is performed on video encoder as according to the network delay. Latency measurements are done before the launch of the system, but also periodically during the whole process. This latency evaluation makes possible the detection of network congestion and then the ability to take necessary actions to adapt the stream. In [11], they use a cloud gaming application, with an aim to guarantee fluidity and responsiveness of the system. The proposed solution is to reduce the quantization parameter (among all macroblocks) and the necessary bitrate. In [12], the assumption between importants objects to the user and their position in the depth map is done. In other words, more the object is close to the user, more it is important. To reduce the necessary bitrate without loosing in quality, they refine the $Qp$ parameter, acting at macroblock level.

This approach seems to be better suited for outside games environment, i.e. for scenes with an important depth map amplitude. In indoor games, range of depth map values is much smaller, in consequence take a decision on each macroblock is more complex and error prone. Additionnaly, the depth map criterion is not a so good one: a defect can be pushed in this approach, especially when the player tries to eliminate enemies far from his position. In this case, despite the fact that the player is actually focusing on these enemies, corresponding macroblocks will therefore be compressed with a greater $Qp$ value. In fact, from the depth map perspective, these macroblocks are considered as not important. This scenario thus degrades the quality in an important area of the image.

In the previous sections, various ways to optimize the compactness of a video stream were reviewed. To adjust the video compression, some are based on network related metrics whereas others use empirical considerations. The interest around cloud gaming is still increasing, many researchers are interested in improving the different parts of the system, mainly using objective metrics. But in a cloud gaming application, another parameter as to be taken into consideration: the player himself. It is therefore interesting to analyze the behavior of the player during a game session. Once important data for the player are known, it becomes easier to adjust the compression, acting for example on some non important areas. This type of approach acting on the perceived quality (commonly known as QoE) is related to subjective judgement. Assessment of QoE is a hot topic in the media world [13], and it has been recently demonstrated that the perceived quality is a very personal data [14].

As an exemple, in [15] an eye-tracker is used to highlight a correlation between the ease of use of a website and the data collected by the eye tracker. In the cloud gaming field, only a few papers are available, these include the work presented in [16]. Authors introduced a conceptuel model for attention evaluation, based both on saliency models and game logic. However the used model for visual attention estimation on each picture is not design for games, it as been design for static picture or video content. Moreover, although the authors suggest that their system operates in real time, no study on the impact of the proposed model as been presented.

Nevertheless, there is a common thread between all these solutions: they always use a set of pixel to encode and adapt the video coding. All presented solutions are using a standard version of H.264, We will use an optimized one using each I and P pictures (B pictures are not used in cloud gaming video compression systems: they introduce latency). Adaptive technologies are largely used, but they are all the time confined to the pixel world. We will use an other type of encoding system, which is based on vectorization. In order to effectively manage the various encoders, we choose to study the user behavior while palying different games, and more particularly where his visual attention was focused. We did intensive gaming tests by appealing several players acting on several games in order to generate attention maps, which will subsequently be used by the algorithm to finely manage encoders.

## 3   Transmodality

We introduce a new way of encoding a video stream using so called *modalities*. A modality is a set of areas to be compressed regarding a specific encoder. Each modality refers to (a) specific(s) part(s) in a frame, regarding an encoder especially well suited for compressed corresponding areas in a picture. According to our experiments we conclude that using more than one encoder will achieve a better compression rate than using only one, while preserving the same quality in terms of Peak Signal to Noise Ratio (PSNR). Conventional encoding approaches consider a video as a set of pixels and use a single encoding scheme for the whole picture. Our approach is based on the assumption that a dynamic partitioning of the video frames and the approximation of some regions with a parametric representation will reduce the video bitrate. Splitting a video stream into objects and encoding them separatly is the basis of MPEG-4 part 2, but the way of doing this work on a video stream is not covered by this standard.

### 3.1   Transmodality Definition

We define the Tansmodality as the fact of using several specific encoders to compress the same video file. The aim is to use a well-suited encoder to each region and using different modalities for video encoding. In other words, a modality is defined as being the compression of an area set by an encoder. We define a class as a set of areas, each class being encoded using one specific encoder. Using one or more modalities is not known by advance but it belongs to the processed video itself. The decision to use 1, 2 or $n$ modalities is taken in real time during multimodal encoding, which means that shapes and area size are potentially different for each frame. For instance, Fig. 1 is made of five areas $z_1$ to $z_5$ which are grouped into three classes $m_1$ to $m_3$. An area is a contiguous set of pixels, contiguity of two pixels is defined using the Kronecker operator (V4 neighborhood).

In the following section we focus on the transmoder whose role is to process the video compression with multi-modalities.

### 3.2   Transmoder *vs* Transcoder

A transcoder is a software or hardware element which aims to modify the way how a video file or stream is compressed. It first decodes a video file or stream, and encodes it again using new parameters. This enables the application to modify the way this video will be transformed including three majors trends: the

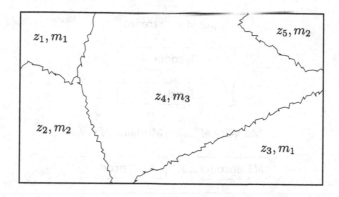

**Fig. 1.** Areas and modalities in a sample picture.

output video size (spatial resolution), the frame rate (temporal resolution) and the quality (resolution in PSNR). In this work, we introduce a new adjustable parameter called modality. Doing so, we define a new application called transmoder, which is a transcoder with an ability of using *modalities*, as described in previous sections. Our Transmoder as compared to transcoder uses an additional parameter that increase the output range of possible bitrates and thus make it possible to distribute the video to a larger number of people. A transmoder is also able to conduct simple transcoding operations, so with regard to our definition, the transcoder is a particular case of the transmoder.

In this work, we focus on implementing a transmoder that can handle two modalities, the pixel and the vector ones. What follows therefore presents our bimodal transmoder approach. In order to simplifiy, following parts of this article will rely on a transmoder working on two modalities. The multimodal process is then limited to a bimodal approach.

## 4   Transmoder Process

Our transmoder is built on three separated parts: a decoder, an encoder and a *sunder*. The whole architecture is presented in Fig. 2. The decoder decodes frames from a video file or stream. The sunder part is in charge of the partitioning of each frame into $n$ modalities, while taking into account attention maps. As depicted in Fig. 2, the sunder output is a combination of $n$ modalities denoted M1 to M$n$. Finally, the encoder uses the processed results of sunder as its input and encodes the whole video in a transmoded stream. The remaining systems blocks are explained in the following sections.

### 4.1   Attention Maps Generation

The state-of-the-art has shown that cloud gaming applications start to consider attention (from a general point of view) to perform a compression adaptation.

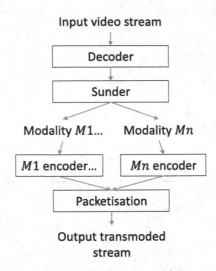

**Fig. 2.** Synoptical transmoder scheme.

Given this trend, we offer a new approach to refine attention models with the aim of making them better.

The goal is firstly to determine which areas are important, depending both on the game and on the player. In order to answer this question, we customized our cloud gaming research plateform. It is now able to manage an eye-tracker so when each picture is displayed, corresponding data (eyes position) is recorded in a specified file. For our first expermiments, two games are available: Doom 3 and 0 A.D. First one is a First-Person Shooter (FPS) while the second belongs to Real-Time Strategy (RTS) video game genre. The first phase of testing is performed using a conventional video compression (no adaptation, constant $Qp$) to make sure that the player's attention is not disturbed. This stage will allow the construction of visual attention maps for each game and each player. The protocol to follow is quite simple: after calibration of the eye-tracking device, users are ask to play one hour each game. To maintain consistency, all tests are performed in the same room, with the same environment. Our tester panel consists of three experienced players, who have completed three time the same test with available games.

Before going further, consistency between the three tests made by a user with a game is checked. This is done by computing the Pearson correlation coefficient for each test, two by two. Our first conclusions show that players behave similarly for the same game, so visual attention is game related. In order to reflect this conclusion, per game final attention maps are built using all available player data. These maps are considered as baselines for future quality evaluation.

## 4.2   The Sunder

The aim of Sunder is to take the decision of splitting (or not) the frame in several modalities. All the required steps for such functionality as depicted in Fig. 2 are explained later. But at this point we consider that the input of this whole process is an uncompressed picture, typically in an Red Green Blue (RGB) raw format. Some image processing treatments is first applied, then the picture is splitted into modalities (see section "Modality Splitting"). Once both modalities are splitted, respective encoding is conducted and some optimizations are applied on the pixel encoding part (see section "Analysis"). The ouput of this process is a so-called bimodal picture. While all necessary informations are available, the video stream can be recorded. This is done by using packets, which are usually containing one frame. Packetisation process is described in details later (see section "Packetisation" of Sect. 4.3).

**Modality Splitting.** Modality splitting involves with splitting operation by exploiting well known image processing filters. Previously, we explained our choice to split a picture into two modalities. To operate efficiently, an image processing filter appears to be the best choice. Our approach splits an image, based on the level of details which can be performed using an edge detector filter. There are various filters available for such requirements including Canny, Laplace an Sobel. For scalability reasons, we require an algorithm that exhibits a good trade-off between performance an computation time. Under these conditions, [17] and more recenlty [18] concludes that the Canny filter is the filter of choice. Furthermore, this choice is affirmed by [3] in which the authors processed videos. It should be noted that this process (and later described sub processes) is not applied on the whole picture but only on non important regions, according

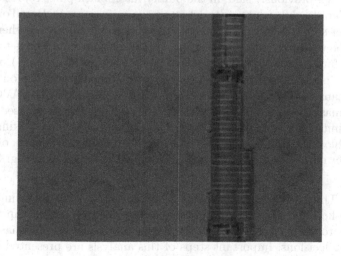

Fig. 3. Sample input picture.

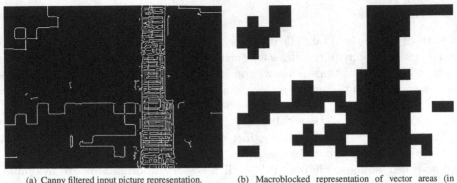

(a) Canny filtered input picture representation.

(b) Macroblocked representation of vector areas (in white).

**Fig. 4.** Canny filtered picture and its macroblocked version, based on 3 input picture.

to the game's attention map. As an exemple, lets take the picture presented in Fig. 3 as an input picture. After the edge detector process, we obtain a binary picture as displayed in Fig. 4(a). As the reader can see, details in the picture are spotted in white, and more uniform areas are in black. Some morphological operations are now necessary to clean this mask (remove single points, close holes...).

At this point, we need to make a choice regarding modality encoding. We choose to use one encoder from the pixel world and another one from the vector one. Chosen pixel encoder is the well-known MPEG-4 AVC, the state-of-the-art reference. As literature does not provide any efficient library for a raster to vector conversion, we thus employ our own vectorization module. This one is designed to suit our specific needs and is further described in section "Vectorization" of Sect. 4.3. As we previously said, in the binary mask black parts represents a high amount of details while white parts depicts more uniform areas. Based on the characteristics of selected encoders, Black parts may be pixel coded whereas white parts may be vector coded. At this point, white areas are candidates to be vector coded, but further analysis (as described in see section "Analysis") may downgrade them in the pixel world to ensure a good compacity in the output video stream. Because we choose to compress a modality using a MPEG-4 AVC encoder, the binary mask needs to be adapted since this kind of encoder is based on a macroblock definition (a $16 \times 16$ pixels size). This is simply done in checking each picture macroblocks: if all pixels are black, then the macroblock is black otherwise it is white. The corresponding new macroblock mask is depicted in Fig. 4(b).

**Analysis.** This concludes as the most important step of transmoding. All decisions made here are based on parameters set by the user at startup time. Currently a macroblock mask is present, the aim is now to process this mask and take appropriate decisions. Important steps of this analysis are presented in Fig. 5.

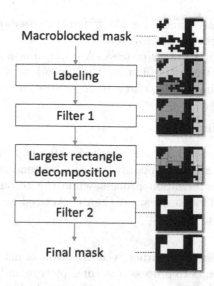

**Fig. 5.** Logic analysis process in the sunder.

*Labeling.* The first operation involves a V4 neighbourhood labelling of white areas. This will ensure that each vector area is separated from the others, and provides an internal data structure easy to manipulate.

*First Filter.* Filter 1 as described in Fig. 5 is responsible of the deletion of some area, based on surface size criterion as according to the threshold set by the user (or by the default value). Consequently, some little areas which were planned to be vector encoded is in place pixel encoded, because in this case a pixel encoder offers better results. As an exemple, Fig. 5 shows a possible output result.

*Largest Rectangle Decomposition.* According to Fig. 5, we can now consider two vector areas. These areas can have any shape, including holes. To make the decoding stage possible, we will need to know two things: covered areas and their respective definitions.

We need now to think on how to store efficiently the binary mask. We can consider a lot of different solutions but in all cases, we need to keep a very good compacity. In order to fulfill this need, we choose to decompose any vector area into a set of largest rectangles. This kind of operation is known as a rectangle decomposition of binary matrix, henceforth DBMR problem. More information on this subject can be found in [19]. Most of the time, taking into account the first two or three biggest rectangles is enough to keep a good approximation of the intial shape.

*Second Filter.* Our second filter aims at deleting little areas (user set thresold) that are moved in the pixel modality. At the end of this analysis, only important large rectangle areas are candidate for a parametrized representation. This process is detailed in section "Vectorisation" of Sect. 4.3.

This is the last step of sunder process. A binary mask specifies if each area has to be compressed using the first or the second modality. Thus encoding operations, related optimizations, and stream generation can be conducted.

## 4.3   Stream Encoding

The modality splitting step is now finished. All pixel and vector areas are known and respective encoding operations can be conducted. The first paragraph describes our vectorization process while the second one is devoted to optimizations. Bimodal video stream is then packetized and dumped in an output video file or stream.

**Vectorization.** As described earlier, vectorization is not a trivial task, especially when the user wants to process a natural picture and expect good quality results. The main problem of such encoding scheme includes complexity of such a project, necessary time to process pictures and output obtained sizes. All these parameters are intimately related to the picture content. The desirable objectives at this point is the implementation of specific software that meets our need along with a fast processing and a good quality (in term of PSNR). Because as the previous operations provides only a specific texture type and in order to achieve a uniform one, we can utilize a simple vectorization approach. As a first implementation we choose to simply use a polynomial based approach, inspired by what has been done in [3]. In order to vectorize an area, we used sequence of retangles as graphic primitives, and a polynomial based colour profil. Each polynomial expression is based on a static template of the form: $Z = a + bx + cy + dx^2 + exy + fy^2$, computed using a least square based regression. Each vector area have three unique polynomials, one for each picture color channel. To control the quality of color profiles, respective correlation coefficients are computed. If their values are too low (thus implies a poor modeling quality), the corresponding area will fall back in the pixel mode.

**Encoding Optimizations.** Encoding a single video using a per area optimized compression is not such a tedious task. The most difficult part is to use them correctly while avoiding redundancy in the data stream and trying to limit the impact on the encoding time. However, the only fact of adding some new lines of code will inevitably increase the necessary computing power.

Starting from this fact, we tried to minimize the impact of the sunder in optimizing the way encoder works. Both vector and pixel parts have been optimized. After all areas are vectorized, a process checks if some of them can be modeled using a same polynomial definition. Special treatment is reserved for writing vector data: for example, the number of digits is limited and all the data is compressed. The sunder process gives us some useful informations, which can be directly sent to the vidoeo encoder. We can denote two optimizations: the first one (O1) directly indicates to the encoder macroblocks to skip, and the second (O2) manipulates the $Qp$ parameter. Each of these two optimization is macroblock based. The aim of O1 is to directly provide a list of macroblocks to encoder that have to be skipped. Thus the analysis cost is reduced (minimize the encoding time) and the stream is more compact, regardless the chosen encoding *preset*. This optimization is only applied on P frames. O2 optimization is related to I and P frames. Per macroblock $Qp$ is modified to force the encoder to skip some macroblocks (thus which are not used by the pixel modality). These two optimizations can be used separately but also at the same time. They do not impact the quality of the output stream.

**Packetisation.** For being able to add our vectorization data part, we modify the way packetisation is done. Each vector data is just positionned after the picture data, hence a frame is a combination of pixel and vector data. As the splitting is done live in an automatic manner, some packets may have only a pixel part, some others only a vector part. This stream is written in such a way that any compliant MPEG-4 AVC decoder will be able to read it, however only the usual pixel modality will be correctly displayed on the screen. In order to get the full picture correctly constructed, a suitable decoder is necessary: final decoded picture is a combination of the rendered vector part *and* of the traditional pixel representation.

# 5  Performance Evaluation

We evaluate our solution using the Doom3[3] game. This video game is a First-Person Shooter (FPS), so it comports a lot of action and rapid scenes. For testing purpose, video is dumped in a raw file (RGB format) while the user is playing. The obtained videos raw files are the result of different gaming sessions, there are all different. We use our transmoder through our remote rendering chain. As a lot of parameters can be tuned and will inevitably lead to different results, we choose to use static parameters for testing. Both modalities coding parameters are fixed to make comparisons possible. Furthermore the pixel video encoding strategy uses a constant quantization parameter, which is set by default at $Qp = 20$. All testing movies have been a $720p$ resolution, frame number varies from 300 to 500 pictures. Optimizations presented in section "Encoding Optimizations" of Sect. 4.3 are used. Our transmoder implementation outputs XML files with all necessary information, like frame sizes, made decisions... Results between a classical approach (transcoder) and our approach are then analyzed. These first tests results only use an objective metric (PSNR) but further assessment will use subjective evaluation methods based on attention maps.

## 5.1  Implementation

Video encoding is a quite heavy task even on most recent computers. The choice of a native programming language is then obvious. Because of code source

---

[3] http://www.idsoftware.com/games/doom/doom3.

portability but also external available libraries, the preferred choice for our implementation is C/C++. In order to accelerate the developping time and reduce the source code size to maintain, some well known multimedia libraries were used, such as FFmpeg and libx264 for decoding, encoding and manipulate the different kind of codec and containers. Image processing related operations are done by OpenCV, and our basic vectorization software uses the GNU Scientific library (GSL). The whole program is available as a standalone executable capable of transmoding any kind of videos, or as a library for direct splitting and encoding. Obviously the transmoder is also capable of simple transcoding operations. Although our model is designed for any number of modalities, our current implementation is limited to two: a pixel modality and a vector one.

## 5.2   Results

Table 1 presents obtained results in size between transcoded and transmoded versions of a same input raw video. These experiments have been done using the *veryfast* preset and the *zerolatency* tune. Column TC indicates the transcoded file size, while TM(1) and TM(2) are transmoded output file size with differents settings (those are presented in section "Analysis" of Sect. 4.2). In TM(1) experiment, both filters have been set to 1 and in the second test, TM(2) both filters have been set to 2. Our transmoder outperforms transcoding operations in all tested cases. Obviously, one can notice than chosen parameters influence the final result. Gains in size ranging from 0.1% (Doom 3 D video) to 2.6% (Doom 3 A video). A sample snapshot is presented in Fig. 6.

**Quality Assessement.** Quality assessment is not a trivial job. Usually for this task, some metrics as well-known PNSR or MSSIM are used to complete surveys, but this is not sufficient. For now we need to take care of subjective meaning and not only objective ones. First conducted tests used a PSNR metric for quality assessment, with some particularities. Indeed, we choose to calculate a per modality and a per framne PSNR value, aiming to preserve a maximum amount of information for later analysis.

Table 2 outputs PSNR results for all tested videos, using a per picture computing. We can notice that two times (Doom 3 A and Doom 3 D videos) out of four, transmoding PSNR results are better than transcoding equivalent operation. When the transcoding operation is better in PSNR, the relative difference is negligible.

**Table 1.** Obtained transcoded and transmoded file sizes (in bytes).

| Video name | TC | TM(1) | TM(2) |
|---|---|---|---|
| Doom 3 A | 9907403 | **9824570** | **9644114** |
| Doom 3 B | 13178506 | **13133818** | **13077405** |
| Doom 3 C | 14912310 | **14876477** | **14831883** |
| Doom 3 D | 13151625 | **13145306** | **13134501** |

**Table 2.** Obtained transcoded and transmoded PSNR values (in dB).

| Video name | 0-TC | O-TM(1) |
|------------|---------|-------------|
| Doom 3 A   | 31.8201 | **31.8211** |
| Doom 3 B   | 32.3262 | 32.3253     |
| Doom 3 C   | 35.4112 | 35.4086     |
| Doom 3 D   | 31.0368 | **31.0379** |

**Table 3.** Per modality PSNR values (in dB) compared to original video.

| Video name | TC-P    | TM(1)-P     | TC-V    | TM(1)-V |
|------------|---------|-------------|---------|---------|
| Doom 3 A   | 34.142  | **34.1514** | 31.7812 | 31.7811 |
| Doom 3 B   | 38.3652 | 37.8888     | 32.0904 | 32.0904 |
| Doom 3 C   | 39.1548 | 39.1019     | 33.9563 | 33.9562 |
| Doom 3 D   | 32.08   | 32.0538     | 31.1088 | 31.1088 |

For a better understanding of the process, and to make sure that PSNR are similar in vector and pixel parts, we computed PSNR values per modality. All PSNR computations have been done between the original raw video and obtained transcoded and transmoded videos. Table 3 summarizes results for all videos. One of the first observations is that vector modality PSNR is very similar, which means that our vectorization software is able to compete a pixel-based encoder in such regions. In vector areas, differences between a transcoded and a transmoded area is negligible. This last remark is also applicable to respective pixel areas.

**Fig. 6.** A Doom 3 final rendered picture.

## 5.3  Real Time Processing

Our first tests reveals that real time processing is possible with videos assuming quite little spatial resolutions (320 × 240). In order to overcome this limitation, we first optimize the whole architecture of the software, especially by adding threading support in appropriate source code parts. Another way of increasing performance, especially in the image processing world is to use the GPU. This aspect has been brought to our program using OpenCV GPU related functions.

**Table 4.** Necessary time for transcoding and transmoding operations (in ms).

| Experiment | Doom 3 A | Doom 3 B |
|---|---|---|
| TC 1 | 7062 | 6906 |
| TM(1) | 57078 | 57672 |
| TM(2) | 67766 | 63921 |
| TM(1)-8T | 16015 | 15937 |
| TM(2)-8T | 19703 | 20328 |

Table 4 outputs necessary time to conduct transcoding and transmoding operations, without any software optimization. In this case, one can see that transmoding operations take 7 to 8 times than simple transcoding. If we activate the multithreading support, using 8 threads significantly reduces necessary time (8T suffix in the table). As doom 1 and doom 2 videos include 500 frames, we can say that our system is able of live transmoding ($\approx$ 40 ms per frame).

A 2 % improvement is quite little one, but this preliminary work comfort us in exploiting other optimizations. Some optimizations have been done on both encoders, but they can be further improved (accuracy, bitstream format...). In the mean time, the decoding process can also be improved. For exemple, at the moment no image processing is done to reduce visual artifacts between pixel and vector areas while decoding. Results have to be analyzed in the light of the used cloud game - a FPS - which brings by definition a lot of action. Further work on other kind of games will be conducted.

## 6  Conclusions and Future Works

In this paper, we presented a new type of video encoding system called transmoder. The video stream is splitted into regions that are encoded using several modalities depending on the regions characteristics. We proposed an overall system architecture for transmoding, that we implemented using two modalities, pixel and vector encoding. Corresponding streaming architecture is presented. We first split each frame into regions using an edge detector. We then determine the more relevant encoder for each region. We output a bimodal video stream combining vector and pixel frames. We tested our approach in a cloud

gaming use case, using a FPS game. Performance analysis shows that our approach outperforms state-of-the-art encoder for a large majority of testbed videos.
Although immature with respect to the transcoder baseline, the system could
compete with state-of-the-art solutions while other optimizations are still possible. This comfort us in continuing the exploration of transmoder algorithm
and architecture. Conducted tests present a reduction of the necessary bitrate
up to 2 %, based on objective metrics. Future research will allow us to optimize
even more our system, using for example GPU optimized algorithms (aiming
at reduce necessary processing time), but also per game attention maps profiles
to know precise locations of important and non important picture parts. In the
frame of our research on cloud gaming systems, we aim to integrate this multimodal coding scheme in the realtime rendering chain. We therefore adapt our
approach for distributed processing in a cloud architecture.

# References

1. Sun, J., Liang, L., Wen, F., Shum, H.Y.: Image vectorization using optimized
   gradient meshes. In: ACM SIGGRAPH 2007 papers. SIGGRAPH 2007. ACM,
   New York, NY, USA (2007)
2. Lai, Y.K., Hu, S.M., Martin, R.R.: Automatic and topology-preserving gradient
   mesh generation for image vectorization. ACM Trans. Graph. **28**, 85:1–85:8 (2009)
3. Zhang, S.H., Chen, T., Zhang, Y.F., Hu, S.M., Martin, R.: Vectorizing cartoon
   animations. IEEE Trans. Vis. Comput. Graph. **15**, 618–629 (2009)
4. Orzan, A., Bousseau, A., Winnemller, H., Barla, P., Thollot, J., Salesin, D.: Diffusion curves: a vector representation for smooth-shaded images. ACM Trans. Graph.
   **27**, 92:1–92:8 (2008)
5. Chaudhury, S., Mathur, M., Khandelia, A., Tripathi, S., Lall, B., Roy, S.D.,
   Gorecha, S.: System and method for object based parametric video coding. U.S.
   Classification: 375/240.16; 375/240.25; 375/E07.027; 375/E07.076 (2011)
6. Khandelia, A., Gorecha, S., Lall, B., Chaudhury, S., Mathur, M.: Parametric video
   compression scheme using AR based texture synthesis. In: Sixth Indian Conference
   on Computer Vision, Graphics Image Processing, 2008. ICVGIP 2008, pp. 219–225
   (2008)
7. Szummer, M., Picard, R.W.: Temporal texture modeling. In: 1996 Proceedings
   of the International Conference on Image Processing, vol. 3, pp. 823–826. IEEE
   (1996)
8. Zhu, C., Sun, X., Wu, F., Li, H.: Video coding with spatio-temporal texture synthesis. In: ICME, pp. 112–115 (2007)
9. Tripathi, S., Mathur, M., Dutta Roy, S., Chaudhury, S.: Region-of interest based
   parametric video compression scheme. Communicated to the IEEE Transactions
   on Circuits and Systems for Video Technology (2012)
10. Felzenszwalb, P.F., Huttenlocher, D.P.: Efficient graph-based image segmentation.
    Int. J. Comput. Vis. **59**, 167–181 (2004)
11. Tizon, N., Moreno, C., Cernea, M., Preda, M.: MPEG-4-based adaptive remote
    rendering for video games. In: Proceedings of the 16th International Conference on
    3D Web Technology. Web3D 2011, pp. 45–50. ACM, New York, NY, USA (2011)
12. Tizon, N., Moreno, C., Preda, M.: ROI based video streaming for 3D remote render-
    ing. In: 2011 IEEE 13th International Workshop on Multimedia Signal Processing
    (MMSP), pp. 1–6 (2011)

13. Vankeirsbilck, B., Verslype, D., Staelens, N., Simoens, P., Develder, C., Demeester, P., De Turck, F., Dhoedt, B.: Platform for real-time subjective assessment of interactive multimedia applications. Multimedia Tools Appl. **72**, 749–775 (2013)
14. Lavignotte, A., Gravier, C., Subercaze, J., Fayolle, J.: Quality of experience, a very personal experience!. In: 2013 24th International Workshop on Database and Expert Systems Applications (DEXA), pp. 231–235. IEEE (2013)
15. Ehmke, C., Wilson, S.: Identifying web usability problems from eye-tracking data. In: Proceedings of the 21st British HCI Group Annual Conference on People and Computers: HCI... but not as we know it, vol. 1, pp. 119–128. British Computer Society (2007)
16. Ahmadi, H., Khoshnood, S., Hashemi, M.R., Shirmohammadi, S.: Efficient bitrate reduction using a game attention model in cloud gaming. In: 2013 IEEE International Symposium on Haptic Audio Visual Environments and Games (HAVE), pp. 103–108. IEEE (2013)
17. Heath, M., Sarkar, S., Sanocki, T., Bowyer, K.: Comparison of edge detectors: a methodology and initial study. In: 1996 Proceedings of the IEEE Computer Society Conference on Computer Vision and Pattern Recognition, CVPR 1996, pp. 143–148 (1996)
18. Maini Raman, D.H.A.: Study and comparison of various image edge detection techniques. Int. J. Image Process. 1–11 (2009)
19. Ferrari, L., Sankar, P., Sklansky, J.: Minimal rectangular partitions of digitized blobs. Comput. Vis. Graph. Image Process. **28**, 58–71 (1984)

# STAR: Speech Therapy with Augmented Reality for Children with Autism Spectrum Disorders

Camilla Almeida da Silva[1], António Ramires Fernandes[2(✉)],
and Ana Paula Grohmann[3]

[1] Faculdade de Computação e Informática, Universidade Presbiteriana Mackenzie,
São Paulo, Brazil
camilla.sil@gmail.com
[2] Centro Algoritmi, Universidade do Minho, Braga, Portugal
arf@di.uminho.pt
[3] Associação para a Inclusão e Apoio ao Autista, Braga, Portugal
apaulaf@gmail.com

**Abstract.** Graphics based systems of Augmented and Alternative Communication are widely used to promote communication in people with Autism Spectrum Disorders. This study discusses an integration of Augmented Reality in communication interventions, by relating elements of Augmented and Alternative Communication and Applied Behaviour Analysis strategies. An architecture for an Augmented Reality based interactive system to assist interventions is proposed. STAR provides an Augmented Reality tool to assist interventions performed by therapists and support for parents to join in and participate in the child's intervention. Finally we report on the usage of the Augmented Reality tool in interventions with children with Autism Spectrum Disorders.

**Keywords:** Autism spectrum disorder · Augmented reality · Augmented and alternative communication · Human-computer interaction

## 1 Introduction

Children with Autism Spectrum Disorders (ASD) are affected with various impairments in communication, social interaction and imagination, three major components of self-development. Regarding communication issues, these range from the total absence of language, 20 % to 30 % [1], to the lack of effectiveness in the communication process, reinforcing the need to promote initiatives to improve communication skills.

Applied Behaviour Analysis (ABA) interventions for autism in early childhood are an effective practice to improve socially relevant behaviours and teach new skills, through several established teaching tools and positive reinforcement strategies. Augmented and Alternative Communication (AAC) based approaches, in particular those based on graphics, are the most used in interventions for children with ASD. These interventions are considered to be highly

© Springer International Publishing Switzerland 2015
J. Cordeiro et al. (Eds.): ICEIS 2014, LNBIP 227, pp. 379–396, 2015.
DOI: 10.1007/978-3-319-22348-3_21

relevant in communication promotion, reduction of behavioural problems, and environmental awareness [2].

The graphics based system usage is supported by the strong visual processing ability seen in many children with ASD. Nevertheless, imagination impairments caused by rigidity and lack of imagination can prevent the usage of some symbols [3]. In [3] it is argued that some children with ASD, when confronted with a symbol, only capture a set of lines, shapes and colours, and the usage of communication symbols would lead to memorization and context association. The authors show that changes in the background or width of the lines are sufficient to prevent recognition on a previously learned symbol. Hence, they conclude that these symbols are meaningless to those children. In [2] it is stated that the lack of symbolic capacity is one of the main handicaps in communication, reflecting the difficulty in learning conventional or shared meanings of symbols. To achieve communication, symbols must be meaningful to the child [4].

Computer animations, 3D graphics, and sounds, may provide deeper engagement for children in their activities, gains in learning, and reduction of behavioural problems, as suggested in several studies on the benefits of Information Technologies in interventions with children with ASD [5–7]. The use of tangible interfaces has also been suggested by [8] to promote alternative ways of collaboration and communication, engaging the children for longer periods of time than with regular interventions.

Augmented Reality (AR), merging virtual objects into real environments, can be explored in some intervention areas for ASD children, such as self-awareness, augmented communication, emotion awareness and identification, social commitment and concept development [9]. These visually oriented approaches are highly suitable due to the remarkable ability of most autistic people to excel at visual spatial skills [10].

Considering the relevance of AAC approaches, and the impact of symbols to promote communication, we performed a study on the usage of AR to assist interventions and expand language with children with ASD. The interactive AR system developed in this study uses both AAC and ABA principles to support interventions focused on facilitating graphic symbol comprehension. The system reinforces the communication symbols superimposing virtual objects and animations over the real environment screen view.

The system's human-computer interaction was previously discussed with speech-language therapists to ensure its suitability for both therapists and children. The system's features include the creation of activities with AR graphics and sound to enrich the symbol's meaning, with both visual and audio reinforcements. The system is adaptable to each individual child, allowing to have multiple activity configurations, and supports a number of different activity templates to increase the options for the therapist.

In order to evaluate the system, the application was tested in speech-language sessions with four children with ASD. The tests fulfilled the framework proposed by Moore [5], where computer assisted learning systems for ASD children should focus on at least one on the major impairments; the projects should be based on current established practices; and evaluation should be performed in cooperation with actual therapists.

In Sect. 2 we provide some background information on ASD. Related work is described in Sect. 3. The architecture of our proposed system is described in Sect. 4, and the working prototype is presented in Sect. 5. The evaluation of the prototype is discussed in Sect. 6. Conclusion and possible avenues for future work are presented in Sect. 7.

# 2   Autism Spectrum Disorder

ASD is a group of developmental brain disorders affecting individuals from all races, cultures and socio-economic groups. It presents a wide range of possible symptoms and varying degrees of severity, the common feature being an early developmental disruption in socialization processes [1]. Impairments in communication, social interaction, and imagination - the triad of impairments [11] - causes difficulties in understanding and using verbal and non-verbal communication, to relate and empathize with other people, and rigidity and inflexibility in thinking, language and behaviour.

The Centers for Disease Control and Prevention [12] estimate that about 1 % of individuals have ASD in Europe, Asia, and North America. ASD is more common among boys than among girls, with a ratio of 5 to 1.

## 2.1   The Triad of Impairments and Behavioural Issues

The difficulty of socialization is the most remarkable feature, being more evident in the first years of life. Even in the first few months of life, many infants with ASD do not interact and avoid eye contact, in contrast to neurotypical infants [13]. Social behaviour is not absent, but is developed with absolute lack of social and emotional reciprocity response [14]. One of the consequences of this difficulty is the lack or decline to imitate, one of the crucial prerequisites for learning and a pre-linguistic skill to language development.

The imagination impairment is manifested by obsessive and ritualistic behaviours, literal understanding of language, resistance to changes in routine or environment, inability to simulate, imagine and participate in pretend games. The consequences of this inability affect several areas of thought, language and behaviour, preventing, for example, the development of skills of social reciprocity, language construction, and acquisition of the word.

The difficulty in coordinating attention between people and objects - shared attention - and the difficulty of learning the conventional meaning of symbols - symbolic capacity - are the core deficits of communication.

The behavioural issues are the most influential regarding the social integration of a children with ASD. These include hyperactivity, lack of focus, mood variability, unexpected movements, and uncommon reaction to sensory stimuli.

## 2.2  Interventions

The main goal of an intervention is to promote functional and spontaneous communication, social interaction and symbolic play, in order to increase functional independence and quality of life. These interventions address communication, social skills, unsuitable behaviours, among other common issues caused by ASD [15]. Intervention programs require a multidisciplinary base, involving behavioural therapy, educational programs, speech-language and communication therapy [16].

Applied Behavioural Analysis methods, such as intense behavioural interventions, directed towards long term behaviour modification, have as goals to increase and maintain adequate behaviours, reduce maladaptive behaviours, teach new skills, and enhance the generalization ability to new contexts [15]. These methods have a short duration and are effective in both adults and children [2]. Discrete Trial Training (DTT) is also an ABA method to enhance skills such as attention, compliance, imitation, and discrimination learning, among others [17]. It consists of a structured learning method whereby a complex learning sequence is divided in small steps, with reinforcements and assistance by the therapist where required.

Regarding ASD, the main goal of AAC is to enhance symbol acquisition, since the development of mental models provides the ability to create abstractions from concrete situations and use them when communicating [18].

The American Speech-Language-Hearing Association defines AAC as an area of clinical practice focused on impairment and disability patterns of individuals with severe expressive communication disorders [19]. AAC methods and tools are also highly adaptable to the autistic child needs and personality.

Graphics based systems take advantage of the strong visual processing skills found in many individuals with ASD, and have been proven effective, through functional communication training, in increasing communication reception in small children, and to replace disruptive behaviour such as aggression, self-aggression and crying [2]. The environment, space, and time concepts are other examples where AAC can be used.

The Picture Exchange Communication System (PECS), developed by Bondy and Frost in 1985 [20], is an AAC method for functional communication based on picture exchange. PECS follows ABA principles being structured in a sequence of six steps, each with specific goals, instructions, and training procedures. Initially the child is taught to initiate requests through figures. Later the child will start building sentences, and answering questions. Later stages require the child to make comments. Several studies [21–23] have shown the benefits of PECS, resulting in vocabulary acquisition and social behaviour improvements.

## 3  Related Work

In [6] the impact of an educational software in vocabulary acquisition is discussed. The software was designed to parallel the existing behavioural program, adding audio reinforcements and object motion. The authors conclude that the usage of the software enhanced the children's focus, motivation and vocabulary acquisition.

3D Virtual Environments and AR techniques have also been used extensively to assist interventions for children with ASD.

Project INMER-II [24] was designed based on a serious game in a virtual environment related to shopping activities. The results show increased levels of functional, symbolic comprehension, and imagination. Furthermore, one child was able to successfully generalize the experience to a real environment.

Project AS Interactive was developed to support people with ASD to improve social skills through 3D virtual environments simulating a cafeteria and a bus [25]. Environments and learning objectives were designed in cooperation with the participants' teachers. User interaction is performed with a joystick and mouse. The participants were able to successfully navigate in the virtual environment and interacted with the system effortlessly. The study performed with teenagers with ASD led to the conclusion that these simulated environments could be successfully used to help people with ASD to engage in social interactions.

Virtual avatars with emotional facial expressions were used in project Virtual Messenger [26]. The goal was to help users to relate emotions to facial expressions. In the first stage, the user would be asked to select the emotion corresponding to the avatar presented on screen, or to select a facial expression that corresponds to an emotion. The second level requires the user to select an emotion that is appropriate for a scenario presented on screen. When in the third level, the user is presented with an avatar's facial expression, and is required to select a scenario that could cause the avatar's expression. The results show that people with ASD were able to increase their level of understanding of emotions based on facial expressions.

Joint attention is one key issue in ASD. According to [27], joint attention is a social interaction in which two people use gestures and gaze to share attention with respect to a third object or element of interest. Joint attention seems to be related to communication as a requirement for its development. Interventions that rehabilitate joint attention have shown correlated improvements in the communication skills of the children, such as social initiations, positive affect, imitation, play, and spontaneous speech [28]. In [29] a system that combines VR simulation with an EEG data acquisition to evaluate the cognitive detection of joint attention stimuli was proposed. Two tasks to explore joint attention were developed: to identify joint attention clue; and follow joint attention clue. Although the work is being developed considering people with ASD as the target, a preliminary evaluation was performed with four people with no disorders for proof-of-concept with encouraging results presenting 90 % classification accuracy.

Mobis is a mobile AR system that aims to redirect the attention of children to the objects used during therapy [30]. The system superimposes digital contents, including text and visual shapes, on top of physical objects. The evaluation was taken with seven teachers and twelve low-functioning children with autism, between the ages of 3 and 8. Children rapidly learn how to manipulate the mobile devices and used Mobis to explore their environment. The results indicate that low-function children with autism can use AR technologies and a mobile device as a visor, and that Mobis helped children to discriminate between and identify new objects. Results also lead to the conclusion that Mobis has a positive effect on the time the child remains on tasks, including when distractions are present, and increased student engagement with people and objects.

In [9] a system based on AR with infrared markers was described. The system superimposes the card symbols on the user's image in real time aiming at enhancing symbol understanding. However, this prototype was never tested on children with ASD. Later, in [3] the Pictogram Room, a AR system using Microsoft Kinect, was proposed having as main goals teaching self-consciousness, body scheme and postures, communication and imitation, using serious games to promote interaction with the children.

An AR marker-base system that substitutes real objects by virtual/imaginary objects was proposed in [31] to promote pretend play based on common practices. The virtual objects simulate appropriate behaviours when the real objects are moved, like rotating wheels. Furthermore, a set of theme-related augmentations are added into scene to reinforce pretence and encourage situational appropriate responses. The same set of real objects can be replaced by different pretend virtual objects to promote flexibility in pretend play. This work is still at an early stage and therefore no testing with children with ASD has been performed.

Tentori and Hayes proposed the Mobile Social Compass framework for the development of mobile AR systems. The Social Compass Curriculum is a behavioural and educational curriculum for social skills training, based on stories and visual paper clues to guide the child in both active and passive social interactions. The framework focuses in the concept of Interaction Immediacy, providing a set of visual clues to assist the child in anticipating situations [32].

MOSOCO is a mobile application implemented using the above described framework, using AR and visual guidance, to assist children with ASD in social interactions in real life. The system guides children in the basic social skills defined in The Social Compass curriculum, encouraging them through interactive resources. The systems evaluation was performed with three children and the results show an increased social interactions, both in quantity and quality, mitigating behavioural and social disruptions. The system also promoted social integration of these children in neurotypical groups.

Another mobile AR application, Blue's Clues, was proposed in [33], to help children with ASD moving from one place to another. Blue's Clues concept was developed for a school environment, aiming at providing the necessary mobility instructions, visual and audio clues, to guide students with ASD.

In [34] the authors have created an AR application where students handle plant entities such as fruits leaves, flowers and seeds. Students are required to match a template page where several fruits are presented with all the above items. The system uses AR to match 3D and 2D plant entities, and provides visual cues, surrounding the entities with red or blue circles as feedback to show if the markers are correctly placed. Auditory and olfactory cues are also provided. The study was performed with a large group of children including 11 cognitive disabled children, some of them with ASD. According to the authors, all the children, including disabled, easily handled the markers and had no difficulty with technical elements. Also, the perception and understanding of the 2D and 3D virtual entities, was effective for all children including the disabled ones. During evaluation the authors have observed that disabled children were very enthusiastic when using the application and showed a high motivation compared to most other pupils. Moreover, autistic and trisomic children were able to express some positive emotions when confronted to the application.

Artifact-AR [35] is an AR cognitive artifact for retraining and cognitive skill development, that explores identification, memorization, comparison, and association of pictures and sounds. The user interacts with markers to perform the tasks. To take full advantage of this system some sort of VR glasses are required. Otherwise, the user must interact with the physical device, while the system responds on a different location (the computer screen). This implies that the user must be concentrated on the physical device to point at the right areas, while at the same time checking the computer screen to see the system's response. The customization of the application can be done adding or removing sound and images in a specific directory and edit some of the of the configuration files, hence, the user doesn't need programming skills to expand or personalize the application. The system was tested by ten therapists to analysing the usability aspects with encouraging results regarding its usability.

## 4   STAR's Architecture

In this section we propose an AR based system that allows the creation of interactive activities based on behaviour principles to assist interventions with children with ASD.

STAR (Speech Therapy with Augmented Reality) design took the needs and characteristics of children in ASD into account. We held meetings and applied questionnaires to parents and experts in order to understand the activities undertaken with children with ASD and identify the potential applications of AR technology in interventions.

As result of this process, and literature review, we defined the requirements of the system, namely providing:

- A broad enough range of AR activities templates to avoid repeating the same task over and over again;
- A GUI activity manager where the therapist can define activities and system behaviours according to needs and characteristics of each child. The therapist does not have to be a programmer nor edit text or configuration files;
- Data generated from the sessions should be gathered and stored in a database containing the history for each child;
- Video recording and annotation;
- Parent participation.

The AR subsystem and the GUI activity manager will be described in more detail in Sect. 5.

Data gathered during the AR sessions can be of assistance to the therapist to plan new sessions, namely by recalling the session history, and specific details of each session, which activities were performed, for how long, where the child had more difficulties, among other items.

While most of these items can be found abundantly in the literature, having participating parents is not so common. The system would allow the parents, in their own homes, to see the videos of the interventions by the therapist, thereby being more aware of the work being developed with their children. The video annotation becomes extremely useful as the therapist can use this resource to provide parents with additional information, or direct their attention to a particular detail on a session.

Session viewing, together with therapist coaching, could ultimately enable parents to perform sessions with their children, acting as co-therapists. Participating parents, acting as co-therapists, has been reported in [36–38]. In [38], the authors claim that parent training has been shown to be a very effective method for promoting generalization and maintenance of skills in children with autism.

These sessions, between a parent and the child, could be streamed live to the therapist who could guide the parents as the session progresses, or viewed later and annotated by the therapist as feedback for the parents. This dual feedback system, where parents access videos recorded in the therapist own sessions, and the possibility of real time guidance, or at least feedback from the therapist based on the parents sessions could provide a richer experience to everybody, strengthening bonds between therapist, parents, and most importantly, the child.

The GUI activity manager would allow the therapist to elaborate and manage activities. The therapist could then select a subset of these activities and make them available to the parent's software client, so they can act as co-therapists. Data gathered during the parent-child session would then be sent back to the central system, registered under the child's history, and made available to the therapist.

This proposal aims to fulfil the main characteristics of successful behaviour intervention in ASD [39]:

- Training in various settings (house, school, clinics);
- Multiples facilitators (parents, teachers, therapists);
- Prompting, reinforcement and fading;
- Transparency and predicable structure of training/environment.

Note, however, that the system should only be seen as a facilitator, not as an enforcer. The therapist should always be in charge and it is up to the therapist to decide, on a child by child basis, whether, and which of these features should be made available to the parents.

# 5   The Prototype

In this section we propose an AR based system that allows the creation of inter-active activities supported on AAC and ABA principles to assist interventions with children with ASD, aided by a therapist. This system has been implemented and tested with children with ASD, as detailed in Sect. 6.

The goal was not to impose a new methodology to the therapist, but to offer a supporting tool that could enrich the current daily activities in the speech-language sessions. Hence, all the development was initially discussed with speech-language therapists, to ensure that the prototype would fit painlessly in the current activities, and that its interface was clear and intuitive for both the therapist and the children.

The prototype allows the design of activities for each individual child attend-ing to the difference in degree of the ASD, the individual personality, and the previous activities developed by the therapist. Within each activity, we aimed at providing as much flexibility as possible. Several templates were provided for this initial evaluation to guide the therapist in designing the individual activities.

The usage of AR is directed towards superimposing 3D models and anima-tions on cards with communication symbols that the child holds or places on the table. This creates a richer experience, and takes advantage of the visual skills found in many children with ASD.

The selection of AR as the underlying technology for this project aims at:

- Promote a natural interaction with the computer through the use of tangible interfaces;
- Facilitate the generalization of the acquired knowledge;
- Allow the enrichment of traditional interventions based on communication symbols without imposing a new methodology on the therapy;
- Eliminate the distractions caused by traditional interfaces such as mouse and keyboard.

In [40] is suggested that for the use of tangible interfaces to be intuitive and natural, it is recommended that the selection of physical objects and interaction metaphors should be familiar to users, allowing them to interact with the system relying on previous skills and experiences. In our project we use communication symbol cards which are already familiar to the children. The child interfaces with the system by showing cards with communication symbols, which is a natural behaviour for the child under intervention. Furthermore, the acquired knowledge is implicitly associated with the communication symbols, hence, the child should be able to recall its experiences afterwards.

The prototype was built with open software tools and APIS such as irrKlang for audio, ARToolkit for the AR component and MySQL. These options aim at providing a low cost solution, and multi-platform future support.

## 5.1   GUI Activity Manager

The activity construction process takes place in a simple support application where the therapist can select a template and design interactive activities to explore with the children.

Initially the therapist associates words with symbol cards, 3D graphics, sounds and animations, and builds phrases with word sequences. The words can be further defined as belonging to user-defined categories such as actions, fruits, or animals.

The data set of words, phrases, and their associated media, is then used to construct the activities based on the available templates. Each template provides full parameterization including reinforcement definition, and error management. Activity parameterization includes:

- Interaction procedure: choose between display or occlude markers to interact with application;
- Interaction events behaviour: choose from (a) superimpose a virtual object, (b) reproduce an audio (c) both or (d) none of them;
- Audio and visual reinforcements: In "beginning of activity", "success on task" and other events, the therapist can select to reproduce an audio file and/or a selectable colour square to surround the mark;
- Sequence management: define when to proceed to next task in activity. Can choose from (a) proceed only on attempt success; (b) proceed even on attempt fails; or (c) proceed on success or after a configurable number of attempts.

## 5.2   Activity Templates

The available templates are: Free, Category, Discriminate, and Phrase. These are based on stages I (Free), III (Category and Discriminate), and IV (Phrase) of PECS. The possibility to use different templates also seeks to avoid having the autistic child engaging in repetitive tasks for long periods of time.

The basic procedure consists in showing a card in the field of view of the web cam. The recognition of the pattern in the card will trigger an action.

The Free template, the simplest one, allows both, child and therapist, to interact freely with the prototype. When designing an activity with this template the therapist can associate the action to be triggered when the card is shown or occluded. This action, which can be a graphic, an animation, or a sound, can act as a positive reinforcement depending on the intervention context, or just be used to engage the child into exploring the system. Additional actions can be specified when the card is occluded. As an example assume an activity based on cards with animals. When the child shows a card the system may display on screen a 3D model of the animal on top of the card. If the child covers the card with the hand then the animal sound can be played.

In the Discriminate template the child is required to identify an object based on a clue provided on screen, and present the card that matches the clue. Positive and negative reinforcements can be associated with each individual clue.

The system supports the configuration for special cards that the therapist can include in the activity. A 'hint' card will trigger a user-defined hint when shown to the system. A 'next' card tells the system to move on to the next object. Finally the 'end' card will end the activity. These cards, if provided by the therapist, allow for a freer interaction from the child, since the child can control the activity when possessing all three special cards, or some subset. The special cards can also be used by the therapist to control the activity.

The Category template can be configured in two different ways. Initially the system will present a hint on screen, namely a graphic or sound. The child is then requested to select and show a card either with the respective category or with an item in the same category. Positive reinforcements, applied when the answer is correct, are configurable, as well as the actions to be triggered for showing the wrong card.

In the Phrase template the child is requested to show a sequence of cards, which represent the subject, verb and noun in a phrase, see Fig. 1 for an example using symbols from the ARASAAC collection (available at http://www.catedu. es/arasaac/descargas.php). When each card is placed on the table a reinforcement can be triggered by the system. This reinforcement will hint the child if the right card is being used, and also if the card is in the correct position within the phrase. The system will detect when a phrase is complete and trigger the user-defined positive reinforcement.

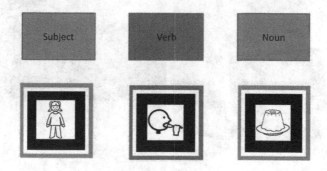

**Fig. 1.** An example of a phrase

## 6   Testing the Protopype

The test was performed in an association that supports children with ASD, the Associação para a Inclusão e Apoio ao Autista, located in Braga, Portugal (http://www.aia.org.pt/).

The prototype was tested by a speech-language therapist, the third author, that performs interventions regularly with children, and four children diagnosed with ASD. The goal was to test if the software was clear to the therapist, and to evaluate its usage as a supporting tool in the interventions performed.

The therapist had 13 sessions with four boys diagnosed with ASD. The children were between the ages of 6 and 10, had some level of orality, and attended school.

Some children were previously assessed as participative in the speech-language sessions, while others have an extremely passive behaviour and barely engaged in spontaneous interaction and communication with the therapist. One child had several verbal and motor stereotypies and expressed himself mainly through echolalia.

A qualitative study was performed with data gathered through observation by the team, including the therapist, in order to evaluate the suitability of the software usage by the children, namely what behaviours were triggered by the usage of AR, and if the children had benefited from the interaction with the software. To support the study we recorded the sessions in video, and filled observation grids with the interaction stages as well as observations that emerged in the sessions with the children (Fig. 2).

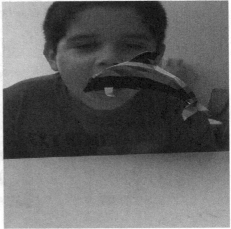

**Fig. 2.** Children interacting with the prototype

## 6.1   Strategies

Based on the previous history with the children, as well as the existing intervention plan for each child, the therapist set the following scripts for these sessions.

For three children the goal was set to: (1) identify animals, nutrients, and daily objects; (2) Identify and designate gender; (3) Identify and designate actions; (4) Discriminate and identify sounds; (5) Answer yes/no questions, together with the respective head nod or shake; and (6) Build sentences with subject, verb and noun.

The other child had as goals to: (1) Enhance declarative skills; (2) Improve language skills; and (3) Create and imagine using language.

The therapist created six activities based on the four available templates to achieve these goals.

## 6.2 Evaluation

In general the children were highly motivated by the usage of AR. Superimposed 3D models and computer animations on top of cards displaying familiar symbols caused a higher degree of engagement in the activities, and had the children requesting the therapist to 'play' with the software when arriving.

The child with stereotypies, when in traditional interventions, used to keep asking to go to the window to watch for cars passing by, and kept repeating out of context phrases. After the AR based session had ended, when they were ready to start a different activity (not related to this project), the child asked the therapist for the dog marker and autonomously presented it to the system. A joyfully expression emerged when the dog's bark was heard.

A child defined by the therapist as passive, regarding communication and behaviour, revealed to be highly motivated, repeating everything the computer 'said'.

Another child, with high functioning ASD, offered an initial resistance to any activity that didn't involve creating stories. Since he had an interest in animals, the therapist started to use the animal markers, and asked the child to show one to the computer. When the system superimposed the 3D model of the animal on the card the child was holding, the child became very interested in the application. In particular, the child showed more enthusiasm for markers associated with 3D models than those associated with sounds only. The therapist took advantage of the sudden child's interest and suggested that he could create a story with the markers. The child selected only markers which were associated with 3D models. During the session the child created two stories, one with insects, and another with sea animals using the 3D models as characters. When the session was over, the child asked for a photo of him playing with the animals to show to his father.

The activities were easily grasped by the children, possibly due to the use of tangible interfaces based on the cards with symbols, something which was highly familiar to these children. The prototype did not require any new form of communication, showing cards was something that was already present in the sessions prior to this test. Hence, the interaction with the computer presented itself as familiar to the child.

After 13 sessions the therapist reported her impressions. On a positive note, the therapist stated that the children kept the interest on the activities for a longer period of time, and inclusively that children had the initiative to ask and use the software on their own. The children acquired new vocabulary and consistently managed to perform correctly the proposed activities.

However, the therapist also noted that a particular child would sometimes disregard everything else concentrating only on his image on the screen. The joint attention was not as high and eye contact occurred less often, suggesting that a balance must be achieved between the several different types of interventions and activities.

The therapist concluded that an AR based approach has the potential to present benefits in speech-language therapy although the social area may be neglected with some children.

## 6.3   Detected Issues

Some issues came up during the test which are worth mentioning in this report. First we had some situations where a card would be incorrectly recognized, triggering an inappropriate action. Other times an action was triggered without having any card on display. These issues came up due to the variations in lighting during the day.

One child actually enjoyed the fact that the system made 'mistakes' and was eager to correct these mistakes. The therapist also took these system misclassifications and explored them within the intervention leading to an even more engaging session. These unintended recognition failures must be fixed, as children with more rigid cognitive processes may be unable to deal with these situations. Nevertheless, this obviously leads to the question: should the system fail occasionally on purpose? Should this feature be introduced in the configuration?

On another session when the system triggered a sound without a card being shown, the child immediately sought for the associated card and showed it to the system. Again, while these unattended failures must be avoided, they may become part of an activity with some children, introducing an element of surprise and breaking the pattern of the activity.

The team also noted that the Phrase template needed to be redesigned to include variations and more reinforcements. The system should be able to provide hints regarding the type of the missing elements and their relative position. Furthermore, the system should allow reinforcements when, although all the correct cards are in the table, the order is not correct. Another option to explore is to start with incomplete phrases and ask the child to identify the type of the missing element, as well as the specific missing card.

The last issue is related to the childs interaction when motor stereotypies are present. In our study a child needed assistance from the therapist to be able to show the cards. This can be solved in the context of the application if the cards are laid on the table. Nevertheless, this issue also suggests a need for a different form of interaction.

## 7   Conclusions

The present work has proposed an approach, relating elements from AAC and ABA, to apply AR in communication and language interventions with children with ASD to mitigate the issues caused by the impairments in communication skills and imagination. We exploited visual and auditory sensory stimulation, combining immediate reinforcement and enrichment of the environment with virtual objects and audio, in order to attract and motivate children.

The resulting prototype has been qualitatively evaluated in an association that supports children with ASD and has therapists conducting interventions in many areas. The sessions were conducted by a therapist and the behaviours of the children and their interaction with the system was recorded on video and using observation grids.

A common issue in qualitatively evaluations relates to the generalization of results to the remaining population. We have no intention of suggesting that the data presented in here can be generalized. This is particularly relevant in the case of ASD due to the wide range of disorders and their varying degrees. This study presents only a contribution to the development of technological systems to support interventions.

Our study shows that the usage of information technologies, in particular AR based systems, in speech-language interventions, complementing and supporting the traditional approaches is an option that must be further explored. The results suggest that the system usage could represent an added value since we could observe greater motivation, word acquisitions, and commitment in performing correctly, as observed by the therapist.

Due to the use of AR and tangible interfaces, familiar physical objects, and an interaction procedure similar to the used in previous AAC sessions, where cards are exchanged between child and therapist, the system was easily grasped by the children. As expected, the children were able to use their past experience to interact effortlessly with the system and hopefully they will be able to generalize the acquired knowledge.

We believe that the positive results obtained in this study are, to some extent, due to the engaging environment provided by the application, and its tangible interface. These factors stimulate cognitive processing and lead to visual learning.

These results illustrate the potential of AR systems to be used in linguistic skill development due to the significant increase in interaction and communication initiated by the children.

While technologies such as the ones in our prototype can provide very positive results, we must pay particular attention to avoid having the child completely immersed on some application details and neglecting social interaction. The therapist plays a fundamental role in these 'augmented' interventions.

## 7.1 Future Work

We believe that the results presented show the need for deeper and further studies, adding more interaction templates, extending their configuration, and testing the system with more children.

Game oriented activity templates could provide an extra level of engagement for the children. Making use of the markers as characters, one child was encouraged to telling stories. Templates with more customizations options could provide a suitable environment to training symbolic play.

Adding templates should be explored to increase the range of possibilities for the therapist to conduct the interventions. The phrase template, as mentioned before, would also benefit from a subdivision or at least more configuration options.

The card recognition subsystem also needs to be fine-tuned to increase robustness, hence suppressing unintentional card misclassification. These system errors, due to the way children reacted to them, raise an interesting question that we believe is worth pursuing: Would a system that intentional provides a wrong answer be a way of further engaging at least some children? What is a 'good' wrong answer?

Children with motor stereotypies also require a different interaction procedure. This condition makes it harder for the system to correctly classify the cards when the child is holding the card, requiring the card to be placed on the table. This is an important issue since a significant number of children with ASD suffer from motor stereotypies.

In this study we focused on speech-language interventions, nevertheless, the designed approach, combining behavioural methods and AR features, could make this system suitable to support other interventions, such as sensorial and motor based intervention or even music therapy.

Finally, the limited number of participating children does not reflect the broad range of the spectrum, nor do they allow for any generalization in a particular subset of these disorders. While the generalization for the whole spectrum of disorders is an impossible task, more participating children would allow for a more relevant analysis, regarding the significance of the contribution of a system such as the one presented in here when used in interventions.

**Acknowledgements.** Work partially funded by National Funds through FCT - Fundação para a Ciência e a Tecnologia (Portuguese Foundation for Science and Technology) within project UID/CEC/00319/2013 and by Conselho Nacional de Desenvolvimento Científico e Tecnológico (CNPq-Brazilian National Council for Scientific and Technological Development) within program Ciência sem Fronteiras (Science without Frontiers), grant 225248/2012-3.

# References

1. Klin, A.: Autism and asperger syndrome: an overview. Rev. Bras. Psiquiatr. **28**, S3–11 (2006)
2. Committee on Educational Interventions for Children with Autism, N.R.C.: Educating Children with Autism. The National Academies Press (2001)
3. Herrera, G., Casas, X., Sevilla, J., Luis, R., Pardo, C., Plaza, J.: Pictogram room: natural interaction technologies to aid in the development of children with autism. Annuary Clin. Health Psychol. **8**, 39–44 (2012)

4. Avila, B.C.: Comunicao Aumentativa e Alternativa para o Desenvolvimento da Oralidade de Pessoas com Autismo. Master's thesis, Universidade Federal do Rio Grande do Sul, Porto Alegre, Brasil (2011)
5. Moore, D., McGrath, P., Thorpe, J.: Computer-aided learning for people with autism; a framework for research and development. Innovations Educ. Training Int. **37**, 218–228 (2000)
6. Moore, M., Calvert, S.: Brief report: vocabulary acquisition for children with autism: teacher or computer instruction. J. Autism Dev. Disord. **30**, 359–362 (2000)
7. Goldsmith, T.R., LeBlanc, L.A.: Use of technology in interventions for children with autism. J. Early Intensive Behav. Interv. **1**, 166–178 (2004)
8. Raffle, H., Farr, W., Yuill, N.: Collaborative benefits of a tangible interface for autistic children. ACM SIGCHI (2009)
9. Herrera, G., Jordan, R., Gimeno, J.: Exploring the advantages of augmented reality for intervention in asd. In: Autism Safari 2006-2nd Word Autism Congress (2006)
10. Grandin, T.: Thinking in Pictures. Bloomsbury Publishing, London (2009)
11. Wing, L.: The Autistic Spectrum: A Guide for Parents and Professionals. Constable and Robinson, London (2002)
12. Centers for Disease Control and Prevention: Autism spectrum disorders (2013). Accessed 15 October 2013. http://www.cdc.gov/ncbddd/autism/data.html
13. Strock, M.: Autism spectrum disorders (pervasive developmental disorders). National Institute of Mental Health (NIMH) (2007)
14. Wing, L.: The continuum of autistic characteristics. In: Schopler, E., Mesibov, G.B. (eds.) Diagnosis and Assessment in Autism. Current Issues in Autism, pp. 91–110. Springer, Heidelberg (1988)
15. Myers, S.M., Johnson, C.P.: The council on children with disabilities: management of children with autism spectrum disorders. Pediatr. **120**, 1162–1182 (2007)
16. Gadia, C.A., Tuchman, R., Rotta, N.T.: Autism and pervasive developmental disorders. J. Pediatr. **80**, 83–94 (2004)
17. Smith, T.: Discrete trial training in the treatment of autism. Focus Autism other Dev. Disabil. **16**, 86–92 (2001)
18. Hobson, R.P.: Autism and the Development of Mind (Essays in Developmental Psychology). Psychology Press, UK (1995)
19. Sevcik, R., Romski, M.: A.A.C.: More Than Three Decades of Growth and Development (2000). http://www.asha.org/public/speech/disorders/AACThreeDecades/. Accessed: 15 October 2013
20. Bondy, A.S., Frost, L.A.: The picture exchange communication system. Focus Autism Other Dev. Disabil. **9**, 1–19 (1994)
21. Charlop-Christy, M.H., Carpenter, M., Le, L., LeBlanc, L.A., Kellet, K.: Using the picture exchange communication system (pecs) with children with autism: assessment of pecs acquisition, speech, social-communicative behavior, and problem behavior. J. Appl. Behav. Anal. **35**, 213–231 (2002)
22. Kravits, T.R., Kamps, D.M., Kemmerer, K., Potucek, J.: Brief report: increasing communication skills for an elementary-aged student with autism using the picture exchange communication system. J. Autism Dev. Disord. **32**, 225–230 (2002)
23. Ganz, J.B., Simpson, R.L.: Effects on communicative requesting and speech development of the picture exchange communication system in children with characteristics of autism. J. Autism Dev. Disord. **34**, 395–409 (2004)
24. Belen, S.O.: INMER-II: Sistema de Inmersin en Realidad Virtual para Personas con Autismo. Tecnoneet 2004: Retos y realidades de la Inclusin Digital (2004)

25. Parsons, S., Leonard, A., Mitchell, P.: Virtual environments for social skills training: comments from two adolescents with autistic spectrum disorder. Comput. Educ. **47**, 186–206 (2006)
26. Fabri, M., Moore, D.: The use of emotionally expressive avatars in collaborative virtual environments. In: Virtual Social Agents, p. 88 (2005)
27. Charman, T.: Why is joint attention a pivotal skill in autism? philosophical transactions of the royal society of London. Ser. B: Biol. Sci. **358**, 315–324 (2003)
28. Kasari, C., Freeman, S., Paparella, T.: Joint attention and symbolic play in young children with autism: a randomized controlled intervention study. J. Child Psychol. Psychiatry **47**, 611–620 (2006)
29. Simões, M., Carvalho, P., Castelo-Branco, M.: Virtual reality and brain-computer interface for joint-attention training in autism. In: Proceedings 9th International Conference Disability, Virtual Reality and Associated Technologies, pp. 507–510 (2012)
30. Escobedo, L., Tentori, M., Quintana, E., Favela, J., Garcia-Rosas, D.: Using augmented reality to help children with autism stay focused. IEEE Pervasive Comput. **13**, 38–46 (2014)
31. Bai, Z., Blackwell, A.F., Coulouris, G.: Making pretense visible and graspable: An augmented reality approach to promote pretend play. In: 11th IEEE International Symposium on Mixed and Augmented Reality, ISMAR 2012, Atlanta, GA, USA, 5–8 November 2012. IEEE Computer Society (2012)
32. Tentori, M., Hayes, G.R.: Designing for interaction immediacy to enhance social skills of children with autism. In: Proceedings of the 12th ACM International Conference on Ubiquitous Computing, pp. 51–60. ACM (2010)
33. Escobedo, L., Tentori, M.: Blues clues: An augmented reality positioning system. In: Child Computer Interaction Workshop (CHI) (2011)
34. Richard, E., Billaudeau, V., Richard, P., Gaudin, G.: Augmented reality for rehabilitation of cognitive disabled children: a preliminary study. In: Virtual Rehabilitation, pp. 102–108. IEEE (2007)
35. Kirner, C., Kirner, T. G.: Development of an interactive artifact for cognitive rehabilitation based on augmented reality. In: 2011 International Conference on Virtual Rehabilitation (ICVR), pp. 1–7. IEEE (2011)
36. Schopler, E., Reichler, R.J.: Parents as cotherapists in the treatment of psychotic children. J. Autism Child. Schizophr. **1**, 87–102 (1971)
37. Krantz, P.J., MacDuff, M.T., McClannahan, L.E.: Programming participation in family activities for children with autism: parents'use of photographic activity schedules. J. Appl. Behav. Anal. **26**, 137–138 (1993)
38. Ingersoll, B., Dvortcsak, A.: Including parent training in the early childhood special education curriculum for children with autism spectrum disorders. J. Positive Behav. Interv. **8**, 79–87 (2006)
39. Bölte, S.: Computer-based intervention in autism spectrum disorders. Focus Autism Res. **9**, 247–260 (2005)
40. Billinghurst, M., Grasset, R., Looser, J.: Designing augmented reality interfaces. SIGGRAPH Comput. Graph. **39**, 17–22 (2005)

# Interpretation of Construction Patterns for Biodiversity Spreadsheets

Ivelize Rocha Bernardo[1]([✉]), Michela Borges[2], Maria Cecília Calani Baranauskas[1], and André Santanchè[1]

[1] Institute of Computing - Unicamp, Avenida Albert Einstein, 1251, Cidade Universitária, Campinas, Brazil
{ivelize,cecilia,santanche}@ic.unicamp.br
[2] Institute of Biology – Unicamp, Zoology Museum, Rua Charles Darwin, s/n, Cidade Universitária, Campinas, Brazil
borgesm@unicamp.br

**Abstract.** Spreadsheets are widely adopted as "popular databases", where authors shape their solutions interactively. Although spreadsheets are easily adaptable by the author, their informal schemas cannot be automatically interpreted by machines to integrate data across independent spreadsheets. In biology, we observed a significant amount of biodiversity data in spreadsheets treated as isolated entities with different tabular organizations, but with high potential for data articulation. In order to automatically interpret these spreadsheets we exploit construction patterns followed by users in the biodiversity domain. This paper details evidences of such patterns and how they can lead to characterize the nature of a spreadsheet, as well as, its fields in a domain. It combines an automatic analysis of thousands of spreadsheets, collected on the Web, with results from a survey conducted with biologists. We propose a representation model to be used in automatic interpretation systems that captures these patterns.

**Keywords:** Pattern recognition · Spreadsheet interpretation · Semantic mapping · Biodiversity data integration

## 1 Introduction

When producing spreadsheets, end-users have autonomy and freedom to create their own systematization structures, with few formal requirements. However, the product is driven to human reading, causing a side effect: programs provide poor assistance in performing tasks, since they are unable to recognize the spreadsheet structure and to discern its implicit schema – hidden in the tabular organization – from the instances and consequently the semantics of this schema. Therefore, it is difficult to combine and coordinate data among spreadsheets using conventional methods, because each new different schema cannot be interpreted.

But, how much different they are in fact? We present in this paper evidences that similarities in spreadsheets can indicate patters followed by groups. We consider that it is possible to map these patterns to a respective semantic description, through the

© Springer International Publishing Switzerland 2015
J. Cordeiro et al. (Eds.): ICEIS 2014, LNBIP 227, pp. 397–414, 2015.
DOI: 10.1007/978-3-319-22348-3_22

recognition of structural reasons which leads a user to interpret a spreadsheet in one way and not another.

Thus, our strategy focuses on the detection of patterns to recognize similar spreadsheets. We argue that the specific way authors build their spreadsheets – i.e. the criterion to define elements, the approach to spatially organize them and the relationship between these elements – is directly related their daily experience in the community they belong.

The challenge of this research is to consider a computer system as a consumer of spreadsheets besides the user. Our approach involves achieving a richer semantic interoperability for data from spreadsheets through pattern recognition.

Most of the related work disregard these patterns to implement strategies for seeking interoperability of tabular data. This paper argues that the structure, i.e. the organization of spreadsheet elements, must be considered, since it leads to the identification of construction patterns, which is related to the user intention/action. This technique allows us to go towards the pragmatic interoperability layer [1].

This article is an extension of a previous work [2], in which we showed evidences of spreadsheet construction patterns adopted by biologists based on an application implemented by us, able to automatically recognize these patterns in the implicit spreadsheet schemas. To support our thesis we collected and analyzed approximately 11,000 spreadsheets belonging to the biodiversity domain.

In this paper we confront previous results with an exploratory observation of these construction patterns based on a survey answered by 44 biologists.

The next sections are organized as follows: Sect. 2 gives an overview of some basic concepts and our research, Sect. 3 details the process of collecting and analyzing spreadsheets employed by biologists, as well as research hypotheses and their evaluation; Sect. 4 highlights evidences of construction patterns followed by biologists; Sect. 5 introduces our model to represent construction patterns; Sect. 6 presents Related Work and Sect. 7 our concluding remarks and the next steps of this research.

## 2  Research Scenario

According to Syed et al. [3], a large amount of the information available in the world is represented in spreadsheets. Despite their flexibility, spreadsheets were designed for independent and isolated use, and are not easily articulated with data from other spreadsheets /files.

For this reason, there is a growing concern to make spreadsheet data more apt to be shared and integrated. The main strategies convert them into open standards to allow software to interpret, combine and link spreadsheet data [4–10].

Related work address this problem mainly by manual mapping to Semantic Web open standards or by automatic recognition, relating spreadsheet elements to concepts available on Web knowledge bases such as DBpedia (http://dbpedia.org).

Systematic approaches for data storage, such as databases, predefine explicit schemas to record data. These schemas can be considered as semantic metadata for the stored data. Spreadsheets, on the other hand, have implicit schemas, i.e. metadata and data merged in the same tabular space.

The central thesis behind our approach is that we can detect and interpret the spreadsheet's schema by looking for construction patterns shared by research groups. We propose in this paper a representation model able to capture such patterns, as well as to be processed by machines. Results of our analysis in thousands of spreadsheets and in a survey indicate the existence of such recurrent patterns and that they can be exploited to recognize implicit schemas in spreadsheets.

There are several aspects that hinder the spreadsheet recognition and its implicit schema, such as differences between columns order, the label used to identify fields and their respective semantics etc.

Although related work explore a subset of the common practices in tabular data – sometimes taking into account their context [11–13] – they do not define a mechanism or model to independently represent these patterns. Since the knowledge about how to recognize patterns is mixed with the programs, they cannot be decoupled from their code. We claim here that a representation to materialize the knowledge about these patterns as artefacts, independently of specific programs and platforms, enables to share, reuse, refine and expand such patterns among users and applications.

This research is driven by a larger project that involves cooperation with biologists to build biodiversity bases. We observed that biologists maintain a significant portion of their data in spreadsheets and, for this reason, this research adopted the context of biology as its specific focus.

We propose a model to represent construction patterns, departing from observations conducted through incremental steps, including spreadsheets collecting/catalog, formulating hypotheses/models, exploratory observation of biology survey and evaluation. These steps will be detailed in next sections.

## 3   Methodology

As previously mentioned, our approach to represent construction patterns was based on a study of related work and field research in the biology domain.

Based on an initial analysis of how biologists of the Institute of Biology (IB) at Unicamp created their spreadsheets, we defined a set of hypothesis and designed experiments and a survey to validate them. These data were also the basis to produce our first model adopted in a process to automate the recognition of construction patterns, whose design involved:

(i)   preliminary collection and analysis of spreadsheet data: in a first moment, we discussed with biologists of the Institute of Biology (IB) at Unicamp about the practices applied when they work with spreadsheets, starting from their creation until their reuse and manipulation;

(ii)  formulation of hypotheses about spreadsheet construction patterns: departing from the spreadsheets, we performed a visual analysis looking for commons elements able to be identified by a system;

(iii) design and implementation of an automatic recognizer for these spreadsheets: we implemented a systems – the SciSpread [2] – which was validated in three progressive groups of spreadsheets: 9 spreadsheets belonging to IB at Unicamp; 40

spreadsheets from the Web selected manually; 11,000 spreadsheets from the Web automatically selected by a crawler script;

(iv) exploratory observation of biology survey: we deployed an online form (available in goo.gl/b1iEvl) to biology students, professors, researchers and professionals, in order to verify according our hypothesis – formulated in (ii) – how biologists classify and arrange their data. This step plus step (iii) were designed to evaluate and refine the hypothesis. The results of both steps are confronted in the next section.

### 3.1 Initial Data Collection and Analysis

Our analysis started with 9 spreadsheets belonging to the IB, in which we identified two main construction patterns, related to the nature of the spreadsheet: catalogs of objects – e.g., specimens in a museum – and event related spreadsheets, e.g., a log of samples collected in the field. We further will refer to these spreadsheet natures as catalog and event.

In order to address the significant differences among spreadsheet types we classified each field in six exploratory questions (who, what, where, when, why, how) [14]. It enabled us to represent and recognize patterns in a higher level of abstraction, e.g., a catalog spreadsheet has as initial fields the taxonomic identification – classified as what question – on the other hand, a collection spreadsheet has as initial fields: date and locality – classified as when and where questions, as illustrated in Fig. 1.

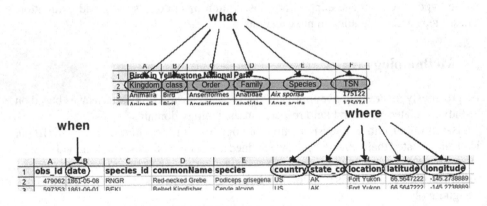

**Fig. 1.** Fields characterization.

The next step involved collecting more 33 spreadsheets on the Web to compose our sample. To search spreadsheets belonging to the biology domain, we applied domain related keywords as criterion.

### 3.2 Hypothesis

According to the observation of these spreadsheets, we proposed the following pattern-related hypotheses:

H1:  most of the spreadsheets organization follows the pattern of columns as fields and rows as records;

H2:  most of the spreadsheets organization follows the pattern of columns as fields and rows as records;

H3:  the first fields of a spreadsheet often define its nature, e.g., catalog or event, as well as its construction pattern.

We developed a system – SciSpread – to automatically recognize schemas based on these hypotheses (see details at [2]). We found evidences, based on our hypothesis, that patterns can drive the recognition of the spreadsheet nature in a context, to make its schema explicit and to support its semantic annotation.

# 4  Evidences of Construction Patterns

The evidences of Construction Patterns are based in two steps. The first was based in an automatic interpretation did by SciSpread system [2], and the second is an exploratory analysis of a survey conducted with biologists.

Thus, the next subsections explain (i) the considerations about the scenario that we implemented the system and observed the evidences, (ii) the survey conducted with biologists in order to verify and refine the hypothesis, and (iii) the comparative results about (i) and (ii).

## 4.1  Evidences Based on Automatic Recognition of Web Spreadsheets

Based on our preliminary assumptions presented in Sect. 3, we looked for patterns concerning: schema layout (e.g., column labels), order and grouping of spreadsheet fields etc. A set of hypotheses – presented in the previous section – was defined and we developed an initial version of the automatic recognition system to validate these hypotheses [2].

The system was tuned to recognize all spreadsheets of this initial sample, whose nature fit in our context. We further randomly collected more 1,914 spreadsheets on the Web, finding them through the Google search engine, based on keywords extracted from previous spreadsheets: kingdom, phylum, order, biodiversity, species, identification key etc. The system recognized 137 spreadsheets (7 %) of all 1,914 spreadsheets collected. The manual analysis of these spreadsheets showed that the system correctly recognized 116 spreadsheets and incorrectly recognized (false positives) 21 spreadsheets. Even though the latter spreadsheets have the expected construction pattern, they do not address the focus of our study, which are spreadsheets used for data management.

Increasing our sample size to 5,633 spreadsheets, the system recognized 7 %; subsequently, increasing to about 11,000 spreadsheets, the system recognized 10.4 %, which corresponds to 1,151 spreadsheets, in which 806 were classified in the catalog and 345 in the event.

We selected a random subset of 1,203 spreadsheets to evaluate the precision /recall of our system. The percentage of automatic recognition of the spreadsheets in the subset was approximately the same as the larger group. Our system achieved a precision of

0.84, i.e. 84 % of retrieved spreadsheets were relevant; are call of 0.76, i.e. the system recognized 76 % of all relevant spreadsheets; and an F-measure of 0.8. The accuracy was 93 % and the specificity 95 %, i.e. among all spreadsheets that the system does classified as not relevant, 95 % were in fact not relevant.

The recognition rate of approximately 10.4 % of the spreadsheets must consider that they were collected through a Web search tool. According Venetis et al. [12], these search tools treat tabular structures like any piece of text, without considering the implicit semantics of their organization and thus causing imprecision in the search results. We further show an analysis of the data extracted from spreadsheets.

### 4.2  Exploratory Analysis Based on a Survey Conducted with Biologists

The survey was performed with 44 biologists, where 36 are from Brazil, 4 are from France, 3 are from EUA and 1 is from Colombia, Denmark and England.

The distribution about their main activity is 11 % are professors, 23 % are researchers, 5 % work in companies, 20 % are post-doctoral students, 25 % are PhD students and 17 % are master students, where 79,5 % work with spreadsheets always or often, 14 % work sometimes and 2 % never use spreadsheets.

We developed an online form with 10 questions to analyze: how biologists organize their specimens' catalogs or samples collected in the field; if the arrange of the fields in a spreadsheet influences its nature; which fields work like identifiers according to the spreadsheet nature; and, if it is possible to capture and map the patters biologist behavior when producing an spreadsheet through a survey with exploratory questions (this survey is available in goo.gl/b1iEvl).

The questions were divided in 2 blocks, in the first block we would like to know the vocabulary which describes catalog and collection spreadsheets. Thus, the biologists chose 8 elements from a list of 17 (author, altitude, collector, common name, date, field number, group, latitude, life stage, locality, longitude, museum, note, species, source, taxonomy identification, time, other) ranked by relevance. In the second block, we presented 3 spreadsheet images and asked to biologists to classify them according to: catalog, field sampling, both types, neither and other. If the option was "other", an extra text field must be filled with the description of the type more adequate to the image.

Compared to spreadsheets retrieved from the Web, the characteristics analyzed in the survey indicated a more specialized set of spreadsheets, i.e. some spreadsheets types retrieved from the Web and classified by the system as catalog or event (field sampling), cannot be related to a specific context as a museum catalog or a research field sampling. Therefore, the results of the survey refined our hypothesis about construction patterns and in a future work we will increase the sampling with more biologists.

In the following subsections, we will confront results obtained from the automatic recognition of Web spreadsheets by our SciSpread system introduced in Sect. 4.1 – which we will refer in abbreviated form as *SciSpread* abbreviated form – and those obtained from the survey introduced in this section – which we will refer in abbreviated form as *Survey*.

## 4.3   Comparative Results: Scispread X Survey

**Pattern for Schema Location.** Our SciSpread system identifies the schema of a spreadsheet guided by the adopted vocabulary, which varies according to the type of the spreadsheet: catalog or event. The scatter chart in Fig. 2 shows the percentage of terms extracted from a given spreadsheet recognized in a vocabulary against the row in the spreadsheet they were recognized. We observe that the spreadsheets schemas were concentrated on the initial lines, since the percentage of matching terms per line decreases exponentially as we move away from the initial lines and the most of the terms are located in the initial lines. Therefore, there is a tendency of positioning schemas at the top followed by their respective instances.

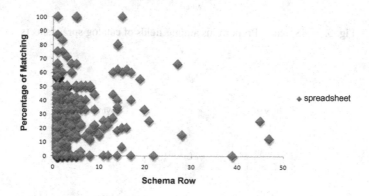

**Fig. 2.** Terms by schema of initial lines.

Even though we did not design a specific experiment to validate this hypothesis in the survey, we assumed this pattern in its examples, when we asked to biologists to recognize spreadsheet images. No biologist reported having difficulty to recognize the schema and the answers indicate they successfully recognized it.

**Predominance of Terms and Spatial Distribution.** In this stage of the analysis, we verified how much the predominant terms and their disposition in the schema can indicate the spreadsheet nature: catalog or event (see explanation of these natures in Sect. 3.1). In order to perform a comparative analysis among proportions and positions of the fields in spreadsheets of the catalog type, we present a radar chart in Fig. 3 (SciSpread) and Fig. 4 (Survey).

While fields and their positions were automatically recognized in SciSpread, in the survey we requested to the interviewee to select and sort fields for a catalog spreadsheet schema. The schema fields were grouped in one of the six exploratory questions and they were weighted according to their position in the schema – the weight has the value one in the leftmost field and decreases to half of its value for each field position towards the right.

In catalog spreadsheets, we observed that, charts have smaller differences and both have a strong tendency to "what" questions, validating that spreadsheets recognized as catalog tend to have many fields that answer the "what" question appearing in the initial positions of the schema. The quantities of the other five questions were no significant

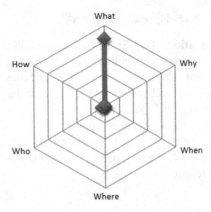

**Fig. 3.** SciSpread - Proportions among fields of catalog spreadsheets.

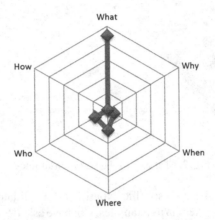

**Fig. 4.** Survey - Proportions among fields of catalog spreadsheets

in the SciSpread spreadsheets and were a bit more significant in the survey spreadsheets, with emphasis to "who" and "where" fields. It delineates a pattern for catalog spreadsheets, which tend to have more fields to identify and detail objects – specimens in this case – in the beginning.

We interpret the increase in the provenance questions (who, where and when) due to the specialization of spreadsheets in the survey, i.e. while we do not have control of the context of the SciSpread spreadsheets and it is not possible to attest the purpose of its catalog spreadsheets, the survey spreadsheets were clearly directed to museums, requiring a more strict control of provenance.

Following the same approach, in Fig. 5 (SciSpread) and Fig. 6 (survey) we show the proportions of fields in event spreadsheets. We can note that there are differences among the proportions of the fields. As in the previous case, our interpretation is that the differences are due to the specialization in the survey spreadsheets. While in the SciSpread spreadsheets the provenance fields – mostly the "when" fields but also the "who" fields – are highly predominant, appearing in the beginning, in the survey spreadsheets the difference compared to "what" fields is less remarkable, but still exists.

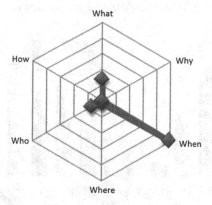

**Fig. 5.** SciSpread - Proportions among fields of event spreadsheets

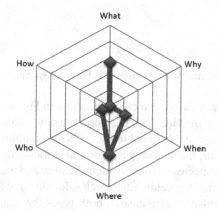

**Fig. 6.** Survey - Proportions among fields of event spreadsheets

The predominance of provenance fields, comparing event to catalog spreadsheets, is enough in both cases (SciSpread and survey) to distinguish their nature. In the survey, we had the opportunity of discussing about the relationship among fields related to "when" and "where" questions. For biologists these fields usually appear together and there is an extra field – usually named field number – which works as an index for a "when" and "where" specification. The relationship among these fields/questions can be considered as a sub-pattern in an automatic analysis.

The previous charts show that it is possible to distinguish between catalog and event spreadsheets, but we need identify which words are the most used by the biologists. In the previous paper [2] we presented detailed observations about the distribution of fields identified by the SciSpread, in this paper we will present values based on the Survey – first block questions.

Thus, the next bar chart (Fig. 7) show which fields are more used by biologists in each spreadsheet nature. The vertical axis describe the quantity of biologists that answered the question and the horizontal axis describe the fields that they chose, according catalog or event spreadsheets.

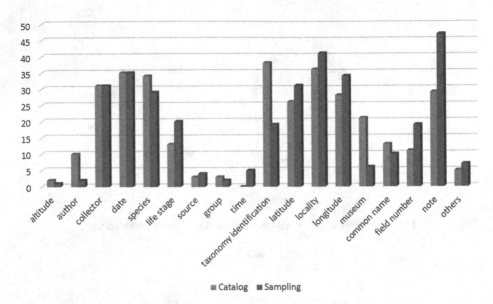

**Fig. 7.** Comparative terms quantities between spreadsheets nature.

Using the result of the previous bar chart, we show in Fig. 8 the distribution of these fields in the columns, i.e. if the biologists must create a new catalog or event spreadsheet, how they will arrange these fields in columns? This distribution indicates that, considering the western behavior, the tendency is to organize most import things from the left to the right. We infer that species, taxonomy identification and museum can be identifiers of catalog spreadsheets, and the fields date, species, locality and field number can be the identifiers of event spreadsheets, because in both types the respective fields appear in greater amount in the first columns.

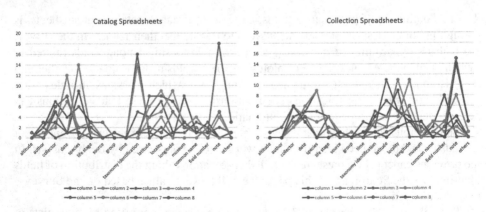

**Fig. 8.** Comparative terms location between spreadsheets nature.

After we consider the vocabulary and the structural organization of the fields – first block questions, it is important analyze how the biologist classifies the spreadsheets – second block questions. According to the spreadsheet shown in Fig. 9, 48 % of the biologists considered this spreadsheet as catalog. The explanation to the decision is due to the detailed information and complete taxonomy identification.

In the second image, we copied the same spreadsheet and we changed the order of the fields, aiming at identifying if the arrangement of the fields is important to characterize the nature of a spreadsheet. The modified spreadsheet is shown in Fig. 10.

The charts in Fig. 11 show in the vertical axis the percentage of biologists that answered the questions and in the horizontal axis the possible choices to classify the spreadsheet images. According to these charts, 40 % of the biologists continue classifying as catalog spreadsheet, but analyzing these charts, we observed that, even though most of the biologists do not consider the second spreadsheet as event, there is a significant number of biologists who changed their opinion to event, and this was due to the simple fact that we changed the fields disposition.

| | A | B | C | D | E | F | G | H | I | J | K | L | M |
|---|---|---|---|---|---|---|---|---|---|---|---|---|---|
| 1 | | | | | Qualitative multiple habitat macroinvertebrates present at the 7 Mile Bridge site (USGS site ID 12424500) on the Spokane River, July 1999; L, larvae; P, pupae. | | | | | | | | |
| 2 | Phylum | Class | Order | SubOrder | Family | SubFamily | Tribe | Genus | Species | Lifestage | Date | Lat | Long |
| 3 | Annelida | Oligochaeta | | | | | | | | | 1861-05-08 | 66.5647222 | -145.27389 |
| 4 | Arthropoda | Insecta | Coleoptera | Polyphaga | Elmidae | | | Optioservus | | A | 1861-06-01 | 66.5647222 | -145.27389 |
| 5 | Arthropoda | Insecta | Coleoptera | Polyphaga | Elmidae | | | Optioservus | Optioservus divergens | A | 1861-06-01 | 66.5647222 | -145.27389 |

**Fig. 9.** Spreadsheet 1 - used in the Survey

| | A | B | C | D | E | F | G | H | I | J | K | L | M |
|---|---|---|---|---|---|---|---|---|---|---|---|---|---|
| 1 | | | | | Qualitative multiple habitat macroinvertebrates present at the 7 Mile Bridge site (USGS site ID 12424500) on the Spokane River, July 1999; L, larvae; P, pupae. | | | | | | | | |
| 2 | Date | Lat | Long | Phylum | Class | Order | SubOrder | Family | SubFamily | Tribe | Genus | Species | Lifestage |
| 3 | 1861-05-08 | 66.5647222 | -145.27389 | Annelida | Oligochaeta | | | | | | | | |
| 4 | 1861-06-01 | 66.5647222 | -145.27389 | Arthropoda | Insecta | Coleoptera | Polyphaga | Elmidae | | | Optioservus | | A |
| 5 | 1861-06-01 | 66.5647222 | -145.27389 | Arthropoda | Insecta | Coleoptera | Polyphaga | Elmidae | | | Optioservus | Optioservus divergens | A |

**Fig. 10.** Spreadsheet 2 - used in the Survey.

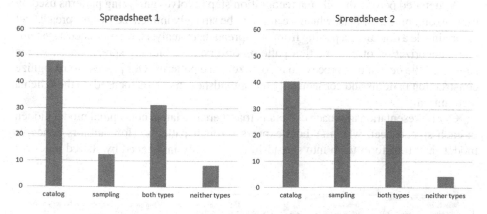

**Fig. 11.** Comparative results about spreadsheets classification.

Therefore, we consider that the order of the fields is important to decide the nature of the spreadsheet, and we add the observation that there is a common understanding among biologists that if a spreadsheet has many fields and complete information, this spreadsheet is more related to a catalog than about events. On the other hand, if the information is synthetic and objective, this spreadsheet is about events. This differentiation is due to the context. Biologists do not have time to detail information and classify specimens during the collection in the field; therefore the conditions limit the answers.

The third spreadsheet, shown in Fig. 12, was classified by biologists classified as event. According to our hypothesis, this spreadsheet must be classified as catalog, considering only the fields. We concluded that the biologists classified as collection despite the lack of date and location fields, due to the quantity of fields, which is limited, characterizing a sample collection in the field.

This information is important since we were not considering in the automatic interpretation of this data type of spreadsheet the relevance of the detail level of the fields. Another point to consider in an automatic interpretation of catalog spreadsheets is that they never start with a "common name" field.

Through this comparative results, we verified that: the schema usually appear on the top of spreadsheets; the fields arrangement influenced in a spreadsheet characterization; the identifiers of catalog spreadsheets can be a taxonomy identifier or a museum number and of event spreadsheets can be a date plus locality information or field number.

## 5  Representation of Construction Patterns

This section details the model, proposed in this paper, to capture and represent construction patterns in spreadsheets, which can be interpreted and used by machines. The characteristics of this model were based on field observations reported in the previous section. Therefore, even though we intend to conceive a generic model to represent patterns in spreadsheets for data management in general, in the present stage our analysis is focused in biology spreadsheets.

As detailed before, the schema recognition step involves analyzing patterns used by users to organize their data, which we argue to be strongly influenced by the spreadsheet nature inside a domain. Departing from our spreadsheet analysis, we produced a systematic categorization of construction patterns observed in biology spreadsheets, which supported the design of a process to recognize these patterns. Our process to recognize construction patterns and consequently the spreadsheet nature is focused on the schema recognition

Our representation approach considers that there is a latent conceptual model hidden in each spreadsheet, which authors express through patterns. How authors conceive models and transform them into spreadsheets is highly influenced by shared practices

**Fig. 12.**  Spreadsheet 3 - used in the survey.

of the context in which the author is inserted, e.g., a biologist author cataloging specimens from of a museum. Her reference to build the catalog will be the specimens themselves, but also the usual strategy adopted by biologists of her community to tabulate data from specimens. Thus, the construction patterns and the respective hidden conceptual models to be represented here reflect community or domain patterns and models. Our analysis shows that a catalog spreadsheet contains taxonomic information of a specimen ("what" question) concentrated in the initial positions, defining their role as identifiers. On the other hand, an event spreadsheet contains temporal and location fields in the initial positions.

A visual analysis of the spreadsheet structure gives us directions of how the pattern is organized, e.g., schema up /instances down; identifier on the left, as a series of progressively specialized taxonomic references. To express these characteristics of the pattern in a computer interpretable representation, we represent them as qualifiers [2] identified by the prefix "q", and they are categorized as follows:

Positional qualifier – characterizes an element in a pattern according to its absolute position within a higher level element. There are four positional qualifiers: left (q ←), right (q →), top (q↑) and bottom (q↓).

Order qualifier (q#) – characterizes an element in a pattern according to its relative order regarding its neighboring elements.

Label qualifier (q@) – indicates that the label characterizes the element. In the example, the label species identifies that this column refers to species.

Data type qualifier (q$) – characterizes the predominance of one data type in the instances of a given property.

Range qualifier – specify if neighbor elements have generalization /specialization relations. The qualifier (q>) indicates that the left one is more general than the right one and (q<) the opposite.

Classified qualifier – characterizes instances of a given property that are arranged in ascending order (q +) or descending order (q-).

Redundancy qualifier (q =) – characterizes redundancy of information in instances of a property. Such redundancy is typical, for example, in non-normalized relations among properties and composite properties, in which the values of a sub-property are broader or more generic of a related sub-property – usually the value of one sub-property embraces the value of the other.

Besides the qualifiers, we associate the relation of elements with one of the six exploratory questions (who, what, where, when, why, how). This association will subsidize the characterization of construction patterns in a more abstract level. For example, looking at other kinds of catalog spreadsheets, outside the biology domain, we observed they define "what" fields as identifiers and they appear in the leftmost position (q ←).

## 5.1 Formalizing the Model to Represent Patterns

In this subsection, we will present a more formal representation, to be stored in digital format and to be read and interpreted by machines. This representation takes as a starting point the conceptual model implicitly expressed through the pattern. Figure 13 shows

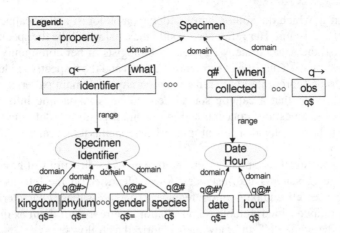

**Fig. 13.** Conceptual model for catalog spreadsheets annotated with qualifiers.

the representation of the construction pattern. The model is based on the OWL Semantic Web standard. The ovals represent classes (owl:class) and rectangles represent properties (owl:ObjectPropertyorowl:DatatypePropert).

The root class –Specimen in the figure –is related to the spreadsheet nature; in this case, instances of the Specimen class represent the instances of the spreadsheet, which catalogs specimens. A class will have a set of applicable properties, represented by a domain edge (rdfs:domain). Properties of this model are related to fields extracted from the spreadsheet. Range edges (rdfs:range)indicate that values of a given property are instances of the indicated class. For simplicity, the diagram omits details of the OWL representation.

Properties in our model are annotated by qualifiers presented in the previous section. Properties can be annotated in OWL through the owl:AnnotationProperty. In this case, annotations are objects that specify the qualifier and the pattern they are related. Qualifiers as annotations are depicted above and/or below the properties they qualify. A qualifier above a property indicates that it is applied to the relationship between the property and the class to which it is applied by the domain relation. For example, the qualifier q ← (left positional qualifier) is represented above the identifier property, indicating that when this property is used as a field in a spreadsheet describing a Specimen, we expect that it will appear in the left position.

A qualifier below the property means that it applies to property values – instances in the spreadsheet. For example, the qualifier q$ = below the kingdom property indicates that a specific type (string) and redundancy are observed in the values of this property in the instances.

Properties are also annotated as answering one of the six exploratory questions. These annotations are depicted in Fig. 13 inside brackets. There are additional concerns in the OWL model that are necessary to bridge it to the implicit spreadsheet schema, which are also represented as annotations: the order of properties and their relation with labels. This OWL representation allows us to digitally materialize building patterns of spreadsheets, to be shared by users and applications.

# 6    Related Work

As discussed in Sect. 5, a fundamental characteristic of spreadsheets used for data management is the separation between schema and instances. The schema is presented above (q↑) or left (q ←) and instances is below (q↓) or right (q →).

This observation appears in all the papers of related work, whose purpose is to recognize the implicit schema of spreadsheets. Syed et al. [3] point out that this challenge leads to a more general problem of extracting implicit schemas of data sources – including databases, spreadsheets etc. One approach to make the semantics of spreadsheets interoperable, promoting the integration of data, is the manual association of spreadsheet fields to concepts in ontologies represented by open standards of the Semantic Web.

Han et al. [6] adopt the simplest approach to devise a schema and its respective instances, called entity-per-row [4]. In this approach, besides the schema, each row of the table should describe a different entity and each column an attribute for that entity, for example, each column corresponds to an attribute – e.g., Date, Genus, Species etc. – and each row to an event – a collection of a specimen. Han et al. [6] and several related work assume the entity-per-row organization to support the process of manually mapping attributes, to make them semantically interoperable. Initially, the user must indicate a cell whose column contains a field which plays the role of identifier–equivalent to the primary key of a database.

Langegger and Wob [15] propose a similar, but more flexible, solution to map spreadsheets in an entity-per-row organization. They are able to treat hierarchies among fields, when a field is divided into sub-fields, for example, fields Date, Latitude and Longitude refer to when and where the species was collected. It is usual that authors create a label spanning the entire range above these columns – e.g., labelled as "Field Number" – to indicate that all these fields are subdivisions of the larger field. This hierarchical perspective can be expressed in our model, since a property can be typed (rdfs:range) by a class, which in turn has properties related to it.

RDF has been widely adopted by related work as an output format to integrate data from multiple spreadsheets, since it is an open standard that supports syntactic and semantic interoperability. Langegger and WOB [15] propose to access these data through SPARQL [16] – a query language for RDF. Oconnor et al. [4] propose a similar solution using OWL.

Abraham and Erwig [10] observed spreadsheets are widely reused, but due to their flexibility and level of abstraction, the reuse of a spreadsheet by people outside its domain increases errors of interpretation and therefore inconsistency. Thus they propose a spreadsheet life cycle defined in two phases: development and use, in order to separate the schema of its respective instances. The schema is developed in the first cycle, to be used in the second cycle. Instances are inserted and manipulated in the second cycle guided by the schema, which cannot be changed in this cycle.

Another approach to address this problem is automating the semantic mapping using Linked Data. Syed et al. [3] argue that a manual process to map spreadsheets is not feasible, so they propose to automate the semantic mapping by linking existing data in the spreadsheets to concepts available in knowledge bases, such as DBpedia (http://dbpedia.org) and Yago (http://www.mpi-inf.mpg.de/yago-naga/yago/). Yago is a large knowledge base, whose data are extracted, among others, from Wikipedia and WordNet (http://wordnet.princeton.edu). The latter is a digital lexicon of the English language, which semantically relates words.

Among the advantages of the last approach, there is the fact that such bases are constantly maintained and updated by people from various parts of the world. On the other hand, the search for labels without considering their contexts can generate ambiguous connections, producing inconsistencies. Thus, there are studies that stress the importance of delimiting a scope before attempting to find links.

Venetis et al. [12] exploit the existing semantics in the tables to drive the consistent manipulation operations applicable to them. The proposal describes a system that analyzes pairs of terms heading columns and their relationship, in order to improve the semantic interpretation of them. Authors state that a main problem in the interpretation of tabular data is the analysis of terms independently. This paper tries to identify the scope by recognizing a construction pattern, which is related to a spreadsheet nature inside a context.

Jannach et al. [11] state that the compact and precise way to present the data are primarily directed to human reading and not for machine interpretation and manipulation. They propose a system to extract information from web tables, associating them to ontologies. They organize the ontologies in three groups: 1. core: concepts related to the model disassociated from a specific domain; 2. core + domain: domain concepts of a schema related to the information to be retrieved; 3. instance of ontology: domain concepts of instances. These ontologies aim at gradually linking the information to a semantic representation and directed by the user's goal.

Among these solutions, we note that some of them address individual pieces of information inside spreadsheets – devoid of context – and others consider the importance of identifying and characterizing the context. Even though all approaches rely on construction patterns of spreadsheets, none of them proposes a model to represent, exchange, reuse and refine these patterns, which is one of the main contributions of this work.

## 7   Conclusions and Future Work

This paper presented our thesis that it is possible, from a spreadsheet structure, to recognize, map and represent how users establish construction patterns, which are reflected in the schema and data organization. One of our main contributions here is an exploratory observation of these patterns through a survey with biologists, as well as the refinement of hypothesis for construction patterns.

Our process also involves the comparative analysis between the SciSpread system and survey results. None of the related work departs from the characterization of the underlying conceptual models and their association with construction patterns, to categorize spreadsheets according to the nature of information they represent, and to recognize them.

Our studies presented here have focused in the area of biodiversity. We intend to investigate its generalization to other domains of knowledge, extending this strategy to a semiotic representation.

**Acknowledgements.** Work partially financed by FAPESP (2012/16159-6), the Microsoft Research FAPESP Virtual Institute (NavScales project), the Center for Computational Engineering and Sciences - Fapesp/Cepid 2013/08293-7, CNPq (grant 143483/2011-0, MuZOO Project and PRONEX-FAPESP), INCT in Web Science (CNPq 557.128/2009-9), CAPES, as well as individual grants from CNPq.

# References

1. Tolk, A.: What comes after the Semantic Web - PADS Implications for the Dynamic Web, pp. 55–62 (2006)
2. Bernardo, I.R., Santanchè, A., Baranauskas, M.C.C.: Automatic interpretation spreadsheets based on construction patterns recognition. In: International Conference on Enterprise Information Systems (ICEIS), pp. 1–12 (2014)
3. Syed, Z., Finin, T., Mulwad, V., Joshi, A.: Exploiting a Web of Semantic Data for Interpreting Tables, pp. 26–27 (2010)
4. O'Connor, M.J., Halaschek-Wiener, C., Musen, M.A.: Mapping master: a flexible approach for mapping spreadsheets to OWL. In: Patel-Schneider, P.F., Pan, Y., Hitzler, P., Mika, P., Zhang, L., Pan, J.Z., Horrocks, I., Glimm, B. (eds.) ISWC 2010, Part II. LNCS, vol. 6497, pp. 194–208. Springer, Heidelberg (2010)
5. Zhao, C., Zhao, L., Wang, H.: A spreadsheet system based on data semantic object. In: 2010 2nd IEEE International Conference on Information Management and Engineering, pp. 407–411 (2010)
6. Han, L., Finin, T.W., Parr, C.S., Sachs, J., Joshi, A.: RDF123: from spreadsheets to RDF. In: Sheth, A.P., Staab, S., Dean, M., Paolucci, M., Maynard, D., Finin, T., Thirunarayan, K. (eds.) ISWC 2008. LNCS, vol. 5318, pp. 451–466. Springer, Heidelberg (2008)
7. Yang, S., Bhowmick, S.S., Madria, S.: Bio2X: a rule-based approach for semi-automatic transformation of semi-structured biological data to XML. Data Knowl. Eng. **52**(2), 249–271 (2005)
8. Ponder, W.F., Carter, G.A., Flemons, P., Chapman, R.R.: Evaluation of Museum Collection Data for Use in Biodiversity Assessment. **15**(3), 648–657 (2010)
9. Doush, I.A., Pontelli, E.: Detecting and recognizing tables in spreadsheets. In: Proceedings 8th IAPR International Workshop Document Analysis System - DAS 2010, pp. 471–478 (2010)
10. Abraham, R., Erwig, M.: Inferring templates from spreadsheets. In: Proceeding 28th International Conference on Software Engineering - ICSE 2006, vol. 15, p. 182 (2006)
11. Jannach, D., Shchekotykhin, K., Friedrich, G.: Automated ontology instantiation from tabular web sources—The AllRight system☆, Web Semant. Sci. Serv. Agents World Wide Web **7**(3), 136–153 (2009)
12. Venetis, P., Halevy, A., Pas, M., Shen, W.: Recovering semantics of tables on the web. Proc. VLDB Endow. **4**, 528–538 (2011)
13. Mulwad, V., Finin, T., Syed, Z., Joshi, A.: Using linked data to interpret tables. In: Proceedings of the International Workshop on Consuming Linked Data, pp. 1–12 (2010)

14. Jang, W., Seiie, Ko, Eun-Jung and Woo: Unified user-centric context: who, where, when, what, how and why. In: Proceedings of the International Workshop on Personalized Context Modeling and Management for UbiComp Applications, pp. 26–34 (2005)
15. Langegger, A., Wöß, W.: XLWrap – querying and integrating arbitrary spreadsheets with SPARQL. In: Bernstein, A., Karger, D.R., Heath, T., Feigenbaum, L., Maynard, D., Motta, E., Thirunarayan, K. (eds.) ISWC 2009. LNCS, vol. 5823, pp. 359–374. Springer, Heidelberg (2009)
16. Pérez, J., Arenas, M., Gutierrez, C.: Semantics and complexity of SPARQL. ACM Trans. Database Syst. 34(3), 1–45 (2009)

# Enterprise Architecture

# Integrating Business Information Streams in a Core Banking Architecture: A Practical Experience

Beatriz San Miguel[✉], Jose M. del Alamo, and Juan C. Yelmo

Center for Open Middleware (COM), Universidad Politécnica de Madrid,
Campus de Montegancedo, E-28223 Pozuelo de Alarcón, Madrid, Spain
{beatriz.sanmiguel,jose.delalamo,
juancarlos.yelmo}@centeropenmiddleware.com

**Abstract.** Traditional commercial and retail banks are under great pressure from new competitors. They must rise to the challenges of understanding their customer actions and behaviors, and be ready to meet their expectations even before they explicitly express them. But the ability to know customers' demands in nearly real-time requires the evolution of existing architectures to support the detection, notification, and processing of business events to manage business information streams. This paper describes a practical experience in evolving a core banking enterprise architecture by leveraging business event exploitation, and includes the definition of business events; the design of a reference architecture and its integration points with the legacy architecture, as well as the description of an initial governance approach. Furthermore, as the core banking architecture is a critical infrastructure we have evaluated the performance of the evolved architecture so as to understand whether or not it can meet the banks' quality levels.

**Keywords:** Enterprise Architecture (EA) · Event-Driven Architecture (EDA) · Event · Core banking · Business information · Middleware

## 1 Introduction

Business information has become a critical asset for companies and it of even more value when obtained and exploited in nearly real time. The correct distribution of this information to all interested parties and its accurate, subsequent use and processing by different applications allow companies and organizations to react quickly to changes in their environment and obtain multiple profits.

In order to fulfill the aforementioned requirements, Event Driven Architecture (EDA) was devised. EDA allows systems and applications to deliver and respond to real time information (events), helping to support business needs from an IT management point of view [1]. Thus, it has associated both technological benefits and business advantages. As regards the former, EDA provides a loose coupling between its components, which reduces dependencies and allows modifications without giving rise to side effects. A many-to-many communication pattern is also applied, facilitating the reusability of information and the freedom to act independently with the received information. All of the above creates an adaptive and flexible architecture that results in business

© Springer International Publishing Switzerland 2015
J. Cordeiro et al. (Eds.): ICEIS 2014, LNBIP 227, pp. 417–433, 2015.
DOI: 10.1007/978-3-319-22348-3_23

advantages. EDA enables faster, more agile and more responsive business processes, enhancing the informed decision-making model and the automation, processing and motoring of operational activities, among other business advantages.

Companies can follow different strategies to introduce the EDA approach and thus exploit the streams of business information. However, these strategies obviously have to coexist and comply with the existing software architecture solutions and legacy systems. In this paper we describe our experience in evolving a core banking Enterprise Architecture (EA), leveraging real time business information processing and exploitation.

The work presented in this paper has been carried out in the context of the Center for Open Middleware (COM), a joint technology center created in 2011 by Santander Bank (together with its technological and operational divisions ISBAN and PRODUBAN) and Universidad Politécnica de Madrid. COM is the incubator of an open software ecosystem aiming at developing middleware solutions and experimenting with new software architecture approaches.

There are different technologies hosted under the COM umbrella and one of the key ones is an EA called BankSphere (BKS). Created by the Santander Group, BKS is a set of integrated design tools, and a deployment and runtime environment that speeds up the development of new bank software such as applications for customers, call center staff or bank branch workers. It provides great flexibility and control, thus saving time, resources and money. Since its introduction, BKS has constantly evolved to fulfil Santander requirements, and it is now required to enhance the generation and exploitation of real time business information.

In this paper we present our findings on how to introduce an event-oriented approach, architectures, tools and technologies and their potential application and integration into a core banking EA. Specifically, we describe how to incorporate and use real time business information in the BKS context, identifying the key elements necessary and integrating them into BKS, while minimizing interference with the existing architecture and procedures.

The remainder of this paper is structured as follows. Section 2 covers related work and puts our work in perspective. Section 3 gives an overview of the background of EDA's main concepts. In Sect. 4 we present a high level description of the BKS characteristics and architecture. Then, we address and detail the proposed solutions to introduce EDA in BKS in Sect. 5. It includes the definition of business events; the design of a reference architecture, which identifies the integration points with the specific EA, and the description of the initial governance approach to manage the new elements. Section 6 describe an operational validation though a case study and a non-functional validation focussing on performance. Specifically, we describe the evaluation of two main metrics: throughput (messages per second supported) and latency (delay experienced by the messages). Finally, Sect. 7 concludes the paper and introduces areas of future research.

## 2 Related Work

Diverse studies have tackled the introduction of business events in existing architectures of different domains. Most of them describe general approaches for EDA and SOA integration such as [1, 2] or [3], while others address only the specific issues of EDA integration such as modelling, simulation, methodologies, performance, etc. For example, [4] proposes an EDA modelling notation and its associated simulation language; [5] describes a unified event ontology and a methodology for event-driven business processes; and [6] explains a business-oriented development methodology for event processing.

The papers reviewed provide the theoretical basis to evolve EAs towards the EDA paradigm. Most of them include a validation exercise through a case study in the field of application. However, these case studies are usually academic or simplified examples, not practical experiences for real-world EAs, since most companies, and banks in particular, do not usually publish the evolution experiences of their core EA.

Our contributions focus on this last point, a real-world EA evolution and its associated solutions, which we think are of the utmost interest for engineers and practitioners.

## 3 Event Driven Architecture

EDA is a software architecture style based on multiple entities communicating asynchronously via announcements or notifications, known as events [7]. Instead of the traditional synchronous, request-response interaction model, where a requestor asks for services or messages and waits for an answer from a replier; in EDA, events are transmitted in a fire-and-forget mode. In other words, events are communicated without a previous request and without being concerned about what happens with them afterwards.

Basically, an event is a change in a state within a particular system or domain that merits attention from other systems [2]. The term has been given other meanings, depending on the context. It can refer to the actual occurrences (the things that have happened), which are also known as instances of a particular type of event. On the other hand, we can use 'event' or 'notification' to specify the particular communication of an event instance. Generally, the word 'event' is used in both cases without distinction. We will use 'event instance' or 'event notification' where its distinction is relevant.

We can think about different types of event taking place in a company, such as events related to low-level technical information, software activity, user actions or business data. Furthermore, we may also consider events happening outside the company (e.g. stock markets, social networks or any other data sources). By way of example, low-level technical events can be information from sensors, ATM status, network data or activity in many other devices. Software events can indicate calls to methods, execution of services or exceptions in the execution of a program or a process. We may understand user events as actions or information generated by both customers and workers of a company. Finally, this paper focuses on business events.

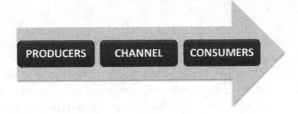

**Fig. 1.** Generic EDA layers.

These events are generated by the core company activities and represent relevant information that has an impact on its economic development and management. For instance, in a financial institution, business events can derive from the registration of new customers, canceling of services, money withdrawals, or the contracting of products such as credits, mortgages, etc.

A generic EDA is made up of three core layers: producers, channel and consumers (Fig. 1). The process begins at the producer layer, detecting, creating and sending events through a channel, and ends when consumers receive these event notifications and carry out a specific task (automatically or with human intervention).

Producers can contain a software subcomponent called preprocessor to add intelligence to the event publication. It can carry out different tasks such as, filter, prioritize or homogenize the produced events. Thus, only the most relevant events will be sent or all event notifications will have the same format.

The channel is responsible for transporting event notifications between producers and all associated consumers. It usually takes the form of a Message Oriented Middleware (MOM) [8], which is a software infrastructure that can send and receive messages between distributed systems, regardless of platforms, technologies and resources used.

A MOM can use different messaging models such as point-to-point or publish/subscribe. In the first model, only one consumer receives a particular event notification, while in the second, more than one consumer may express their interest in a set or subset of event types, in order to be notified when a producer generates their registered interest [9]. Technically, it is usually achieved thanks to an intermediary entity known as broker that receives all event notifications from producers and routes them to the subscribed consumers, using queues that store event notifications if necessary.

There are three characteristic examples of standards for MOM that implement the publish/subscribe model: the Data Distribution Service for Real-Time Systems (DDS) [10]; the Java Message Service (JMS) [11]; and the Advanced Message Queuing Protocol (AMQP) [12].

DDS was created by the Object Management Group (OMG) and is the first middleware standard that defines publish/subscribe messaging model for real time and embedded systems. It supports a lot of Quality of Service (QoS) policies to control many aspects of data delivery and quality and provides a robust architecture. However, DDS has few open source implementations. For its part, JMS is a widely used Java MOM API from Sun Microsystems but it is not a messaging system in itself. JMS only defines the interfaces and classes needed to communicate two Java applications and does not include the specification of brokers or queuing systems. Finally, AMQP is an open standard protocol for MOM, originated in the financial services industry in 2006. It enables client applications to communicate (sent or received messages) with messaging brokers, using messaging queues.

On the other hand, consumers can be any entity such as software components, applications or systems that react to the received notifications. For example, consumers can create new event notifications, invoke a service, initialize a business process, increase a value or notify humans to carry out manual tasks. There is a special kind of consumer that is known as an event processing engine, which encompasses the set of computational procedures to carry out operations with events such as reading, creation, transformation, deletion or correlation [13]. Because of its importance, it is frequently considered as an independent layer in EDA.

There are three styles of event processing which may be used together [14]: simple, stream and complex. The former is the most basic process: an event is received and it produces an action. On the other hand, Event Stream Processing (ESP) [15] continually receives all kinds of events (ordinary and notable) and, through established rules or queries on the flow of data, it decides whether or not to forward events (or information on them) to other consumers. Finally, Complex Event Processing (CEP) [16] relates different event types from various sources to produce new events or extract relevant information.

# 4  BKS Banking Service Platform

BKS is a set of development tools created by the Santander Group that allows programmers to create new banking applications quickly. It includes a design framework integrated with the Eclipse IDE, and a deployment and runtime environment based on Java Enterprise solutions and web technologies.

BKS has been designed to allow the reuse of software components and simple, fast programming. The former is achieved through its Service Oriented Architecture (SOA)-like approach, where pieces of software are developed and exposed to be reused by other components. The latter is carried out by using a visual programming environment which allows programmers to design applications through usable graphical user interfaces (GUI). It hides the code details and lets programmers to use graphic symbols that represent software components.

Simply put, BKS programmers can create presentation and business flows by reusing previously implemented software components. The business flows are exposed by a facade and can be used to create banking applications. An application is usually constituted by a main presentation flow that calls different business flows, which in turn call backend operations or services.

A BKS application is typically turned into a Java Enterprise Edition application, exposing the application through a web module (WAR) and implementing the business logic through various Enterprise Java Beans (EJB). It is then executed in a runtime environment provided by BKS.

The execution of BKS applications at runtime is as follows (Fig. 2). First, a request for an application is detected and redirected to the operation container. It invokes different initial operations and the states defined by the presentation flow. These states can call business flows through a common facade. At this point, the execution entails invoking backend operations and external components defined by the business logic. Finally, the request ends when all presentation states have been executed and the control is returned to the user.

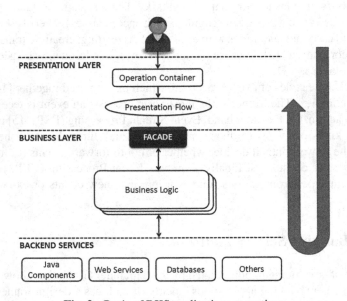

**Fig. 2.** Basis of BKS applications at runtime.

# 5    Proposed Solutions

In the previous sections we have reviewed the foundations of EDA and the main features of BKS. Converging on a solution that brings the best of these architectures requires extending current BKS capabilities and identifying the key integration points that interfere minimally in the existing architecture and the associated procedures.

We include the proposed solutions to evolve an EA towards the EDA paradigm in the following subsections. The specific results are: the definition of the new banking business events; the design of a reference architecture to integrate EDA that allows business event generation and exploitation and identifies the specific integration points with BKS; and finally, a description of the initial governance approach to manage the new EDA elements.

## 5.1    Business Event Definition

The event definition entails deciding what semantic and data each event instance must contain, and which data-exchange format is assigned to event notifications. Given that there is no standard or a generally adopted event format, and there is a huge variety of business event types with different meanings and aims, the event definition is one of the most problematic issues in EDA integration.

We have carried out a study with the possible alternatives that are used or can be used to communicate and later, process business events, concluding with the following:

- There is a wide range of event definitions in different formats that addresses specific issues in a company and changes depending on the purpose of the event, the domain, or the business layer [17].
- Event notifications can be implemented by any data-exchange format such as XML, JSON, Google Protocol Buffers, CSV, ASN.1 or Hessian [18] and [19].
- Event processing engines can use Java Objects, expressions or JSON-based or tag-delimited languages to represent events [13].

Moreover, we have examined several initiatives proposed in the field of web services, such as the WS-EventDescription [20] or the WS-Notification [21]. They are not specific event definitions and cover the description of communication protocols between web services. Events in other domains, for example the specification Activity Streams [22] for social web application, have also been reviewed.

Clearly, there is no agreement on how to represent event-related information and some solutions can be used either jointly or separately. However, there is a trend towards formats that allow the inclusion of two differentiated parts: header and body [13, 14]. The header includes metadata information: generic event information such as the name, identifier, occurrence time or producer identification, or can describe the event type. On the other hand, the body or payload contains the specific data on the event instance.

We have decided to follow the aforementioned structure using XML as the representation format. We have defined a general XML Schema Definition (XSD) that contains the basic structure for all the event types we are managing (Fig. 3).

In our structure, the header has three basic elements common to all events:

- eventType: indicates the type of event according to the hierarchy of the Santander Group's business event catalogue. It has an attribute denominated as a category that specifies the nature or domain of the event and the value is a text string that contains two parts separated by a dot, indicating the business area and the specific type.
- createdTime: contains the timestamp of an event occurrence.
- createdBy: identifies the event producer that generates the event.

The body is limited by an element called logRecordAppData that contains a reference to other separated XSD. There is an XSD for each event type and each of them describes the specific data of an event type. It is important to highlight that we have divided the header and body definitions into different XSDs to allow specialized actors to handle a specific part.

## 5.2   Reference Architecture

An EDA process starts with the detection and creation of events. Although BKS does not include any EDA layers, it uses relevant business information that can be mapped to banking business events. As a result, event producers have been detected as the only integration point between EDA and BKS architectures (Fig. 4).

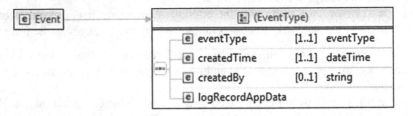

**Fig. 3.** XML event definition.

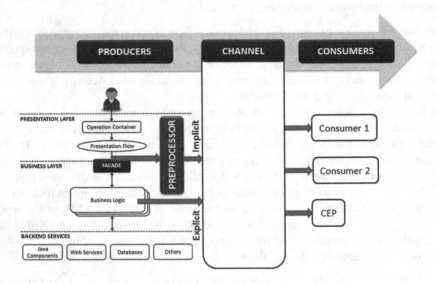

**Fig. 4.** EDA integration with BKS.

We have detected two main ways of incorporating event producers in BKS applications: explicit and implicit.

– *Explicit.* BKS programmers must include a call to an event producer component to generate business events, configuring the exact values for the business event instance. In other words, they have to decide where to include the creation of the event within the business logic and moreover, obtain the context data that corresponds to event instances.

This solution has several drawbacks. First, programmers have to acquire new responsibilities and understand new concepts related to business areas that differ from their daily technical work. Secondly, this incorporation into existing banking applications, which are currently in production, implies their modification and can entail risks in stable applications.

– *Implicit.* Here, the incorporation of event producers is almost transparent for programmers. They are strictly limited to defining the business logic and the business event generation is associated with calls to business flows.

The main disadvantage of this solution is the low quality of the generated events. They correspond to calls to functional business methods but they do not necessarily tie in with business event definitions. To solve this last point, a preprocessor can be included. It can create real business events based on execution traces obtained from calls to the facade. However, it requires an in-depth analysis of the context and each functional component to be related to business events.

Both alternatives can coexist in BKS. We have specifically proposed to use explicit business event generation for new BKS applications and implicit generation for existing applications.

The remaining of the EDA layers (channel and consumers) will be new elements in BKS. At present, BKS already incorporates a stable commercial messaging system for logging the application. It allows execution traces to be stored in a database to be batch processed. Therefore, a MOM that allows the publish/subscribe model to distribute business events in real time has to be incorporated.

## 5.3  Governance Approach

The incorporation of EDA elements in BKS entails the creation of new operational and organizational processes that allow the Santander Bank to govern business events. Governance is a wide discipline that can be applied on multiple perspectives of a company such as that related to EA, IT, data, business or SOA [23]. Basically, it seeks to define a global structure for establishing and ensuring how the company resources sustain and extend the organization strategies. To begin with, we have identified the organizational processes involved in the creation, use and reuse of business events in the BKS context. This new process has been called event lifecycle and has been defined according to the existing procedures in the bank.

The event lifecycle (Fig. 5) describes the different activities or tasks that must be carried out in design time to define, incorporate and use business events generated by applications. In previous sections, we noticed that BKS programmers know the functional specification and logical model of their applications. However, they ignore the business value of their components. Consequently, other stakeholders must participate.

We have identified four main actors in the event lifecycle: the project leader of an event-oriented application that wants to use a specific event, the project leader responsible for the BKS application that generates the event and the corresponding programmers of each project. Members of the quality department participate in approving the different stages.

The lifecycle starts with an identification stage: the event-oriented project leader detects the need to consume a specific business event to take advantage of it and examines whether the specific banking business event exists. If it is already incorporated into any BKS application, a subscription to this event is made. Otherwise the new event is defined.

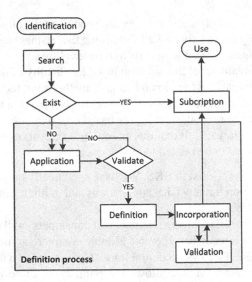

**Fig. 5.**  Event lifecycle.

The definition process begins with a formal request for the incorporation of a new business event (application stage). The request goes through a validation stage and if approved, the event is defined and incorporated into a BKS application. The quality department validates this last step again. The definition process ends with the event subscription and use.

# 6  Validation

In order to validate the previous solutions, we have developed a proof-of-concept test bed in an open source environment. It incorporates several event producers, a MOM, a CEP, and different event consumers that give shape to a banking case study. The case study supports the operational validation of our contributions as well as the evaluation of some non-functional aspects, such as performance.

## 6.1  Case Study

The case study consists of a wire transfer scenario whose aim is to demonstrate the feasibility of the proposed solutions and the value added to the business by EDA. The scenario takes into account Santander customers who are sending and receiving money from the same bank or others. It must incorporate the technologies and mechanisms that allow the detection, distribution and use of the associated business events. Moreover, it must show any of the multiple possibilities for exploiting these events in real time.

We have identified two main business event types: sent wire transfer and received wire transfer. The former represents the events of orders that Santander customers carry out to transfer a certain amount of money to other bank institutions. Conversely, received wire transfers are orders from customers of other banks to Santander customers. Each event type contains the specified header and the following information in the body: session identification, IP address, source account, target account and amount of the transfer.

Our scenario includes the following logical entities (Fig. 6):

- Two event producers. Each of them generates a different business event for wire transfers and publishes it through a MOM.
- One MOM distributes the received events to all the associated consumers.
- A CEP acts as a consumer and receives all the previous events. It extracts relevant information and displays it in a visualization dashboard. Moreover, if applicable, it generates a new event type that indicates that an individual (not a corporate entity) has received a wire transfer above a threshold. This new event type is called user alert.
- An application displaying a wire transfer dashboard that shows relevant information on the business events of sent and received wire transfers.
- Two consumers that react to the user alert event. One of them is a simulation of a Customer Relationship Management (CRM) that displays records of the wire transfers received by Santander users. Moreover, it can manage, assign and create alerts to call-center software with the aim of carrying out commercial actions. The other consumer is a user notification system that sends mails and/or Short Message Service (SMS) to Santander users that have activated the real time notification service to be informed about their transactions.

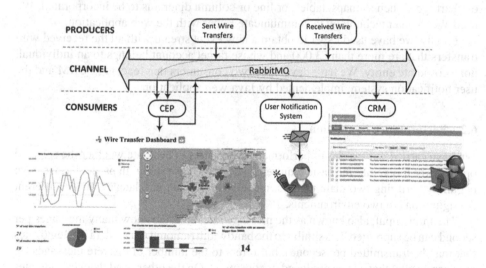

**Fig. 6.** Architecture of the case study.

We have developed the previous components using open source tools and applications, and the Java programming language. Event producers have been entirely implemented as Java preprocessors that use information from different BKS applications. They generate event notifications based on the proposed XML event definition for sent and received wire transfers and publish them through a channel.

The channel is implemented by an open source MOM called RabbitMQ [24] that supports the AMQP in its 0.9.1 version. AMQP covers different messaging models such as publish/subscribe. Its main advantage is to be interoperable, thus allowing consumers and producers to use any programming language or data format.

As regards the CEP consumer, we have selected an open source solution available for Java such as Esper, and for.NET such as NEsper [25]. It allows large volumes of events to be processed by applying ESP and CEP. Basically, Esper allows applications to store queries and run the event streams through to obtain information or new event streams. Queries are written using Event Processing Language (EPL) [13] and [26] that is similar to the Structure Query Language (SQL) of databases. The differences are: the queries are carried out through an event stream, the data available for querying within the stream is defined by views and the basic units of data are events and their specific information.

We have obtained information on the received events with EPL queries such as the total number of sent or received transfers, the accumulated amount or the amounts per second for each event type. We also have drawn up a ranking of the top five banks for the most sent accumulated amounts. We extract extra information on the received events by carrying out an enrichment process. Thus, we have located the source of the transfers. In particular, the associated Santander bank branches that are the source or destination of transfers.

All the previous information has been displayed in a web application called Wire Transfer Dashboard. We have implemented it using the Google Charts that allow a lot of chart types such as maps, tables, or line or column diagrams to be incorporated. We used WebSocket technology to communicate Esper with the web application.

Finally, we have used Esper to obtain a new event stream with all the received wire transfers that are more than €3,000 and whose target account belongs to an individual, not a corporate entity. We have developed two consumers that react to it: CRM and the user notification system, implemented by Java web applications.

## 6.2 Performance Evaluation

We have carried out a series of performance measures to evaluate whether the selected open source tools fulfil the basic requirements for our case study. In particular, we have begun by verifying two main metrics, namely throughput and latency, using different configurations in two environments.

The throughput, also known as the message rate, measures how many messages per second can be supported. It is similar to the bandwidth (amount of raw data in MegaBytes that may be transmitted per second), but refers to the number of discrete messages (in our case events) that can be produced or consumed. On the other hand, latency indicates the delay experienced by messages from producers to consumers. Generally, latency is explained from the channel point of view, but producers and consumers can also interfere, depending on how the environment is configured. In our performance evaluation, we have considered production and consumption rates of throughput and latency.

The measures were repeated using different persistency configurations. Specifically, we dealt with persistent and non-persistent messages. The former guarantees that a message will not be lost, and so it could survive a crash in the EDA layers. To ensure it, producers have to flag the messages as persistent before publishing, and the broker components have to be configured as durable [27]. Durability is a similar concept to persistence but applied to RabbitMQ components. By default, these components are transient or non-durable and therefore, they do not survive reboots and could be lost on failovers.

We have compared the performance of the two types of message in different scenarios. First, we considered a real time scenario, in which one producer publishes events and one consumer reacts to them as soon as they arrive. We have called it *scenario 1:1*. Moreover, we have also defined a *scenario 1:n* in which more than one consumer has participated. In this case, the variable n indicates the number of consumers in the different tests.

We have worked with two different environments to compare the results. First, we used two virtual machines, one hosts the messaging broker and another hosts the consumers and producers. In this environment each machine has an Intel Xeon E5520 @2.27 GHz × 4 core processor, running 2 GB RAM, 30 GB disk capacity and Ubuntu 12.04 LTS, 64 bit server. The virtual machines are hosted in a shared network of the university. The second environment includes two physical machines with greater features, an Intel Core i7-3720Q @2.60 GHz × 8 core processor, 16 GB RAM and 80 GB disk capacity, running in an isolated network.

In the following subsections we will describe the different tests carried out in each scenario and the results obtained. It is important to point out that each test was run three times and that the measures obtained were averaged.

**Scenario 1:1.** It is the more general case in which there is only one producer and one consumer, publishing and receiving messages, respectively.

We have carried out different tests to check how the production and consumption throughput varies with the message size in the described environments. First, we performed an in-depth test in which a producer sent bursts of ten thousand messages through the broker to a producer. We repeated the test increasing the message payload

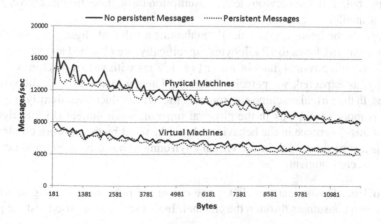

**Fig. 7.** Throughput for producers in scenario 1:1.

from 181 bytes to 12 kilobytes with a 120 byte interval. The tests were repeated for both the persistent and non-persistent configurations, and in both the virtual and physical environments.

Figure 7 summarizes the results for the throughput of producers, which are very similar but a little lower for consumers. The observed throughput decreases when the message size increases. There is also a notable difference between using virtual or physical machines.

Based on the analysis of the business events managed by Santander, we estimated that the payload of our messages (event notifications) would be between 2 and 5 kilobytes. For these figures, we observe that the throughput is greater than 4,000 messages per second in both cases (virtual and physical environments), doubling the amount in the physical machines.

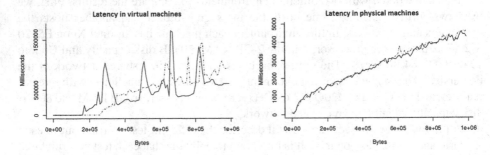

**Fig. 8.** Latency in the different environments, scenario 1:1.

In addition to the previous tests, we continued increasing the message size until the saturation throughput was reached. In the virtual-machine environment, we observed steady values of around 100 messages per second, for message sizes of 100 kilobytes and over. For the case of physical machines, we identified the message size of 600 kilobytes as the saturation point. Here, the throughput falls to 200 messages per second and it is almost stable for bigger messages. The previous values are production throughput but, as in the previous test, consumption throughput figures are very similar but with a smaller difference.

As regards the latency, it practically maintains a value of slightly above 100 ms in the range from 181 bytes to 12 kilobytes. Specifically, we obtained an average delay of 119–125 ms with physical machines and 148–158 ms with virtual machines.

Finally, as expected, we perceived that the latency increases with the size of the messages. In the virtual machine environment the latency fluctuates sharply (Fig. 8, left) while it is more continuous in the physical machine environment (Fig. 8, right). We think that this difference in the behavior is brought about by the network configuration, since it is a shared network in the virtual environment but it is an isolated network in the physical environment.

**Scenario 1:n.** This scenario includes one consumer publishing messages, which are delivered to n consumers through the channel. In this scenario we used just the physical machine environment, since the goal was to understand how many consumers can be hosted in the same machine.

As in the previous scenario, we varied the size of the messages and calculated the throughput and latency in each consumer. However, we have reduced the number of sizes and increased the number of sent messages for each size. Specifically, the producer published 40,000 messages for each of the four message sizes tested, namely 1 byte, 1 kilobyte, 10 kilobytes, and 1 megabyte.

We started by executing a test with one producer and one consumer, and we increased the number of consumers iteratively at the end of each test. We detected the saturation of the scenario with 6 consumers, when the machines crashed.

The throughput drops when a consumer is added to the scenario. It is more pronounced in the case of using persistent messages (Fig. 9, right) than non-persistent messages (Fig. 9, right).

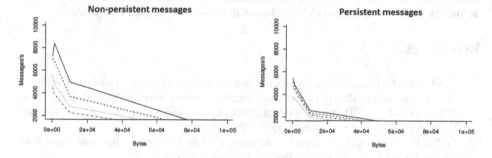

**Fig. 9.** Throughput for consumers, scenario 1:5.

The results obtained are within the target range of message payload (2-5 kilobytes) and therefore, they suggest that RabbitMQ can be applied in BKS. Moreover, although using physical machines would cover larger amounts of events, virtual machines do also meet our requirements, providing greater flexibility and adaptation to variable conditions.

# 7  Conclusions

We have analyzed how to introduce business event streams in a legacy, core banking architecture, and have described our practical experience on this journey. Supporting business event processing at an architectural level, would allow programmers to create software bank applications quickly, efficiently and proving high performance. In turn, this architectural evolution would support traditional commercial and retail banks in dealing better with new entrants in the banking domain by leveraging business event exploitation.

We have analyzed the technical challenges that this integration involves, and have proposed a set of solutions to meet them, including a business event definition based on an XML structure with our own semantic; a reference architecture to integrate business events generation, notification and processing that identifies the specific integration points with the core banking EA; the definition of an event lifecycle that allows the incorporation and use of business events without interfering with the existing legacy infrastructure; and the related governance processes. These solutions have been successfully validated in a proof-of-concept test bed that uses open source tools. Furthermore, we have carried a performance evaluation of the selected tools to understand whether they would meet the bank quality requirements.

Since our first results have demonstrated the workability of our approach, the future points towards a further analysis the governance approach. A core banking architecture requires solutions that allow the cataloguing and managing of events to optimize their production, reuse and consumption. The monitoring of events and their lifecycle will also ensure the consistency of the solution.

**Acknowledgements.** The work presented in this paper has been carried out in the context of the Center for Open Middleware (COM), a joint technology center created by Universidad Politécnica de Madrid, Banco Santander and its technological divisions ISBAN and PRODUBAN.

# References

1. Malekzadeh, B.: Event-Driven Architecture and SOA in collaboration - A study of how Event-Driven Architecture (EDA) interacts and functions within Service-Oriented Architecture (SOA). Master of Thesis in IT-Management, Department of Applied Information Technology, University of GothenBurg (2010)
2. Taylor, H., Yochem, A., Phillips, L., Martinez, F.: Event-Driven Architecture: How SOA Enables the Real Time Enterprise. Pearson Education, Boston (2009)
3. Marechaux, J.L.: Combining Service-Oriented Architecture and Event-Driven Architecture using an Enterprise Service Bus. Technical report, IBM Developer Works (2006)
4. Clark, T., Barn, B.S.: A Common basis for modelling service-oriented and event-driven architecture. In: 5th India Software Engineering Conference, pp. 23–32. ACM, New York (2012)
5. Weigand, H.: The pragmatics of event-driven business processes. In: 7th International Conference on Semantic Systems, pp. 211–218. ACM, New York (2011)
6. Vidackovic, K., Kellner, I., Donald, J.: Business-oriented development methodology for complex event processing: demonstration of an integrated approach for process monitoring. In: 4th ACM International Conference on Distributed Event-Based Systems, pp. 111–112. ACM, New York (2010)
7. Levina, O. H., Stantchev, V.: Realizing event-driven SOA. In: 4th International Conference on Internet and Web Applications and Services, pp. 37–42. IEEE, Washington (2009)
8. Snyder, B., Bosanac, D., Davies, R.: ActiveMQ in Action. Manning Publications, Stamford (2011)
9. Eugster, P., Felver, P., Guerraoui, R., Kermarrec, A.: The many faces of publish/subscribe. J. ACM Comput. Surv. **35**(2), 114–131 (2003)
10. Data Distribution Service Portal. http://portals.omg.org/dds/
11. Oracle, Java Message Service Specification - version 1.1. http://www.oracle.com/technetwork/java/docs-136352.html
12. AMQP, Advanced Message Queuing Protocol. http://www.amqp.org/
13. Etzion, O., Niblett, P.: Event Processing in Action. Manning Publications, Greenwich (2010)

14. Michelson, B.M.: Event-Driven Architecture Overview – Event-Driven SOA Is Just Part of the EDA Story. Technical report, Patricia Seybold Group (2006)
15. Cugola, G., Margara, A.: Processing flows of information: From data stream to complex event processing. J. ACM Comput. Surv. **44**(3), 15 (2012)
16. Hurwitz, J., Nugent, A., Halper, F., Kaufman, M.: Big Data For Dummies. Wiley, For Dummies (2013)
17. Becker, J., Matzner, M., Müller, O., Walter, M.: A review of event formats as enablers of event-driven BPM. Bus. Inf. Process. **99**, 433–445 (2012)
18. Aihkisalo, T.: A performance comparison of web service object marshalling and unmarshalling solutions. In: 2011 IEEE World congress on Services, pp. 122–129. IEEE, Washington (2011)
19. Maeda, K.: Performance evaluation of object serialization libraries in XML, JSON and binary formats. In: 2st International Conference on Digital Information and Communication Technology and it's Applications, pp. 177–182. IEEE, Bangkok (2012)
20. Davis, D., Malhotra, A., Warr, K., Chou, W.: Web Services Event Descriptions (WS-EventDescriptions). W3C Recommendation, World Wide Web Consortium (2011)
21. OASIS Web Services Notification (WSN) TC. https://www.oasis-open.org/committees/tc_home.php?wg_abbrev=wsn
22. Activity Streams. http://activitystrea.ms/
23. Brown, W.A., Laird, R.G., Gee, C., Mitra, T.: SOA Governance. Pearson Education, Boston (2009)
24. RabbitMQ, Messaging that just works. http://www.rabbitmq.com/
25. EsperTech, Event Series Intelligence: Esper & NEsper. http://esper.codehaus.org/
26. Davis, J.: Open Source SOA. Manning Publications, Greenwich (2009)
27. Videla, A., Williams, J.W.: RabbitMQ in Action: Distributed Messaging for Everyone. Manning Publications, New York (2012)

# PRIMROSe: A Graph-Based Approach for Enterprise Architecture Analysis

David Naranjo$^{(\boxtimes)}$, Mario Sánchez, and Jorge Villalobos

Universidad de los Andes, Bogotá, Colombia
{da-naran,da-naran,jvillalo}@uniandes.edu.co
http://ticsw.uniandes.edu.co/

**Abstract.** Enterprise Models are the central asset that supports Enterprise Architecture, as they embody enterprise and IT knowledge and decisions. Static analysis over this kind of models is made by inspecting certain properties and patterns, with the goal of gaining understanding and support decision making through evidence. However, this is not a straightforward process, as the model in its raw form is rarely suitable for analysis due to its complexity and size. As a consequence, current approaches focus on partial views and queries over this model, leading to partial assessments of the architecture. In this paper, we propose a different approach to EA analysis, which consists on the *incremental* assessment of the architecture based on the interaction of the user with visualizations of the whole model. We implemented our approach in a visual analysis tool, PRIMROSe, where analysts can rapidly prototype custom functions that operate on topological or semantic properties of the model, combine partial insights for sounder assessments, associate these findings to visual attributes, and interact with the model using multiple visualization techniques.

**Keywords:** Enterprise architecture · Visual analysis · Enterprise models · Model analysis

## 1 Introduction

Thirty years since its inception, Enterprise Architecture (EA) has evolved from a method for reconciling business and IT to a relatively mature discipline. Enterprise Modelling is one of the subjects where EA can deliver real value on the organization, and consists on the development of Enterprise Models (EMs), which are the embodiment of all the collected information about the enterprise under several perspectives. Building EMs typically comes with a high price tag that is payed for when they are analyzed, that is, when additional knowledge is created by processing and reworking previously defined facts [1]. The knowledge gained from analyzing EMs serves to support decision making processes in architectural and stakeholders boards, and to lower risk.

A very important concern with analysis is that it is far from being a trivial task. Most of the times, analyzing an EM involves the formulation and reformulation of hypotheses, as well as the composition of different insights in order to get

© Springer International Publishing Switzerland 2015
J. Cordeiro et al. (Eds.): ICEIS 2014, LNBIP 227, pp. 434–452, 2015.
DOI: 10.1007/978-3-319-22348-3_24

to sound assessments. Furthermore, the scope of analysis processes is arbitrary and not necessarily known *a priori*. It may range from a full-fledged impact analysis over the entire model, to an in-depth analysis on a specific domain where issues were detected during the early stages of the analysis process. For instance, if an analyst needs to assess the business process architecture of an enterprise, he would use a pertinent and proven method (e.g. Flow Analysis) for this evaluation, which differs from say, a security (e.g. vulnerability) assessment. Furthermore, it would be a good idea to use a combination of several methods, in order to arrive to more powerful insights.

On top of that, the reasoning process behind an analysis is rarely expressed and documented because it heavily depends on the experience of the analyst. This lack of a traceability mechanism forces the analyst to guess the rationale behind past decisions.

Also, we have to take into account that EA modelling tools offer different features and thus restrict the kind of analysis that they support [2]. Some of the characteristics that result in limitations include (a) the modelling approach, (b) the metamodels supported, and (c) their analytical capabilities, which range from model conformity checks to generation of pre-defined views and the possibility to query the model.

Given known and important characteristics of EMs, such as being large, complex, typed, and structural in nature [3], visualizations are becoming more and more used to support analysis methods. However, most modelling tools only provide the capacity to visualize (by means of diagrams or views) partial models that are subsets of an EM. While there is the notion of an integration of these views to form an unified model, it is rarely possible to apply analysis techniques over the whole EM.

The problem with this, as evidence suggests, is that applying analysis without an overview of the whole model can possibly lead to information loss and reaching false conclusions [4]. Furthermore, interactive exploration of the large volumes of data by visual means, appears to be "... useful when a person simply does not know what questions to ask about the data or when the person wants to ask better, more meaningful questions" [5]. This precisely reflects what precedes most ad-hoc analyses and explains why visualizations are progressively considered less as a product (diagrams) than a medium.

Taking into account the issues discussed above, we consider that a platform that enables structural analysis of EMs, and is supported by its visual exploration and interaction, can facilitate the tasks of an analyst. Thus, we can formulate our research question as follows: *How can we provide an useful and flexible method for inspecting facts on an Enterprise Model, and what is the architecture behind an analysis tool that supports the visualization of the whole model, displaying these facts incrementally?*

The goal of this paper is to present a conceptual framework –and a tool that implements it– that addresses these issues. This framework supports the formulation of analytical functions that enrich the model, and allows their visualization through an extensible set of visualization techniques. This work is based on the usage of Overview Visualizations that display the underlying topology of an Enterprise Model and help the analyst to incrementally find new structural properties and patterns. This conceptual framework was implemented in PRIM-ROSe, an advanced platform for the analysis of metamodel-independent EMs, which provides feedback continuously as new insights are generated during an analysis process.

The structure of this paper is as follows: First, in Sect. 2, we make a short literature review of similar approaches. Section 3 offers an overview of our approach, followed by Sect. 4, which provides its conceptual framework. Section 5 describes the architecture and implementation of PRIMROSe, and Sect. 6, illustrates the use of the tool with an ArchiMate model. Finally, Sect. 7 will discuss results and future steps.

## 2    Related Work

In general, EA Visual Analysis is grounded in the wide array of previous work in Software Visualization. Of interest is the work of Panas et al. [6], where the authors describe a framework and architecture for the configuration of model-to-view and view-to-scene transformations using a graph-based approach. Based on the relation between visual attributes and views, the authors start from a model graph, which is translated almost directly to a view graph by filtering unused properties from the model. The authors also introduce Visual Metaphors as a collection of common Visual Representations, i.e. families of visual objects fitting together. These metaphors are used to visualize properties of a model, using techniques such as graphs, trees, or more complex 3D representations (e.g. city maps).

This framework, however, only deals with visualization: it requires a pre-processing of the model that is left to the user. Moreover, its focus lies on the visual analysis of vertices of the graph, giving edges the same importance. This is a downside, taking into account that EA Analysis is pretty much based on relationships [3]. Finally, the process is one-way: it is not clear how to travel the way back from visualization to further analysis.

Chan et al. [7] describe a Visual Analysis tool for bottom-up enterprise analysis, based on the incremental reconstruction of hierarchical data. Analysis is made by the exploration of the model, starting with an initial view of an entity, and adding elements to a graph visualization by selecting concepts and relations in the metamodel. This is complemented with a set of filtering, searching, and abstraction methods. This bottom-up exploration is useful to manage the complexity of models, and can be a complement to top-down analysis. A downside of this approach is that it assumes that the analyst knows where to start, which is a problem in models that span thousands of elements. Furthermore, earlier processing and analysis is again a prerequisite, and there is no integration with graphical frameworks.

In the field of Model Driven Engineering, the Eclipse Foundation presents Zest [8], a library that aims to amplifiy the visual capabilities of modeling editors. Built on top of the Graphical Editing Framework, it offers a family of graph layouts, such as Spring, Tree, Radial and Grid algorithms. The library allows the processing of a model graph, operating in terms of the attributes of the model elements. Also, it can selectively highlight elements and relations by developing *view operations* that modify visual attributes. A disadvantage, however, is that each view must be developed from scratch. While the authors focus on an easily to program framework, there is no explicit way to compose and process independent view operations depending on the outcome of an analysis.

Recent approaches on the Visual Analysis of EA focus on view-based modelling and analysis. Buckl et al. and Schaub et al. [9,10] describe the conceptual framework and requirements behind the generation of domain independent interactive visualizations that comply to predefined stakeholder Viewpoints, linking an abstract View Model with the EA Information Model. With a focus on non-technological stakeholders, the authors provide a tool [11] that allows the design of *ad hoc* visualizations that filter the model taking into account aspects such as access rights of a stakeholder to the information.

In [12], Roth et al. further enhance this framework with a pattern matching algorithm that supports the mapping of information and view models, based on the information demand and offering. The tool provides a set of configurable visualization techniques, such as a Gantt Charts, Matrices, Bubble Charts, and Cluster Maps. While this allows the analysis of the Enterprise Model by non-technical business experts, it makes difficult to provide flexible and specialized analysis to architects. As described in Sect. 1, the generation of these views deal with the communication of the architecture.

In summary, there are some aspects that current research is not addressing, leaving a gap in the field of Enterprise Model Analysis:

- We could not find approaches that allow the composition/combination of different analysis methods, i.e. incremental processing of the model by operating on previous analysis routines.
- Approaches seldom provide a clear division between analysis and visualization, the latter commonly being just a product of the analysis, e.g. diagrams, instead of a medium for interactive analysis.
- Support for *ad-hoc* analysis is limited, and often implies the development of tailored analysis tools from scratch.
- We could not find approaches that take full advantage of the several topological properties of Enterprise Models seen as networks/graphs, such as the differentiation of relations between elements, discovery of paths, clusters, or graph metrics.
- Current approaches are often tied to a concrete graphical library/framework, offering a limited set of visualization techniques. In addition, the composition of several techniques on the same representation is not possible.

## 3   Visual Analysis of EA Models

Visual Analysis takes advantage of the ability of people to discover patterns easily, and revolves around giving shape - or *Finding the Gestalt* [13]- of information, in order to uncover outliers, bad smells, and interesting or unusual groups/clusters. In this aspect, the human visual system is one of the most sophisticated in nature, and shape is one of the most important visual attributes to characterize objects [14].

On the other hand, the complexity of Enterprise Models demands new methods for inspecting their properties and finding interesting facts about them. Thus, Visual Analysis appears as a valuable field with several ideas that we can take advantage of. This section will describe the Visual Analysis process that starts with an Enterprise Model and ends with the results of analysis that derive on assessments about the architecture. This kind of analysis is incremental, and it is guided by the interaction of the analyst with the model.

### 3.1   Visual Exploration and Interaction

In their study about the interactive nature of visualizations, Chi and Riedl [15] provide a conceptual model and a classification of interactive tasks. They propose the notion of operators that transform a data model under a series of stages in a *Visualization Pipeline* (see Fig. 1). This results on a *view* of the data, mediated by *Analytical* and *Visualization* models.

Wickam et al. [16] take this idea further, asserting that any visualization technique has the (often implicit) notion of a pipeline. However, they also mention the fact that this pipeline metaphor breaks down when user interaction is considered: on each transformation stage of the process, user interaction (e.g., grouping, collapsing, zooming) can take the visualization to another transformation step. Thus, instead of being sequential, the Visual Analysis processes operate in a *sense-making loop*, or dialog, between the user and the data in a visual form.

In the context of EA, Schaub et al. [10] describe a conceptual framework with requirements for interactive visualizations of EA models. In particular, the interaction type is selected depending on the type of analysis required. For example, in order to perform 'what-if' analyses, the framework provides the means to generate dynamic views conformant to a viewpoint metamodel, thus aligned to the concerns of a stakeholder and his access to information.

### 3.2   A Process for EA Visual Analysis

At this point we want to make a parallel with the field of Visual Analytics, which can be regarded as the transformation from data to insights by a concatenation of several sub processes, such as visualizing data sets and generating hypothetical models from them.

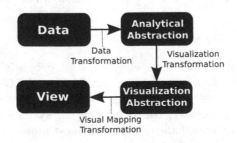

**Fig. 1.** Visualization pipeline from [15].

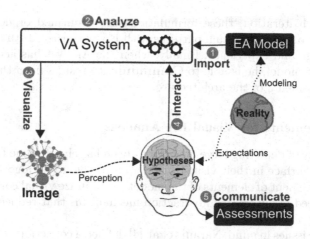

**Fig. 2.** The EA visual analysis process.

Visualization is a semi-automated analytical process, where humans and systems cooperate using their respective distinct capabilities for the most effective results [17]. The user modifies visualization parameters repeatedly [18], allowing the analyst to gain insights by directly interacting with the data, and coming up with new hypotheses that can be validated, again with visual interaction [19].

This process is based on the economic model of visualization proposed by van Wijk [5,20], where a visualization is a time-dependent image (instead of a static one), and a gain in knowledge is based on the perception of the image and knowledge acquired from previous interactions. Inspired by this model, we define EA Visual Analysis as an iterative process between an *Analyst* and a *Visual Analysis System*, where hypotheses are generated and refined by the means of interaction with *Visualizations*.

This process, described in Fig. 2, begins with an **Import** of the Enterprise Model, which is transformed into a graph structure (part of the Analytical Abstraction - see Fig. 1). This model can be **Analyzed**, i.e. processed under a series of *Analytical Functions* that operate in terms of its structure and semantics, adding new knowledge that was not explicitly present in the model. For the first iteration of the process, this stage will be a lightweight processing, as our priority is to visualize and explore the model in its totality.

Posterior to this processing, the analyst is able to **Visualize** the model structure with several *Visualization Techniques*. We use these visual representations as a memory aid to amplify cognition - that means, we transform data into images to derive insights, using pattern recognition from the human visual system to process visual information.

As the analyst starts to **Interact** with visualizations of the model, Hypotheses (which start as expectations, i.e. weak formulations) get refined over time. This interaction modifies the parameters of a visualization, both with view and data operators. These last operators parametrize and activate the Analytical Functions for further processing of the model.

Within each iteration, these formulations are confirmed or denied, as the analyst starts to associate visual patterns with EA patterns [21] that are present from knowledge and experience. Finally, when the Analyst has acquired sound insights on the model, he is able to **Communicate** results from the analysis in terms of Assessments of the architecture.

### 3.3 Requirements for Visual EA Analysis

The complexity of depicting large models has been largely examined, and two key concerns that surface in their visualization are: (a) the use of algorithms for the automatic placement of elements of the model to minimize visual complexity [22], and (b) the need of automated abstraction mechanisms that reduce information overload [23].

With these issues in mind, Naranjo et al. [4] defined a collection of requirements from the Visual and EA Analysis perspectives. By exploring the concept of 'holistic' or 'total' overview visualizations, and in the context of Visual Analysis applied to Enterprise Models, these requirements were used to evaluate the gap between what is currently offered by popular EA modelling tools, and what is possible with general purpose visualization toolkits. EA Analysis Requirements provide the guidelines that complement and support the process described in Sect. 3.2.

Another important, but often overlooked issue, is to maximize the effectiveness of these visualizations, that means, to provide an overview of the model that is expressive enough to support the tasks of an analyst. In [3], the authors examine the effectiveness of four overview visualization techniques: Force-directed graphs, Radial graphs, Sunbursts and Treemaps, and further prescribe use cases (i.e. Analytical Scenarios) for EA Visual Analysis. These cases include the *diagnosis* of Enterprise Models, that is, to discover anomalies in their structure, such as isolated sub-graphs of the model. This preemptive aspect of analysis is largely unexplored, but we consider that it is where valuable insights are generated, in the same manner as a physician can identify pathologies with a view to a MRI scan.

## 4    PRIMROSe: Conceptual Framework

The goal of this section is to present the conceptual framework at the base of PRIMROSe, and the way it is structured to support the application of analysis and visualization functions.

Figure 3 presents a trivial model that will be used throughout this section to illustrate our conceptual framework. This figure represents a small excerpt of an Enterprise Model that relates elements from domains such as Strategy, Infrastructure, or Business Process Architecture. In this model, A and C are Business Processes, while B is an Application Component and D is a Macro Process that references processes A and C. For the purpose of illustrating an analysis over this model, we will try to assess the consequences of removing process A. This should have an impact on B, C and D, and also implies the removal of relations a, b and e.

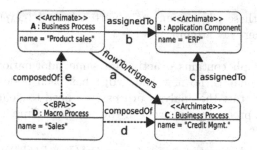

**Fig. 3.** Small fragment of an enterprise model.

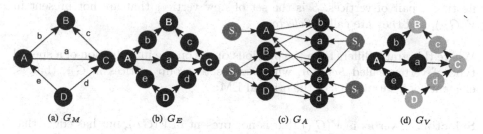

**Fig. 4.** Transformation stages of the enterprise model, from the model graph to a visual graph.

In order to support even simple analysis such as the one presented in the previous section, it is necessary to have the capacity to identify or select, and group, individual elements in the model. Taking into account that in Enterprise Architecture analysis working with the relations is as important as working with the elements, the underlying data structures for the analysis are not the raw Enterprise Models. Instead of that, our approach is based on graphs that are an *homeomorphism* on the EM, which means that they are topologically equivalent to it [24], but make relations first-level elements. We now describe these graphs and the way in which they are built, starting from what we call a *Model Graph* (see Fig. 4(a)).

**Model Graph.** A directed graph $G_M = (V(G_M), E(G_M))$, where $V(G_M)$ is a set of vertices and $E(G_M)$ is a set of edges. Each vertex in $V(G_M)$ references one element of the original Enterprise Model, along with its attributes. Each edge in $E(G_M)$ references a relationship in the model between the corresponding pair of elements.

The second data structure, which can be built directly from the Model Graph, is what we call an *Expanded Graph* (see Fig. 4(b)):

**Expanded Graph.** A directed and *bipartite* graph $G_E = (V(G_E), E(G_E))$, where $V(G_E) = V(G_M) \bigcup E(G_M)$ is the set of vertices, and $E(G_E)$ is the set of edges. Each of these edges connects a vertex from $V(G_M)$ and an edge on $E(G_M)$, or the other way around.

The Expanded Graph contains exactly the same information as the original Enterprise Model, that is, no new knowledge has been added. In order to do so, and thus really start the analysis process, we need to define the third data structure, which is precisely what we call the *Analysis Graph*:

**Analysis Graph.** A directed graph $G_A = (V(G_A), E(G_A))$, where $V(G_A) = V(G_E) \bigcup S$ is the set of vertices, and $E(G_A)$ is the set of edges, each one connecting a pair of vertices. $S$ is the set of new vertices that are not present in $V(G_E)$, and they are called *Selectors*.

Where this graph differs from the previous one is on the introduction of a special type of vertex called *Selector*, which serves to group vertices in $G_E$, that is, elements or relationships of the original EM:

**Selector.** A vertex in $V(G_A)$ that is not present in $V(G_E)$, but has edges that point to vertices of $V(G_E)$.

Ultimately, selectors are the elements in an Analysis Graph that reify the knowledge acquired through an analysis process. Within the proposed framework, selectors are added by means of the application of functions that operate over Analysis Graphs:

**Analysis Function.** Is a graph rewriting function $f_A \colon G_A \times P \to G_A$, with $P = \{p_0, p_1, ..., p_n\}$ the set of parameters, which vary depending on the specific function. These functions have an unique identifier, and can be either (1)Generic, i.e. can be applied to any Enterprise Model, or (2)Metamodel specific. An Analysis Function may add additional attributes to existing vertices.

Considering these functions and the available data structures, we can now illustrate the analysis process applied to the sample model. For this, we now define 5 atomic operations which incrementally process $G_A$ (see Fig. 5) and ultimately result in a graph where it is trivial to answer the question "which elements will be affected by the removal of process A (Product Sales)?".

- $f_0$ is a function that adds the domain of an element as an attribute. In the example, elements $A, B$, and $C$ are grouped in the same domain because they represent ArchiMate [25] concepts, while element $D$ is classified in another domain.
- $f_1$ is a function that adds a selector $(S_1)$ which groups edges that connect elements from different domains.
- $f_2$ is a function that adds a selector $(S_2)$ to vertices that satisfy an expression entered as a parameter. In this case, the only element selected is $A$, which refers to the Process where the attribute **name** equals "Product Sales".

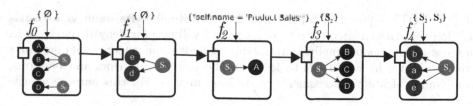

**Fig. 5.** Analysis pipeline for the example.

- $f_3$ is a function that selects neighbors of a given vertex. In this case, it selects the elements $B, C$, and $D$, that are pointed by $A$, and introduces the selector $S_3$ to reference them.
- $f_4$ is a function that selects the relations between elements in groups of elements defined by selectors. In this case, it selects $a, b$, and $c$, which are the relations between elements selected by $S_2$ and $S_3$.

After all the sequence of Analysis Functions is executed, we have $G_A$ with all the additional facts added, and affected vertices pointed by selectors. Now we have to translate this data into visual information. To do this, we use *Visual Rules*, that are pairs of (1) a Visual Attribute (e.g. color, shape, position) and (2) a function that returns the value of such attribute for a given vertex:

**Visual Rule.** A rule $R_i = \{A, f_R\}$ is a pair of $A$ a Visual Attribute, and $f_R : V \rightarrow X$ a function, where $V \in V(G_A)$ and $X$ is a value of $A$.

A Visual Rule returns the value (e.g. 'red') of a visual property (e.g. color) when an attribute of a vertex holds certain condition. In order to apply multiple rules to a set of vertices pointed by a selector, we use a *Visual Decorator*:

**Visual Decorator.** A function $f_V: G_A \times S_i \times R \rightarrow G_A$, with $S_i$ a given selector, that removes $S_i$ and its associated edges, and applies a set of visual rules $R = \{R_0, ..., R_n\}$ to all target nodes of such edges.

This function effectively removes the selector, and enriches the selected nodes with visual information. However, we need a final structure that embodies the translation of an Analysis Graph to a *Visual Graph*:

**Visual Graph.** A directed graph $G_V = (V(G_V), E(G_V))$ that is a subgraph of $G_A$, where $V(G_V)$ is a set of $n$ vertices, such that $n = |V(G_V)| = |V(G_E)|$. Each vertex contains only visual properties.

Having $G_V$ with all the information needed to visualize the analyzed model, we can generate all the necessary graphic files of a given format (e.g. GraphML,

JSON, DOT) required by a particular graphical toolkit. Its result is a Visualization that the architect uses to propose and validate (or deny) hypotheses in a sense-making loop. Finally, as the architect finds some evidence that supports his suspicions, he would like to focus on the relevant elements and relations, and communicate his assessments to decision makers. For this purpose we use *Filters*:

**Filter.** A function $f_F \colon G_V \times Pr \to G_V$, that removes vertices (and their respective edges) of $G_V$ that satisfy a predicate $Pr$.

These filters are applied sequentially, and the resulting graph is exported to a model, which is a View of the original Enterprise Model.

## 5   PRIMROSe: Application Framework

Before presenting the architecture that realizes the conceptual framework, we highlight some aspects to bear in mind:

**Incremental Analysis.** As described by the process in Fig. 2, EA Visual Analysis is incremental, starting with lightweight processing in the initial stage of analysis, and with the application of additional processing on demand, given by the interaction of the user with the tool. In this order of ideas, Analysis Functions should be applied in a composite manner, e.g. as a *pipeline* (see Sect. 6.2), with functions given in terms of Selectors created on previously applied functions (see $f_3$ and $f_4$ of Fig. 5).

**Reusable and Extensible Functions.** One of the pillars of PRIMROSe are analysis functions described in terms of elements of the model and/or metamodel, complemented with basic graph functions that are independent of the EM and its metamodel.

**Non-destructive Analysis.** As it could be noted by the reader in Sect. 4, Analysis Functions cannot remove nodes from the Analysis Graph. Filtering is made explicit by the user in terms of the visualization, not the data, i.e. elements are visually hidden, but present in the Analysis Graph.

**Independence from the Visualization Toolkit.** Currently, there is no general-purpose graphical toolkit that satisfies all of the visual requirements for the Visual Analysis of EMs [4]. Each one has its own strengths in various aspects, so the user should select which one to use, depending on the visualization technique and capabilities needed for a specific analysis, or design their own graphical library for EA-specific visualizations.

**Customizable Visualizations.** Selectors of the Analysis Graph must be mapped to visual attributes of a visualization. This mapping has to be translated into toolkit-specific code and input data.

## 5.1 Architecture

The PRIMROSe architecture is divided into four main components, and four stages (**Analysis, Mapping, Visualization,** and **Filters**) that conform the global pipeline (see Fig. 6):

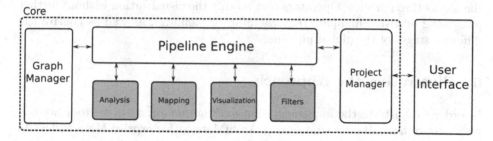

**Fig. 6.** PRIMROSe architecture.

**Graph Manager.** This component is responsible of translating the Enterprise Model into an Expanded Graph $G_E$ through the transformations defined in Sect. 4.

**Project Manager.** This component administers the different projects of an user. A *Project* is composed of an Enterprise Model, as well as the aggregate descriptors needed for the analysis. A *Pipeline Descriptor* is a sequence of *Operations*, each one with its own parameters. For instance, an operation of the *Analysis Pipeline* contains an instance of an Analysis Function to be executed, as well as the parameters needed for the function. The *Visual Pipeline*, on the other hand, contains the Visual Decorators. Finally, the *Filter Pipeline* is a sequence of Filters.

**Pipeline Engine.** Its purpose is to manage and apply the different stages of the global pipeline. For each stage, that also is a pipeline, the engine composes and applies the respective operations sequentially.

1. **Analysis:** Involves the transformation of the Analysis Graph using the Analysis Functions referenced in the Analysis Pipeline.
2. **Mapping:** Processes the Visual Decorators in the Visual Pipeline and builds the Visual Graph.

3. **Visualization:** Taking into account that each toolkit 'knows' how to visualize a graph (or a similar structure) in its own fashion, the Visualization stage translates the processed graph $G_V$ into tool-specific artifacts, such as code and/or input files, e.g. a GraphML or a JSON file that contains the data to be visualized.
4. **Filters:** Transforms the Visual Graph by removing vertices and edges with the Filters in the Filter Pipeline.

**User Interface.** This component serves both as an editor for the Pipeline Descriptors, and also as a workbench for visual Analysis. The user can explore the model through View Operators that modify the visualization without further processing or visual mapping (e.g. zooming or panning), as well as control the different stages of the global pipeline.

## 6   Illustrating the Approach

In order to illustrate the implementation and interaction with the tool, we will make use of a small case study using ArchiMate as Enterprise Metamodel. As described by its authors in [26], the ArchiSurance case study is an example of a fictitious insurance company, which has been formed as the result of a merger of three previously independent companies, and describes the baseline architecture of the company and then a number of change scenarios.

We start by creating a Project containing the model, which is imported by the Graph Manager (see Fig. 7). Until now, we have not done much.

We would want to analyze this model in order to acquire new knowledge. For instance, and for the sake of a small example that fits in this paper, we asked ourselves some questions: *What is the relative importance of each element in the model?* Also, related to this, *what is the impact of a change in the model?*,

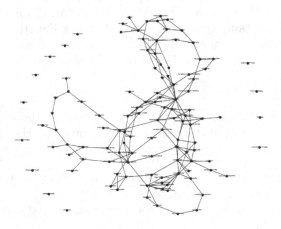

**Fig. 7.** ArchiSurance model graph

e.g. the removal of the *Customer* Business Role. In order to perform this kinds of analyses, we need (1) A function that finds the connectivity degree of each node, (2) A function that finds paths and neighbors of a given model element.

## 6.1 Analysis Functions

Each Analysis Function comes with an unique identifier, and receives as input the Analysis graph, in addition to custom parameters defined by the creator of the function. Its output is the modified graph, with additional selectors, and even new attributes.

This *selection* of relevant vertices is the backbone of Analysis Functions. In order to select subsets of vertices of the graph, the Pipeline Engine exposes some methods to Analysis Functions that allow them to query the model.

In order to elucidate the definition of Analysis Functions, we created two very simple functions that operate with the topology of the model:

**Degree Calculator.** Adds an attribute –*degree*– to every vertex that represents an element of the model. Its value is the number of incoming and outgoing edges. Finally, it adds a selector for all the modified vertices of the Analysis Graph.

**Impact Analysis.** Given the id of a vertex, it adds a selector to adjacent vertices and their respective edges. It also adds a selector to the source element.

The following snippet of code shows the Java class that is used to implement the Impact Analysis function:

```java
public class ImpactAnalysis extends AnalysisFunction{

    private PipelineEngine engine;
    ...
    public static Collection<Selector> execute(Collection<Parameter>
            parameters) {
        ArrayList<Selector> selectors = new ArrayList<Selector>();
        Long source = parameters.iterator().next().getValue().asLong();

        List<Vertex> neighbors = engine.getNeighbors(source,
                pipelineEngine.getAnalysisGraph());
        List<Vertex> relations = engine.getIncomingEdges(source);

        Vertex s0 = new Selector();
        s0.addAttribute("name","sourceElement",String.class);
        selectors.add(s0);

        Vertex s1 = new Selector();
        s1.addAttribute("name","impactedElements",String.class);
        selectors.add(s1);
```

```
AnalysisGraph graph = engine.getAnalysisGraph();
Long id = graph.addVertex(s1);

for(Vertex v : neighbors){
    graph.addEdge(id, v.getId());
}

for(Vertex v : relations){
    graph.addEdge(id, v.getId());
}
}
...
}
```

## 6.2 Analysis Pipeline

As described in Sect. 3, analysis is a dynamic process where the flow of control is constantly changing between the user and the system, with incremental processing oriented by the addition of operations to the Analysis Pipeline. At the same time, analysis is also incremental, where insights are obtained progressively.

This is the Analysis Pipeline for our example, in JSON format:

```
[
    {
        "id": "o1",
        "function": "org.primrose.functions.DegreeCalculator",
        "parameters": []
    },
    {
        "id": "o2",
        "function": "org.primrose.functions.ImpactAnalysis",
        "parameters":  [{"source","9"}]
    }
]
```

The pipeline starts by executing the DegreeCalculator function, which does not require any parameter. After the execution finishes, we run the Impact Analysis function, that receives the ID of the source vertex as a parameter.

We can create more complex pipelines, where we would like to combine different functions. However, at the same time, we would like to preserve the encapsulated nature of each function. For these reasons, the Pipeline Engine also has a registry of the selectors created on each function, and a method that returns them given a function ID.

## 6.3 Visual Pipeline

The Visual Pipeline is a series of Visual Decorators. Each one of them is in control of a Visual Attribute, is assigned to a selector, and has its respective set of Visual Rules:

```
[
    {"id": "v1",
        "function": "elementSize",
        "parameters":
        [
            {"selector":"degreeElements"},
            {"attribute":"size"},
            {"rules":[{"expression":"allElements",
                            "value":"attribute(degree)"}]}
        ]},
    {"id": "v2",
        "function": "impactedElementsColor",
        "parameters":
        [
            {"selector":"impactedElements"},
            {"attribute":"color"},
            {"rules":[
                {"expression":"allElements","value":"#FF4D4D"},
                {"expression":"allRelations","value":"#FF4D4D"}
            ]}
        ]
    }
]
```

The Mapping component works over the Visual Graph, which is a graph that only contains visual information, despite having the same structure as the Expanded Graph. In this case, we are inserting visual attributes defined on each Visual Decorator:

First, we obtain all the elements of the Analysis Graph pointed by the selector *degreeElements*, which is the selector added by the DegreeCalculator function, and then insert the value of the attribute *degree* into the **size** attribute of the Visual Graph.

For the second Visual Decorator, we obtain all the elements of $G_A$ pointed by the selector *impactedElements*, which is the selector added by the ImpactAnalysis function, and then insert the value *#FF4D4D*, a shade of red, into the **color** attribute of the Visual Graph.

## 6.4   Results

Figure 8(a) is the visualization when we execute the first function, DegreeCalculator, and Fig. 8(b) is the final visualization, where we have executed both functions. Here we can identify clearly both questions that we formulated at the beginning of this section (see Fig. 9).

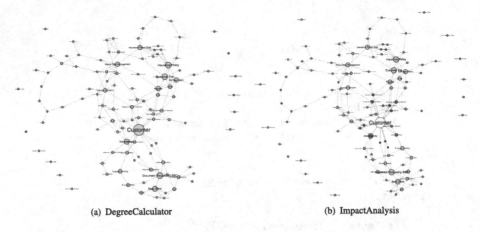

(a) DegreeCalculator                    (b) ImpactAnalysis

**Fig. 8.** Incremental appliance of analysis functions.

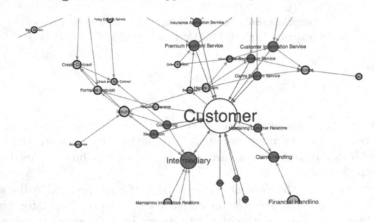

**Fig. 9.** Detail of Fig. 8(b)

# 7    Conclusion

This paper delineates the Visual Analysis of Enterprise Models, emphasizing on the interactive nature of this activity, and taking into account that there is a reasoning process – which goes in parallel– in the brain of the analyst.

Seeing this analysis more as a dialogue than the production of automated and partial results, the contribution of this paper lies in the conceptual framework and architecture that enables the incremental production and refinement of hypotheses that end in assessments that support decision making.

We designed this PRIMROSe framework (and tool architecture) supported by a set of requirements from various perspectives, also taking into account the structural properties of Enterprise Models. Analysis over these models is made with non-destructive functions that select and decorate an analytical abstraction. This Analytical Model is then mapped to a Visual Graph, which is transformed

Into the necessary artifacts that are needed to depict the results on a given visualization toolkit. The user interacts with the visualization and returns the flow of control to the system, allowing the user to deepen on more detailed analyses.

We omitted the last stage of the process, **Communicate** (see Fig. 2), which deals with the transformation of a visualization and its associated insights into a view by using filters. We think this is the meeting point between PRIMROSe and similar approaches (see Sect. 2) that complement and enhance analysis.

Extension points for the framework include the traceability of the whole process, which seems a promising field for complementing and enhancing EA documentation, as it would provide evidence of the rationale behind analysis. Moreover, the Analysis Graph should be preserved throughout the lifecycle of the Enterprise Model, as it allows the preservation of the additional facts that are introduced.

On the other hand, we are currently evaluating and augmenting the tool with more complex scenarios involving different EMs of large enterprises that span several thousands of elements and relations. As with every Visual Analysis tool, user feedback shapes the supported functionality, as well as design considerations that involve its usability. This evaluation consists of a given Enterprise Model and a set of Analytical Scenarios, which are complex questions that require some method of analysis to answer. Users will be invited to use PRIMROSe and fill a questionnaire addressing both the Analysis Component and the Visualization Component, in functional (e.g. accuracy, efficiency) and usability (e.g. location of elements, interactive operations) aspects. This will help us shaping the limitations of the tool, measure its effectiveness, and assess the minimal set of basic functions that are useful for the different kinds of EA Analysis.

# References

1. Buckl, S., Gulden, J., Schweda, C.M.: Supporting ad hoc analyses on enterprise models. In: EMISA. GI, vol. 172, pp. 69–83. LNI (2010)
2. Schekkerman, J.: How to Survive in the Jungle of Enterprise Architecture Frameworks: Creating or Choosing an Enterprise Architecture Framework. Trafford, Victoria (2006)
3. Naranjo, D., Sánchez, M., Villalobos, J.: Connecting the dots: examining visualization techniques for enterprise architecture model analysis. In: Grabis, J., Kirikova, M., Zdravkovic, J., Stirna, J. (eds.) PoEM of Short Paper Proceedings of the 6th IFIP WG 8.1 Working Conference on the Practice of Enterprise Modeling, CEUR-WS, vol. 1023, pp. 29–38 (2013)
4. Naranjo, D., Sánchez, M., Villalobos, J.: Visual analysis of enterprise models. In: Workshops Proceedings of the 16th IEEE International Enterprise Distributed Object Computing Conference, EDOCW 2012. IEEE Computer Society, September 2012
5. Fekete, J.-D., van Wijk, J.J., Stasko, J.T., North, C.: The value of information visualization. In: Kerren, A., Stasko, J.T., Fekete, J.-D., North, C. (eds.) Information Visualization. LNCS, vol. 4950, pp. 1–18. Springer, Heidelberg (2008)

6. Panas, T., Lincke, R., Lwe, W.: Online-configuration of software visualizations with vizz3d. In: Naps, T.L., Pauw, W.D. (eds.) SOFTVIS, pp. 173–182. ACM (2005)
7. Chan, Y.H., Keeton, K., Ma, K.L.: Interactive visual analysis of hierarchical enterprise data. In: Proceedings of the 12th IEEE International Conference on Commerce and Enterprise Computing. CEC 2010, pp. 180–187. IEEE Computer Society, Washington (2010)
8. The Eclipse Foundation: Zest: The eclipse visualization toolkit (2013). http://www.eclipse.org/gef/zest/. Accessed 15 October 2013
9. Buckl, S., Ernst, A.M., Lankes, J., Schweda, C.M., Wittenburg, A.: Generating visualizations of enterprise architectures using model transformations. In: EMISA. GI, vol. P-119, pp. 33–46. LNI (2007)
10. Schaub, M., Matthes, F., Roth, S.: Towards a conceptual framework for interactive enterprise architecture management visualizations. In: Modellierung. GI, pp. 75–90, vol. 201. LNI (2012)
11. Hauder, M., Roth, S., Pigat, S., Matthes, F.: A configurator for visual analysis of enterprise architectures. In: ACM/IEEE 16th International Conference on Model Driven Engineering Languages and Systems (MODELS 2013), Miami (2013)
12. Roth, S., Hauder, M., Zec, M., Utz, A., Matthes, F.: Empowering business users to analyze enterprise architectures: structural model matching to configure visualizations. In: 7th Workshop on Trends in Enterprise Architecture Research (TEAR 2013), Vancouver (2013)
13. Buja, A., Cook, D., Swayne, D.F.: Interactive high-dimensional data visualization. J. Comput. Graph. Stat. 5(1), 78–99 (1996)
14. Backes, A.R., Casanova, D., Bruno, O.M.: A complex network-based approach for boundary shape analysis. Pattern Recognit. 42(1), 54–67 (2009)
15. Chi, E.H.-h., Riedl, J.: An operator interaction framework for visualization systems. In: Proceedings of the 1998 IEEE Symposium on Information Visualization. INFOVIS 1998, pp. 63–70. IEEE Computer Society, Washington (1998)
16. Wickham, H., Lawrence, M., Cook, D., Buja, A., Hofmann, H., Swayne, D.: The plumbing of interactive graphics. Comput. Stat. 24, 207–215 (2009)
17. Kohlhammer, J., May, T., Hoffmann, M.: Visual analytics for the strategic decision making process. In: De Amicis, R., Stojanovic, R., Conti, G. (eds.) GeoSpatial Visual Analytics. LNCS, pp. 299–310. Springer, Heidelberg (2009)
18. Jankun-Kelly, T., Ma, K.L., Gertz, M.: A model and framework for visualization exploration. IEEE Trans. Vis. Comput. Graph. 13(2), 357–369 (2007)
19. Keim, D.A.: Information visualization and visual data mining. IEEE Trans. Vis. Comput. Graph. 8(1), 1–8 (2002)
20. van Wijk, J.: The value of visualization. In: (2005) Visualization VIS 2005, pp. 79–86. IEEE, October 2005
21. Buckl, S., Ernst, A., Lankes, J., Matthes, F., Schweda, C.: Enterprise architecture management patterns - exemplifying the approach. In: (2008) 12th International IEEE Enterprise Distributed Object Computing Conference EDOC 2008, pp. 393–402, September 2008
22. Fruchterman, T.M.J., Reingold, E.M.: Graph drawing by force-directed placement. Softw. Pract. Exper. 21, 1129–1164 (1991)
23. Egyed, A.: Automated abstraction of class diagrams. ACM Trans. Softw. Eng. Methodol. 11, 449–491 (2002)
24. Ray, S.: Graph Theory with Algorithms and its Applications. In Applied Science and Technology. Springer, Heidelberg (2012)
25. The Open Group: ArchiMate 2. 0 Specification. Van Haren Publishing (2012)
26. Jonkers, H., Band, I., Quartel, D.: Archisurance case study. Accessed 4 April 2014

# A Review and Evaluation of Business Model Ontologies: A Viability Perspective

A. D'Souza[1](✉), N.R.T.P. van Beest[3], G.B. Huitema[2],
J.C. Wortmann[2], and H. Velthuijsen[1]

[1] School of Communication, Media and IT, Hanze University of Applied Sciences,
Zernikeplein 11, Groningen, The Netherlands
{a.d.souza,h.velthuijsen}@pl.hanze.nl
[2] Department of Operations, University of Groningen, Nettelbosje 2,
Groningen, The Netherlands
{g.b.huitema,j.c.wortmann}@rug.nl
[3] Software Systems Research Group, NICTA Queensland, 70-72 Bowen Street,
Spring Hill, 4000 Brisbane, Australia
nick.vanbeest@nicta.com.au

**Abstract.** Organisations are increasingly becoming interdependent in order to create and deliver superior value to their customers. The resulting business models of such organisations are becoming increasingly complex and difficult to design, because they have to deal with multiple stakeholders and their competing interests, and with dynamic and fast paced markets. Hence, in order to ensure the long-term survival of such firms, it is crucial that their business models are viable. Business model ontologies (BMOs) are effective tools for designing and evaluating business models. However, the viability perspective has largely been ignored, and the current BMOs have not been evaluated on their capabilities to facilitate the design and evaluation of viable business models. In order to address this gap, current BMOs have been assessed from the viability perspective. To evaluate the BMOs, a list of 26 criteria is derived from the literature. This list of criteria is then applied to assess six well-established BMOs. The analysis reveals that none of the BMOs satisfies all the criteria. However, the e3-value satisfies most of the criteria, and it is most appropriate for designing and evaluating viable business models. Furthermore, the identified deficits clearly define the areas for enhancing the BMOs from a viability perspective.

**Keywords:** Business model ontology · Business model assessment · IS alignment · Viability

## 1 Introduction

Organisations operate in an increasingly dynamic and networked setting that involves many stakeholders. The resulting business complexity requires new business models. Consequently, this also requires a change in the corresponding enterprise architecture (EA).

© Springer International Publishing Switzerland 2015
J. Cordeiro et al. (Eds.): ICEIS 2014, LNBIP 227, pp. 453–471, 2015.
DOI: 10.1007/978-3-319-22348-3_25

An important example of the increased complexity is the energy industry. The influx of new technologies, changing customer needs, environmental concerns, and government policies, is causing a shift towards a decentralised energy industry. This also implies a shift from a centralised monopolistic or linear logic of value creation to a decentralised non-linear logic of value creation. The decentralised energy industry is characterised by cleaner decentralised energy generation assets (e.g. solar panels), smart grids, and new stakeholders, such as the prosumers (both large and small scale). The traditional consumers are taking on the role of prosumers, who not only consume energy, but also produce energy with the help of technologies such as solar panels. Consequently, the traditional simplistic and linear business models have to be changed to deal with such new stakeholders and technologies. Furthermore, new services are needed to support such new stakeholders. For example, the amount of energy delivered to the grid by the prosumers will have to be metered and they have to be compensated for it. This means that the appropriate metering, billing, and accounting services will have to be designed and implemented. In addition, the energy industry is a heterogeneous mix of stakeholders with conflicting interests. For example, the system operator (responsible for maintaining the grid infrastructure) is interested in maintaining a robust infrastructure at minimal cost; the political stakeholders are interested in promoting green energy in order to reduce $CO_2$ emissions, and in creating new jobs; the prosumers are interested in a sustainable lifestyle, and at the same time want lower energy bills. Hence, this shift towards a decentralised energy system increases the technical and business complexity [1]. Consequently, the enterprise architecture[1] (EA) as well as the physical technologies (e.g., solar panels, windmills) that support this new market setting are highly distributed. Furthermore, its components are owned and managed by different stakeholders.

It is essential that such complex enterprise architectures (comprising the business processes, enterprise information system (EIS) infrastructure, and the physical technologies) are derived from a viable business model. That is, all the participating organisations and stakeholders are able to capture value, such that they are committed to the overall business model [3]. In addition, the envisioned business model should be technologically viable [4]. However, this new way of doing business in a networked setting dramatically increases the complexity of designing viable business models, due to the competing interests of stakeholders and the new technologies that enable new ways of creating value [3]. Moreover, the technology infrastructure not only has to align with the overall business model [4], in some cases it is an explicit part of the business model.

The design and evaluation of business models is supported by business model ontologies (BMOs). BMOs can also be used to conceptualise and communicate business models [5]. The existing BMOs are conceived from different perspectives and are used for different purposes. However, the viability perspective has been largely neglected. As such, the capabilities of BMOs to support the design and

---

[1] An enterprise architecture is defined as "a coherent whole of principles, methods, and models that are used in the design and realisation of an enterprise's organisational structure, business processes, information systems, and infrastructure" [2].

evaluation of viable business models remains unclear, particularly in complex business settings.

Therefore, this paper presents a list of fundamental criteria to which a BMO should comply in order to facilitate the design and evaluation of viable business models and, therefore, enterprise architectures. These criteria are subsequently used to assess six well-established BMOs. Out of the six ontologies, four were specifically conceived to represent business models (e3-value, VNA, BMC, and EBMS), while the other two (VSM and REA) were conceived for different purposes. The VSM was developed for reorganising production systems from the lean manufacturing perspective [6]. The REA was originally proposed as a generalised accounting framework, which allows accountants and non-accountants to maintain information about the same set of phenomena in terms of resources exchanged, events (economic exchanges), and the agents involved in the exchanges [7]. However, they could possibly be used as BMOs (for more details we refer to Sect. 4.2). Therefore, we refer to these modelling ontologies as BMOs.

The BMOs are assessed against the derived criteria, in order to select the most appropriate BMO, and to identify the deficits and areas for improvement from a viability perspective. This will allow future research to enhance BMOs to fully support viability as an explicit design focus of business models.

Accordingly, the paper is structured as follows. Section 2 provides a discussion on related work. Section 3 describes the criteria as provided in literature. Subsequently, Sect. 4 applies the criteria to assess current BMOs. Finally, the paper is concluded in Sect. 5, along with some directions for future research.

## 2   Related Work

The boundaries of traditional enterprises are shifting from a single organisation to a network of organisations [2]. This has led to enterprise architectures being developed, owned, and operated in a highly distributed manner, which in turn has lead to misaligned and inflexible enterprise architectures [4,8]. Furthermore, for an enterprise architecture to be effective, it has to enable the business strategy. However, the distance between strategy and enterprise architecture is very large, because it is hard to conceive and design enterprise architectures based on general strategy statements [8,9]. Therefore, scholars have argued that the business model concept helps to address these challenges by conceptualising and translating the strategy into a blueprint that describes how business is carried out [8,10–12]. The business model, as shown in Fig. 1, is the linking pin between strategy and the enterprise architecture [10–12]. As such, it is critical that the enterprise architectures (i.e., the business processes, technical infrastructure – both ICT and the physical technological infrastructure –, and the organisational structure) are derived from or aligned with a viable business model.

The business model concept is relatively young, and scholars are constantly debating the meaning and scope of the concept [11,13]. They are debating the scope of business models on several fronts such as strategy and operational detail

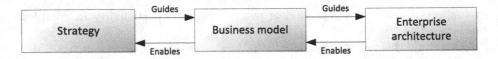

**Fig. 1.** Business model in relation to strategy and enterprise architecture.

[13]. However, since we consider business models to be a linking pin between strategy and enterprise architecture, we make the following distinction between them. A business model translates the strategy into a blueprint that describes how value is created, exchanged, and captured among the stakeholders. In addition, it also describes the organising logic of the key components of a business model. Strategy is concerned with how to create and maintain competitive advantage [11,14,15]. At a meta level, the enterprise architecture describes the process of designing and implementing the organisational structure, business processes, technology (ICT and physical technologies), and infrastructure. Furthermore, scholars from different disciplines are studying the concept of business models, which makes it difficult to agree on a common definition. There has been considerable interest in integrating the multidisciplinary views and arriving at a common definition [11,13]. It is important to distinguish between business models and the individual components of the EA in particular, business process models, because in the past, business process models have been used wrongly to represent business models [16]. Looking at business models from the viability perspective they should focus on value and viability. The business process models focus on describing how the business model should be implemented. It describes the activities, the sequence of activities, and the actors performing them. Business models and business process models are closely related, but they are not the same. According to [4] modelling business processes is the next logical step in designing enterprise architectures, after a viable business model has been designed. Therefore, the business process models should align with the business model, especially in terms of viability.

Scholars are also interested in the design of viable business models. They focus on identifying the factors, characteristics, and conditions that lead to viable business models. Furthermore, they provide guidelines and evaluation criteria for business models [17–19]. The viability of business models is mainly studied from two perspectives. Some use a qualitative approach to conceptualise and analyse viable business models [17,18], whereas others use BMOs to conceptualise, design, analyse, and evaluate viable business models [4,20]. BMOs are a reliable way of conceptualising, designing and evaluating business models [11]. They provide a common language to conceptualise and represent business models, and leave little room for misinterpretation of the business model.

BMOs and business models are closely related. A BMO is a language, which can be used to conceptualise and communicate any number of business models. For example, e3-value can be used to conceptualise and communicate business models of companies [14].

There has been some interest in the past to compare BMOs for different purposes. In [5], a framework is proposed to compare BMOs to find similarities and differences with the goal of integrating BMOs. In [21], a framework is proposed to assess BMOs from a taxonomical perspective. However, no attempts have been made to assess existing BMOs from a viability perspective.

# 3 Derivation of Criteria

This section describes the research design, and how it is applied to distil a set of criteria, which are subsequently used to assess the BMOs.

## 3.1 Research Design

Figure 2 visualises the research design. The Conceptual Model Analysis Framework (CMAF) [22] is proposed to help researchers to compare and analyse the BMOs. The CMAF is a generic and flexible framework, which we will use to derive the criteria from literature in a systematic manner. The literature review will yield a list of criteria that we subsequently use to compare, assess, and select the most appropriate BMO for designing and evaluating viable business models. Furthermore, the revealed deficits can be used to enhance the BMOs in context of designing and evaluating viable business models.

However, the CMAF framework assumes that the process of comparing and analysing BMOs will automatically lead to the selection of an appropriate BMO. This implies that the user is required to come up with a set of preferences (and

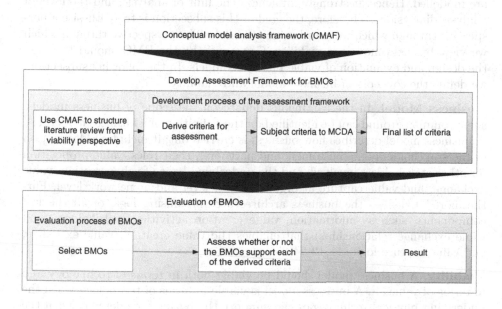

**Fig. 2.** Research design.

hence a subset of relevant criteria) based on which the user will select a BMO. Consequently, there is a need for a set of criteria specifically tailored to assess a BMO on its capabilities to facilitate the design and evaluation of viable business models.

The CMAF framework consists of three dimensions, namely conceptual focus, unit of analysis, and level of analysis. These dimensions will be used to distil a set of criteria to assess the BMOs. In addition, we have also made use of the existing literature in the strategic management domain and the business model domain (also including BMO literature). Following [23], we analyse the literature from the domains mentioned above, and distil a set of criteria that are relevant, understandable, complete and concise, and judgementally independent (i.e. the preference for one criterion should not be dependent on other criteria). Furthermore, the criteria are distilled in such a way that they are operational, which means that they are readily applicable to BMOs. Additionally, attention is paid to the simplicity versus complexity condition. In order to ensure simplicity (without sacrificing the complexity) of the criteria and to ensure the criteria are operational, some of the criteria are further decomposed into a set of lower level criteria. Finally, in Sect. 4.1 the criteria are checked to ensure that they comply with the redundancy condition.

### 3.2 Conceptual Focus

The conceptual focus dimension helps to synthesise a perspective through which we view business models. It defines the functionality of the BMOs, the components that should be modelled and analysed, and the granularity at which they are modelled. Hence, it strongly influences the unit of analysis, and the level of analysis dimensions. Therefore, the goal of this subsection is to synthesise a perspective through which we view business models. The perspective through which we view business models is viability. Consequently, the BMO should focus on the design and evaluation of viable business models. In the following subsection, we define the concepts of business model and viability.

**Business Model.** In the continuous debate on the scope of business models, some common ground can be identified on the definition of a business model [11]. A business model describes how business is carried out; it includes a description of the stakeholders (e.g. customers and partners), their roles, value proposition for other stakeholders involved, and the underlying logic of value creation, value exchange, and value capture at organisational level and at network level. Furthermore, it defines the business architecture (organising logic of all the key components, such as information, value creation activities, stakeholders, and value exchange relationships) that enables the value creation, value exchange, and value capture logic [11, 12, 24, 25].

**Viability.** A business model should be viable both in terms of technology and in terms of value [4]. A business model is viable in terms of technology when the underlying physical technologies can support the business model and when the

ICT infrastructure can support the information services required by the business model to work. This can be achieved by considering which type of information services (and, therefore, the ICT infrastructure) and physical technology infrastructure is needed to support the business model. In addition, the capabilities of new technologies should be considered to determine how they could lead to better and new ways of doing business [8]. For example, if the value proposition of a business model is self-sufficiency in terms of energy use, the underlying technological infrastructure should support the creation and delivery of this value proposition. If the underlying technologies are unable to supply the energy demand then the business model is not technologically viable. Consequently, the customer will not be self-sufficient and as a result the business model will fail. A business model is viable in terms of value when all the participating organisations/stakeholders are able to capture value, such that they are committed to the business model [3].

**Value.** Value is the core component of a business model, and it plays an important role in making business models viable [12]. Figure 3 shows that value is composed of *exchange value* (e.g. euros, dollars etc.) and *use value* (e.g. benefits of a product or service enjoyed by a customer, benefits derived by other stakeholders) [26,27]. Use value concerns the desired benefits end users derive out of a product or a service. The concept of use value was extended by [26] to include benefits realised by stakeholders other than end users, such as governmental organisations and society. This implies that the business model could include a broader set of stakeholders other than end users and the company selling the product or a service. This is especially evident in the energy industry. For example, let us consider a community-owned small-scale solar farm in the Netherlands. The business model of the solar farm involves several stakeholders, such as the community members, solar farm operators, local municipality, and the subsidising agency. These stakeholders are interested in different types of value. For instance, the solar farm operator is purely interested in exchange value (profits), while the community members are interested in exchange value (return over investment) as well as use value (reduction of $CO_2$, jumpstarting

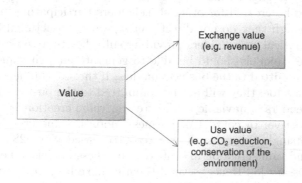

**Fig. 3.** Composition of value.

the local economy by hiring local suppliers and installers). Similarly, the local municipality and the subsidising agency are interested in use value, i.e. reducing $CO_2$ emissions to meet the EU sustainability goals, and at the same time in boosting the local economy.

### 3.3  Unit of Analysis

The unit of analysis describes the functionality of the BMOs and the components to be modelled and analysed. BMOs can model and analyse business models at organisational level as well as at business network level. The organisational level analysis includes the components within the organisation, such as value creation activities. The business network analysis includes the components within the business network, such as organisations and relationships among them. The functionality and the components to be modelled are derived from literature, and are directly influenced by the conceptual focus. In addition, the functionality and the components that should be modelled and analysed are presented as a list of criteria.

Based on the definition of the business model, we posit that the BMOs should conceptualise, encompass, and model the following concepts, functionality, and components. BMOs should conceptualise and model business models at two levels: at organisational level and at network level [22,28]. Further, they should conceptualise the stakeholders within the network, and how they create, exchange, and capture value. Additionally, they should be able to represent the business model architecture of viable business models and the business rules that govern them.

Business models have been studied from different perspectives [11]. Hence, we further explore these concepts below, to gain a better understanding of the concepts it encompasses from the perspective of viability and what it means to BMOs.

**Value Creation.** Value creation is a central concept in management literature. It is the increased value (exchange value and use value) that two or more parties enjoy when they engage in mutually beneficial transactions [27]. Furthermore, value could also be created for other stakeholders participating in the business model, even though they do not directly engage in transactional relationships, for example, political stakeholders providing subsidies to green energy producers [26]. Business models should be able to generate enough value to keep the stakeholders committed to the business models. If the stakeholders are unable to capture enough value, they will not be committed to the business model, which consequently renders it unviable [3]. Therefore, value creation is crucial from a viability perspective. In context of business models, value creation cannot be explained by a single theory, such as a resource based view [28]. Therefore, to truly understand value creation in context of business models, a nexus of several theories is necessary [3]. Hence, several theories have been reviewed that utilise different units of analysis to explain value creation [28]. Further, it is argued that the units these theories analyse are the sources of value creation [3,28].

Following the lead of [3, 28], we posit that the BMO should model and analyse the different sources of value creation, because by definition of business models, it is crucial to understand how value is created. Table 1 highlights the theories and the sources of value creation they analyse.

We acknowledge Schumpeters theory of entrepreneurship, which posits that an entrepreneur is the source of value creation [28]. However, we do not review this theory in context of this research, because the conceptual focus used to view viability of business models is at the organisational and the network level, and not at the entrepreneur level. An overview of the criteria concerning value creation is shown in Table 2.

**Value Capture.** Value capture is the amount of value retained by each stakeholder within the business model [26]. The amount of retained value is conceptualised in terms of use value and exchange value. The value captured in terms of exchange value is the total amount of revenue a stakeholder is able to retain

**Table 1.** Sources of value creation.

| Theory | Source of value creation |
| --- | --- |
| Value chain framework | Value creation activities |
| Resource based view | Resources |
| Business networks | Business networks |
| Transaction cost economics | Transactions (value exchange relationships) |

**Table 2.** Assessment criteria concerning value creation.

| No | Criteria | Sources |
| --- | --- | --- |
| 1. | Value creation | [27] |
| 1.1. | Model value creation by each stakeholder | [25] |
| 1.2. | Model sources of value creation | [28] |
| 1.2.1. | Value creation activities | [28] |
| 1.2.2. | Resources | [28] |
| 1.2.3. | Business network | [28] |
| 1.2.4. | Transactions | [28] |

**Table 3.** Assessment criteria concerning value capture.

| No | Criteria | Sources |
| --- | --- | --- |
| 2. | Value capture | [27] |
| 2.1. | Model value captured by each stakeholder | [3] |
| 2.2. | Model captured value in terms of use value | [27] |
| 2.3. | Model captured value in terms of exchange value | [27] |

(i.e. profit) [27]. The value captured in terms of use value is the total benefits realised by a stakeholder from a product and/or a service, or by participating in a business model [26].

Successful business models ensure that the stakeholders participating in the business models are able to capture value, such that they are committed to the business model. If not, the business model will not be able to attract and retain competitive stakeholders. Hence, this could lead to the business model being rendered unviable. Consequently, the BMO should be able to model and analyse the amount of value captured by each stakeholder. An overview of the criteria concerning value capture is shown in Table 3.

**Value Exchange.** Value exchanges are relationships formed among stakeholders to exchange value. At the organisational level, these relationships can be analysed within the organisations, and at a dyadic level. Organisations form dyadic relationships with partners, such as channel partners and customers [3]. Adopting the business network approach implies that the value exchange relationships are among the basic building blocks of the business network [20]. Consequently, it calls for a systemic approach, where the value exchanges are analysed not only from a focal organisations perspective, but also from a business networks perspective. This involves the analysis of the entire business network formed to produce, govern, and deliver the products and services to the end user [3]. Hence, this implies that the BMO should be able to conceptualise and model the value exchanges at organisational level and at network level. An overview of the criteria concerning value exchange is shown in Table 4.

**Table 4.** Assessment criteria concerning value exchange.

| No | Criteria | Sources |
|--------|------------------------------------------------------|---------|
| 3. | Value exchange | [3] |
| 3.1. | Model value exchanged at organisational level | [3] |
| 3.1.1. | Use value at organisational level | [27] |
| 3.1.2. | Exchange value at organisational level | [27] |
| 3.2. | Model value exchanged at business network level | [20] |
| 3.2.1. | Use value at business network level | [27] |
| 3.2.2. | Exchange value at business network level | [27] |

**Business Model Architecture.** Business model architecture is the organising logic of how the key components that enable value creation, value capture, and value exchange relationships are organised [29]. Visualising the business model architecture helps in gaining a deeper insight into the business model. Further,

**Table 5.** Assessment criteria concerning the business model architecture.

| No | Criteria | Sources |
|----|----------|---------|
| 4. | Represent the business model architecture | [29] |

it is a useful and effective technique used to brainstorm and identify alternative configurations of the business model. Hence, in context of designing viable business models, visualising the business model architecture of the business models is an effective tool in organising the components in such a way that it enables viability [20]. Therefore, the BMOs should be able to visualise the business model architecture. An overview of the criteria concerning the business model architecture is shown in Table 5.

**Design of Viable Business Models.** The design of viable business models is an iterative process. Therefore, the ontology should also allow for the manipulation of the business model to achieve viability [20]. Moreover, it is crucial to consider the capabilities of the underlying technologies (ICT technologies and physical technologies) while designing business models. For example, let us consider a business model where a prosumer produces electricity using a solar panel. The produced electricity is delivered to the electricity grid, and the prosumer is compensated for it. For this business model to work, two layers of technology are necessary namely the physical technology layer, and the ICT layer. The physical technology layer consists of technological infrastructure such as the solar panel, the cables that carry the electricity, the meters that measure how much electricity is delivered to the grid. The ICT layer consists of technologies, which collect data and processes it into information. The information is necessary to support the business processes and decision making such as the billing process and trade decisions [30].

Modelling the underlying technological infrastructure alongside business models is a good way of improving the business and technology alignment [4]. Modelling the required information services, ICT infrastructure, and the physical technology infrastructure in essence is a cross-domain exercise, which involves professionals from the business domain and technological domain. Therefore, they need a common language in order to be effective. Additionally, talking about ICT in terms of information services gives technologists and business professionals a common language. It facilitates the discussion about business models and their underlying need for information and, therefore, ICT [31]. Hence, it is important to conceptualise and model the underlying information services needed to support the business model. Further, conceptualising the underlying information services helps technologists to draft requirements for the ICT architecture. The ICT architecture in turn supports the information services [31]. This also helps improve the alignment between business models and ICT [32]. Therefore, the BMOs should be able to model the underlying information services of a business model. Furthermore, business models often embody multiple commodities and include multiple stakeholders [1]. Consequently, the BMOs should also be able to model multiple commodities and multiple stakeholders. Business models span multiple organisations; as a result, a systemic approach should be adopted to design business models. The systemic approach entails designing business models at an organisational level, which involves analysing and modelling the value created and contributed by each individual organisation. It also entails designing business models at a network level, which entails configuring the organisations and the value exchanges among them in a way that enables viability. Therefore, the BMOs should be able to design business modelsat an organisational level as well as at the business network level. Table 6 provides an overview of the criteria concerning business model design.

**Table 6.** Assessment criteria concerning business model design.

| No | Criteria | Sources |
|----|----------|---------|
| 5. | Design business models | [20] |
| 5.1. | Ability to manipulate business models | [20] |
| 5.2. | Model underlying information services | [30,31] |
| 5.3. | Model ICT necessary to support the information services | [4,30] |
| 5.4. | Model underlying physical technologies | [33] |
| 5.5. | Model multiple commodities | [1] |
| 5.6. | Model multiple stakeholders/roles | [1] |
| 5.7. | Ability to design business models at organisational level | [25] |
| 5.8. | Ability to design business models at the network level | [25] |

**Evaluation of Viable Business Models.** The BMO should facilitate the evaluation of viability in terms of exchange value and use value. One of the ways it could help evaluate the viability in terms of value is by generating reports on the value captured by each stakeholder. Furthermore, technologists can evaluate the modelled informationservices and the corresponding ICT, and the physical technologies for technological viability. Table 7 shows the assessment criteria concerning viability.

**Table 7.** Assessment criteria concerning viability.

| No | Criteria | Sources |
|----|----------|---------|
| 6. | Evaluation of business models for viability | [11] |
| 6.1. | Evaluate use value captured by the stakeholders | [20] |
| 6.2. | Evaluate exchange value captured by the stakeholders | [20] |
| 6.3. | Visualise the information services | [30,31] |
| 6.4. | Visualise ICT | [4] |
| 6.5. | Visualise the physical technologies | [33] |

**Business Rules.** Business rules define constraints, conditions, and policies that govern a business model. A business rule can be defined as a statement that affects the value creation, value capture, value exchange, and the underlying business model architecture of a business model [29]. Business rules internalise the external requirements put on the business models, such as governmental regulations and technological limitations [29]. In addition, the business rules include the internal requirements on the business model, such as requirements of the strategy on the business model [29]. In context of viability, the business rules can hamper or facilitate the viability of a business model. Hence, it is important that the BMO considers the business rules. An overview of the criteria concerning business rules is shown in Table 8.

**Table 8.** Assessment criteria concerning business rules.

| No | Criteria | Sources |
|----|----------|---------|
| 7. | Embodies business rules | [29] |

## 3.4 Level of Analysis

Level of analysis corresponds to the level of abstraction or granularity at which the business models are conceptualised. BMOs conceptualise business models on a continuum, which ranges from a high level of granularity to a low level of granularity. The BMOs that conceptualise and analyse business models at a high level represent less information, and the business models are usually generalisable. Contrarily, BMOs that conceptualise and analyse business models at a low level represent more information, while the business models are specific to an organisation or a business network. Consequently, they are not generalisable [22]. It is clear from the evaluation criteria derived thus far, that the design and evaluation of viable business models requires large amounts of information. Therefore, the BMOs should model the business models at a relatively low level [22]. Table 9 shows the assessment criteria concerning level of analysis.

**Table 9.** Assessment criteria concerning level of analysis.

| No | Criteria | Sources |
|----|----------|---------|
| 8. | Model BMOs at low level of granularity | [22] |

# 4 BMO Assessment

The criteria presented in the previous section can be used to assess how well BMOs support the design and evaluation of viable business models. The criteria can be applied qualitatively to assess the characteristics of the BMOs. The challenge of assessing BMOs based on a set of criteria can also be framed as a classic multi-criteria decision analysis (MCDA) problem [23, pp. 1–2]. Therefore, we have subjected the criteria to MCDA conditions. The following section elaborates on how the conditions impact the list of criteria.

## 4.1   Restructuring the Criteria

As mentioned previously, for the criteria to be usable they have to meet the following conditions [23, pp. 55–58]: value relevance, understandable, measurable, non-redundant, judgementally independent, complete and concise, operational, and simple (without sacrificing the complexity).

We reviewed the criteria in light of the above conditions. To satisfy the condition of non-redundancy, we have eliminated the criteria of business network and transactions (1.2.3 and 1.2.4). The business network concept emerges under the category of design of business models, where we assess whether the business model is conceptualised at the organisational level and at the business network level. Similarly, the idea of transactions (value exchange) appears under the concept of value exchange.

## 4.2   Selected BMOs

Our search led to six well established BMOs that focus on value. The following BMOs will be assessed using the criteria described above.

**e3-Value.** The e3-Value adopts a value constellation (business network approach), where business models span multiple organisations. e3-Value aims at conceptualising business models and evaluating them for viability [20]. Further, it aims to create a common understanding of the business models among collaborating firms (multi-stakeholder environment) by explicitly visualising the business models. It aims to improve the alignment between business and ICT. e3-Value has its roots in computer science and management science [5].

**Value Network Analysis (VNA).** VNA is rooted in the principles of living systems. It views business models as a pattern of exchanges between stakeholders. It focuses on both the tangible (e.g. money, and products) and the intangible (e.g. knowledge) value exchanges among stakeholders [34]. VNA aims to incorporate a systemic view (business network) of business models, and the intangible values into the mainstream business model analysis.

**Business Modelling Canvas (BMC).** The BMC views business models in terms of 9 building blocks. The BMC conceptualises business models on the level of a single organisation and not on the level of a business network. However, the BMC does identify key partners [35]. The BMC is rooted in information systems and management science. Their main goal is to help companies conceptualise how they create, deliver and capture value [5].

**Value Stream Mapping (VSM).** VSM is based on the concept of lean manufacturing. It conceptualises the flow of value in a value stream. VSM adopts a supply chain approach to map the demand back from customers to raw materials. Their main goal is to help managers shift their attention from individual processes to a larger perspective. It is an attempt to shift the focus from individual processes to the system of interconnected processes required to deliver the product to the customer [36].

**Resource Event Agent (REA).** REA is a domain specific (accounting domain) modelling ontology, which focuses on conceptualising economic resources, economic events, economic agents, and the relationships among them. These are conceptualised from the perspective of a single organisation [7]. It is rooted in information science and management science. It aims to design flexible accounting systems that are better integrated with other enterprise systems and decision support systems [7].

**e-Business Modelling Schematics (EBMS).** The EBMS adopts a business network approach to business models, aiming at e-business initiatives. It adopts a focal organisation perspective to describe business models that span multiple organisations. It is rooted in management science and information science. EBMS was conceived with the aim of helping business executives to conceptualise and analyse new e-business initiatives [31].

### 4.3 Assessment

Each of the BMOs is assessed against the criteria. The assessment is carried out such that if the BMOs fully support the criteria a ✓ sign is assigned, and if it does not or partially support the criteria the criteria a ✗ sign is assigned. We adopt this method of evaluating the BMOs, because even if the BMOs partially support the criteria it will not lead to an accurate conceptualisation and analysis of viability. Therefore, it could lead to unreliable design and evaluation of viable business models. Table 10 shows how the six BMOs perform on the viability criteria derived from literature. It is clear that not all the BMOs conceptualise business models in the same way. Furthermore, it is evident that certain important viability criteria are ignored. None of the BMOs conceptualise value capture and evaluation of business models in terms of use value. Similarly, none of them conceptualise and evaluate the underlying information services, ICT, and physical technologies. The business model architectures are only represented to a certain extent, but not satisfactorily. Therefore, we have rated them as not supporting the criteria "represent the business architecture".

Based on Table 10, we observe that none of the BMOs perform satisfactorily on all criteria. However, e3-value satisfies most of the criteria except for the 9 criteria, namely model captured value in terms of use value, represent the business architecture, model underlying information services, model underlying ICT, model underlying physical technologies, evaluate use value captured by the stakeholders, visualise the information services, visualise the ICT, and visualise the physical technologies. The reason why some of the BMOs perform well against the criteria and some do not could be attributed to the reason that

**Table 10.** Assessment of BMOs.

| No | Criteria | e3-value | VNA | BMC | VSM | REA | EBMS |
|---|---|---|---|---|---|---|---|
| **1.** | **Value creation** | | | | | | |
| 1.1. | Model value creation by each stakeholder | ✓ | ✗ | ✗ | ✓ | ✗ | ✗ |
| 1.2. | Model sources of value creation | | | | | | |
| 1.2.1. | Value creation activities | ✓ | ✗ | ✓ | ✓ | ✓ | ✗ |
| 1.2.2. | Resources | ✓ | ✓ | ✓ | ✓ | ✓ | ✗ |
| **2.** | **Value capture** | | | | | | |
| 2.1. | Model value captured by each stakeholder | ✓ | ✗ | ✗ | ✗ | ✗ | ✗ |
| 2.2. | Model captured value in terms of use value | ✗ | ✗ | ✓ | ✗ | ✓ | ✓ |
| 2.3. | Model captured value in terms of exchange value | ✓ | ✗ | ✓ | ✗ | ✓ | ✗ |
| **3.** | **Value exchange** | | | | | | |
| 3.1. | Model value exchanged at organisational level | | | | | | |
| 3.1.1. | Use value at organisational level | ✓ | ✗ | ✓ | ✓ | ✓ | ✗ |
| 3.1.2. | Exchange value at organisational level | ✓ | ✗ | ✓ | ✓ | ✓ | ✗ |
| 3.2. | Model value exchanged at business network level | | | | | | |
| 3.2.1. | Use value at business network level | ✓ | ✓ | ✗ | ✗ | ✗ | ✓ |
| 3.2.2. | Exchange value at business network level | ✓ | ✓ | ✗ | ✗ | ✗ | ✓ |
| **4.** | **Represent the business architecture** | ✗ | ✗ | ✗ | ✗ | ✗ | ✗ |
| **5.** | **Design business models** | | | | | | |
| 5.1. | Ability to manipulate business models | ✓ | ✓ | ✓ | ✓ | ✓ | ✓ |
| 5.2. | Model underlying information services | ✗ | ✗ | ✗ | ✗ | ✗ | ✗ |
| 5.3. | Model underlying ICT | ✗ | ✗ | ✗ | ✗ | ✗ | ✗ |
| 5.4. | Model underlying physical technologies | ✗ | ✗ | ✗ | ✗ | ✗ | ✗ |
| 5.5. | Model multiple commodities | ✓ | ✓ | ✓ | ✓ | ✓ | ✓ |
| 5.6. | Model multiple stakeholders/roles | ✓ | ✓ | ✗ | ✓ | ✓ | ✓ |
| 5.7. | Ability to design business models at organisational level | ✓ | ✗ | ✓ | ✓ | ✓ | ✗ |
| 5.8. | Ability to design business models at the network level | ✓ | ✓ | ✗ | ✓ | ✗ | ✓ |
| **6.** | **Evaluation of business models for viability** | | | | | | |
| 6.1. | Evaluate use value captured by the stakeholders | ✗ | ✗ | ✗ | ✗ | ✗ | ✗ |
| 6.2. | Evaluate exchange value captured by the stakeholders | ✓ | ✗ | ✗ | ✗ | ✗ | ✗ |
| 6.3. | Visualise the information services | ✗ | ✗ | ✗ | ✗ | ✗ | ✗ |
| 6.4. | Visualise the ICT | ✗ | ✗ | ✗ | ✗ | ✗ | ✗ |
| 6.5. | Visualise the physical technologies | ✗ | ✗ | ✗ | ✗ | ✗ | ✗ |
| **7.** | **Embodies business rules** | ✓ | ✗ | ✗ | ✓ | ✓ | ✗ |
| **8.** | **Model BMOs at low level of granularity** | ✓ | ✗ | ✗ | ✓ | ✓ | ✗ |

not all of them were exclusively conceived to represent business models. Furthermore, even the ones that were conceived to represent business models were not designed from the perspective of designing and evaluating viable business models, except for e3-value. This shows that the viability perspective has been largely ignored in context of BMOs.

# 5   Conclusions

Viable business models are vital to businesses. However, due to the increased complexity, the design and evaluation of viable business models has become very hard. Therefore, we need appropriate tools to reliably design and evaluate viable business models. BMOs are effective tools for designing and evaluating business models.

In the past, different frameworks have been proposed to compare BMOs. However, none of these frameworks compare BMOs from the perspective of design and evaluation of viable business models. We have addressed this gap by assessing BMOs on their capabilities to support the design and evaluation of viable business models. A list of criteria is derived from literature for evaluating BMOs from a viability perspective. We have subsequently applied these criteria to evaluate six well-established BMOs, and identified a BMO which is best suited for the design and evaluation of business models from a viability perspective.

Our analysis reveals that none of the BMOs satisfy all the criteria. Furthermore, each of the BMOs conceptualises business models differently. Our findings suggest that e3-value is the most appropriate BMO for designing and evaluating business models from a viability perspective. However, it fails on 9 criteria: model captured value in terms of use value, represent the underlying business architecture, model underlying information services, model underlying ICT, model underlying physical technologies, evaluate use value captured by the stakeholders, visualise information services, visualise ICT, and visualise physical technologies.

Furthermore it is hard to assess the viability of business models, as current BMOs have a number of deficits that are particularly important for complex, distributed business settings. Consequently, these identified deficits provide clear areas for improvement of each assessed BMO. However, the derived criteria are relying on our conceptualisation of the term viability and influenced by the assumption that business models rely on technology (ICT and physical technology) for execution.

Our analysis shows that the gap between BMOs and strategic management is large. Accordingly, future research should work towards enhancing BMOs to fully support viability as an explicit design focus of business models for dynamic and complex settings. However, this increases the risk of creating overly complex BMOs, which are very hard to use and understand. Care should be taken not to overcomplicate BMOs. Future research should also explore the possibility of combining the strengths of different BMOs and other modelling ontologies, for example by using BMC, e3-value, and business process modelling complementarily to design and evaluate business models from a viability perspective, and to improve the alignment between business models and EAs. In addition, future research can also involve the direct application of enhanced BMOs to design and evaluate the highly complex business models in a distributed setting, and to improve their alignment with the supporting distributed EAs.

Another interesting direction for future research is to extend the enterprise architecture modelling techniques (in particular business process modelling techniques) to incorporate the viability perspective in order to better align strategy, business models, and enterprise architecture. It is logical to incorporate the viability perspective into business process modelling techniques, because it helps conceptualise and design business processes that align with business models in terms of value. By doing this, we minimise the risk of designing business processes that do not add value to the business models. Consequently, this will lead to better and more effective EISs.

**Acknowledgements.** This research has been financed by a grant of the Energy Delta Gas Research (EDGaR) programme. EDGaR is co-financed by the Northern Netherlands Provinces, the European Fund for Regional Development, the Ministry of Economic Affairs and the Province of Groningen, the Netherlands. NICTA is funded by the Australian Government through the Department of Communications and the Australian Research Council.

# References

1. Adhikari, R.S., Aste, N., Manfren, M.: Multi-commodity network flow models for dynamic energy management-smart grid applications. Energy Procedia **14**, 1374–1379 (2012)
2. Lankshorst, M.: Enterprise Architecture at Work-Modelling, Communication and Analysis. Springer, Heidelberg (2009)
3. Chesbrough, H., Vanhaverbeke, W., West, J.: Open Innovation: Researching a New Paradigm. Oxford University Press, New York (2006)
4. Kraussl-Derzsi, Z.: OPerationalized ALignment: Assessing Feasibility of Value Constellations Exploiting Innovative Services. Vrije Universiteit, Amsterdam (2011)
5. Gordijn, J., Osterwalder, A., Pigneur, Y.: Comparing two business model ontologies for designing e-business models and value constellations. In: Proceedings of the 18th Bled eConference, pp. 6–8, Bled (2005)
6. Lasa, I.S., Laburu, C.O., De Castro Vila, R.: An evaluation of the value stream mapping tool. Bus. Process Manag. J. **14**, 39–52 (2008)
7. McCarthy, W.E.: The rea accounting model: a generalized framework for accounting systems in a shared data environment. Account. Rev. **57**, 554–578 (1982)
8. Ross, J.W., Weill, P., Robertson, D.C.: Enterprise Architecture as Strategy: Creating a Foundation for Business Execution. Harvard Business Press, Boston (2006)
9. Engelsman, W., Wieringa, R.: Goal-oriented requirements engineering and enterprise architecture: two case studies and some lessons learned. In: Regnell, B., Damian, D. (eds.) REFSQ 2011. LNCS, vol. 7195, pp. 306–320. Springer, Heidelberg (2012)
10. Osterwalder, A., Pigneur, Y.: An e-business model ontology for modeling e-business. In: 15th Bled Electronic Commerce Conference, pp. 17–19, Bled (2002)
11. Pateli, A.G., Giaglis, G.M.: A research framework for analysing eBusiness models. Eur. J. Inf. Syst. **13**, 302–314 (2004)
12. Al-Debei, M.M., Avison, D.: Developing a unified framework of the business model concept. Eur. J. Inf. Syst. **19**, 359–376 (2010)
13. Lambert, S.: A Review of the Electronic Commerce Literature to Determine the Meaning of the Term 'Business Model'. Flinders University of South Australia, School of Commerce (2003)

14. Osterwalder, A., Pigneur, Y.: Clarifying business models: origins, present, and future of the concept. Commun. Assoc. Inf. Syst. **16**(1), 1–25 (2005)
15. Porter, M.: Competitive Advantage: Creating and Sustaining Superior Performance. Free Press, New York (1985)
16. Gordijn, J., Akkermans, H., van Vliet, H.: Business modelling is not process modelling. In: Mayr, H.C., Liddle, S.W., Thalheim, B. (eds.) ER Workshops 2000. LNCS, vol. 1921, p. 40. Springer, Heidelberg (2000)
17. Sharma, S., Gutiérrez, J.A.: An evaluation framework for viable business models for m-commerce in the information technology sector. Electron. Mark. **20**, 33–52 (2010)
18. De Reuver, M., Haaker, T.: Designing viable business models for context-aware mobile services. Telemat. Inform. **26**, 240–248 (2009)
19. Keen, P., Qureshi, S.: Organizational transformation through business models: a framework for business model design. In: Hawaii International Conference on System Sciences, 2006, Proceedings of the 39th Annual HICSS 2006, vol. 8, p. 206b. IEEE (2006)
20. Gordijn, J., Akkermans, J.M.: Value-based requirements engineering: exploring innovative e-commerce ideas. Requir. Eng. **8**, 114–134 (2003)
21. Mäkinen, S., Seppänen, M.: Assessing business model concepts with taxonomical research criteria: a preliminary study. Manag. Res. News **30**, 735–748 (2007)
22. Lambert, S.: A conceptual model analysis framework: Analysing and comparing business model frameworks and ontologies. Ph.D. thesis, International Business Management Association (IBMA) (2010)
23. Belton, V., Stewart, T.: Multiple Criteria Decision Analysis: An Integrated Approach. Springer, Heidelberg (2002)
24. Tapscott, D., Lowy, A., Ticoll, D.: Digital capital: Harnessing the Power of Business Webs. Harvard Business Press, Watertown (2000)
25. Zott, C., Amit, R., Massa, L.: The business model: recent developments and future research. J. Manag. **37**, 1019–1042 (2011)
26. Lepak, D.P., Smith, K.G., Taylor, M.S.: Value creation and value capture: a multilevel perspective. Acad. Manag. Rev. **32**, 180–194 (2007)
27. Bowman, C., Ambrosini, V.: Value creation versus value capture: towards a coherent definition of value in strategy. Br. J. Manag. **11**, 1–15 (2000)
28. Amit, R., Zott, C.: Value creation in e-business. Strateg. Manag. J. **22**, 493–520 (2001)
29. Eriksson, H.E., Penker, M.: Business modeling with UML. Wiley, Chichester (2000)
30. Davenport, T.H., Prusak, L.: Information Ecology: Mastering the Information and Knowledge Environment. Oxford University Press, Cary (1997)
31. Weill, P., Vitale, M.: What it infrastructure capabilities are needed to implement e-business models. MIS Q. Exec. **1**, 17–34 (2002)
32. Henderson, J.C., Venkatraman, N.: Strategic alignment: leveraging information technology for transforming organizations. IBM Syst. J. **32**, 4–16 (1993)
33. Baden-Fuller, C., Haefliger, S.: Business models and technological innovation. Long Range Plan. **46**, 419–426 (2013)
34. Allee, V.: A value network approach for modeling and measuring intangibles. In: Transparent Enterprise, Madrid (2002)
35. Osterwalder, A., Pigneur, Y.: Business Model Generation: A Handbook for Visionaries, Game Changers, and Challengers. John Wiley & Sons, Hoboken (2010)
36. Rother, M., Shook, J.: Learning to See: Value Stream Mapping to Create Value and Eliminate Muda.-Version 1.3. Learning Enterprise Institute, Cambridge (2003)

# Enterprise-Specific Ontology-Driven Process Modelling

Nadejda Alkhaldi[1(✉)], Sven Casteleyn[1,2], and Frederik Gailly[3]

[1] Vrije Universiteit Brussel, Pleinlaan 2, 1050 Brussels, Belgium
nadejda.alkhaldi@vub.ac.be, sven.casteleyn@uji.es
[2] Universitat Jaume I, Av. De Vicent Sos Baynat s/n, 12071 Castellon, Spain
[3] Ghent University, Tweekerkenstaart 2, 9000 Ghent, Belgium
frederik.gailly@ugent.be

**Abstract.** Different process models are created within an enterprise by different modelers who use different enterprise terms. This hinders model interoperability and integration. A possible solution is formalizing the vocabulary used within the enterprise in an ontology and put this ontology as bases for constructing process models. Given that an enterprise is an evolving entity, the ontology needs to evolve to properly reflect the domain of the enterprise. This paper proposes an enterprise-specific ontology-driven process modelling method which tackles the two aforementioned issues by assisting the modeller in creating process models using terminology from the ontology and simultaneously supporting ontology enrichment with feedback from those models. When the modeller creates a model, matching mechanisms incorporated in the method are working together to suggest a list of ontological concepts that have a high potential to be useful for a particular modelling element. When the model is created, its quality is first evaluated from different perspectives to make sure that it can be used within the enterprise, and second to discover whether its feedback can be useful for the ontology. When the feedback is extracted, the proposed method incorporates guidelines on how to use this feedback.

**Keywords:** Business process modeling · Enterprise ontology · Ontology-driven modelling · BPMN · UFO

## 1 Introduction

When different models within an enterprise are created by different modelers, integrating those models is hard. A possible solution for this integration problem is providing modelers with a shared vocabulary formalized in an ontology [1] and [2]. Over the last 30 years, different domain ontologies have been developed which describe the concepts, relations between concepts and axioms of a specific domain. In a business context, a particular type of domain ontologies are so-called enterprise ontologies. They describe the enterprise domain and consequently provide enterprise domain concepts that can be reused by different enterprises. Example of enterprise ontologies include the Enterprise Ontology [3], TOVE [4] and the Resource Event Agent enterprise ontology [5]. Two different approaches have been proposed to incorporate enterprise ontologies into the modeling process. Some authors consider enterprise ontologies to be reference models

© Springer International Publishing Switzerland 2015
J. Cordeiro et al. (Eds.): ICEIS 2014, LNBIP 227, pp. 472–488, 2015.
DOI: 10.1007/978-3-319-22348-3_26

that support the creation of different kind of models. For instance, [6] suggests developing the Generic Enterprise Model as an ontology that is later used as a reference for creating both data and process models. Other authors developed an enterprise-specific modelling language which is based on the concepts, relations and axioms described in the enterprise ontology [7].

In this paper we focus on using enterprise-specific ontologies (ESO) during the development of business process models. Enterprise-specific ontologies are domain ontologies that differ from enterprise ontologies in the fact that their Universe of Discourse is a specific enterprise, rather than the enterprise domain. They may have their origin in an established domain ontology or in an enterprise ontology, but their main goal is describing the concepts, relations and axioms that are shared within a particular enterprise. Enterprise-specific ontologies are getting increasingly important in the context of data governance and knowledge representation [1]. Supporting tools, such as IBM InfoSphere[1] or Collibra Enterprise Glossary[2] allow enterprises to specify their own enterprise glossary/ontology. Such an enterprise-specific ontology, once available, can subsequently be deployed to help enterprise modellers in creating compatible, enterprise-specific models, such as requirements, data or process models. This paper focuses on business process models. Additionally the ESO ontology needs to be maintained and enriched while the enterprise evolves. Enriching ESO from the process models is very practical because it will reflect processes that were introduced recently within the enterprise, or processes that where adjusted.

The work described in this paper is a process model-specific instantiation of a framework for ontology-driven enterprise modeling aimed to facilitate model construction based on an enterprise-specific ontology on one hand, and support enterprise-specific ontology creation and evolution based on feedback from the modelling process on the other hand. This framework also proposes criteria to evaluate the quality of resulting models to ensure that their feedback is potentially useful. To illustrate our work, we use the Unified Foundational Ontology as core ontology, OWL as ontology representation language and BPMN as business process modelling language.

## 2    Enterprise-Specific Ontology Engineering and Process Modelling Method

The method that is proposed in this paper in an instantiation of the meta-method which can be used for different enterprise modeling languages and which was proposed in previous work [8]. As displayed in Fig. 1, the ontology and modeling method consists of two parallel cycles, which in turn consist of different phases. For a general description of the different phases we refer to [8]. In this paper we will focus on describing the different phases specifically for process modeling using BPMN.

---

[1] http://www-01.ibm.com/software/data/infosphere/.
[2] http://www.collibra.com/.

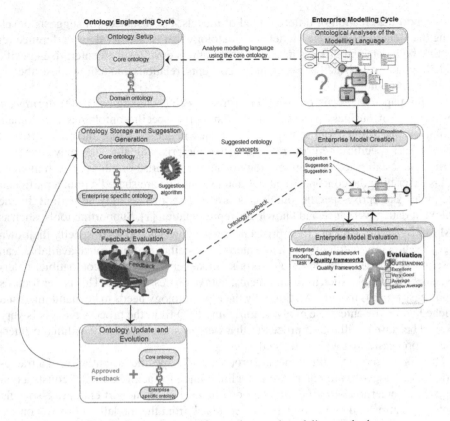

**Fig. 1.** Enterprise specific ontology and modeling method.

## 2.1   Ontology Setup Phase

This is the first phase of the Ontology Engineering cycle. It includes pre-processing of the selected enterprise-specific ontology (ESO) so that matching mechanisms can be applied in the later phases to derive useful suggestions. Pre-processing in this case implies mapping concepts from the selected ESO to a core ontology. A core ontology is an ontology that describes universally agreed upon, high level concepts and relations, such as objects, events, agents, etc. [9]. Constructs of the selected modelling language will also be mapped to this core ontology in the next phase of the proposed method. The core ontology thus forms a bridge between the ESO and the selected modeling language, and incorporates shared semantics.

The Unified Foundational Ontology (UFO) was selected as a core ontology in this work for three reasons: 1/ the benefits of grounding domain ontologies in UFO are well motivated [10], and several such UFO-grounded domain ontologies are available, e.g., [11] 2/ UFO is specifically developed for the ontological analysis of modelling languages, and 3/ BPMN was chosen as modelling language in this work and analysis of BPMN using UFO is available in literature [12].

UFO has different layers of which here only UFO-U is used, as this is sufficient for finding construct-based matches between the selected modeling language (explained later) and ESO. However, it can be further investigated if using (full) UFO is beneficial to refine the proposed algorithms. The top level element in UFO-U is a Universal. It represents a classifier that classifies at any moment of time a set of real world individuals and can be of four kinds: Event type, Quality universal, Relator universal and Object type.

For the purpose of this demonstration, we have selected as ESO an existing ontology in financial domain.[3] This ontology contains static concepts related to finance, such as Branch, Customer, Loan, Insurance, etc., which can be used as a reference for models constructed in the financial domain. A sample of the mapping between the ESO and UFO-U is presented in Table 1.

**Table 1.** Mappings between ESO and UFO-U.

| ESO concept | UFO-U | ESO concept | UFO-U |
|---|---|---|---|
| AddedValue | Quality_ Universal | Liability | Relator Universal Mediates Customer and mediates Branch |
| Adminstrative | Role_Type | Loan | Relator Universal Mediates Customer and mediates Branch |
| Asset | Mixin Type | Mortgage-Loan | Relator Universal Mediates Customer and mediates Branch |
| Branch | Base_Type | Castomer | Mixin Type |

## 2.2 Ontological Analyses of the Modeling Language

The selected modeling language also needs to be analyzed because the core ontology forms a intermediary through which modeling constructs are mapped to the concepts of ESO. Although our meta-method support any kind of core ontology, it is important that the used modelling languages are analysed using the selected core ontology because the suggestion generation process relies hereupon. Table 2 represents mappings between BPMN and UFO-U.

---

[3] http://dip.semanticweb.org/documents/D10.2eBankingCaseStudyDesignandSpecificationofApplicationfinal.pdf.

**Table 2.** Mappings between BPMN and UFO-U.

| BPMN construct | UFO-U | BPMN construct | UFO-U |
|---|---|---|---|
| Pool | Object type | End event | Event Type |
| Lane | Object type | Event noun | Base type, Mixin type, Relator universal |
| Task Noun | Relator universals or quality universal | Condition Exclusive Gateway | Quality universal |
| Noun Sub Process | Relator universals or quality universal | Data object | Relator universal,, Base type |
| Start event | Event Type | Message flow label | Relator universal |
| Intermediate event | Event Type | | |

## 2.3   Ontology Storage and Suggestion Generation Phase

Every time the modeler places a modeling element on the canvas, several matching mechanisms are cooperating in order to rank the ESO concepts to display the most relevant of them on the top of a suggestions list. Given the potentially extensive amount of ESO concepts, relevance ranking of suggestions is a critical feature.

Depending on the type of modelling construct that is added, the position of the construct relevant to other elements (i.e., its neighborhood) in the model, and the label entered by the modeller, the order of the suggestion list is prioritized so that ontology concepts with a higher likelihood to be relevant in the current context appear first. To achieve this, four different suggestion generation mechanisms are used. These mechanisms are partly inspired by ontology matching techniques [13], but are specifically focused to fit within our framework, where the semantics of the modelling language can be exploited.

Every matching technique calculates a relevance score (between 0 and 1) for each ESO concept, which is stored. Subsequently, the overall relevance score is calculated using a weighted average of all individual scores. This corresponds to the formula below:

$$ConceptRelevanceScore = \frac{S_s W_s + S_{syn} W_{syn} + S_c W_c + S_{nb} W_{nb}}{W_s + W_{syn} + W_c + W_{nb}}$$

Where:
$S_s W_s$: the score and weight of string match
$S_{syn} W_{syn}$: the score and weight of synonym match
$S_c W_c$: the score and weight of construct match
$S_{nb} W_{nb}$: the score and weight of neighborhood based match

The weights for each matching mechanism are thus configurable. In our demonstration (see Sect. 3), we assigned a higher weight to string matching as we expect that, within a particular enterprise context, a (quasi) exact string match has a high possibility of representing the intended (semantic) concept. The lowest weight is assigned to construct matching, because it typically matches very broadly, and thus delivers a large amount of suggestions. Further experimentation with the distribution of weights over the individual relevance scores should be performed to determine an optimal overall score calculation. This is considered future work. As a final result, the suggestion list, a descending ordered list of ESO concepts according to relevance, is generated and presented to the modeller. In the next four subsections the different mechanisms are described in more detail. The implementation of the mechanisms can be consulted via our Github repository: https://github.com/fgailly/CMEplusBPMN.

### 2.3.1 String Matching Mechanism

The goal of the string matching algorithm is to find ESO concepts whose label is syntactically similar to the label of modeling elements entered by the modeller. If these two strings are syntactically the same, there is a high possibility that they have the same semantics, especially as both reside within the same enterprise and business context.

Currently Jaro-Winkler distance [14] is used to calculate the edit distance between the given BPMN element label, and the label of each concept in the enterprise-specific ontology. The Jaro-Winkler distance was chosen because this hybrid technique takes into account that the text entered by the modeller can contain spelling errors, and additionally favours matches between strings with longer common prefixes (i.e., a substring test, which is very useful in our context because matching is executed each time a character is added to the label). Jaro-Winkler distances are between 0 (no similarity) and 1 (exact match), and are thus immediately useable as a relevance score.

### 2.3.2 Synonym Matching Mechanism

The synonym matching mechanism aims to detect synonyms of the given BPMN element label (or part of it) in the ESO. To realize this, WordNet [15] is used. WordNet is an online lexical database that organizes English nouns, verbs, adjectives and adverbs into sets of synonyms (so-called synsets). It is thus ideal to find synonyms. For each synonym of the modeling element label, the previously described string matching algorithm is performed on all ESO concepts, thereby generating a relevance score between 0 (no match) and 1 (exact synonym match).

### 2.3.3 Construct Matching Mechanism

This matching mechanism operates based on the mapping performed in "ontology set up" and "ontological analyses of the modeling language" phases described previously. Consequently, BPMN modeling constructs can be mapped to ESO concepts through the UFO core ontology. During the matching process, this mechanism assigns a score of 1 to all ESO concepts mapped to the same UFO-U construct as the modeling language construct created. All the other ESO concepts are assigned relevance score of 0. In our implementation, the mappings between the ESO and UFO, and BPMN and UFO, are each represented in an OWL file. OWL reasoning is then used to perform the mappings between the ESO concepts and BPMN constructs based on the two aforementioned OWL files.

### 2.3.4   Neighborhood – Based Matching Mechanism

Neighborhood-based mechanism calculates relevance scores for ESO concepts based on the location of the newly added modeling element, the type of modeling element that is added, and the relationships between the ESO concepts corresponding to the modeling elements surrounding the newly added element. The neighborhood of a BPMN element is determined by the connectivity objects (i.e. sequence flow, message flow, association), and which pool (or lane) the BPMN element is located in. In other words, for every element we can determine which pool or lane it is a part of, and which other element(s) is/are connected to this element using either a sequence, message flow or association. Next, the relationships (which are specified in terms of the UFO-U relationships through the ESO-UFO-U mappings) between the ESO concepts are exploited. According to [10] there are two types of relations: formal and material. A *formal relation* between entities holds directly, without any further intervening individuals. A *material relation* has material structure by itself. It includes relations such as *working at, being treated at*, etc. Entities related by this type of relation are mediated by individuals called relators. In Sect. 3 we will demonstrate how the UFO-U relators can be used to suggest concepts from the ESO.

Finally, using both the relative position of the new element and the material relations between the ESO concepts, the element neighborhood-based mechanism can now derive relevance scores for ESO concepts in relation to some BPMN modeling elements (for examples, see Sect. 3):

1. To create a pool construct when another pool already exists, the suggestions (relevance score 1) are UFO-U object types that are related by a material relationship with the ESO concept with which the existing pool(s) was/were annotated (i.e., the ontology annotations of the pool(s)).
2. To create a lane construct within a pool, the suggestions (relevance score 1) are UFO-U role types that are related by a material relationship with the ontology annotation of the pool(s)
3. To create a message construct that results in transmitting a message between a task or event of a pool and another pool, the suggestions (relevance score 1) are UFO-U relators mediating material relations connecting objects that annotate respectively the noun of the task and the ontology annotation of the pool.
4. To create a conditional gateway, there are two ways to derive suggestions (both receive relevance score 1):
- ESO concepts annotated by the task label preceding the gateway. This can work very well for tasks that are performing evaluation or calculation, after which the gateway is used to make a decision based on the results. In this case, the condition on the gateway will use the same concept as used in the task. This concept is most likely to be a quality, especially if the task at hand is performing calculations. Nevertheless, it can also be a relator, such as for example verifying if the contract is ok or not.

- Qualities associated with the UFO-U object type annotation of the pool where the gateway is located. Or UFO-U qualities associated with UFO-U object types participating in material relations with Object type annotation of the pool where the gateway is located.
5. For creation of a task construct, the suggested concepts are most likely to be related through material relations to the pool where the task is located. The suggestions can be either quality types of the concept annotating that pool or relators mediating those material relations.

## 2.4  Enterprise Model Creation Phase

During this phase the modeler proceeds with creating the process model utilizing suggestions derived by the matching mechanisms described in the previous section. With every modeling element placed on the canvas the modeler is advised to select ESO concept from the suggestions list to annotate the modeling element. This annotation implies maintaining a link between the modeling element and the corresponding concept of the ESO. With the help of the annotation, the modeling element is semantically connected to the ESO concept even if they have different labels. In our implementation, the annotation is realized by creating an OWL file where a URI of the OWL ESO concept is added to the corresponding modeling element using the OWL annotation mechanism. A portion of the annotation OWL file is presented below. It shows that pool construct "Participant_1" has a label "Customer" and is annotated by "Customer" concept of the bank ontology (our ESO).

```
<ClassAssertion>
<Class IRI = "http://www.mis.ugent.be/ontologies/bpmn.owl#Pool"/>
<NamedIndividual IRI = "#Participant_1"/>
</ClassAssertion>
<AnnotationAssertion>
<AnnotationProperty abbreviatedIRI = "rdfs:isDefinedBy"/>
<IRI > #Participant_1 </IRI>
<Literal datatypeIRI = "http://www.w3.org/2001/XMLSchema#string">
http://www.mis.ugent.be/ontologies/bank#Customer
</Literal>
</AnnotationAssertion>
```

## 2.5  Enterprise Model Evaluation Phase

Within the Enterprise-Specific Ontology and Modeling framework, the model quality evaluation phase has two main goals: (1) it ensures that the model can be used within the enterprise and (2) that the feedback extracted from the creation of the model is useful and potentially worth incorporating into the ESO. Literature provides a plethora of frameworks for quality evaluation of different kinds of models. For an overview of how process model quality can be evaluated we refer to [16]. A well-known scheme for classifying quality dimensions is the Lindland et al. framework [17] which makes a distinction between syntactic, semantic and pragmatic quality dimensions. *Syntactic quality* implies correspondence between the model and the modelling language. *Semantic quality* measures how compliant the model is to the domain. And *pragmatic quality* is the correspondence between the model and the user interpretation of it.

The first goal of the model evaluation phase can be satisfied by focusing on measures that fall within the syntactic and pragmatic dimension because for the model to be used within the enterprise it needs to be correct and understandable. The second goal can be achieved by focusing on measures that fall within the semantic quality dimension. More specific the developed process model has to reflect the process it was designed for. Hence, the three quality dimensions postulated by [17] are well suited for this phase of the meta-method.

### 2.5.1  Syntactic Quality

This dimension stipulates that the created model must be syntactically correct in order to be used within an enterprise. If the model has syntactic flows, its process cannot be correctly implemented. Syntactic quality is achieved using syntactic correctness criterion. According to [18] verification of the syntactic quality of a process models focuses on two properties: static property and behavioral property. Static property is the related to the elements of the model and how they are used and connected. For example, in BPMN it is not allowed to have sequence flow between two pools. The static syntactic quality can be verified by the modeling tool itself while the model is being created. Behavioral property relates to the behavior of the process model. For example, the process cannot reach a deadlock and proper process completion is guaranteed. This is evaluated automatically by computer programs after the model is created.

### 2.5.2  Semantic Quality

Semantic quality of a process model is typically evaluated by means of completeness and validity measures. Completeness is defined in [16] as a degree to which a model has all the necessary and relevant information. Following the work of [19] completeness of a process model can be measured by: 1. Counting the number of items in BPMN model that do not correspond to the description of the actual process 2. counting the number of requirements that are present in model description, but are not reflected in the model itself. It is advisable to document the process to be constructed so that this document can serve as a reference for model evaluation. But when no description is available, the quality evaluation metrics can be executed by another stakeholder familiar with the process, or by the modeler himself. According to [18] the model is valid when all its statements are correct and relevant to the problem. In order to verify validity, one must know the meaning of modeling elements and the process that the model is representing.

### 2.5.3  Pragmatic Quality

Pragmatic quality is about the correspondence between the process model and users' comprehension of it. This quality dimension is not relevant when the modeler himself is the only user of the model because he obviously will understand the model he made.

But if the model will be presented to other stakeholders, it is very important that they understand it.

The literature contains several propositions on how to evaluate understandability. [16] proposes using structural complexity metrics suggested by [20] (which is specific to BPMN) as an indication of the degree of model understandability. If the model is complex, it is likely to be less understandable. In the context of the proposed method it is possible to use a complexity metric to make sure that the model is not exceeding complexity limits.

### 2.6   Community-Based Ontology Feedback Evaluation Phase

The method only proceeds to this phase if the model satisfies the expected semantic quality, meaning that it correctly reflects the process it was designed for, and all the statements in the model are valid within the process. When the process model is complete, an OWL file representing this model and the ESO concepts selected for the model annotation is stored. This file is processes in order to extract any possible feedback which is potentially useful and can be incorporated into the ESO. A possible feedback is a listing of the elements from the model that were not annotated by ESO concepts. As they were not annotated, the reason might be that there is no equivalent for them in the ESO. This feedback is made available for other community members and is subject to discussion, until finally a consensus is reached whether or not the proposed change(s) should be included (such as new concepts added) in the new version of the ontology. The community will discuss the proposed concepts such as their usage, definition and usefulness within the enterprise. Community members are other people working in the same business domain. As community members are typically not co-located at the same physical location, and we are aiming to progressively reach a consensus about what is needed by the community, the Delphi approach [21] is used. This approach is perfectly suited to capture collective knowledge and experience of experts in a given field, independently of their location, and to reach a final conclusion by consensus. More specifically, consensus is reached by commenting on the feedback in 3 cycles. Three cycles were chosen because studies show that most changes in responses occur in the first 2 rounds [21]. In every cycle comments are assigned a score, and when all three cycles are accomplished, a decision is taken whether to incorporate feedback or discard it. Only in case the community is not able to reach a consensus, the final decision is made by community members with a high level of trust. A system for assigning trust credits to community members is foreseen.

If negotiation upon the feedback progresses slowly, the process may be terminated without accomplishing predefined number of cycles. In this case highly trusted, authorized community members are responsible to make a decision.

### 2.7   Ontology Update and Evolution Phase

After the feedback verification is performed, ontology expert incorporate its results into the enterprise ontology. It is worth mentioning that ontology experts do not interfere in feedback verification. Their mission is limited solely to incorporating the final results into the ontology in a syntactically correct way. Once a considerable amount of feedback is incorporated, a new ontology version is proposed. The new ontology incorporates new concept/relationships, updates lacking/incomplete ones, and/or removes irrelevant once, as the domain evolves or new insights are reached by the expanding community.

## 3   Demonstration

This section illustrates the suggestions generation phase of the method explained in the previous sections by means of a lab demonstration in which the modeller constructs a process model in BPMN notation in the financial domain using an existing financial domain ontology[4] as enterprise-specific ontology.

Once the ESO is grounded in the core ontology (as mentioned, this only needs to be done once, and can subsequently be re-used for any model created within the enterprise), the modeller can start creating the process model. He selects a construct to be added, places it on the canvas and starts typing the construct's desired name. As he selects the construct, and as he is typing, the mechanisms described in the previous section derive suggestions from the ESO and present them to the modeller. If an ESO concept in the suggestion list appropriately corresponds to the intention of the modeller for this particular BPMN construct, he selects this concept, and the BPMN construct is (automatically) annotated with the chosen ESO concept.

The process model to be created in our lab demonstration represents the loan application assessment process in a bank, and is taken from [22]. By using an existing specification, we avoid bias towards our method. The process starts when the loan officer receives a loan application from one of the bank's customers. This loan application is approved if it passes two checks: the first check is the applicant's loan risk assessment, which is done automatically by the system after a credit history check of the customer is performed by a financial officer. The second check is a property appraisal check performed by the property appraiser. After both checks are completed, the loan officer assesses the customer's eligibility. If the customer is found to be not eligible, the application is rejected. Otherwise, the loan officer starts preparing the acceptance pack. He also checks whether the applicant requested a home insurance quote. If he did, both the acceptance pack and the home insurance quote are sent to the applicant. If the insurance was not requested, only the acceptance pack is sent. The process finally continues with the verification of the repayment agreement.

Figure 2 represents the BPMN model of the loan application process. Constructs that are surrounded by a thick red square are annotated with ESO concepts.

---

4  http://dip.semanticweb.org/documents/D10.2eBankingCaseStudyDesignandSpecificationofApplicationfinal.pdf.

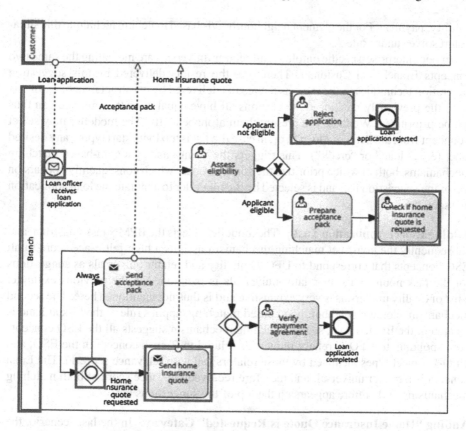

**Fig. 2.** BPMN model describing loan application.

**Adding Branch Pool:** The modeller selects the pool construct to be created. Based on the construct matching mechanism all ESO concepts corresponding to UFO-U object type are given a relevance score of 1 for this matching mechanism. Among those concepts the modeller can find Branch which is classified as UFO-U base type. If there is already a "Customer" pool, based on the construct neighbourhood matching mechanism, this case corresponds with rule 1. As the already existing pool is the Customer pool, the mechanism looks for ESO concepts related to the Customer concept through material relationships. There is only one concept satisfying this requirement: Branch. As a result, the Branch concept is listed in the beginning of the suggestion list, as it scored for both the construct and neighbourhood matching mechanisms (and no other concept scored equal or higher). Note that in this scenario, string and synonym matching cannot contribute to the overall relevance score yet, as the modeller did not (yet) type any label.

**Adding Message Flow "Loan Application":** According to the construct matching mechanism, message flow corresponds to the relator universal. Therefore, all ESO concepts corresponding to the UFO-U relator universal will be selected. Those concepts are: Channel, loan, mortgage loan, current mortgage loan, future mortgage loan, invoice, liability, payment. For the element neighbourhood- based matching technique this situation resolves under rule 2.

In our enterprise-specific ontology, all relator universals are mediating the same two concepts Branch and Customer. Therefore, the results delivered by this suggestion generation technique are the same as the results delivered by construct matching. In this case, the previously mentioned suggestions all have equal overall score, and can thus not be prioritized. We therefore present them alphabetically. The modeller may select a concept from the list (i.e., "loan"), or, in case the list is too long, start typing any desired label (e.g., "loan" or "credit"). This triggers the string- and synonym-based matching mechanisms, both of which prioritize the concept Loan, which consequently appears on top of the suggestion list, and is selected by the modeller to annotate the loan application message flow.

**Adding Reject Application Task:** The modeller selects the BPMN task construct, and subsequently the construct matching mechanism assigns a high relevance score to all ESO concepts that correspond to UFO-U quality and relator universals as suggestions for the task noun. A list of relator universals is mentioned in the previous example; a list of quality universals is very exhaustive and is thus not mentioned here. The second mechanism, element neighbourhood based matching, applies rule 3: the task at hand is located in the Branch pool, so this matching mechanism suggests all the ESO concepts corresponding to UFO-U relator universals related to Branch concept in the ESO, and UFO-U object types mediated by those relators (all with relevance score 1). The Loan concept is a relator universal, and therefore received relevance score of both matching mechanisms; it therefore appears on the top of the suggestions list.

**Adding "Home Insurance Quote is Requested" Gateway:** In the last scenario, the modeller draws an inclusive decision gateway on the canvas. Based on construct matching mechanism, all quality universals will be assigned a priority score of 1. The element neighbourhood-based mechanism classifies this situation under rule 4, which suggests ESO concepts that were used to annotate a task construct preceding the gateway. In this case it is the "check if home insurance quote is requested" task, which is annotated with the Home Insurance concept. This concept thus receives relevance score 1 for the gateway, and is prioritized in the suggestion list. It perfectly matches our needs.

To start the discussion, we note that the scenarios elaborated here were chosen to illustrate the more complicated cases. As a result, string- and synonym-based matching mechanism are underrepresented. Evidently, when no or few BPMN elements are already on the canvas, neighbourhood-based matching will be unable to sufficiently differentiate between potential suggestions (as in scenario 2), and string- and synonym-matching will become important. Equally, when the modeller has a certain label already in mind, string and synonym matching will dominate the suggestion list, as the modeller is typing the label he had in mind. Having made this comment, we note that in general, it was possible to derive suggestions based on the construction and element neighbourhood matching mechanisms for all model constructs for which the related concepts existed in the ontology. In fact, as can be seen in the scenarios, construct and neighbourhood based matching complement each other well. The majority of the concepts required by the model, but missing from the ontology were also correctly classified under the assumptions of neighbourhood-based matching mechanism, and would have been assigned a high relevance score if they would have been present in the ontology. However, there was one case where the neighbourhood-based matching mechanism was not very accurate. While creating the last message flow "Home insurance quote", based on the second assumption of the neighbourhood-based matching mechanism and the construct matching mechanism, relator universals must be suggested. But in reality, it was annotated with a quality universal HomeInsurance, instead of a relator. Further fine-tuning of the suggestion generation mechanism should avoid this type of mismatches.

The lab demonstration was used here to demonstrate viability of our method, to detail the different steps and provide a concrete case. It shows that the suggestion generation algorithm indeed provides useful suggestions to the modeller, and allows (automatic) annotations of the model, thereby semantically grounding them and facilitating model integration. It needs to be mentioned that the lab demonstration was done using a single modeller, and that therefore the aforementioned positive indications of using our method cannot be statistically proven. We are currently performing a more elaborate empirical validation, where a group of test users is divided in three different groups: one group is given an ESO and our method, the second group is only given the ESO but without support of our method, and the last group is not given an ESO and thus needs to model without any ontology or method support. The experiment is specifically designed to show the impact of our model on modelling efficiency, consistency in the use of terminology, and the semantic grounding of the resulting models.

After the model is created, it is time to perform model quality evaluation. Syntactic quality is measured by counting the amount of violations of BPMN syntax. From the static perspective, the model in Fig. 2 is syntactically correct which is expected as the modeling tool itself prevents some basic violations. From the behavioral aspect it is important to look into different scenarios of model completion. This model will always reach a valid completion independently of which paths are selected at the gateway. There are no tasks in the model that can never be executed. To evaluate semantic quality, we need to look back to the model description in the beginning of this demonstration section. Because within the context of this method, this description represents the domain to which the model needs to correspond. There are two requirements in the description that are not reflected in the process model in Fig. 2. The first requirement is: "applicant's loan risk assessment, which is done automatically by the system", and the second requirement is: "credit history check of the customer is performed by a financial officer". Those requirements need to be incorporated before the feedback from the model is taken.

To evaluate the pragmatic quality, structural complexity is calculated based on measures presented in [16] presented in Table 3. According to [23] those measures are directly related to understandability. The thresholds suggested for those values are: number of nodes between 30 and 32, Gateway mismatch is between 0 and 2, depth is 1, connectivity coefficient is 0.4. With those values the model is considered to be 70% understandable. The values obtained in evaluating the model in Fig. 2 are close to the proposed threshold, and therefore the model is potentially understandable.

**Table 3.** Structural complexity measurements of the model in Fig. 2.

| Metric | Result |
|---|---|
| Number of nodes in the model | 15 |
| Gateway mismatch (sum of gateway pairs that do not match with each other) | 1 |
| Depth (maximum nesting of structure blocks) | 0 |
| Connectivity coefficient (Ratio of the total number of arcs in a process model to its total number of nodes) | $13/15 = 0.9$ |

## 4    Conclusions and Future Work

This paper presented an overview of an enterprise-specific ontology-driven process modeling method. On the one hand, this method improves semantic consistency of process models by relying in ESO in model construction. On the other hand, it supports the evolvement of the ESO according to practical needs of the enterprise by taking feedback from the process models. While constructing models, the modeler is aided by a list of suggestions extracted from the ESO. ESO concepts are ranked in a suggestions list using four matching mechanisms. Two of them, the string and synonym matching mechanisms, are based on the label of the newly created BPMN element, which is systematically compared with concepts in the ESO. The other two, namely construct matching and neighbourhood-based matching, depend on the type of the BPMN construct and the position (relative to other modelling elements) where it is added.

Another benefit of the proposed method is that it facilitates maintenance and improvement of the ESO by means of feedback from the process models. This feedback is only accepted if the resulted model properly reflects the process it is representing. The proposed method incorporates guidelines on model quality evaluation. When a model is created, an OWL file containing all modeling elements is stored. This file is processed by ontology expert and all the elements representing potential feedback. This feedback is subject to community discussion and if approved, it will be incorporated in the new ontology version.

Future work will follow different directions. Concerning model creation based on the ESO, first, we are currently performing further empirical validation of the benefits of our method. Second, suggestions towards the ontology (e.g., missing concepts) based on the modelling process, and subsequent community-based ontology evolution, needs to be explored. Finally, we also plan to apply the method for other modelling languages (i.e. i*, KAOS), and using other core ontologies. Concerning ESO maintenance and amelioration, we are planning to set up a forum where the community will discuss model feedback. Clear definition of guidelines for discussion and voting is also very essential.

# References

1. Bera, P., Burton-Jones, A., Wand, Y.: Guidelines for designing visual ontologies to support knowledge identification. MIS Q. **35**(4), 883–908 (2011)
2. Di Francescomarino, C., Tonella, P.: Supporting ontology-based semantic annotation of business processes with automated suggestions. In: Halpin, T., Krogstie, J., Nurcan, S., Proper, E., Schmidt, R., Soffer, P., Ukor, R. (eds.) Enterprise, Business-Process and Information Systems Modeling. LNBIP, vol. 29, pp. 211–223. Springer, Heidelberg (2009)
3. Uschold, M., King, M., Moralee, S., Zorgios, Y.: The enterprise ontology. Knowl. Eng. Rev. Spec. Issue Putting Ontol. Use **13**(1), 31–89 (1998)
4. Fox, M.S.: The TOVE project: towards a common-sense model of the enterprise. In: Belli, F., Radermacher, F.J. (eds.) Industrial and Engineering Applications of Artificial Intelligence and Expert Systems, pp. 25–34. Springer, Germany (1992)
5. Geerts, G.L., McCarthy, W.E.: An accounting object infrastructure for knowledge based enterprise models. IEEE Intell. Syst. Their Appl. **14**, 89–94 (1999)
6. Fox, M., Gruninger, M.: On ontologies and enterprise modelling. In: Kosanke, K., Nell, J.G. (eds.) Enterprise Engineering and Integration, pp. 190–200. Springer, Heidelberg (1997)
7. Sonnenberg, C., Huemer, C., Hofreiter, B., Mayrhofer, D., Braccini, A.: The REA-DSL: A domain specific modeling language for business models. In: Mouratidis, H., Rolland, C. (eds.) CAiSE 2011. LNCS, vol. 6741, pp. 252–266. Springer, Heidelberg (2011)
8. Gailly, F., Casteleyn, S., Alkhaldi, N.: On the symbiosis between enterprise modelling and ontology engineering. In: Ng, W., Storey, V.C., Trujillo, J.C. (eds.) ER 2013. LNCS, vol. 8217, pp. 487–494. Springer, Heidelberg (2013)
9. Doerr, M., Hunter, J., Lagoze, C.: Towards a core ontology for information integration. J. Digit. Inf. **4**(1) (2006)
10. Guizzardi, G., Wagner, G.: What's in a relationship: an ontological analysis. In: Li, Q., Spaccapietra, S., Yu, E., Olivé, A. (eds.) ER 2008. LNCS, vol. 5231, pp. 83–97. Springer, Heidelberg (2008)
11. Barcellos, M.P., Falbo, R., Dal Moro, R.: A well-founded software measurement ontology. In: 6th International Conference on Formal Ontology in Information Systems (FOIS 2010), vol. 209, pp. 213–226 (2010)
12. Guizzardi, G., Wagner, G.: Can BPMN be used for making simulation models? In: Barjis, J., Eldabi, T., Gupta, A. (eds.) EOMAS 2011. LNBIP, vol. 88, pp. 100–115. Springer, Heidelberg (2011)
13. Euzenat, J., Shvaiko, P.: Ontology Matching. Springer, Berlin (2013)
14. Winkler, W.: String comparator metrics and enhanced decision rules in the Fellegi-Sunter model of record linkage. In: Proceedings of the Section on Survey Research Methods, American Statistical Association (1990)
15. Miller, G.: WordNet: a lexical database for English. Commun. ACM **38**(11), 39–41 (1995)
16. Sánchez-González, L., García, F., Ruiz, F., Piattini, M.: Toward a quality framework for business process models. Int. J. Coop. Inf. Syst. **22**(01), 1350003 (2013)
17. Lindland, O., Sindre, G., Sølvberg, A.: Understanding quality in conceptual modeling. IEEE Softw. **11**(2), 42–49 (1994)
18. Reijers, H.A., Mendling, J., Recker, J.: Business Process Quality Management. In: vom Brocke, J., Rosemann, M. (eds.) Handbook on Business Process Management 1, pp. 167–185. Springer, Berlin (2010)
19. Moody, D.L.: Metrics for evaluating the quality of entity relationship models. In: Ling, T.-W., Ram, S., Li Lee, M. (eds.) ER 1998. LNCS, vol. 1507, pp. 211–225. Springer, Heidelberg (1998)

20. Rolón, E., Ruiz, F., Garcia, F., Piattini, M.: Applying software metrics to evaluate business process models. CLEI-Electron. J. **9**(1) (2006)
21. Gupta, U.G., Clarke, R.E.: Theory and applications of the delphi technique: a bibliography (1975–1994). Technol. Forecast. Soc. Chang. **53**, 185–211 (1996)
22. Dumas, M., La Rosa, M., Mendling, J., Reijers, H.: Fundamentals of Business Process Management. Springer, Heidelberg (2013)
23. Sánchez-González, L., Garcia, F., Mendling, J., Ruiz, F.: Quality assessment of business process models based on thresholds. In: Meersman, R., Dillon, T.S., Herrero, P. (eds.) OTM 2010. LNCS, vol. 6426, pp. 78–95. Springer, Heidelberg (2010)

# Author Index

Printed in the United States
by Bookmasters

Printed in the United States
By Bookmasters